A Monetary and Fiscal History of Latin America, 1960–2017

The Monetary and Fiscal History of Latin America project was launched in 2013 by the University of Chicago's Lars Peter Hansen in his former capacity as the director of the Becker Friedman Institute (BFI) and as part of its fiscal policy initiative. Upon the advice of Thomas Sargent, New York University and former distinguished fellow of the BFI, and Fernando Alvarez, University of Chicago, the institute provided funding and other support for this vibrant project initiated and led throughout by the University of Minnesota's Timothy Kehoe and the Federal Reserve Bank of Minneapolis's Juan Pablo Nicolini. In supporting and hosting this project, the institute envisioned an intensive research program to produce a comprehensive monetary and fiscal history of the ten largest countries of South America plus Mexico since 1960. Under Kehoe's and Nicolini's leadership and with the extensive efforts of a large number of scholars with expertise on the macroeconomic experiences of Latin American countries, this project delivered with great success on its initial ambition. The authors of the chapters are country experts who participated in numerous meetings over six years to discuss and receive feedback on their findings that were framed in ways to facilitate comparisons and open the door to novel insights applicable more broadly. Along with the scholarship represented in this book, these economists worked with BFI to create a dynamic database for the eleven Latin American countries under review (https://mafhola.uchicago.edu/), which will inform and inspire scholarship for years to come.

Becker Friedman Institute
FOR ECONOMICS AT THE UNIVERSITY OF CHICAGO

A Monetary and Fiscal History of Latin America, 1960–2017

Timothy J. Kehoe

and

Juan Pablo Nicolini, *Editors*

University of Minnesota Press
Minneapolis
London

The University of Minnesota Press gratefully acknowledges financial assistance for the publication of this book from the Becker Friedman Institute and the University of Chicago.

Frontispiece: La Paz, Bolivia, 2015. Photograph by Anabella Maudet.

Published by the University of Minnesota Press
111 Third Avenue South, Suite 290
Minneapolis, MN 55401-2520
http://www.upress.umn.edu

A Cataloging-in-Publication record for this book is available from the Library of Congress.

ISBN 978-1-5179-1136-2 (pb)
ISBN 978-1-5179-1198-0 (hc)

Printed in the United States of America on acid-free paper

The University of Minnesota is an equal-opportunity educator and employer.

30 29 28 27 26 25 24 23 22   10 9 8 7 6 5 4 3 2

El desarrollo es un viaje con más náufragos que navegantes.
Development is a voyage with more shipwrecks than navigators.

—Eduardo Galeano, *Las venas abiertas de América Latina* (1971)

¿En qué momento se había jodido [América Latina]?
At what precise moment had [Latin America] screwed itself up?

—Mario Vargas Llosa, *Conversación en la catedral* (1969)

Contents

Foreword xi
François R. Velde

Acknowledgments xiii

Detecting Fiscal-Monetary Causes of Inflation 1
Fernando Alvarez, Lars Peter Hansen, and Thomas J. Sargent

A Framework for Studying the Monetary and Fiscal History of Latin America 19
Timothy J. Kehoe, Juan Pablo Nicolini, and Thomas J. Sargent

Argentina

The History of Argentina 45
Francisco Buera and Juan Pablo Nicolini

Discussion of the History of Argentina 1 71
Guillermo Calvo

Discussion of the History of Argentina 2 75
Andrew Powell

Bolivia

The History of Bolivia 83
Timothy J. Kehoe, Carlos Gustavo Machicado, and José Peres-Cajías

Discussion of the History of Bolivia 127
Manuel Amador

Contents

Brazil

The History of Brazil. 133
Joao Ayres, Márcio Garcia, Diogo Guillen, and Patrick Kehoe

Discussion of the History of Brazil 1. 191
José A. Scheinkman

Discussion of the History of Brazil 2. 195
Teresa Ter-Minassian

Chile

The History of Chile 199
Rodrigo Caputo and Diego Saravia

Discussion of the History of Chile 231
Sebastian Edwards

Colombia

The History of Colombia 243
David Perez-Reyna and Daniel Osorio-Rodríguez

Discussion of the History of Colombia 271
Arturo José Galindo

Ecuador

The History of Ecuador 277
Simón Cueva and Julián P. Díaz

Discussion of the History of Ecuador 315
Alberto Martin

Mexico

The History of Mexico 323
Felipe Meza

Discussion of the History of Mexico 355
Alejandro Werner

Paraguay

The History of Paraguay 361
Carlos Javier Charotti, Carlos Fernández Valdovinos, and Felipe González Soley

Discussion of the History of Paraguay 1 387
Roberto Chang

Discussion of the History of Paraguay 2 391
Pablo Andrés Neumeyer

Peru

The History of Peru 401
César Martinelli and Marco Vega

Discussion of the History of Peru 1 435
Mark Aguiar

Discussion of the History of Peru 2 443
Saki Bigio

Uruguay

The History of Uruguay 451
Gabriel Oddone and Joaquín Marandino

Discussion of the History of Uruguay 1 479
Eduardo Fernández-Arias

Discussion of the History of Uruguay 2 485
Carlos A. Végh

Venezuela

The History of Venezuela 495
Diego Restuccia

Discussion of the History of Venezuela 1 525
Luigi Bocola

Discussion of the History of Venezuela 2 529
Fabrizio Perri

Contents

Lessons from the Monetary and Fiscal History of Latin America . . . 537
Carlos Esquivel, Timothy J. Kehoe, and Juan Pablo Nicolini

Contributors 567

Foreword

Era el solitario y lúcido espectador de un mundo multiforme,
instantáneo y casi intolerablemente preciso.
He was the solitary and lucid spectator of a multiform, instantaneous
and almost intolerably precise world.

—Borges, "Funes el memorioso"

Almost every word in Jorge Luis Borges's description of a man who cannot forget anything carries advice for those who want to learn from the past rather than merely chronicle it.

The title of this volume states its ambition and reveals its origin. Milton Friedman's famous history of the United States was monetary and so were many histories of other countries that it inspired. The work remains a classic, and this volume pays it due homage in inspiration and in method. The editors and authors are moved by a deep concern that prosperity has eluded Latin America and by a strong suspicion that macroeconomic policies are in part to blame.

The question is complex, and the first task is to assemble and organize the evidence. The contributors to this volume do so as social scientists, guided by theory but not blinded by it. As with Friedman, the work remains a history in which theory suggests what facts to look for and how to organize them. The process is one of selection and simplification, to make the world less multiform. But it cannot be one of reduction or obliteration: the goal is to bring the picture down to a tolerable level of precision and make the world less instantaneous.

As social scientists, we must believe that there is both accumulation and progress in ideas. The theory that guides this project shares deep insights with Friedman's work but also relies on what economists have developed in the decades since. This is a monetary *and fiscal* history. The government's budget constraint, a simple but powerful equation (if its terms are properly defined and measured), was imposed on each chapter. In that constraint, the title's two adjectives are yoked, and it becomes impossible to see one without looking for the other. This volume demonstrates how fruitful is that discipline, if sensibly abided.

At this stage, however, imposing more structure would be unwise. The facts do not speak for themselves, but they must speak first. Other ideas must be in our minds as we read this history, as themes ready to fall into consonance with it at various turns: uncertainty and how agents deal with it, the expectations or beliefs they form, the nature and timing of debt obligations, multiple equilibria lurking in the background. The introductory chapters should be carefully rehearsed and our minds readied.

Writing a *monetary and fiscal history* is in itself a first. But writing that of a *continent*? The project's leaders believe that, multiform as they are, the countries of Latin America are similar enough that their dissimilar histories will be revealing. Macroeconomists don't run experiments, quasi or otherwise: they spot patterns. When formulated with the underlying rigor of theory, the patterns can be described and shown to others. Then, even if we remain spectators, we need not be solitary.

But we want to be more than spectators. The editors' and authors' deep concern over the past is also a project for a better future, and their suspicion about policy's past role is also optimism about its future role. As social scientists, we must hope that ideas lead to progress in outcomes, even if learning from history makes us wonder at times how much learning shapes history.

François R. Velde
Federal Reserve Bank of Chicago
March 2019

The views presented here do not necessarily reflect those of the Federal Reserve of Chicago or the Federal Reserve System.

Acknowledgments

This project is the result of three shocks. The first one was in 1998 when the Inter-American Development Bank decided to fund a series of simultaneous studies on public debt for several Latin American countries under their Red de Centros research program. The study of Argentina was done by Paco Buera and Juanpa Nicolini, both at the Universidad Di Tella at the time. Their interest in the subject largely transcended the scope of the role of public debt as defined in that project, which was mostly descriptive. Their working paper became a first rough attempt to understand the macroeconomic history of Argentina as driven by the fiscal policies the country adopted in the last few decades, at a time when Argentina was already visibly walking toward one of the worst economic crises in its history.

The second shock was in 2006. Juanpa Nicolini was invited to discuss a paper by Tom Sargent, Noah Williams, and Tao Zha in which they estimated a learning model to study several hyperinflations in Latin America during the 1980s. In the paper, the authors chose to estimate the model using only price-level data for each country, disregarding data on monetary aggregates even though the additional data would have provided increased precision in the estimation. The main reason for that approach, the authors argued, was the lack of consistent, good-quality data for monetary aggregates. Out of those discussions with Tom, an idea was born: to make an effort to build a consistent data set for a few Latin American countries, using a common theory that could be used to understand the multiple macroeconomic crises that had plagued the region for decades.

The third shock occurred in 2009 during lunch at the Minneapolis Fed, where Juanpa mentioned the vague ideas discussed with Tom a few years before. His comments immediately caught the attention of Tim Kehoe, given his ever-present interest in Latin America and his experience as editor—together with Ed Prescott—of a book on great depressions of the twentieth century, published by the Federal Reserve Bank of Minneapolis.

Soon enough, the idea to host a conference at the Minneapolis Fed and discuss the history of several Latin American countries took shape, and Kei-Mu Yi, then research director, immediately supported it.

The conference took place in August 2010 and included the existing working paper for Argentina, plus drafts for Bolivia, Brazil, Ecuador, Mexico, Peru, and Venezuela. Tim got his hands dirty doing monetary policy analysis working with Carlos Gustavo Machicado in writing the first draft of the Bolivia paper.

In our view, the conference was a success. We were able to interest highly qualified economists to act as discussants, and the presentations and discussions generated lively and fruitful debates. Nevertheless, there was still much work to do. Most of the countries had major data problems, and more importantly, we had not managed to converge to a common conceptual framework. The conference was closer to a sequence of papers than to the systematic application of a common set of ideas to all the countries.

It became clear to us that we needed to strengthen the theory and to make sure that every case study applied it in the same way. On the other hand, we also needed to allow for enough flexibility so as to acknowledge episodes in which the data could not be explained by the theory. After a first pass, we borrowed from the macroeconomics literature and further specialized the theory to capture some of these apparently puzzling episodes. These multiple steps from theory to data and back to theory would take time, which we had, and money, which we did not.

Our search for funding was quickly over when we got in touch with Lars Peter Hansen, who at the time was the director of the Becker Friedman Institute (BFI) at the University of Chicago. The generosity and encouragement shown by Lars were his two most important contributions, and patience was a close third. Finishing the project took us at least twice the time we estimated initially, mostly because the iteration between sharpening the conceptual framework and applying it to the eleven countries became more interesting over time. At each iteration, our ambition would only grow. Soon enough, our relationship with the BFI started, and Fernando Alvarez joined efforts with Lars in helping us shape the project to its final form.

As part of that iteration, we organized a second conference, this time in Chicago, in April of 2014. At that time, we were able to incorporate a new country into the list: Chile. After that conference, we decided to organize one-day workshops in each of the participating countries. At each workshop, the case study for each country would be presented to an audience of local economists, academics, and former policy makers, who would act as discussants. We ran the first workshop at Universidad Di Tella in Buenos Aires in August 2015. Later that same year, we organized the workshops at the Universidad Católica Boliviana in La Paz, the Central Bank of Chile in Santiago, and the Pontifícia Universidade Católica in Rio de Janeiro.

In October 2015, we also held a conference in Barcelona, hosted by MOVE (Markets, Organizations and Votes in Economics), the Universitat Autònoma de Barcelona, and the Barcelona Graduate School of Economics, where we reviewed some of the country cases that needed more work and added three new countries: Colombia, Paraguay, and Uruguay.

During 2016, we organized the workshops at the Universidad Católica del Perú in Lima, the Banco de la República in Bogotá, the Central Bank of Uruguay in Montevideo, and the Central Bank of Paraguay in Asunción. Finally, during 2017, we organized the workshops at ITAM in Mexico, at Universidad de las Americas in Quito, and at the BFI in Chicago to discuss the case of Venezuela.

After a new round of revisions, we held a three-day conference during which all the cases were presented and discussed at the BFI in Chicago, in December of 2017. Three final conferences were held in 2018, at the Banco de México in June, at the Central Bank of Chile in August, and at the Inter-American Development Bank in September, to complete a final revision of some of the cases and to discuss the main lessons of the project.

In the last three years of the project, Carlos Esquivel provided outstanding research assistance to the point of becoming coauthor of the final chapter in this book. Funding for Carlos's efforts was generously provided by the Heller-Hurwicz Economics Institute at the University of Minnesota.

The BFI at the University of Chicago provided both funding and behind the scenes staff support for many of the conferences that were held to support this venture. Initially, the BFI staff support was overseen by Suzanne Riggle and later by Sam Ori, with the important direct staff inputs by Amy Lee Boonstra, and more recently, by Diana Petrova. In the latter stages of this project, Diana worked with the individual contributors of the various components of this volume to shepherd this project to completion and to make its contributions accessible to a broader community of scholars and central bank researchers. Joan Gieseke provided invaluable help editing all the chapters. Carlos Esquivel, then at the University of Minnesota, provided extensive support in generating the graphs and figures associated with the chapters and related discussions, as well as in converting the material into the appropriate formats. Karen Anderson, BFI's senior director of policy, communications, and external affairs, played a key role in overseeing the launch of the Monetary and Fiscal History of Latin America project website in 2018 along with Diana Petrova and Eric Hernandez, senior digital media manager, who worked on the content migration for this online repository to serve as a historical account of this multiyear project.

Finally, Tim Kehoe would like to thank his wife, Jeani, and Juanpa Nicolini would like to thank his wife, Anabella, for their encouragement and support.

We would also like to thank the discussants and organizers of all the conferences and local workshops:

For their participation in the Minneapolis conference of 2010, we thank Narayana Kocherlakota, Rodolfo Manuelli, Kjetil Storesletten, Lee Ohanian, Cristina Arellano, Harold Cole, Fabrizio Perri, and Luis Jácome.

For their participation in the Chicago conference of 2014, we thank Manuel Amador, Fernando Alvarez, Rodolfo Manuelli, Andrew Powell, Gerardo Della Paolera, Nancy Stokey, and Veronica Guerrieri.

For their participation in the Barcelona conference of 2015, we thank Albert Marcet, Fernando Broner, Roberto Chang, Alberto Martin, and Omar Licandro.

For their participation in the Chicago conference of 2017, we thank Marco Bassetto, Randy Kroszner, Manuel Amador, Enrique Mendoza, Rodolfo Manuelli, Saki Bigio, Mark Aguiar, José De Gregorio, Pedro Videla, Fabrizio Perri, Luigi Bocola, Andrew Powell, Ariel Burstein, Andy Neumeyer, Ricardo López Murphy, Marcelo Veracierto, Paulina Restrepo-Echavarria, Fernando Alvarez, Cristina Arellano, and François Velde.

For their participation in the Chile conference of 2018, we thank Joaquín Vial, Álvaro Saieh, Fernando Alvarez, Andy Neumeyer, José Scheinkman, Arnold Harberger, Andrés Velasco, Sara Calvo, Carlos Végh, and Guillermo Calvo.

For their participation in the Inter-American Development Bank conference of 2018, we thank Alejandro Izquierdo, Andrew Powell, Alejandro Werner, Joaquim Levy, Teresa Ter-Minassian, Carmen Reinhart, Miguel Castilla, Adrian Armas, Eduardo

Fernández-Arias, Carlos Végh, Eduardo Borensztein, Arturo Galindo, Leandro Gastón Andrian, Jorge Roldós, and Sebastián Edwards.

For their participation in the local workshop in Argentina, 2015, we thank Andy Neumeyer, Roberto Cortés Conde, Pablo Gerchunoff, Roque Fernández, José Luis Machinea, Mario Vicens, Pablo Guidotti, Daniel Artana, José María Fanelli, Gerardo Della Paolera, Domingo Cavallo, Carlos Alfredo Rodríguez, and Alieto Guadagni.

For their participation in the local workshop in Bolivia, 2015, we thank Gonzalo Chávez, Oscar Vega, Rolando Morales, Horst Grebe, Ivan Finot, Juan Antonio Morales, Juan Carlos Requena, Luis Carlos Jemio, Flavio Machicado, Armando Pinell, Fernando Candia, and Ramiro Cavero.

For their participation in the local workshop in Brazil, 2015, we thank Marcelo Abreu, Affonso Pastore, Claudio Jaloretto, Edmar Bacha, Gustavo Franco, Murilo Portugal, Alfonso Bevilaqua, Eduardo Loyo, Amaury Bier, Rogério Werneck, Pedro Malan, Pérsio Arida, and Tiago Berriel.

For their participation in the local workshop in Chile, 2015, we thank Rodrigo Vergara, Roberto Álvarez, Daniel Tapia de la Puente, Manuel Agosin, Raimundo Soto, Gabriel Palma, Rolf Lüders, Patricio Meller, and Felipe Morandé.

For their participation in the local workshop in Colombia, 2016, we thank Hernando Vargas, Daniel Osorio-Rodríguez, Fabio Sánchez, Hernán Rincón, Mauricio Avella Gómez, Roberto Junguito, Rudolf Hommes, Juan José Echavarria, Guillermo Perry, Miguel Urrutia, and Andrés Álvarez.

For their participation in the local workshop in Paraguay, 2016, we thank Carlos Rodríguez Báez, Alberto Cáceres Ferreira, José Cantero, Ovidio Otazú, Carlos Knapps, Reinaldo Penner, Blas Chamorro, Marcos Lezcano Bernal, Marciano Charotti, Roland Holst, Carlos Carvallo, Hugo Eligio Caballero, Aníbal Insfrán, Jorge Schreiner, Raúl Vera, Dionisio Coronel, Gabriel González, Álvaro Caballero Carrizosa, Hermes Gómez Ginard, Santiago Peña, Manuel Ferreira, Miguel Mora, César Barreto, Ernst Bergen, Alberto Acosta Garbarino, Jorge Corvalán, and José Molinas.

For their participation in the local workshop in Peru, 2016, we thank José Rodríguez, Efraín Gonzales de Olarte, Gonzalo Llosa, Bruno Seminario, Oscar Dancourt, Renzo Rossini, and Waldo Mendoza.

For their participation in the local workshop in Uruguay, 2016, we thank Julio de Brun, Ariel Davrieux, Carlos Sténeri, Alejandro Végh Villegas, Isaac Alfie, Alberto Bensión, Javier de Haedo, Luis Mosca, Mario Bergara, Andrés Masoller, Azucena Arbeleche, Fernando Barrán, and Pablo Rosselli.

For their participation in the local workshop in Ecuador, 2017, we thank Javier Díaz Cassou, Pablo Lucio Paredes, Jorge Gallardo, Joaquín Morillo, Vicente Albornoz, Jaime Morillo, Abelardo Pachano, Francisco Swett, Magdalena Barreiro, Pablo Better, Miguel Dávila, Augusto De La Torre, and Rodrigo Espinosa Bermeo.

For their participation in the local workshop in Mexico, 2017, we thank Diego Alejandro Domínguez Larrea, Enrique Cárdenas Sánchez, Ignacio Trigueros Legarreta, Germán Rojas Arredondo, Alejandro Hernández Delgado, Jesús Marcos Yacamán, Jaime Serra Puche, Manuel Sánchez González, Francisco Gil Díaz, and Manuel Ramos Francia.

For their participation in the local workshop to discuss Venezuela in Chicago, 2017, we thank Pedro Palma, Pablo Druck, Ramón Espinasa, Manuel Toledo, Omar Bello, Felipe Pérez, and José Pineda.

Finally, the Becker Friedman Institute would like to acknowledge the generous financial support we received for this project throughout the years from Edward R. Allen, AM '85, PhD '92, and Donald R. Wilson Jr., AB '88, which ultimately led to the publication of this book and furthered research on fiscal studies more generally. BFI could not possibly have published this volume summarizing the important contributions made during this multiyear project without their generous contributions.

We would also like to thank in advance the exceptional young scholars who will take on this important body of work in the future and use it as a resource to continue exploring the important fiscal and monetary interactions in Latin America, Central America, and the world. We are also immensely thankful to the University of Minnesota Press for taking on the publication of this project and bringing this volume to fruition.

Detecting Fiscal-Monetary Causes of Inflation

Fernando Alvarez
University of Chicago

Lars Peter Hansen
University of Chicago

Thomas J. Sargent
New York University and Hoover Institution

Introduction

Latin American countries have experimented with a wide variety of macroeconomic policies and have experienced diverse and sometimes adverse consequent outcomes. The Monetary and Fiscal History of Latin America (MFH) project has collected and organized systematic evidence consisting of comparable data sets from these varied historical experiences to construct a knowledge base for studying the origins and effects of alternative monetary and fiscal policies. Instances of these diverse policies were themselves caused by various political and economic events, so they can't easily be viewed as "experiments" purposefully conducted to learn the general equilibrium effects of alternative policies. Indeed, the study of macroeconomic policies explores not only their direct effects on individuals' behaviors and their indirect effects on altered market prices but also the responses of future policies to changes created by the policies that preceded them. Such interactions are central focuses of policy analysis.

While many economists emphasize the importance of evidence-based policy analysis, the evidence won't speak for itself; we require a conceptual framework to organize and interpret evidence. Decades ago, Koopmans (1947), while at the Cowles Commission at the University of Chicago, wrote "Measurement without Theory," a critical review of extensive research by Burns and Mitchell (1946) that measured business cycles from macroeconomic data. Koopman's review sparked a debate (for instance, see Vining 1949) that continues to this day as we struggle to put data science and machine learning methods to scientific use. Marschak (1953), Hurwicz (1966), and Lucas (1976) are classic expositions of the case for using structural econometric models to do policy analysis.

The architects of the MFH project, Tim Kehoe and Juan Pablo Nicolini, are keenly aware of the interplay between evidence and theory. They aimed to design the project to facilitate the use of multicountry data to compare and contrast alternative models of fiscal and monetary interactions.

As macroeconomists, we find this study to be particularly promising because of the varied institutional structures, policy experiences, and macroeconomic outcomes presented. The countries have different degrees of separation between responsibilities for designing and executing monetary and fiscal policies. These separation conventions influence how these policies are ultimately coordinated and the extent to which one policy authority dominates the other. Such institutional conventions matter for alternative models of macroeconomic impacts. Whether fiscal or monetary policies are dominant or the extent to which they act in unison with common ambitions can have important consequences for macroeconomic performance. Studies like the MFH project promote understanding of the impacts of monetary-fiscal policy interactions.

Intellectual History

As background, we recall how Milton Friedman encouraged his students Eugene Lerner (1956) and Phillip Cagan (1956) to study big inflations that accompanied the Civil War in the United States and that followed both World War I and World War II.[1] Friedman recognized that these episodes contained sources of data variations that would let Lerner and Cagan isolate fundamental monetary-fiscal causes of inflation and private behavioral responses to it that can be confounded by many other forces that also affect the price level. Thus Friedman and his students aimed to sidestep the complex interactions of monetary and fiscal policy and avoid taking account of various general equilibrium effects by focusing on data for which monetary policy would dominate macroeconomic effects.

Specifically, Friedman's students sought

1. a single behavioral relationship—an aggregate demand function for money linking real balances inversely to an expected rate of inflation,
2. measures of the supply of nominal money balances, and
3. links between time series of measured inflation and an estimate of the public's expected rate of inflation suitable for plugging into the demand function for real balances.

Friedman's hunch was that the episodes studied by Lerner and Cagan could be treated as though they were "natural experiments." Specifically, explosive money supply series were "uncaused events," the sources of which need not be analyzed in order to understand the main force driving the price level and real balances. During the episodes studied by Lerner and Cagan, the three items on Friedman's list would overwhelm a long list of confounding forces that in tranquil times also affect the price level and make the quantity-theoretic sources of inflation more difficult to detect.

The MFH project led by Kehoe and Nicolini aims to extend the quantity-theoretic tradition pursued by Friedman and his students in ways that can help us understand the histories of inflation in a set of Latin American countries. All the countries studied experienced a variety of inflationary episodes, though usually at rates substantially below those in the short European hyperinflation episodes studied by Cagan.[2] And while the three identification pillars of Friedman's students' analyses play roles in these new studies, variations in the rates of money creation and inflation are sufficiently lower that other forces confound their influences. The studies in the MFH project thus also pay attention to other data that the researchers hope will allow them to detect those other causes of inflation.

Explicitly dynamic equilibrium analyses of economies are vital for understanding how macroeconomic policies operate. The analyses avoid the "measurement without theory" criticism stated by Koopmans. While this approach makes macroeconomic policy analysis challenging, the results can be enlightening. We should not expect the data and analyses from this project to settle all modeling and measurement challenges, although the authors and architects of the study have taken important steps forward.

The main hypothesis explored by Kehoe and Nicolini is that sustained inflation rates, as opposed to short bursts of hyperinflation, are outcomes of particular monetary and fiscal regimes and the associated (perhaps rational) expectations about future policy actions that they cause. This is what led Kehoe and Nicolini to stress a common measurement of the consolidated budget constraint faced by monetary and fiscal authorities, together with the institutional backgrounds in which they are managed. Importantly, interrelated monetary and fiscal policies sometimes lead to indeterminate outcomes in the form of multiple equilibria that offer potential sources of variations in macroeconomic outcomes. One example is that economies can be pulled in different directions at different points in time. For example, Sargent (1999) and Sargent, Williams, and Zha (2009) illustrated how a multiplicity of self-confirming equilibria in conjunction with an adaptive learning mechanism present a dynamic pull toward and escape from these equilibria. Finally, a point that is usually deemphasized or ignored in models in the rational expectations tradition is that people inside economic models (e.g., consumers, entrepreneurs, and even policy makers) are exposed to macroeconomic ambiguity as they wrestle with uncertain policies. (For example, see the discussion in Hansen 2014.) Sometimes adaptive learning is motivated by agents' awareness of potential model misspecifications. It is worth noting that "control theory" counterparts can also be used to understand how people inside our models perceive the complex uncertainty that they confront and that affects both markets and policy making. We will elaborate on some existing work that features adaptive learning as a way to model potentially shifting environments.

This introduction presents and explores a list of theories about forces that help us understand equilibrium responses to alternative macroeconomic policy configurations. To interpret evidence, we find it compelling to push beyond the identification approach used in the empirical monetarist approach of Friedman and his former students Cagan and Lerner. This approach is needed to refine inferences about those basic forces to be drawn from the types of episodes studied by the team of researchers contributing to the MFH project. In so doing, model builders and econometricians are compelled to

1. refine models of expectations,
2. make components endogenous that Friedman and his colleagues took to be exogenous, and
3. add more "realistic" components of government budget constraints, such as risk-free real debt, risk-free nominal debt, and defaultable debt.

Challenges to "Exogenous" Money Supply

In this section, we review three empirical-econometric paths that refined and extended the money demand model used in the classic studies by Friedman and his former students.

BROADENING THE MEASUREMENT OF MONEY

Encouraged by Friedman and others, an extensive empirical literature refined theoretical specifications and estimates of the demand for money. An empirical challenge in such studies is how to construct the most appropriate counterpart to "money." The aim has been to produce a measure of money that discovers the most "stable" demand for money function. Advances in transactions technologies have created close substitutes for cash in its transactional role. There were two research responses to these developments. One sought to broaden the definition of money, while the other substantially reduced the role of money in many macroeconomic models applied to developed economies.

Very recently, Lucas and Nicolini (2015) and Benati et al. (2016) embraced the first perspective and argued for a long-run stable demand for money by adjusting the measure of money based in part on regulatory considerations. For the United States, Lucas and Nicolini modified the M1 measure to include money market accounts, while Benati et al. found that the standard definition sufficed for a stable long-run demand for money function for many other countries. Inventing a monetary aggregate leading to a stable long-run demand for money function potentially inserts interesting additional linkages between money demand and monetary policy. While Lucas and Nicolini (2015) dismiss this as a serious concern for M1 or their modified version of it, we remain open to this notion and see endogenous responses as interesting in their own right and potentially important quantitatively. Moreover, Lucas and Nicolini's use of low-frequency characterizations would seem to put aside the notion of using such broader definitions of money for high-frequency fine-tuning of monetary policy.[3]

DETECTING DYNAMIC FEEDBACKS

A second refinement has its origins in the applied time series to empirical macroeconomics that traces back to Yule (1927), Slutsky (1927), and, importantly, Frisch (1933) in his research on "impulse and propagation." Subsequently, Sims (1980) and others saw the importance of extending time series methods to multivariate settings through what are referred to as vector autoregression (VAR) methods. Early research in the VAR tradition discovered that the notion of an exogenous money supply specification was untenable in postwar data. Sims (1972) had previously linked the exogeneity of money to Granger's notion of causality in a dynamic setting. But by extending a bivariate analysis of money and income to a larger collection of variables represented as a VAR, the endogeneity of money became expressed in the VAR system as feedback effects from other variables, such as short-term interest rates, that had been omitted in the bivariate analysis. These analyses used post–World War II data and were outside the realm of hyperinflations. By emphasizing the importance of dynamic feedbacks among variables, this empirical finding undermined the practice of estimating money demand via a simple single equation time series regression. This evidence was from post–World War II economies in which inflationary episodes were very modest in comparison to the hyperinflation episodes studied by Cagan (1956) and Lerner (1956).

EMBRACING RATIONAL EXPECTATIONS

A third refinement emerged from reassessing the econometric specification of Cagan's original model (Cagan 1956). His model featured (1) a demand function for real balances, linking real balances to expected inflation, and (2) an equation linking the expected rate of inflation to a geometric average of current and past inflation (adaptive expectations). Cagan took the money supply as exogenous. This ruled out feedback effects that the previously mentioned VAR literature subsequently sought to characterize. In extending Cagan's analysis, Sargent and Wallace (1973) and Sargent (1977) found an alternative rationale for refining the exogeneity restriction by asking under what circumstances Cagan's specification of private-sector beliefs would be rational. By solving the implied inverse optimal prediction problem, Sargent and Wallace were led to a money supply process in which the process for money depended on past inflation, violating the Granger-Sims time series notion of exogeneity. In their specification, the only variable needed to forecast future inflation is current and past inflation, not money supply. This prediction-theoretic endogeneity of money could be only loosely motivated by saying that "maybe the feedback from inflation to money creation" somehow reflected the workings of a government budget constraint that made money creation endogenous. This thought can be viewed as leading to theoretical advances that involved adding economic forces to make money creation endogenous.

By looking at the relationships between monetary and fiscal policy from three different vantage points, these studies represent a central theme of the MFH project.

Inflation Theories under Cagan Demand

We now explore some initial extensions of the Friedman-Cagan money demand approach with explicit fiscal-monetary interactions. To begin, suppose that the government budget constraint is financed entirely by printing money. This happened to be one of Friedman's recommendations for coordinating monetary and fiscal policy (see Friedman 1948).

Interestingly, Friedman wrote that proposal a few years before the accord between the Treasury and the Federal Reserve that granted the Federal Reserve independence from the Treasury. Friedman's proposal recommends complete fiscal dominance over monetary policy. Within such a monetary-fiscal setup, we explore alternative ways of modeling private-sector beliefs.

SENSITIVITY TO EXPECTATIONS

Sargent and Wallace (1987) and Imrohoroglu (1993) explored the implications of rational expectations for a fiscal version of a Cagan-type model. The models have a continuum of equilibria, including many with sunspots. Nevertheless, data on money creation and inflation strongly overidentify free parameters, including one that indexes which, if any, sunspot equilibrium prevails. Imrohoroglu (1993) extracted estimates from the German hyperinflation data by using the method of maximum likelihood. Looking across the multiplicity of equilibria, we see that two types have attracted special interest—namely, "stationary" ones on each side of the Laffer curve in the inflation tax rate. Of particular interest is that rational expectations dynamics can drive the economic system toward a steady state on the bad side of a Laffer curve—that is, toward the stationary perfect foresight equilibrium that has the higher steady-state inflation rate. This outcome is disturbing because the comparative dynamics at that steady state imply that a *higher* sustained deficit financed by money creation is associated with lower steady-state inflation. That finding belies the "old-time religion" that asserts that bigger deficits financed by money creation lead to higher inflation. This is a rather dramatic illustration of how interactions between monetary-fiscal policy and private-sector expectations formation play a prominent, and in this case surprising, role in determining inflation.

Bruno and Fischer (1990) studied inflation dynamics in a similar model but under Cagan-style adaptive expectations. By altering the assumption about how the private sector forms beliefs, they found that the dynamic economic system, absent uncertainty, always converged to a perfect foresight steady state in which inflation is on the *good* side of the Laffer curve. Thus their findings resurrected the old-time religion by departing from rational expectations along transition paths. This line of research illustrates how private-sector expectations play a critical role in determining the manner in which monetary and fiscal policies, as intermediated through private-sector expectations, jointly affect inflation. These contributions also opened the door to studies that investigate how more flexible models of learning affect inflation as well as real variables, the topic we turn to next.

ADAPTIVE LEARNING

Researchers probed the stability of rational expectations under least squares learning. The resulting approach is an example of what Bray and Kreps (1987) call learning *about* an equilibrium in contrast to learning *within* an equilibrium. Adaptive versions of least squares learning allow discounting past observations as a flexible way to cope with possible changes over time in an economic environment. The resulting equation systems are examples of so-called self-referential systems in which behavior today depends on beliefs about where the system will be in the future. This structure provided a framework for studying the stability of a rational expectations equilibrium. Within this framework, Marcet and Sargent (1989a) showed that under some regularity conditions, forces push the dynamical economic system toward the rational expectations equilibria, where convergence is punctuated with infrequent expectations-driven escapes toward other belief-outcome combinations. Marcet and Sargent (1989b) applied this approach to the study of hyperinflations in Cagan-type models with 100 percent deficit monetization. Like Bruno and Fischer (1990), Marcet and Sargent (1989b) found environments in which outcomes converged to a rational expectations equilibrium on the good side of the Laffer curve in the inflation tax rate. Technically, the system's "mean dynamics" (the dynamics averaged over the contributions from shocks) drive it toward this good outcome. But they also found positive probability "escape routes" in which there occur expectations-driven explosions in inflation not driven by money-creation-financed deficits.

Marcet and Sargent (1989b) noted that what they call a "projection facility" is needed to push the system back into the region of the good Laffer equilibrium. To Marcet and Sargent, the explosive inflation escape dynamics are a technical annoyance that they wanted to sidestep. But for Marcet and Nicolini (2003), those explosive escape paths provided a tool that could help in understanding the puzzling episodes in Latin American inflation histories in which inflation paths seemed to come unhinged from money-growth causes. Specifically, Marcet and Nicolini added an economic interpretation to Marcet and Sargent's "projection facility." In particular, Marcet and Nicolini interpreted this facility as a form of direct policy actions that reset expected inflation via exchange-rate interventions or price controls. These interventions are all cosmetic in the sense that they leave unchanged the government deficit to be financed by money creation.

Marcet and Nicolini (2003) used a calibration strategy to partition stabilizations in several Latin American episodes into ones that resulted from fundamental corrections—associated with reductions in the government deficit to be financed by money creation—and others resulting from cosmetic measures that left the government deficit unchanged. Sargent, Williams, and Zha (2009) extended this approach by using a maximum likelihood strategy to estimate a hidden Markov version of the Marcet and Nicolini model and to infer Markov movements in the government deficit, treated as a hidden state. In this way, they inferred whether various inflation explosions and stabilizations were driven by movements in fundamentals or by escape dynamics and subsequent cosmetic (and necessarily temporary) stabilizations.

Overall, this literature exposes the sensitivity of inflation dynamics to seemingly minor but sensible relaxations of pure rational expectations. The least squares dynamics involve expectations that are typically "wrong" only in subtle and hard-to-detect ways. This approach does not, however, allow for investors (or policy makers) to express aversion to potential misspecifications. Amplifying agents' reactions to concerns about those misspecifications could have an important impact on market and social valuation, an important topic that future research should explore.

Models without Full Debt Monetization

In the preceding models, government deficits are financed entirely by money creation. This structure serves as a pedagogically revealing example of the interplay between monetary and fiscal policy, but it is too special a case for understanding macroeconomic policies and their outcomes in many countries at many times. The unpleasant monetarist arithmetic of Sargent and Wallace (1981) adds one-period government debt to a model with perfect foresight and a demand for real balances like Cagan's. This simple setting frames the need to coordinate a monetary policy that determines a rate of money creation process with a fiscal policy that determines a net-of-interest government deficit process. Because seigniorage is a source of real government revenues and hence affects the equilibrium present value of these revenues, the "independence" of monetary authorities is a fiction (or said more politely, a "convention"). Sargent and Wallace stated conditions on fiscal policy and equilibrium real rates of interest under which a monetary authority could fight inflation in the short run only by making it worse in the long run.

Sargent and Wallace's unpleasant arithmetic also opened the door to a "fiscal theory of the price level" developed subsequently by Sims (1994), Woodford (1995), Leeper (1991), and others. (See Leeper and Leith [2016] for a comprehensive survey and Loyo [1999] for application to Brazilian inflationary episodes.) In a simple instance, imagine an environment in which real discount factors (potentially stochastic) are determined by an external economy and in which a real net-of-interest government surplus series is specified exogenously. The real value of debt is pinned down by a present-value relation. Since nominal debt is predetermined, the nominal price follows from a formula for the equilibrium present-value relation. This gives a rather stark example of the impact of fiscal policy on price determination. Of course, this is a (typically too) simple specification of the dynamic economic system. More generally, we expect more endogeneity, and this present-value relation is one among a system of equations that must hold in equilibrium.[4]

As in the example economies with full monetization, there is a multiplicity of equilibria, and the details of the monetary and fiscal rules matter and can appear as alternative types of regimes in which either monetary policy or fiscal policy dominates. By allowing for more than one-period debt, Cochrane (2001) explored policy ramifications for the full term structure. Recently, Chen, Leeper, and Leith (2015) and Bianchi and Ilut (2017) contributed an econometric exploration of regime-shift models between so-called fiscal dominance and monetary dominance. As an alternative, employing the Marcet and Sargent (1989a) type approach, in which the private sector embraces adaptive learning, opens the door to expectations-based escape dynamics with different forces pushing toward alternative equilibria.

Overall, these models point out the potential importance of the rules of engagement between fiscal and monetary authorities, as well as the crucial role of expectations formation in determining macroeconomic outcomes. They further demonstrate the need to study monetary and fiscal history together, as well as the value of a common measurement framework for the interpretation of the varied economic experiences in Latin America.

Models with Risky Nominal Government Debt

Pushing fiscal policy to the forefront puts a focus on the tools and consequences of debt management. To frame this discussion, we start with the classic benchmark model of Lucas and Stokey (1983) describing an optimal policy analysis under commitment when there exists a rich (complete) set of financial markets. Lucas and Stokey explored monetary-fiscal interactions in several revealing ways. Parts of the paper are tied to the Ramsey enterprise of constructing an optimal monetary-fiscal policy mix under well-posed rules of the game. The model has become a standard reference point for analyzing the consequences of risky government debt and for demonstrating how inflation can make nominal government debt mimic risky real government debt when managed appropriately. But because they recover a version of a Friedman rule of a zero nominal interest rate as a Ramsey policy, Lucas and Stokey's normative analysis requires modification in developing the positive description needed to understand various Latin American high-inflation episodes.

Extensions of potential value for interpreting evidence include

1. introducing explicit forms of market incompleteness,
2. allowing for default, and
3. adding tractable forms of heterogeneity across sectors, external investors, and individuals within the countries under investigation.

Such extensions put inflation and deflation into the arsenal that a Ramsey planner could use to redistribute among nominal debtors and creditors in response to macro-shocks. Moreover, the planner could denominate debt in either local or foreign currency as part of the policy design.[5]

SOVEREIGN DEFAULTS

Models of sovereign debt retreat from a complete markets specification and build on the insight that partial defaults provide possibly useful state contingency as part of the government's debt. Models in the Eaton and Gersovitz (1981) and Arellano (2008) tradition solve Ramsey plans in which a benevolent government chooses if and when to default. In these models, governments honor their debts only when they want to. To make governments want to honor their debts, the model builder adds adverse consequences in the form of punishments that creditors impose on the government in the event of a default.[6] Specifications of punishments are important determinants of the quantitative implications of these models. Attempts have been made to directly measure costs that creditors impose on governments for defaulting, as surveyed by Tomz and Wright (2013) and more recently by Hébert and Schreger (2017). These models typically deliver unique processes of endogenous sovereign default premia that can be informative in calibration.

MULTIPLE EQUILIBRIA WITH SOVEREIGN DEFAULT

In models of multiple equilibria with distinct default premia, high default premia worsen a government's fiscal prospects by augmenting its interest burden (via a sophisticated kind of unpleasant arithmetic), thereby increasing the probabilities of default. Low default premia, on the other hand, ease a government's fiscal situation and make default less likely. An early example with such forces is Calvo (1988), who analyzes both outright defaults and implicit defaults induced by large inflationary episodes. Ayres et al. (2018) further explore the role of expectations in sovereign defaults. Cole and Kehoe (2000), who presented a fully dynamic version of a related problem, emphasize coordination problems associated with rolling over short-term debts. Chang and Velasco (2001) analyze a default model with a different sort of coordination problem, one driven by the potential illiquidity of banks, as in a classic Diamond and Dybvig (1983) setup. A growing literature explores alternative justifications for default, an understanding of which seems of vital importance in interpreting the varied experiences in Latin America.

DEFAULTS AND TERM STRUCTURE

While the contributions of Calvo (1988), Cole and Kehoe (2000), and Chang and Velasco (2001) all emphasize the perils of rolling over short-term debt, in practice there is typically a nontrivial term structure of outstanding government debts. Governments face trade-offs between issuing long- or short-term debts that interact with potential consequences of default. Quantitative analyses that have investigated these trade-offs include Hatchondo and Martinez (2009) and Arellano and Ramanarayanan (2012), who study hedging benefits brought by short- versus long-term debt. Aguiar et al. (2019) provide a theoretical framework for characterizing these trade-offs and their impact on nominal prices.

Besides being realistic, long-term debt introduces other possibilities. Multiple equilibria can emerge, including ones in which debt crises unfold gradually (see Lorenzoni and Werning 2013). Also, there is a term structure of default premia for bonds that is affected by variability in the underlying nominal interest rates, as featured in Tourre (2017). The term structure of default premia for fixed-rate bonds became particularly relevant for sovereign debt issued under the Brady Plan and had important implications for decisions to default on short-term obligations. For several chapters of the MFH, a salient instance was the rise in U.S. interest rates in the early 1980s, which arguably contributed to the wave of defaults in Latin American countries.

Much of the literature on defaults was motivated by events that occurred in Latin American countries during the time span of the MFH project. With better and more comparable data, we now have a better opportunity to assess the quantitative impacts of default through the lenses of competing and complementary models. The forward-looking nature of sovereign default and the potential for multiplicity in equilibria open the door to more in-depth probes into the impact of expectations and the social and private consequences of model uncertainty.

SUDDEN STOPS AND BALANCE OF PAYMENT CRISES

Guillermo Calvo (1998) made popular the term "sudden stops" to refer to rapid changes in capital flows to developing countries that are associated with large contractions in economic activity. Sudden stops are different from, but related to, traditional balance of payments crises. During both types of events, there are nominal depreciations of currencies and reversals of current accounts; however, the two events are set off by different triggers. Sudden stops have spawned an array of models that emphasize diverse mechanisms, all of which are relevant for understanding several episodes studied in the MFH.[7] Mendoza (2010) is an early example of a model of sudden stops induced by exogenous changes in borrowing limits. The observed countercyclicality of the current account motivated Aguiar and Gopinath (2007) to use a version of the Eaton and Gersovitz (1981)–Arellano (2008) models in which the volatility of trend growth is a critical cause of the extreme fluctuations found in emerging economies. The observed sudden stops also inform studies of macroprudential policy options, as in Bianchi and Mendoza (2018). Atkeson (1991) authored a notable model of sudden stops and repudiation risk by deploying tools from the theory of optimal recursive contracts. His model offers a sense in which sudden stops are part of an optimal arrangement for disciplining the allocation of resources in the face of information and enforcement problems that affect public borrowing.

Bailouts, either contemporaneous or anticipated, provide a link between fiscal and monetary policy distinct from the ones that occur during balance of payments crises. This topic arises naturally when interpreting some of the MFH evidence. Burnside, Eichenbaum, and Rebelo (2001) studied bailouts in the context of the Asian currency crises that occurred in 1998, and Schneider and Tornell (2004) investigated how sectoral differences and bailout policies contribute to sudden-stop crises.

Phillips Curve Dynamics

The classic Friedman-Lerner-Cagan studies shut down Phillips curve dynamics by taking aggregate supplies of goods and aggregate employment as exogenous. A number of the subsequent contributions mentioned previously followed in this tradition by shutting down exploitable or permanent trade-offs between inflation and real outputs (e.g., the unpleasant monetarist arithmetic of Sargent and Wallace [1981] and the Lucas and Stokey [1983] investigation of state-contingent debt and taxation). Macroeconomic analyses of developed economies often embrace "sticky prices" to activate exploitable Phillips curve dynamics that at low or moderate inflation rates disguise the inflationary forces isolated by Cagan and Lerner.

Most current research modeling of Phillips curve dynamics in developed economies relies on Calvo's (1983) exogenously specified price-setting mechanism. Imposing this structure dramatically simplifies calculations, often with little sacrifice of insights that would come from a deeper theory of price stickiness. Nevertheless, in the case of persistent high inflation or large nominal shocks, Calvo's modeling device can have quantitatively counterfactual implications. Moreover, the Calvo price-setting Poisson coefficients cannot plausibly be transported across economies with very different monetary-fiscal policies. Embracing a more primitive starting point to model price setting opens the door to a better understanding of economies that experience higher levels of inflation. An attractive alternative is to use a model price setting with menu costs, as in Sheshinski and Weiss (1977), or its general equilibrium version with idiosyncratic shocks, as in Golosov and Lucas (2007). Alvarez et al. (2019) obtain theoretical predictions for this class of models and showed that they are in line with data for large inflation rates, including findings from earlier research by Gagnon (2009) based on evidence from Mexico. Exploring the conceptual underpinnings of price sluggishness promises to provide a unified framework for better understanding the evidence and its implications across the varied inflationary experiences in Latin America as studied in the MFH.

Putting Things Together

Cagan (1956) was able to do a good job of explaining a set of spectacular hyperinflations by using a simple model. Relative to Cagan's model, we have added complications that seem vital for understanding Latin American macroeconomic histories. Because the monetary-fiscal events studied by the Kehoe-Nicolini team are less extreme than those studied by Cagan, the Kehoe-Nicolini team cannot neglect the confounding forces that Cagan could ignore. Prime among these are government debts. For example, by the time the German hyperinflation got rolling, the German government had defaulted on virtually all its domestic debt, so for better or worse, Cagan could ignore government debt.

For many of the episodes studied by the Kehoe-Nicolini team, government debts and how and whether they were paid, rescheduled, or defaulted on are big parts of the story. But limitations on how governments and central banks account for government debts present substantial measurement difficulties. The budget constraints of macroeconomic theory are about government debts that are priced to market, while government accounts typically report par values and do a poor job of accounting for coupon payments, let alone default premia. Even the best government accounting systems, such as those of the United States and the United Kingdom, report measures of government debt that can deviate markedly from the objects in a macroeconomist's government budget constraint (for example, see Hall and Sargent 2011).

Institutions delimiting the conduct of monetary and fiscal policy are vital to understanding the origins of inflation and its macroeconomic consequences. Societies are prone to revisit arrangements that set the scope of central bank independence, so these arrangements are naturally subject to controversy and stress. Former President Trump's 2019 public comments about the conduct of monetary policy in the United States are only one example among many instances. Arrangements, rules, and their evolution have contributed to successes in the control of inflation in countries such as Brazil, Chile, Colombia, and Paraguay as well as to the failures in Argentina and Venezuela.

The aim of our project has been to compare arrangements and outcomes across countries, to recognize patterns, and to generalize; in doing so we have necessarily ignored some important country-specific details and episodes. We strive to describe different regimes using a framework within which policy was conducted. On the other hand, there is scope for future research to probe deeper into the determinants of the different policy regimes. We see ours as a deliberate and defensible choice, but we acknowledge that it leaves many gaps. Indeed, we see this project as opening the door to investigations that will widen our appreciation of a broader set of long- and short-term economic and political forces that account for and explain experiences of the countries we have studied and, we hope, of other countries too.

While the MFH project offers valuable new data, it does not justify a "just let the data speak for themselves" approach. It is important to use formal models to interpret evidence and reason about the consequences of alternative government policies. While the modeling advances surveyed here are promising, their quantitative and empirical importance remains to be investigated fully. Thus the chapters in this volume provide information and ideas that promise not only to enhance our understanding of past Latin American experiences but, going forward, to evaluate more generally the relevance of alternative models and to suggest improvements in those models.

Notes

We wish to thank Juan Pablo Nicolini for helpful feedback on this essay.

1 These essays are two of the chapters in *Studies in the Quantity Theory of Money* (Friedman 1956).

2 Sargent (1982) subsequently used these same episodes to investigate how commitment to fiscal balance without seigniorage could end hyperinflations.

3 Lucas and Nicolini's focus on long-run relations is reminiscent of Friedman's characterization of the "long and variable" lags in the monetary transmission mechanisms about which he was cautious to theorize or estimate (see Friedman 1960).

4 This "in equilibrium qualification" skirts some important considerations. A more primitive analysis begins by thinking formally about a game between monetary and fiscal authorities and with rules of the game spelled out that limit the strategic

interactions. See Bassetto (2002) for such a formulation and its implications.

5 Interestingly, a substantial part of Lucas and Stokey (1983) investigates how to implement the Ramsey policy without commitment to a tax policy, provided that there is no default and that a debt management authority appropriately chooses maturities of both nominal and real debts. Their analysis also has interesting implications for the choice of debt maturities denominated in different currencies.

6 In these models, the government is a principal acting as an agent for its citizens.

7 Models range from the first-generation currency attack models of Salant and Henderson (1978) and Krugman (1979) that emphasize the inconsistency of fiscal and monetary policy (e.g., pegging a nominal exchange rate while expanding central bank financing of the Treasury) to the purely belief-driven balance of payments crises described by Obstfeld (1986).

References

Aguiar, Mark, Manuel Amador, Hugo Hopenhayn, and Ivan Werning. 2019. "Take the Short Route: Equilibrium Default and Debt Maturity." *Econometrica* 87 (2): 423–62.

Aguiar, Mark, and Gita Gopinath. 2007. "Emerging Market Business Cycles: The Cycle Is the Trend." *Journal of Political Economy* 115 (1): 69–102.

Alvarez, Fernando, Martin Beraja, Martín Gonzalez-Rozada, and Pablo Andrés Neumeyer. 2019. "From Hyperinflation to Stable Prices: Argentina's Evidence on Menu Cost Models." *Quarterly Journal of Economics* 134 (1): 451–505.

Arellano, Cristina. 2008. "Default Risk and Income Fluctuations in Emerging Economies." *American Economic Review* 98 (3): 690–712.

Arellano, Cristina, and Ananth Ramanarayanan. 2012. "Default and the Maturity Structure in Sovereign Bonds." *Journal of Political Economy* 120 (2): 187–232.

Atkeson, Andrew. 1991. "International Lending with Moral Hazard and Risk of Repudiation." *Econometrica* 59 (4): 1069–89.

Ayres, Joao, Gaston Navarro, Juan P. Nicolini, and Pedro Teles. 2018. "Sovereign Default: The Role of Expectations." *Journal of Economic Theory* 175 (C): 803–12.

Bassetto, Marco. 2002. "A Game-Theoretic View of the Fiscal Theory of the Price Level." *Econometrica* 70 (6): 2167–95.

Benati, Luca, Robert E. Lucas Jr., Juan P. Nicolini, and Warren Weber. 2016. "International Evidence on Long Run Money Demand." Working paper 22475, National Bureau of Economic Research, Cambridge, Mass.

Bianchi, Francesco, and Cosmin Ilut. 2017. "Monetary/Fiscal Policy Mix and Agent's Beliefs." *Review of Economic Dynamics* 26:113–39.

Bianchi, Javier, and Enrique G. Mendoza. 2018. "Optimal Time-Consistent Macroprudential Policy." *Journal of Political Economy* 126 (2): 588–634.

Bray, Margaret, and David M. Kreps. 1987. "Rational Learning and Rational Expectations." In *Arrow and the Accent of Modern Economic Theory*, edited by George R. Feiwel, 597–625. New York: New York University Press.

Bruno, Michael, and Stanley Fischer. 1990. "Seigniorage, Operating Rules, and the High Inflation Trap." *Quarterly Journal of Economics* 105 (2): 353–74.

Burns, Arthur F., and Wesley C. Mitchell. 1946. *Measuring Business Cycles.* New York: National Bureau of Economic Research.

Burnside, Craig, Martin Eichenbaum, and Sergio Rebelo. 2001. "Prospective Deficits and the Asian Currency Crisis." *Journal of Political Economy* 109 (2): 1155–97.

Cagan, Phillip. 1956. "The Monetary Dynamics of Hyperinflation." In *Studies in the Quantity Theory of Money*, edited by Milton Friedman, 25–117. Economics Research Studies of the Economics Research Center of the University of Chicago. Chicago: University of Chicago Press.

Calvo, Guillermo A. 1983. "Staggered Prices in a Utility-Maximizing Framework." *Journal of Monetary Economics* 12 (3): 383–98.

Calvo, Guillermo A. 1988. "Servicing the Public Debt: The Role of Expectations." *American Economic Review* 78 (4): 647–61.

———. 1998. "Capital Flows and Capital-Market Crises: The Simple Economics of Sudden Stops." *Journal of Applied Economics* 1 (1): 35–54.

Chang, Roberto, and Andres Velasco. 2001. "A Model of Financial Crises in Emerging Markets." *Quarterly Journal of Economics* 116 (2): 489–517.

Chen, Xiaoshan, Eric M. Leeper, and Campbell Leith. 2015. "US Monetary and Fiscal Policies—Conflict or Cooperation?" Technical report, University of Glasgow, Glasgow.

Cochrane, John H. 2001. "Long-Term Debt and Optimal Policy in the Fiscal Theory of the Price Level." *Econometrica* 69 (1): 69–116.

Cole, Harold L., and Timothy J. Kehoe. 2000. "Self-Fulfilling Debt Crises." *Review of Economic Studies* 67 (1): 91–116.

Diamond, Douglas W., and Philip H. Dybvig. 1983. "Bank Runs, Deposit Insurance, and Liquidity." *Journal of Political Economy* 91 (3): 401–19.

Eaton, Jonathan, and Mark Gersovitz. 1981. "Debt with Potential Repudiation: Theoretical and Empirical Analysis." *Review of Economic Studies* 48 (2): 289–309.

Friedman, Milton. 1948. "A Monetary and Fiscal Framework for Economic Stability." *American Economic Review* 38 (3): 245–64.

———, ed. 1956. *Studies in the Quantity Theory of Money.* Economics Research Studies of the Economics Research Center of the University of Chicago. Chicago: University of Chicago Press.

———. 1960. *A Program for Monetary Stability.* New York: Fordham University Press.

Frisch, Ragnar. 1933. "Propagation Problems and Impulse Problems in Dynamic Economics." In *Economic Essays in Honour of Gustav Cassel*, edited by Karin Koch, 171–205. London: Allen and Unwin.

Gagnon, Etienne. 2009. "Price Setting during Low and High Inflation: Evidence from Mexico." *Quarterly Journal of Economics* 124 (3): 1221–63.

Golosov, Mikhail, and Robert E. Lucas Jr. 2007. "Menu Costs and Phillips Curves." *Journal of Political Economy* 115 (2): 171–99.

Hall, George J., and Thomas J. Sargent. 2011. "Interest Rate Risk and Other Determinants of Post-WWII US Government Debt/GDP Dynamics." *American Economic Journal: Macroeconomics* 3 (3): 192–214.

Hansen, Lars P. 2014. "Nobel Lecture: Uncertainty Outside and Inside Economic Models." *Journal of Political Economy* 122 (5): 945–87.

Hatchondo, Juan Carlos, and Leonardo Martinez. 2009. "Long-Duration Bonds and Sovereign Defaults." *Journal of International Economics* 79 (1): 117–25.

Hébert, Benjamin, and Jesse Schreger. 2017. "The Costs of Sovereign Default: Evidence from Argentina." *American Economic Review* 107 (10): 3119–45.

Hurwicz, Leo. 1966. "On the Structural Form of Interdependent Systems." In *Logic, Methodology and Philosophy of Science: Proceedings of the 1960 International Congress*, edited by Ernest Nagel, Patrick Suppes, and Alfred Tarski, 232–39. Vol. 44, *Studies in Logic and the Foundations of Mathematics.* Amsterdam: Elsevier.

Imrohoroglu, Selahattin. 1993. "Testing for Sunspot Equilibria in the German Hyperinflation." *Journal of Economic Dynamics and Control* 17 (3): 289–317.

Koopmans, Tjalling C. 1947. "Measurement without Theory." *Review of Economics and Statistics* 29 (3): 161–72.

Krugman, Paul. 1979. "A Model of Balance-of-Payments Crises." *Journal of Money, Credit and Banking* 11 (3): 311–25.

Leeper, Eric M. 1991. "Equilibria under 'Active' and 'Passive' Monetary and Fiscal Policies." *Journal of Monetary Economics* 27 (1): 129–47.

Leeper, Eric, and Campbell Leith. 2016. "Understanding Inflation as a Joint Monetary and Fiscal Phenomenon." In *Handbook of Macroeconomics*, vol. 2, edited by John Taylor and Harald Uhlig, 2305–415. Amsterdam: Elsevier.

Lerner, Eugene M. 1956. "Inflation in the Confederacy, 1861–65." In *Studies in the Quantity Theory of Money*, edited by Milton Friedman, 163–177. Economics Research Studies of the Economics Research Center of the University of Chicago. Chicago: University of Chicago Press.

Lorenzoni, Guido, and Ivan Werning. 2013. "Slow Moving Debt Crises." Working paper 19228, National Bureau of Economic Research, Cambridge, Mass.

Loyo, Eduardo. 1999. "Tight Money Paradox on the Loose: A Fiscalist Hyperinflation." Technical report, John F. Kennedy School of Government, Harvard University, Cambridge, Mass.

Lucas, Robert E., Jr. 1976. "Econometric Policy Evaluation: A Critique." *Carnegie-Rochester Conference Series on Public Policy* 1 (1): 19–46.

Lucas, Robert E., Jr., and Juan P. Nicolini. 2015. "On the Stability of Money Demand." *Journal of Monetary Economics* 73 (C): 48–65.

Lucas, Robert E., Jr., and Nancy L. Stokey. 1983. "Optimal Fiscal and Monetary Policy in an Economy without Capital." *Journal of Monetary Economics* 12 (1): 55–93.

Marcet, Albert, and Juan P. Nicolini. 2003. "Recurrent Hyperinflations and Learning." *American Economic Review* 93 (5): 1476–98.

Marcet, Albert, and Thomas J. Sargent. 1989a. "Convergence of Least Squares Learning Mechanisms in Self-Referential Linear Stochastic Models." *Journal of Economic Theory* 48 (2): 337–68.

Marcet, Albert, and Thomas J. Sargent. 1989b. "Least-Squares Learning and the Dynamics of Hyperinflation." In *International Symposia in Economic Theory and Econometrics*, edited by William Barnett, John Geweke, and Karl Shell, 119–37. Cambridge: Cambridge University Press.

Marschak, Jacob. 1953. "Economic Measurements for Policy and Prediction." In *Cowles Commission Monograph 14: Studies in Econometric Methods*, edited by William C. Hood and Tjalling C. Koopmans, 1–26. New York: Wiley.

Mendoza, Enrique G. 2010. "Sudden Stops, Financial Crises, and Leverage." *American Economic Review* 100 (5): 1941–66.

Obstfeld, Maurice. 1986. "Rational and Self-Fulfilling Balance-of-Payments Crises." *American Economic Review* 76 (1): 72–81.

Salant, Stephen, and Dale Henderson. 1978. "Market Anticipations of Government Policies and the Price of Gold." *Journal of Political Economy* 86 (4): 627–48.

Sargent, Thomas J. 1977. "The Demand for Money during Hyperinflations under Rational Expectations: I." *International Economic Review* 18 (1): 59–82.

———. 1982. "The Ends of Four Big Inflations." In *Inflation: Causes and Effects*, edited by Robert E. Hall, 41–98. Chicago: University of Chicago Press.

———. 1999. *The Conquest of American Inflation.* Princeton, N.J.: Princeton University Press.

Sargent, Thomas J., and Neil Wallace. 1973. "Rational Expectations and the Dynamics of Hyperinflation." *International Economic Review* 14 (2): 328–50.

———. 1981. "Some Unpleasant Monetarist Arithmetic." *Federal Reserve Bank of Minneapolis Quarterly Review* 5 (3): 1–17.

———. 1987. "Inflation and the Government Budget Constraint." In *Economic Policy in Theory and Practice*, edited by Assaf Razin and Efraim Sadka, 170–207. London: Palgrave Macmillan.

Sargent, Thomas J., Noah Williams, and Tao Zha. 2009. "The Conquest of South American Inflation." *Journal of Political Economy* 117 (2): 211–56.

Schneider, Martin, and Aaron Tornell. 2004. "Balance Sheet Effects, Bailout Guarantees and Financial Crises." *Review of Economic Studies* 71 (3): 883–913.

Sheshinski, Eytan, and Yoram Weiss. 1977. "Inflation and Costs of Price Adjustment." *Review of Economic Studies* 44 (2): 287–303.

Sims, Christopher A. 1972. "Money, Income, and Causality." *American Economic Review* 62 (4): 540–52.

———. 1980. "Macroeconomics and Reality." *Econometrica* 48 (1): 1–48.

———. 1994. "A Simple Model for Study of the Determination of the Price Level and the Interaction of Monetary and Fiscal Policy." *Economic Theory* 4 (3): 381–99.

Slutsky, Eugen. 1927. "The Summation of Random Causes as the Source of Cyclic Processes." [In Russian.] *Problems of Economic Conditions* 3 (1). Revised English version published in 1937, *Econometrica* 5 (2): 105–46.

Tomz, Michael, and Mark L. J. Wright. 2013. "Empirical Research on Sovereign Debt and

Default." *Annual Review of Economics* 5 (1): 247–72.

Tourre, Fabrice. 2017. "Macro-Finance Approach to Sovereign Debt Spreads and Returns." Working paper, Becker Friedman Institute for Research in Economics, University of Chicago, Chicago.

Vining, Rutledge. 1949. "Koopmans on the Choice of Variables to Be Studied and of Methods of Measurement." *Review of Economics and Statistics* 31 (2): 77–86.

Woodford, Michael. 1995. "Price-Level Determinacy without Control of a Monetary Aggregate." *Carnegie-Rochester Conference Series on Public Policy* 43 (1): 1–46.

Yule, G. Udny. 1927. "On a Method of Investigating Periodicities in Disturbed Series, with Special Reference to Wolfer's Sunspot Numbers." *Philosophical Transactions of the Royal Society of London; Series A, Containing Papers of a Mathematical or Physical Character* 226:267–98.

A Framework for Studying the Monetary and Fiscal History of Latin America

Timothy J. Kehoe
University of Minnesota, Federal Reserve Bank of Minneapolis,
and National Bureau of Economic Research

Juan Pablo Nicolini
Federal Reserve Bank of Minneapolis and Universidad Torcuato Di Tella

Thomas J. Sargent
New York University and Hoover Institution

Introduction

It has been almost half a century since Eduardo Galeano published the first edition in 1971 of *The Open Veins of Latin America* as *Las venas abiertas de América Latina*, quoted in one of this book's two epigraphs. Since then, more than seventy-five editions have been launched, and the book has been translated into more than a dozen languages. Galeano's book has a major virtue: it is an intellectual project that provides a diagnosis of a painful Latin American reality and attempts to build an explanation for the region's underperformance. In addition, it was the first such attempt to become part of the popular culture: the term *open veins*, or *las venas abiertas* in Spanish, went beyond the limits of its readers, its argument, and its ideology and came to occupy its own place in songs and newspaper articles. It became a popular icon all across the region, representing a generalized sense of failure.

Galeano's book is the product of a particular time, and it provides an explanation for Latin America's failure that we do not accept. Nevertheless, Galeano's diagnosis of the underperformance of the region is uncontroversial: the great homeland that Simón Bolívar imagined at the dawn of the nineteenth century has been a profound disappointment for José Artigas, Miguel Hidalgo, Bernardo O'Higgins, José de San Martin, Antonio Sucre, Túpac Amaru II, and many others who devoted their lives to independence, hoping for freedom and prosperity for the region. Two hundred years later, Latin America continues to be a region with very high income inequality and low social mobility. Only sub-Saharan Africa surpasses Latin America in terms of economic stagnation.

A similar view on the performance of the region can be found in the writings of Mario Vargas Llosa. His famous novel *Conversation in the Cathedral*, published in 1969 as *Conversación en la catedral*, immortalized in its opening paragraph the sentence forming this book's second epigraph: "At what precise moment had Peru screwed itself up?" (or in Spanish, "En qué momento se había jodido el Perú?"). That sentence summarizes a view of decadence that Vargas Llosa ascribed to Peru in many of his novels and for all of Latin America in his later writings after he had moved into politics. Regarding the reasons for the decadence, Vargas Llosa has very different views from the ones expressed in *Las venas abiertas*, but the general sense of disappointment is common to both writers.

Good and comparable data across the region for the first century following independence are not available. Data for the twentieth century, however, can be used to illustrate the economic stagnation emphasized by Galeano and Vargas Llosa. For this chapter, we chose as a starting point the year 1935, so as to leave out the First World War and the start of the Great Depression, which were unusual events for the world as a whole.

We describe the data in more detail below but provide here a brief overview. During the period from 1935 to 1973, when Vargas Llosa and Galeano had just published their books, the region had enormous difficulty bridging the income gap with rich countries. For example, the average income of the region grew from 21 percent relative to the United States in 1935 to 26 percent in 1973—a growth of only 5 percent in thirty-eight years. (We focus on the ten largest countries in South America plus Mexico.) In comparison, we note that in the same period, average income in the twelve countries of Western Europe (the EU 12, the twelve original members of the European Union) —went from 58 percent to 76 percent relative to the United States—a growth of 18 percent—with a terrible war in the middle of that period.

These numbers represent averages for the Latin American region. If one cares about the most vulnerable groups in society, the situation is even worse, given that levels of economic inequality are greater in Latin America than in the United States. Therefore, the differences between the poor in Latin America and the poor in the United States are substantially greater than those mentioned above. The most evident symptom of this situation is the systematic migratory flow of workers from the south to the north. The bitter consolation for societies that have failed to generate opportunities for the most vulnerable is that many of them have successfully managed to find those opportunities in different societies.

This reality takes on a more dramatic dimension if we review the years from the publication of *Las venas* and *Conversación* to the end of the century. Data comparable to those discussed above reveal a strong deterioration relative to the United States in the final three decades of the twentieth century. On average, the region declined from the 26 percent that it had reached in 1973 down to 23 percent by 2000. It took the region the first decade and a half of the twenty-first century to bring its average back to the 26 percent it had reached in 1973.

The obvious and immediate question that arises is, Why? What went wrong in Latin America? The only honest answer is that we do not know. As a profession, we economists do not have the policy answers that would have guaranteed convergence of Latin America to the income level of the richest countries in the world. Coincidental with the periods of poor economic performance, however, countries in Latin America have been plagued by economic crises. The specific symptoms of each crisis have been very different: high inflation rates, balance of payments crises followed by large devaluations, banking crises, defaults on government debt, deposit confiscations, and so on.

Our fundamental hypothesis is that, despite their different manifestations, all economic crises in Latin America have been the result of poorly designed or poorly implemented macrofiscal policies. The prototypical scenario for a crisis is that, because of social pressures, the government increased expenditures without a compensating increase in revenues. Initially, the government financed the resulting deficit by borrowing, with a large fraction of the borrowing done abroad. When the debt reached a certain level, however, lenders were unwilling to lend more, and a crisis unfolded. This process continued until there was a reform. In a number of countries, the process leading to a crisis occurred more than once. A reasonable conjecture is that the prevalence of crises is at the root of a sizable fraction of the stagnation of Latin America.

The first aim of the series of chapters in this book is to collect systematic and comparable data on several macroeconomic variables for the eleven countries included. We believe these variables are key to understanding the main causes of the sequence of crises that prevailed in the region. The second aim is to use this data set to construct narratives for each country, so the crises and the evolution of the main variables can be jointly understood within the economic environment of the time and the macroeconomic policy decisions made in each country at different points in time.

As economists, we use theory to organize and understand the data. We need to abstract from details and particular idiosyncrasies to try to unravel general patterns. It is therefore a requirement for us that the narratives for all countries follow a unified theoretical framework, which is developed in detail in the third section of this chapter. The authors of the studies of our set of eleven countries then use our theoretical framework to link the data to the sequence of the main macroeconomic events for each of the countries and to assess the role of the different macroeconomic policies enacted, whenever possible.

We keep the conceptual framework as simple as possible, following the detailed discussion in the preceding chapter, "Detecting Fiscal-Monetary Causes of Inflation." We hope that the framework allows us to capture the principal forces behind the sequence of events that our narratives describe. Therefore, by construction, we are not able to capture the effect of forces that arise only sporadically or in only a few of the countries. The theoretical framework cannot therefore be applied dogmatically. We use it systematically, but we need to acknowledge the cases in which it fails to provide a convincing explanation of the facts. The following chapters provide several examples of events that do not conform to the logic of the theory. Some qualifications to the basic conceptual framework, which we briefly discuss, can go a long way toward explaining some of the initial anomalies, as the following chapters argue. Finally, the narratives that follow also highlight events that challenge the conceptual framework and eventually will suggest avenues for further work.

The conceptual framework focuses on the relationship between the joint determination of fiscal and monetary policies and their interaction with nominal instability, as discussed above. It therefore lacks any theory of the determination of total average real economic activity. As such, the conceptual framework is unable to link economic crises with the poor economic performance that is evident in Figure 1. The narratives that follow therefore limit themselves to establishing the time coincidence of economic crises with the large and persistent recessions—and even great depressions—that were so common in the region during this period. Thus we fall short of providing a summary of policies that can lead to sustainable growth and bring prosperity to the region. Nevertheless, we hope that the database and the narratives we provide can be used by policy makers as laboratory experiments from which to draw useful lessons, from both the lost decades at the end of the twentieth century and the better decade experienced at the dawn of the twenty-first. We also hope that this sequence of studies will motivate others to pursue the quest for policy rules that can help break the vicious cycle of crisis and stagnation in Latin America.

In the second section of this chapter, we very briefly describe the macroeconomic performance of the eleven countries since 1960. We also summarize the macroeconomic instability that reigned in the region, particularly during the interim period. Finally, as noted, in the third section we describe the framework that serves as the guiding theoretical apparatus to organize the data and construct the narratives for each of our eleven countries.

Economic Performance and Macroeconomic Instability

We now describe the evolution of the income per capita of the Latin American countries included in the study, relative to the income per capita of the world frontier. The data are from the Maddison Project Database, version 2018 (Bolt et al. 2018). We use real GDP per capita measured in 2011 U.S. dollars, based on multiple benchmark comparisons of prices and income across countries that make the data more suitable for cross-country income comparisons. (See Bolt et al. 2018 for a more extensive explanation of the construction of this variable.)

Standard practice is to use the income per capita in the United States as a proxy for the world frontier. In doing so, however, the measure is affected by idiosyncratic events in the United States, like the severity of the Great Recession and the expansion during World War II. In contrast, we use a trend growth for the United States, which grows at 2 percent per year and which is equal to the observed income per capita in the United States in 1960. The year 1960 has the advantage that the observed value was very close to a trend computed for the period 1985–2012. That is, the 2 percent per year growth line for the United States that runs through 1960 is essentially the same line as the regression trend line for 1985–2012. We then calculate the relative income of each of the eleven countries and the regional average by dividing its observed real GDP per capita by the U.S. trend and plot the results in Figure 1.

Each patterned line in the figure represents a different country, and the solid line represents the average for all countries, weighted by population. The top The top panel depicts the data from 1935, right after the Great Depression, to 1973, the year in which

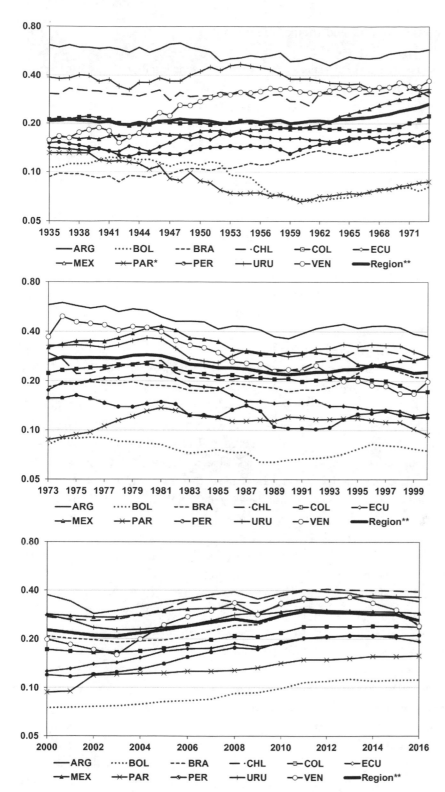

Figure 1. Real GDP per capita relative to the United States: top panel: 1935–73; middle panel: 1973–2000; bottom panel: 2000–2016

*The data for Paraguay starts in 1939, the graph assumes 2% annual growth between 1935 and 1939.

**Average, weighted by population.

nominal instability, measured as the average volatility of the inflation rate, starts to grow (see the discussion below). The figure shows a very modest but positive convergence for the average of the region to the levels of income per capita of the United States, particularly at the end of the sample. The weighted average of the relative income per capita that was 21 percent in 1935 grew a modest 5 percent by 1973, amounting to an incremental growth of about 0.13 per year.

This convergence is the combination of three different experiences. First, there is divergence of the three initially richest countries: Argentina, Chile, and Uruguay. In addition, there is also divergence for two of the initially very poor countries: Bolivia and Paraguay. These are the only countries that had in 1973 a lower value for relative income per capita than the value they had in 1935. These effects, however, are more than compensated for by a substantial convergence of the initially middle-income countries and by Brazil, which was initially the poorest. Notice also that two remarkable success stories occur in the two largest countries measured by population, Brazil and Mexico. The third success story is Venezuela.

The middle panel in Figure 1 depicts the data from 1973 to 2000. Notice that the vertical axis is exactly the same as in the top panel. This figure depicts the substantial failure of Latin America to continue to develop economically. By 2000, the average GDP per capita had diverged back to 23 percent of the U.S. growth trend—a number barely above the one in 1935. Had the region kept the pace of convergence of the previous period—about 0.13 per year—the ratio would have been almost 30 percent. That is equivalent to an income per capita that is about 30 percent higher than it was in 2000—a sizable lunch. Only two countries—Brazil and Paraguay—end the period with values above the ones in 1973, and only barely so.

Finally, in the top panel of Figure 1, we show the data for the first years of this century. This period reflects better performance, showing a resumption of the slow convergence of Latin America to the United States to an average of 26 percent by 2016.

As mentioned above, the reasons that Latin America lags behind in terms of economic growth still remain somewhat of a puzzle for economists. Many hypotheses have been analyzed, but no systematic and comparative analysis has been performed that could orient policy in a systematic and predictable way. A lack of understanding, however, does not mean that the problem has not been acknowledged. The revival of studies on economic growth that started in the 1980s included a series of papers pioneered by Barro (1991) that attempted to establish empirically the existence of economic convergence, a common prediction of standard neoclassical growth models. Prominently significant in cross-country studies that included countries in Latin America was the so-called "Latin American dummy," which identified a negative effect on the growth rate between 1960 and 1985 for countries in Latin America, even when a series of controls were added to the regressions. The systematically poor performance of the region, which is detected by the dummy in those regressions, can clearly be appreciated in Figure 1; although this set of countries was significantly poorer than the United States in the early 1960s (the initial year for the Barro regressions), they had failed to maintain convergence to the United States by 1985 (the final year in those same regressions). The purpose of this book is to shed light on the underlying causes of the Latin American dummy.

Coincidental with poor growth outcomes, the lost decades of the 1970s and 1980s were the years in which the region went through the highest macroeconomic instability of its history. Latin America during that period is plagued by chronic inflation, balance of payments crises, financial crises, defaults, hyperinflations, major confiscations of assets, and bailouts of private-sector debts.

To illustrate this coincidence of poor growth outcomes with macroeconomic instability, Figure 2 shows the average inflation for the eleven countries at a monthly frequency.

We choose to plot monthly inflation rates because, at the more standard yearly frequency, the two peaks in 1986 and 1991 blur the scale of the figure. We plot average inflation for the eleven countries included in this study, separated into two groups. The first group (whose inflation rates correspond to the scale on the left axis) includes the five countries with higher average inflation: Argentina, Bolivia, Brazil, Chile, and Peru; the second group (whose inflation rates correspond to the scale on the right axis) includes the other six countries—that is, Colombia, Ecuador, Mexico, Paraguay, Uruguay, and Venezuela. We also plot two vertical lines corresponding to 1973 and 2000, the years that correspond to the subperiods in Figure 1.

In Figure 3 we graph rolling volatilities of the inflation rates over time. Specifically, for each country we consider windows of eight years for the inflation rate and compute, for those years, the standard deviation of the inflation rate. We then plot, for each year, the corresponding volatility, starting in 1968. Clearly, the worst years in terms of economic performance correspond to the periods of higher and more volatile inflation rates.

A closer look at the behavior of each country shows that five of them (Argentina, Bolivia, Brazil, Chile, and Peru) suffered one or more hyperinflations between 1973 and

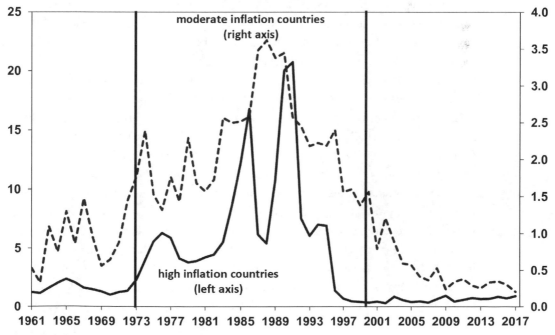

Figure 2. Average monthly inflation

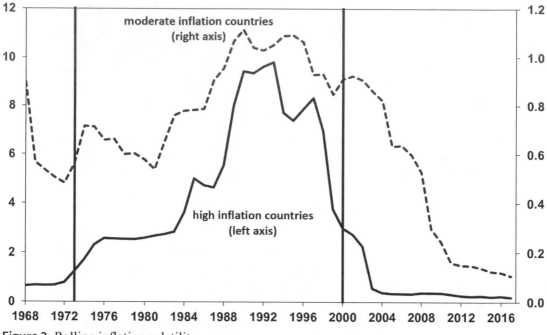

Figure 3. Rolling inflation volatility

1994; Venezuela is going through another one as we finish this book. Runs against the domestic currency that led to balance of payments crises were almost too common to count, and many countries in the region defaulted on their government debt, in several cases more than once. The wave of defaults around the world in the early 1980s that jeopardized the health of several large U.S. banks has been named the Latin American default crisis, even though default was also declared by some countries that are not part of Latin America. Nevertheless, it was labeled as a Latin American default crisis because most of the heavy borrowing was done by governments in that region. Massive banking crises, with bailouts that amounted to several percentage points of GDP, have occurred in almost all countries between the late 1970s and the early years of the current century. Again, some countries experienced more than one crisis. All sorts of different policies have been tried, including dual exchange rates (in every country), a currency board that ended in a major crisis (in Argentina), and full dollarization (in Ecuador), a policy that has lasted to this day. There were also several periods of floating exchange rates, a policy still prevailing today in many countries of the region. Banking crises have been dealt with in different ways in different countries and periods. Default renegotiations have also varied across countries and time periods. Banks have been nationalized and privatized.

The coincidence over time between these dramatic policy decisions, macroeconomic instability, and the economic decadence of Latin America makes its recent history a very rich experiment to analyze. As we mentioned above, however, as a profession, economists still lack good theories that associate macroeconomic instability with economic performance—at least theories that can be subject to serious quantitative scrutiny. Nevertheless, a substantial literature associates bad macroeconomic fiscal and monetary policies with macroeconomic instability: balance of payments crises, financial crises, defaults, hyperinflation, and so on. We now briefly describe a conceptual framework that summarizes the many contributions to that literature, contributions that serve as the theoretical framework to support the eleven narratives constituting the core of this book.

Conceptual Framework

To develop a framework to evaluate the impact of sets of monetary and fiscal policies implemented in our eleven Latin American countries over the period 1960–2017, we start by describing the framework developed by Sargent (1986) to evaluate the impact of the set of monetary and fiscal policies implemented in the United States in the early 1980s. This framework consists of two main ideas: a budget identity for the consolidated government and a demand for real money.

The budget identity classifies all sources of government financing into three groups: tax revenues, interest-bearing debt, and non-interest-bearing debt, or money. As such, it imposes a constraint between four different dimensions of macroeconomic policy: total government expenses, total revenues, increases in government debt, and increases in the money supply. The constraint implies that the four different policy decisions cannot be made independently. Once three of them are decided, the fourth has to adjust to satisfy that constraint. In what follows, we combine two of the policy variables into one by netting our total revenues from total expenditures to obtain a measure of the deficit or surplus in case it is negative. We take this approach because the government budget constraint does not independently restrict spending and revenues, only its difference, as will become clear below. A direct implication of this constraint is that a deficit implies an increase in government debt, an increase in the money supply, or a combination of both. To study the fiscal-monetary linkages, the analysis in this collection of studies takes the fiscal deficit as the exogenous driving force. That Latin American countries have larger levels of inequality and social tensions than many other countries could explain the large levels of government spending and deficits. We leave these issues for research.

The demand for real money establishes a systematic relationship between the general price level, short-term nominal interest rates, total real income, and some measure of money. It implies that systematic increases in the money supply generate inflation.

The combination of these two main ideas does not imply that sustained deficits cause inflation, since they can be financed by increases in government debt. Nevertheless, debt implies a promise of future government surpluses to be used to pay for that debt. To the extent that these promises lack credibility, the government may face a limit on its ability to borrow. If this is the case, the combination of the two ideas implies a direct connection between fiscal deficits and inflation. Thus the size of interest-bearing debt relative to total production plays a key role.

As many of the cases studied illustrate, the framework just described cannot rationalize some of the crises that the region experienced during the period under study. This should not be surprising, since Sargent's object of study was the macroeconomy of the

United States in the early 1980s, where moderate inflation was the only macroeconomic problem. The difference between Latin America and the United States in the early 1980s does not lie exclusively with the much higher and more volatile inflation rates observed in Latin America during the period. As mentioned before, the region experienced other types of crises, and we need to adapt the framework to study them.

We first consider an open economy version of Sargent's (1986) framework to study balance of payments crises. We then briefly discuss models that exhibit default in equilibrium, a policy option that is not considered in the basic framework, since it did not seem to be an issue for the U.S. government, but that was a policy option chosen by several of the Latin American countries during the period under study. We then move to models in which not only the size but also the characteristics of total debt matter for the determination of equilibria. We review models where the size of short-term debt or the units in which debt is denominated, or both, can determine the outcome in the economy. In particular, we review models that address the possibility of multiple equilibria. In these models, a crisis may occur driven by expectations alone, in spite of the fundamentals of the model being right. The discussion of these variations is self-contained by using very simple versions of those models.

At the end of this section, we briefly mention (but do not discuss) other theoretical results derived from the theory of optimal dynamic contracts with enforcement constraints. These models complement the basic framework in a natural way and may be useful in thinking about limits to total debt. Those models raise several interesting questions that we briefly address.

THE ECONOMICS OF BUDGET CONSTRAINTS

The first building block of the conceptual framework is the government budget identity. In describing sources of financing, we separately specify, when possible, domestic currency denominated debt, inflation indexed, and foreign currency denominated debt. Specifically, we let B_t, b_t, and B_t^* be total nominal, indexed, and dollar-denominated debt and D_t be the deficit of the governments in real terms, measured as expenditures and normal transfers minus taxes. We also let M_t be the stock of money, P_t be the domestic price level (that is, the GDP deflator), and E_t the nominal exchange rate. Furthermore, we let R_t, r_t, and B_t^* be the gross returns on nominal, inflation indexed, and foreign currency bonds. Then the budget constraint of the government is

$$B_t + P_t b_t + E_t B_t^* + M_t = P_t(D_t + T_t) + B_{t-1}R_{t-1} + P_t b_{t-1}r_{t-1} + E_t B_{t-1}^* R_{t-1}^* + M_{t-1}. \tag{1}$$

Unless explicitly mentioned, the stock of debt, B_t, does not include the assets and liabilities of the central bank. These can be important for some countries and in some periods of time and will be mentioned explicitly in the case studies that follow.

Notice that on the right-hand side of equation (1) we have added a term T_t to the deficit. We do this because we have independent measures for all the other terms in the equation, and we can measure T_t as a residual. Specifically, we choose the value for T_t that makes the budget constraint hold, given the values for all the other terms. In many cases, the variable T_t allows us to identify off-the-book expenses, particularly in times of crisis. To fix ideas, we can provide two examples drawn from the experiences of several countries. Following banking crises, governments in many circumstances chose to bail out the financial sector, typically by issuing government bonds. These would be accounted for as a positive value for T_t. In some cases, the government also provided subsidies through state-owned development banks or state-owned companies and, on many occasions, used seigniorage from the central bank to cover those losses. These off-the-book expenses would also show up as positive values for T_t. As many of the chapters in this book illustrate, the accumulated effect of these computed transfers can be very large over time. In some cases, the narratives help identify the economic forces that created these large transfers.

The real exchange rate is

$$\xi_t = \frac{E_t P_t^W}{P_t},$$

(2)

where P_t^W is the price level for dollar-denominated debt—that is, the U.S. GDP deflator. Then

$$\xi_t \left(\frac{B_t^* / P_t^W}{y_t} \right) = \frac{E_t P_t^W}{P_t} \left(\frac{B_t^* / P_t^W}{y_t} \right) = \frac{E_t B_t^*}{P_t y_t}$$

(3)

is the value of dollar-denominated debt as a fraction of nominal GDP, $P_t y_t$. If we let

$$\theta_t^N = \frac{B_t}{P_t y_t}, \quad \theta_t^r = \frac{b_t}{y_t}, \quad \theta_t^* = \frac{B_t^* / P_t^*}{Y_t}, \quad m_t = \frac{M_t}{P_t Y_t}, \quad d_t = \frac{P_t D_t}{P_t y_t}, \quad \tau_t = \frac{P_t T_t}{P_t y_t},$$

and

$$\xi_t = \left(\frac{E_t P_t^*}{P_t} \right), \quad g_t = \frac{Y_t}{Y_{t-1}}, \quad \pi_t = \frac{P_t}{P_{t-1}}, \quad \pi_t^W = \frac{P_t^W}{P_{t-1}^W},$$

we can write the budget constraint in terms of changes as fractions of GDP as

$$\left(\theta_t^N - \theta_{t-1}^N \right) + \left(\theta_t^r - \theta_{t-1}^r \right) + \left(\xi_t \theta_t^* - \xi_t \theta_{t-1}^* \right) + \left(m_t - m_{t-1} \right) + m_{t-1} \left(1 - \frac{1}{g_t \pi_t} \right)$$

$$= \theta_{t-1}^N \left(\frac{R_{t-1}}{g_t \pi_t} - 1 \right) + \theta_{t-1}^N \left(\frac{r_{t-1}}{g_t} - 1 \right) + \xi_t \theta_{t-1}^* \left(\frac{R_{t-1}^*}{g_t \pi_t^W} - 1 \right) + d_t + \tau_t$$

. (4)

A detailed derivation of this equation is in appendix A to this chapter. The first three terms on the left-hand side of our budget accounting equation (4) represent increases in debt-to-output ratios in the three different types of debt: nominal, indexed, and foreign currency. The fourth term represents increases in high-powered money, and the last one measures seigniorage. The first three terms on the right-hand side represent the service costs on each of the three debt types. Notice that we discount each of these terms by growth of GDP, and we discount the nominal debt service costs by domestic inflation and the foreign debt service costs by U.S. inflation. These adjustments account for the reductions in ratio of debt to GDP caused by GDP growth and inflation. The final two terms on the right-hand side represent the fiscal deficit—including the extraordinary transfers T_t—as a fraction of output.

All eleven of the countries that we study in this volume imposed dual or multiple exchange rates during the 1970s or 1980s or both. What exchange rate should we use for the nominal exchange rate E_t in the budget constraint (1) and to construct the real exchange rate x_t in equation (2)? Ideally, we should use the rate that corresponds most closely to a market rate. If there is a real devaluation, using the market rate—rather than a lower official rate or preferential rate—better captures the magnitude and the timing of the increase in the burden of foreign debt implied by the devaluation. To the extent that the central bank exchanges foreign currency for local currency at the lower official rate for some importers, for example, it is subsidizing purchases of imports by these agents. Conversely, to the extent that the central bank exchanges local currency for foreign currency for some exporters at the official rate, it is taxing the exports by these agents. Typically, we do not have information on the purchases or sales of foreign currency at different exchange rates, which means that these implicit subsidies and taxes are included in the transfer term.

The second building block is a demand for real money balances, which we write as

$$\frac{M_t}{P_t} = \gamma - \delta\left(\frac{P_{t+1}}{P_t}\right),$$

(5)

where M_t is the outstanding stock of money, P_t is the price level, and $\gamma > \delta$. This money demand equation arises in a simple overlapping-generations general equilibrium model, as in the ones described in Sargent (1986) and Marcet and Nicolini (2003) and as we show in appendix B to this chapter. In a stochastic model, we would replace the inflation factor P_{t+1}/P_t with its expected value, but here we keep our discussion simple by focusing on the deterministic model. The linearity of the money demand equation is not essential to our arguments, but it makes the discussion simple. Notice that neither real output nor the real interest rate appears in equation (5), because in the above-mentioned models, both of those variables are constant over time and are embedded in the parameters γ and δ. The assumption of constant real output is without loss of generality, since the variable M_t can be interpreted as the ratio of money balances to output. The assumption of a constant real interest rate is less innocuous, but nothing essential in what follows hinges on that assumption.

We can solve forward the difference equation defined in (5) and write the unique nonbubble solution for the price level as

$$P_t = \frac{1}{\gamma} \sum_{j=0}^{\infty} \left(\frac{\delta}{\gamma} \right)^j M_{t+j}.$$

(6)

This equation implies that sustained increases in money growth generate sustained increases in prices.

The government budget constraint implies that sustained deficits lead either to sustained increases in the quantity of money or to sustained increases in government debt. The first option implies sustained inflation, as it does for the money demand equation. The second option implies that the government may eventually face constraints in its ability to borrow.

Fiscal deficits do not necessarily imply that inflation needs to increase because of the possibility of issuing bonds. As does Sargent (1986), however, we assume that there is a limit on the ability to borrow, which, as a first approximation, should be related to the ability of the government to generate future surpluses. Specifically, we assume that there is a debt limit,

$$\theta_t^N + \theta_t^r + \xi_t \theta_t^* \leq \Theta,$$

(7)

where Θ is an exogenously specified number. We summarize some models that attempt to understand the value of Θ below.

To the extent that the debt constraint (7) is not binding, governments can use fiscal policy as a tool to smooth shocks that affect the business cycle without creating inflation. All adjustments required to satisfy the budget constraint can be done by properly managing the debt. This regime is a very good approximation of the way the governments in the United States and the United Kingdom financed their war efforts in the last century. (See, for example, Hall and Sargent 2011.) These circumstances may appear to be ones in which monetary and fiscal policy can be designed independently from each other. This is not true, however: debt financing does not eliminate the interdependence between fiscal and monetary policy; it only postpones the debate. This is the central message of the analysis in Sargent (1986). While debt financing is available, deficits may not interfere with the design of monetary policy. Eventually, however, once the debt is high enough—that is, the debt constraint (7) is binding—the debate naturally arises, and a game of chicken arises between the monetary authority and the fiscal authority.

This situation is characterized by fiscal dominance when the winner of the game of chicken is the fiscal authority and the central bank monetizes the deficits. The reverse case, in which the fiscal authority generates surpluses, is one of monetary dominance. As it turns out, in the United States, monetary dominance prevailed as fiscal surpluses in the 1990s followed the Reagan deficits. In contrast, the dramatically high inflation rates observed in Latin America are evidence of all-too-frequent periods of fiscal dominance. High inflation rates followed once a specific country had already reached its debt limit and the financing requirements, given by the right-hand side of equation (4), were positive. In these cases, the budget constraint becomes

$$
\left(m_t - m_{t-1} \right) + m_{t-1}\left(1 - \frac{1}{g_t \pi_t} \right)
$$

$$
= d_t + \tau_t + \theta^N_{t-1}\left(\frac{R_{t-1}}{g_t \pi_t} - 1 \right) + \theta^N_{t-1}\left(\frac{r_{t-1}}{g_t} - 1 \right) + \xi_t \theta^*_{t-1}\left(\frac{R^*_{t-1}}{g_t \pi_t^W} - 1 \right), \tag{8}
$$

and inflation is unavoidable.

The debt constraint (7) would naturally bind during the years immediately following a default, as it did for many countries in Latin America at the beginning of the 1980s. A direct implication of this analysis is that the countries that defaulted and ran deficits in the following years ought to experience inflation. This is indeed the case in the studies that follow.

This positive relationship between deficits and inflation rates over time is a direct implication of the model above, which can be solved using perfect foresight: notice that the future price level in the money demand equation is the same as the equilibrium price level. As shown in Marcet and Nicolini (2003) and Sargent, Williams, and Zha (2009), however, the joint equilibrium dynamics of the deficit and the inflation rate can be different if one allows for small departures from rational expectations. Interestingly, the model dynamics in these papers closely resemble many features of the data. We ignore those details in the narratives that follow. The interested reader can consult the papers just mentioned for details.

As we have mentioned, Latin American experiences feature events that are apparently much more complicated than those of the United States experience, for which Sargent (1986) designed the conceptual framework. We now describe some relatively minor modifications to the framework that will help us interpret those events.

BALANCE OF PAYMENTS CRISES

The framework above can also accommodate balance of payments crises when countries chose to fix the devaluation rate, as most countries in Latin America did at some points during the period that we study. We briefly describe how to introduce the sort of balance of payments crisis studied by Krugman (1979).

We assume that purchasing power parity holds

$$
P_t = E_t P_t^W. \tag{9}
$$

By successfully fixing the rate of depreciation of the nominal exchange rate, E_{t+1}/E_t, and given foreign inflation, the government pins down the domestic inflation rate. Under these conditions, the money demand equation (5) determines the path for the money supply.

Consider now a country where debt has reached its debt constraint (7) and that chooses to fix the devaluation rate. The relevant budget constraint in this case is given by equation (8), where the left-hand side is given by the evolution of inflation together with the money demand equation, as explained above. Given a value for the primary deficit and the interest payments, the only variable left to satisfy the government budget constraint (8) is the transfer t_t. The natural interpretation is that the reserves at the central bank adjust to satisfy the budget constraint, and this is one rationale for the key role played by the central bank's stock of reserves in fixed exchange rate regimes.

A balance of payments crisis unfolds after a sequence of positive deficits that are financed with those reserves. While this occurs, the exchange rate regime suppresses domestic inflation through the mechanism described above at the cost of a systematic decline in the stock of reserves. Eventually, agents foresee that, if there were a speculative attack, the central bank would not have enough reserves to support the exchange rate regime. A devaluation ensues, which, through the budget constraint (8), pushes domestic prices upward. Thus exchange rate regimes may delay the inflationary consequences of chronic deficits. The delay is paid for by the reduction in the stock of foreign reserves held at the central bank. Again, the inability to borrow is a key component of the theory.

EQUILIBRIUM DEFAULT

The model above has an exogenous borrowing constraint, so to the extent to which that constraint binds for a particular country, access to the debt market is restricted, and the connection between deficits and inflation becomes tight. In that model, however, default never occurs.

A large body of literature developed following the contributions of Aguiar and Gopinath (2006) and Arellano (2008), who build on Eaton and Gersovitz (1981), to address that issue. This literature assumes that government debt is noncontingent and that governments are sovereign in the sense that they cannot commit to repaying, so default is always an option, and there is either no or very limited ability to collateralize the debt. Default is assumed to be costly in terms of lost output, so the models do exhibit default in equilibrium. The implications of these models will be taken into account in the narratives that follow, and the data and the narratives can narrow down the theories and discipline the parameters to deepen our understanding of these dramatic episodes.

THE MATURITY PROBLEM

More recent papers developed after the 1994–95 Mexican crisis, such as Calvo (1998) and Cole and T. J. Kehoe (1996, 2000), that have emphasized the maturity structure of debt rather than the total value of the debt. These papers develop models in which debt crises can be touched off by the expectations of investors in government bonds—that is, investors' expectations of a crisis are self-fulfilling—but in which the possibility of such crises can be reduced or eliminated by having debt of a long enough maturity.

To understand how these models work, we consider a simple two-period economy based on Calvo (1998). The government inherits debt B and has the budget constraint

$$B = s_1 + \frac{s_2}{R},\qquad(10)$$

where $s_t = -d_t$ is the primary surplus of period t, and R is the (gross) international interest rate. The debt is positive, so the government will need positive surpluses to pay it back.

In this simple model, we impose three assumptions to ensure expectations-driven multiplicity. First, we assume away any enforcement problems. Second, we assume that $\bar{s}$ is the maximum surplus that the government can raise without provoking a recession. Finally, we assume that a recession means that in the following period, no surplus can be raised, and consequently the government must default on any remaining debt.

We now develop conditions on B, R, and s for which there is no debt crisis if investors do not expect a crisis but there is a crisis if investors expect one. Given our assumptions, if

$$B \leq \bar{s},$$

then all the debt can be paid in period 1, and a recession can be avoided in both periods. That is one way to pay for the debt; but clearly, any pair of surpluses that satisfies (10) can also achieve that goal without creating a recession.

On the other hand, if

$$B > \bar{s} + \frac{\bar{s}}{R},$$

then the debt cannot be paid without avoiding a recession. A debt crisis necessarily occurs in the first period and the government defaults.

Now we consider the more interesting case of intermediate values of the debt:

$$\bar{s} < B \leq \bar{s} + \frac{\bar{s}}{R}.\qquad(11)$$

Imagine that all the debt is due in the first period. This case has two possible equilibria. In the first equilibrium, there is a positive surplus in the first period, close enough to, but less than or equal to, $\bar{s}$, that covers part of the debt, while a share of the debt is refinanced for repayment in period 2. Then, a surplus can be generated in period 2 that is enough to pay back all the remaining debt. Clearly, both of the surpluses can be less than or equal to $\bar{s}$, so recessions are avoided. This equilibrium depends on investors being willing to refinance $B - s_1$ from period 1 to period 2.

In the second equilibrium, none of the debt gets refinanced, so the government is forced to raise a surplus that is higher than $\bar{s}$. This provokes a recession, implying that the government in the second period is unable to raise a surplus, making it rational for the lenders not to refinance the debt. In this second equilibrium, the government may be forced to default in the first period if it is unable to raise a surplus that is large enough to pay all the debt. Whether the government defaults in period 1 and suffers whatever default penalty we specify or it generates the surplus necessary to pay back the debt and suffers the recession depends on how we specify the costs of recessions and defaults.

This case is interesting because the maturity of the debt can be managed to eliminate the second equilibrium. If an amount equal to $\bar{s}$ is due in the second period, then the government has automatic refinancing, does not need to raise a surplus larger than the maximum, and thus avoids a recession.

The model that we have outlined has two equilibria. We can think of the determination of which equilibrium occurs as being determined by a randomization device, a sunspot. Cole and T. J. Kehoe (1996, 2000) develop an infinite horizon model with sunspots. This model has richer implications but is more complex. The probability of a negative sunspot now determines a risk premium on government debt, and this risk premium feeds back into the determination of the crisis zone—the set of debt levels that satisfy the analogue of condition (11)—that is, the set of debt levels for which there are a repayment continuation equilibrium and a default continuation equilibrium. The higher the risk premium, the more difficult the government finds it to pay back its debt even if there is no negative sunspot, and the crisis zone shrinks. Cole and T. J. Kehoe (1996) also show that the longer the maturity of debt, the smaller the crisis zone. In the case of debt in perpetuities, the crisis zone disappears. The lesson from analyzing high probability crises and long maturity debt is the same: it is not the total amount of debt that is crucial in determining whether or not a crisis can occur but the amount of debt service required every period.

THE DENOMINATION PROBLEM

The chapters that follow are replete with stories of Latin American governments having debt crises because they issue debt denominated in dollars. We can use a simple version of alternative multiple equilibrium developed by Calvo (1988), however, to illustrate the benefits of issuing debt denominated in a foreign currency like U.S. dollars. Assume that a government launches a stabilization plan that fixes the nominal exchange rate. For simplicity, assume that the foreign interest rate is fixed at R^*. If the investors who buy the bonds expect the government to keep the exchange rate fixed, then the expected devaluation is zero, and the domestic interest rate is also R^*.

This government can modify fiscal policy to generate primary fiscal surpluses, but some uncertainty is involved. In particular, we assume the surplus will be a random variable, and, to keep our discussion simple, we assume that it can take on two values, $s_t = \underline{s} < 0$ with probability π and $s_t = \bar{s} > 0$ with probability $1 - \pi$.

Given the stock of government debt, B_t, the government's financing needs are

$$B_t R_t - s_t \in \{B_t R_t - \bar{s}, B_t R_t - \underline{s}\}.$$

We again assume that there is a maximum $\bar{B}$ that the market is willing to lend to this government in a given period. If financing needs in a given period are larger than this maximum, then we assume that the government has to use its international reserves, a balance of payments crisis occurs, and the government then devalues at the rate $e = E_t/E_{t-1} > 0$.

If the maximum $\bar{B}$ is larger than $B_t R^* - \underline{s}$, then there is an equilibrium with $R_t = R^*$ and no devaluation. In fact, if investors expect devaluation to be zero, then the probability that financing needs will be higher than the maximum is zero, and thus the probability of a devaluation is zero. On the other hand, if investors expect a balance of payments crisis to occur with positive probability, then they demand a higher interest rate on the bonds, $R_t > R^*$. In the equilibria that we examine, investors assign devaluation either the probability 0 or the probability π because they expect devaluation to occur only if the government runs a deficit. It is worth mentioning that, if the maximum $\bar{B}$ is smaller than $B_t R^* - \bar{s}$, then the unique equilibrium is one in which the government devalues.

If investors are risk neutral, they require the expect discounted value in period t of the bonds that they bought in period $t - 1$ to satisfy the arbitrage equation

$$1 = \beta \left(\pi \frac{R_t}{e} + (1-\pi)R_t \right). \tag{12}$$

Notice that if $\pi = 0$, then the country can borrow at the risk-free rate $R_t = R^* = 1/\beta$ as we have explained. If, however, investors expect the government to devalue with probability π, then the arbitrage equation (12) tells us that

$$R_t = \frac{1}{\beta} \frac{1}{\pi \frac{1}{e} + (1-\pi)} = R^* + \frac{R^* \pi (e-1)}{e - \pi(e-1)} > R^*. \tag{13}$$

Can risk premium $R_t - R^*$ in equation (13) be part of a rational expectations, self-fulfilling balance-of-payments crisis equilibrium? For this to be the case, we require that

$$B_t R_t - \underline{s} > \bar{B} \geq B_t R^* - \underline{s}. \tag{14}$$

The crisis zone is defined by condition (14) and depends on the parameters $\bar{B}$, $\underline{s}$, β, π, and e. In this case, the multiplicity is due to a denomination problem: since the debt is denominated in domestic currency and a devaluation can reduce the value of the debt, there is a low interest rate equilibrium, where the debt maintains its value with probability 1, and a high interest rate equilibrium, where the debt devalues with positive probability.

More recently, Lorenzoni and Werning (2013) show that a similar type of multiplicity can arise with debt of long maturities. Ayres et al. (2018) do the same in models in which the economy faces the likelihood of relatively long periods of stagnation.

These models suggest that the total size of government debt may not be the unique determinant of the ability of the government to borrow and that market expectations can play an independent role. The extent to which these theoretical considerations can explain some of the default episodes during the period will be addressed in the studies that follow.

REPUTATION AND ENFORCEMENT

In this subsection, we discuss two theoretical developments that may be useful in explaining why developing countries, like our eleven Latin American countries, find it more difficult to borrow than do more developed countries, like those in Western Europe and the United States and Japan. In the first set of theories, governments in developing countries pay back their debts to establish good reputations, which allow them to borrow in the future. Bad luck in the past can lead to countries having bad reputations, which can persist over time. In the second, governments in developing countries are limited in their ability to borrow by their incentives to repay in the future. Governments that have only recently gained access to international credit markets may have fewer incentives to repay, which translates into a lower ability to borrow.

A large body of literature models the importance of reputation in access to foreign loans (for a survey, see Cole and P. J. Kehoe [1997]). Amador and Phelan (2020) develop a model in which a government's hidden type randomly switches back and forth between a commitment type, which cannot default, and an optimizing type, which defaults with a positive probability. The type of the government can be interpreted as a statement about the persons currently in office or the quality of institutions that help discipline their behavior. In their model, lenders have beliefs about the probability that the government is the commitment type and update them based on its actions. These beliefs can be interpreted as the government's reputation; thus lenders are more willing to pay a higher price for the government's debt—or offer a lower interest rate—the higher its reputation. The government's type changes stochastically, and the government is also subject to random shocks. It is only in situations where the government is of the optimizing type and where it has a negative shock that the government defaults. Because the lenders update their beliefs through Bayesian updating, the government's reputation evolves over time. In equilibrium, the model features a "graduation date," which is a finite amount of time since the last default, after which the interest rates are not affected by the level of the debt.

Reputation models focus on problems of incomplete information. In contrast, in models with enforcement constraints, information is complete, and both the government of the borrowing country and its creditors know that in some situations the government will not want to repay its debt—that is, situations where the debt contract is not enforceable. In equilibrium, the creditors do not offer debt contracts to the government if they know that the government will not repay. Kehoe and Levine (1993) develop a general equilibrium theory with enforcement constraints. Albuquerque and Hopenhayn (2004) incorporate enforcement constraints into a model of firm dynamics. In their model, a young firm borrows to build up its capital stock. The young firm is constrained, however, because creditors know that it has a limited ability to repay. As the firm gets older, it accumulates capital, which relaxes the enforcement constraint. Eventually, the firm is able to reach the optimal size where it is no longer constrained. In a sense, this model also rationalizes a "graduation date." An interesting direction for research would be to model a government as being like a firm in the Albuquerque-Hopenhayn (2004) model. When it enters international capital markets for the first time, it faces enforcement constraints and borrows to build up infrastructure. After some time participating in international capital markets, the government has potentially accumulated enough infrastructure so as to have more incentives to repay. This mechanism makes enforcement constraints less binding in the future.

Most models of enforcement constraints allow state contingent debt and borrowers to honor all commitments. This does not mean that there are no equilibrium outcomes that can be interpreted as defaults. In the Albuquerque-Hopenhayn (2004) model, one outcome is what they call liquidation, in which a firm shuts down and pays its creditors less than they would have received if the state were more favorable. Similarly, Kehoe and Levine (2008) show that there are equilibria in which borrowers pay nothing on their debts and forfeit their collateral. This is just the equilibrium outcome that the enforcement constraints require.

In some of the equilibria in these models, the maximum amount that the government is able to borrow depends on the history of shocks and changes over time. Many times, the borrowing constraint is either binding or close to the bound. It is therefore possible that even if a government has a relatively low debt-to-GDP ratio, it could be unable to borrow a few percentage points of GDP in a single period.

We hypothesize that these sorts of models can rationalize the distinction between "emerging" governments (the ones that only recently entered the international capital markets) and "developed" governments (the ones that have used the debt markets for a long time). In these setups, it is interesting to reconsider the liberalization of capital markets and financial systems. Experience shows that liberalizing the financial sector substantially increases contingent debt, and if a shock is realized that causes the government to bail out banks, then the need for debt runs discontinuously high, which may not be consistent with the credit constraints of the problem. The discussion suggests that a good part of the debt crisis in the early 1980s may be explained by the crackdown in financial sectors and the substantial increase in government debt due to the deposit insurance. Thus the combination of an emerging government together with a liberalization of capital flows may be explosive because the emerging government could find itself limited in the amount of credit that it can obtain in the market. The emerging nature of the government implies that it will be credit constrained for a time. On the other hand, financial liberalization substantially increases the contingent debt. Tension seems to be present between opening the country to foreign capital and early financial liberalization. This is the central message of Diaz-Alejandro (1985).

These considerations will be relevant in trying to understand some of the crises experienced by the Latin American region during this period. They may help shed light on questions such as these: Why is there a debt limit to begin with? Does it make a difference if you arrive at that limit smoothly or by a discrete jump in the debt? To put it differently, should the constraints on debt be related to the total amount of debt in a given period or to the net change in the total amount of debt in a given period? How relevant are incentives rather than ability to repay in determining credit limits? We will fall short of providing clear answers to these difficult and very important questions, but we are convinced that the case studies that follow in this book bring us closer to these answers.

Appendix A

The government's budget constraint in units of domestic currency is

$$B_t + P_t b_t + E_t B_t^* + M_t = P_t(D_t + T_t) + B_{t-1} R_{t-1} + P_t b_{t-1} r_{t-1} + E_t B_{t-1}^* R_{t-1}^* + M_{t-1},$$

where the notation has been defined in the third section above.

Dividing the equation by GDP in current prices, we obtain

$$\frac{B_t}{P_t y_t} + \frac{P_t b_t}{P_t y_t} + \frac{B_t^* E_t}{P_t y_t} + \frac{M_t}{P_t y_t} =$$

$$\frac{P_t D_t}{P_t y_t} + \frac{P_t T_t}{P_t y_t} + \frac{B_{t-1} R_{t-1}}{P_t y_t} + \frac{P_t b_{t-1} r_{t-1}}{P_t y_t} + \frac{E_t B_{t-1}^* R_{t-1}^*}{P_t y_t} + \frac{M_{t-1}}{P_t y_t}.$$

We can rewrite this equation as

$$\frac{B_t}{P_t y_t} + \frac{P_t b_t}{P_t y_t} + \left(\frac{E_t P_t^W}{P_t}\right) \frac{B_t^* / P_t^W}{y_t} + \frac{M_t}{P_t y_t}$$

$$= \frac{P_t D_t}{P_t y_t} + \frac{P_t T_t}{P_t y_t} + \left(\frac{P_{t-1} y_{t-1}}{P_t y_t}\right) \frac{B_{t-1} R_{t-1}}{P_{t-1} y_{t-1}} + \left(\frac{P_{t-1} y_{t-1}}{P_t y_t}\right) \frac{P_t b_{t-1} r_{t-1}}{P_{t-1} y_{t-1}}$$

$$+ \left(\frac{E_t P_t^W}{P_t}\right)\left(\frac{P_{t-1}^W y_{t-1}}{P_t^W y_t}\right) \frac{B_{t-1}^* R_{t-1}^* / P_{t-1}^W}{y_{t-1}} + \frac{M_{t-1}}{P_t y_t}.$$

Now let

$$\theta_t^N = \frac{B_t}{P_t y_t}, \quad \theta_t^r = \frac{b_t}{y_t}, \quad \theta_t^* = \frac{B_t^* / P_t^*}{Y_t}, \quad m_t = \frac{M_t}{P_t Y_t}, \quad d_t = \frac{P_t D_t}{P_t y_t}, \quad \tau_t = \frac{P_t T_t}{P_t y_t}$$

and

$$\xi_t = \left(\frac{E_t P_t^*}{P_t}\right), \quad g_t = \frac{Y_t}{Y_{t-1}}, \quad \pi_t = \frac{P_t}{P_{t-1}}, \quad \pi_t^W = \frac{P_t^W}{P_{t-1}^W}.$$

We can write the budget constraint as

$$\theta_t^N + \theta_t^r + \xi_t \theta_t^* + m_t = d_t + x_t + \frac{R_{t-1}}{g_t \pi_t} \theta_{t-1}^N + \frac{r_{t-1}}{g_t} \theta_{t-1}^N + \xi_t \frac{R_{t-1}^*}{g_t \pi_t^W} \theta_{t-1}^* + \frac{1}{g_t \pi_t} m_{t-1}.$$

Subtracting θ_{t-1}^N, θ_{t-1}^r, $\xi_t\theta_{t-1}^*$, and $m_{t-1}/(g_t\pi_t)$ from both sides of this equation, we obtain

$$\left(\theta_t^N - \theta_{t-1}^N\right) + \left(\theta_t^r - \theta_t^r\right) + \left(\xi_t\theta_t^* - \xi_t\theta_{t-1}^*\right) + m_t - \frac{1}{g_t\pi_t}m_{t-1}$$

$$= d_t + \tau_t + \theta_{t-1}^N\left(\frac{R_{t-1}}{g_t\pi_t}-1\right) + \theta_{t-1}^N\left(\frac{r_{t-1}}{g_t}-1\right) + \xi_t\theta_{t-1}^*\left(\frac{R_{t-1}^*}{g_t\pi_t^W}-1\right),$$

which is equivalent to our budget accounting equation (4), since

$$m_t - \frac{1}{g_t\pi_t}m_{t-1} = \left(m_t - m_{t-1}\right) + m_{t-1}\left(1 - \frac{1}{g_t\pi_t}\right).$$

Appendix B

In this appendix, we solve a deterministic small open economy version of a simple, two-period-lived overlapping-generations model in which there is a demand for money like that in equation (5).

Each cohort has a unit mass of household members that live for two periods. There is one type of consumption good in every period. The utility function of the representative household of the generation born in period t is

$$\log c_t^t + \lambda \log c_{t+1}^t, \tag{15}$$

where c_t^t is the consumption of this household when young and c_{t+1}^t is the consumption when old. The representative household is endowed with 1 unit of the good when young and e consumption when old, where $1 > e > 0$.

There are two assets in the economy: domestic and foreign currency. To ensure that there are equilibria in which domestic currency is used, we impose a cash-in-advance constraint for local currency on net purchases of consumption:

$$M_t \geq P_{t+1}(c_{t+1}^t - e). \tag{16}$$

This condition makes foreign currency less valuable to households than domestic currency. To finance expenditures, the government levies lump sum taxes τ_t on the young in generation t.

The budget constraint of the household born in t when young is

$$P_t c_t^t + M_t = P_t - P_t\tau_t. \tag{17}$$

The household maximizes utility (15) subject to budget constraint (17), the cash-in-advance constraint (16), and a nonnegativity constraint on money holdings $M_t \geq 0$. The solution is

$$
c_t^t = \begin{cases} \dfrac{P_t(1-\tau_t)+P_{t+1}e}{(1+\lambda)P_t} & \text{if } \dfrac{P_{t+1}}{P_t} \leq \dfrac{\lambda(1-\tau_t)}{e} \\[4mm] 1 & \text{if } \dfrac{P_{t+1}}{P_t} \geq \dfrac{\lambda(1-\tau_t)}{e} \end{cases} .
$$

$$
c_{t+1}^t = \begin{cases} \dfrac{\lambda(P_t(1-\tau_t)+P_{t+1}e)}{(1+\lambda)P_{t+1}} & \text{if } \dfrac{P_{t+1}}{P_t} \leq \dfrac{\lambda(1-\tau_t)}{e} \\[4mm] e & \text{if } \dfrac{P_{t+1}}{P_t} \geq \dfrac{\lambda(1-\tau_t)}{e} \end{cases}
$$

$$
\dfrac{M_t}{P_t} = \begin{cases} \dfrac{\lambda(1-\tau_t)}{1+\lambda} - \dfrac{e}{1+\lambda}\left(\dfrac{P_{t+1}}{P_t}\right) & \text{if } \dfrac{P_{t+1}}{P_t} \leq \dfrac{\lambda(1-\tau_t)}{e} \\[4mm] 0 & \text{if } \dfrac{P_{t+1}}{P_t} \geq \dfrac{\lambda(1-\tau_t)}{e} \end{cases} .
$$

Notice that the money demand function (5) has exactly this form, where

$$
\gamma = \frac{\lambda(1-\tau_t)}{1+\lambda}, \quad \delta = \frac{e}{1+\lambda} .
$$

Note

The views expressed herein are those of the authors and not necessarily those of the Federal Reserve Bank of Minneapolis or the Federal Reserve System.

References

Aguiar, Mark, and Gita Gopinath. 2006. "Defaultable Debt, Interest Rates and the Current Account." *Journal of International Economics* 69 (1): 69–83.

Albuquerque, Rui, and Hugo A. Hopenhayn. 2004. "Optimal Lending Contracts and Firm Dynamics." *Review of Economic Studies* 71 (2): 285–315.

Amador, Manuel, and Christopher Phelan. 2020. "Reputation and Sovereign Default." Unpublished paper, University of Minnesota, Minneapolis and Saint Paul.

Arellano, Cristina. 2008. "Default Risk and Income Fluctuations in Emerging Economies." *American Economic Review* 98 (3): 690–712.

Ayres, João, Gaston Navarro, Juan Pablo Nicolini, and Pedro Teles. 2018. "Sovereign Default: The Role of Expectations." *Journal of Economic Theory* 175 (C): 803–12.

Barro, Robert J. 1991. "Economic Growth in a Cross-section of Countries." *Quarterly Journal of Economics* 106 (2): 407–43.

Bolt, Jutta, Robert Inklaar, Herman de Jong, and Jan Luiten van Zanden. 2018. "Rebasing 'Maddison': New Income Comparisons and the Shape of Long-Run Economic Development." Maddison Project Working Paper 10, Groningen Growth and Development Centre, University of Groningen, Netherlands. https://www.ggdc.net/maddison.

Calvo, Guillermo A. 1988. "Servicing the Public Debt: The Role of Expectations." *American Economic Review* 78 (4): 647–61.

———. 1998. "Varieties of Capital-Market Crises." In *The Debt Burden and Its Consequences for Monetary Policy*, edited by Guillermo A. Calvo and Mervyn King, 181–207. Proceedings of a conference held by the International Economic Association at the Deutsche Bundesbank, Frankfurt, Germany. Houndmills, Basingstoke, Hampshire, UK: Palgrave Macmillan/International Economic Association.

Cole, Harold L., and Patrick J. Kehoe. 1997. "Reviving Reputation Models of International Debt." *Federal Reserve Bank of Minneapolis Quarterly Review* 21 (1): 21–30.

Cole, Harold L., and Timothy J. Kehoe. 1996. "A Self-Fulfilling Model of Mexico's 1994–1995 Debt Crisis." *Journal of International Economics* 41 (3–4): 309–30.

———. 2000. "Self-Fulfilling Debt Crises." *Review of Economic Studies* 67 (1): 91–116.

Diaz-Alejandro, Carlos. 1985. "Good-Bye Financial Repression, Hello Financial Crash." *Journal of Development Economics* 19 (1–2): 1–24.

Eaton, Jonathan, and Mark Gersovitz. 1981. "Debt with Potential Repudiation: Theoretical and Empirical Analysis." *Review of Economic Studies* 48 (2): 289–309.

Galeano, Eduardo. 1973. *Open Veins of Latin America: Five Centuries of the Pillage of a Continent.* New York: Monthly Review. First published 1971, as *Las venas abiertas de América Latina*, Mexico City: Siglo XXI Editores.

Hall, George J., and Thomas J. Sargent. 2011. "Interest Rate Risk and Other Determinants of Post-WWII US Government Debt/GDP Dynamics." *American Economic Journal: Macroeconomics* 3 (3): 192–214.

Kehoe, Timothy J., and David K. Levine. 1993. "Debt Constrained Asset Markets." *Review of Economic Studies* 60:865–88.

———. 2008. "Bankruptcy and Collateral in Debt Constrained Markets." In *Macroeconomics in the Small and the Large: Essays on Microfoundations, Macroeconomic Applications, and Economic History in Honor of Axel Leijonhufvud*, edited by Roger E. A. Farmer, 99–114. Cheltenham, U.K.: Edward Elgar.

Krugman, Paul. 1979. "A Model of Balance-of-Payments Crises." *Journal of Money, Credit and Banking* 11 (3): 311–25.

Lorenzoni, Guido, and Ivan Werning. 2013. "Slow Moving Debt Crises." Working paper 19228, National Bureau of Economic Research, Cambridge, Mass.

Marcet, Albert, and Juan P. Nicolini. 2003. "Recurrent Hyperinflations and Learning." *American Economic Review* 93 (5): 1476–98.

Sargent, Thomas J. 1986. *Rational Expectations and Inflation*. Princeton, N.J.: Princeton University Press.

Sargent, Thomas, Noah Williams, and Tao Zha. 2009. "The Conquest of South American Inflation." *Journal of Political Economy* 117 (2): 211–56.

Vargas Llosa, Mario. 1974. *Conversation in the Cathedral*. New York: HarperCollins. First published in 1969, as *Conversación en la catedral*, Barcelona: Editorial Seix Barral, S.A.

Argentina

The History of Argentina

Francisco Buera
Washington University in St. Louis

Juan Pablo Nicolini
Federal Reserve Bank of Minneapolis and Universidad Torcuato Di Tella

Major fiscal and monetary events, 1960–2017

1962 Balance of payments crisis	**1990** Mandatory swap of short-term bank deposits for long-term government bonds (Bonex Plan)
1975 First hyperinflation	
1978 Stabilization plan with crawling peg (*tablita*)	
	1991 Currency board
1981 Balance of payments crisis	**1993** Brady Plan (Par Bond)
1982 Banking crisis and default on government debt	**1995** Banking crisis Currency board maintained
1985 Second hyperinflation Stabilization plan with fixed exchange rate (Austral Plan)	**2001** Banking crisis Abandonment of currency board Default on government debt
1988 New stabilization plan (Spring Plan)	**2005** First debt renegotiation
1989 Third hyperinflation	**2010** Second debt renegotiation
	2016 Third and final debt renegotiation

Introduction

In this chapter, we review the monetary and fiscal history of Argentina from 1960 to 2017, a period that witnessed the highest level of macroeconomic instability in Argentina's history. During that time, the economy was characterized by very disappointing growth performance, particularly during the three intervening decades: per capita income in 2003 was roughly the same as it was in 1973. This growth performance can be seen in Figure 1, which plots the logarithm of income per capita along with the logarithm of a trend that grows at 2 percent per year. The vertical lines in this figure, and in the figures that follow, visually divide the period we analyze into four subperiods, which we use to organize the discussion of Argentina's macroeconomic history. We explain this choice of subperiods below. The economy did reasonably well until 1974, keeping pace with the 2 percent trend, the long-run growth rate of per capita output in the United States. But

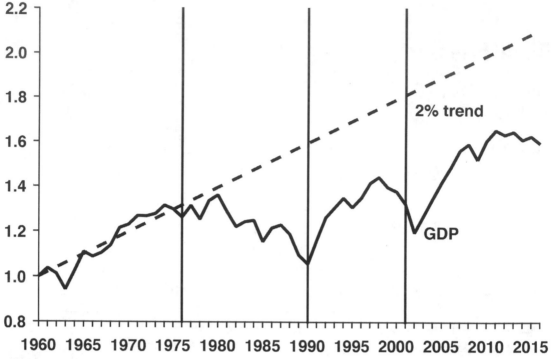

Figure 1. Log of per capita GDP

afterward it entered into a three-decades-long stagnation with highly volatile growth rates. Sustained growth resumed in 1991 but was stopped by a major depression that started in 1998 and bottomed out in 2002. The recovery from the depression was fast, and several years of high growth followed until 2010, when the economy again stagnated until 2017, the last year of the period we study.

Figure 2 plots the inflation rate for the period. Owing to the magnitudes of the rates, and as was done in this volume for other countries that experienced periods of hyperinflation, we plot the equivalent monthly rate that, being constant, would imply the same yearly rate as the one observed in the data.[1] Inflation, chronic for the first decade but moderate, became uncontrollable for a decade and a half and was terminated in 1991, the year in which a currency board was imposed. The following decade was the only one in which the inflation rate was the same as in developed countries, averaging 2.7 percent per year. It then jumped up, following the traumatic ending of the currency board in early 2002, but remained at low levels, similar to those of the late 1960s.

Figure 3 depicts the fiscal deficit for the period as a fraction of total output. It includes the deficits of both state-owned enterprises and the provinces. Chronic but relatively low deficits characterize the first decade and a half, with an average value of 3.2 percent from 1960 to 1973.

But the trend changes in 1973, and a sequence of higher and more volatile deficits accompanied the high-inflation period, averaging 6 percent from 1974 to 1990. In 1991,

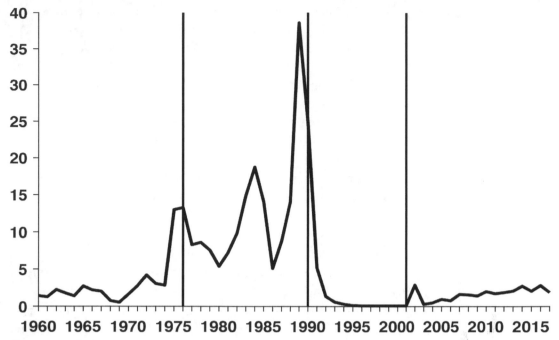

Figure 2. Inflation, average monthly inflation rate per year

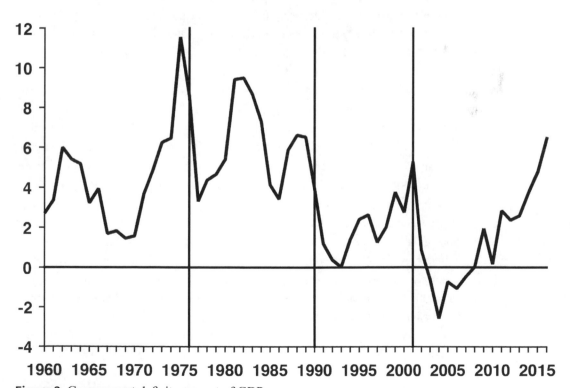

Figure 3. Government deficit, percent of GDP

inflation abruptly ends. That year coincides, as implied by the conceptual framework discussed in the preceding chapter, "A Framework for Studying the Monetary and Fiscal History of Latin America," with the year in which a structural break occurred in the behavior of the deficit. While the deficit was almost always above 2 percent from 1960 to 1990 and averaged 4.7 percent in that period, it was almost always below 2 percent from 1991 to 2010 and averaged 0.6 percent. This finding is remarkable, given that the period includes the massive crisis Argentina endured between 1998 and 2002. Starting in 1998, Argentina entered into a recession that transformed into a depression by 2001, with an output drop of almost 20 percent from peak (1998) to trough (2002). The crisis included a major banking crisis, a default on debt, and, as mentioned above, the traumatic end of the decade-long currency board. Despite all these events, the deficit in those years was remarkably low, reaching a peak of slightly above 4 percent in the midst of the worst recession in decades. The years that followed the crisis were characterized by sustained fiscal surpluses, a feature unseen in Argentina not only during the period we study but also since World War II, which is when credible data became available. But this surplus did not last long: the fiscal deficit gradually worsened, increasing by 2017 to levels that had not been seen since the hyperinflation years. As Figure 2 makes clear, though, the impact on inflation has been very moderate, at least until 2017, the final period we study.

A comparison of Figures 2 and 3 clearly shows that from the beginning of the sample until 1973, the deficit was moderately low, as was inflation. Healthy growth characterizes this period. In contrast, the period of very high deficits and high inflation that started in 1973 and ended in 1991 coincides with the worst experience in terms of output growth, as Figure 1 makes clear: per capita GDP, which had grown by around 30 percent from 1960 to 1973, went back in 1991 to the same level it was in 1960. After the sudden and very successful end of inflation in 1991, the economy ran for a decade with low inflation rates, a period that coincided with a remarkable convergence of output to the trend. Both the low inflation and the convergence to the trend ended abruptly with the 2001 crisis. The economy very quickly recovered from the crisis by 2003 and, at the same time, managed to keep inflation at very low rates until 2010. This period is accompanied, as Figure 3 makes clear, by the lowest deficits for the whole period, averaging −0.4 percent and including six consecutive years with fiscal surpluses. This period coincided with a strong convergence of per capita GDP to the 2 percent trend. Then, after 2010, inflation started rising again, and per capita income stopped growing. Both events coincided with the worsening of the fiscal deficit.

In what follows, we explain in more detail the evolution of the deficit and the way it was financed. In this way, we explain the evolution of government debt during the period, as well as the different policies that were implemented at various points. As we argue, the discussion will help us understand the roots of all the main macroeconomic events that unfolded in Argentina during the period, including several balance of payments crises, periods of hyperinflation, banking crises, and defaults. All the analysis will follow the conceptual framework described in "A Framework for Studying the Monetary and Fiscal History of Latin America." As the framework makes clear, the way a given deficit is financed is crucial to understanding the evolution of the main macroeconomic variables. However, the ability to finance the deficit with debt depends on the government's access to either domestic or international markets. Therefore, the government's ability to borrow is the main element we consider when choosing the starting and ending years for each subperiod.

The first subperiod we will analyze starts in 1960 and runs until 1976. During these years, the economy was closed to capital movements. The domestic credit market was heavily regulated and not very developed. Therefore, the government's ability to borrow was rather limited.

The second subperiod is from 1977 to 1990. This period witnessed the first liberalization of domestic financial markets, with a market-determined interest rate and a substantial entry of new financial institutions. At the same time, the capital account was opened, so the credit market was integrated with the world markets. This integration allowed the government to borrow in international markets, which it did. Within a few years, the government's foreign debt increased rapidly. But in 1982, Argentina defaulted on its foreign debt, as did many other countries in the region. A natural consequence of this default was that the only remaining source of financing for the government was printing money. A decade of very high inflation followed, which ended when the currency board was adopted in 1991.

This is the starting point of the third subperiod, 1991–2001, characterized by a second liberalization of financial and international markets and a successful debt renegotiation process. This process allowed the government to borrow in international markets again. A decade of low inflation and high growth ensued. However, the debt kept growing and a new crisis developed in 2001, a year that saw the currency board collapse in the midst of a banking crisis and a new default on government debt.

The final subperiod starts in 2002, with Argentina excluded again from international markets because of the default during the previous year.[2] A bargaining round with bondholders was held in 2005, when around 75 percent of the debt was renegotiated. A second round took place in 2010, and the proportion of the debt renegotiated went up to 93 percent. The remaining bondholders went to court and were finally paid in 2016. Thus this period is characterized by the government's inability to borrow abroad. The recovery from the 2001 crisis was fast, leading to high growth rates in per capita income, with higher inflation rates than in the 1990s, but very moderate and stable relative to the Argentinean experience of the second half of the twentieth century. This discussion rationalizes the vertical lines in Figures 1 to 3.

The rest of the chapter evolves as follows. In the second section we discuss the evolution of the debt of the Argentinean government, as well as some of its characteristics. The third to sixth sections describe in detail the main macroeconomic events of each of the subperiods. In each of those sections, we also discuss how well the events can be understood using the conceptual framework in "A Framework for Studying the Monetary and Fiscal History of Latin America." In the seventh section we present the budget constraint decomposition discussed in "A Framework," and in the final section, we provide some concluding remarks.

The Evolution of Government Debt

The value of Argentina's government debt in 1996 U.S. dollars is depicted in Figure 4. The figure represents total federal government debt, including bonds, banking debt, and debt with other governments and financial institutions, as well as the debt of the provinces and public enterprises when information is available.[3]

The level of the debt was small and relatively stable during the first subperiod. However, starting in 1975 and until the default of 1982, the yearly average growth rate of the debt was close to 30 percent. From the time of the default until the end of the decade, the debt remained roughly constant again, its movements essentially explained by two factors: first, by the arrears that resulted from the default, and second, by the liabilities that resulted from the balance of payments and banking crisis of 1981, which were gradually accounted for as they matured. Starting in the early 1990s, as the government regained access to international capital markets, the debt started to grow again, at the average yearly rate of 10 percent. This persistent increase in debt continued until the 2001 crisis. At that point, the evolution of debt is characterized by a sharp increase from 2002 through 2004 and a drastic reduction in 2005. These fluctuations represent the fiscal cost of the crisis and the subsequent debt renegotiation that included a substantial haircut on capital. By 2011, government debt was at the value it had been prior to the 2001 crisis. Then debt rose again as the fiscal deficit grew. Since a fraction of the debt defaulted on in 2001 was still in default until 2016, most of the new debt issued was domestic. After the final agreement in early 2016, the government regained wide access to foreign

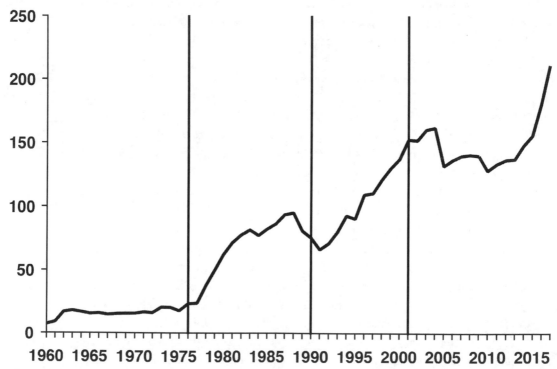

Figure 4. Total public debt, 1996 billion U.S. dollars

borrowing, and the increase in the deficit in the last years explains the corresponding sharp increase in total debt.

Figure 5 depicts the debt-to-GDP ratio. Two main developments affect this figure relative to the one before. The first one—GDP growth—is obvious. The second, which is very important for Argentina during the period, is real exchange rate movements between the peso and the dollar. GDP as well as peso-denominated debt are deflated using peso price indexes, while the dollar-denominated debt is deflated using the U.S. price indexes and the nominal exchange rate between the peso and the dollar. Any movements in the real exchange rate will affect the figure. This is important to consider because it implies movements in the debt-to-GDP ratio that are associated not with the evolution of the deficit but with relative price changes, and substantial relative price changes took place in Argentina during the period considered here, as we now show.

To decompose the effect of real exchange rate changes in the evolution of debt, Figure 6 depicts a counterfactual value of the debt-to-GDP ratio. The simulation is made assuming a value for the real exchange rate that is, for the whole period, equal to the value it had in 1991. This real exchange rate is used to value the fraction of total debt that was denominated in dollars.[4] The differences between the two curves are very large, making evident the role of the real exchange rate in explaining changes in the debt-to-GDP ratio.[5] Thus, while the debt-to-GDP ratio could be low by international standards, a large and sudden real exchange rate appreciation can substantially modify this ratio. As it turns out, large and sudden real appreciations are not uncommon events.

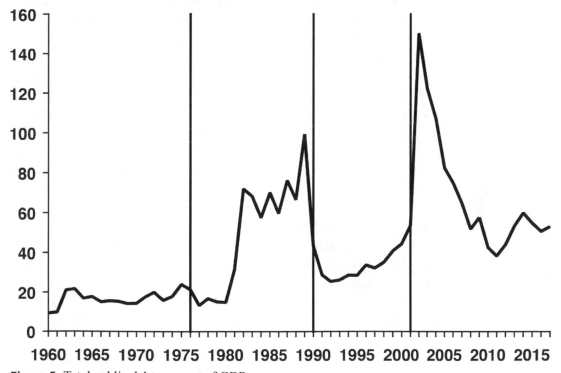

Figure 5. Total public debt, percent of GDP

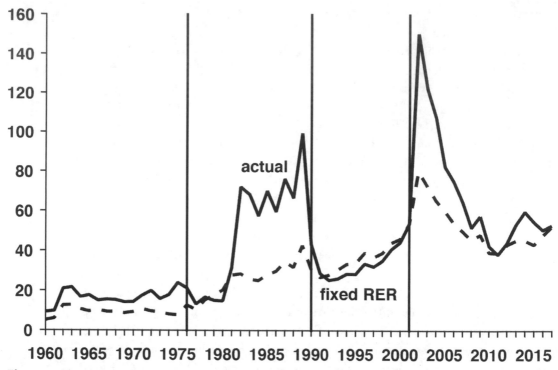

Figure 6. Simulated public national debt fixing the real exchange rate (RER), percent of GDP

To further understand the previous two figures, in Figure 7 we plot the ratio of total debt denominated in pesos to total debt denominated in foreign currency, as well as the ratio of nonindexed debt to indexed debt, starting only in 1962, the first period for which we have data. The share of peso-denominated debt was important (about a third of total debt) during the 1960s and vanished during the high-inflation period. It then had a modest increase in the 1990s and only became significant again after the 2001 crisis. Most of the peso-denominated debt issued during the 1990s is nonindexed debt, while in the 2000s the opposite was true. Figures 5, 6, and 7 together show that while the debt-to-GDP ratio was low in normal times, albeit trending up, the exposure of this number to real exchange rate fluctuations was very important. For most of this period, around 90 percent of the debt was dollar denominated, which means that a real exchange rate depreciation would substantially affect that ratio. For instance, to increase the debt-to-GDP ratio from 25 percent to 40 percent, the government should have a deficit (including interest payments) three points higher than the growth rate of output sustained for ten years. A crisis that conveys a 50 percent real depreciation—a modest number given the recent experience—would achieve that change instantaneously.

Another feature of the debt that is relevant for the discussion that follows is its maturity structure, as discussed in "A Framework for Studying the Monetary and Fiscal History of Latin America." Figure 8 depicts the evolution of the maturity of government debt, as measured by the share of debt maturing in one year. As shown in the figure, substantial changes have taken place over the years. The stabilization period of the late 1970s

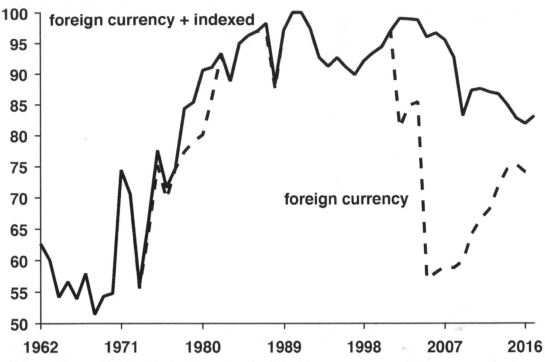

Figure 7. Types of public debt, percent of total public debt

inherits a distribution of maturities that are highly biased toward short-term debt. Almost a third of the debt was due within a year. The bias toward short-term debt continues up to the default, suggesting that rollover risk may have been a key aspect of the debt crisis. Following the debt restructuring under the Brady Plan, less than 10 percent of the debt was due in a year. This is a reflection more of the negotiations between the government and the creditors that took into account the government's inability to quickly generate surpluses to pay the debt than of an explicit policy to manage the maturity of the debt.

However, the debt expansion of the 1990s evident in Figure 4—most of it voluntary debt floated by the government in international capital markets—managed to preserve a favorable maturity structure. Thus by 1997 less than 40 percent of the debt was due in the following four years, and only 8 percent was due in the following year. By 2000 the maturity problem worsened somewhat. The fraction of debt due in the following year increased to 14 percent of GDP. Nevertheless, while substantial, the maturity problem was less significant than it had been prior to the 1982 crisis. By 2009 the structure was similar to that in 2000 and worsened somewhat by 2017: the debt maturing in one year was then slightly less than 20 percent of the total stock of debt, which is equivalent to roughly 12 percent of GDP, a relatively large number that needed to be rolled over during the following year.

A final factor that determines the evolution of the debt is the real interest rate faced by the country. Movements in that rate can be explained by changes in the international risk-free rate or in the default risk; this last component may be driven by fundamentals or

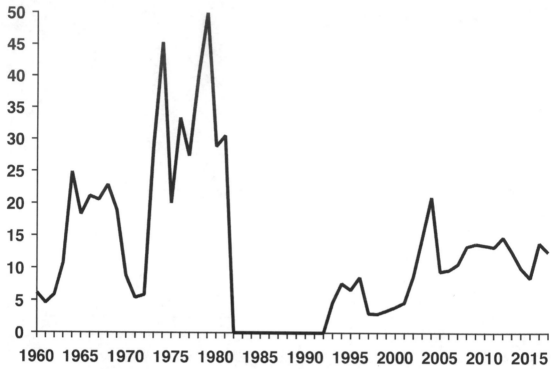

Figure 8. Short-term public debt, percent of total

multiplicity, as explained in "A Framework for Studying the Monetary and Fiscal History of Latin America." In Figure 9, we plot total interest payments over GDP. As the figure shows, in both default episodes, interest payments to GDP reached very high values. In the first case, 1981, it coincides with high real interest rates in the United States. But in the second, 2001, it is less obvious that the international risk-free rate had a spike, suggesting that default risk may have played an important role. While movements in the interest rate can explain the behavior in Figure 9, another factor should be considered, one related to the nature of the bonds issued and the accounting practices that were followed. The total interest paid on the accounts corresponded to the interest that actually accrued. Thus the amount of interest paid depended on coupons paid by the type of bond that was issued. At the time of the debt renegotiation in the early 1990s, some of the bonds were structured to back-load the interest payments, a feature that also explains part of the sharp increase shown in the figure during the second half of the 1990s.

1960–76

During the first decade and a half of the period we study, Argentina was closed to international capital movements. At the same time, the domestic financial market was heavily regulated. The interest rate was fixed by the government, and credit intermediation was

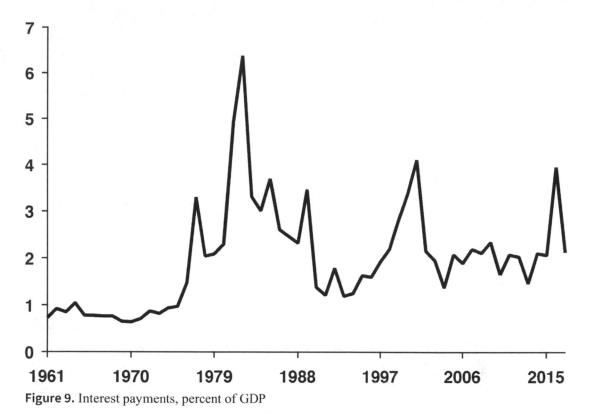

Figure 9. Interest payments, percent of GDP

mostly done through government-owned banks. As a result, there was very little room for financing fiscal deficits with debt. In 1960, the ratio of government debt to GDP was a mere 9.8 percent.

The period we discuss in this section starts in the middle of a stabilization plan that had been launched in 1959, the objective of which was to reduce the inflation rate. The nominal anchor chosen was the exchange rate. But, as Figure 3 makes clear, the required fiscal adjustment did not complement the stabilization efforts and rose from 2 percent in 1960 to around 5 percent by 1962. As a result, and as explained in "A Framework for Studying the Monetary and Fiscal History of Latin America," because of the difficulties of borrowing, part of that deficit was financed by monetary expansion from the central bank. We show this expansion in Figure 10, which plots two components of the monetary base: the international reserves and the credit to the domestic market.[6] The figure shows that, starting in early 1961, the increase in domestic credit is accompanied by a reduction in international reserves, to the point where half of the reserves had been lost by the end of the year. This trend lasted until February 1962, when the fixed exchange rate policy was abandoned and a devaluation of 60 percent followed in the subsequent three months, pushing inflation all the way up to 30 percent by the end of 1962. Figure 10 is a transparent example of the mechanics of a balance of payments unraveling due to a monetary financing of the deficit, as described in "A Framework for Studying the Monetary and Fiscal History of Latin America."

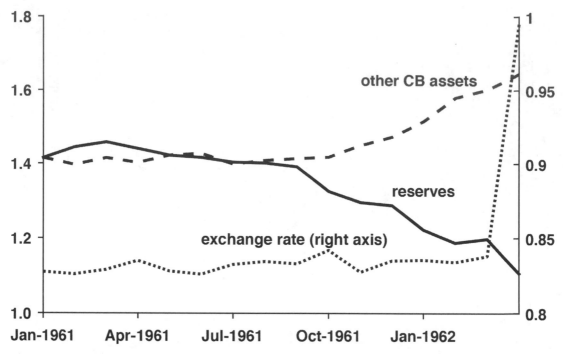

Figure 10. 1962 BoP crisis, Reserves and other Central Bank assets, billion U.S. dollars, ER in pesos/US dollar

The rest of the decade showed a gradual adjustment of the deficit, followed by a similar gradual adjustment in the inflation rate, which reached a one-digit yearly rate in 1969. Argentineans had to wait more than two decades, until 1993, to live in a one-digit-inflation economy again.

Starting in 1970, the healthy downward trend in the deficit reverted, and it started growing again every year, reaching a record high of 11 percent of GDP by 1975. Given the difficulties of borrowing, our conceptual framework implies that inflation should also increase, which is exactly what happened (see Figure 2), consistent with the fact that total government debt barely changed during this fifteen-year period. An apparent contradictory feature between Figures 2 and 3 is the drop in the inflation rate in 1973 and 1974 in spite of the rampant deficits. These years were characterized by policies of price controls that at times generated shortages of products. These price controls were eliminated in July 1975, and the first outburst of inflation ensued, reaching values between 300 percent and 700 percent annually during several months of 1975 and 1976.

Total public debt dropped substantially between the crisis of 1962 and 1968, in both constant dollars and as a fraction of GDP. We conjecture that part of this reduction can be explained by negative ex post returns on peso-denominated debt, induced either by unexpected inflation or by direct controls in the nominal interest rate. As we mentioned, during the period, the domestic financial sector was heavily regulated, including the imposition of ceilings on nominal interest rates. Note that by 1975, more than 90 percent of the debt was either indexed or in dollars (see Figure 7). This result was very likely the outcome of past experiences during which the government inflated away part of its debt.

In summary, this period matches the analysis in "A Framework for Studying the Monetary and Fiscal History of Latin America" remarkably well. The government did not have access to international credit markets, and the domestic market offered limited financing. Thus the fiscal deficit was driving inflation during this period. As the fiscal deficit went out of control by 1975, so did the inflation rate.

1977–90

The early years of the period 1977–90 are marked by widespread deregulation of the economy. Trade barriers were substantially reduced, and the capital account was liberalized, allowing for both private and public borrowing. This allowed the government to finance its deficit abroad at a time of highly liquid international markets. In addition, the domestic credit market was also deregulated. Entry restrictions for private financial institutions were relaxed, and the interest rate was left to be market determined. As is customary in many countries, the government decided to provide deposit insurance.

Following these changes, many banks entered the market, and the size of the financial sector as a proportion of GDP increased dramatically. This is reflected in Figure 11, where we plot the total liabilities of the financial sector, minus the international reserves of the central bank, divided by GDP.[7] The measure in Figure 11 represents the contingent liabilities held by the government, which are not recorded in the debt measures—as long as a banking crisis docs not occur. In this case, where there was deposit insurance, the figure represents explicit contingent liabilities. Because Argentina experienced three major banking crises during the period we study, this measure will help us understand the behavior of total government debt on some occasions, as we discuss below.

A final feature relevant to understanding the early years of this period is that the government also adopted a crawling-peg system as a way to gradually stop inflation. The scheme, which was very similar to the ones adopted by Chile and Uruguay at the same time, involved a sequence of preannounced and decreasing rates of devaluations of the peso versus the U.S. dollar. This system would gradually reduce the inflation rate, which had been over 700 percent in 1976. With the hope of making the exchange rate mechanisms more credible, the government offered exchange rate insurance in the event that a devaluation occurred.

The behavior of the deficit in 1977 was consistent with this gradual dis-inflationary approach, since it was brought down from over 8 percent in 1976 to less than 4 percent in 1977. However, as can be seen in Figure 3, it immediately started rising again, to above 8 percent in 1981. The crawling-peg system was successful at the beginning, so inflation continued to decline until 1981. This could happen, in spite of the increasing deficits, because the government could access the foreign debt markets in those years (see Figure 4). However, as Figure 12 shows, starting in 1980 the central bank began financing the rampant deficit by increasing the domestic credit component of the monetary base. Therefore, the international reserves started declining, just as they did during the

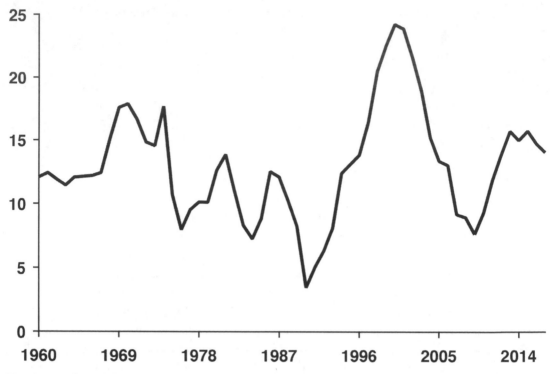

Figure 11. Financial exposure as a fraction of GDP

1962 crisis discussed above and in line with the discussion in "A Framework for Study-ing the Monetary and Fiscal History of Latin America." The devaluation in 1981 and the consequent burst in inflation were thus unavoidable.

The devaluation triggered the two mechanisms discussed above. First, the exchange rate insurance contracts had to be paid. Second, because of a currency mismatch in the assets and liabilities, the devaluation affected the banking sector. On top of this, very weak regulation of financial institutions, coupled with deposit insurance, created a systemic moral hazard problem, inducing a high fraction of nonperforming loans on financial institutions' balance sheets. This explosive combination generated a massive banking crisis and a decision to nationalize the debts of the banking sector. The rampant deficits, plus the realization of these contingent liabilities, led to a very high level of debt, high inflation, and the default on government debt in 1982.

The theory that emphasizes maturity is an attractive way to understand this episode. As mentioned above, the government accumulated contingent debt through the exchange rate and deposit insurance mechanisms. The deposits of the financial sector were of very short maturity, mostly a few months. The foreign exchange rate guarantee started for debts of over a year and a half but was rapidly extended to short-term liabilities too, so this bailout also included short-term debt. At the same time, the maturity of the existing debt in 1982 had an important bias toward the short term. According to Figure 8, more than 40 percent of the debt was due within a year. Thus 1982 and 1983 were years in which substantial amounts of liabilities were due.

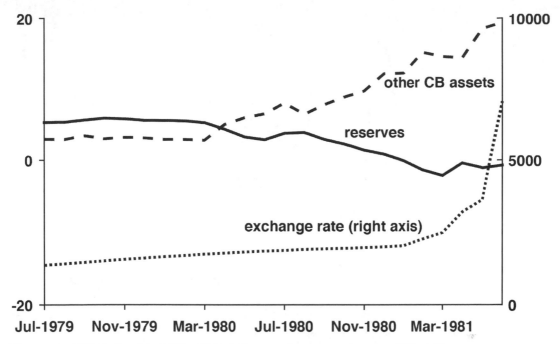

Figure 12. 1981 BoP crisis, billion U.S. dollars, exchange rate in pesos/U.S. dollar

The 1982 default forced the government out of the international capital markets until the early 1990s; hence, the fiscal imbalances had to be financed by seigniorage. The budget constraint discussed in "A Framework for Studying the Monetary and Fiscal History of Latin America" has a direct implication: deficits imply inflation, and that is the dominant characteristic of Argentina during this period. The hyperinflation of 1985 is the result of a declining but still high deficit.[8] The Austral Plan of June 1985 immediately brought down inflation, and a fiscal effort drove the deficit down to 3.7 percent and 2.9 percent of GDP in 1985 and 1986, respectively. But this effort reversed, and the deficit grew to around 5 percent in the following three years. Consequently, a new hyperinflation period developed by 1989. This decade is perhaps the most dramatic and clearest example of the forces behind the conceptual framework of the government budget constraint discussed in "A Framework for Studying the Monetary and Fiscal History of Latin America."[9]

The lack of access to credit markets is reflected in the flat portion of total debt exhibited during the 1980s (see Figure 4). In fact, during this period, the only source of financing for the government, other than printing money, was through the financial system, by increases in the reserve requirements of commercial banks deposited at the central bank. These reserves were remunerated at market-determined interest rates. In this way, an important fraction of domestic savings in the form of deposits financed the central government. The central bank was thus effectively acting as the financial arm of the Treasury. As we discuss below, this mechanism created a short-maturity, peso-denominated debt that planted the seeds for a high-cost debt problem that led to the Bonex Plan in December 1989.

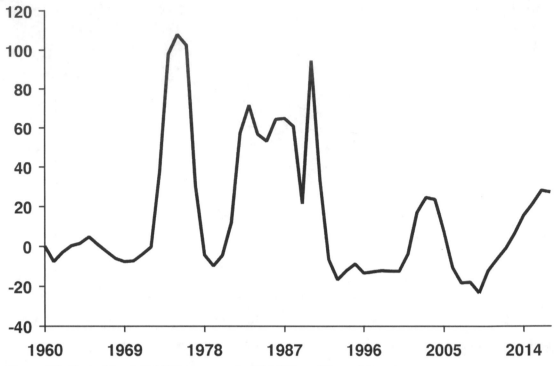

Figure 13. Central bank liabilities, percent of liabilities of financial sector

Figure 13 depicts the interest-bearing liabilities of the central bank, net of the international reserves, as a fraction of the total liabilities of the financial sector.[10] This is a key element in understanding some developments of the period 1989 to 1991. The implicit maturity structure of this debt is the maturity structure of the financial system liabilities, mainly deposits. During the period, the most common maturity for deposits was a week, almost never above a month. Thus the government was indebted to the private sector through the financial system at very low maturities for deposits. This form of financing—at very short maturities and very high interest rates—is the genesis for another episode involving rollover risk: the Bonex Plan of December 1989.

In order to understand the main forces behind this plan, let us go back to Figure 13. By 1989, almost 90 percent of the lending capacity of the banking sector went toward financing the government. Because of the extreme instability of the time, with highly volatile inflation rates, the most common maturity of deposits was a week. Thus the liabilities of the central bank represented very short-term maturity debt. On the verge of a stabilization plan, this very short-term, peso-denominated debt represented both a maturity and a denomination overhang, which can both be understood by using the conceptual framework of "A Framework for Studying the Monetary and Fiscal History of Latin America." The Bonex Plan was a swap of maturities and a swap of denomination. It mandatorily changed the peso-denominated short-term deposits of the private sector to dollar-denominated bonds with a ten-year maturity. The effect of the plan can be seen in Figure 11, which shows the large drop in the liabilities of the banking sector in 1989.

The Bonex Plan swap may have prevented bad equilibria, in which high interest rates justify a higher probability of default (either explicit or through future inflation), and the higher probability of default justifies those higher interest rates. This is one potential implication of the models in Calvo (1988), Cole and Kehoe (1996, 2000), and Calvo (1998) reviewed in "A Framework for Studying the Monetary and Fiscal History of Latin America." The reason is that the plan changed the denomination and the maturity of the debt the government had when the currency board was launched the following year. Thus the plan was in all likelihood an important ingredient in taming the high inflation in Argentina during the last decade of the last century. The deposits were swapped with Bonex, domestically issued dollar-denominated bonds. Several series of Bonex bonds were in circulation at the time, and the government never defaulted on them. The Bonex issued for this plan were fully paid by the government in due time. However, in the week immediately after the plan, the newly issued debt was selling at thirty cents per dollar. Thus it implied a substantial wealth redistribution from deposit holders, for whom their (one-week) term deposits were transactional assets and who needed to liquidate these deposits to pay incoming obligations, to deposit holders with deep pockets and no liquidity constraints.

1991–2001

The Bonex bonds may have been instrumental in improving the characteristics of the debt by 1990. However, besides the effort to lower the fiscal deficits that averaged 6.5 percent of GDP from 1987 to 1989, by 1990 the deficit was still 4 percent of GDP, inconsistent with low inflation rates, given the lack of access to foreign credit. A new burst of inflation, reaching a monthly rate of almost 100 percent in March 1990, was a dramatic beginning for a year that ended with an overall inflation rate exceeding 700 percent, and it paved the way for the currency board adopted in April 1991, the starting point of the third subperiod. The currency board established a fixed exchange rate between the U.S. dollar and the newly created peso at a price of 1. It also, by law, changed the mandate of the central bank of Argentina and imposed a 100 percent U.S. dollar backing of the monetary base.[11] In this way, the central bank could only print pesos to buy U.S. dollars, shutting down monetary financing of the deficit. The logic of the currency board was simple: by law, it made the inflation tax term in the budget constraint equal to zero. Thus any remaining deficit ought to be financed by issuing debt. This was a new attempt to end the policy regime of fiscal dominance that had prevailed in Argentina for decades and to begin a new regime of monetary dominance. Consistent with that notion, Congress passed a law that gave independence to the central bank—a law that has also been modified after the 2002 crisis.

The government was in default at the time, however, so the ability to borrow abroad was severely limited; that was why inflation was unavoidable during the 1980s, given the high fiscal deficits. Thus the currency board strategy was to put all eggs in the same basket: only fiscal surpluses would make the currency board viable. And so it was. As can be seen in Figure 3, the deficit was practically eliminated in 1991 and 1992, and a surplus was generated in 1993. One factor that explains this behavior is the privatization of state-owned companies in the beginning of the decade, which directly added to available resources.[12] The government accepted its own bonds as a means of payment in the auctions, so to some extent, the privatization process was a state company stocks-bond swap.

There is a sense in which the logic of the currency board had a substantial impact. As mentioned, it was designed to force a dramatic reduction in fiscal deficits, and along that dimension it was successful: monetary dominance prevailed in the years that followed. As can be seen in Figure 3, between 1960 and 1990, the deficit was below 2 percent only from 1966 to 1970. All other years it was above 2.5 percent, and during those thirty-one years, it averaged 4.7 percent of GDP. On the other hand, since 1991 it was above 2 percent (but barely so) in 1996, 1999, and 2001 and more recently in 2011 and 2013, but again, barely so. From 1991 until 2013, it averaged 0.75 percent. It seems apparent that the year of the structural break is 1991.

The fiscal effort is more radical than the numbers in Figure 3 suggest, since in 1993 Argentina reformed the social security system, which transitioned from a pay-as-you-go system to a fully funded one with private accounts. This transition had an important effect on the fiscal deficit, since the obligations to the current pensioners had to be partially absorbed with regular taxes.[13]

By 1993, with the economy growing at high rates, the government signed on to the Brady Plan, which was intended to restructure the debt in default—mostly bank debt—and transform it, after some debt forgiveness, into sovereign bonds. Following the plan, the government was able to borrow again in international markets, and this explains the expansion of the debt during the 1990s, which is clear in Figure 4. The natural reading of this event, using the budget constraint, is that the Brady Plan allowed the government to run the deficits from 1994 onward.

In early 1995, a severe bank run began, during which total deposits of the banking sector fell by almost 20 percent in five months. The same year, output dropped by 4 percent. The 1995 banking crisis was particularly difficult, since the currency board implied that the central bank was severely limited in acting as a lender of last resort. Had the banking crisis been much more severe, it would have forced the government to increase financing because of the existing contingent liabilities. Figure 11 shows that total financial exposure was around 13 percent of GDP. In the same period, the ratio of total debt to GDP was around 25 percent. It is unclear whether the government could have borrowed abroad to face additional liabilities equivalent to the total financial exposure. But, as it turned out, it did not need to: by mid-1995, the run on deposits was over. As we will see, this problem was substantially more severe in 2001.

Starting in 1994, deficits were positive, so debt started rising, doubling in about ten years. However, the size of the reported deficits, shown in Figure 3, does not seem to justify such a large increase in debt. As we show in the seventh section of this chapter, part of the increase in debt can be explained by unrecorded liabilities from the previous decade that were recognized later during this time period.

Starting in 1998, the country faced a sudden reversal of its current account, following the financial crisis of Southeast Asia in 1997 and the Russian default of 1998. A recession started in 1998 that ended a strong recovery with GDP growth rates that had been around 6 percent a year. This effect interacted with a feature that responded to the Brady negotiations of half a decade earlier. At the time, the debt payments, in terms of both capital and interest, had been back-loaded, and an important fraction of the debt was maturing starting in 2001, a year in which interest payments alone were above 4 percent of GDP (see Figure 9). The apparent difficulties in dealing with the payments on the foreign debt, together with the prolonged recession, started weakening the credibility of the currency board. As the financial system was highly dollarized, this raised doubts regarding the soundness of the banks, and a run on deposits started in early 2001. By then, as Figure 11 shows, the total exposure of bank liabilities was over 16 percent of GDP. Thus while the currency board implied that the central bank could back 100 percent of the monetary base, it could certainly not act as a lender of last resort unless it could obtain foreign borrowing in those amounts. But this banking crisis was unraveling at the time of a major credit crunch!

The deposit run lasted almost the whole year, mostly owing to the heavy capital requirement and liquidity provisions imposed on the banking sector by the central bank. But by November 2001, over 27 percent of the deposits had left the banking system. The inability of some banks to respond to their depositors led to a deposit freeze by the end of November. The freeze lasted only a few weeks, however, and the crisis, which implied the fall of the acting administration, ended in default on foreign debt and the abandonment of the currency board by January 2002, in the midst of the worst depression Argentina had experienced in decades.

During the decade we are considering, the values for inflation, the deficit, and the debt-to-GDP ratio for Argentina all satisfied the values required in the Maastricht Treaty, which established conditions for entry in the Eurozone. During the few years following the treaty, none of the European countries that signed the treaty satisfied those conditions. In spite of this, the country risk that the Argentinean government faced on the bonds it issued was on average around 6 percent a year. This country risk implied (assuming one-period debt, just to simplify) an extra payment during the decade of more than 15 percent of GDP. A counterfactual in which Argentina faced zero country risk, where those funds were used to cancel debt, would have left the country a debt-to-GDP ratio in 2000 equal to 25 percent instead of the 40 percent it had. Would Argentina have defaulted with that debt-to-GDP ratio? The models with multiple equilibria discussed above suggest that this may have been a critical factor during the 1990s.[14]

2002–17

The bottom of the recession was the first quarter of 2002, after a drop in GDP since 1998 of close to 18 percent. Unemployment reached unprecedented levels, and poverty rates rose above 40 percent. The crisis was very expensive in terms of its effect on public debt, as the jump in 2002 in Figures 4, 5, and 6 shows. Three factors are important in explaining this jump. The first was a bailout to the banking sector, which was bankrupt because of an asymmetric conversion of bank assets and liabilities to pesos. Indeed, while the dollar-denominated deposits were transformed to pesos at a 1.4 exchange rate, the dollar-denominated loans were transformed to pesos at the value of 1.0. The second factor is that by 2002, several provincial governments had debts that were absorbed by the federal government. The third was the launching of ad hoc social programs designed to cope with the impact of the crisis on the poorest share of the population. The 2005 debt renegotiation explains the large drop in debt in that year. The offer made in 2005 was accepted by a fraction of bondholders that was large enough to amount to almost three-quarters of the total owed. A second round of renegotiation in 2010 took that figure to 93 percent. The remaining 7 percent won the right in court to be paid in full, and a final agreement with creditors was reached in 2016.

It is worth mentioning that even after the debt forgiveness of 2005, total debt in 1996 dollars (Figure 4) and the debt-to-GDP ratio (Figure 5) were higher in 2006 than the value of 2001, just before the default. An important ingredient in many theoretical models of default like the ones revisited in "A Framework for Studying the Monetary and Fiscal History of Latin America" is that countries that go through a default episode may pay costs arising from different sources, but they end up with substantially lower levels of debt. At least in the case of Argentina, this does not seem to be the case.

The recovery from the Great Recession of 1998–2002 was very fast and was accompanied by six consecutive years of fiscal surpluses—a completely unprecedented event in Argentina. Those surpluses implied that the natural exclusion from credit markets that followed the default did not have any consequences for the inflation rate: there was no need to raise seigniorage. As a result of those surpluses, inflation remained mostly at a one-digit level from 2003 to 2007, and the dollar value of the debt in 2010 was very similar to what it had been in 2006, the year following the first and larger step in the long debt renegotiation process.

Things changed between 2008 and 2010. The healthy surpluses started to disappear and became a 2 percent fiscal deficit by 2013. The deficit then continued to increase, reaching a worrying value of close to 6 percent by 2017. Given the lack of access to foreign borrowing that lasted until 2016, the deficits had to be financed by seigniorage, and inflation rose again, to an average close to 25 percent a year, remaining around that value until the end of the sample. Not all the deficit was financed by the central bank during the period: domestic debt instruments were issued, explaining the upward trend in debt since 2010. Finally, the agreement with all bondholders by 2016 allowed the government to again borrow abroad, which explains why the large deficits of 2016 and 2017 did not put pressure on seigniorage but rather were financed by foreign debt, as Figure 4 makes clear.

The structural change in the behavior of the deficit in 1991, visible in Figure 3, did revert sometime between 2008 and 2010, and it has gone back to levels that resemble the period before 1991 and all the way to 2017, the last year covered by this study. One implication of the theories discussed in "A Framework for Studying the Monetary and Fiscal History of Latin America" is that if this deficit process is not modified, macroeconomic instability may eventually resume in Argentina. As we finish the last version of this chapter at the end of 2018, those signs of instability are already clearly visible, as discussed in the conclusions.

Budget Constraint Decomposition

In this section, we present the decomposition of the budget constraint discussed in "A Framework for Studying the Monetary and Fiscal History of Latin America," which is the basis for our summary and conclusions in this section. Table 1 presents each of the main components for the four subperiods studied. The top two rows are the sources of financing: change in debt and seigniorage. The bottom two rows are the needs for financing that is, the primary deficit and interest payments.

As discussed in "A Framework for Studying the Monetary and Fiscal History of Latin America," we have used independent measures for all the components of the budget constraint. Thus the numbers will not necessarily match in any particular period. We mentioned above several reasons why this may be the case. For example, the payments made for deposit and exchange rate insurance in the early 1980s were contingent liabilities that became explicit liabilities. At the same time, the resolution of the banking crisis in 2002, in which dollar-denominated assets and liabilities of the banking sector were transformed to pesos at different rates, involved the issuance of bonds to recapitalize the banks.

To make progress in quantifying these off-the-books measures, we then use the government budget constraint to compute a transfer, as explained in "A Framework for Studying the Monetary and Fiscal History of Latin America." This transfer measures the excess spending in that period if it turns out to be positive. And it measures unrecorded taxes or confiscations when it is negative. The average value of this transfer for each of the subperiods is depicted in the bottom row of Table 1.[15]

The first subperiod is characterized by sizable primary deficits of 3.6 percent and small interest payments. As we mentioned above, given the lack of access to credit markets, it was hard for the government to finance them with debt, which is reflected in the slow average increase in debt during the period. On the other hand, monetary financing was important in that seigniorage net of money creation was a large fraction of financing,

Table 1. Budget constraint decomposition

	1960–75	1976–90	1991–2001	2002–17
Change in debt (A)	0.9%	2.9%	0.4%	−0.1%
Change in real money (B)	−0.4%	−0.3%	0.1%	0.2%
Seigniorage (C)	2.4%	3.8%	0.3%	1.8%
Primary deficit (D)	3.6%	3.1%	0.0%	−0.5%
Interest payments (E)	0.1%	2.3%	−0.3%	−0.3%
Transfers $= (A + B + C) − (D + E)$	−0.8%	1.0%	1.2%	2.7%

which explains why inflation was high during the period. Finally, this is the only subperiod in which the transfer is negative—probably explained by the fact that many of the local debt instruments were denominated in pesos, so increases in inflation diluted the real value, which is equivalent to a confiscation of private-sector assets. As shown in Figure 7, Argentineans quickly learned this lesson, and the ability of the government to issue peso-denominated nonindexed debt was very limited from then on.

The second subperiod is also characterized by high primary deficits—though a bit lower than the previous decade and a half—but substantially larger interest payments. This reflects the large increase in government debt (see the top row of Table 1) during the early years of this period. Seigniorage was substantially higher than the period before, which also explains the higher inflation rates in this subperiod. Notice, however, that overall, inflation allowed the government to collect an additional 1.6 percent of GDP, compared with the previous fifteen years. The price paid during times of higher inflation seems to be excessively high, as Figure 2 makes clear.

The radical change in the behavior of the primary deficit starting in 1991 can also be seen in Table 1. Seigniorage became negligible in the 1990s because of the currency board. All increases in the debt are explained by positive transfers. Most of these transfers arose in the years immediately after the inflation rate was stabilized and can be explained by a series of bonds issued to pay unrecorded debts, mostly with pension holders, that had been taken to court.

The final period is characterized by the resurgence of seigniorage as a major source of revenue, as was the case in the first two periods. The primary deficit is negative on average, but, as we mention in the text, worsens during the last years. The very large value of the transfers can be explained mostly by the large increase in debt during the 2002 crisis, as can be seen in Figure 4. The off-budget expenses of those years were so large that they more than compensated for the write-off obtained in the first step of the debt renegotiation process in 2005, which can also be seen in Figure 4.

An alternative way to evaluate the overall impact, throughout the period, of these off-budget expenses is to simulate what total debt would have been in each year if these transfers had been zero every year.[16] The result can be seen in Figure 14, where we plot the result of the simulated debt-to-GDP ratio, together with the observed value. As expected, during the first subperiod, the simulated debt is higher than the observed one. This pattern started changing in the early 1980s, and the difference was likely the result of the deposit and exchange rate insurance that had to be paid in 1982. The difference then becomes larger in the early 1990s, related to the issuance of bonds to pay for unrecorded debts, as mentioned above. It then becomes very large during the crisis, moderating the year of the debt renegotiation but increasing again after that year. Our interpretation of the difference between the true values for the debt and the simulated values is precisely those off-the-books expenses created by the contingent liabilities.

Overall, the picture describes a dramatic fact. By the end of 2017, the debt-to-GDP ratio of Argentina was somewhat above 50 percent. This calculation shows that if it had been based only on the recorded deficits, the ratio should have been just 20 percent. Thus more than 60 percent of the total debt can be explained by "accidents" rather than conscious and agreed-upon decisions to change government spending.

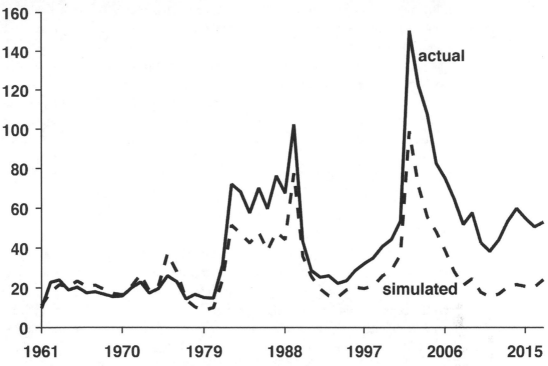

Figure 14. Simulated vs. actual debt, percent of GDP

Conclusions

Our analysis strongly supports the view that from 1960 to 1990, a systematic imbalance between government revenues and outlays explains the chronic and high inflation rates that Argentina experienced during those three decades. At the same time, the economic performance of the country during the fifteen years of the highest inflation rates was extremely disappointing: per capita income in 1990 was essentially the same as in 1960 (see Figure 1). The analysis also explains why, starting in 1991 and until 2001, Argentina used over 2 percent of its output, on average, to service its debt, since its primary deficit was zero on average. The increase in the debt incurred to pay that interest explains most of the debt increase during the 1990s that led to the 2001 debt crisis. The debt crisis was very expensive fiscally, and the government ended with a higher level of debt, even taking into account the haircut agreed upon in 2005, in the first step of the debt renegotiation process. That debt burden remains today, and it has been exacerbated by a substantial deterioration of the primary deficit, with values that resemble the ones that prevailed during the times of high inflation and bad economic performance. As we finish writing this chapter, at the end of 2018, some of the potential risks of that deterioration of the primary deficit, together with the debt burden, have already been realized, and their impact has become visible. The inflation rate has been higher than the government anticipated, and there was a run on the dollar that generated a doubling of the exchange rate in just a few weeks, leading to two changes in central bank authorities during 2018. At the same time, the interest rate charged on Argentinean bonds has increased dramatically, to the point where the government has been forced to ask for financial assistance from the International Monetary Fund (IMF).

The last half century of Argentina's macroeconomic history is infamously rich in terms of extraordinary events. These events have offered the average Argentinean only misery and pain, and, we argue, all seem symptoms of the same disease: the government's inability to restrict spending to genuine tax revenues. The disease became active again around 2010, and its symptoms worsened dramatically in 2018. A cure has been proposed by the government, with the support of the IMF. Whether this effort will be the final cure remains to be seen.

It may be the case that the Argentine society has not learned its lesson, and as too often in the past, the disease will spread and a new macroeconomic crisis will unravel, repeating the alternating cycle of optimism and frustration.

But if it is the final cure, we may be witnessing the end of macroeconomic instability in Argentina for good. And to the extent that this instability is responsible for some sizable fraction of the difference between the evolution of income per capita and the 2 percent trend in Figure 1, one could even hope that, if the cure works, several years of high growth rates and economic prosperity await the average Argentinean as income per capita closes a fraction of the wedge with that trend. The American dream that many immigrants were after when they came to the country in the first half of the twentieth century may eventually come true, albeit delayed by only a few generations.

Notes

The views expressed herein are those of the authors and not necessarily those of the Federal Reserve Bank of Minneapolis or the Federal Reserve System.

1 Specifically, we computed the ratio of the price level at year $t + 1$ over the price level at t. Then we raised that ratio to 1/12 and subtracted 1.

2 The default occurred in the last days of December 2001, a few days before the abandonment of the currency board.

3 The figure includes the external debt of the public enterprises and provinces for the period 1962–77. The total debt of the provinces is included for the period 1996–2017. We also included the external debt of the central bank and its issues of domestic bonds net of its holding of international reserves.

4 We have data on dollar-denominated, indexed, and peso-denominated debt only starting in 1975. To make the adjustment for the first fifteen years, we assumed that the fraction of dollar-denominated debt during those years was similar to the value in 1975, about 70 percent of the total.

5 In Figure 5c of the online appendix (http://manifold.bfi.uchicago.edu), we show the debt-to-GDP ratio together with the real exchange rate, where the comovement is transparent.

6 Total domestic credit and reserves are in billions of U.S. dollars. To have a scale that facilitates comparison in the figure, we added US$1 billion to the reserves data.

7 This measure is a variation of the one proposed by the Calvo (1996) ratio, which expresses M2 as a proportion of central bank reserves.

8 The calendar inflation rate in Figure 2 for 1984 is higher than in 1985. However, the highest monthly inflation rate was in May 1985. In June of that year, a stabilization plan was launched that substantially lowered inflation from that month through the rest of the year. This makes the calendar inflation rate in 1985 lower than in 1984.

9 A comparison of Figures 2 and 3 reveals a striking feature. The comovement between inflation and the deficit is clear: the three local maxima in the deficit correspond to the three spikes in inflation. But it is not the case that higher deficits imply higher inflation spikes. Quite the contrary: while the local maxima in the deficit go down over time, the inflation spikes go up over time. For an attempt at explaining this behavior, see Marcet and Nicolini (2003) and Sargent, Williams, and Zha (2009).

10 Among the interest-bearing liabilities of the central bank, we include the domestic bonds issued by the central bank, the deposits of the financial system during the period of nationalization of deposits (1973–76), and the bank reserves, which for various subperiods were remunerated.

11 Technically, a fraction of the requirement could be fulfilled with dollar-denominated domestic assets, making the true backing less than 100 percent.

12 The income from privatizations added an extra 0.7 percent of GDP a year from 1991 to 1993 on average.

13 In 2008, the reform ended, and Argentina reverted to the old pay-as-you-go system. The extra revenues the government obtained by reverting the reform make the fiscal expansion that started in 2010 even more dramatic.

14 For a theory along this direction, see Ayres et al. (2015).

15 In the online appendix, we present the time series of all the rows in Table 1. See http://manifold.bfi.uchicago.edu.

16 The details of this computation are explained in "A Framework for Studying the Monetary and Fiscal History of Latin America."

References

Ayres, Joao, Gastón Navarro, Juan Pablo Nicolini, and Pedro Teles. 2015. "Sovereign Default: The Role of Expectations." Working paper 723, Federal Reserve Bank of Minneapolis.

Calvo, Guillermo A. 1988. "Servicing the Public Debt: The Role of Expectations." *American Economic Review* 78 (4): 647–61.

———. 1996. "Capital Flows and Macroeconomic Management: Tequila Lessons." *International Journal of Finance and Economics* 1 (3): 207–23.

———. 1998. "Varieties of Capital-Market Crises." In *The Debt Burden and Its Consequences for Monetary Policy*, edited by Guillermo A. Calvo and Mervyn King, 181–207. London: Palgrave Macmillan.

Cole, Harold L., and Timothy J. Kehoe. 1996. "A Self-Fulfilling Model of Mexico's 1994–1995 Debt Crisis." *Journal of International Economics* 41 (3–4): 309–30.

———. 2000. "Self-Fulfilling Debt Crises." *Review of Economic Studies* 67 (1): 91–116.

Marcet, Albert, and Juan P. Nicolini. 2003. "Recurrent Hyperinflations and Learning." *American Economic Review* 93 (5): 1476–98.

Sargent, Thomas, Noah Williams, and Tao Zha. 2009. "The Conquest of South American Inflation." *Journal of Political Economy* 117 (2): 211–56.

Discussion of the History of Argentina 1

Guillermo Calvo
Columbia University

The main contribution of these essays is to view a variety of experiences within the bare-bones framework spelled out in this volume's "A Framework for Studying the Monetary and Fiscal History of Latin America." The effort is especially valuable for the case of Argentina because the large number of trees that history throws in our way threatens to rapidly occlude the view of the bush. The authors are able to offer a narrative that helps give a rationale for the variety of facts and policies discussed in "The History of Argentina." The chapter covers the period 1960 to 2017, which starts in the midst of an inflation stabilization program that saw the annual rate of inflation hover around 100 percent in 1959, the highest since the beginning of the century. But this record was not going to last. As shown in Figure 2, inflation reached hyperinflation levels (according to Phillip Cagan's [1956] definition) in the late 1980s. These facts could lead the reader to quickly sympathize with the authors' conclusion that "from 1960 to 1990, a systematic imbalance between government revenues and outlays explains the chronic and high inflation rates that Argentina experienced during those three decades." But soon she will realize that the imbalance that the authors refer to could hardly be captured by conventional variables. For example, Figure 3 shows a clear downward trend in the government deficit as a share of GDP. Thus if the government deficit were taken as a measure of "imbalance"—and few economists would raise an eyebrow at that choice—the implication would be that inflation increases as imbalances go down, which goes against the chapter's conclusions. An important contribution of the chapter is to show that the excess of outlays over revenues is caused by factors that are not directly under the control of government, such as terms of trade, the sharp rise in the real exchange rate, liability dollarization, and the tightening of international credit conditions, all of which in several cases go far beyond government deficits. These factors become increasingly relevant as the economy became more financially integrated with the international capital market and as the latter suffered major shake-ups, dramatically exemplified by Volcker's stabilization plan in the early 1980s. Figure 5, for instance, shows that fiscal deficits alone would be wide of the mark for explaining the sharp rise in government debt in the 1980s and early 2000s.

Let me now take a bird's-eye view of "imbalances" in the period covered by the chapter. The government deficit is relevant for the early 1960s, given that the public sector had limited access to the bond market and expenditure shocks needed to be financed by the central bank, increasing the money supply. This established a tight link between deficits and inflation, and inflation was easy to rein in by tighter fiscal policy. However, that situation changed in the 1970s when governments relied on price controls to keep inflation in check. This generated a break in the link between deficits and inflation, a clear instance in which fiscal imbalance does not lead to inflation (as measured by the statistical office). But that was not to last long. When controls were lifted, the price level rose steeply in a rush, giving rise to a phenomenon that I like to call "inflation explosion." An episode of that sort that is deeply imprinted in Argentineans' collective conscience is the so-called *Rodrigazo* in 1975 (in reference to Celestino Rodrigo, the minister of the economy in charge), in which the dollar exchange rate increased by around 150 percent, far exceeding the rise in the wage rate, and which not long afterward led to the ousting of the president in charge.

The new administration took a sharp turn toward free market policies and liberalized the banking and financial sectors, resulting in a large expansion of quasi-monies. As pointed out in the chapter, one implication of this was to make the central bank's contingent liabilities grow, since the central bank was expected to bail out failed financial institutions. Thus a sensible definition of "imbalance" would have to take these new contingent liabilities into account. Being contingent, these liabilities do not increase government expenditure and the fiscal deficit as long as financial institutions are not subject to runs. But the inflationary impact could be large and unexpected when they do. This threatens governability and can generate chronic inflation, as economic agents lose trust in the central bank's ability to stabilize the price level. For instance, the latter may lead price setters to keep updating prices at a high tick, giving rise to *price inertia* and increasing the cost of inflation stabilization. This is the sort of phenomenon behind the Austral/Primavera episodes that ended in the 1989 hyperinflation while the government deficit (especially the primary deficit) showed no dramatic rise, as I will show below.

As pointed out in the chapter, access to capital markets improved considerably in the 1990s. The Brady Plan probably contributed to this by placing in the market bonds that were previously on lenders' balance sheets. This gave incentives for the creation of emerging market economies (EMs) desks in investment banks, which further facilitated access to the international capital market by private and public operators in EMs. The dismal outcome that followed is well known, and Argentina was not absent from the crises that started to occur from 1994 to 1995 (the Tequila crisis). These crises are associated with sudden stops—that is, large and largely unexpected cuts in capital inflows (see Calvo 2016). Sudden stops give rise to imbalances because, whatever the prior fiscal policy stance, the associated credit drought tends to turn sustainability into unsustainability in the fiscal sphere. Culprits are hard to find because EMs were mostly innocent bystanders, and investment banks were just doing their business (losing their shirts, sometimes, as the Lehman Brothers crisis demonstrated in 2008). But, again, in the final analysis, when Argentina was involved, the "imbalance" mentioned by the authors was always present. For example, the 2001 crisis, the costliest crisis since the beginning of the twentieth century for Argentina, occurred not because Argentina went on a crazy shopping spree but because the interest bill skyrocketed and terms of trade with respect to Brazil (a large trading partner) sharply deteriorated (see Figure 13 and Calvo, Izquierdo, and Talvi 2004).

Argentina's inflation explosions are worth exploring in greater detail. I call them "explosions" because they exhibit inflation rates that are orders of magnitude higher than those occurring shortly before and, as a general rule, are cases in which financial and other considerations dominate primary fiscal deficits. Figure 2 very clearly shows the 1989 and 2001 explosions that seem to come from nowhere. This is not the place to elaborate on these episodes at length, but some broad brushstrokes offer interesting insights. The Austral program, for instance, starts in June 1985 after what I like to call the Volcker Bomb (i.e., the large increase in the Federal Reserve's interest rate in 1982 that had deleterious effects on indebted less-developed economies and triggered the lost decade of the 1980s). The rise in the interest bill had a large impact on the government deficit. Believing that the situation was getting out of hand, the Argentinean government decided to change the unit of account from peso *to* austral *and* define the interest rate in austral in such a way that it was free from the high inflation expectations involved in the peso interest rate (a clever trick called *desagio*), a subterfuge that prevented the emergence of a wave of inefficient bankruptcies and helped initially stabilize inflation expectations. The program was very successful in the short run. Inflation fell as though stricken by a thunderbolt. The primary deficit improved to the point of turning into a sizable surplus, due partly to the Olivera-Tanzi effect. However, the lack of credibility regarding the government's ability to stick to price stability and other factors once again increased the burden of the interest bill on the government budget, which, combined with the fact that elections took place at the end of 1989—and that the winner campaigned on promising a big salary increase (*salariazo*) and hinted at debt default—led to a sharp rise in prices that the central bank had to accommodate to prevent a politically costly increase in unemployment. This set up conditions under which price inertia dominated, and even though a new program was put in place in August 1988 (the Primavera plan), it was not sufficient to assuage inflationary expectations, a situation that eventually ended up in a couple of brutal hyperinflation episodes (annual inflation reached 16,000 percent), while, as shown in Figure 3, the government deficit shows a clear downward trend from 1975 to 1989, totally oblivious to the monetary tragedy that was going around!

In sum, the authors are right in pointing to imbalances as key factors behind the dismal outcome of Argentina's economy. After reading the chapter, I felt much wiser but, at the same time, eager to learn more about these fascinating episodes. Questions about fundamental issues that may help explain the coexistence of imbalances with low growth, for example, popped up in my mind. Are low growth and a propensity to be caught in financial crises parts of the same tree? I think the issue of low saving rates deserves further study in this respect. Argentina's current saving rate is around 12 percent of GDP, much lower than the average for Latin America—not a high bar, since Latin America's saving rates look like pygmies relative to Asia's. Following Feldstein and Horioka (1980), one is tempted to conjecture that low saving is a possible explanation for slow growth, but there is also the question of whether low saving rates also make economies more susceptible to balance of payments and financial crises. After all, given technology, the smaller the saving rate, the greater will likely be dependence on external saving, thus possibly making the economy more sensitive to episodes of systemic sudden stops that are typically external to the economy in question and accompanied by balance of payments or financial crises. Moreover, repeated systemic sudden stops, as has been the case since the Volcker Bomb in the early 1980s, are likely to undermine the reliability of domestic financial intermediaries and depress the propensity to save, especially for individuals and small and medium enterprises that do not have easy access to the international capital market and can hardly keep their savings in a safe place. Therefore, there could be a vicious circle in which low saving triggers a high incidence of balance of payments and financial crises and the latter feeds back into lower propensities to save.

I will be eagerly looking forward to future volumes of this project!

References

Cagan, Phillip. 1956. "The Monetary Dynamics of Hyperinflation." In *Studies in the Quantity Theory of Money*, edited by Milton Friedman, 25–117. Chicago: University of Chicago Press.

Calvo, Guillermo A. 2016. *Macroeconomics in Times of Liquidity Crises: Searching for Economic Essentials*. Cambridge, Mass.: MIT Press.

Calvo, Guillermo A., Alejandro Izquierdo, and Ernesto Talvi. 2004. "Sudden Stops, the Real Exchange Rate, and Fiscal Sustainability: Argentina's Lessons." In *Monetary Unions and Hard Pegs*, edited by Volbert Alexander, Jacques Mélitz, and George M. von Furstenberg, 151–82. Oxford: Oxford University Press. First published in July 2003 as working paper 9828, National Bureau of Economic Research, Cambridge, Mass.

Feldstein, Martin, and Charles Horioka. 1980. "Domestic Saving and International Capital Flows." *Economic Journal* 90 (358): 314–29.

Discussion of the History of Argentina 2

Andrew Powell
Inter-American Development Bank

Writing on recent Argentine economic history is no easy task. There is much to discuss, and much has been said. The authors of this chapter are assisted by clear terms of reference and a well-defined approach. Following closely the methodological stance of the project, they are able to condense fifty-seven turbulent years of Argentine economic history into just twenty or so pages. This is an incredible feat; the authors deserve hearty congratulations! The chapter gives an excellent, succinct description of the main events and clearly illustrates the association between Argentina's fiscal and monetary travails. In these brief comments, I will not attempt to be comprehensive but rather will limit myself to just three main takeaways from the chapter where I hope I can add value.

The first takeaway relates to the strong view that Argentina's woes were essentially fiscal and that monetary instability and high inflation, including the bouts of hyperinflation, in the end boil down to fiscal impropriety. Overall, I have sympathy for this perspective, but there is surely a richer set of dynamics, and there is a danger of pushing the "it's all fiscal" doctrine too far. The main equation defining the government's budget constraint provides a clear link between the fiscal and the monetary but does not ascribe causality. The causal mechanism in mind seems to consider spending as set, but then if financing through taxes or debt is not available, residual financing through money creation drives inflation. But high (and uncertain) inflation may have an impact on activity and tax revenues, affecting the level of funding. In the case of Argentina, high and uncertain inflation, as well as the actions to lower inflation, surely had an impact on activity and revenues.

The authors place emphasis on the fact that the 1976–90 period was the one with the highest fiscal deficits. It was also the period of lowest growth. The authors' estimate of trend growth pre-1980 was more or less reestablished after that decade. Arguably, the 1980s account for why Argentina continues to lie below that trend today. I won't repeat everything leading up to the lost decade, but the 1977 financial liberalization seems key. Coupled with weak regulation and supervision, severe financial vulnerabilities arose. At the end of the 1970s, commodity prices fell and then U.S. interest rates rose and the dollar appreciated. A banking crisis ensued. The first major bank to fail was in March 1980, followed quickly by the failure of three more banks, all before the 1981 devaluation—which then deepened the crisis. Decisions to resolve the crisis proved expensive. Exchange rate guarantees, full deposit insurance, and the liquidation of seventy-one banks increased fiscal woes.[1] The above contributed to the 1982 default, but the causal links are not obvious. The fiscal problems surely played an important role in Argentina's subsequent inflation trajectory, but like most airplane accidents, many things went wrong: weak banking oversight, poorly sequenced liberalization, exogenous shocks, decisions taken to resolve the crisis and default, all with growth, revenue, and availability-of-financing—in addition to spending—implications.

The second takeaway on which I wish to comment is the authors' view that, because there was a structural break in inflation, as fiscal deficits fell and debt stabilized, the currency board "worked."[2] While this is one definition of "worked," ultimately the project failed; I would argue that it did not produce the fiscal discipline needed to guarantee its survival, given a set of significant shocks. There has been much discussion of late regarding de facto dollarization and consequent vulnerabilities. I don't want to rehash those discussions and would point the interested reader to meta-analyses on the origins of the crisis.[3] Suffice to say, I think the authors are broadly right to focus on the fiscal. After the Tequila shock, Argentina grew at 5.5 percent in 1996 and over 8 percent in 1997 but ran a 1 percent primary deficit in the first year and just scraped a primary surplus (around 0.3 percent) in 1997.[4] To withstand negative shocks that would surely emerge at some point, Argentina should have saved more, as the International Monetary Fund (IMF) argued at the time.

Argentina was hit by strong negative shocks, such as the November 1997 attack on the Hong Kong currency board, the August 1998 Russian default, falling commodity prices, and the January 1999 Brazilian devaluation. One fascinating discussion that recently came back to the fore regards full dollarization in early 1999. What didn't happen might be of interest, as well as what did. President Menem asked the president of the central bank, Pedro Pou, to consider the options to dollarize. The advice provided by the central bank was (a) *against* unilateral dollarization, (b) that a monetary union with an Argentine seat on the Federal Open Market Committee (FOMC) would not be palatable to the U.S. authorities (!), but (c) that if Argentina wished to dollarize, the option to consider would be in the context of a U.S.–Argentina monetary treaty. The treaty would state that the United States would *not* be a lender of last resort, that the U.S. authorities would *not* regulate Argentine banks or markets, but that the treaty would advance a seigniorage-sharing scheme.[5] Warnings *against* dollarizing without wide support from Congress and the population were also included. Two missions to the United States ensued. Despite resistance at the Federal Reserve and mixed views at the U.S. Treasury, Larry Summers (U.S. Treasury secretary at the time) gave a speech with remarkable resonance to the Argentine technical position. However, Floridian Republican Senator Connie Mack put forward hasty legislation in favor of seigniorage sharing. The bill was unacceptable to the U.S. executive branch, and Democrats voted it down. There was also no widespread support in Argentina, and the idea was shelved.

What would have happened if Argentina had dollarized? Would the scheme have survived 2002? Would the cost of having had no monetary policy have exceeded the benefits of lower interest rates? Any answer would be a judgment call. More generally, the relative merits of dollarizing decrease if monetary shocks can be contained, if an alternative credible nominal anchor can be developed, and (hence) when an independent monetary policy can provide a floating exchange rate that stabilizes rather than destabilizes. The experience of the currency board is only partially informative regarding the possible success of dollarizing. While dollarizing may reduce interest rates, without fiscal discipline, debt can spiral, requiring debt restructuring from time to time.[6] And dollarizing does not prevent a new currency being introduced. If, as the authors suggest, the bottom line is fiscal profligacy, then, while dollarization is not orthogonal, it may not solve the underlying problem. Other countries in the region have successfully developed alternative credible nominal anchors and contained fiscal excesses to some degree.[7] In the case of Argentina's excesses, there is clearly more work to be done to attain this objective.

Despite the negative shocks of the late 1990s and their impacts on economic activity, the required fiscal adjustment and the required adjustment in the current account to ensure that the currency arrangement was sustainable were not large.[8] Even as late as the first quarter of 2001, there seemed to be no technical reason to prevent them from being attained. But policies tended to be reactive rather than proactive, and then they became counterproductive, and politics appeared to often get in the way.

This brings me to comment number three regarding multiple equilibria stories. The authors appear drawn to one particular possibility, following Calvo (1988) and Ayres et al. (2018). But they offer no real evidence in favor versus a simpler alternative of higher interest costs due to a rising risk of default. And there are also alternative multiple equilibria hypotheses to consider. Of particular importance was the trajectory of bank deposits (critical to rolling over the public debt) and the role of the IMF. The authors state that there was a continuous outflow of deposits through 2001, but on closer inspection there were four distinct runs, the first starting in 2000.[9] The authors could have explained more regarding Argentina's "systemic liquidity policy," consisting of high bank liquidity requirements, international reserves in excess of the two-thirds backing required by the Convertibility Law, and an innovative US$6 billion-plus Contingent Repo Facility signed with a group of international banks and supplemented by loans totaling US$1 billion from the Inter-American Development Bank and the World Bank.[10] Arguably, the strong liquidity position allowed the currency board to survive so long. The third run, in June–July 2001, was the most serious to that point but was halted, temporarily, by the IMF agreement signed in August 2001.

The role of the IMF as a type of lender of last resort has come under close scrutiny. But in such circumstances, the IMF is placed in a tough spot. If the IMF agrees to support a country without reservation, then this may prevent a run, ruling out a no-rollover bad equilibrium. But there is a danger of "moral hazard"—in other words, the country may choose riskier strategies (or *gamble for resurrection*) that the IMF would disapprove of and that for a systemic country may risk international financial instability. On the other hand, if the IMF does not support the country without reservation, the country may be vulnerable to the bad equilibrium and, to avoid that outcome, may be forced into a safe strategy, which the IMF should be happy to support. This simple logic suggests that in a one-shot game, there may be no equilibrium in pure strategies, and the only feasible equilibrium is in mixed strategies where the IMF may support with some probability (not without reservation) and there is little clarity about whether the country is playing safe.[11] This is my interpretation of what was going on through much of 2001.

Formally, Argentina had an IMF program. But there were doubts about whether each subsequent set of quantitative targets would be met, whether the program would continue, and whether the next disbursement would arrive. And Argentine policy making became difficult to interpret.[12] Then came the IMF agreement of August 2001. While this agreement did stop the bank run temporarily, it also signaled that Argentina needed to renegotiate its debt, providing neither advice nor sufficient financing to do so. The zero-deficit policy then failed, the IMF withdrew, a new run commenced, and the currency board fell.[13]

Let me make one comment on the resolution of the 2002 crisis that often seems to go unquestioned. Namely, I would suggest that there were many potential ways to exit the currency board, each with associated costs, benefits, and distributional consequences. The policy of a system-wide *asymmetric pesification* (where deposits were converted from dollars to pesos at 1.4 to 1, and dollar loans were converted to pesos at 1 to 1), coupled with the depreciation to over 4 pesos to 1 dollar from the currency board's 1:1, was not the only way, and the choice was not random. One alternative would have been to float with guidelines on how banks and firms should renegotiate loan contracts.[14] The blanket rule inflicted losses on private banks that had significant dollar loans and deposits and protected public banks whose balance sheets were largely in pesos, such as the Banco de la Provincia de Buenos Aires, which had a weak balance sheet at that time. In contrast, the private banks had substantial capital. Indeed, I suspect if they had had more capital, then pesification would have been more asymmetric; the objective appeared to be to redistribute bank capital. Moreover, while Argentina's public sector was short "external" dollars (public external debt exceeded reserves), the private sector was substantially long.[15] Any owner of a business with dollar debt with the local financial system and money saved abroad received a huge transfer. And consumers with dollar local loans received transfers irrespective of their "needs." The policy appeared to be designed to hit private banks and protect certain public ones, and local businesses received transfers. Following the money makes the political economy of the exit policy clearer. The result was a dismantling of the private financial system, likely deepening the collapse. It did, however, allow the economy to recover quickly from the crisis with very little bank credit.

Given the various banking crises in Argentina (1982, 1995, and 2002) and in other countries, follow-up work on banking could nicely complement this project. Not all banking crises have fiscal origins, so this would provide nuances to the "it's all fiscal" doctrine. Moreover, the region has come a long way in managing financial system risk. First, the quality of regulation and supervision to control risks ex ante has improved. Second, after interesting experiments, most countries now have some type of deposit insurance in place. In the case of Argentina, the contagion within the system during the Tequila crisis amply illustrated the risks of its elimination. Finally, bank resolution techniques have improved. Argentina's novel system implemented after the Tequila crisis is a case in point. The authors' preferred measure of banking sector contingent liabilities is M2/GDP, but according to this measure, the 2015 contingent liabilities of banks in the European Union were about 24 trillion euros, or some 146 percent of EU GDP, dwarfing those of Argentina, which at most were a modest 20 percent of GDP. This measure essentially values all bank assets at zero. If ex ante risks can be contained and resolution techniques can minimize losses, this appears too crude a measure. A wider project might be entitled "The Fiscal, Monetary, and Banking History of Latin America" and could focus on better measures of financial sector risks and how they were and can be managed.

To conclude, this is a fascinating story succinctly told, in part owing to the benefit of a strong methodological choice. A tremendous amount of information is summarized, and yet it leaves the reader wanting more. It is akin to an award-winning short documentary with a strong message from the director(s). And despite the issues I have raised, if countries had actually followed the advice implicit in this chapter and the other country chapters, I have no doubt that economic stability would have been enhanced and the region would be considerably more prosperous today. The project has been an extremely valuable endeavor, and I have greatly enjoyed acting as a commentator.

Notes

1 See especially Diaz Alejandro (1985), Baliño (1987), and D'Amato and Katz (2018) on the lead-up to the 1980 banking crisis and its resolution.

2 It's worth detailing that the "currency board" was not a "pure currency board." International reserves only had to be 80 percent of the monetary base in 1991, falling to two-thirds, although there was also a restriction on the growth in Argentine dollar bonds on the central bank's balance sheet that made up the residual backing. Also, at the start, the currency could fluctuate in a very fine band (this was shut down after the Tequila shock), and several currencies could compete for transaction purposes within the country.

3 See Cline (2003), International Monetary Fund (2004), and Powell (2002) for evaluations of several theories about the crisis.

4 Data from the International Monetary Fund's World Economic Outlook, October 2018.

5 For further discussion on dollarization and the idea of a monetary treaty, see Guidotti and Powell (2003).

6 See Powell and Sturzenegger (2000) for a discussion of the impact of dollarization on interest rates.

7 See Mariscal, Powell, and Tavella (2018) on how the "credibility" of Latin America's inflation targets developed.

8 See the estimates in Powell (2002).

9 In Powell (2002), I discuss the four runs.

10 See Calomiris and Powell (2000) for a description of various elements of banking oversight introduced in the post-Tequila period. I normally like to describe these measures as seat belts, very useful in 30 mph crashes. But such rules will not protect passengers if the truck is driven off a cliff!

11 See Powell and Arozamena (2003) for a game theoretic model that encapsulates these ideas.

12 Such measures included the use of "monetary policy" under the currency board (i.e., the relaxation of liquidity requirements to promote bank credit), a move from the dollar to a basket as the exchange rate reference currency, a system of export subsidies and import taxes to simulate a devaluation, and the zero-deficit law.

13 The policy of announcing a zero planned deficit turned out to be counterproductive. One argument was that while many knew Argentina was in a tough spot, this was not common knowledge. When Argentina announced the policy, every investor then knew that all

the others were refusing to provide any additional financing. See Mussa (2002) for a critical examination of the 2001 IMF agreement.

14 For example, in Ecuador after a maxi depreciation (followed by dollarization), small loans were restructured by extending loan maturities and gradually introducing increasing payment schedules, and there was a largely voluntary scheme for large borrower workouts avoiding large transfers or bailouts (see International Monetary Fund 2000, para. 49).

15 On public versus private sector balance sheets, see Powell (2002).

References

Ayres, Joao, Gaston Navarro, Juan P. Nicolini, and Pedro Teles. 2018. "Sovereign Default: The Role of Expectations." *Journal of Economic Theory* 175 (C): 803–12.

Baliño, Thomas J. T. 1987. "The Argentine Banking Crisis of 1980." Working paper WP/87/77, International Monetary Fund, Washington, D.C.

Calomiris, Charles W., and Andrew Powell. 2000. "Can Emerging Market Bank Regulators Establish Credible Discipline? The Case of Argentina." In *Prudential Supervision: What Works and What Doesn't*, edited by Frederic Mishkin, 147–91. Chicago: University of Chicago Press.

Calvo, Guillermo A. 1988. "Servicing the Public Debt: The Role of Expectations." *American Economic Review* 78 (4): 647–61.

Cline, William R. 2003. "Restoring Economic Growth in Argentina." Policy Research Working Paper 3158, World Bank, Washington, D.C.

D'Amato, Laura, and Sebastian Katz. 2018. "Una constante en la evolución macroeconómica Argentina: Dinero, deuda y crisis (1945–2015)." In *Nueva historia económica de la Argentina: Temas, problemas, autores. El último medio siglo. Ensayos de historiografía económica desde 1810 a 2016*, edited by Roberto Cortés Conde and Gerardo Della Paolera, 141–76. Buenos Aires: Edhasa, Ciudad Autónoma de Buenos Aires.

Diaz Alejandro, Carlos. 1985. "Good-Bye Financial Repression, Hello Financial Crash." *Journal of Development Economics* 19 (1–2): 1–24.

Guidotti, Pablo, and Andrew Powell. 2003. "The Dollarization Debate in Argentina and Latin America." In *International Financial Markets: The Challenge of Globalization*, edited by Leonardo Auernheimer, 175–220. Chicago: University of Chicago Press.

International Monetary Fund. 2000. "Ecuador: Selected Issues and Statistical Annex." Staff Country Report 00/125, International Monetary Fund, Washington, D.C.

———. 2004. "Report on the Evaluation of the Role of the IMF in Argentina, 1991–2001." Independent Evaluation Office (IEO) of the IMF, IEO Publications, Washington, D.C.

Mariscal, Rodrigo, Andrew Powell, and Pilar Tavella. 2018. "On the Credibility of Inflation-Targeting Regimes in Latin America." *Economia* 18 (2): 1–24.

Mussa, Michael. 2002. *Argentina and the Fund: From Triumph to Tragedy. Policy Analyses in International Economics* (Book 67). Washington, D.C.: Institute for International Economics.

Powell, Andrew. 2002. "Argentina's Avoidable Crisis: Bad Luck, Bad Economics, Bad Politics, Bad Advice." *Brookings Trade Forum* (January):1–58.

Powell, Andrew, and Leandro Arozamena. 2003. "Liquidity Protection versus Moral Hazard: The Role of the IMF." *Journal of International Money and Finance* 22 (7): 1041–63.

Powell, Andrew, and Federico Sturzenegger. 2000. "Dollarization: The Link between Devaluation and Default Risk." Unpublished paper, Universidad Torcuato Di Tella, Buenos Aires.

Bolivia

The History of Bolivia

Timothy J. Kehoe
University of Minnesota, Federal Reserve Bank of Minneapolis,
and National Bureau of Economic Research

Carlos Gustavo Machicado
Institute for Advanced Development Studies

José Peres-Cajías
University of Barcelona

Major fiscal and monetary events, 1960–2017

1969	Nationalization of the Bolivian Gulf Oil Company	**1986**	Tax reform
1972	First devaluation of the Bolivian peso since 1958	**1995**	Independence of central bank
		1996	Pension reform
1979	Balance of payments crisis	**2005**	Beginning of multilateral debt relief initiatives
1982	De-dollarization program	**2006**	Nationalization of hydrocarbon companies
1985	Hyperinflation Stabilization plan: New Political Economy/Nueva Política Económica	**2011**	Beginning of de facto nominal fixed exchange rate
		2014	Fiscal balance turns to deficits

Introduction

In the early seventeenth century, Bolivia was so famous for its mineral wealth that Miguel Cervantes in his *Don Quixote* used the phrase "valer un Potosí" (to be worth a Potosí) to indicate something of great worth, referring to the Bolivian silver mining city of Potosí. The phrase had become popular in Spain in the late sixteenth century, and its use by Cervantes cemented it into the Spanish language, where it is still used today, often with a small *p*. Unfortunately, Bolivia's exports of its proverbial wealth in natural resources—first silver, then tin, and now natural gas—have not prevented it from becoming the poorest country in South America in 2017, according to the World Bank's World Development Indicators.[1]

We study Bolivia's poor economic performance, focusing on its modern economic history, from 1960 to the present. Figure 1 presents a graph of the evolution of real GDP

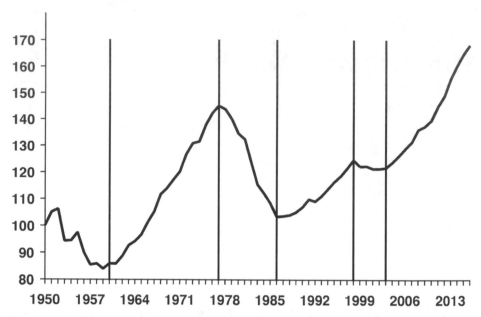

Figure 1. Real GDP per working-age person, 1960 = 100
Sources: Maddison Project, ECLAC, Instituto Nacional de Estadística, UN Population Center

per working-age (fifteen to sixty-four years) person (WAP) in Bolivia, in which we divide its modern economic history into five distinct periods. The first period runs from 1960 to 1977 and is characterized by the most rapid economic growth that Bolivia has experienced. It is followed by the second period of debt crisis and hyperinflation, which runs from 1977 to 1986. The third period is a slow recovery that extends from 1986 to 1998. The fourth period is the 1998–2002 financial crisis. The fifth and final period starts in 2002 and runs to 2017. This period is characterized by growth—although not as rapid as that from 1960 to 1977—and, starting in 2006, by an increase in the participation of the state in the economy through the nationalization of enterprises in key economic sectors.

We develop a narrative for the uneven economic development depicted in Figure 1 that focuses on monetary and fiscal policies, particularly on the external debt and the finances of state-owned enterprises. Our narrative is compatible with other theories for Bolivia's uneven development. The most common narrative for Bolivia's economic problems stresses that the country's continuing dependence on the export of a few natural resources makes its economy sensitive to external shocks (see, for instance, Peñaloza Cordero 1985). Tin has accounted for at least 50 percent of total exports from 1904 to 1985. After a short period of export diversification, natural gas has accounted for at least 40 percent of total exports at the end of the twentieth century and throughout the twenty-first century. Many economists have stressed the country's dependence on foreign aid, in terms of debt, grants, and foreign direct investment (Huber Abendroth et al. 2001; Peres-Cajías 2014). Other economists point to the low level of industrialization (Rodríguez Ostria 1999; Seoane 2016). Production of manufactured goods has been stagnated at about 15 percent of GDP since the early 1940s.

Although these narratives differ in their focus, they agree that government intervention in the economy has been the driving force in either promoting or impeding economic development. This took the form of excessive intervention in production activities in the 1960s, 1970s, and recent years and of intervention in the allocation of resources through regulations in the 1990s and early 2000s. Given this common agreement about the centrality of government policies, we stress the need for a comprehensive analysis of these policies that focuses on the government's intertemporal budget constraint.

A special feature of Bolivia's modern economic history is that it has received subsidized loans. It has also defaulted frequently. Although it has been in default on some loans during every year in the period 1960–2009, Bolivia nevertheless has continued receiving loans. In fact, it is the only country in South America that has benefited from the joint International Monetary Fund–World Bank programs to reduce the debt of very poor countries: the Heavily Indebted Poor Countries (HIPC) Initiative and the Multilateral Debt Relief Initiative (MDRI).

Our general argument runs as follows: After the economic reforms that followed the National Revolution of the 1950s, Bolivia was well positioned for sustained growth. Indeed, Bolivia achieved unprecedented growth during the period 1960–77. Mistakes in economic policies, especially the rapid accumulation of debt seen in Figure 2, which was due to persistent deficits, coupled with a fixed exchange rate policy during the 1970s, led to a debt crisis that began in 1977. From 1977 to 1986, Bolivia lost almost all the gains in GDP per working-age person that it had achieved from 1960 to 1977. In 1986, Bolivia started to grow again, albeit slowly, interrupted only by the financial crisis of 1998–2002, which was the result of a drop in the availability of external financing.

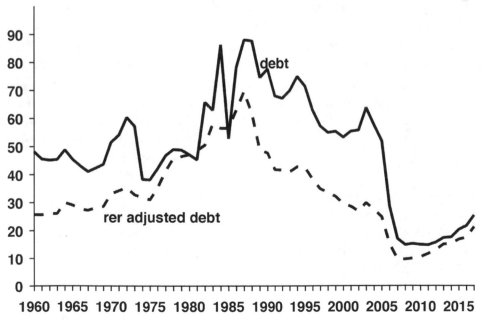

Figure 2. External debt and fixed real exchange rate (RER) debt, percent of GDP
Source: Banco Central de Bolivia

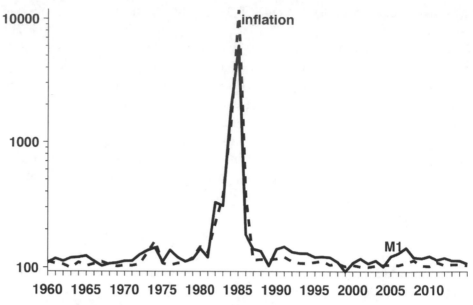

Figure 3. Inflation and money supply growth, factors (100 + rate) in log scale
Source: Banco Central de Bolivia

Bolivia has grown since 2002, but government policies since 2006 are reminiscent of the policies of the 1970s that led to the debt crisis. Particularly troubling have been the accumulation of external debt and the drop in international reserves due to a de facto fixed exchange rate since 2013.

As Figure 3 shows, Bolivia has experienced only one period of hyperinflation, whereas other countries, such as Argentina and Brazil, have experienced multiple episodes of hyperinflation.[2] In contrast to Argentina and Brazil, Bolivia adopted a fixed exchange rate policy over long periods, which has allowed it to maintain inflation at low levels.

We carry out a systematic data analysis of Bolivian monetary and fiscal policies and their effects on the economy. We use Kehoe and Prescott's (2007) growth accounting analysis to identify the real impact of government policies, and we use the government budget accounting analysis in "A Framework for Studying the Monetary and Fiscal History of Latin America" to identify changes in government policies.

In the second section, we perform the growth accounting analysis. The third section describes the different periods or cycles of Bolivia's modern economic history between 1960 and 2017. In the fourth section we perform the budget accounting analysis. Our conclusions appear in the fifth section. We also provide an appendix presenting a brief historical overview of Bolivia's economic history before 1960, focusing on the National Revolution of the 1950s and its aftermath.

Growth Accounting

Figure 4 summarizes the macroeconomic history of Bolivia from 1960 to 2017 with the results of a growth accounting exercise based on those in Kehoe and Prescott (2007). We use a Cobb-Douglas production function for real GDP:

$$Y_t = A_t K_t^{\alpha} L_t^{1-\alpha}, \tag{1}$$

where we cumulate investment deflated by the GDP deflator to measure capital and number of workers to measure labor. We employ a value of 0.42 for the capital share in the production function, following the estimate of Carlos Gustavo Machicado (2012).[3]

The capital stock series is calculated using the perpetual inventory method, based on the law of motion for capital,

$$K_{t+1} = (1-\delta)K_t + I_t, \tag{2}$$

where δ is the depreciation rate that we assume is equal to 0.05, a standard value for yearly data.

Our growth accounting rewrites the production function (1) as

$$\frac{Y_t}{N_t} = A_t^{\frac{1}{1-\alpha}} \left(\frac{K_t}{Y_t}\right)^{\frac{\alpha}{1-\alpha}} \left(\frac{L_t}{N_t}\right), \tag{3}$$

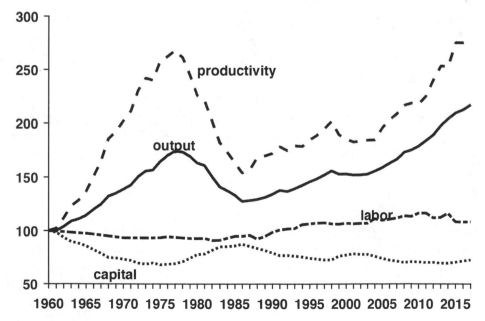

Figure 4. Growth accounting for Bolivia, 1960 = 100
Source: Authors' calculations

where N_t is the number of working-age persons. The advantage of this growth accounting is that, in a balanced growth path, $\left(K_t / Y_t\right)^{\alpha/(1-\alpha)}$ and L_t / N_t are constant, and growth in Y_t / N_t is driven by growth in $A_t^{1/(1-\alpha)}$. Kehoe and Prescott (2007) apply this composition to data for the United States and use it to show that the U.S. growth path is close to balanced: in particular, the growth in Y_t / N_t is close to that in, $A_t^{1/(1-\alpha)}$ and $\left(K_t / Y_t\right)^{\alpha/(1-\alpha)}$ and L_t / N_t are close to constant.

In Figure 4, four features are worth noting. First, fluctuations in GDP per working-age person in Bolivia are driven mostly by fluctuations in total factor productivity (TFP). Second, during the 1960s and early 1970s, we observe a remarkable expansion in TFP that is almost completely lost during the debt crisis period. Third, although there was devaluation in 1972 and 1973, TFP continued growing; it is in 1978 that it starts to fall. Fourth, TFP falls in 1999 to 2001 because of the financial crisis.

The beauty of this growth accounting is that we can identify the deviations from balanced growth. In fact, in the rest of this chapter, we attempt to relate the major deviation from balanced growth in Bolivia to shocks, both internal and external, and to monetary and fiscal policy. Our hypothesis is that Bolivia followed economic policies up through 1985 that left it very vulnerable to shocks. Starting in 1985 with its new economic policy (NPE, Nueva Política Económica), the Bolivian government implemented a series of reforms that successfully isolated the economy from shocks, at least until 1998.

Periods of Economic Development in Modern Bolivia

STABILIZATION AND GROWTH (1960–77)

In 1956, the Bolivian government enacted the Eder Plan.[4] The plan intended to reduce the liquidity available in the economy by cutting public expenditures and loans and by liberalizing prices, beginning with the exchange rate and then prices for goods. The plan also modified budget procedures by including the deficit of public enterprises, established a mining royalty and new tariffs, and restructured the tax system.

The Eder Plan planted the seeds for the rapid growth that the Bolivian economy experienced subsequently because it managed to control inflation, reducing it from 178 percent in 1956 to 11.5 percent in 1960. In fact, between 1960 and 1969, the Bolivian economy grew by 3.0 percent in terms of GDP per capita, a rate higher than those of Brazil and Chile (2.6 percent). An important feature of this period is that external debt increased, mainly to finance macroeconomic stability and the fiscal deficit but particularly to finance the expenditures of public enterprises. Overall, external debt increased from US$181.5 million in 1960 to US$1,476.9 million in 1977. Figure 2 depicts the evolution of the ratio of external debt over GDP. This ratio increased from 48.2 percent in 1960 to 60.3 percent in 1972 and then decreased to 46.7 percent in 1977.

As we can see in Figure 5, between 1960 and 1970 private lending represented the largest source of external credit, although it fell during this period. In 1960, bilateral lending represented 30 percent of total debt, but in 1970 it represented only 22 percent.

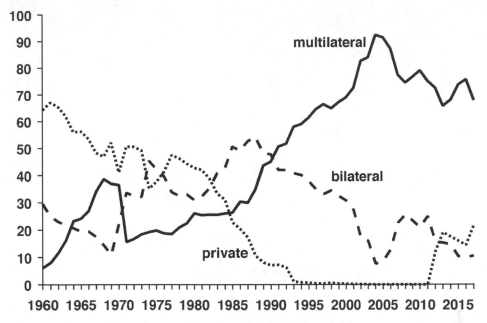

Figure 5. Composition of external creditors, percent of total debt

Source: Banco Central de Bolivia

Multilateral lending increased during the 1960s but then decreased in 1970. In fact, during the 1970s and mid-1980s, multilateral lending was not very important and was below bilateral lending and far below private lending.

During the period 1960–77, external financing was employed primarily in maintaining macroeconomic stability. In addition, the sustained net disbursements of debt generated a sustained positive balance in the capital account of the balance of payments, which was larger than the deficit of the current account. Therefore, there were net international reserve gains, as seen in Figure 6. From 1964 to 1978, net international reserves as a share of GDP were positive, with its highest value of 8.1 percent in 1974.

In Figure 7, we see that net transfers from international creditors were always positive and large, although very volatile, during the 1960s and 1970s. They increased from 3.9 percent in 1969 to 9.9 percent in 1970 and then fell to 0.2 percent in 1973, increasing again to 8.8 percent of GDP in 1977. According to Figure 8, this was a period in which sovereign debt in default was low. There were some bonds in foreign currency that were in default during the 1960s, but then, between 1970 and 1977, the amount of foreign currency bonds in default was on average only US$5 million, an amount so small that it is difficult to see in Figure 8.

The Bolivian government maintained a fixed exchange rate regime during the Bretton Woods period, up until 1971. It devalued in 1972, but then maintained a fixed exchange rate again from 1973 to 1978. In Figure 9, we see that during the fixed exchange rate regime there was a steady real appreciation, with the exception of the 1972–73 devaluation. We do not catalog the 1972 devaluation as a balance of payments crisis because it was not accompanied by a fall in international reserves, as seen in Figure 6.

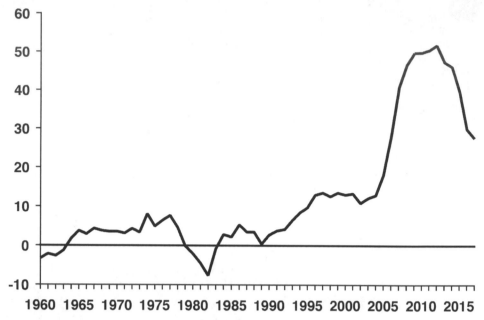

Figure 6. Net international reserves, percent of GDP
Source: Banco Central de Bolivia

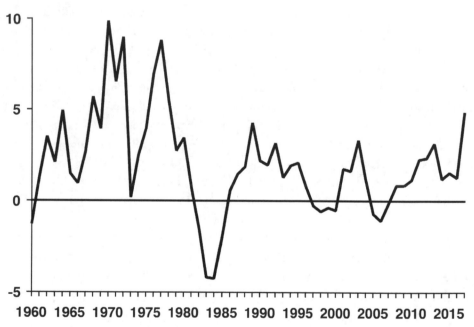

Figure 7. Net transfers from external lenders, percent of GDP
Source: Banco Central de Bolivia

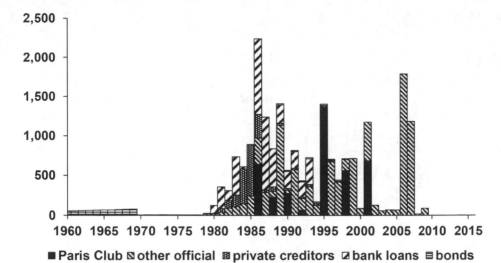

Figure 8. Sovereign debt in default by issuer, million US$
Source: Bank of Canada

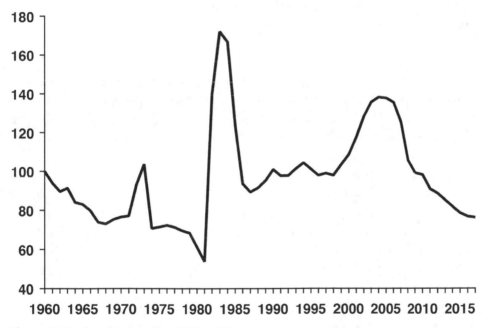

Figure 9. Real exchange rate, 1960 = 100
Source: International Monetary Fund

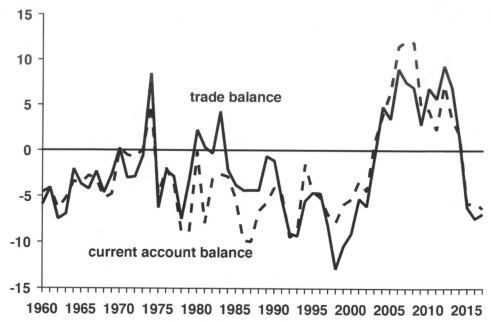

Figure 10. Trade balance and current account balance, percent of GDP
Source: World Bank

In the 1970s, Bolivia enjoyed favorable economic conditions that provided a basis for sustained growth. The country had access to vast foreign credit, and the export prices of mining and oil—the most important economic sectors—were high. According to Figure 10, the trade balance had a surplus of 8.5 percent of GDP in 1974. Unfortunately, Bolivia did not take advantage of these favorable conditions because it failed to reverse the historical trend of being a producer and an exporter of raw materials. In fact, during this period, there was active criticism of fiscal policy, in part because most of the external resources were used to finance public enterprises and not to reduce social inequality.

Between 1960 and 1970, current revenues of the general government increased from 5.9 percent of GDP to 9.4 percent, while expenditures increased from 8.1 percent of GDP to 10.3 percent, as seen in Figure 11. This allowed the fiscal deficit to decrease as a share of GDP. It decreased from 2.1 percent of GDP in 1960 to 0.9 percent of GDP in 1970.

In the 1970s, the trend of reduction of the deficit of the general government reversed. We see in Figure 12 that the fiscal deficit as a share of GDP increased from 2.4 percent in 1971 to 4.4 percent in 1977. The data in Figure 13 show that, in the 1970s, the Bolivian government started running primary deficits when external conditions were favorable. In Figure 13, the terms of trade are measured as the ratio of the export price index to the import price index—that is, the relative price of exports to imports. During the period 1974–96, the correlation of the primary surplus with the terms of trade was −0.66, while during the other years that we study, 1960–73 and 1997–2017, this correlation was 0.60. During 1986 through 1996, the government struggled to run primary surpluses as it recovered from the debt crisis even as the terms of trade deteriorated, as we discuss

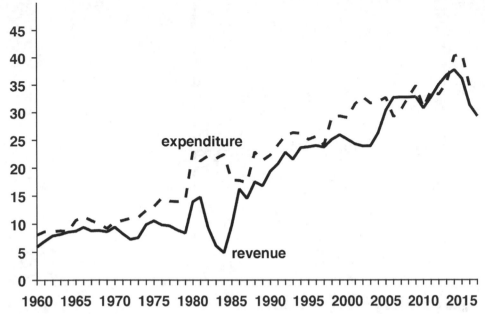

Figure 11. General government expenditure and revenue, percent of GDP
Source: Banco Central de Bolivia

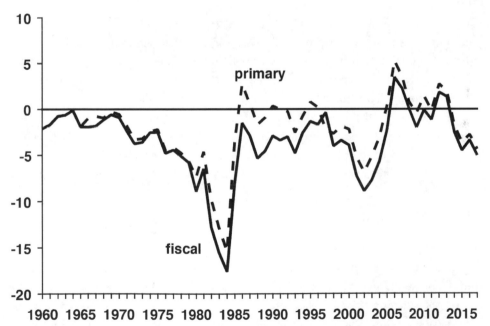

Figure 12. Fiscal and primary surplus of the general government, percent of GDP
Sources: Banco Central de Bolivia, UDAPE (Unidad de Análisis de Políticas Sociales y Económicas)

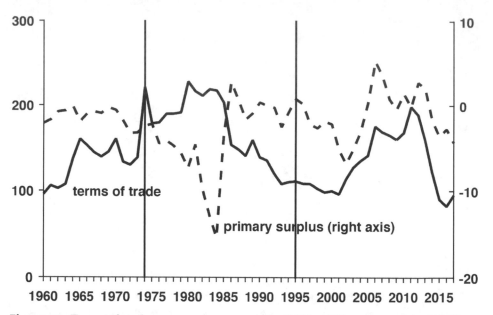

Figure 13. Terms of trade versus primary surplus, 2000 = 100, and percent of GDP
Sources: ECLAC (Economic Commission for Latin America and the Caribbean), Banco
Central de Bolivia, UDAPE

subsequently. During 1974 through 1985, however, the government ran primary deficits
even as the terms of trade improved. The large fiscal deficits and primary deficits in the
1970s are explained mostly by a boom in public investments financed by a large inflow
of external resources. According to Otalora (2002), during the years 1975–79, there were
currency surpluses that financed only a minor part of the public investments.

In Figure 14 we can see that, while the general government reduced its debt during
the 1960s and mid-1970s, public enterprises increased their debt from 8.4 percent of GDP
in 1969 to 24.7 percent in 1973, remaining at around 19 percent of GDP in the 1970s. We
interpret this as indicating that the fiscal problems came mostly from public enterprises.

DEBT CRISIS (1977–86)

Between 1977 and 1986, Bolivia suffered an economic crisis of extraordinary proportions. During the 1970s, Bolivia, like other Latin American countries, enjoyed large
inflows of credit, mostly from foreign currency loans from international banks. In the
1980s, the situation reversed, and external credit was severely constrained or cut off.
This period was also characterized by internal political chaos between 1978 and 1982,
overlapping with the onset of high interest rates and a global recession. Between 1982 and
1985, Bolivia experienced a democratic opportunity, but with a political crisis in which
the new administration, led by Hernán Siles Zuazo from the Democratic and Popular
Union (UDP), had little internal support; therefore, it had to rely on external support. The
main internal opposition that confronted the government came from the Bolivian Labor
Union (Central Obrera Boliviana), which was not just a confederation of guilds, with

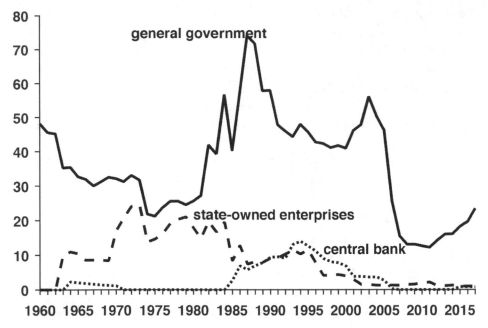

Figure 14. Composition of borrowers, percent of GDP
Source: Banco Central de Bolivia

wage demands and stability of employment, but also viewed itself as a political party with the aspiration to control the government (Toranzo 2009). Its main demand was a minimum wage that was 100 percent indexed to past inflation. By the end of the period, the average annual consumer price index inflation rate was above 11,000 percent, and the fiscal deficit was around 18 percent of GDP. Morales (1988) and other authors attribute the hyperinflation to the financing of the fiscal deficit by increased money printing. The data in Figure 3 support their assertion.

External debt doubled from US$1,476.9 million in 1977 to US$3,642.5 million in 1986. As a share of GDP, debt jumped from 45.1 to 100.4 percent in one year (1981–82), as seen in Figure 2. Most of the increases in the external-debt-to-GDP ratio between 1977 and 1983 were due to real exchange rate (RER) depreciation, as seen in Figure 2. The figure shows what the debt-to-GDP ratio would have been if the real exchange rate had been constant over 1960–2017 at its 1980 value. For example, we interpret the fact that in 1983 the RER-adjusted debt-to-GDP ratio was only 36 percent of the debt-to-GDP ratio as indicating that 64 percent of the debt-to-GDP ratio in 1983 was due to the real exchange rate devaluation between 1980 and 1983, with the remaining 36 percent due to accumulated fiscal deficits.

The crisis that started in July 1978 with the resignation of President Hugo Banzer Suárez was a balance of payments crisis of the sort analyzed by Krugman (1979): the government had no other option than to devalue in 1979, as net international reserves were falling. Figure 6 shows that net international reserves as a share of GDP started falling in 1978, and by 1979 they were negative. The government fixed the nominal exchange rate again in 1980–81, but reserves continued to fall, so there was no other option than to devalue. Inflation and dollarization followed.

In 1982, Bolivia ended a period of several military dictatorships. Democratic openness was accompanied by a severe economic, political, and social crisis. The disinvestment of large public enterprises and the sharp increase in financial obligations, related to servicing the external debt, were the main sources of the most severe crisis that Bolivia experienced in 1985. The crisis was characterized by hyperinflation, unemployment, and a worsening of living conditions.

The prevailing conditions in the international financial markets allowed Bolivia to increase its external debt by a factor of 1.8 between 1978 and 1985. The stock of external debt was US$1,799.7 million in 1978 and US$3,294.4 million in 1985. The data in Figure 8 indicate that sovereign debt in default also increased sharply during this period, from US$6.6 million in 1978 to US$2,236.69 million in 1986. In 1986, Bolivia defaulted on all debt with all types of creditors, but most of this debt was in foreign currency bank loans and bilateral debt.

The political uncertainty involved in the return to democracy that characterized the early 1980s was reflected in the government's debt policy. Even though there was an international movement in favor of a suspension of the service of debt, the Bolivian government renounced this possibility. International creditors, in particular the international banks, implemented a policy to solve the payment limitations of the large debtors, Mexico, Brazil, and Argentina, but they did nothing to solve the problems of the small debtors like Bolivia. In this setting, the Bolivian government decided to impose discipline on its external financial obligations to avoid punishment by the international creditors and to maintain its internal legitimacy. Notice in Figure 7 that net transfers were negative between 1982 and 1985. This means that, while Bolivia defaulted with some creditors, it paid others. In fact, this is a particular feature of Bolivia's debt policy. It seems that it managed its debt portfolio by paying some creditors while acquiring new debts, possibly using some of the new debt to pay old debts.[5]

Figure 5 shows that there is also a change in creditors between 1982 and 1985. The relative weight of private creditors dropped to 22.8 percent because the government initially paid this debt. Simultaneously, the relative weight of bilateral creditors rose to 50.7 percent, which is explained by the support that the Bolivian government and other official organizations gave toward the democratic process initiated in Bolivia. Of course, the decision to pay as much debt service as possible had drastic implications for the economy. The ratio of debt service to exports of goods and services plus factor income from abroad reached 63 percent in 1984, which was an unsustainable level. We also observe in Figure 10 that between 1978 and 1983, the trade balance increased from −7.5 percent of GDP to 4.3 percent of GDP and then fell abruptly. Rather than an abrupt sudden stop, the Bolivian economy went through a painful five-year cutoff of most foreign lending.

In 1985, the most severe economic crisis in Bolivia's history occurred, characterized by a hyperinflation of unprecedented magnitude that occurred as a direct consequence of money printing to finance the fiscal deficit. Notice in Figure 3 that the inflation rate reached 11,750 percent (the corresponding inflation factor is 11,850 percent). As Milton Friedman stated, "Inflation is always and everywhere a monetary phenomenon in the sense that it is and can be produced only by a more rapid increase in the quantity of money than in output" (Friedman 1963). Figure 3 shows that hyperinflation coincided with a large increase in the rate of growth of the monetary aggregate M1. Thus hyperinflation was a monetary phenomenon in Friedman's sense, but the need to print this money came from fiscal problems and problems with external debt, as we have discussed. Notice, however, that M1 did not increase as much as did the price level, nor, except for 1985, the year of the hyperinflation, did the increases in M1 exactly coincide with the increases in the price level.

The decline in tax revenue—that is, of current revenue—and the increase in current expenditures during the years 1978–79 pushed up the fiscal deficit. The increase in the fiscal deficit coincided with a decline in exports as a percentage of GDP driven by a decline in quantities exported rather than a decline in export prices, since we can see in Figure 13 that this was a period in which the terms of trade were improving. Because most Bolivian exports were produced by public enterprises, the decline in the quantities exported is a clear sign of their inefficiency.[6] At the same time, there was also an increase in external debt service and a decrease in disbursements of external debt. All these factors contributed to the deterioration of the financial position of the National Treasury (TGN), which drove the increases in primary deficits not only in the later years of the 1970s but also during the following years. Notice how the fiscal and primary deficit rose in the early 1980s, reaching levels of 17 percent and 15 percent of GDP, respectively, in Figure 12.

In Figure 15, we observe that the deficit of the nonfinancial public sector (NFPS) increased after 1982. In 1983, it was 17.0 percent as a share of GDP, and after a year it rose to 21.2 percent of GDP. The growth in the deficit is explained in part by the Olivera-Tanzi

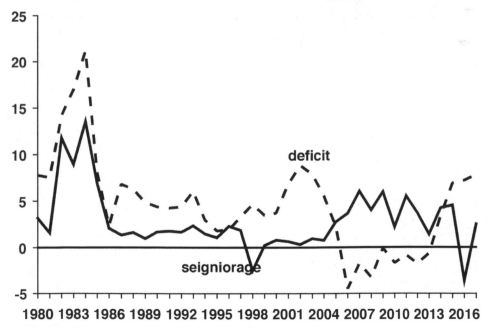

Figure 15. Seigniorage and deficit of the NFPS, percent of GDP
Sources: UDAPE, Banco Central de Bolivia

effect (see Tanzi 1977) and also by an increase in government spending due to the wage policy that was implemented. In the figure we can also see that seigniorage allowed the government to cover most of its deficit.[7]

Two aspects are worth noting concerning the economic instability in the late 1970s and early 1980s. First, as the crisis deepened and external financing options were limited as foreign lending was cut off, the government developed a greater confidence in the inflation tax as a mechanism of financing. This reliance on seigniorage encouraged outflows of capital and the public's use of foreign currency, especially dollars. Second, because the banks had guaranteed access to dollars, they rejected payments in national currency for foreign currency–denominated debt, thus creating a parallel exchange market where borrowers kept buying dollars, which they kept as a store of value to protect against devaluation and inflation (see Antelo 1996).

The lack of fiscal discipline led the government to eliminate deposits in foreign currency in the domestic financial system and to impose capital controls. By the end of 1982, several attempts were made to stabilize the exchange rate. An official exchange rate was established with state control of foreign exchange based on controls on foreign trade and compulsory delivery of foreign currency to the state. In addition, the Foreign Exchange Policy Commission was created to allocate the scarce foreign exchange according to criteria and rules determined by the government.

One of the measures to restrict the use of dollars was the "de-dollarization" program, which consisted of converting all obligations contracted in dollars or with value maintenance into national currency, including deposits in the banking system, at the exchange rate determined by the government on a given day. This measure created a mismatch in the banking system, hurting creditors and those with deposits in foreign currency in the banking system but favoring debtors. The policy of de-dollarization failed because dollar transactions actually increased, and the government had to refinance debts and

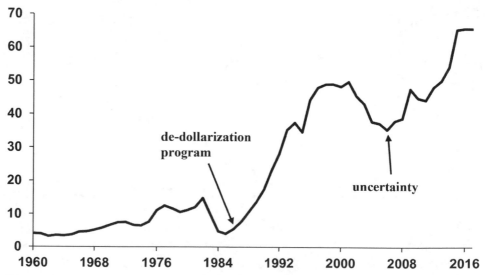

Figure 16. Deposits in the banking system, percent of GDP
Source: Banco Central de Bolivia

deposits in dollars with currency creation, thus increasing inflation (see Cariaga 1996). This program also generated a bank run and a subsequent government bailout of the banks, as seen in Figure 16. Deposits in banks as a share of GDP fell from 14.8 percent in 1982 to 4.0 percent in 1985.

Morales (2012) argues that the de-dollarization program produced a liquefaction of the government's short-term debt, insofar as the foreign currency (or value maintenance) reserves of the banking system in the Banco Central de Bolivia had been used to partially finance the fiscal deficit. According to Antelo (1996), the de-dollarization program had four goals: first, to reduce the demand for dollars by giving back to the government control over the money supply and to concentrate the stock of dollars in external debt repayments; second, to restore the government's ability to raise funds through inflation; third, to encourage sectors stifled by their dollar debts; and, fourth, to lower investment costs in industry, whose debts denominated in dollars increased with real exchange rate depreciation. The de-dollarization program failed to accomplish these objectives, however, and financial disintermediation and informal dollarization followed.

RECOVERY AND SLOW GROWTH (1986–98)

The year 1986 marked the beginning of a period of recovery and growth and the replacement of the state by the market.[8] In fact, in the second half of 1985, a restructuring process was initiated that had two main objectives: first, to stabilize the economy and, second, to implement structural reforms in which national or foreign enterprises would be the main economic actors. According to Antelo (2000), the structural reforms implemented in Bolivia were framed in line with the Washington Consensus. This period lasts until 1998 and included different subperiods of structural reforms: economic stabilization and first-generation reforms (1986–89), deepening of the first-generation reforms (1990–93), and second-generation reforms (1994–97).[9] The seed of these reforms was the new economic policy, the Nueva Política Económica (NPE). The NPE was a stabilization plan whose primary objective was to reduce inflation and generate foreign resources. The structural reforms included the liberalization of goods and financial markets, capitalization through privatization, a tax reform, commercial policies in favor of exports and foreign direct investment (FDI), and fiscal decentralization among municipalities. It was a period characterized by slow growth; GDP per WAP growth was on average 1.1 percent per year between 1986 and 1998.

The NPE was implemented in August 1985, with Supreme Decree 21060. This stabilization plan was enacted to confront the crisis, stop hyperinflation, and stabilize the economy. It was part of a broader structural adjustment program aimed at changing the whole function of the economy by reducing the influence of the state on production; increasing reliance on the price system in the markets for goods, labor, and capital; and promoting private-sector initiatives. As Jemio (2001) indicates, the framework of incentives adopted under the NPE included free convertibility of foreign exchange, elimination of price controls, reduced government intervention in labor contracts, financial liberalization, and commitment to price stability. All these actions were designed to encourage greater private-sector participation in the economy. The core of this stabilization program was based on exchange rate unification, drastic measures to control the fiscal deficit, and a very tight monetary policy.

Starting in 1981, the Bolivian government had maintained a system of dual exchange rates: an official exchange rate and a parallel—that is, market—exchange rate. In 1986, the government unified these exchange rates with the liberalization of the exchange market, accompanied by restrictive monetary and fiscal policies, and an ingenious mechanism of intervention by the Banco Central de Bolivia, known as "El Bolsín." In the Bolsín, the demand for foreign exchange that could not be satisfied by private operators was covered by the Banco Central de Bolivia through an American auction with a base or reserve price. The price resulting from this operation served to define the official exchange rate. Once the exchange market was controlled, the devaluation rate of the parallel exchange rate with the U.S. dollar was reduced from almost 7,300 percent in 1985 to 13 percent in 1987. After that, a crawling-peg regime was adopted with minidevaluations, as seen in Figure 9. This regime lasted until 2005, when a real appreciation recurred.

The NPE allowed the possibility of transacting in U.S. dollars within the financial system, and with the reestablishment of foreign currency deposits, a formal financial system based on the U.S. dollar was established. A bimonetary system was established where transactions could be made in dollars or in local currency. This, in combination with the crawling-peg regime, generated the incentives for an increase in dollarization from 48.3 percent in 1986 to 90.1 percent in 1997, as seen in Figure 17.

Macroeconomic stabilization was achieved in two years. Antezana (1988) explains that stabilization was achieved by a combination of fiscal and monetary policy. Fiscal

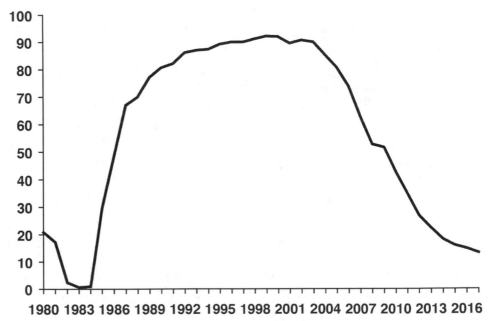

Figure 17. Dollarization in Bolivia, percent of total deposits

Source: Banco Central de Bolivia

policy reduced public expenditure and increased revenues by raising prices and taxes on goods and services sold by the public sector, mainly fuels. Monetary policy aimed to control the money supply by tightly restricting net lending to the public sector and to development banks. The inflation rate was reduced from more than 11,000 percent in 1985 to 276.3 percent in 1986 and to 14.6 percent in 1987, as seen in Figure 3.[10]

Monetary policy was fundamental in stabilizing prices. Supreme Decree 21060 required the Banco Central de Bolivia to submit a monetary program to the Ministry of Finance with reports every ten days to allow the Ministry of Finance to closely monitor the money supply. This mechanism made it possible to coordinate efforts to reduce the fiscal deficit with control of fiscal credit, both to the National Treasury and to decentralized entities, public companies, and departmental and local administrations. Although the Ministry of Finance monitored the monetary management, the Banco Central de Bolivia defined its operational objectives independently. In this way, monetary policy ceased to be subordinated to fiscal financing needs.

Hyperinflation left the country with no way to pay its external debt. Therefore, the NPE aimed to promote exports so as to generate foreign resources. The orientation of the NPE in terms of its relationship to the multilateral organizations was linked to a solution of this incapacity to pay the debt. As the general government was the main debtor, as seen in Figure 14, one of the first objectives of the NPE through the Structural Adjustment Program (Programas de Ajuste Estructural; PAE) was to reduce and control the fiscal deficit. Therefore, in May 1986, a new tax structure was imposed.[11]

A priority of the NPE was the reduction and payment of the accumulated foreign debt. In February 1987, the 131 creditor banks of Bolivia approved a refinancing agreement (Enmienda al Convenio de Refinanciamiento) from 1981, in which these banks had the opportunity to purchase bonds in the secondary market and also exchange the debt for investment bonds. The solution consisted of the buildup of a fiduciary fund administered by the International Monetary Fund so that it could collect resources donated by the developed countries and move them to the secondary market to acquire debt at a lower price. In this way, Bolivia reduced its commercial debt by purchasing it in the secondary market at 11 cents per dollar. This form of reduction was also supported by the approval of the Brady Plan. Between 1987 and 1989, Bolivia reduced its external debt by US$797.4 million.[12]

The success of this repurchase of debt led to a second round. Between 1992 and 1993, external debt was bought in the secondary market at a value of 16 cents per dollar. This operation also allowed exchanging debt for short- and long-term bonds. In sum, these operations contributed to reducing the external debt by US$170 million. Furthermore, in 1989 the Banco Central de Bolivia issued investment bonds with the aim of exchanging them with international private debt. The bonds had a present value of 11 cents per dollar, and they were redeemed in twenty-five years.[13]

In terms of bilateral debt, the Bolivian government appealed several times to the Paris Club to reschedule its debt with governments and official organizations. Due to the fiscal crisis, in July 1988, the government entered into an agreement with the International Monetary Fund called the Servicio Reforzado de Ajuste Estructural (SRAE).

Table 1. Debt negotiations according to creditors

Private	Bilateral	Multilateral
1988 (buyback)	1986 (Paris I)	1998 (HIPC-1)
1992 (buyback)	1988 (Paris II)	1999 (HIPC-2)
	1990 (Paris III)	2005 (MDRI)
	1992 (Paris IV)	
	1995 (Paris V)	
	1996 (Paris VI)	

Source: Banco Central de Bolivia

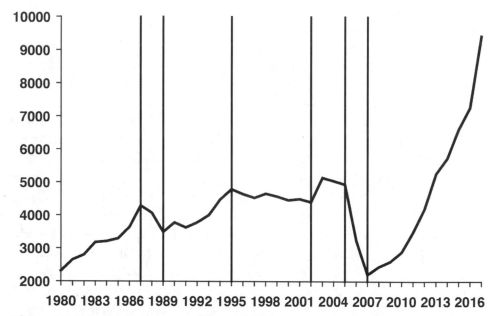

Figure 18. Debt renegotiations, millions of US$
Source: Banco Central de Bolivia

This program allowed the Bolivian government to continue to reschedule its debt with the Paris Club. As a result of all these negotiations, which started in 1986 and ended in 1996, Bolivia managed to reduce its external debt significantly. Table 1 presents a summary of the debt negotiations according to the type of creditors, and Figure 18 shows the debt reductions achieved by these two types of renegotiations.

As a result of the structural reforms, in particular the privatization of public enterprises, in the 1990s, there was a large inflow of foreign resources in the form of foreign direct investment (FDI). The entry of foreign enterprises in strategic sectors such as oil, energy, and telecommunications allowed the economy to resume its growth. On average, the economy grew by 2 percent between 1990 and 1997 in terms of GDP per capita. In 1994, the rate of growth was 2.3 percent as a result of capitalization, but the ratio of external debt to GDP reached a maximum value of 75.1 percent. This ratio then declined to 57.3 percent in 1997, a value that was still high for a country that needed to reverse its poverty levels. Nevertheless, the state-owned enterprises reduced their debt as a percentage of GDP, due to the capitalization program, from 11.6 percent in 1995 to 1.2 percent in 2005.

The composition of debtors also has changed dramatically since the implementation of the Programas de Ajuste Estructural (PAE), as seen in Figure 14. Since 1985 the general government, and in particular the central government, appears as the principal debtor, absorbing 74 percent of total debt in 1997. The central government allocated these resources primarily to public investment because the tax policy thus far did not generate sufficient internal resources to cover capital and current expenditures. The financial public sector (Banco Central de Bolivia and specialized banks) appears as the second debtor. Its relative weight doubled in ten years, and it represented 18.7 percent of total debt in 1997.

During this period, sovereign debt in default was also large. In particular, we see in Figure 8 that in 1995 Bolivia defaulted in US$1,363 million of its bilateral debt, and in 1996 and 1997, it defaulted in US$669.1 million and US$417 million, respectively, of its multilateral debt. By that time, multilateral debt represented 40 percent of GDP, and it was already the largest component of total debt.

The NPE allowed a reduction of the fiscal deficit of the nonfinancial public sector (NFPS) from 8.1 percent in 1985 to 2.3 percent in 1986, with the reversion of the Olivera-Tanzi effect, because inflation was drastically reduced. In 1987, however, the fiscal deficit of the NFPS increased again to 6.8 percent of GDP, as seen in Figure 15. Therefore, a tax reform was implemented with the goal of achieving fiscal balance. Between 1989 and 1997, the fiscal deficit was on average 3.8 percent of GDP. During the 1990s, the privatization programs that the Bolivian government implemented helped reduce the deficit to 1.8 percent and 1.9 percent of GDP in 1995 and 1996, respectively.[14]

FINANCIAL CRISIS (1998–2002)

From 1998 to 2002, the economy entered a slowdown phase, induced by external shocks: a deterioration in the terms of trade and the reversal in capital flows. During this period, financial flows, with the exception of FDI, reversed significantly. FDI remained at relatively high levels (US$770 million on average per year) because the capitalized companies were still accomplishing their investment commitments.

Public external debt increased to finance the growing fiscal deficit resulting from the economic slowdown and the implementation of structural reforms. Among them, pension reform implemented in 1996 had a significant fiscal impact. Bolivia passed from a system of mutual funds to a system of individual capitalization. In 1999, the fiscal deficit of the NFPS was 3.0 percent of GDP, but the fiscal deficit without pensions was indeed a surplus of 0.7 percent of GDP. In 2002, the fiscal deficit was 8.5 percent, from which half represented pensions.

In September 1996, the International Monetary Fund and the World Bank created the Heavily Indebted Poor Countries (HIPC) Initiative to give financial support to a limited number of countries characterized by poverty and with medium-term external financial obligations in terms of debt service that were higher than what these countries were able to afford. The argument was that reducing the external debt for these countries would free up greater resources that could be used to attack poverty. This was the first time that a debt forgiveness program included multilateral debt, which, as we have seen in Figure 5, accounted for most of Bolivia's debt by the end of the 1990s.

The International Monetary Fund and World Bank imposed conditions in terms of macroeconomic policies and structural reforms as part of the concession of the HIPC debt reduction. Bolivia met all these conditions and, being a poor country, was selected to participate in this initiative. Through the HIPC I program, implemented in 1998, the accorded reduction of multilateral debt was equivalent to 24 percent of the stock debt by the end of 1998 in the next forty years, although the largest part of this reduction would be effective in the first years. The application of this program managed to reduce the debt service over exports to 25.5 percent in 1999. Nevertheless, the negative external shocks that began in 1999 offset the beneficial results of the HIPC I. The service of the external debt and the worsening of the terms of trade drastically reduced the level of national savings. There was a huge drop in output and exports, and the negative balance of the current account could be compensated only with the inflow of FDI. As can be seen in Figure 2, the debt as a share of GDP remained constant during these years at an average of 55 percent.

The HIPC II initiative made it possible for Bolivia to obtain additional resources through the forgiveness of the debt with the approval of the so-called Bolivian Strategy for Poverty Reduction. The HIPC II strategy consisted of the reduction of multilateral debt in fifteen years, starting in 2001. The application of the HIPC I and HIPC II initiatives allowed an increase in forgiveness of the average debt of 1999–2000 by 44 percent. This initiative allowed a reduction of external debt of US$50 million between 1999 and 2000, which represented 2 percent of GDP, but this reduction was not sufficient. Indeed, in 2001 the external debt represented the same proportion of GDP as it did in 1999, as seen in Figure 2.

The data in Figure 12 show that fiscal problems worsened at the beginning of the 2000s. The fiscal deficit shot up between 2000 and 2001. The fiscal deficit increased from 3.9 percent to 7.2 percent of GDP, and the primary deficit increased from 2.2 percent to 5.2 percent. These fiscal problems made it impossible for the government to continue paying its debt obligations; therefore, in 2001 we also observe large amounts of sovereign debt in default. Bolivia defaulted by US$685 million in its bilateral debt and by US$488.4 million in its multilateral debt, as seen in Figure 8.

The period 1998–2002 is characterized as a financial crisis. Jemio (2006) explains that, starting in 1998, the Bolivian economy experienced a drop in the growth rate, high unemployment, and financial disintermediation. The financial sector suffered the most, experiencing a credit crunch due to the contagion effects of the international financial crisis through lower capital and commercial flows and policies followed by other countries.

The contraction of international demand reduced prices of the main export commodities, affecting the income of the exporting companies and deteriorating their cash flows and their capacity to service the debts contracted. The trade balance as a share of GDP fell to −12.9 percent in 1998, as seen in Figure 10. Additionally, the economy was affected by a lower availability of external financing, since in the years before the crisis there had been an outflow of capital, especially capital intermediated by the financial system.

This situation resulted in a fall in international reserves and a contraction in the money supply. Figure 6 shows that net international reserves fell from 13.2 percent to 10.8 percent of GDP between 2001 and 2002. The lack of liquidity accentuated the fall in the pace of economic activity. Finally, the devaluation of the Brazilian real represented a loss of competitiveness of the traded goods sector and exerted pressure on the exchange rate. The rate of depreciation of the real exchange rate was 5.0 percent in 2000, but it increased to 8.1 percent and 9.2 percent in 2001 and 2002, respectively, as seen in Figure 9.

Monetary and fiscal policies were procyclical. Monetary policy tried to maintain stable growth through payments by using open market operations, domestic credit, and, to a lesser extent, the level of bank reserves. Fiscal policy restricted public investment as a way to reduce the deficit, amplifying the effect of real shocks. The financial system responded to this situation by rationing credit, and this was encouraged by the enactment of a stricter prudential regulation by the Superintendency of Banks and Financial Institutions (SBEF) in November 1998. This resulted in portfolio declines; increases in the reserves of banks; lower interest rates, deposits, and loans; and an increase in bank spreads.

The regulations in force until 1998 allowed an overexpansion of bank credit during the 1990s, but this increased the risk of the financial system and was one of the main causes for the subsequent contraction of credit since 1998. Although the change in regulations introduced by the SBEF in November 1998 was aimed at correcting this contraction by obliging banks to increase their loans, it had the opposite effect because it was too late. According to Morales (2012), between 1999 and 2003, the banking system had reduced its deposits by 24.6 percent and its loans by 43.4 percent.

NATIONALIZATION AND GROWTH (2002–17)

The slowdown that began in 1999 created a climate of social and political conflict, which became critical after 2002 when a new president was elected.[15] The economic and social crisis that the new president inherited created uncertainty for investment and deposits. Morales (2012) explains that the unexpected results of the elections increased the nervousness of the depositors in the financial system. As a result, there was a huge outflow of deposits between June and July 2002. In six weeks, the financial system lost 23 percent of total deposits. In fact, deposits as a share of GDP fell from 49.0 percent in 1998 to 35.4 percent in 2006, as seen in Figure 16.

In 2002, indicators pointed to a worsening of the crisis as neighboring countries were having serious financial problems. According to Morales (2012), the abandonment of the convertibility and the moratorium on the Argentinean debt, the Uruguayan banking crisis, and the rapid depreciation of the Brazilian real, together with the instability within Bolivia, posed serious threats to the financial system. The structural reforms that had been made in the 1990s, however, endowed Bolivia with an unexpected robustness, and, consequently, economic collapse was avoided.

What could not be avoided was political collapse. In 2003, when the fiscal deficit had reached unsustainable levels—8.9 percent of GDP in 2002 according to Figure 12—the government decided to implement an income tax, which had never previously existed (nor does it today) in the Bolivian economy. This policy generated a resounding rejection by the entire population. Political turmoil ensued. In October 2003, after having lost its legitimacy and having serious conflicts in the city of El Alto, the government elected in 2002 was forced to resign.

International economic conditions began to recover in 2003, but most importantly, Bolivia increased its natural gas exports to Brazil. The value of natural gas exports increased from US$265.5 million in 2002 to US$389.5 million in 2003. In addition, an increase in the prices of Bolivian exports produced an export boom. The trade balance had a large surplus between 2004 and 2014, as seen in Figure 10. GDP growth also increased, although not to the levels of 1960–77. Between 2002 and 2017, growth in GDP per WAP averaged 2.6 percent per year.

Even though the economy was showing signs of recovery, the social and political instability continued because the presidents who followed Sánchez de Lozada did not have sufficient support in the Congress. In addition, the export boom, mainly from the hydrocarbon industry, led to political debate about how incomes were distributed. Recall that the hydrocarbon sector was controlled by international companies, and the government received only taxes from exports.

In 2005 there were new elections, won by Evo Morales, who became president in January 2006. With his administration, a new economic vision was implemented. The year 2006 began a period characterized by a return to an economy in which the state played the leading role through the nationalization of the main companies in strategic sectors such as oil, electricity, and telecommunications. These companies were previously under private ownership.

The extremely favorable international conditions of high commodity prices, along with the nationalization of the hydrocarbon sector, allowed Bolivia to experience, for the first time in its modern economic history, a continuous nonfinancial public-sector surplus between 2006 and 2013. Figure 12 shows that the fiscal surplus was 4.5 percent of GDP in 2006 and that it remained at an average of 1.8 percent until 2013.

The stock of foreign debt as a share of GDP declined from 55.4 percent in 1999 to 51.9 percent in 2005, as seen in Figure 2. The largest decrease in debt occurred after 2006, however, when the stock of debt was reduced to 28.4 percent of GDP in 2006 and to 16.8 percent of GDP in 2007. This decline represented US$2,732.9 million. Starting in 2008, the stock of foreign debt remained around 15 percent of GDP, but, starting in 2015, it has increased, reaching 25.3 percent of GDP in 2017.

In 2005, during a meeting of the G8 countries, a complete forgiveness of debt was announced for the HIPC countries (Bolivia included). This program, called the Multilateral Debt Relief Initiative (MDRI), explains the large reduction of Bolivia's multilateral debt. To this we have to add the change in the external economic conditions since 2005 that coincided with the end of the social crisis that Bolivia experienced between 2000 and 2003 and the end of the so-called neoliberal period, when the economy was based in the free market.

The windfall of funding received by the nonfinancial public sector (NFPS) and the external surplus allowed the Banco Central de Bolivia to accumulate reserves to amounts never seen before. Net international reserves increased from 12.0 percent of GDP in 2003 to 51.8 percent of GDP in 2012. Since then, reserves have started to decrease, coinciding with a reversal of these favorable conditions, as seen in Figure 6.

The large current account surpluses that the Bolivian economy started to experience in 2004 generated an excess of dollars in the economy that caused the nominal exchange rate to appreciate. In 2005, the nominal exchange rate reached a value of 8.08 boliviano (BOB)/US$, and it appreciated further to 8.05 BOB/US$ in 2006. Figure 9 shows that the real exchange rate has experienced a real appreciation since 2005 that continues today. In fact, in November 2011, the Banco Central de Bolivia adopted a de facto fixed exchange rate policy. Since then, the nominal exchange rate has been fixed at 6.96 BOB/US$. This policy explains the fall in international reserves observed in recent years in Figure 6.

By 2017, international reserves were 27.5 percent of GDP, there was a fiscal deficit of 7.8 percent of GDP, and the current account deficit was 7.0 percent of GDP. External debt has increased to US$9,427.9 million, and, although it is an amount larger than Bolivia's debt in 2005—US$4,941.6 million—it represents only 25.3 percent of GDP.

The policies being implemented today have the following features in common with policies that were implemented in the 1970s:

- nationalization of the enterprises in strategic sectors (oil and energy)

- economy based on the role of the state as producer (state capitalism in the 1970s), where the surplus generated by strategic enterprises was used (or was intended to be used) to finance other enterprises

- adoption of a fixed exchange rate policy that led to an overvaluation of the local currency

- ambitious investment plans that did not clearly identify the sources of financing or the profitability of projects

- increasing fiscal deficits, mainly due to the increase in the deficit of public enterprises

- fall in reserves due to an expansion of domestic credit

These similarities in policies lead us to ask, Is the Bolivian economy heading toward a balance of payments crisis?

Budget Accounting Analysis for Bolivia

Our analysis of budget accounting for Bolivia uses debt data from the Banco Central de Bolivia because they cover a longer period than alternative sources such as the World Bank's International Debt Statistics.

Recall that during the 1970s, Bolivia borrowed large amounts from private lenders. The capacity for negotiation with these creditors fell as the country increased its debt. Therefore, Bolivia had no other option but to contract loans with more severe conditions, which means that interest rates were higher and maturities were lower. This is exactly what happened in the early 1980s: there was a rise in world interest rates, and most of the loans that Bolivia contracted in the 1970s reached their maturity. This fact, associated with the incapacity of the country to generate foreign resources and large fiscal deficits, set the stage for the subsequent crisis.

In the 1990s, with the consolidation of structural reforms and the change in international creditors, maturities started to rise, and interest rates decreased. By the end of the decade, interest rates were on average 3 percent and maturity was fifteen years on average. It is important to mention also that these credit conditions changed to conditions even more favorable for the Bolivian government with the debt forgiveness and reductions that benefited Bolivia during the 1990s.[16]

Between 1988 and 2000, there was an increase in debt contracted under multiple currencies, but most of this debt was contracted in U.S. dollars. In 2005, 75 percent of total debt was in dollars. Debt contracted in deutsche marks never reached more than 10 percent of total debt, and debt contracted in yen reached its highest share of 13.7 percent in 1994.

We have modified the budget equation in "A Framework for Studying the Monetary and Fiscal History of Latin America" to incorporate not only nominal and indexed internal debt but also dollar internal debt, as Bolivia has a bimonetary system, and the Banco Central de Bolivia as well as the National Treasury can issue debt in dollars or in bolivianos.

The government began to issue internal debt in 1988, which became important in 1996 after the pension reform. With the new pension system, the newly created pension funds used Treasury bonds as the major way to invest their funds. In fact, the pension system was thought of as a system that could serve as a source of financing for the government as well as a system that could generate the incentives for creating a stock market in Bolivia. Currently, the pension funds not only serve as a major source of financing for the government, as they have bought around 25 percent of the government sovereign bonds issued in 2017, but also now represent the main source of liquidity for the financial system.[17]

Between 1988 and 2000, most of the internal debt was also debt from the Banco Central de Bolivia, issued to sterilize the monetary effects of the high accumulation of international reserves through open market operations. In Bolivia, a significant share of internal debt in local currency is issued not for financing needs but to control excessive liquidity.

Figure 19 depicts the evolution of internal and external debt as a share of GDP since 1993. Notice that, since 2003, the stock of external debt as a share of GDP decreased,

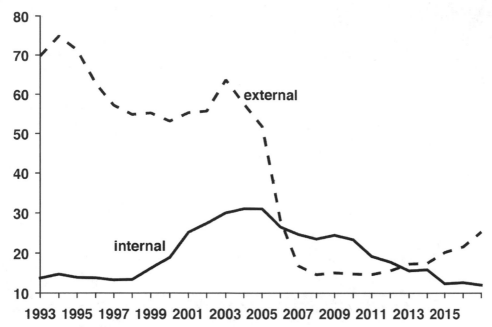

Figure 19. External versus internal debt, percent of GDP
Source: Banco Central de Bolivia

while the stock of internal debt as a share of GDP increased until 2004. Internal debt was even larger than external debt between 2007 and 2012.

Our budget accounting starts with the year-by-year budget constraint of the government in nominal domestic currency:

$$B_t + b_t P_t + B_t^d E_t + B_t^* E_t + M_t =$$
$$(D_t + X_t)P_t + B_{t-1}R_{t-1} + b_{t-1}r_{t-1}P_{t-1} + B_{t-1}^d R_{t-1}^d E + B_{t-1}^* R_{t-1}^* E + M_{t-1}, \qquad (4)$$

where B_t is nominal internal debt, M_t is the stock of money, b_t is indexed internal debt, B_t^d is dollar-indexed internal debt, and B_t^* is the dollar external debt; P_t is the price level, E_t is the nominal exchange rate, R_t, r_t, and R_t^d are the gross returns on nominal, indexed, and dollar-denominated internal debt; and R_t^* is the gross return on external debt, D_t is the deficit of the general government, and X_t is the residual. We are not sure what the residual exactly includes, but it certainly includes the deficit of the public enterprises.

If we assume that X_t represents only the deficit of public enterprises, we can consider $D_t + X_t$ as the deficit of the nonfinancial public sector, for which we only have information since 1980. Since we have information on the central and general government since 1960, however, we calculate X_t as a residual. Unfortunately, this residual—which represents a measure of our ignorance—is large in some periods.

We can write the budget constraint in terms of real GDP as

$$(\theta_t^N - \theta_{t-1}^N) + (\theta_t^r - \theta_{t-1}^r) + \xi_t(\theta_t^d - \theta_{t-1}^d) + \xi_t(\theta_t^* - \theta_{t-1}^*) + (m_t - m_{t-1}) + m_{t-1}\left(1 - \frac{1}{g_t\pi_t}\right) =$$

$$d_t + x_t + \theta_{t-1}^N\left(\frac{R_{t-1}}{\pi_t g_t} - 1\right) + \theta_{t-1}^r\left(\frac{r_{t-1}}{g_t} - 1\right) + \xi_t\theta_{t-1}^d\left(\frac{R_{t-1}^d}{g_t\pi_t^W} - 1\right) + \xi_t\theta_{t-1}^*\left(\frac{R_{t-1}^*}{g_t\pi_t^W} - 1\right), \tag{5}$$

where the first four terms on the left-hand side measure the issuance of debt compared to GDP in the three different types of internal debt and the issuance of foreign debt. Here

$$\theta_t^N = \frac{B_t}{P_t Y_t} \tag{6}$$

is the ratio of nominal internal debt to GDP and θ_t^r is defined similarly, and

$$\xi_t\theta_t^* = \frac{E_t B_t^*}{P_t Y_t} = \left(\frac{E_t P_t^W}{P_t}\right)\left(\frac{B_t^* / P_t^W}{Y_t}\right) \tag{7}$$

is the ratio of external debt to GDP and $\xi_t\theta_t^d$ is defined similarly. In both of these terms, we factor out the real exchange rate, ξ_t. The last two terms on the left-hand side of equation (5) represent increases in high-powered money and seigniorage. The first two terms on the right-hand side represent the deficit of the general government and the residual as a fraction of output, respectively, and the final four terms measure the real net service costs on all types of debt adjusted by GDP growth.[18]

To understand better the debt issuance terms for dollar-indexed internal debt and external debt in budget accounting equation (5), we decompose the issuance term for external debt as

$$\xi_t(\theta_t^* - \theta_{t-1}^*) = (\xi_t\theta_t^* - \xi_{t-1}\theta_{t-1}^*) - \theta_{t-1}^*(\xi_t - \xi_{t-1}). \tag{8}$$

Of course, an analogous decomposition applies to dollar-indexed internal debt. The first term in this decomposition tells us how much the value of external debt as a fraction of GDP changed from year $t-1$ to year t. The second term tells us how much of this change in value was due to the change in the real exchange rate. As we have seen in Figure 2, much of the year-to-year changes in the ratio of external debt to GDP are due to real exchange rate fluctuations, and our term for the issuance of external debt factors this out. As we have discussed, the value of external debt increased from 45.1 percent of Bolivian GDP in 1981 to 100.4 percent in 1982. Of this increase of 55.3 percentage points (pp), we account for 51.4 pp by the revaluation ter— $(\xi_t\theta_t^* - \xi_{t-1}\theta_{t-1}^*)$, that is, by the real exchange rate depreciation. Our debt issuance term is the difference, 3.9 pp. Bolivian external debt increased by 5.7 percent in dollar terms between 1981 and 1982. Our external debt

Table 2. Budget accounting results across periods

Period	1960–71	1971–77	1960–77	1977–86	1986–98	1998–2002	2002–17	2006–17	1960–2017
(1) Issuance of local currency internal debt	0.00	0.00	0.00	0.00	0.08	0.24	0.45	0.53	0.16
(2) Issuance of indexed internal debt	0.00	0.00	0.00	0.00	0.25	1.14	-0.07	-1.54	0.09
(3) Issuance of dollar internal debt	0.00	0.00	0.00	0.00	0.70	1.05	-1.02	-0.28	-0.02
(4) Issuance of external debt	0.70	1.31	0.90	4.59	-2.47	-2.65	-1.31	-1.13	-0.24
(5) Money issuance	0.25	0.07	0.13	-0.72	0.05	-0.64	1.16	1.38	0.29
(6) Seigniorage	1.07	2.27	1.55	6.01	1.31	0.54	1.65	1.96	2.17
Total	2.02	3.65	2.58	9.87	-0.09	-0.31	0.85	0.92	2.45
Obligations									
(1) General government primary deficit	1.05	3.08	1.80	6.53	0.50	3.75	0.75	-0.22	2.14
(2) Service of local currency internal debt	0.00	0.00	0.00	0.00	0.03	0.08	-0.41	-0.54	-0.10
(3) Service of indexed internal debt	0.00	0.00	0.00	0.00	-0.04	-0.10	-0.27	-0.52	-0.09
(4) Service of dollar internal debt	0.00	0.00	0.00	0.00	0.07	0.29	-0.08	-0.02	0.02
(5) Service of external debt	-2.78	-3.79	-3.14	1.63	-1.40	-0.75	-1.03	-0.79	-1.36
(6) Residual	3.75	4.36	3.92	1.71	0.77	-3.59	1.88	3.02	1.84
Total	2.02	3.65	2.58	9.87	-0.09	-0.31	0.85	0.92	2.45

Source: Authors' calculations.

issuance adjusts this term downwards because of U.S. inflation of 6.2 percent and adjusts it upwards because of −4.4 percent Bolivian real GDP growth.[19]

For each year, we compute the terms in equation (5), and the accounting results are reported in Table 2. The numbers in Table 2 are in units of percentage of GDP per year. That is, we calculate the terms in equation (5) for every year in the period 1960–2017 and then average over periods and subperiods.

Table 2 highlights the role of seigniorage as a source of financing. In the period 1960–77, it covered 60 percent of financing needs, and in the period 1977–86, it covered 61 percent. During the debt crisis, increases in external debt compared to GDP accounted for 4.59 pp of financing needs on average, but, as we have discussed above, this number factors out the enormous increase in the value of debt compared to GDP caused by real depreciation.

Notice that, during most of the entire period, the contribution to obligations of the net service costs on external debt has been negative, except between 1977 and 1986, the period of the debt crisis, when Bolivia defaulted several times and with different creditors. These negative service costs on debt mean that, except during the period from 1977 to 1986, U.S. inflation and Bolivian GDP growth were higher than the interest rate on external debt. In fact, interest rates were subsidized in the sense that there were concessional terms on much of the external debt, mainly multilateral. Thus the real interest payments of Bolivia were negative, as we have already seen in the data in Figure 7.

It is noteworthy that the deficits of public enterprises—if we assume that they make up most of the residual—were the largest component of financing needs for the government between 1960 and 1977. By dividing this period in two, we can see that the deficit of the general government was not important between 1960 and 1971, but it became more important between 1971 and 1977. This is a sign that changes in government policies during the rapid growth period of 1960–77 explain much of the debt crisis of the mid-1980s.

During the debt crisis, the deficit of the general government became the most important component of obligations, representing 6.53 pp of financing needs. The deficits of the public enterprises—that is, the residual—represented only 1.72 pp because the general government absorbed the obligations of the public enterprises, as most of them were on the edge of bankruptcy.

The fiscal reform implemented in 1986 managed to reduce the importance of the deficit of the general government in financing needs between 1986 and 1996. In fact, the deficit of the general government fell to only 0.50 pp between 1986 and 1998, but then it increased to 3.75 pp during the financial crisis. As we mentioned in the third section, the increase in the fiscal deficit was a major cause of the financial crisis. This increased contribution was offset by an increasing contribution of the surpluses of public enterprises—the residual of 3.59 pp—between 1998 and 2002. In fact, these surpluses are mostly explained by the privatization policy that the different governments implemented during the 1990s, which reduced current expenditures and revenues.

Notice that in the period of recovery and growth of 1986–98 and the period of the financial crisis of 1998–2002, financing needs were negative: −0.09 pp and −0.31 pp, respectively. This reinforces our conclusion that the structural reforms implemented

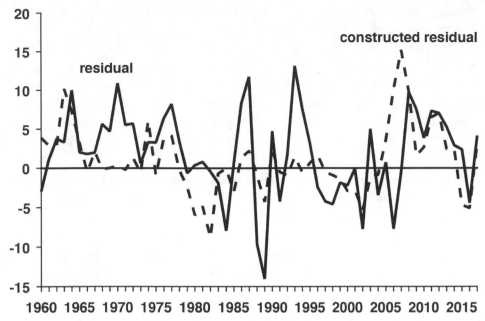

Figure 20. Budget accounting residual, percent of GDP
Source: Authors' calculations

between 1986 and 1998 helped mitigate the impact of the financial crisis of the late 1990s: although the government deficit was high, public enterprises had a surplus, and therefore the financing needs were negative.

External debt as a source of financing turned negative in 1986 because Bolivia started to pay its debt to different types of creditors, as already seen in Table 1. External debt fell by approximately 20 pp between the years 1989 and 2006, which is mainly explained by the Multilateral Debt Relief Initiative (MDRI). During the period of nationalization and growth of 2002–17, the residual, which we interpret as mostly the net income from public enterprises, shows a deficit of 1.88 pp in contrast to the period 1998–2002, when it showed a surplus. Moreover, the deficit of public enterprises increased to 3.02 pp in the period 2006–17 (see Linares Calderón 2018). This large deficit is compensated by a surplus of the general government of 0.22 pp and also by the other obligations (internal and external debt service) that have negative signs. That is why we observe only a small increase in total obligations from 0.85 pp in 2002–17 to 0.92 pp in 2006–17.

In the period 2006–17, we can also observe that there is an increase in money issuance (1.38 pp) as a source of financing. This is explained not only by "bolivianization" (the opposite of dollarization), which allowed real money demand to increase (see Cerezo and Ticona 2017), but also by an increase in income due to economic growth. Bolivianization also allowed the government to increase internal debt in local currency as a source of financing. In the period 1986–98 it represented only 0.08 pp, whereas in the period 2002–17 it represented 0.45 pp. The issuance of internal debt indexed to the cost of living was an important source of financing during the financial crisis period, but in the next period, it was reduced and represented a negative source of financing. The same occurred with the internal debt in dollars, which represented −1.02 pp during the last period.

Until now, we have described the results using the residual as the public enterprises deficit, but being a residual, it can and does include other things. Figure 20 shows the comparison between the residual and a constructed residual, which is the sum of variables that we think the residual includes: the reported deficits of public enterprises, changes in international reserves, capital transfers, unidentified expenses, and the negative of donations received. Notice in Figure 20 that the fit between the residual and the constructed residual is very good at the beginning and at the end of the period. In particular, the constructed residual explains most of the residual between 1960 and 1967 and between 2008 and 2017. Over the entire period 1960 to 2017 the correlation between the residual and the constructed residual is 0.33. The average value of the residual over the entire period 1960 to 2017 is 1.84 pp, while the average value of the constructed residual is 1.03 pp. Consequently, the part of the residual that we are unable to explain averages 0.81 pp per year. This means that, on average, there were expenditures or transfers or losses of public enterprises that were not recorded that amounted to 0.81 percent of GDP per year on average.

This residual includes transfers or contingent liabilities. In the Bolivian case, we hypothesize that four are of particular interest:

- The deficits of the public enterprises were not computed correctly. Much of the time, investment was not accounted for—only the flows of income and expenditures. Often the sales income of these enterprises was used to finance the general government expenditures, and these transfers were also not accounted for in the balance sheets of these enterprises. Another problem was that most of these enterprises suffered corruption problems, and their balances did not reflect the true situation of the enterprises.[20]

- Since 2002, Bolivia has accumulated international reserves as never before: from 10.8 percent of GDP in 2002 to 40.5 percent in 2007. This accumulation of reserves reached its maximum point in 2012 at 51.4 percent of GDP.

- Bolivia has always received donations from foreign governments and from international organizations such as the United States Agency for International Development. Most of the time, these donations were aimed at attacking poverty through specific projects and programs.

- Some expenses appear as unidentified in the balance of the nonfinancial public sector. These are also potential contingent liabilities.

In Figure 20, we see that our attempts to account for the residual with our constructed residual do particularly poorly during the periods from 1968 to 1973, from 1986 to 1987, from 1992 to 1996, and from 2006 to 2007. During the early 1970s, we cannot do much in accounting for the residual because we do not have any data for public enterprises. In

1986 and 1987, the problem could be that different exchange rates (the official rate and the parallel rate) were used in different accounts. Between 1992 and 1996, the problem was probably in accounting for the receipts of privatizations. In 2006 and 2007, the problem was probably in accounting for the costs of nationalizations. Here are some of our hypotheses:

- The net income of public enterprises is not very well measured. The accounts of public enterprises are not transparent because of corruption or because the government wanted to hide the true state of the public companies. For instance, many public enterprises report their cash flows, but they do not report their investment or capital expenditures.[21] It is noteworthy that the press release summarizing the International Monetary Fund (IMF) executive board's 2018 article IV consultation with Bolivia concludes, "[The directors] encouraged further reforms, including . . . reforming the legislative framework governing state-owned enterprises and including the activities of all subsidiaries in the fiscal accounts of the non-financial public sector" (International Monetary Fund 2018).

- The receipts of privatizations during the 1990s should have been accounted for as a decrease in assets and therefore as an increase in net liabilities. In the accounts of the NFPS, however, they cannot be identified, and it seems that they were not accounted for, at least not in that way. Conversely, the nationalization process in recent years did not involve a confiscation of the private companies; rather, they were bought by the state. For instance, in the hydrocarbon sector, the nationalization of strategic companies began on May 1, 2006, with the approval of Supreme Decree 28071, which allowed the Bolivian state, through YPFB (the public oil company), to recover "ownership, possession and total and absolute control" of the country's hydrocarbon resources. For this purpose, the decree forced the purchase of the total or majority shareholding in the companies Chaco, Andina, Transredes, Petrobras Bolivia Refining (PBR), and Compañía Logística de Hidrocarburos de Bolivia (CLHB). The same mechanism was applied in the other sectors, and therefore, until 2010, the state had already paid US$476 million. These costs are also not accounted for in the NFPS accounts.

- During the 1970s, the government's operations of three state banks—Banco Minero, Banco Agrícola, and Banco del Estado—were not well accounted for. These banks were intended to give credit to producers but were captured by special interest groups that siphoned off the loans for their own use. These banks granted loans without sufficient guarantees, and, of course, most of them were not repaid. It has yet to be determined how many of these unpaid liabilities were effectively assumed by the Bolivian central government or by the Banco Central de Bolivia.[22]

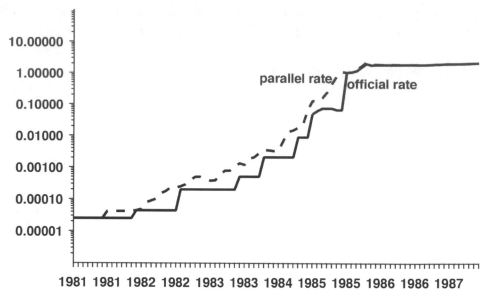

Figure 21. Nominal exchange rates, bolivianos per US$, log scale
Source: UDAPE

- From 1981 to 1986, the Bolivian government, like many other Latin American
  governments during this period, used a system of dual exchange rates.
  Figure 21 depicts the behavior of the official exchange rate and the parallel
  exchange rate determined by the market. The parallel rate was 85 percent
  higher than the official rate on average from 1981 to 1986. During 1985, it
  was 383 percent higher on average and was 1,616 percent higher in August
  1985. In our budget accounting, we have used the parallel exchange rate
  for the nominal exchange rate E_t in the budget constraint (4) and used it to
  calculate the real exchange rate ξ_t in the budget accounting equation (5). If the
  government forced exporters or foreign investors to buy domestic currency
  at the official rate, this was an implicit tax on exports or foreign investment. If
  the government allowed some importers to buy dollars at the official rate, this
  was an implicit subsidy on their imports. We do not have data on these taxes
  and subsidies, so they end up in the residual. If we redo the budget accounting
  using the official exchange rate rather than the parallel exchange rate, we
  find that the only differences in Table 2 occur during the period 1977–86:
  both sources and obligations decline from 9.87 pp to 8.80 pp. In sources, this
  decrease is accounted for by the contribution of external debt decreasing from
  4.59 pp to 3.52 pp; in obligations, it is accounted for by the contribution of
  the external service costs decreasing from 1.63 pp to 0.69 pp and the residual
  decreasing from 1.71 pp to 1.58 pp. We prefer to use the budget accounting
  with the parallel exchange rate because it gives us a more accurate measure of
  how external debt increased compared to GDP. The difference in the residual
  between the budget accounting using the parallel rate and that using the official

rate, 0.13 pp, gives us a rough idea of the net of the implicit subsidies minus implicit taxes imposed by the dual exchange rates. Notice that this is the average yearly net subsidy over the entire period 1977–86. It was much higher in 1983, when it was 3.79 pp.

- During the 1990s, there was something called *gastos reservados* (reserved expenditures), which were intended to be used in the battle against drug trafficking. Later, these reserved expenses were also used as a way to give special but unofficial payments to public servants.[23] Perhaps part of these expenditures are accounted for in the so-called unidentified expenses. We do not know what these unidentified expenses represent today.

- The deficit depicted in Table 2 represents the primary deficit of the general government, but the data for the internal debt represent only the internal debt of the National Treasury. In addition, we have data for internal debt only since 1993. We lack data for internal debt after 1993 for local and regional governments.

Conclusions

In this chapter, we have analyzed the modern economic history of Bolivia, with an emphasis on the monetary and fiscal policies implemented between 1960 and 2017. We have identified five distinct periods. The first period, one of stabilization and rapid growth, runs from 1960 to 1977. The second period, characterized by a debt crisis and hyperinflation, runs from 1977 to 1986. The third period runs from 1986 to 1998 and is a period of recovery and slow growth. The fourth period runs from 1998 to 2002 and is characterized by a financial crisis. The final period runs from 2002 to 2017 and is one of growth but is also notable for the nationalizations that the government implemented. In a brief description of the fiscal policies implemented in these periods, it has been possible to identify the close relation between fiscal policy and external debt. In fact, we have described the evolution of the external debt in Bolivia because it has determined the interaction between fiscal and monetary policy in Bolivia.

In addition, we have performed a growth accounting exercise for the whole period, which has enabled us to identify total factor productivity (TFP) as the main element that explains the deviations from the balanced growth path. A goal for future research is to analyze how fiscal and monetary policies could explain these deviations and what their effects have been on TFP in the different periods of analysis. As a conclusion, we can say that if the evolution of debt has determined the way fiscal and monetary policies were conducted in Bolivia, it might be important to explain the evolution of the growth rate. For example, the constraints that the debt policy implied in the mid-1980s might have dampened growth in the period after the crisis. We need a model and data analysis to show this, as growth could also explain the evolution of debt as well as the evolution of fiscal and monetary policy.

The budget accounting exercise carried out in the previous section allows us to see that the fiscal deficit and the accumulation of debt in the period of stabilization and growth (1960–77) explains much of the debt crisis of the 1980s. In particular, we see that in the 1970s the deficit of public companies became important, and at the same time, external debt grew in importance as a source of financing. We also see that governments frequently resorted to seigniorage as a source of financing.

We hope that this study will contribute to the analysis of economic history in Bolivia. Currently, we lack a detailed and comprehensive analysis of the country's modern economic history based on a rigorous analysis of data and on quantitative models.[24]

The current economic situation in Bolivia displays troubling similarities to that of the policies of the 1970s. There is a fixed exchange rate, international reserves are falling, and the fiscal deficit is growing. If the government does not take corrective measures, this situation could end up in a balance of payments crisis as agents begin to perceive that international reserves are running out and that the Banco Central de Bolivia will not be able to sustain the de facto fixed exchange rate.

Appendix: Economic History of Bolivia before 1960

Bolivia became an independent republic in 1825 and was one of the last countries in Latin America to achieve its independence from Spain. As a Spanish colony, Bolivia—in particular, its city of Potosí—was economically important. In 1650, Potosí had 160,000 inhabitants and was larger than Paris or New York. Its main economic activity was mining, particularly silver extraction (Bakewell 1985; Menegus Bornemann 1999).

Despite the economic importance of Potosí and the surrounding region (Assadourian 1982), Bolivia emerged as a country with many difficulties and a lack of integration, with the majority of its population being indigenous and poor (Klein 2011a; Pentland 1975). During the following decades, the country was characterized by political instability (Barragán 2002). Although this instability was tamed by the end of the nineteenth century, the country lost significant pieces of its original territory up until the early 1930s through wars with its neighbors (Fifer 1972). Furthermore, despite having vast natural resources, particularly minerals, Bolivia did not manage to consolidate a national market until 1952, when the National Revolution took place (Peres-Cajías 2017; Rodríguez Ostria 1994; Sandoval et al. 2003). The most important economic features of the National Revolution were the nationalization of mineral extraction and the distribution of agricultural lands to peasants.

The process of market integration in both geographic and social terms was accompanied by other radical economic transformations that, in turn, were related to sweeping political changes (Zondag 1966). These transformations had long-lasting, persistent effects (Grindle and Domingo 2003). Economic historians traditionally date Bolivia's modern economic history as starting with the economic transformation that followed the 1952 National Revolution. For the sake of consistency with the other chapters in this volume, however, we start our history in 1960. Bolivia is a clear example of a "reversal of fortune" (Acemoglu, Johnson, and Robinson 2002): it was among the most important economic territories during colonial times and today is among the poorest countries in the region. For example, the Bolivian GDP per capita as a share of U.S. GDP per capita has declined from 20 percent in 1950 to 12 percent currently; likewise, it has declined from 51 percent of the Chilean GDP per capita to 24 percent during the same time span. The rate of decline, however, has not been constant throughout time (Herranz-Loncán and Peres-Cajías 2016). Indeed, the economic gap between Bolivia and the most dynamic economies in the Americas increased during the nineteenth century and during two specific periods in the twentieth century: the 1950s and the 1980s.

This concentration of the Bolivian divergence in certain periods can clearly be seen in the distinct periods of Bolivian economic history. In the nineteenth century, the existence of a constant low economic dynamism stands out. For instance, the available evidence on Bolivian GDP per capita shows an annual average growth rate around 0.7 percent from 1846 to 1900. Alternative indicators, such as population growth and levels of urbanization, also point to (absolute and relative) low economic dynamism. Up to the 1870s, this process seems to be explained by the difficulties in overcoming the economic and political instability brought about by the direct and indirect costs of independence (Langer 2009; Mitre 1981; Prado 1995; Prados de la Escosura 2009). From the 1870s onward, backwardness is related to the relatively small size of the mining export sector, the most dynamic sector of the economy.

Economic growth accelerated during the first third of the twentieth century, thanks to the constant expansion of tin exports. The consolidation of tin as the main export product was in turn related to infrastructure expansion and state support for export activities (Contreras 2003; Mitre 1993; Peres-Cajías 2017). This period also featured major political changes, such as the centralization and expansion of education spending and the progressive centralization of money issuance (Peres-Cajías 2014). In spite of this progress, economic imbalances were noticeable: export concentration in a single product and few producers increased the negative effects of commodities volatility and the dependence on very specific economic agents (Peres-Cajías and Carreras-Marín 2017); the economic dynamism in the western part of the country sharply contrasted with the stagnation in the east (Rodríguez Ostria 1994); the modernization of the export sector was contemporaneous to a backward agrarian sector dominated by few landowners and dispersed Indigenous communities (Larsson 1988); and political voice as well as economic rights were unfairly distributed (Klein 2011b). After the economic crisis generated by the Great Depression and the Chaco War of 1932–35, economic dynamism resumed, thanks again to tin exports and industrial production, which for the first time in Bolivian history became relevant. The war and postwar political instability, however, increased the political pressure toward state involvement in the economy. Because of this and the inability to increase revenues in the short term, macroeconomic instability increased in the late 1930s and early 1940s. Moreover, in spite of the resumption of positive economic growth, economic imbalances persisted.

The National Revolution of 1952 sought to overcome these imbalances through radical reforms: it nationalized the three biggest mining companies and created a new state-owned mining company (COMIBOL); it pursued an agrarian reform that radically changed land ownership in the western part of the country by distributing land to farmers and releasing farmers from debts to landowners; it redistributed state resources to the eastern part of the country, in the form of infrastructure investment (mainly roads), state-owned companies, and soft loans; and it promoted industrial production through the redistribution of cheap foreign exchange (Sandoval et al. 2003; Zondag 1966). Initially, however, these structural reforms generated an economic downturn. On the one hand, economic agents had to adjust to the new economic structure. For instance, small farmers did not have the same skills as landowners regarding agricultural production (Dirección Nacional de Informaciones 1962). On the other hand, the heterodox financing state expansion had negative consequences: the Bolivian government applied an overvalued exchange rate on COMIBOL revenues that were redistributed to other economic agents through an undervalued exchange rate. This measure, as well as the determination to increase the wages of miners (key political allies) and to contract those miners who lost their jobs in the previous years, widened the company deficits. Thereafter, these deficits were financed through direct loans from the Banco Central de Bolivia, which were backed by inorganic emission—that is, by printing domestic currency not backed by accumulating foreign reserves. This, in turn, increased inflation to rates that were higher than 100 percent in 1953 and 1956, higher than 50 percent in 1954 and 1955, and close to hyperinflation rates in some months during these years (Peres-Cajías 2014).

The initial macroeconomic shake-up of the 1952 revolution was tamed by an orthodox stabilization plan pursued with the close cooperation of the U.S. government and the International Monetary Fund at the end of 1956. The stabilization plan comprised the elimination of price controls, the unification of the exchange rate, a tax reform, and a plan of wage setting in public companies. Thanks to these changes, the structural reforms of the revolution were not reversed, and state intervention continued, but with stable macroeconomic backing.

Notes

The views expressed herein are those of the authors and not necessarily those of the Federal Reserve Bank of Minneapolis or the Federal Reserve System.

1 It is difficult to compare GDP per capita in Venezuela with that in Bolivia. The International Monetary Fund's World Economic Outlook Database estimates that GDP per capita in Venezuela was US$12,388 in 2017, compared to US$7,543 in Bolivia, but the Venezuelan number is subject to a lot of uncertainty. The World Bank has not been willing to publish any estimates for Venezuelan GDP per capita since 2014.

2 Notice that the data in Figure 3 are in terms of percentage growth factors—where the percentage growth factor is 100 + percentage growth rate—rather than growth rates. This allows us to plot data with both positive and negative growth rates with a logarithmic scale. With this scale, 100 indicates a zero inflation rate or a zero growth rate of the money supply, depending on the series.

3 Other estimations for Bolivia include that of Humérez and Dorado (2006) with a value of 0.35 and that of Jemio (2008) with a value of 0.69.

4 The plan was named after George Jackson Eder, an economist sent by the United States as part of the technical assistance provided to Bolivia.

5 At the conference "La Historia Monetaria y Fiscal de Bolivia: 1960–2014," one of the presidents of the Banco Central de Bolivia during this period, when asked whether Bolivia intended to pay its debt, answered, "We wanted to pay, but we were not able to."

6 According to Requena et al. (1989), the fiscal deficit of the Bolivian public sector from 1980 to 1985 was mostly driven by the nonfinancial deficit, and this deficit was mostly driven by the fall in the quantities exported by public enterprises.

7 The Olivera-Tanzi effect is a situation in which an increase in inflation reduces fiscal revenues in real terms because of the lag in the payment of taxes.

8 Up until 2000, ninety-four public enterprises were privatized (see Garrón, Capra, and Machicado 2003).

9 See Barja Daza (2000) for a detailed explanation of the specific reforms that occurred in each period.

10 Once stabilized, the currency, the Bolivian peso (BOP), was replaced by the boliviano (BOB), where one boliviano was worth one million Bolivian pesos. This modification took effect on January 1, 1987 (Law 901, November 1986).

11 This tax reform (Law 843) reduced the tax structure to seven taxes, among which the value-added tax was the most important. This law, in its 1986 version, did not include a tax on labor or capital income, and even today the labor income tax is absent from the Bolivian tax structure.

12 A critique of this form of debt reduction can be found in Bulow and Rogoff (1988).

13 They were equivalent to Triple A bonds. The sale of these bonds was intermediated by Merrill Lynch. This company bought fiduciary documents from international organizations—the World Bank and the International Monetary Fund—and from the Federal Reserve.

14 See Garrón, Capra, and Machicado (2003) for a review of the three waves of privatization in Bolivia.

15 Gonzalo Sánchez de Lozada became president for the second time, after going to a runoff with Evo Morales.

16 For a complete review of Bolivia's debt history, see Huber Abendroth et al. (2001).

17 Bolivia issued sovereign bonds in 2012, 2013, and 2017 for US$1,000 million each.

18 The term π_t^W is the inflation in the dollar price level of traded goods consumed in Bolivia; as we do not have that information, we have used the inflation of the United States.

19 The adjustments work out additively to one decimal point, $3.9 = 5.7 - 6.2 - (-4.4)$, but this is a matter of luck and of the adjustments being small. The adjustments for growth and foreign inflation are multiplicative, not additive.

20 Almost reliable, or at least consistent, data for public enterprises can be found starting in 1980.

21 See UDAPE (1986) for a discussion of these issues for public enterprises during the 1970s. See Linares Calderón (2018) for an analysis of current intragovernmental transfers that are neither properly measured nor publicly presented.

22 In theory, the debt of these banks was assumed by the Banco Central de Bolivia, following Supreme Decree 21660. In 1989, and according to Supreme Decree 22194, the debts of the Banco del Estado, Banco Minero, and Banco Agrícola were around US$46 million, US$32 million, and US$116 million, respectively. This was a debt of around US$194 million, without

Timothy J. Kehoe, Carlos Gustavo Machicado, and José Peres-Cajías

considering judiciary costs and charges for defaulted payments (Peres Arenas, Antezana, and Peres-Cajías 2013).

23 These expenditures were used to eradicate the coca plants under the Plan Dignidad. Some estimates indicate that this plan caused an outflow of US$500 million from the economy.

24 Most of the recent literature on Bolivian economic history focuses on a description of economic events, but not with an appropriate analysis of data that could substantiate these descriptions. For example, Flavio Machicado (2010) describes modern economic history, but from the point of view of policy makers.

References

Acemoglu, Daron, Simon Johnson, James A. Robinson. 2002. "Reversal of Fortune: Geography and Institutions in the Making of the Modern World Income Distribution." *Quarterly Journal of Economics* 117 (4): 1231–94.

Antelo, Eduardo. 1996. "La dolarización en Bolivia: Evolución reciente y perspectivas futuras." *Análisis económico* 15:113–38.

———. 2000. "Políticas de estabilización y de reformas estructurales en Bolivia a partir de 1985." In *Quince años de reformas estructurales en Bolivia: Sus impactos sobre inversión, crecimiento y equidad*, edited by Luis Carlos Jemio and Eduardo Antelo, 15–98. La Paz, Bolivia: CEPAL-IISEC.

Antezana, Oscar. 1988. *Análisis de la nueva política económica*. La Paz, Bolivia: Los Amigos del Libro.

Assadourian, Carlos Sempat. 1982. *El sistema de la economía colonial: Mercado interno, regiones y espacio económico*. Lima, Peru: Instituto de Estudios Peruanos.

Bakewell, Peter. 1985. *Miners of the Red Mountain: Indian Labor in Potosi, 1545–1650*. Albuquerque: University of New Mexico Press.

Barja Daza, Gover. 2000. "Las reformas estructurales Bolivianas y su impacto sobre inversiones." In *Quince años de reformas estructurales en Bolivia: Sus impactos sobre inversión, crecimiento y equidad*, edited by Luis Carlos

Jemio and Eduardo Antelo, 99–144. La Paz, Bolivia: CEPAL-IISEC.

Barragán, Rossana. 2002. "El estado pactante. Gouvernement et peuples. La configuration de l'état et ses frontieres, Bolivie (1825–1880)." PhD diss., École des Hautes Études en Sciences Sociales, Paris.

Bulow, Jeremy, and Kenneth Rogoff. 1988. "The Buyback Boondoggle." *Brookings Papers on Economic Activity* 2:675–704.

Cariaga, Juan. 1996. *Estabilización y desarrollo*. La Paz, Bolivia: Los Amigos del Libro.

Cerezo, Sergio M., and Ulises A. Ticona. 2017. "Bolivianización, demanda de dinero y señoreaje en Bolivia: Evidencia empírica y una propuesta teórica." *Revista latinoamericana de desarrollo económico* 27:7–38.

Contreras, Manuel E. 2003. "Bolivia, 1900–1939: Minería, ferrocarriles y educación." In *La era de las exportaciones latinoamericanas de fines del siglo XIX a principios del XX*, edited by Enrique Cardenas, José Antonio Ocampo, and Rosemary Thorp, 259–96. México: Fondo de Cultura Económica.

Dirección Nacional de Informaciones. 1962. *Bolivia: 10 años de revolución, 1952–1962*. Vol. 1. La Paz, Bolivia: Dirección Nacional de Informaciones.

Fifer, J. Valerie. 1972. *Bolivia: Land, Location and Politics since 1825*. New York: Cambridge University Press.

Friedman, Milton. 1963. *Inflation: Causes and Consequences*. Bombay: Asian Publishing House for the Council for Economic Education.

Garrón, Mauricio, Katherina Capra, and Carlos Gustavo Machicado. 2003. "Privatization in Bolivia: The Impact on Firm Performance." Research Network Working Paper R-461, Inter-American Development Bank, Washington, D.C.

Grindle, Merilee S., and Pilar Domingo, eds. 2003. *Proclaiming Revolution: Bolivia in Comparative Perspective*. Vol. 10, David Rockefeller Center for Latin American Studies Series. London: Institute of Latin American Studies.

Herranz-Loncán, Alfonzo, and José Alejandro Peres-Cajías. 2016. "Tracing the Reversal of Fortune in the Americas: Bolivian GDP Per Capita since the Mid-nineteenth Century." *Cliometrica* 10 (1): 99–128.

Huber Abendroth, Hans, Mario N. Pacheco Torrico, Carlos Villegas Quiroga, Alvaro Aguirre Badani, and Hugo Delgadillo Barca, eds. 2001. *La deuda externa de Bolivia—125 años de renegociaciones y cuantos más? Desde la operación secreta del gobierno y los meiggs hasta la iniciativa HIPC*. La Paz, Bolivia: CEDLA/OXFAM.

Humérez, Julio, and Hugo Dorado. 2006. "Una aproximación de los determinantes del crecimiento económico en Bolivia 1960–2004." *Análisis económico* 21:1–39.

International Monetary Fund. 2018. "IMF Executive Board Concludes 2018 Article IV Consultation with Bolivia." IMF Press Release 18/453. https://www.imf.org/en/News/Articles/2018/12/06/pr18453-imf-executive-board-concludes-2018-article-iv-consultation-with-bolivia?cid=em-COM-123-38070.

Jemio, Luis Carlos. 2001. *Debt, Crisis and Reforms in Bolivia: Biting the Bullet*. International Finance and Development Series. Houndmills, Basingstoke, Hampshire, UK: Palgrave Macmillan.

———. 2006. "Volatilidad externa y el sistema financiero en Bolivia." Informe de consultoría elaborado para la Corporación Andina de Fomento (CAF), La Paz, Bolivia.

———. 2008. "La inversión y el crecimiento en la economía Boliviana." Documento de Trabajo No. 01/08, Instituto de Investigaciones Socioeconómicas, IISEC, Universidad Católica Boliviana, La Paz, Bolivia.

Kehoe, Timothy J., and Edward C. Prescott, eds. 2007. *Great Depressions of the Twentieth Century*. Minneapolis: Federal Reserve Bank of Minneapolis.

Klein, Herbert S. 2011a. *A Concise History of Bolivia*. 2nd ed. Cambridge Concise Histories. Cambridge, UK: Cambridge University Press.

———. 2011b. "The Emergence of a Mestizo and Indigenous Democracy in Bolivia." In *A Concise History of Bolivia*, 2nd ed., edited by Herbert S. Klein, 264–96. Cambridge Concise Histories. Cambridge: Cambridge University Press.

Krugman, Paul. 1979. "A Model of Balance-of-Payments Crises." *Journal of Money, Credit and Banking* 11 (3): 311–25.

Langer, Erick D. 2009. "Bringing the Economic Back In: Andean Indians and the Construction of the Nation State in Nineteenth-Century Bolivia." *Journal of Latin American Studies* 41 (3): 527–51.

Larsson, Brooke. 1988. *Colonialism and Agrarian Transformation in Bolivia: Cochabamba, 1550–1900*. Princeton, N.J.: Princeton University Press.

Linares Calderón, and Julio Héctor. 2018. *Más ruido que nueces: Análisis de los emprendimientos empresariales del proceso de cambio*. La Paz, Bolivia: CEDLA.

Machicado, Carlos Gustavo. 2012. "Determinantes del crecimiento económico nacional en el largo plazo." In *Factores que inciden en el crecimiento y el desarrollo en Bolivia*, coordinador Carlos Gustavo Machicado. La Paz, Bolivia: Fundación PIEB y Plural Editores.

Machicado, Flavio. 2010. *Historia económica de la república de Bolivia, 1952–2009*. La Paz, Bolivia: Plural Editores.

Menegus Bornemann, Margarita. 1999. *Dos décadas de investigación en historia económica comparada en América Latina: Homenaje a Carlos Sempat Assadourian*. México, DF: Colegio de México.

Mitre, Antonio. 1981. *Los patriarcas de la plata: Estructura socioeconómica de la mineria Boliviana en el siglo XIX*. Lima, Peru: Instituto de Estudios Peruanos.

———. 1993. *Bajo un cielo de estaño: Fulgor y ocaso del metal en Bolivia*. Vol. 6, Biblioteca Minera Boliviana. La Paz, Bolivia: Asociación Nacional de Mineros Medianos.

Morales, Juan Antonio. 1988. "Inflation Stabilization in Bolivia." In *Inflation Stabilization: The Experience of Israel, Argentina, Brazil, Bolivia, and Mexico*, edited by Michael Bruno, Guido di Tella, Rudiger Dornbusch, and Stanley Fischer, 307–46. Cambridge, Mass.: MIT Press.

———. 2012. *La política económica Boliviana, 1982–2010*. La Paz, Bolivia: Plural Editores.

Otalora, Carmen Rosa. 2002. "La política fiscal Boliviana entre 1975 y 1989." Documento de Trabajo 02/90, Instituto de Investigaciones Socioeconómicas, IISEC, Universidad Católica Boliviana, La Paz, Bolivia.

Peñaloza Cordero, Luis. 1985. *Nueva historia económica de Bolivia. El estaño*. Enciclopedia boliviana. La Paz, Bolivia: Los Amigos del Libro.

Pentland, Joseph Barclay. 1975. *Informe sobre Bolivia*. Potosí, Bolivia: Editorial Potosí.

Peres Arenas, José Antonio, Sergio Antezana, and Jose Alejandro Peres-Cajías. 2013. *Historia de la regulación y supervisión financiera en Bolivia*. Vol. 2, *1750–2012*. La Paz, Bolivia: Autoridad de Supervisión del Sistema Financiero.

Peres-Cajías, José Alejandro. 2014. "Bolivian Public Finances, 1882–2010: The Challenge to Make Social Spending Sustainable." *Revista de Historia Económica—Journal of Iberian and Latin American Economic History* 32 (1): 77–117.

———. 2017. "Bolivian Tariff Policy during the Late Nineteenth and Early Twentieth Centuries: High Average Tariff and Unbalanced Regional Protection." *Journal of Latin American Studies* 49 (3): 433–62.

Peres-Cajías, José Alejandro, and Anna Carreras-Marín. 2017. "The Bolivian Export Sector, 1870–1950." In *Latin America's First Export Era Revisited*, edited by Sandra Kuntz-Ficker, 73–110. London: Palgrave.

Prado, Gustavo. 1995. "Efectos económicos de la adulteración monetaria en Bolivia, 1830–1870." *Revista de humanidades y ciencias sociales* 1:35–76.

Prados de la Escosura, Leandro. 2009. "Lost Decades? Economic Performance in Postindependence Latin America." *Journal of Latin American Studies* 41 (2): 279–307.

Requena, Juan Carlos, Gualberto Guarachi, Gover Barja, and Ernesto Cupe. 1989. "Determinantes del déficit del sector público en Bolivia (período 1980–1987)." Munich Personal RePEc Archive, MPRA Paper 4751. Munich University Library, Munich.

Rodríguez Ostria, Gustavo. 1994. *Elites, mercado y cuestion regional en Bolivia*. Quito: Facultad Latinoamericana de Ciencias Sociales FLACSO.

———. 1999. "Industria: Producción, mercancías y empresarios." In *Bolivia en el siglo XX: La formación de la Bolivia contemporánea*, edited by Fernando Campero, 291–328. La Paz, Bolivia: Harvard Club Bolivia.

Sandoval, Carmen Dunia, Ada Vania Sandoval, Marco Antonio del Rio, Franz Sandoval, Carlos Mertens, and Claudia Parada. 2003. *Santa Cruz: Economía y poder, 1952–1993*. Investigaciones Regionales. La Paz, Bolivia: Fundación Pieb.

Seoane, Alfredo. 2016. *Industrialización tardía y progreso técnico: Un acercamiento teórico-histórico al proyecto desarrollista Boliviano*. La Paz, Bolivia: CIDES-USMA.

Tanzi, Vito. 1977. "Inflation, Lags in Collection, and the Real Value of Tax Revenue." *IMF Staff Papers* 24 (1): 154–67.

Toranzo, Carlos. 2009. "Partidos políticos y think tanks en Bolivia." In *Dime a quién escuchas . . . think tanks y partidos políticos en América Latina*, edited by Enrique Mendizabal and Kristen Sample, 209–39. Lima, Peru: IDEA Internacional and ODI.

UDAPE. 1986. *Las estadísticas fiscales de Bolivia, 1970–1985*. La Paz, Bolivia: UDAPE.

Zondag, Cornelius H. 1966. *The Bolivian Economy, 1952–65: The Revolution and Its Aftermath*. Praeger Special Studies in International Economics and Development. New York: Praeger.

Discussion of the History of Bolivia

Manuel Amador
University of Minnesota and Federal Reserve Bank of Minneapolis

The chapter on Bolivia by Timothy Kehoe, Gustavo Machicado, and José Peres-Cajías presents an illuminating analysis of Bolivia's economic history since 1960. As the authors tell us, this history is, unfortunately, characterized by extremes. During this time, Bolivia experienced episodes of both dismal economic growth and economic expansions. On the monetary side, it featured episodes of hyperinflation as well as periods during which inflation was moderate. On the fiscal side, Bolivia's government accumulated extreme levels of external debt, with several defaults throughout this period.

The chapter's starting point is that, in order to explain the uneven economic performance of Bolivia, it is necessary to take into account its fiscal and monetary policies, as well as the large accumulation of external public debt by the Bolivian government. Another important point raised by this chapter is that this debt accumulation was not just the result of actions taken by the central government; public enterprises also contributed significantly to the dynamics of the stock of publicly guaranteed debt.

The authors divide the history into several periods. To begin with, Bolivia entered the late 1970s with a significant amount of external public debt (see Figure 1). The global shocks that followed severely limited the financing choices of the government, resulting in a large reduction in GDP per capita, which was accompanied by a major debt crisis as well as a dramatic hyperinflation episode. In the subsequent period, from 1986 to 1998, Bolivia's government implemented several domestic reforms and received significant external help, which allowed the economy to recover. Important elements were a debt renegotiation, an increase in foreign direct investment inflows, and the privatization of several public enterprises. External public debt continued to be an issue, and Bolivia defaulted again in 1995, 1996, and 1997. At the end of this period, Bolivia became part of the Heavily Indebted Poor Countries (HIPC) Initiative by the International Monetary Fund and the World Bank—a debt forgiveness program that ended up significantly reducing Bolivia's external obligations by 2007. During the 2000s, another remarkable feature of the public finances is the large foreign reserve accumulation undertaken by the Central Bank.

The authors focus much of their attention on the behavior of Bolivia's fiscal deficit and the accumulation of external public debt, and they are right to take this approach.

The theory of debt overhang emphasizes that high levels of external public borrowing can lead to subsequent low investments and growth. The dismal performance of Bolivia during the Latin American debt crisis, as well as its recovery afterward, is broadly consistent with this theory, as is the behavior of foreign direct investment (FDI) flows, which did not become significant until after the external debt public stock had been significantly reduced. The theory of debt overhang also provides a justification for Bolivia's inclusion in the HIPC Initiative: the reduction in external indebtedness could be a source of subsequent economic growth and stability.

In addition to the effects of debt overhang on investment and growth, external public borrowing can have other costs. First, a large accumulation of debt distorts the spending allocation toward the present while shifting its costly repayment toward the future. By allowing the government to borrow in good times rather than bad, access to external borrowing may make government policies procyclical—amplifying rather than mitigating shocks. Finally, high levels of external debt also expose the country's citizens to the risk of future costly default episodes. Given all these costs, why would the governments of poor countries borrow large amounts externally? Political economy models point out that political turnover may generate myopic decision-making, and as a result, policy makers may borrow too much from the perspective of their citizens. Weak governance and institutions make this problem worse, as external borrowing may be channeled toward low return projects or foreign bank accounts.

In this context, debt reduction initiatives may provide valuable relief. Their effects may be temporary, however, if the political economy problems that led to the high external levels of borrowing in the first place are not permanently resolved. In Bolivia's case, the

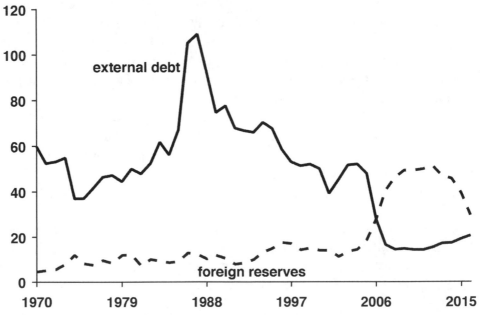

Figure 1. External debt and foreign reserves in Bolivia
Source: World Bank, World Development Indicators

HIPC Initiative appears to have been successful up to 2012. Debt was reduced to levels under 20 percent of GDP. In addition, international reserves were accumulated at a rapid pace, reaching 50 percent of GDP by 2012. But did these facts represent a permanent shift away from debt financing in Bolivia? Or were they just the result of a temporary combination of favorable external conditions, as highlighted in the chapter? One would hope that it is the first that holds true, and that the lessons from past overborrowing have been learned. But the last few years offer a note of caution. Since 2012, Bolivia's government has increased its external borrowing while reducing its international reserves. If the trend continues, the negative effects of external borrowing could again become part of Bolivia's economic history.[1]

This chapter contains a comprehensive description and analysis of Bolivia's economic performance and policies. It collects and aggregates data from several sources. And it documents the dynamics and characteristics of Bolivia's external debts (including the several ways in which Bolivia and its creditors tried to manage that debt: through debt renegotiations, buybacks, and forgiveness). As the authors make clear, there is a lot to learn from Bolivia's complex economic history. This chapter provides a much needed and helpful guide.

Note

1 This note of caution is further strengthened when we compare Bolivia with other countries that also obtained debt relief within the HIPC Initiative and found themselves facing external debt problems soon afterward. For example, the Republic of Congo also reduced its external debt and accumulated large foreign reserves (reaching 40 percent of GDP in 2010). But soon afterward, with the decrease in oil prices, foreign reserves were reduced (down to 5 percent of GDP), the external public debt was increased, and default occurred once more.

Brazil

The History of Brazil

Joao Ayres
Inter-American Development Bank

Márcio Garcia
Pontifical Catholic University of Rio de Janeiro, Brazilian National
Council for Scientific and Technological Development, and
Fundação de Amparo à Pesquisa do Estado do Rio de Janeiro

Diogo Guillen
Itau-Unibanco Asset Management

Patrick Kehoe
Stanford University, Federal Reserve Bank of
Minneapolis, and University College London

Major fiscal and monetary events, 1960–2017

1964	Stabilization plan (PAEG)		**1994**	Stabilization plan (Real Plan)
	Establishment of central bank			Adoption of crawling-peg regime
1982	Default			End of hyperinflation
1986	Stabilization plan (Cruzado)		**1999**	Currency crisis
1987	Stabilization plan (Bresser)			Adoption of floating exchange
1989	Stabilization plan (Summer Plan)			rate regime
1990	Stabilization plan (Collor Plan I)			Inflation targeting
	Temporary freezing of private		**2000**	Fiscal reform (Fiscal
	assets			Responsibility Law)
1993	External debt renegotiation		**2014**	Fiscal balance turns to deficits
	(Brady Plan)			

Introduction

This chapter presents the monetary and fiscal history of Brazil between 1960 and 2016, with emphasis on the hyperinflation episodes. It describes the evolution of the Brazilian monetary and fiscal policy institutions and how they relate to episodes of macroeconomic instability and growth experience, focusing on the high-inflation period (pre-1994) and two stabilization plans: the Government Economic Action Plan (PAEG, Plano de Ação

Econômica do Governo) and the Real Plan. The PAEG, in 1964, stabilized inflation around 100 percent per year, whereas the Real Plan, in 1994, stabilized inflation around 90 percent per month after six failed attempts in over a decade. The analysis follows the conceptual framework in "A Framework for Studying the Monetary and Fiscal History of Latin America" by focusing on the government budget constraint.

A summary of the period is illustrated in Figure 1, which shows the evolution of real GDP per capita, inflation, and government deficits for the 1960–2016 period.[1] Three subperiods are identified: (1) 1960–80: fast economic growth with high inflation and moderate deficits; (2) 1981–94: slow growth with hyperinflation and high deficits; and (3) 1995–2016: moderate growth with low inflation and low deficits.[2] The 1981–94 subperiod stands out not only for its poor growth performance and hyperinflation but also for the severe balance of payments problems, a common feature among highly indebted Latin American countries affected by the increase in international interest rates and the slowdown in international economic growth.

When relating the episodes of macroeconomic instability to the government fiscal and monetary policies, we observe the following: (1) both stabilization plans, PAEG in 1964 and the Real Plan in 1994, included measures to improve fiscal balances and were followed by increased access to debt financing; (2) the government policy to increase public investment in the wake of the first oil shock in 1973 explains the rapid increase in external debt that preceded the external debt crisis of 1983 seen in Figure 2; and (3) the high-inflation periods (pre-1994) were characterized by the combination of fiscal deficits, passive monetary policy, and constraints on debt financing, while the transition to the low-inflation period (1995–2016) was associated with improvements in government fiscal balances, higher de facto independence of the monetary authority (as of this writing, Brazil still lacks a formally independent central bank), as well as much greater access to debt financing.

In comparison to other Latin American countries, the following two characteristics make the Brazilian experience stand out: (1) a long period of high inflation, with annual inflation rates above 100 percent between 1980 and 1994; and (2) modest levels of deficits for very high underlying inflation rates. We discuss two features that may explain these unique characteristics of the Brazilian hyperinflation. The first is a poor institutional framework in which other public entities besides the monetary authority had indirect control over money issuance. We discuss that framework in the fourth section. The second is the combination of a high degree of indexation in the economy to past inflation with a passive monetary policy.[3] Together, these features created what was called at the time *inflation inertia*, which could explain why the Brazilian hyperinflation was a much more protracted process than elsewhere and gave many the illusion that it could be cured without major improvements in the fiscal stance. We also discuss that factor in the fourth section.

This chapter is organized as follows: in the second section we present a summary of the government budget constraint, and in the third section we provide a historical description of each of the subperiods 1960–80, 1981–94, and 1995–2016. In the fourth section we discuss the evolution of the institutional framework involving both fiscal and

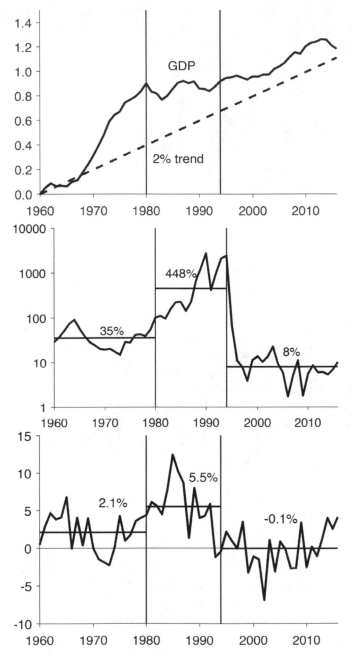

Figure 1. Real GDP per capita, inflation, deficit, 1960–2016: top panel: log of real GDP per capita; middle panel: annual inflation rate, log scale; bottom panel: deficit, percentage of GDP

Sources: Brazilian Institute of Geography and Statistics, Central Bank of Brazil

Note: Inflation rates are computed using the general price index, IGP-DI, from the Getulio Vargas Foundation. See the online appendix available at http://manifold.bfi.uchicago.edu/ for a description of how we construct the deficit series and the series of nominal GDP. Numbers correspond to the (geometric) average of inflation rates in each subperiod in Figure 1 (middle panel) and to the (arithmetic) average of the deficits as a percentage of GDP in each subperiod in Figure 1 (bottom panel).

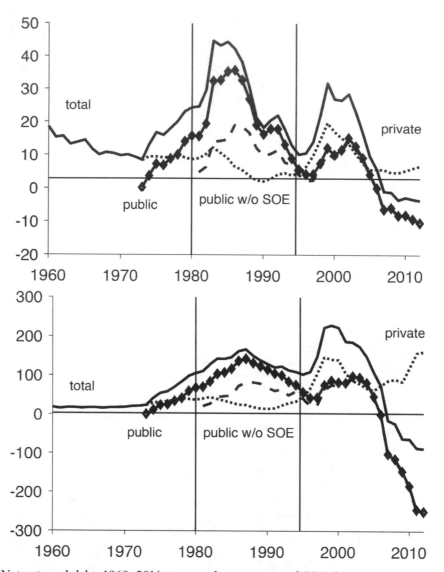

Figure 2. Net external debt, 1960–2016: top panel: percentage of GDP; bottom panel: constant US$
Sources: Brazilian Institute of Geography and Statistics, Central Bank of Brazil (CBB)
Note: Net private external debt represents the series of registered private external debt (code 3566) from
the CBB. Public net external debt is computed as the registered public external debt (code 3564)
minus the foreign reserves (code 3566), both from the CBB. The external debt of state-owned enterprises
represents the series of net debt of the public-sector, state-owned companies from IPEADATA. The
total external debt is computed as the sum of net public external debt and net private external debt
after 1973 and by subtracting foreign reserves from the series of total registered external debt from
IBGE before that. Exchange rates represent end-of-period values (code 3691). See the appendix for a
description of how we compute the nominal GDP series. We use the U.S. GDP deflator from the Bureau
of Economic Analysis to compute constant US$ values. The series codes correspond to the codes used
on the website of the CBB (https://www3.bcb.gov.br/sgspub/localizarseries/localizarSeries.do?method=
prepararTelaLocalizarSeries).

Table 1. Government budget accounting (percentage of GDP)

Sources	1960–64	1965–72	1973–80	1981–94	1995–2002	2003–11	2012–16
(1) Domestic debt	0.0	0.8	−0.2	−0.3	−0.6	1.1	3.5
(2) External debt	0.0	0.0	1.7	−1.8	0.0	−2.3	0.0
(3) Real monetary base	−0.4	−0.2	−0.2	−0.1	0.1	0.1	−0.1
(4) Seigniorage	4.1	1.9	2.4	3.2	0.4	0.4	0.3
Uses							
(5) Interest on domestic debt	0.3	0.4	1.3	0.4	2.0	1.7	3.2
(6) Interest on external debt	0.0	0.0	0.7	1.9	0.3	0.3	0.1
(7) Primary deficits	2.9	1.0	0.2	3.1	−3.0	−2.7	−1.1
(8) Transfers (residual)	0.5	1.1	1.6	−4.5	0.7	−0.1	1.5
Other measures							
(9) Primary deficits + transfers	3.4	2.2	1.8	−1.4	−2.3	−2.8	0.4
(10) Fiscal deficits	3.2	1.5	2.1	5.5	−0.8	−0.6	2.1
(11) Fiscal deficits + transfers	3.7	2.6	3.7	1.0	0.0	−0.8	3.6

Sources: Brazilian Institute of Geography and Statistics, Central Bank of Brazil

Note: See the online appendix available at http://manifold.bfi.uchicago.edu/ for a description of the budget constraint. Transfers are computed as (8) = (1) + (2) + (3) + (4) − (5) − (6) − (7). The fiscal deficit is computed as (10) = (5) + (6) + (7).

monetary authorities and the genesis of inflation inertia; the fifth section presents our final remarks and conclusion.

The Government Budget Constraint

We are interested in analyzing the evolution of the government budget constraint for Brazil in 1960–2016. We attempt to match the variation in stocks (debt figures) with flows (fiscal deficits), duly accounting for valuation effects.[4] Table 1 presents a summary of the results. In order to finance interest payments and primary deficits, the government can either issue domestic and external debt or issue money and receive seigniorage revenues. Transfers account for the residual.[5]

We divide the 1960–80 subperiod into three parts: 1960–64, 1965–72, and 1973–80. In 1960–64, markets for government debt securities were still underdeveloped, and the government faced restrictions on both domestic and external debt financing. Interest payments were low, but primary deficits were on the rise and had to be financed with seigniorage revenues. In 1964–67, the stabilization plan PAEG implemented both fiscal and financial reforms, which reduced primary deficits and allowed the government to issue domestic debt securities. Those reforms account for the increase in domestic debt financing and the reduction in seigniorage revenues that we observe in the 1965–72 period. In 1973–80, on the other hand, we observe a rise in both debt financing in external markets and seigniorage revenues, which were associated with higher interest payments on external debt and a significant rise in transfers, the residual.[6] Fortunately, in this case, we can explain what most of these transfers are. In the wake of the first oil crisis of 1973, the government implemented policies aimed at boosting investment through external borrowing, and that was done mainly through state-owned enterprises (SOEs). The debt series that was used to compute the government budget constraint includes SOEs, but the primary deficit series does not. The increase in investment by SOEs, documented in Table 2, accounts for a large fraction of the increase in transfers.[7] Therefore, we argue that deficits at the time are better represented by adding the transfers to the reported primary deficits; this is reported in row 9 of Table 1, labeled "primary deficits + transfers."[8]

In 1981–94, debt financing in external markets decreased sharply, and interest payments on external debt increased as a reflection of the debt crisis that followed the increase in international interest rates. In that period, seigniorage revenues were used to finance the payments of both principal and interest of the external debt as well as the primary deficits.

The 1995–2002 period followed the agreement on the external debt renegotiations and the end of the hyperinflation in 1994. It showed a significant reduction in seigniorage revenues and a large improvement in primary and fiscal balances. Interest payments on external debt decreased, whereas interest payments on domestic debt increased. The 2003–11 period continued to show primary and fiscal surpluses and low seigniorage revenues, and the external debt was replaced by domestic debt. As we will discuss, the pattern that we observe in 1994–2011 reflects changes in both monetary and fiscal policy institutions, with higher de facto independence of the central bank and greater control over the government budget. However, in the most recent period, 2012–16, we observe a deterioration in fiscal balances that have been financed by a rapid increase in domestic debt.

In the sections that follow, we provide a detailed historical background that describes the fiscal and monetary policies adopted in the 1960–2016 period and that accounts for the evolution of the government budget constraint.

Table 2. Investment by state-owned enterprises (percentage of GDP)

	Subperiod			
	1960–72	*1973–80*	*1981–94*	*1995–2000*
All sectors	**2.2**	**4.7**	**2.7**	**1.3**
Manufacturing	1.0	1.5	0.6	0.3
Energy	0.4	1.0	0.8	0.2
Transportation	0.3	0.9	0.3	0.0
Communication	0.1	0.8	0.6	0.5

Source: Brazilian Institute of Geography and Statistics, *Estatísticas do Século XX* (https://seculoxx.ibge.gov.br/economicas.html)

Historical Description

1960–80: FAST GROWTH WITH MACROECONOMIC INSTABILITY

Brazil went through important transformations during the first subperiod of our analysis. It moved from being a rural society, in which 55 percent of the population lived in rural areas, to an urban society, with 68 percent of the population living in cities. Its production structure shifted toward the manufacturing sector, which increased its fraction of GDP from 32 to 41 percent, while the agricultural sector saw its fraction of GDP reduced from 18 to 10 percent.[9] It was a period of fast economic growth, with real GDP per capita increasing 4.6 percent per year on average (Figure 1, top panel). It was also a period of macroeconomic instability, however, with a deep recession in the early 1960s, increasing external indebtedness following the first oil crisis in 1973, and nominal instability. Inflation rates rose in the beginning and reached levels around 100 percent in 1964, when the stabilization plan PAEG was implemented after a military coup.[10] Inflation rates fell significantly but started to accelerate again around the first oil crisis in 1973, returning to three-digit levels in 1980.[11]

To understand the fiscal and monetary policy institutions that were in place during these years, one should note that it was a period of heated debate regarding the role of the state in promoting economic development and during which the government undertook major national development plans, such as the Targets Plan in 1956–61, the National Development Plan I in 1972–74, and the National Development Plan II in 1975–79. That process also led to a surge in the number of public banks, with nine out of twenty-three states creating their own banks between 1960 and 1964 to finance their fiscal deficits, and to the creation of some of the largest Brazilian SOEs, such as Eletrobras in 1962 and Telebras in 1972.[12] As we discuss below, they would all play an important role in explaining the dynamics of the government budget constraint.

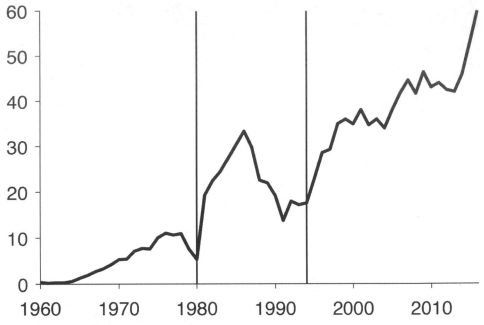

Figure 3. Domestic debt, percentage of GDP

Sources: Brazilian Institute of Geography and Statistics, Central Bank of Brazil

Note: Before 1981, domestic debt consists of the federal and state governments' debt securities, together with the Dívida Publica Fundada, available from *Estatísticas do Século XX*, IBGE. After 1981, it is the net debt of the public sector computed by the Central Bank of Brazil plus the balance of the Bank of Brazil accounts on the balance sheet of the central bank. See the online appendix available at http://manifold.bfi.uchicago.edu/ for an explanation of why we adjust the debt series for the Bank of Brazil accounts at the central bank and for a description of how we compute the series of nominal GDP.

1960–64

Before 1964, the government Treasury had direct control over money issuance through the Bank of Brazil (BB), which was both the bank of the government and a commercial bank.[13] The main monetary policy instruments in use were the control over the monetary base, subsidized credit to the industrial and agricultural sectors, and interventions in the foreign exchange market. Some of those interventions aimed to protect the local industry by imposing restrictions on the imports of products that were also produced locally—that is, they were used to implement import-substitution policies.[14] There was no centralized market in which one could trade government debt securities in Brazil. Debt contracts were very heterogeneous and faced legal limits on the nominal interest rates that could be charged (12 percent per year).[15] With rising inflation and primary deficits, that led to a decrease in the stock of domestic debt before 1964 (Figure 3), and seigniorage revenues became the main source of funds for the government to cover its fiscal deficits, as Table 1 shows. Access to external debt was restricted in that period. Brazil had a balance of payments crisis in 1952 and faced balance of payments problems again in the late 1950s.[16]

On the fiscal side, Brazil already had a diverse set of tax instruments, such as income, import, and consumption taxes, amounting to around 17 percent of GDP (Figure 4). Taxes on production were cumulative instead of value added; that is, revenues and not the value added were taxed. There were no fiscal rules such as limits on fiscal deficits, and the government could adopt expansionary policies without explicitly indicating how to finance them.

During 1956–61, President Juscelino Kubitschek launched the first major national development plan, the Targets Plan, which had ambitious goals to create the necessary infrastructure to facilitate the industrialization process in Brazil. The transportation and energy sectors were the main targets, and the country exhibited a rapid expansion of its highway and electric energy systems. That plan also became famous for the creation of the new capital city, Brasília. Besides relying on government funds, that plan also relied on large foreign direct investment, especially in the automotive industry. During its implementation, Brazil experienced high growth rates in real GDP per capita but entered a recession in the following years, 1962 and 1963, accompanied by rising fiscal deficits and inflation. That crisis was followed by a military coup in 1964 and by the implementation of an economic stabilization program in 1964–67, PAEG, which aimed to stop the inflationary process and resume growth through fiscal and financial reforms.

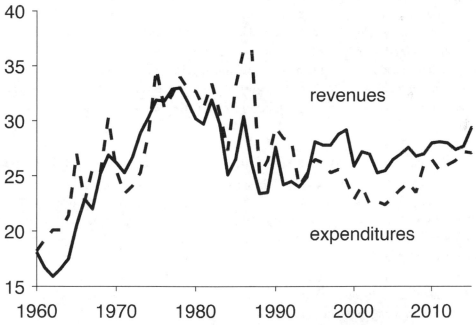

Figure 4. Government revenues and expenditures, percentage of GDP
Sources: Brazilian Institute of Geography and Statistics, National Treasury Secretariat, Central Bank of Brazil
Note: Revenues correspond to direct and indirect taxes. See the online appendix available at http://manifold.bfi.uchicago.edu/ for a description of how we compute the revenues and expenditures of the public sector and the nominal GDP series.

PAEG was launched in November 1964. At that time, there was a clear relationship between inflation and the expansion of the monetary base (Figure 5, top panel), and the government understood that it should find ways to finance its expenditures and investment projects other than seigniorage revenues. The government tackled that problem on two fronts: a fiscal reform to decrease government deficits and a financial reform to create other financing options. On the fiscal side, the government increased its tax revenues to around 23 percent of GDP (Figure 4) and managed to reduce its fiscal deficits, as documented in Table 1, subperiod 1965–72. That was achieved through the creation of new taxes, increases in existing tax rates, and modernization of the tax system with the introduction of a value-added tax. On the financial side, the main changes were the introduction of monetary correction (indexation) to circumvent the legal limits on nominal interest rates, the creation of the Central Bank of Brazil (CBB), and the adoption of a banking system with a clear-cut separation between commercial banks and nonbank institutions. These changes would have important implications for the inflationary process.

Regarding the Central Bank of Brazil, it is important to mention that upon its creation, the government established an account between the central bank and the Bank of Brazil, the Conta de Movimento, that ended up providing the Bank of Brazil with the power to issue money. The Bank of Brazil could withdraw funds from that account whenever prompted to further extend financing to sectors or firms targeted by economic policy, and the central bank would automatically provide those funds through an expansion of the monetary base.[17] In addition, the government created the National Monetary Council, which would rule over the central bank. Both of these changes served to impose constraints on the control of the monetary base expansion by the monetary authority, as the fourth section explains in detail. With respect to the monetary correction, the existence of indexed public debt held by private savers on a voluntary basis was critical for the development of financial markets in Brazil in the following years.

1965–72

Figure 6 illustrates how successful PAEG was in controlling the inflation process. After 1964, primary deficits decreased, and the government was able to reduce its seigniorage revenues, which explains the reduction in inflation and money growth rates that followed. The reforms also led to an increase in debt financing. The 1968–73 period became known as the years of the economic miracle in Brazil, with annual GDP growth rates in excess of 10 percent. That led to the optimistic view that the Brazilian state had created a wholesome mechanism to capture private savings and channel them toward public investment. The idea that public and private investment were complementary led many to argue that, by borrowing to pay for large public projects, the government could spur private investment. During those years, the government implemented the National Development Plan I (1972–74), focused on improving the country's infrastructure. It included large projects such as the Itaipú Dam, Trans-Amazonian Highway, and Rio-Niterói Bridge. The country also experienced higher investment by SOEs and an increasing supply of credit by public banks, such as the Bank of Brazil and the National Bank for Economic Development (BNDE).[18]

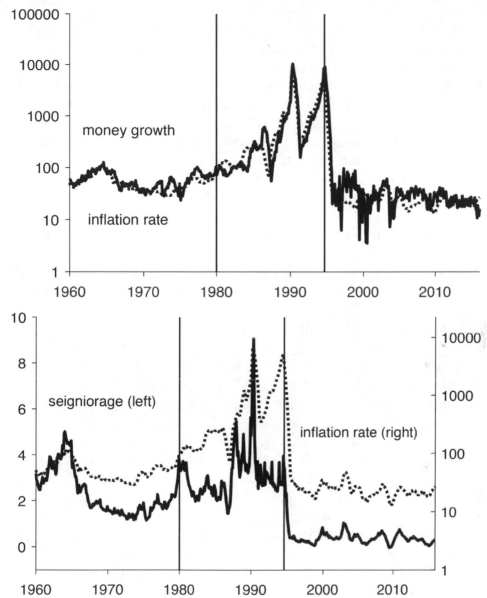

Figure 5. Inflation, seigniorage, and money growth, 1960–2016: top panel: money growth and inflation, logscale; bottom panel: seigniorage and inflation

Sources: Brazilian Institute of Geography and Statistics, Central Bank of Brazil

Note: For the inflation and money growth series, we plot the transformation log $(15 + X)$, in which X denotes the annual percentage rate. We sum 15 to avoid taking logs of negative numbers. Inflation rates are computed using the general price index, IGP-DI, from the Getulio Vargas Foundation. See the online appendix available at http://manifold.bfi .uchicago.edu/ for a description of how we compute the seigniorage and nominal GDP series.

1973–80

When the first oil crisis in 1973 presented challenges to the feasibility of the high-growth path, the Brazilian government kept its long-run strategy in the President General Ernesto Geisel years (1974–79) to grow its way out of the first oil crisis, even if it had to rely on further increasing public indebtedness by borrowing from abroad. That explains the rapid increase in external debt in Figure 2 and also accounts for the rise in external debt financing in the 1973–80 period shown in Table 1. One of its main goals was to reduce the country's dependence on oil imports through higher investment in domestic oil production and the exploration of other sources of energy, such as ethanol and nuclear power. As part of this strategy, the government launched the National Development Plan II during 1975–79, which focused on the manufacturing, energy, transportation, and communication sectors (Table 2). It had the SOEs as its main implementation vehicle, and that accounts for their increasing investment and debt accumulation.

The external debt series does not allow us to distinguish SOEs from the rest of the public sector before 1981, but in that year, the external debt of SOEs represented 72 percent of the total, which indicates that they accounted for a large fraction of the increase in public external debt after 1973 (Figures 2 and 7, top panel). The same holds for the domestic debt, although in that case the concentration of SOEs was less pronounced. They accounted for 35 percent of the total domestic debt in 1981, while 25 percent was from states and municipalities, and 40 percent was from the federal government (Figure 7, bottom panel). These figures also show how the deficits at the subnational level accounted for a large fraction of the increase in public domestic debt.

The change in economic policy that took place after the first oil crisis is clearly illustrated in Figure 6. After 1973, Brazil was back to a scenario of rising deficits, rising seigniorage revenues, and rising inflation and money growth rates. That period was also characterized by the poor management of the government budget, so it is important to take into account the off-budget transactions when analyzing the dynamics of the government budget constraint. As an example, at that time the government operated at least three budgets: one that was discussed in Congress and presented in the official statistics, the monetary budget that was controlled by the National Monetary Council (see section 4), and the budget of the SOEs.

The main off-budget transactions we identified were the transfers from the central bank to the Bank of Brazil and the operations of SOEs. The transfers between the central bank and the Bank of Brazil are approximated by variations in the Conta de Movimento, the dashed line in Figure 8 referred to as "variation in the balance of BB accounts."[19] The figure shows the rise in those transfers in the 1973–80 subperiod, which reflects the rise in subsidies and subsidized credit provided by public banks to state and local authorities and to the private sector. The deficits of SOEs are partially captured by the transfers in the government budget constraint, since their debt is included in the external debt series since 1973 and in the domestic debt series since 1981 (see appendix).[20] Figure 9 compares the fiscal deficit series with and without transfers, and it shows that transfers increased significantly during that period.

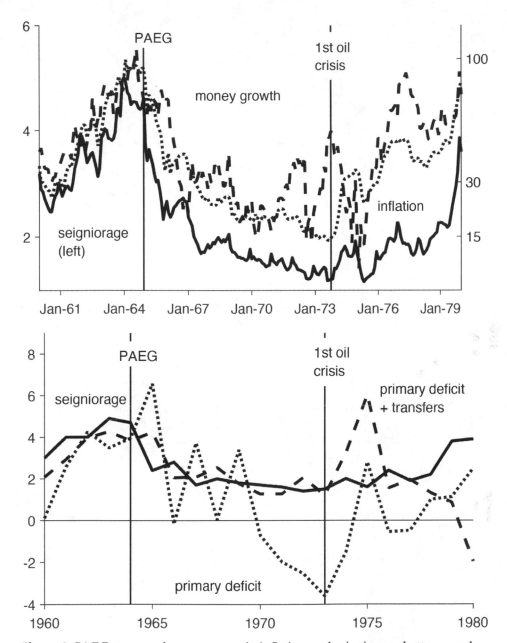

Figure 6. PAEG: top panel: money growth, inflation, and seigniorage; bottom panel: primary deficits and seigniorage, percentage of GDP

Sources: Brazilian Institute of Geography and Statistics, Central Bank of Brazil

Note: Seigniorage is in percentage of GDP. For the inflation and money growth series, we plot the transformation $\log(15 + X)$, in which X denotes the annual percentage rate. We sum 15 to avoid taking logs of negative numbers. Inflation rates are computed using the general price index, IGP-DI, from the Getulio Vargas Foundation. See the online appendix available at http://manifold.bfi.uchicago.edu/ for a description of how we compute the seigniorage and nominal GDP series.

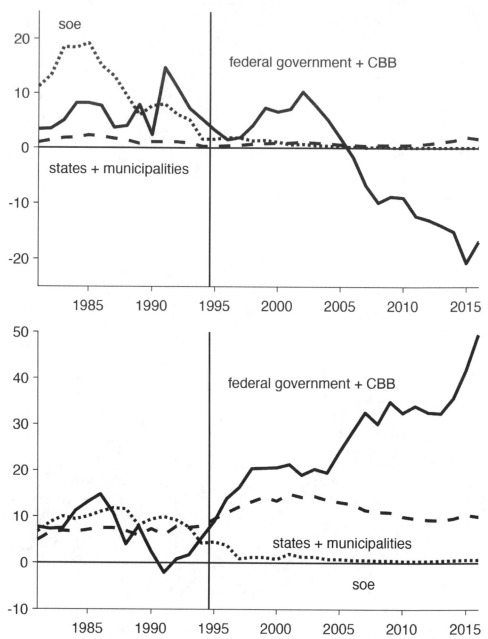

Figure 7. Sectoral composition of the public debt, 1960–2016: top panel: external debt, percentage of GDP; bottom panel: domestic debt, percentage of GDP

Sources: IPEADATA, Central Bank of Brazil, Brazilian Institute of Geography and Statistics

Note: The series of net debt, both external and domestic, of the federal government, state governments, and SOEs are from IPEADATA. We add the balances of Bank of Brazil accounts on the balance sheet of the central bank to the series of net domestic debt of the federal government. See the online appendix available at http://manifold.bfi.uchicago.edu/ for a description of how we compute the nominal GDP series.

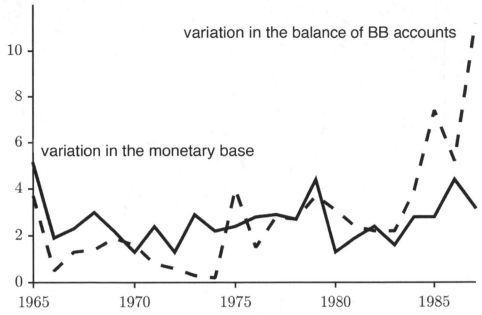

Figure 8. Bank of Brazil (BB) and the central bank, percentage of GDP

Sources: Brazilian Institute of Geography and Statistics, Central Bank of Brazil

Note: The variation in the balance of BB accounts denotes the variation in the balance of the accounts of the Bank of Brazil that are reported on the balance sheet of the Central Bank of Brazil, which comprises the Conta de Movimento and the Conta de Suprimentos Especias. See the online appendix available at http://manifold.bfi.uchicago.edu/ for a description of how we compute the nominal GDP series.

The strategy to sustain growth through external borrowing was successful in the first few years, as the accumulation of public debt was compatible with the maintenance of economic growth at high rates. Continuity of this process, however, relied on other factors: on the growth of private wealth, on the wealth holders' confidence in the capability of the public sector to service its debt, and on the use that was ultimately being made of the savings captured by the government. In the second half of the decade, GDP growth declined sharply, inflation doubled, and controlling the growth of public-sector financial needs became increasingly difficult. In the 1973–80 subperiod, the average maturity of the federal government debt securities reached its peak in 1975 (Figure 10), but the share of nonindexed bonds kept growing (Figure 11) until the end of the decade, as interest rates began to rise in 1976 following the abandonment of the interest rate ceilings, which had prevailed until September 1976.

The first year of President General João Figueiredo's term, 1979, started with a reduction in the real value of public bond debt due to two effects. The first was the decline in real interest rates due to the decline in nominal interest rates promoted by Planning Minister Antônio Delfim Netto in an attempt to stimulate economic activity, which reduced the attractiveness of the debt.[21] The second effect was the increase in exchange rate uncertainty

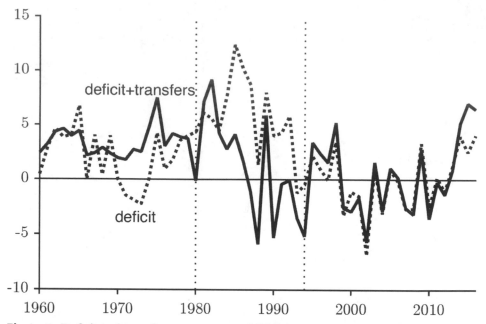

Figure 9. Deficit and transfers, percentage of GDP

Sources: Brazilian Institute of Geography and Statistics, Central Bank of Brazil

Note: Our definition of "deficit" is the primary deficit plus real interest payments on debt discounting for real GDP growth, and transfers represent the residual (the variation in debt that cannot be explained by official deficit statistics). See the online appendix available at http://manifold.bfi.uchicago.edu/ for a description of how we compute the series of deficits, transfers, and nominal GDP.

related to the second oil crisis. Figure 12 shows how interest rates were kept consistently below inflation rates between 1979 and 1981. Both factors led to a decrease in the stock of public domestic debt (Figure 3) and an increase in the fraction of government debt securities that are indexed to inflation (Figure 11). The policies implemented by Delfim Netto, mainly low nominal interest rates and the corresponding increase in the growth rate of the monetary base, had the effect of significantly increasing inflation, from around 50 percent in 1979 to over 100 percent in 1980.

1981–94: NO GROWTH WITH HIGH MACROECONOMIC INSTABILITY

If the previous subperiod was characterized by the number of national development plans that were implemented, the subperiod 1981–94 is famous for its number of stabilization plans, some of which are indicated in Figure 13, and by severe balance of payments problems.[22] In this section, we discuss Brazil's balance of payments crisis and provide a description of its stabilization plans during the 1980s and early 1990s, focusing on their main points and reasons for their failures and trying to find

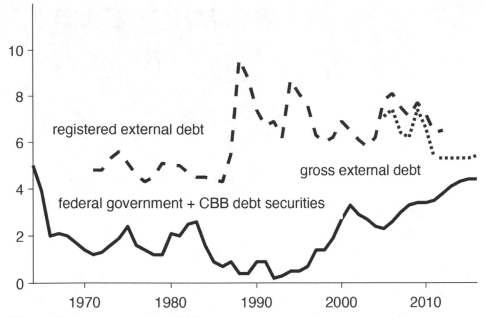

Figure 10. Average maturity of debt, years

Sources: Central Bank of Brazil, National Treasury Secretariat

Note: We use the series of average maturity of the registered external debt (code 3688) from 1971 to 2012 and the series of the average maturity of the gross external debt (code 3689) from 2005 to 2016, both from the central bank. Regarding the maturity of the domestic debt, from 1964 to 2008, we used the average maturity reported in the statistical appendix, table A.4.5, of *Dívida pública: A experiência brasileira*, published by the National Treasury Secretariat in 2009. After 2009, we use the series of average maturity of the federal government debt securities (code 10621) from the central bank. The series codes correspond to the codes used on the website of the CBB.

out the most important differences between them and the ultimately successful plan, the Real Plan.

Even though inflation was increasing to rates above 100 percent per year, in the first half of the 1980s the greater concern was to reduce external imbalances rather than reduce inflation. In 1981 and 1982, the main objective of Brazil's macroeconomic policy was to reduce the need for foreign capital. Figure 14 shows the current account balance, trade balance, and net interest income. We can observe the increasing cost of interest payments on external debt and the trade balance reversal (from deficit to surplus) in those years. There was a large devaluation of the real exchange rate (Figure 15), and real GDP per capita contracted sharply.[23] In 1982, Brazil entered a sequence of episodes in which it accumulated arrears on interest payments of its external debt, illustrated in Figure 16; this period would end only in 1994.[24] These facts account for the drop in external debt financing and the rise in interest payments on external debt reported in Table 1, subperiod 1981–94. During that period, we also observed the nationalization of the external debt.

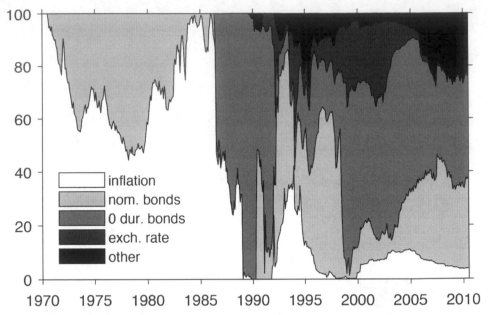

Figure 11. Indexation of federal government debt securities, percentage share

Source: IPEADATA

Note: Debt securities indexed to inflation correspond to those indexed to either IGP-DI or IGP-M. Those indexed to IPCA or other price indexes are included in others. Debt securities that are not indexed correspond to nominal bonds. Finally, debt securities indexed to the interest rate denote those that are indexed to the interest rate that is used by the central bank as its policy instrument, the SELIC. These securities are sometimes referred to as zero-duration bonds.

Foreign debtors would pay the Central Bank of Brazil in domestic currency, and the central bank would retain those funds in the name of the creditors. Any gains or losses resulting from the debt negotiations regarding write-offs and so on would be captured by the central bank. In addition, new foreign debt would be deposited at the central bank, which would then lend those funds to local debtors in local currency. As a result, a large fraction of the external debt became concentrated in the central bank's balance sheet up to 1994, as Figure 17 illustrates.

While the government's attention was focused on the balance of payments crisis, inflation kept increasing. It was only in 1986 that the sequence of stabilization plans began. But before moving to the discussion about each stabilization plan in detail, it is important to put into perspective what was considered to be the cause of high inflation at that time. The first plans were based on the idea that inflation inertia due to the highly indexed economy was the essence of the inflationary process and that breaking that inertia should be the main focus of the stabilization plan. These plans had a neutral shock of freezing prices as one of their main characteristics. However, the staggering of wages and other prices under very high inflation was an extra obstacle to that strategy. At the moment that a price freeze to stop inflation was introduced, agents with similar average

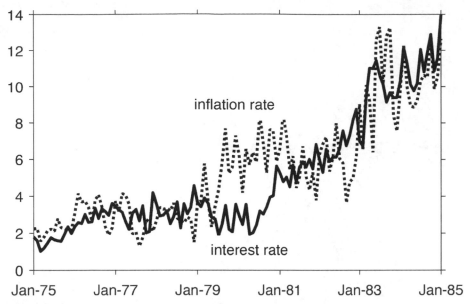

Figure 12. Nominal interest rate and inflation, percentage per month

Source: IPEADATA

Note: Interest rates correspond to the daily averages of the interest rates charged in the overnight operations between the central bank and other financial institutions. Inflation rates are computed using the general price index, IGP-DI, from the Getulio Vargas Foundation.

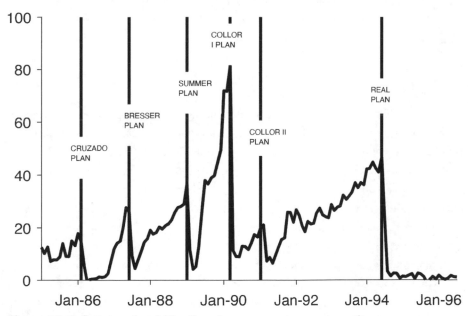

Figure 13. Inflation and stabilization plans, percentage per month

Source: IPEADATA

Note: Inflation rates are computed using the general price index, IGP-DI, from the Getulio Vargas Foundation.

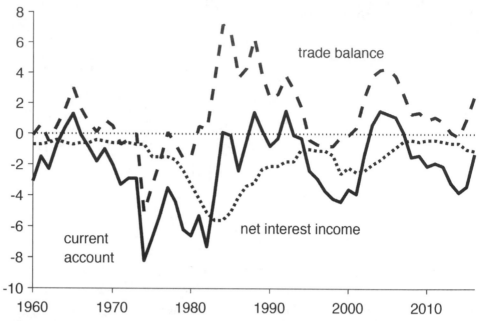

Figure 14. International accounts, percentage of GDP

Source: Central Bank of Brazil

Note: We use the exchange rate series with average purchase values in the year (code 3693) from the central bank to convert dollar values to reais. The current account, trade balance, and net interest income values correspond to the series with codes 2301, 2301, and 2398, respectively. The series codes correspond to the codes used on the website of the CBB. See the online appendix available at http://manifold.bfi.uchicago.edu/ for a description of how we compute the series of nominal GDP.

real wages would have different real wages depending on when the last adjustment was set. Since inflation was supposed to decrease substantially after the plan, the differences in real wages at the moment of the plan would prompt losers to claim rights to be compensated, while the winners would not complain. If the losers were compensated, that would reignite the inflation spiral. To avoid that problem, a conversion table was always mandated at the beginning of each plan, aimed at keeping, in the new low inflationary environment, the same average real wage that had prevailed under the previous high inflationary period.[25]

An alternative and more standard, orthodox theory considers the persistent and large fiscal deficits as the main cause of the inflationary process, since the government had to increase the growth rate of the monetary base to raise seigniorage revenues to finance those deficits. We discuss both theories in the fourth section. As we will see, from the first to the last plan, there was less emphasis on the heterodox part of the plan, which comprised price freezes, and more emphasis on the orthodox part. Fiscal and monetary policies became a major component of the latter plans while maintaining a

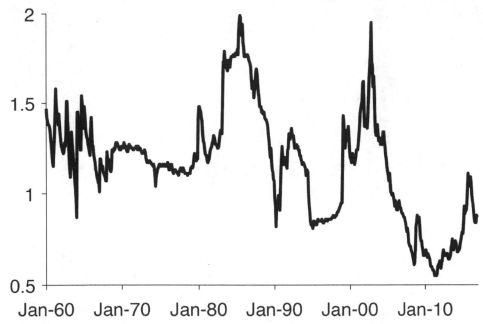

Figure 15. Real exchange rate, index (July 1994 = 1)

Sources: Central Bank of Brazil, IPEADATA, Bureau of Economic Analysis

Note: We consider the bilateral real exchange rate between the United States and Brazil. The real exchange rate is computed as the U.S. price index times the exchange rate divided by the price index in Brazil. We use the U.S. consumer price index (CPI) as the price index for the United States, the exchange rate series (R$/US$) with average purchase values from the central bank, and the general price index, IGP-DI, from the Getulio Vargas Foundation as the price index for Brazil.

device to synchronize the adjustment of nominal variables to avoid threatening the new low inflation level.

Cruzado Plan

In February 1986, the government implemented the Cruzado Plan. As became standard in most Brazilian stabilization plans, the first rule was to change the currency, in that case from cruzeiro to cruzado, which meant cutting three zeros. Prices were frozen, and any indexation clauses for periods shorter than one year were forbidden.[26] Wages were converted into cruzados based on the average purchasing power of the last six months but could be readjusted every time inflation hit 20 percent or during the annual readjustment cycle. Moreover, unemployment benefits were introduced, and the minimum wage was raised by 8 percent in real terms. The exchange rate regime also changed, with the domestic currency now pegged to the U.S. dollar. Fiscal and monetary policies were put under the discretion of the policy makers, but there was an important change: the end of the Conta de Movimento between the central bank and the Bank of Brazil. In practice, however, that only took place after 1988 because another account between the

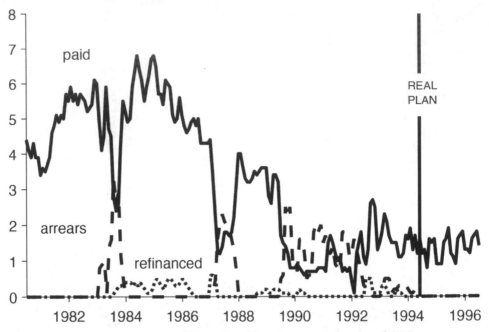

Figure 16. Interest payments refinanced and in arrears, percentage of GDP

Sources: Central Bank of Brazil, IPEADATA

Note: We use the monthly series for interest actually paid (code 2833), in arrears (code 2835), and refinanced (code 2834) relative to the external debt from the central bank. We use the exchange rate series with average purchase values in the month from IPEADATA to convert dollar values to reais. We use accumulated values in three months to smooth the series and report annualized values by multiplying the series by four. The series codes correspond to the codes used on the website of the CBB. See the online appendix available at http://manifold.bfi.uchicago.edu/ for a description of how we compute the series of nominal GDP.

central bank and the Bank of Brazil, the Conta de Suprimentos Especias, replaced the Conta de Movimento until its extinction in 1988 (see the fourth section). Another important measure was the creation of the National Treasury Secretariat, which would take control over both the administration of the domestic public debt and the government budget.[27] At first, the Cruzado Plan was very successful in reducing inflation. The average monthly inflation from March to July of 1986 was 0.9 percent (11 percent per year). Moreover, the claim to freeze prices had a civic impact, since the population was encouraged to "audit" prices; but that led to overheating. Sales increased 23 percent in the first six months of 1986 compared to the first six months of 1985, and real wages increased 14 percent from March to September of 1986 (Figure 18). One story that is consistent with such evidence is that even though prices were not allowed to change, *equilibrium prices* were increasing, which produced overheating, since posted prices were too low. Therefore, production increased to meet the higher demand in the beginning, but then production decreased and stores started to run out of stock. Meanwhile,

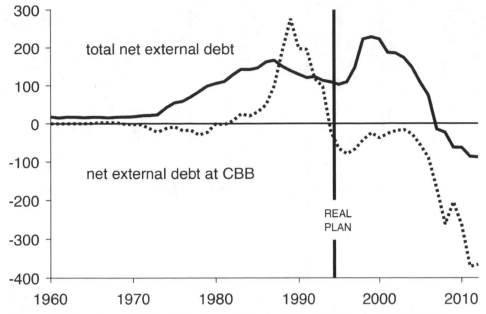

Figure 17. Net external debt of the Central Bank of Brazil, billions of 2009 US$
Source: Central Bank of Brazil
Note: We use data on assets and liabilities denominated in foreign currency on the balance sheet of the central bank to compute the net external debt of CBB. We use end-of-period exchange rates (code 3691) to convert to dollars. See note in Figure 2 for how we computed the series of total external debt. We use the U.S. GDP deflator from the Bureau of Economic Analysis to compute constant US$ values. The series codes correspond to the codes used on the website of the CBB.

the Central Bank of Brazil tried to keep interest rates low to induce low expectations. One huge imbalance was the inconsistency of the plan for inflation and the monetary base: the monetary base was increasing much faster than inflation itself.

In July 1986, the government implemented a timid fiscal package, Cruzadinho, focusing on increasing government revenues. But in reality, Cruzadinho had the opposite result of what policy makers expected. Expecting prices to be allowed to change again, demand increased, and the overheating problem became even more dramatic. Inflation remained low, but it was not truly representative because products were scarce. Because of the high demand, imports kept increasing while exports declined (Figure 19), thereby exacerbating the trade deficit. A rumor of a large devaluation in the near future reinforced that pattern. This expectation led to a postponement of exports and an acceleration of imports, which increased the problems with the balance of payments.[28] Facing all these challenges, in November 1986, the government opted for a fiscal plan, Cruzado II, trying to increase revenues through the readjustment of some public prices and some indirect taxes, which led to a high inflationary shock. Once again, the environment was one of high inflation (17 percent per month in January 1987). Meanwhile, the external crisis was just getting worse. In February 1987, the government suspended interest payments

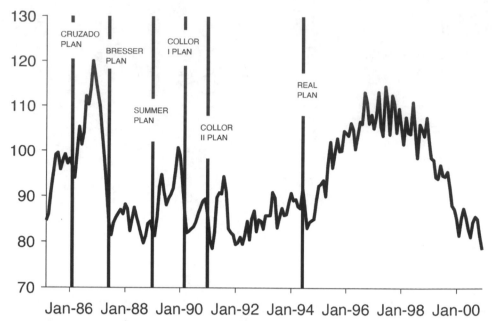

Figure 18. Real wages, index (January 1986 = 1)

Sources: IPEADATA, CBB

Note: Wages correspond to the average remuneration in the metropolitan region of Sao Paulo. Real values are computed using the general price index, IGP-DI, from the Getulio Vargas Foundation. We use a three-month average to smooth the series.

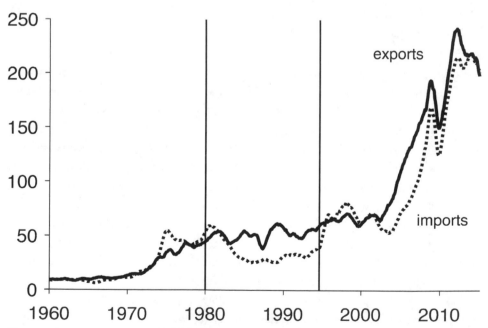

Figure 19. Exports and imports, billions of January 2009 US$

Sources: Central Bank of Brazil, Bureau of Economic Analysis

Note: We use the U.S. consumer price index (CPI) to compute constant dollar values.

on external debt for an indeterminate amount of time (Figure 16). The idea was to stop the losses of international reserves and to start a new phase of the renegotiation of the debt with the support of the population.

Bresser Plan

In July 1987, the government implemented the Bresser Plan, named after Finance Minister Luiz Carlos Bresser-Pereira. It was presented as a hybrid plan, with fiscal and monetary policies as well as aspects to deal with inflation inertia. As in the Cruzado Plan, prices were frozen. As usual, the moment in which the price freeze took place was important because the relative prices would remain stuck and possibly off-equilibrium. Trying to get a better result than the Cruzado Plan in this aspect, after the price freeze there was an increase in the prices of public services and some administered prices to correct for misalignments in relative prices. The extinction of the automatic trigger in wage resetting if inflation surpassed a 20 percent threshold was also perceived as another improvement. But the economic team created another kind of wage indexation, the URP (Price Reference Unit), in which in each quarter the government would specify the readjustment for the next three months based on the average inflation of the period. This would keep a monthly readjustment, but a gap would remain between the readjustment and current inflation. In contrast to the Cruzado Plan, monetary and fiscal policies were active. Real interest rates remained positive in the short term. In the fiscal policy arena, the government aimed to reduce the operational deficit from the expected 6.7 to 3.5 percent of GDP.[29] The plan did not address (or seek to deal with) the consequences of the previous default with creditors. Another interesting aspect of this plan is that it did not target zero inflation but was meant to be just a deflationary shock.

Bresser-Pereira's main purpose was to introduce a fiscal reform to reduce inflation. However, the reform was not successful. In 1987, the deficit was much higher than promised. Unlike the Cruzado Plan, which had popular support, the Bresser Plan was not popular, and in February 1988, some liberalization of prices took place, reducing the effectiveness of the price freeze. A third problem of the plan was that it led to a fall in gross fixed capital formation.

After Minister Bresser-Pereira left, Maílson da Nóbrega, the second in command, took his position. In January 1988, the government adopted an economic policy referred to as the Feijão-com-Arroz policy, which can be translated to English as the "Black-Beans-and-Rice" policy.[30] Instead of freezing prices, its target was merely to keep inflation at 15 percent per month. The deficit was expected to reach 7 to 8 percent of GDP in 1988, and there was a temporary freeze of public-sector wages to reduce it.

At first, this policy succeeded in avoiding an inflationary explosion, and the fiscal stance improved. The default on external debt was suspended, and the government started negotiations with external creditors. However, inflation started rising again, and the target of 15 percent per month was not achieved in the second quarter of 1988.

In October 1988, a new constitution was enacted. The new constitution increased fiscal expenditures, reduced the flexibility of expenditure switching between fiscal accounts, and substantially increased labor costs. It did so by increasing expenditures and increasing the transfers from the central government to states without transferring the corresponding responsibilities, which induced an increase in the deficit of the central government. To put this into perspective, 92 percent of the revenues were earmarked; that is, revenues from different sources were dedicated to specific programs or purposes (or both), reducing the flexibility of fiscal policies. In addition, the new constitution reduced the standard weekly working time from forty-eight to forty-four hours and increased the cost of overtime.

Summer Plan

The government implemented the Summer Plan in January 1989. Again, it was a hybrid plan, but the debate on the need for changes in fiscal and monetary policies was increasing. Like the previous plans, it included a component of price freezing as well as the adoption of a nominal anchor. In this case, a fixed exchange rate (1 cruzado novo = 1,000 cruzados = US$1) was implemented for an indefinite time. Moreover, an attempt was made to end inflation indexation. On the fiscal and monetary side, the plan was to adopt a tight monetary policy and to fight inflation by controlling the public deficit. It intended to control expenditures and increase revenues through the privatization of publicly owned assets and a reduction in the wage bill of the public sector.

Overall, the plan seemed to incorporate everything that was missing in the previous plans. Although it kept a heterodox flavor, it was mostly an orthodox plan aiming to reduce subsidies, close public firms, and fire public employees, with a deindexation plan that was sort of a small default. However, the government did not have the political power to carry it through. Without Congress, privatizations and other unpopular measures, such as the closing of public firms, were canceled. In the end, the reforms were not implemented. Moreover, the tight monetary policy put interest rates at high levels and increased the fiscal deficit of the government. With low credibility and a reform that did not go through, inflation accelerated, and the Summer Plan also failed.

The 1980s ended with inflation rates of about 70 percent a month and with almost 100 percent of the federal bond debt being rolled over in the form of zero-duration bonds.[31] This state of affairs reflected not only the extremely high uncertainty regarding inflation and interest rates but also the fear of an explicit default of the public debt by the incoming administration, headed by President Fernando Collor de Mello. At the time, the credit risk of the public securities was clouded with widespread suspicion, which was indeed validated by the new administration's actions. Collor de Mello was elected president of Brazil after twenty-nine years of either indirect or undemocratic elections. The very day he took office, he launched the first Collor Plan.

Collor Plan I

In March 1990, the government launched the Collor Plan I. Prices and wages were frozen. The plan recognized that a reduction in deficits was necessary to end the hyperinflation, and it implemented both temporary and permanent fiscal policies. Among the temporary measures were the establishment of a tax on financial intermediation and the suspension of tax incentives. But the permanent policies were more important. An effort was made to reduce fiscal evasion (one of the president's trademarks during the presidential campaign) and increase taxes. Other major components included privatizations and an administrative reform. However, that plan became famous for its (controversial) monetary policy. In an attempt to reduce the money supply, the government confiscated deposits in both transaction and savings accounts for a period of eighteen months.[32] Those resources amounted to 80 percent of bank deposits and financial investments, which would be held at the Central Bank of Brazil and invested in federal government bonds. These resources were remunerated while they were kept at the central bank, but their rates of return were decided by the government itself and therefore were subject to partial defaults.

Following the plan's implementation, monetary aggregates fell sharply, especially the higher ones (Figure 20), and real GDP per capita contracted by 5.7 percent in 1990. This reduction in liquidity, however, was not sufficient to control inflation. Regarding the fiscal reform, the threatening behavior of the government toward the public-sector employees made the reform very unpopular. The plan encountered a lot of resistance, and in the end, it could not deliver on what it had promised. While some privatizations succeeded, most of its reforms were short-lived.

Collor Plan II

In January 1991, the same government implemented the Collor Plan II. Just like the previous one, it planned to reduce government expenditures by firing civil servants and closing public services. It also proposed the privatization of state-owned enterprises. As usual, the plan included some price freezes. Wages were converted by a twelve-month average, a new *tablita* was adopted based on the assumption that inflation would fall

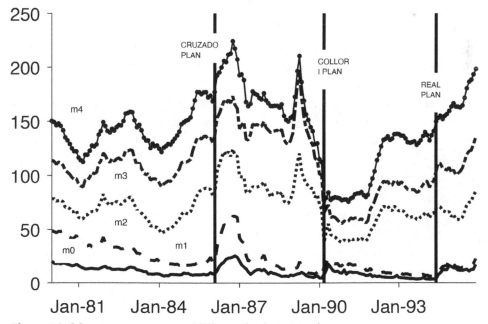

Figure 20. Monetary aggregates, billions of July 1994 R$
Source: Central Bank of Brazil

to zero, and the plan put an end to indexation.[33] Not entirely related to the fight against inflation, this plan had a motif that Brazil had to improve the quality of its products. In the words of the president, Brazil was producing horse-drawn coaches instead of cars. To achieve that goal, the government opened the Brazilian economy to foreign competition and privatized state-owned firms.

Following the plan's implementation, the country experienced a recession. But it recovered afterward, and this recovery is usually attributed to enhanced competition in the economy. Inflation ended up rising again, but this plan did make two important permanent changes. First, it opened up the Brazilian economy and expanded trade, reversing the previous trend (Figure 19). Second, it increased productivity. In the beginning of 1992, when expectations of accelerated inflation did not materialize, the effects of the recovery in investors' confidence started to show up in public debt markets. Those expectations had been based on the combination of price liberalization, corrections of public tariffs, and the devaluation that followed the floating of the exchange rate in October 1991 in face of the strong monetization of the hijacked assets during Collor Plan I.[34] The return of investors' confidence is also confirmed by the recovery of foreign exchange reserves after 1992.

Following the high political turbulence that characterized the months preceding the impeachment of President Collor de Mello (October 2, 1992), the beginning of Itamar Franco's presidency was marked by high uncertainty concerning economic policy. Proposals of another moratorium, and even repudiation of the public debt, were constantly in the press. It was only after the president nominated Fernando Henrique Cardoso, his fourth minister of finance in less than six months, that the recovered confidence materialized in higher external reserves.

Real Plan

In February 1994, the government launched its last stabilization plan, the Real Plan, which would finally put an end to the hyperinflation. The plan that conquered Brazilian inflation did not have the blessing of the International Monetary Fund (IMF), an always troubled relationship in the previous decades. The plan's concepts were different from the previous ones: it aimed to reduce deficits, modernize firms, and reduce the distortions that arose from previous price freezes. An important difference from previous plans is that it was planned in advance, with several measures being taken before its official announcement. Its first stage started in June 1993, when the government launched the Programa de Ação Imediata (Program for Immediate Action), designed to focus on fiscal imbalances that would arise when the seigniorage revenues fell.[35] It included an increase in existing tax rates, such as the income tax; the creation of new taxes, such as the tax on financial intermediation; and the renegotiation of subnational government debt in an attempt to control the deficits of subnational governments.[36] Another fiscal adjustment came in the beginning of 1994, with the Fundo Social de Emergência (Emergency Social Fund), a way to suspend part of the earmarked revenues of states and municipalities, providing more flexibility in the government budget. On the monetary side, a clearly stated intention to limit issuances of the new currency led to the adoption of a high interest rate policy and high reserve requirement ratios (100 percent reserve requirements on new deposits after July 1, 1994). In addition, the plan included changes in the institutional framework in which the central bank operated, such as the transfer of management of the external debt to the National Treasury Secretariat and the reduction of the size and duties of the National Monetary Council. Section 4 discusses those changes in more detail. On top of all these measures, the government also reached an agreement on its external debt renegotiations under the Brady Plan, and in March 1994 its defaulted debt was securitized and the country regained access to international capital markets.[37]

The Real Plan did not involve price freezes itself, but it was able to solve the problems of staggered wages and prices. Actually, this was considered the most controversial aspect of the plan but ended up being very successful. The creation of a new unit of account, the URV—Unidade Real de Valor (Unit of Real Value)—aimed at establishing a parallel unit of value to the cruzeiro real, the inflated currency. The idea was to make the unit temporary. Prices were quoted in both URVs and cruzeiros reais, but payments had to be made exclusively in cruzeiros reais. The URV worked like a shadow currency that had its parity to cruzeiro real constantly adjusted, since it was one-to-one with the dollar. Therefore, a conversion rate of the URV/cruzeiro novo (the old currency) was set every day, and many conversions were left to free negotiation between economic agents, with the government having more interference in oligopolized prices. That would allow agents to observe the low inflation of the parallel currency, therefore breaking the expectations of high inflation once the currency was changed. The URV was created in February 1994 when the Real Plan was officially launched, and in May 1994 the government announced that the real would become the new currency in July 1994. The government kept its plan, and the URV was extinguished on July 1, 1994, when it was converted to the new currency, the real, with the parity being 1 dollar = 1 real = 1 URV = 2,750 cruzeiros reais, and the adoption of a crawling-peg regime followed.

After the currency conversion was implemented, inflation rates fell significantly, and the hyperinflation period in Brazil came to an end. Figure 21 illustrates how the increasing primary surplus since 1993 allowed the government to reduce its seigniorage revenues after the Real Plan was implemented. The drop in seigniorage revenues was associated with a reduction in both inflation and money growth rates. In Table 3 we use the monthly data to compute the government budget constraint around the time the Real Plan was implemented. Note that while the primary surplus increased in May/93–May/94, the government was able to accumulate foreign reserves by 6.3 percent of GDP (which explains the negative 6.3 percent of GDP relative to net external debt in Table 3). Then, between May/93–May/94 and May/94–May/95, seigniorage revenues fell from an average of 2.7 percent to only 0.7 percent of GDP, and that was possible because of the increase in primary surplus, from 2.8 to 4.0 percent of GDP, as a result of the fiscal measures described above. However, in May/95–May/96, after inflation was under control and seigniorage revenues fell, the government showed a deterioration in its primary balance that would be reversed in the subsequent years. That fiscal deterioration was financed through domestic debt issuance, which shows

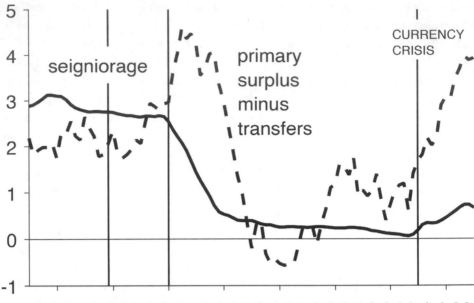

Jul-92 Jul-93 Jul-94 Jul-95 Jul-96 Jul-97 Jul-98 Jul-99

Figure 21. Real Plan, percentage of GDP

Sources: Central Bank of Brazil, Brazilian Institute of Geography and Statistics

Note: In this plot we are using the opposite of *primary deficits plus transfers*. See the online appendix available at http://manifold.bfi.uchicago.edu/ for a description of how we constructed the seigniorage, deficit, and transfers series.

Table 3. Domestic debt, percentage of GDP

	Subperiod			
Sources	*May 1992–93*	*May 1993–94*	*May 1994–95*	*May 1995–96*
(1) Domestic debt	−1.4	−2.6	−4.1	7.8
(2) External debt	−2.1	−6.3	0.6	−4.1
(3) Real monetary base	−0.3	−0.1	1.4	0.1
(4) Seigniorage	2.8	2.7	0.7	0.3
Uses				
(5) Interest on domestic debt	0.8	−3.4	2.7	3.3
(6) Interest on external debt	−0.1	−0.2	−0.1	0.2
(7) Primary deficits + transfers	−1.8	−2.8	−4.0	0.5

Sources: Brazilian Institute of Geography and Statistics, Central Bank of Brazil

Note: See the online appendix available at http://manifold.bfi.uchicago.edu/ for a description of the budget constraint. Transfers are computed as
(8) = (1) + (2) + (3) + (4) − (5) − (6) − (7).

that the credibility of the reforms played an important role, as it allowed the government to keep seigniorage revenues at low levels.

In addition, the increase in real money balances following the Real Plan also contributed to increasing the financing options of the government (Figure 22). Lastly, Brazil started to accumulate external debt again after 1994, but that was done by the private sector (or by public entities that were not included in the fiscal and debt statistics), which borrowed from abroad and, concurrently, financed the government. That accounts for the current account deficits after 1994 (Figure 14), explained by lower trade balances as a result of increasing imports (Figure 19).

Here, it is important to mention that the analysis above used the official *primary deficits plus transfers* as the benchmark measure of government primary deficits. We did so because there are large discrepancies in fiscal statistics around the time the Real Plan was implemented.[38] If instead we considered only the primary deficits from government accounts, without the *transfers*, we would observe a transition from large primary deficits to large primary surplus upon the implementation of the Real Plan, without the subsequent deterioration in primary balances mentioned above. We discuss that in the appendix. We were not able to explain the differences between both series. We chose the *primary deficits plus transfers* as our benchmark measure because it is closer to the primary deficit series reported by the Central Bank of Brazil, and it has been the preferred measure by economists that analyzed the fiscal policy in Brazil at that time (e.g., Giambiagi and Alem [2011] and Portugal [2017]).

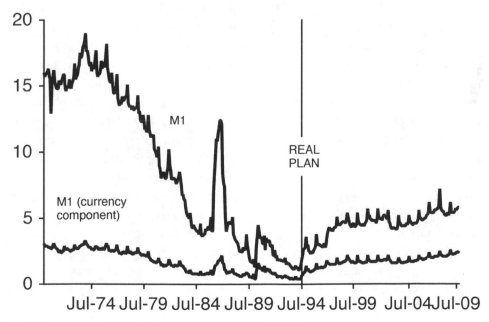

Figure 22. Real money balances, percentage of GDP

Sources: Central Bank of Brazil, Brazilian Institute of Geography and Statistics

Note: See the online appendix available at http://manifold.bfi.uchicago.edu/ for a description of how we constructed the nominal GDP series.

Under our benchmark measure of primary deficits, the fiscal deterioration from May/94–May/95 to May/95–May/96 is usually explained by the increase in wages that resulted from wage negotiations in 1994 and by the Bacha effect, which worked as the reverse of the Olivera-Tanzi effect.[39] The reason is that fiscal revenues in Brazil were very well indexed to inflation, but fiscal expenditures were not.[40] So the executive branch could, and indeed did, cut the real value of expenditures just by disbursing the originally planned nominal amounts with some delay, as higher inflation rates would rapidly erode the real value of those expenditures. Of course, this had the collateral effect of creating large problems, since public hospitals would run out of money at the end of the year, several bridges or roads would stay unfinished for many years, and so on. Guardia (1992) studied the budget for 1990 and 1991 in detail and reported significant differences between total expenditures in the (federal) budget and the actual expenditures. In 1990 and 1991, total expenditures hovered around 63 and 60 percent of the voted expenditures, respectively. Therefore, after inflation was under control, the government had to deal with the large discrepancies between nominal expenditures and revenues in the budget, which could explain the temporary deterioration in fiscal balances in the subsequent years.

The success of the Real Plan in conquering the hyperinflation is indisputable, but many discussions have taken place regarding which were the most important points in accounting for it. As is evident, many important changes were taking place around the implementation of the Real Plan, so it is hard to answer that question. One important condition was the availability of foreign financing, as foreign capital inflows resumed after the government reached an agreement with its foreign creditors under the Brady Plan.[41] That was the end of a long process of foreign debt rescheduling. Another important factor was the fiscal reform that increased primary surpluses (Figure 21). That reform also included other important fiscal measures that, most likely, did not have an immediate impact on government fiscal statistics. Among those measures was the imposition of fiscal constraints on subnational governments, seen as an important achievement of the Real Plan. The deficits of the subnational governments became a big issue in the 1980s and 1990s, and many attempts were made, often including bailouts, to solve that issue. In 1989, for example, a debt renegotiation with the state governments took place, and only two years before the government had renegotiated the debt of ten state banks. The state banks, in particular, were constantly used to finance subnational government deficits. Many of them actually operated with negative reserves, which ultimately pressured the central bank to expand the monetary base (see the fourth section). In 1993, the reforms enabled the federal government to use the fiscal revenues of subnational governments as debt guarantees and also to forbid the state banks from making new loans to their respective state governments. That was the beginning of a sequence of reforms that would culminate in the implementation of the Fiscal Responsibility Law in 2000. Finally, the tightness of monetary policy was an important characteristic of the Real Plan, and it still characterizes monetary policy to this day.

1995–2016: MODERATE GROWTH WITH HIGHER STABILITY

The last subperiod of our analysis represents the period of lowest inflation in Brazilian history. Inflation rates averaged only 8 percent per year, accompanied by the adoption of active fiscal and monetary policy rules. Economic growth resumed, but at moderate rates. Real GDP per capita grew 1.2 percent per year on average. We also observed the process of fiscal consolidation, with primary surpluses in 1995–2002 and 2003–11 averaging 2.3 and 2.8 percent of GDP, respectively (row 9, table 1). Despite all those advancements, the country experienced a big shift in its economic policy at the onset of the international financial crisis in 2008–9, which eventually culminated in a rapid deterioration of its fiscal balances and a deep recession in recent years. These events have raised concerns about the capability of the government to maintain a low-inflation regime in the future.[42]

1995–2002
The years following the implementation of the Real Plan represented a consolidation of the reforms that had begun in the previous subperiod. The government kept the privatization process and promoted both fiscal and banking reforms. Part of these reforms were possible only because of the success of the Real Plan in conquering the hyperinflation, which gave the government the political support to push its agenda of reforms. The value the public bestowed on the new low-inflation scenario became clear in the following presidential elections. Fernando Henrique Cardoso, the finance minister during the elaboration of the Real Plan, was elected president of Brazil in the first round, not only in the presidential elections of 1994 but again in the 1998 elections.[43]

The low-inflation regime, however, also brought some challenges. For example, a banking crisis followed the Real Plan, during which some private and state-owned banks failed. One of the reasons for the failure was that the fall in inflation led to a fall in seigniorage-like revenues (the float) that were partially captured by these banks. Here is an example of how this mechanism works. The Central Bank of Brazil increases the monetary base by $1,000 reais by depositing that amount in the account that holds the bank reserves. Assuming that the banks have no incentives to hold any voluntary reserves, the banking system lends the $1,000 reais to the public. The public borrows that amount, and after spending it, the $1,000 reais return to the banks as deposits. Assuming that the reserve requirement ratio is, for example, 10 percent, the banks keep $100 reais as reserves and now have $900 reais left to lend to the public again. Then the public borrows that amount, and after spending it, the $900 reais return to the banking system as deposits again. The banking system holds $90 reais as reserves and lends the rest. That process continues indefinitely, and the increase in the amount of deposits converges to $10,000 reais (= $1,000 + (1 − 10%) × $1,000 + (1 − 10%)^2 × $1,000 + . . .), which represents ten times (the inverse of the reserve requirement ratio) the initial increase in the monetary base. The ratio of deposits to bank reserves in Brazil is illustrated in Figure 23. Finally, given that banks charge interest when lending money to the public and that deposits are usually not remunerated, that process represents an increase in the revenues of the banking system. So, overall, for inflation to fall, the Central Bank of Brazil must make

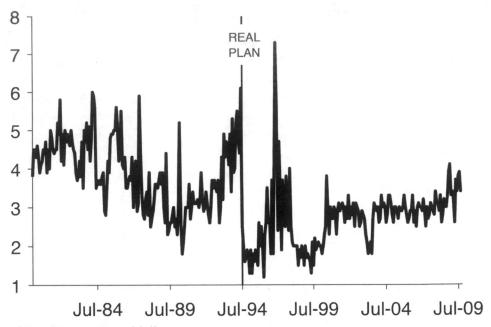

Figure 23. Money multiplier

Source: Central Bank of Brazil

Note: The money multiplier is defined as the ratio of bank deposits over bank reserves.

fewer such increases to the monetary base and thus must collect fewer revenues, as we have just described. That decrease in revenues hurt the balance sheets of banks and, all else being equal, contributed to the banking crisis.

Besides the banking crisis, the government also faced turbulence in international capital markets. The first one was the 1997 Asian financial crisis, which was immediately followed by the 1998 Russian financial crisis. After the latter, there was a speculative attack on the real, and the Central Bank of Brazil experienced a fast deterioration of its international reserves (Figure 24). The IMF stepped in, but the situation was such that the central bank could no longer hold the crawling-peg regime, and in January 1999, a floating exchange rate regime was adopted. This change also culminated in the replacement of the governor of the central bank, but not of the finance minister.[44]

In March 1999, following the adoption of the floating exchange rate regime, Brazil adopted an inflation-targeting regime, an arrangement that holds to this day. Concurrently, the government started to announce fiscal policy targets and took important measures to improve the conduction of its fiscal policy. One important step in that process was the Fiscal Responsibility Law, enacted in 2000, which imposed rigid fiscal constraints on both federal and subnational governments. Those measures led to fiscal surpluses, as illustrated in Figure 9.

However, the government faced another deterioration in the external scenario in 2001, with the recession in the United States and the fall of the Argentine peso. To make matters worse, the country also experienced a major energy crisis. It resulted from the poor management of its infrastructure, and the government ended up imposing mandatory electricity rationing. The government lost its popularity, and during the presidential campaigns of the 2002 elections, the stability of Brazil's macroeconomic policy was put to the test. The polls indicated that Luiz Inácio Lula da Silva, "Lula," would be the new president, and that led to an episode of current account reversal (Figure 14), with a large devaluation of the real exchange rate (Figure 15) and a sharp increase in the interest rates of government debt securities, in both the domestic and external debt markets. The reason behind this new episode is that the leading candidate had advocated for a debt renegotiation of both domestic and external debt in the past, indicating the possibility of an outright default. Under the adverse scenario, the IMF stepped in again, its last intervention in Brazil. Lula ended up announcing that he would keep the main macroeconomic policies that the previous government had implemented. Once elected, he kept his promise, and the financial markets returned to normality.

2003–11

The years following the election of President Lula were characterized by a favorable external scenario, with a worldwide boom in commodity prices. In particular, the period between 2004 and 2008 had the best economic outcomes of the 1960–2016 period. It was characterized by fiscal surpluses, high growth rates of real GDP per capita, current account surpluses, an expansion of international trade, a reduction of the public external debt and the accumulation of international reserves, and the consolidation of the inflation-targeting regime that had been adopted in 1999. In addition, the government implemented large

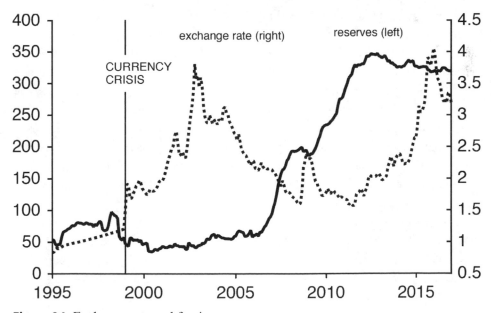

Figure 24. Exchange rate and foreign reserves

Source: Central Bank of Brazil

Note: Exchange rate as R$/US$. Reserves are in units of January 1999 US$ billions.

conditional cash transfer programs, such as the social welfare program Bolsa Família, which led to big improvements in income inequality in the fight against poverty.

Nevertheless, following Lula's reelection in 2006, the government shifted its macro-economic policy toward a larger intervention of the state in the economy, which would eventually lead to a deterioration in fiscal balances. In 2007, for example, the government launched the Growth Acceleration Program (PAC), a major infrastructure program consisting of investment projects and policies that aimed at boosting economic growth. Through BNDES, Brazil's development bank, the government began to invest heavily in large national companies in an attempt to increase its competitiveness in the global market. And through the now state-controlled mixed-capital oil company Petrobras, the government promoted large investments in the exploration of oil in the presalt layer, which had recently been discovered. As expected, some of these policies represented the expansion of fiscal deficits, but since neither BNDES nor Petrobras was included in the public-sector fiscal statistics in that time, they did not show up in the official statistics. In fact, in those years the government started to implement budget maneuvers to artificially inflate its primary surplus to meet the fiscal policy targets, which makes the assessment of the actual fiscal deficit figures even harder for that period. That effort became popularly known as *contabilidade criativa* (creative accounting).

With the global financial crisis in 2008–9, the government started to push those policies even further, seeking to implement a countercyclical policy that would prevent the country from going through a major recession. Initially, the policy seemed to be very successful, as real GDP per capita grew 6.2 percent in 2010. However, it did not last for long.

2012–16

In 2012, the economy was already showing signs of exhaustion, with annual growth rates of real GDP per capita decelerating to only 1 percent. The drop in commodity prices made the situation even worse. The fiscal deterioration accelerated, and the use of *contabilidade criativa* to hide deficit figures became even more pronounced. The government was now also intervening in state-owned enterprises in an attempt to manage inflation through the control of administered prices; that is, the government maintained low prices for goods and services (e.g., fuel and electricity) that were sold by SOEs, even though the other prices in the economy were increasing. The main reason for this intervention is that the government did not want to bear the political burden of reporting higher inflation rates, since it was the government itself that pressured the central bank to reduce nominal interest rates in the first place.

Furthermore, the government also used its public banks (as well as private banks) to hide its deficits. Here is one way that it did so. The government instructed the public banks to pay social security pensions to the public, but then the government never reimbursed the public banks for the full value of those payments. Hence, the public banks registered losses that should have been counted as deficits of the government.

Brazil was now back to a scenario in which the government used public banks and SOEs to hide its deficits while economic growth kept decreasing. These fiscal maneuvers became popularly known as *pedaladas fiscais* (fiscal pedaling) and eventually led to the impeachment of former president Dilma Rousseff in 2015, who had replaced Lula in 2010 and was reelected in 2014.

In 2015 and 2016, real GDP per capita decreased by 4.6 and 2.7 percent, respectively, and fiscal deficits reached levels of around 7 percent of GDP in 2016. The fiscal situation proved to be worse than previously expected. The previous government avoided tackling the reforms that would lead to a fiscal consolidation, such as the reforms to the pension system, and, at the time of this writing, the outstanding question is whether the next president can resolve the current precarious fiscal situation. As Figure 3 shows, public domestic debt is now at record levels, and previous fiscal adjustments were implemented through higher public expenditures and even higher public revenues. But the tax burden in Brazil is already very high, imposing an extra constraint on the capability of the government to raise more revenues.

With this history in mind, we now turn to discussing why inflation rates were so persistently high before the implementation of the Real Plan.

Weak Institutions, Deficits, and Inflation Inertia

WEAK INSTITUTIONS THAT PROVIDED INDIRECT ACCESS TO THE PRINTING PRESS

One of the most striking features of Brazilian monetary and fiscal history is its long period of high inflation pre-1994. Figure 5 shows that inflation rates were closely related to the growth rates of the monetary base and to seigniorage revenues. We argue that the high degree of passiveness in monetary policy due to a weak institutional arrangement, together with persistent and large fiscal deficits during that period, delivers a type of inflation persistence that goes a long way in accounting for these facts. In this section, we present a summary of the history of the Central Bank of Brazil, starting from the discussions surrounding its creation, and provide a description of how the government accessed seigniorage revenues. As will become clear, the Central Bank of Brazil was used many times to perform operations that are not consistent with the current notion of an autonomous monetary authority.

Before 1945, there was no clear separation between monetary and fiscal authorities, in the sense that the government Treasury had total control over money issuance. Rather, that was done through the Bank of Brazil, which held a monopoly over money issuance and operated in many instances as the bank of the government, as a commercial bank, and as a development bank. The debate surrounding the establishment of a central bank started before 1945, but it was only in that year when the first measures took place. The government created the Superintendency of Money and Credit (SUMOC), whose council had regulatory powers over the Central Bank of Brazil's monetary affairs, and this SUMOC was supposed to serve as a stepping-stone toward the creation of a central bank. However, the Bank of Brazil received the majority of seats on that council, which meant that, in practice, there was no disruption in the way monetary policy was conducted. Therefore, instead of establishing a central bank directly, Brazil opted for a two-step approach, in which the first step, SUMOC, lasted for twenty years. That process reflected a political impasse, with many interest groups reluctant to lose privileged access to subsidized credit—that is, their indirect access to money printing.

In 1964, the Central Bank of Brazil was finally established.[45] However, the SUMOC's council was restructured to form the National Monetary Council (CMN), which had regulatory powers over the central bank and still operates today. In the beginning, CMN had nine members: the finance minister, the president of the Bank of Brazil, the president of the National Bank for Economic Development, and six other members with fixed terms of six years each. Four of those six members would compose the board of the Central Bank of Brazil, one being its governor. Although the fixed terms granted some independence to the central bank, it did not last for long. In 1967, during the first transition of power within the military regime, the board of the central bank, including the governor, was forced to resign, and the fixed terms were officially abolished later on. The evolution of the number of members in the CMN and its composition provide an interesting perspective on the passiveness of monetary policy in Brazil because, in practice, that council ended up operating a separate budget from the one approved in Congress, usually referred to as the monetary budget. In the hyperinflation periods, the number of members in the CMN increased to twenty-six, and they came from very different sectors of the government and society, including business leaders and labor union representatives. That process reflected the increasing importance of the monetary budget for the implementation of economic policy. It was only in 1994 that the Real Plan reduced its number of members to the actual three (the governor of the Central Bank of Brazil, the finance minister, and the minister of planning), granting the board of the central bank greater control over monetary policy.[46] Figure 25 shows how

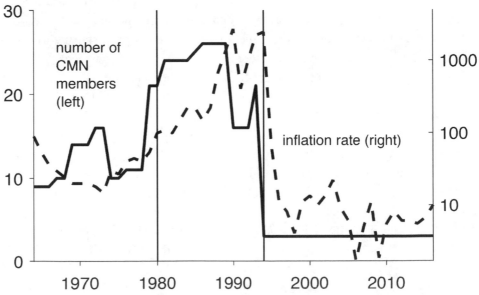

Figure 25. Size of National Monetary Council (CMN) and inflation
Sources: IPEADATA, Franco (2017)

the number of members in that council changed over time. The correlation between inflation rates and the number of members in the National Monetary Council is remarkable. In our reading of history, whenever the council was increased to allow additional groups to play a more prominent role, the desire of the council to pursue anti-inflationary measures with positive long-term consequences but negative short-term consequences was weakened.

With respect to the central bank's operations, Figure 26 shows the evolution of its balance sheet between 1965 and 2016, separating assets from liabilities. The complexity of its balance sheet during the high-inflation period shows that it was used many times to perform operations that normally do not fall to a central bank, and most of the time, these operations were effectively dictated to the central bank by the government. For example, upon its creation, the share of the monetary base in the central bank's liabilities was only 50 percent, with the rest consisting mostly of government funds to implement economic policies. The reason is that, instead of focusing exclusively on monetary policy, the Central Bank of Brazil also played the role of a development bank. For example, the central bank was given the job of providing insurance to agriculture (PROAGRO).

Additionally, the Central Bank of Brazil took on some of the tasks normally reserved for the Treasury, as it was made responsible for managing both domestic and external public debt, which involved issuances and payments of principal and interest. During the external debt crisis, for example, the central bank was one of the main players involved in the negotiations. When the external debt was nationalized, it was forced to absorb all this debt on its balance sheet, as described in the third section. The Real Plan ended that policy in 1994 and transferred the administration of the external debt to the national Treasury, and at the time, the government clearly stated that that action was taken to avoid monetary pressures. Regarding domestic debt, the government created the National Treasury Secretariat in 1986, which became responsible for managing that debt. However, the central bank was still authorized to purchase government debt securities directly from the Treasury under special circumstances, such as in the case of failed auctions. That was forbidden in 1988, but evidence suggests that it kept doing so until the implementation of the Real Plan, which partially accounts for the concentration of federal government debt securities on the Central Bank of Brazil's balance sheet. Figure 27 shows that during the hyperinflation years, the fraction of government domestic debt securities at the central bank reached levels above 80 percent.[47]

Next, when we analyze the central bank's operations during the high-inflation period, we find evidence that the government had access to and was using seigniorage revenues. Up to 1988, that was done mainly through its operations with the Bank of Brazil. As mentioned before, many of the government policies, such as subsidized credit, were initially conducted by the Bank of Brazil, and they continued to be after the central bank was created. In order to facilitate the interaction between both institutions, the government created the Conta de Movimento, an account of the Bank of Brazil that would show up on the central bank's balance sheet as a credit and the balance of which should average zero. In practice, that provided the Bank of Brazil with control over money issuance, since it could automatically withdraw funds from that account, which would automatically be matched with an expansion of the monetary base, of equal value, on the central bank's

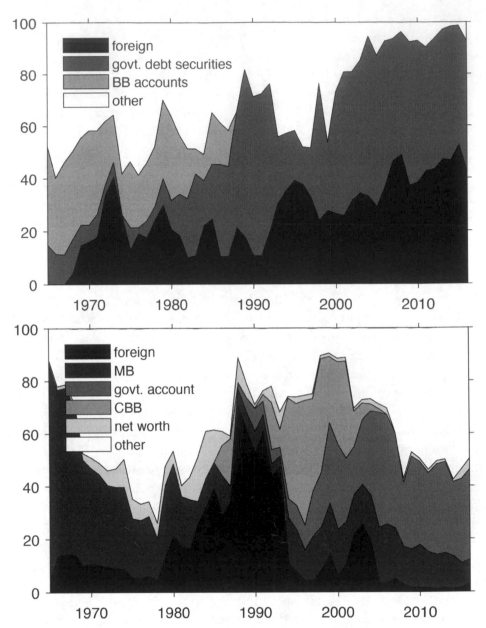

Figure 26. Composition of the balance sheet of the Central Bank of Brazil, percentage share: top panel: assets; bottom panel: liabilities   BB: accounts at Bank of Brazil; MB: monetary base; CBB: bonds issued by Central Bank of Brazil.
Source: Central Bank of Brazil

balance sheet. Not surprisingly, as Figure 28 shows, the correlation between variations in that account's balance over GDP and the variation in the monetary base over GDP was very high, and a large part of seigniorage was, de facto, "spent" by funding credit programs through the Bank of Brazil.[48] Since the Bank of Brazil worked in large measure as the government's banker (Pastore 2014), this should not be a surprise. Note also that

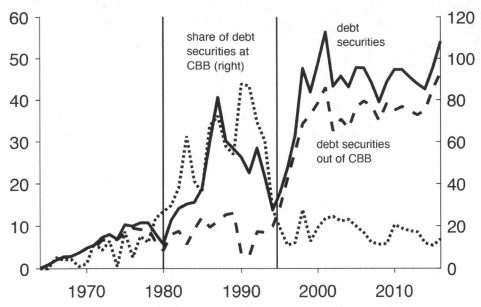

Figure 27. Government debt securities held by the Central Bank of Brazil
Source: IPEADATA
Note: Shares are expressed in percentage points and stocks are in percentage of GDP.

those transfers increased significantly around 1975, which coincides with the period in which government deficits and inflation rates started to rise again. The following quotation from Maílson da Nóbrega (2005), former minister of finance, suggests how little control the central bank had over the expansion of the monetary base and how such seigniorage was used to finance fiscal deficits, especially of subnational governments:

> In 1983, a troublesome fact occurred. Some newly elected state governors realized that their banks could overdraw cash from their accounts at Bank of Brazil (which held the reserves). It would take more than a month for the Central Bank of Brazil to realize that through its financial statements. There was no system that could provide that information in real time. The first one was the governor of Rio de Janeiro. The governors of Goiás, Santa Catarina, and Paraíba followed. The governor of Paraíba, Wilson Braga, was kind enough to let me know about his overdraft in the same day it took place, given that we are friends and from the same state. I warned him that it was very serious, but he replied to me saying that he needed to pay public employees and that the overdraft had already occurred. (Nóbrega 2005)

This quotation also indicates that one should analyze the operations of public banks, such as the Bank of Brazil and state banks, to understand how the seigniorage revenues were ultimately used. These operations were mostly done off-budget, so they must be taken into account when computing public deficits in Brazil, especially during the

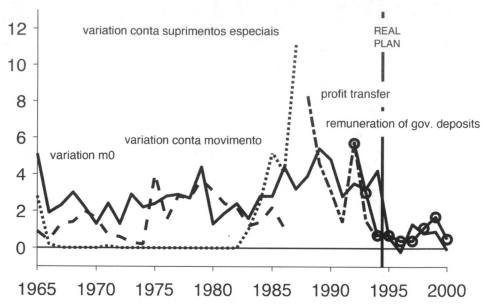

Figure 28. Transfers from the central bank to the Bank of Brazil and to the Treasury, percentage of GDP

Source: Central Bank of Brazil

high-inflation periods. We use the transfers from the central bank to the Bank of Brazil as an approximation of those deficits, and we add those transfers to the deficits data.[49] However, the evidence above suggests that Brazil effectively had multiple monetary authorities during the high-inflation period, so those transfers might not represent all of the deficit that was financed through money issuance. The reason is that given the size of the public financial sector, part of the seigniorage-like revenues (the float) described above in the third section was captured by public banks, so the total revenue of the public financial sector was probably somewhere between the variation of the monetary base over GDP and the variation of M1 over GDP, both illustrated in Figure 29.[50] However, we do not have enough information on those banks, so we restrict our analysis to the transfers between the central bank and the Bank of Brazil.

Initially, the Central Bank of Brazil did not transfer its profits to the government Treasury, so the use of the Conta de Movimento was a direct way the government could access seigniorage revenues. Interestingly, when that account was frozen in 1986, the government started to use another similar account between the Bank of Brazil and the central bank, the Conta de Suprimentos Especias, until its extinction in 1988.[51] When both accounts became unavailable, the government established the transfer of the profits of the central bank to the Treasury.[52] In fact, after 1988, there were two ways in which the government could access seigniorage revenues: through the transfer of profits and through the remuneration of its deposits at the Central Bank of Brazil. The new constitution in 1988 established that the government could not have accounts with commercial banks, only one account, and that account should be at the central bank, the Conta Única do

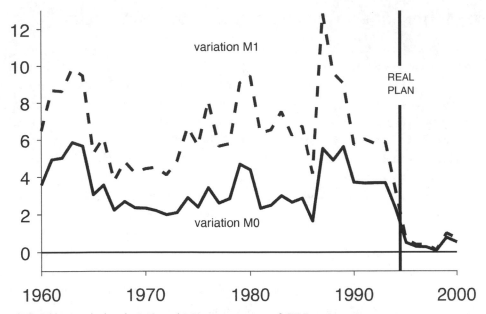

Figure 29. Variation in M0 and M1, percentage of GDP
Source: IPEADATA

Tesouro (Single Government Account), which should be used for all its transactions. A particular feature of this account is that the Central Bank of Brazil became responsible for paying interest on its balances, which were based on the average remuneration of the government debt securities in its portfolio. Since deposits are usually not remunerated, those transfers can also be interpreted as part of the seigniorage revenues. Figure 28 demonstrates that they match well with the series of seigniorage revenues.

The discussion above shows that the persistence and magnitude of the inflation process in Brazil are closely related to the persistence and magnitude of the degree of passiveness of its monetary policy and to the government's fiscal deficits and that important structural changes took place in both the institutional arrangements and fiscal balances in the transition to the low-inflation period. In addition, it also provides an explanation of why the government increased seigniorage revenues in the 1970s despite its access to debt financing. The direct access to the central bank's funds through the Conta de Movimento provided incentives for some groups to use that account instead of going through negotiations with Congress. In this case, the "provinces" effect might have played an important role in accounting for the high and persistent inflation in Brazil. That was the term used by Calvo and Végh (1999) as a possible explanation for chronic inflation episodes, in which different entities of the government chose their deficit level without taking into account its effect on the aggregate deficit, which would lead, in equilibrium, to higher deficits that are financed through higher seigniorage revenues, therefore leading to higher inflation.[53]

INFLATION INDEXATION AND PASSIVE MONETARY POLICY

Another factor that contributed to the Brazilian inflation process is indexation, which was often mandatory and became a widespread phenomenon in Brazil after its introduction in the 1960s. Most prices, wages, taxes, and the exchange rate, as well as asset prices, were indexed to past inflation. That, together with a peculiar form of monetary passiveness, would create the so-called inflation inertia. The main idea is that the widespread indexation would induce agents to expect even higher inflation rates in the future and to demand more money balances, which would then be satisfied by the (passive) monetary policy. So agents' expectations of higher inflation rates would translate into higher growth rates of money balances and higher inflation rates, leading to a vicious circle.

In such an environment, inflationary shocks, like the maxi-devaluations undertaken during external crises, would permanently increase the inflation rate. As the monopsonist in the money market, the central bank could, in theory, opt not to validate such an increase in money demand by not increasing money supply—that is, by substantially increasing the interest rate. However, this was not the monetary policy that was followed during the pre–Real Plan years. Monetary policy at the time was more geared to keeping the ex-ante real interest rate at a low positive level (Pastore 1994, 1996). The adoption of a more active monetary policy by the Real Plan represented a major change in the way monetary policy was conducted, and that could explain part of its success.

This hypothesis regarding inflation inertia gave many economists the illusion that the hyperinflation could be cured without major improvements in the fiscal stance, as discussed in our description of the stabilization plans. This mechanism has been studied by many economists in Brazil (Pastore 2014; Cati, Garcia, and Perron 1999; Garcia 1996), but it has not been completely formalized yet, so we still cannot fully evaluate its importance.[54]

Final Remarks and Conclusion

This chapter has shown that a simple fiscal story goes a long way toward accounting for the inflation dynamics in Brazil, in which inflation rates are highly correlated with both money growth rates and seigniorage revenues. In 1960–73, debt financing was still very restricted, and the government relied mostly on seigniorage revenues to finance its deficits. Then, in 1973–88, even though the government had some access to debt financing, the institutional arrangement was such that seigniorage revenues were being channeled to finance deficits at the Bank of Brazil. During the period with the highest inflation rates, 1989–94, the connection between government financing needs and seigniorage revenues became more complex. The government obtained higher seigniorage revenues, but that was done through the profit transfers from the central bank to the Treasury and also through the remuneration of its deposits at the central bank, which were less direct mechanisms than before. The financial repression during the Collor Plan I also guaranteed that part of household savings was used to finance government deficits and allowed the government to partially default on interest payments given that the remuneration of the confiscated savings was chosen by the government itself. Finally, in the low-inflation period (after 1994), Brazil showed primary surpluses and low seigniorage revenues.

The fiscal story is also consistent with the fiscal adjustments that were implemented by the Plano de Ação Econômica do Governo (PAEG) and the Real Plan, the two successful stabilization plans that managed to reduce inflation in Brazil. In both cases, the drop in seigniorage revenues that followed their implementation was compensated by higher primary surpluses. The credibility of these stabilization plans also played an important role, given that they paved the way for increased access to debt financing by the government, which allowed the adjustments to be implemented more gradually. In the case of the Real Plan, the increased access to debt financing even allowed for a temporary deterioration in fiscal balances in subsequent years, in which increased access to debt financing enabled the government to keep low seigniorage revenues.

On the other hand, the connection between government fiscal deficits and growth performance is much less clear. Even though many of Brazil's recessions were associated with government fiscal imbalances, such as in the early 1960s, early 1980s, and the most recent one, the large reduction in macroeconomic instability that was achieved after the Real Plan in 1994 did not result in much higher growth rates of real GDP per capita. Nevertheless, the periods of fast economic growth in 1968–73 and most recently in 2004–8 were associated with improvements in fiscal balances, so that leads us to conclude that fiscal stability is a necessary but not sufficient condition for sustained growth. That has been shown to be a more difficult task and would have to include, for example, reforms to Brazil's education, tax, political, and judicial systems.

Another lesson from the Brazilian case is that the government often used off-budget transactions, mostly through public banks and state-owned enterprises, to "hide" its fiscal deficits, especially in the high-inflation period (pre-1994). Some recent developments in Brazilian public finances, such as the *pedaladas fiscais*, accounting maneuvers that eventually led to the impeachment of former president Dilma Rousseff, remind us that we should always be aware of the constant attempts to "violate" the intertemporal budget constraint.

Finally, we observed that Brazil's transition to its low-inflation regime beginning in 1994 was associated with the institution of active monetary policy in a context in which fiscal dominance has been avoided with several initiatives to improve the fiscal stance, most notably the Fiscal Responsibility Law. Unfortunately, after this great achievement, and the very substantial improvement in the fiscal stance, especially after the floating of the currency in 1999, Brazil's primary surplus has decreased rapidly in the last few years. To make matters worse, the public-debt-to-GDP ratio accelerated again and now hovers at record levels. With the tax burden also at very high levels, Brazil must finally confront the political challenges required to rein in public expenditures. This major challenge facing the next president of the country will have to be tackled, or the Real Plan will pass into history as a long noninflationary interregnum.

Joao Ayres, Márcio Garcia, Diogo Guillen, and Patrick Kehoe

Appendix

This appendix describes the data and methodology that were used to compute the government budget constraint used in Table 1. Also discussed are the different primary deficit series that are available for Brazil.

We consider the following consolidated budget constraint of the government in units of the domestic currency (in our case, reais):

$$P_t b_t + E_t P_t^* b_t^* + M_t = P_t(D_t + T_t) + P_t r_{t-1} b_{t-1} + E_t P_t^* r_{t-1}^* b_{t-1}^* + M_{t-1}, \qquad (1)$$

where P_t is the price level of the domestic good in local currency, b_t is the real stock of domestic debt in units of the domestic good, E_t is the nominal exchange rate between the foreign (dollar) and local currencies, P_t^* is the price level of the foreign good in foreign currency, b_t^* is the real stock of external debt in units of the foreign good, M_t is the monetary base in units of the local currency, D_t is the real primary deficit in units of the domestic good, r_t is the gross real return on domestic debt, r_t^* is the gross real return on the external debt, and T_t denotes the transfers in units of the domestic good. The transfers, T_t, account for the residual in equation (1).

We follow the same methodology as in "A Framework for Studying the Monetary and Fiscal History of Latin America," with two simplifying assumptions: (1) we assume that the share of the domestic good in the domestic price level is one ($\alpha = 1$), and we express the stock of external debt, b_t^*, in units of the foreign good, so the value of the external debt in units of the foreign currency is $P_t^* b_t^*$; and (2) we assume that all domestic debt is real because most domestic debt in Brazil is indexed to inflation or nominal interest rates (or both), and we do not have data on interest payments that separate real from nominal debt.

Dividing equation (1) by $P_t Y_t$, in which Y_t is real GDP of the domestic country, and after some algebra, we can express the consolidated government budget constraint as

$$\underbrace{(\theta_t - \theta_{t-1})}_{\text{domestic debt}} + \underbrace{\xi_t(\theta_t^* - \theta_{t-1}^*)}_{\text{external debt}} + \underbrace{(m_t - m_{t-1})}_{\text{monetary base}} + \underbrace{\frac{\pi_t g_t - 1}{\pi_t g_t} m_{t-1}}_{\text{seigniorage}}, \qquad (2)$$

$$= \underbrace{\frac{r_{t-1} - g_t}{g_t} \theta_{t-1}}_{\text{interest on domestice debt}} + \underbrace{\xi_t \frac{r_{t-1}^* - g_t}{g_t} \theta_{t-1}^*}_{\text{interest on external debt}} + \underbrace{(d_t + \tau_t)}_{\text{primary deficit + transfers}}$$

where we used the following definitions: $\theta_t = \dfrac{b_t}{Y_t}$, $\theta_t^* = \dfrac{b_t^*}{Y_t}$, $\xi_t = \dfrac{E_t P_t^*}{P_t}$, $m_t = \dfrac{M_t}{P_t Y_t}$, $g_t = \dfrac{Y_t}{Y_{t-1}}$, and $\pi_t = \dfrac{P_t}{P_{t-1}}$.

Next, we describe how we use the available data to compute the government budget constraint in equation (2), whose averages are reported in Table 1. The fiscal deficit, as in

Figure 1 (bottom panel), corresponds to *interest on domestic debt + interest on external debt + primary deficit.*

We start by describing how we compute the price level, real GDP, and exchange rate series.[55] An important issue in our case is that stock values are expressed in units of the domestic currency at the end of the period, while the official price statistics report average prices within the period. In periods of high inflation, the difference between end-of-period and average prices is substantial. To overcome that, we deflate stock values by an estimate of end-of-period prices. In addition, for the most recent period (after 1990), we are able to compute the government budget constraint for each month, so we use the twelve-month sum of the budget constraint to compute the annual sequence of government budget constraints. To do that, we also construct a monthly series of real GDP.

Price index: We use the general price index (IGP) from the Getulio Vargas Foundation. It is composed of three price indexes: 60 percent Producer Price Index (IPA), 30 percent Consumer Price Index (IPC), and 10 percent Construction Price Index (INCC). Prices are collected from day one to day thirty of the reference month. Data are available at the IPEADATA website, *IGP-DI—geral—índice (ago. 1994 = 100).* End-of-period values are computed as the geometric average between t and $t + 1$. We normalize the IGP-DI such that its average is equal to the GDP deflator in 1995. The GDP deflator in 1995 is equal to the nominal GDP in 1995 divided by 100 (we normalize real GDP to 100 in 1995). Data on nominal GDP are from IPEADATA (Produto interno bruto [PIB] a preços de mercado—referência 2000). Regarding the price index of the foreign good, we use the GDP deflator for the United States for the annual series and the U.S. CPI for the monthly series.

Real GDP: Data are from the Brazilian Institute of Geography and Statistics (IBGE), series SCN53. It is annual, from 1947 to 2014. The series shows the percentage variation in volume. We normalize real GDP in 1995 to 100 and use the variation to construct the series of real GDP. We use the annual variation in real GDP (reference year 2010) between 2015 and 2016 to update the series to 2016. It is available at the IPEADATA website. To construct a monthly series, we assume that the annual values correspond to July values and use linear interpolation to compute real GDP for the other months.

Exchange rate: We use the exchange rate (buy price) between the Brazilian currency and US$. Both average and end-of-period series are available at the IPEADATA website.

Subperiod 1960–81
Most series are available at an annual frequency for this subperiod, so we only compute the budget constraint at an annual frequency. We use the sum of three series to compute the stock of domestic debt $P_t b_t$: federal government debt securities out of the central bank, debt securities of states and municipalities, and *dívida pública fundada.* Data are from IBGE, *Estatísticas do Século XX.* We use the series of monetary base, M0 (end-of-period) from IPEADATA, as our measure of M_t.

We use the series of real interest payments on domestic debt divided by nominal GDP as our measure of interest payments on domestic debt $\left[(r_{t-1} - g_t) / g_t \right] \theta_{t-1}$. We avoid manipulating this series in the first subperiods because the series of interest payments and stock of debt come from different sources. The series of real interest payments is computed as the series of nominal interest payments on domestic debt minus the series of monetary correction, multiplied by the fraction of federal debt securities out of the central bank, all from IBGE, *Estatísticas do Século XX.*

Regarding the net external debt, we assume that b_t^* is zero up to 1972. After that, we use the series of registered public external debt (code 3564) minus foreign reserves (code 3566) as the measure of $P_t^* b_t^*$, both from the Central Bank of Brazil.[56] For the series of interest payments on external debt, we only observe the total payments of interest on gross external debt, which includes both public and private debt. We observe both the series of total gross external debt (code 3682) and public gross external debt, so we assume that interest payments are proportional to the stocks, which gives us a series of interest payments on public external debt, $P_t^* r_{t-1}^* b_{t-1}^*$.

The series of primary deficit is computed as expenditures minus tax revenues plus the transfers from the central bank to the Bank of Brazil. Tax revenues include direct and indirect taxes. Expenditures correspond to government consumption, subsidies, transfers, and investment, net of other current net revenues. Data are from IBGE, *Estatísticas do Século XX.* The transfers to the Bank of Brazil are computed as the variation in the balance of the Bank of Brazil accounts at the central bank: the Conta de Movimento and the Conta de Suprimentos Especias. The transfers τ_t are computed as the residual of equation (2).

Subperiod 1982–90

In 1981, the Central Bank of Brazil started to publish the series of the public-sector borrowing requirement, which requires the computation of both net domestic and net external debt series of the nonfinancial public sector. We rely mostly on these series to construct the budget constraint after 1981. As our measure of domestic debt, $P_t b_t$, we use the series of net domestic public debt, available at IPEADATA. However, this series includes the monetary base as liabilities and the accounts of the Bank of Brazil at the central bank as assets, so we adjust the series for that. We subtract the monetary base and add the balance of the Conta de Movimento and the Conta de Suprimentos Especias on the balance sheet of the central bank to the series of net domestic debt.

Regarding the series of net public external debt, the central bank does not distinguish between exchange rate adjustments and inventory adjustments; it reports only the sum. We construct the series of exchange rate adjustments and use the difference as the proxy for inventory adjustments on the external debt. We assume that, for the 1981–90 period, all the adjustments that are made to compute the nominal deficit based on the variation in total net public debt are from adjustments on the net external debt series. The reason is that this period is characterized by a sequence of external debt renegotiations, which could lead to variations in the net external debt figures without being related to nominal deficits.

In order to compute the series of interest payments on external debt, we proceed in a similar fashion as in the previous subperiod, but now we adjust the value of interest payments on external debt for default. We compute the fraction of total interest paid over total interest due relative to total gross external debt and use this fraction to adjust for interest payments that were actually paid. The source of these data is the same as in Figure 16.

Regarding the series of interest payments on domestic debt, we use the same method as before up to 1984. After that, the central bank started to publish the series of nominal interest payments. We then subtract the series of interest payments on external debt described above and use the result as our measure of interest payments on domestic debt.

Subperiod 1990–2018

After 1990, the central bank began to publish its fiscal statistics on a monthly frequency. From that point on, we have all the information that is needed to compute the government budget constraint in (2), except for the primary deficit. At this point, we can only compute the sum of primary deficit plus transfers, corresponding to the residual of (2). This is similar to the primary deficit series that the central bank uses. As mentioned above, we proceed by summing the monthly budget constraints to have an annual series for the government budget constraint. We then use the primary deficit series from IBGE and subtract it from (primary deficit + transfers) to compute the transfers. Finally, note that the series of primary deficits from IBGE is available up to 2000. After that, we use the publications of the consolidated national public-sector accounts available on the website of the National Treasury Secretariat.

PRIMARY DEFICIT SERIES IN BRAZIL

In Brazil, there are two main sources of data on the public-sector primary deficit: the Brazilian Institute of Geography and Statistics (IBGE) and the Central Bank of Brazil (CBB). The data from IBGE are annual and cover the period from 1947 to the present.[57] The IBGE data include the federal government, states, and municipalities and are published in the national accounts—public sector.[58] The data are based on the executed budget of the government. The data on primary deficits from CBB, on the other hand, are available on an annual frequency since 1985 and on a monthly frequency since January 1991. These data include the federal government, states, and municipalities, as well as the central bank and state-owned enterprises (SOEs). We illustrate both (original) series in Figure 30.

There are important differences in the methodology used to compute each of these series. The data from IBGE use the actual data reported on the books of government authorities and can be considered the traditional measure of primary deficit.[59] The CBB, on the other hand, estimates its data based on the public-sector borrowing requirement. That is, the CBB computes the variation of the stock of net debt and money supply from the federal government, central bank, states and municipalities, and state-owned enterprises. That variation gives a proxy for the fiscal deficit of the government, which includes both interest payments and the primary deficit. CBB then estimates the interest payments based on the characteristics of assets and liabilities and computes the primary deficit as a residual.

In Brazil, the preference among economists is to use the deficit series from the CBB after 1985.[60] A few factors explain that preference. (a) At the onset of the external debt crisis in the early 1980s, authorities needed to work with recent data, and the statistics on

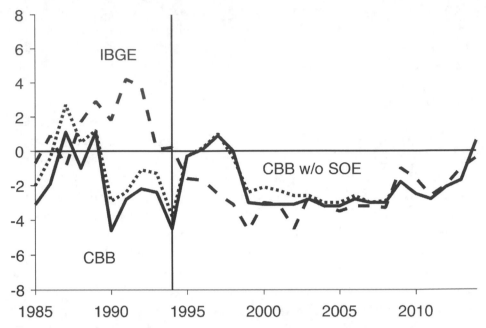

Figure 30. Primary deficit: CBB versus IBGE, percentage of GDP
Sources: Brazilian Institute of Geography and Statistics, Central Bank of Brazil

the primary deficit took a long time to be released. The CBB, on the other hand, had the ability to compile debt information for both domestic and external debt in a timely fashion, so it decided to compute its own fiscal statistics based on the public-sector borrowing requirements. (b) Another factor is the inclusion of SOEs. The debt series used by the CBB covered SOEs, whereas the other deficit series did not. Since SOEs were constantly used by the government to implement its economic policies (see the main chapter), that was considered a significant advantage. (c) Finally, there was lack of confidence in the capability of the government to accurately report its finances. The National Treasury Secretariat, for example, was created only in 1986.

Second, we discuss a few points regarding the primary deficit series of the central bank. (a) The inclusion (or not) of SOEs in the primary deficit series does not make a big difference after 1985, especially after the 1990s, when most privatizations took place (Figure 30). (b) The CBB did not take into account privatizations when estimating primary deficits. In other words, if the government sold some of its assets to finance current expenditures, that would not be captured in the deficit series from the CBB. Figure 31 (top panel) compares both series, with privatization and no privatization, for the period after 1996, which is the year when the data on privatizations used by the CBB became available.

Third, the CBB does not account for defaults. It estimates interest payments on an accrual basis. So if the government defaulted on its interest payments, the CBB would underestimate the primary deficit. The reason is that the CBB assumes that the government paid all the interest that was due. Therefore, it would conclude that the government had the

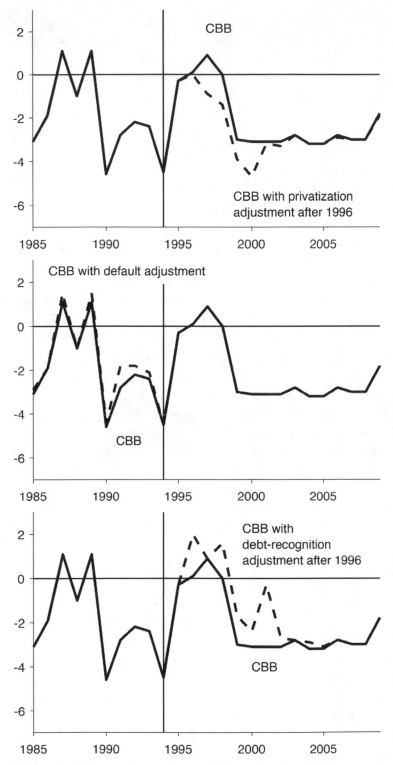

Figure 31. Adjustments to primary deficit series from CBB, percentage of GDP: top panel: privatization adjustment; middle panel: default adjustment; bottom panel: debt recognition adjustment

Sources: Brazilian Institute of Geography and Statistics, Central Bank of Brazil

resources to pay for the interest due, which must have come from lower primary deficits (or higher surpluses) according to the CBB's methodology. Remember that the primary deficit is computed as a residual. But if the government defaulted on the interest payments, then it must be the case that deficits were actually higher than the ones reported by the CBB. As the main text mentions, the country accumulated arrears on interest payments on the external debt for many years, especially in the 1990–94 period. We use the information on the fraction of interest on external debt that was actually paid to correct for both the interest payments and the primary deficit series reported by the CBB. The difference in the primary deficit series is illustrated in Figure 31 (middle panel). Unfortunately, we do not have information regarding defaults on domestic debt.

Fourth, the CBB does not distinguish "bad assets" from the rest of the government's assets. In these cases, the CBB might conclude that the government is saving, since it is accumulating more assets, when in reality those assets are worthless (the extreme case). One example is the accounts from the Bank of Brazil (BB) on the CBB's balance sheet (see main text) that were used to transfer funds from the CBB to the BB. In Figure 32 (top panel) we show the magnitude of those transfers given by the variation in their balances. By looking at its own assets, the CBB would conclude that it is saving, but those funds were never repaid and represented deficits. We did correct the primary deficit series for the transfers between the CBB and BB through those accounts. However, there might be other cases. Imagine, for example, the case in which the government bails out a public bank by exchanging the "bad assets" that they were holding on their balance sheet. The CBB would conclude that there were no surpluses or deficits, since the government is exchanging assets for liabilities in "equal" amounts when, in reality, they were transfers to finance expenditures.[61]

Additionally, in some cases, debt recognitions (skeletons) enter the debt series. The CBB does not include those variations when estimating the primary deficit, but it shows that some previous deficits were not taken into account. They are shown in Figure 31 (bottom panel).

Finally, note that the IBGE series also misses the transactions between the CBB and BB, so we also need to make that adjustment in the IBGE series. See Figure 32 (bottom panel).

IMPLICATIONS

As we can see in Figure 30, the difference between both series is significant, especially around the time of the Real Plan. However, the main conclusion from our analysis does not change, even when we include the adjustments mentioned above. The low-inflation period (after 1994) is characterized by improvements in fiscal balances. Note that both series show primary surpluses after 1998. The main controversy arises in the period surrounding the implementation of the Real Plan. It is usually emphasized that the government switched from large surpluses to large deficits when the plan was implemented, but given the pitfalls in the CBB's series, one cannot be 100 percent sure of it. If we look at the Institute of Geography and Statistics (IBGE) series instead, we observe the opposite: large deficits before the Real Plan and an improvement right after. But again, this series also has its own pitfalls, so one must be careful when drawing conclusions based on these observations.

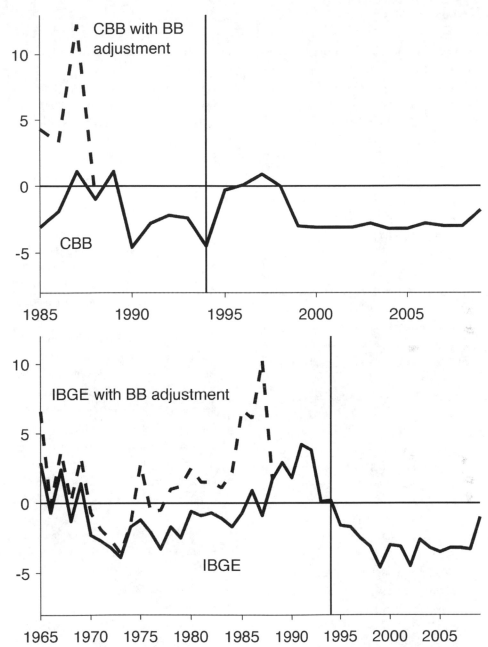

Figure 32. Adjustment regarding Bank of Brazil, percentage of GDP: top panel: CBB + BB; bottom panel: IBGE + BB

Sources: Brazilian Institute of Geography and Statistics, Central Bank of Brazil

Notes

We would like to thank Claudio Considera, Fabio Giambiagi, and Ana Maria Jul. The views expressed herein are those of the authors and not necessarily those of the Federal Reserve Bank of Minneapolis, the Federal Reserve System, or the Inter-American Development Bank.

1 The appendix discusses the data and methodology. Our definition of "deficit" is the primary deficit plus real interest payments on debt discounting for real GDP growth (see "A Framework for Studying the Monetary and Fiscal History of Latin America"), and throughout the chapter we use the general price index from the Getulio Vargas Foundation, IGP-DI, as our benchmark.

2 One must bear in mind that the quality of fiscal statistics decreases as we move back in time.

3 Most prices, wages, taxes, and the exchange rate were indexed to past inflation.

4 Mainly the effect of devaluations on *foreign-currency-denominated* or indexed debt.

5 The sums of primary deficits and transfers are close to the measure of the primary deficit reported by the Central Bank of Brazil starting in 1985, which is based on the public-sector borrowing requirements and is usually referred to as the primary deficit *below the line*. See appendix.

6 Interest payments might be negative because we are discounting for growth rates in real GDP and for the monetary correction of the debt.

7 According to Werneck (1991), the average capital expenditures of SOEs for the 1973–80 period made up 7.4 percent of GDP, so our figures might be underestimating their importance. Nevertheless, both sources of data indicate a rapid increase in investments by SOEs in that period.

8 By doing so, we approximate what the Central Bank of Brazil has done in its fiscal statistics starting in 1985. See appendix.

9 Data from the Brazilian Institute of Geography and Statistics (IBGE).

10 The military dictatorship would last until 1985.

11 For thorough analyses of that period, we refer to Orenstein and Sochaczewski (2014), Mesquita (2014), Lago (2014), and Carneiro (2014).

12 The other well-known Brazilian SOEs, Companhia Siderúrgica Nacional (CSN), Companhia Vale do Rio Doce, and Petrobras, had been created in 1941, 1942, and 1953, respectively.

13 The section titled "Weak Institutions That Provided Indirect Access to the Printing Press" discusses the institutional framework in which the central bank operated at length.

14 That was done through both quantity (restricted access to foreign currency) and price restrictions.

15 See Silva (2009) and Pedras (2009) for the history of Brazilian government debt.

16 Brazil started negotiations with the International Monetary Fund (IMF) in the late 1950s, but the negotiations were suspended when Brazil did not accept the IMF's conditions.

17 We added the variations in the Conta de Movimento to the original primary deficit series to account for the transfers between the Central Bank of Brazil and the Bank of Brazil. See appendix.

18 BNDE was established in 1952, and it was renamed the National Bank for Economic and Social Development (BNDES) in 1982. See Costa Neto (2004) for the history of public banks in Brazil.

19 It can also be considered a proxy for the deficit of the monetary budget.

20 The government did not have control over the budget of its SOEs. Given the deterioration of their accounts and attempts to control that process, the government created the Secretary of Coordination and Governance of State-Owned Enterprises (SEST) in 1979.

21 Delfim Netto replaced Mario Henrique Simonsen in August 1979 as the de facto manager of the economy, less than six months

into the new government of President General Figueiredo.

22 For thorough analyses of that period, we refer to Carneiro and Modiano (2014), Modiano (2014), and Abreu and Werneck (2014).

23 Under our convention for the real exchange rate, a real depreciation happens when the real exchange rate increases.

24 See Cerqueira (2003) for a detailed description of the external debt negotiations during that period.

25 The change of currency allowed for reductions of those wages that had recently been adjusted, in order to keep the same average real wage. Without the change of currency, the reduction in nominal wages would not be possible, since nominal wage reductions are not allowed by Brazilian law.

26 For fixed rate contracts, a schedule for interest rate conversion was set. It was assumed that all nominal interest rates were based on the inflation expectation of 0.45 percent a day (210 percent a year), which had been the average daily inflation in 1985–86. The real rate, then, was the (new) nominal rate in the new currency (cruzado), since the new expected inflation (at least for the government) was zero. For the variable interest rate contracts, which prescribed a nominal rate equal to the sum of the monetary correction and variable (real) interest rates, the new nominal rates in cruzados were set to be the ones above the monetary correction before the plan.

27 Before that, the Central Bank of Brazil managed both the domestic and external public debt, which included issuances, amortizations, and interest payments.

28 The government kept the minidevaluations based on an indicator of the exchange rate–wage (crawling-peg) ratio. However, this same indicator was suggesting that the exchange rate was appreciated.

29 At the time, the government used the public-sector borrowing requirement as a measure of the nominal deficit. However, nominal deficits were very high because of the monetary correction of the value of the debt. In order to overcome that, the operational deficit was adopted as the main deficit measure, which included only the nominal value of real interest payments. See appendix.

30 The policy name reflects the meaning in Brazilian culture of black beans and rice, a dish that Brazilians eat every day. It is considered to be neither very interesting nor very complicated, but it does the job of providing a healthy meal.

31 Zero-duration bonds are bonds that pay ex post the accrual of daily overnight interest rates. Therefore, the price of these bonds is insensitive to interest rate changes. It was a way to separate interest rate risk from maturity risk, thereby somewhat lengthening the very short-term public debt.

32 The government confiscated the amounts exceeding $50,000 cruzados novos. The resources actually became available before the eighteen-month period, as Figure 20 shows.

33 *Tablita* was the name for the interest rate conversion table when the currency changed.

34 The recovery of the stock of public debt in the portfolio of the private sector was a clear demonstration that asset holders were willing to return to business as usual in spite of the disruptions of repeated interventions that had been made in the rules of indexation and the liquidity of public securities during the previous twelve years. One should bear in mind that the majority of economic analysts at the time were forecasting that the government would never again be able to place new debt.

35 The program was announced in June 1993, but many of the reforms were implemented later in that year or even in 1994.

36 See Portugal (2017) for a discussion of the fiscal adjustments that were adopted in that period.

37 The agreement was signed in November 1993.

38 One advantage is that it allows us to make the analysis using monthly data because the official fiscal statistics covering the national

public sector are reported at an annual frequency.

39 See Bacha (2003) and Tanzi (1977).

40 A daily index, the UFIR (Fiscal Reference Unit), was computed based on inflation. Taxes would be denominated in this indexed unit of account and then translated to the nominal hyperinflated currency on the very day that taxes were paid to the banking system.

41 The capital inflows were a main factor in the expansion of the interest-bearing public debt, as the Central Bank of Brazil conducted massive, sterilized purchases of foreign exchange. In 1993, so much capital was flowing into Brazil that the government implemented controls on capital inflows (B. S. de M. Carvalho and Garcia 2008).

42 For thorough analyses of that period, we refer to Werneck (2014a, 2014b).

43 According to the constitution of 1988, the president is elected by a majority voting in a two-round system. If a presidential candidate receives more than 50 percent of the valid votes in the first round—that is, after the exclusion of blank and null votes—then the candidate is elected president without a second round. So far, no other presidential candidate besides Fernando Henrique Cardoso has been elected in the first round after the constitution of 1988 was enacted. Voting is mandatory in Brazil.

44 The Central Bank had eighteen different governors between 1985 and 2016.

45 The Central Bank of Brazil was created on December 31, 1964, and it started to operate in 1965.

46 See Franco (2017) for a complete description of that process.

47 The confiscation of savings during the Collor Plan I and the fact that external debt was being held at the Central Bank of Brazil also account for the increase in that share, since those resources were mostly invested in government debt securities.

48 The funds transferred to the Bank of Brazil from the central bank were technically loans that in practice paid no interest. In a high-inflation environment, these no-interest loans would fall quickly in value and soon lose importance on both balance sheets. This is how a loan became akin to a government expenditure.

49 See appendix.

50 Salviano Junior (2004) also makes that point in his analysis of the process that led to the privatization of the public banks (PROES) that followed the Real Plan.

51 Between 1965 and 1987, the average variation in the monetary base over GDP was 2.6 percent, while the average variation in the Bank of Brazil's accounts over GDP was 2.8 percent. Those figures show that seigniorage revenues were used mostly to finance the operations of the Bank of Brazil.

52 See Carvalho (2017) for a description of the evolution of the institutional framework regarding the relationship between the Central Bank of Brazil and the government Treasury.

53 That issue was formally analyzed in Chari and Kehoe (2007) in the context of a monetary union.

54 Garcia (1996) highlights a distinct aspect of the Brazilian hyperinflation with respect to the causal relation between seigniorage and inflation. He points out that although seigniorage revenues were used to finance fiscal deficits, the causal relation was not a direct one from higher deficits to higher inflation and higher seigniorage. According to his partial equilibrium model, seigniorage was endogenously generated by the interaction between indexation and money demand in the case in which the government provided a currency substitute—that is, inflation-indexed accounts offered by the banks that invested in government bills with daily liquidity. To keep this system from collapsing, the central bank had to match the increase in nominal money demand, thereby generating seigniorage. The central bank, however, could generate neither more nor less. Garcia (1996) calls this the "non-controllability" of seigniorage revenues.

55 Nominal GDP is computed as the price level multiplied by real GDP.

56 Codes denote the series codes on the website of the central bank.

57 From 1947 to 2000, the series can be downloaded from the *Estatísticas do Século XX* from IBGE. We extrapolate it using the annual publications of the public-sector accounts on the website of the National Treasury Secretariat.

58 Data on the federal government deficit and central government are also readily available on the website of the Department of the Treasury for the most recent period.

59 For example, IBGE uses data from the *Balanço Geral da União* (Union General Budget) for the federal government.

60 See Giambiagi and Alem (2011).

61 In other words, the value of those assets on the balance sheet does not represent their true value.

References

Abreu, Marcelo de Paiva, and Rogério L. F. Werneck. 2014. "Estabilização, abertura e privatização, 1990–1994." In *A ordem do progreso: Dois séculos de política econômica no Brasil*, 2nd ed., edited by Marcelo de Paiva Abreu, 313–30. Amsterdam: Elsevier.

Bacha, Edmar L. 2003. "Brazil's Plano Real: A View from the Inside." In *Development Economics and Structuralist Macroeconomics: Essays in Honor of Lance Taylor*, edited by Amitava Krishna Dutt and Jaime Ros, 181–205. Cheltenham, UK: Edward Elgar.

Calvo, Guillermo A., and Carlos A. Végh. 1999. "Inflation Stabilization and BOP Crises in Developing Countries." In *Handbook of Macroeconomics*, vol. 1C, edited by John Taylor and Michael Woodford, 1531–614. Amsterdam: North Holland.

Carneiro, Dionísio D. 2014. "Crise e esperança, 1974–1980." In *A ordem do progreso: Dois séculos de política econômica no Brasil*, 2nd ed., edited by Marcelo de Paiva Abreu, 241–262. Rio de Janeiro: Elsevier.

Carneiro, Dionísio D., and Eduardo M. Modiano. 2014. "Ajuste externo e desequilíbrio interno, 1980–1984." In *A ordem do progreso: Dois séculos de política econômica no Brasil*, 2nd ed., edited by Marcelo de Paiva Abreu, 263–80. Rio de Janeiro: Elsevier.

Carvalho, Antonio C. C. D'Ávila, Jr. 2017. "BC e Tesouro: Um estudo sobre a constituição, leis complementares, leis ordinárias e medidas provisórias." In *A crise fiscal e monetária brasileira*, 2nd ed., edited by Edmar L. Bacha, 153–86. Rio de Janeiro: Civilização Brasileira.

Carvalho, Bernardo S. de M., and Márcio G. P. Garcia. 2008. "Ineffective Controls on Capital Inflows under Sophisticated Financial Markets: Brazil in the Nineties." In *Financial Markets Volatility and Performance in Emerging Markets*, edited by Sebastian Edwards and Márcio G. P. Garcia, 29–96. Chicago: University of Chicago Press.

Cati, Regina Celia, Márcio G. P. Garcia, and Pierre Perron. 1999. "Unit Roots in the Presence of Abrupt Governmental Interventions with an Application to Brazilian Data." *Journal of Applied Econometrics* 14 (1): 27–56.

Cerqueira, Ceres Aires. 2003. *Dívida externa brasileira*. 2nd ed. Brasilia: Banco Central do Brasil.

Chari, V. V., and Patrick J. Kehoe. 2007. "On the Need for Fiscal Constraints in a Monetary Union." *Journal of Monetary Economics* 54 (8): 2399–408.

Costa Neto, Yttrio Corrêa da. 2004. *Bancos oficiais no Brasil: Origem e aspectos de seu desenvolvimento*. Brasilia: Banco Central do Brasil.

Franco, Gustavo H. B. 2017. "O conselho monetário nacional como autoridade monetária: Das origens aos dias actuais." In *A crise fiscal e monetária brasileira*, 2nd ed., edited by Edmar L. Bacha, 39–66. Rio de Janeiro: Civilização Brasileira.

Garcia, Márcio G. P. 1996. "Avoiding Some Costs of Inflation and Crawling toward Hyperinflation: The Case of the Brazilian Domestic Currency Substitute." *Journal of Development Economics* 51 (1): 139–59.

Giambiagi, Fabio, and Ana Claudia Alem. 2011. *Finanças públicas—teoria e prática no Brasil*. 4th ed. Amsterdam: Elsevier.

Guardia, Eduardo R. 1992. "Orçamento público e política fiscal: Aspectos institucionais e a experiência recente–1985/1991." Master's thesis, Universidade Estadual de Campinas, Instituto de Economia, Campinas.

Lago, Luiz Aranha Corrêa. 2014. "A retomada do crescimento e as distorções do milagre, 1967–1974." In *A ordem do progresso: Dois séculos de política econômica no Brasil*, 2nd ed., edited by Marcelo de Paiva Abreu, 213–40. Rio de Janeiro: Elsevier.

Mesquita, Mário M. C. 2014. "Inflação, estagnação e ruptura, 1961–1964." In *A ordem do progresso: Dois séculos de política econômica no Brasil*, 2nd ed., edited by Marcelo de Paiva Abreu, 179–96. Rio de Janeiro: Elsevier.

Modiano, Eduardo M. 2014. "A ópera dos três cruzados, 1985–1990." In *A ordem do progresso: Dois séculos de política econômica no Brasil*, 2nd ed., edited by Marcelo de Paiva Abreu, 281–312. Rio de Janeiro: Elsevier.

Nóbrega, Maílson da. 2005. *O futuro chegou: Instituições e desenvolvimento no Brasil*. Rio de Janeiro: Globo.

Orenstein, Luiz, and Antonio Claudio Sochaczewski. 2014. "Democracia com desenvolvimento, 1956–1961." In *A ordem do progresso: Dois séculos de política econômica no Brasil*, 2nd ed., edited by Marcelo de Paiva Abreu, 157–78. Rio de Janeiro: Elsevier.

Pastore, Affonso Celso. 1994. "Déficit público, a sustentabilidade do crescimento das dívidas interna e externa, senhoriagem e inflação: Uma análise do regime monetário brasileiro." *Brazilian Review of Econometrics* 14 (2): 177–234.

————. 1996. "Por que a política monetária perde eficácia?" *Revista brasileira de economia* 50 (3): 281–311.

————. 2014. *Inflação e crises: O papel da moeda*. Amsterdam: Elsevier.

Pedras, Guillermo B. V. 2009. "História da dívida pública no Brasil: De 1964 até os dias atuais." In *Dívida pública: A experiência brasileira*, edited by Lena Oliveira de Carvalho, Otavio Ladeira de Medeiros, and Anderson Caputo Silva, 57–80. Brasilia: Secretaria do Tesouro Nacional, Banco Mundial.

Portugal, Murilo. 2017. "Política fiscal na primeira fase do plano real, 1993–1997." In *A crise fiscal e monetária brasileira*, 2nd ed., edited by Edmar L. Bacha, 373–400. Rio de Janeiro: Civilização Brasileira.

Salviano Junior, Cleofas. 2004. *Bancos estaduais: Dos problemas crônicos ao PROES*. Brasilia: Banco Central do Brasil.

Silva, Anderson Caputo. 2009. "Origem e história da dívida pública no Brasil até 1963." In *Dívida pública: A experiência brasileira*, edited by Lena Oliveira de Carvalho, Otavio Ladeira de Medeiros, and Anderson Caputo Silva, 33–56. Brasilia: Secretaria do Tesouro Nacional, Banco Mundial.

Tanzi, Vito. 1977. "Inflation, Lags in Collection, and the Real Value of Tax Revenue." *IMF Economic Review* 24 (1): 154–67.

Werneck, Rogério L. F. 1991. "Public Sector Adjustment to External Shocks and Domestic Pressures, 1970–85." In *The Public Sector and the Latin American Crisis, 1970–1985*, edited by Felipe Larrain and Marcelo Selowsky, 53–87. San Francisco: International Center for Economic Growth.

————. 2014a. "Alternância política, redistribuiçãao e crescimento, 2003–2010." In *A ordem do progreso: Dois séculos de política econômica no Brasil*, 2nd ed., edited by Marcelo de Paiva Abreu, 331–56. Rio de Janeiro: Elsevier.

————. 2014b. "Consolidação da estabilização e reconstrução institucional, 1995–2002." In *A ordem do progreso: Dois séculos de política econômica no Brasil*, 2nd ed., edited by Marcelo de Paiva Abreu, 357–430. Rio de Janeiro: Elsevier.

Discussion of the History of Brazil 1

José A. Scheinkman
Columbia University, Princeton University, and
National Bureau of Economic Research

Ayres et al. provide an excellent summary of Brazil's monetary and fiscal history since the 1960s. The analysis emphasizes the government budget constraint following the framework exposited in "A Framework for Studying the Monetary and Fiscal History of Latin America" in this volume. Rather than commenting on every aspect of the chapter, I will focus on two issues raised by this survey. The first is the high rate of inflation in 1980–94 in the presence of relatively modest *measured* fiscal deficits. The second is the low growth in the post–Real Plan period.

Inflation and the Fiscal Deficit

The Chicago PhD dissertation of Yoshino (1993) documents that, despite the very high inflation rates, regulation allowed private banks to collect an inflation tax on demand deposits that in the years between 1980 and 1988 reached between 61 percent and 110 percent of the inflation tax collected by the central bank. The government also imposed a tax on demand deposits by requiring private banks to make subsidized loans to certain sectors (e.g., agriculture) corresponding to a percentage of demand deposits. In this way, what would have been a fiscal expenditure was directly financed by the inflation tax on M1. The remaining revenue from the inflation tax on demand deposits would have been divided between the cost of services provided to attract depositors and profits. The evidence summarized in Carvalho (2003) that financial institutions achieved twice the return on equity that nonfinancial firms obtained in 1981–91 indicates that service competition did not totally eliminate banks' gains from the inflation tax. There was also a large network of federal and state-owned banks in Brazil during that period. Yoshino estimates that these banks collected during the same years (1980–88) an amount that varied between 50 percent and 58 percent of the inflation tax generated by the central bank.[1] In the case of state-owned banks, a large share of loans made before 1994 went to their own state governments at subsidized rates. For instance, at the start of the Real Plan, Banespa, the bank controlled by the state of São Paulo and the largest state-owned bank, had 80 percent of its assets in credits to the public sector.[2]

The obligation to lend a proportion of demand deposits was not the only form of directed credit imposed by the central government. Many other types of deposits and compulsory savings were also affected.[3] The World Bank estimated that, in 1986–87, directed credit programs accounted for 80 percent of the average *stock* of credit in Brazil and placed the implicit subsidy on a sample of the largest directed credit programs, including housing finance, at the equivalent of 80 percent of Treasury revenue, or about 7 to 8 percent of GDP.[4] Since many of the subsidies were in the form of lower nominal interest rates, it is unlikely that the government could have transferred these amounts without a high inflation rate.

Overall, the evidence indicates that the true seigniorage in Brazil in 1981–94 was substantially larger than the 3.2 percent of GDP reported in Table 1 in the appendix of Garcia et al. This observation makes it even harder to explain the nondollarization of the Brazilian economy in the 1980s.

Macroeconomic Stability and Growth

As shown in the appendix of Garcia et al., the Real Plan led to much lower rates of inflation, and, at least during the period 1999–2013, Brazil produced annual primary surpluses. Many observers believed that with the major macroeconomic imbalances eliminated, Brazil could return to the high growth rates it had enjoyed before the first oil shock. Unfortunately, the growth rate, except perhaps in some years of the commodity boom, has been mediocre. According to the World Bank World Development Indicators Series on GDP per person employed (constant 2011 purchasing power parity [PPP]), output per worker employed grew only 18 percent from 1995 to 2017. During this period, Brazil's distance to the frontier increased, and a Brazilian worker went from producing 34 percent of the output of a U.S. worker to 29 percent.[5]

Growth accounting points toward total factor productivity (TFP) as a major contributor to this loss in relative output per worker between Brazil and the United States. TFP calculations are notoriously imprecise, but according to the Total Economy Database, the growth factor in Brazilian TFP in 1995–2017 was only 68 percent of the corresponding U.S. growth factor. In the Penn World Table (PWT) version 9.0, Brazil's TFP at current PPP fell from 61 percent to 48 percent of U.S. TFP between 1995 and 2014. In comparison, the Human Capital Index in Brazil in the PWT increased from 52 percent to 74 percent of the U.S. index.[6]

Possible sources for the continued low performance in productivity include the increase in the tax burden from 25 percent of GDP pre–Real Plan to 33.6 percent in 2017; a complicated tax system that favors specific sectors and even particular firms and also favors smaller firms; an uncertain legal environment that, among other things, discourages private infrastructure investments; and a myriad of policies that make it difficult for new firms to enter certain sectors. However, output per worker in Brazil behaved very differently across major economic sectors. Between 2000 and 2013, output per worker *fell* 5.5 percent in manufacturing, rose only 11.7 percent in services, but rose 105.6 percent in agriculture.[7] TFP in agriculture grew 4.3 percent per year in 1997–2014.[8] Agriculture seems to have benefited from two factors absent in manufacturing or services. The first is public investments in research through the agricultural research corporation Embrapa that, among other things, developed the new techniques that transformed the Cerrado region into an agricultural powerhouse. Second, since 1990, Brazil has had an open agriculture trade policy that contrasts with the high rates of protection in manufacturing. Gasques et al. (2012) estimate that a 1 percent increase in agribusiness exports raised TFP by 0.35 percent. The performance in agriculture indicates that Brazil may need to solve only a few of the problems that depress productivity to achieve much higher growth rates.

Notes

I thank Emilio Garcia for his research assistance.

1 Cysne and Lisbôa (2007) use a different methodology to calculate the inflation tax and do not distinguish private from federal or state-owned commercial banks but arrive at a similar qualitative picture for 1980–94.

2 Dall'Acqua (1997, 80).

3 A World Bank discussion paper (Morris, Dorfman, Ortiz, and Franco 1990) states that "Brazil is probably the Latin American country which uses directed credit to the largest extent. It is also among the countries in the developing world which make more use of these programs and may even be the largest."

4 See Morris et al. (1990).

5 The Conference Board's Total Economy Database (TED), November 2018 version, reports a slightly worse performance, from 33 percent to 26 percent. A third data series, Penn World Table (PWT) version 9.0 (see Feenstra, Inklaar, and Timmer 2015), actually reports an improvement in Brazil's output per worker relative to the United States from 1995 until 2014. The data in the PWT imply a growth rate of 22.9 percent for Brazil's GDP in 1995–96, whereas the other two sources report more reasonable growth rates: 2 percent (World Bank) and 0.02 percent (TED). This single data point explains three-quarters of the difference in output per worker between the PWT and the other sources.

6 The role of TFP in depressing the relative performance of Brazil's output per worker is not a recent phenomenon. Ferreira and Veloso (2015) estimate that in 1990, TFP differences explained more than half the difference in output per worker between Brazil and United States.

7 Arias et al. (2017, 2), using data from Instituto Brasileiro de Geografia e Estatistica, the Brazilian Institute of Geography and Statistics.

8 Arias, Vieira, Contini, Farinelli, and Morris (2017, 7).

References

Arias, Diego, Pedro Abel Vieira, Eliseo Contini, Barbara Farinelli, and Michael Morris. 2017. *Agriculture Productivity Growth in Brazil: Recent Trends and Future Prospects.* Washington, DC: World Bank Group.

Carvalho, Carlos E. 2003. *Bancos e infla cão no Brasil: Da crise dos anos 80 ao plano real.* ABPHE, Associação Brasileira de Pesquisadores em História Econômica (Brazilian Economic History Society), São Paulo.

Cysne, Rubens P., and Paulo C. Lisbôa. 2007. "Imposto inflacionário e transferências inflacionárias no brasil: 1947–2003." *Estudos economicos* 37 (2): 275–91.

Dall'Acqua, Fernando M. 1997. "The State Banks Crisis: The Banespa Case." Technical report, EAESP/FGV/NPP—Núcleo de pesquisas e publica cões, São Paulo.

Feenstra, Robert C., Robert Inklaar, and Marcel Timmer. 2015. "The Next Generation of the Penn World Table." *American Economic Review* 105 (10): 3150–82.

Ferreira, Pedro C., and Fernando A. Veloso. 2015. "O desenvolvimento econômico brasileiro no pós-guerra." Technical report, Fundação Getulio Vargas, Rio de Janeiro.

Gasques, Jorge G., Eliana T. Bastos, Constanza Valdes, and Mirian Rumenos P. Bacchi. 2012. "Produtividade da agricultura brasileira e os efeitos de algumas politicas." *Revista de politica agricola* 21 (3): 83–92.

Morris, Felipe, Mark Dorfman, Jose P. Ortiz, and Maria C. Franco. 1990. *Latin America's Banking Systems in the 1980s: A Cross-country Comparison.* World Bank Discussion Paper No. 81. Washington, D.C.: World Bank Group. http://documents.worldbank .org/curated/en/861371468756991253/Latin -Americas-banking-systems-in-the-1980s-a -cross-country-comparison.

Yoshino, Joe A. 1993. "Money and Banking Regulation: The Welfare Costs of Inflation." PhD diss., University of Chicago, Chicago.

Discussion of the History of Brazil 2

Teresa Ter-Minassian
International Economic Consultant

I would like to thank the organizers of this volume for inviting me to comment on the interesting chapter by Garcia et al. on the fiscal and monetary history of Brazil, 1960–2016.

The chapter covers a long period (more than fifty years) of Brazil's macroeconomic performance, seeking to trace the main causes of its persistently high rates of inflation and the reasons for the failure of various attempts to tame it, until the successful Real Plan of 1994–95. It then discusses how the plan succeeded in achieving sustained disinflation by breaking the inflation inertia due to pervasive indexation mechanisms and ending the prolonged passive stance of monetary policy by strengthening the institutional framework for the conduct of this policy.

I broadly agree with most of the analysis in the chapter; therefore, I will concentrate my remarks on a few areas in which I differ somewhat from it. I will start by noting that, while the Real Plan did indeed represent a major turning point in the conduct of macroeconomic policies in Brazil, it fell short of optimal in a number of respects. The years between its adoption and the end of the century (1995–98) witnessed a significant real appreciation of the exchange rate and related weakening of Brazil's external accounts, a progressive easing of monetary policy, and most importantly, inadequate fiscal adjustment.

Public finances deteriorated significantly during that period, as the growth of real spending, no longer eroded by high inflation, significantly outpaced that of revenues. The primary balance of the consolidated public sector deteriorated significantly, moving into deficit. The overall deficit narrowed initially, reflecting a sharp decline in nominal interest rates, but worsened subsequently, and the public debt rose by nearly 10 percentage points of GDP. To be sure, important structural fiscal reforms were undertaken during those years, including the restructuring of subnational debts and the de-earmarking of a significant portion of revenues (the Fundo de Emergencia Social mentioned in the chapter), but they were insufficient to stem the deterioration in the fiscal accounts.

The substantial weakening of the external accounts, in an international context marked by the Asian and Russian crises, ultimately forced the adoption in early 1999 of a strong adjustment program, supported by large external International Monetary Fund and bilateral official financing. The program included the floating of the real, a substantial tightening of monetary policy and the adoption of inflation targeting, and a range of revenue-raising and public expenditure containment measures. As a result, the primary balance moved into a significant surplus (around 3 percent of GDP), the nominal deficit was substantially reduced, and the growth of the public debt decelerated. Further, the institutional fiscal architecture was much strengthened by the adoption in 2000 of the Fiscal Responsibility Law.

While the fiscal adjustment was substantial and ushered in a prolonged period of significant primary surpluses, I would argue that it remained inadequate in terms of quality and sustainability. It relied mainly on increases in revenue, partly reflecting the adoption of distortive taxes, such as a financial transactions tax, and partly due to cyclical factors related to the commodity price boom of the first half of the 2000s. Spending continued to rise, reflecting increases in public employment and wages, and especially the growth of entitlement programs, as a result of the failure to adopt needed pension reforms.

The fiscal position started to steadily deteriorate in the aftermath of the global financial crisis, first reflecting strong stimulus measures and then a continued expansionary stance, even as the economy quickly recovered from the crisis. Between 2008 and 2016, the public sector's primary balance went from a surplus of 3.3 percent of GDP to a deficit of 2.5 percent of GDP, and the gross public debt rose to 75 percent of GDP. Furthermore, the deterioration during that period was partly masked by accounting stratagems and one-off operations of various sorts, including the use of financial and nonfinancial state-owned enterprises for quasi-fiscal purposes.

The sustained lack of fiscal adjustment has had a number of costs; in particular, it has necessitated the maintenance of high real interest rates and repeated tightening of credit conditions, with an adverse impact on domestic demand, especially in private investment. The failure to adopt needed structural reforms in taxation, pension systems, public expenditure management, and intergovernmental fiscal relations has also led to a compression of public investments and a further deterioration of the country's already inadequate infrastructure, with adverse effects on productivity and growth.

The roots of Brazil's fiscal malaise are deep and extensive and reflect distributive conflicts that the current political system appears unable to resolve. I would agree with the chapter's conclusion that the fiscal challenge facing the next administration "will have to be tackled, or the Real Plan will pass to history as a long noninflationary interregnum." Let us hope that the new government that took office in early 2019 will be able to muster the political consensus needed to effectively tackle the challenge.

Chile

The History of Chile

Rodrigo Caputo
Centre for Experimental Social Sciences, University
of Oxford and Universidad de Santiago

Diego Saravia
Central Bank of Chile

Major fiscal and monetary events, 1960–2017

1962 Balance of payments crisis	**1989** Central Bank independence
1966 Moderate success in inflation stabilization	**1990** Stabilization plan based on exchange rate bands and declining inflation targets
1973 Hyperinflation	
1975 Recession	**1999** Abandonment of exchange rate band
1979 Fixed exchange rate to stabilize inflation	Establishment of inflation targeting
1981 Inflation stabilized to one-digit levels	**2001** Fiscal rule, "Ley de responsabilidad fiscal"
1982 Balance of payments crisis Abandonment of fixed exchange rate regime	**2006** Creation of the Pension Reserve Fund
1983 First debt restructuring episode	**2007** Creation of the Economic and Social Stabilization Fund to substitute the CSF
1985 Treasury transfers to Central Bank due to operational losses	
1987 Creation of the Copper Stabilization Fund (CSF)	

Introduction

Thirty years ago, when referring to the study of the economic history of Chile, Edwards and Cox Edwards (1987) asserted that "the study of Chile's modern economic history usually generates a sense of excitement and sadness. Excitement, because from 1945 to 1983 Chile has been a social laboratory of sorts, where almost every possible type of economic policy has been experimented. Sadness, because to a large extent all these experiments have ended up in failure and frustration." Today, when analyzing the recent economic history of Chile, we still share this sense of excitement: many economic policies, new to the country, have been adopted since then. However, we do not have a sense of sadness, mainly because the economy has been on a stable economic path for the last three decades.[1] Of course, the Chilean economy today faces substantial challenges, and looking into the past may be useful for designing efficient policies and avoiding costly mistakes. In this chapter, we review the economic history of Chile from 1960 to 2017 in order to understand the role of monetary, fiscal, and debt management policies in determining the macroeconomic outcomes in Chile.

In terms of growth, inflation, and fiscal deficits (Figures 1 to 3), we are able to identify four different phases that are homogeneous in terms of outcomes and policies. The first, from 1960 to 1973, is characterized by a very stable growth path: GDP per capita grew around 2 percent a year, with a minor contraction in 1965 (see Figure 1). In this phase, per capita GDP did not deviate significantly from a predetermined trend. In terms of inflation, this phase is characterized by high and persistent inflation rates, as shown in Figure 2. On average, annual inflation was 30 percent, although it increased to 100 percent in 1972. This was not a new phenomenon: inflation had a long history in Chile, becoming entrenched during and after the 1930s.[2] In terms of fiscal policy, this period was characterized by systematic—and mild—fiscal deficits, as shown in Figure 3. Until 1970, these deficits were relatively small: on average, 2 percent of GDP. This trend was broken in 1971 and 1972, years in which fiscal deficits reached 8 percent and 12 percent of GDP, respectively. As with inflation, the existence of mild fiscal deficits was a persistent feature of the Chilean economy, but the figures in 1971 and 1972 were, even for Chilean standards, very high.

The second phase goes from 1974 to 1981 and is characterized by great real and nominal instability. As shown in Figure 1, there is a pronounced bust-boom cycle in which per

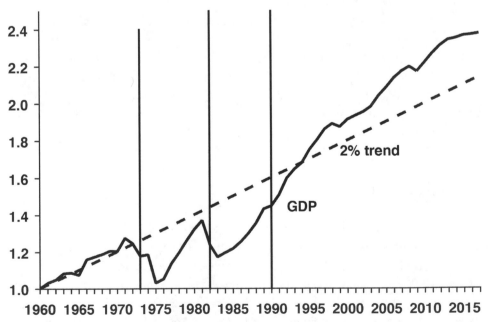

Figure 1. Log of per capita GDP (1960–2017)

Sources: World Bank, Central Bank of Chile, https://www.bcentral.cl

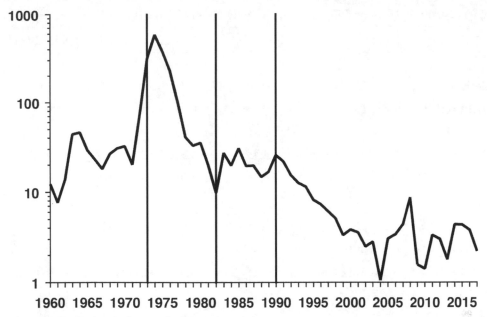

Figure 2. Inflation in log-scale (1960–2017)
Source: Central Bank of Chile

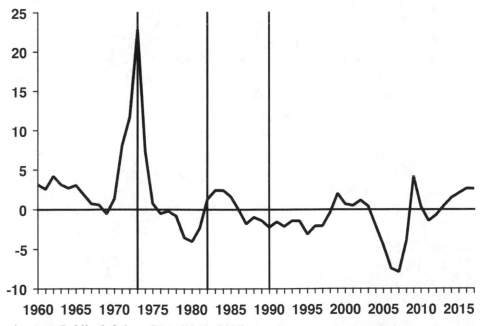

Figure 3. Public deficit to GDP (1960–2017)
Sources: DIPRES (Dirección de Presupuestos, Ministerio de Hacienda), Central Bank of Chile
Note: Includes the deficits of state-owned enterprises.

Table 1. Budget constraint decomposition, 1960–2016 (% of GDP)

Period	1960–73	1974–81	1982–90	1991–2016
Sources				
External debt	0.64	0.33	−0.99	−0.03
Domestic debt (CLP + indexed)	0.23	−0.21	0.16	0.60
Domestic debt (US$)	−0.26	0.36	1.65	−0.69
Seigniorage	4.43	4.53	0.49	0.52
Total	5.04	5.01	1.32	0.40
Obligations				
External debt interest payment	−0.93	0.78	0.63	0.04
Domestic debt interest payment (CLP)	−0.89	−1.35	−2.14	−0.12
Domestic debt interest payment (US$)	−0.25	−0.53	0.26	0.09
Primary deficit	3.44	−0.58	−1.28	−2.11
Partial total	1.37	−1.69	−2.52	−2.10
Implicit transfers (residuals)	3.67	6.70	3.83	2.50
Total	5.04	5.01	1.32	0.40

capita GDP declined in 1975 by almost 30 percent, relative to the predetermined trend. Then it recovered over a period of five years so that by 1981 per capita GDP was almost back to the trend level. In terms of inflation, this period witnessed the exacerbation of inflationary pressures of the previous phase. In 1973 inflation reached 400 percent, and in 1974, after price controls were removed, it reached 600 percent. This was the highest inflation level ever reached in the history of the country. Inflation declined slowly. By 1981 it had reached 20 percent in a context in which the exchange rate was fixed. The fiscal deficit continued to increase from the previous phase: by 1973 it had reached an unprecedented level of 23 percent of GDP.[3] From 1974 onward, an important fiscal adjustment took place. Despite this fact, inflation remained relatively high until the last years of this phase.

The third phase, from 1982 to 1990, is again a severe bust-boom cycle episode. This phase, however, has two features that are different from the previous episode. The first is that the fiscal discipline, implemented in the mid-1970s, was still present for most of the time. As shown in Figure 3, in this phase the fiscal deficit was almost zero: 0.1 percent of GDP on average. The second difference is that inflation increased substantially but did not return to the hyperinflation levels of the early 1970s. As shown in Figure 2, inflation increased from 10 percent in 1982 to 27 percent in 1983. It remained at this level during the whole period. Overall, the main feature of this phase is the deep and long recession that affected the economy. In particular, as a result of the severe balance of payments crisis of the early 1980s, real per capita GDP declined by 20 percent between 1981 and

1983, as shown in Figure 1. Then, it gradually recovered so that in 1990 per capita GDP was at the same level as in 1981.

The last phase goes from 1991 to 2017. This period marks the beginning of a disinflation process that was never reverted and that was unprecedented in Chile. It is the longest period with single-digit inflation rates. As shown in Figure 2, inflation was 22 percent in 1991 and declined gradually to 3.5 percent in 2001. Ten years later, in 2011, inflation was at the same level: 3.3 percent. By 2017 inflation was 2.2 percent. In terms of economic growth, this period is characterized by systematic increases in real per capita GDP each year (two exceptions are the mild contractions of 1999 and 2009). As shown in Figure 1, per capita GDP almost doubled between 1991 and 2017. Also, since 1994 this variable has been growing above the 2 percent trend. Today real per capita GDP is 24 percent higher than the level implicit in the constant trend line. In terms of fiscal behavior, as is clear from Figure 3, the fiscal discipline of the previous decades was maintained: on average, there was a fiscal surplus of 0.9 percent of GDP.

To understand the role of different policies in each of the four phases, we describe the main macroeconomic developments and discuss the policies implemented and the limitations, or unexpected consequences, they may have induced. Of course, because of the length of the chapter, not all developments can be described in detail. When appropriate, we use the contributions in the literature to explain developments observed in the data. In the analysis of the different periods, we use the fiscal budget constraint as described in this volume's "A Framework for Studying the Monetary and Fiscal History of Latin America" as the common conceptual framework. This approach allows us to associate the sources and uses of funds and to relate them to economic outcomes, such as inflationary episodes, for example.

Macroeconomic, Debt Evolution, and Fiscal Adjustment in Chile: 1960–2016

Over the past sixty years, Chile experienced radical economic changes and witnessed real and nominal instability. Policies shifted from an import-substitution strategy, adopted by many Latin American economies in the 1940s, to market-oriented policies, in which the role of the state, as both producer and regulator, greatly diminished. In this period, Chile presented a scenario of a wide range of economic policies and economic outcomes. It experienced almost all definitions of inflation, from moderate to hyperinflation. It had periods of high fiscal deficits and periods of fiscal surpluses, balance of payments crises, banking crises, and successful and unsuccessful stabilization plans, as well as severe economic recessions in the 1970s and 1980s. In political terms, changes were drastic: after a relatively long period of democracy since 1925, the military seized power in 1973, overthrowing Salvador Allende, an elected socialist president. Democracy was recovered in 1990, and since then, seven elected presidents have been in office.

Before discussing in detail the four phases that characterize the Chilean economy, we present the fiscal budget constraint decomposition in Table 1. As stressed in

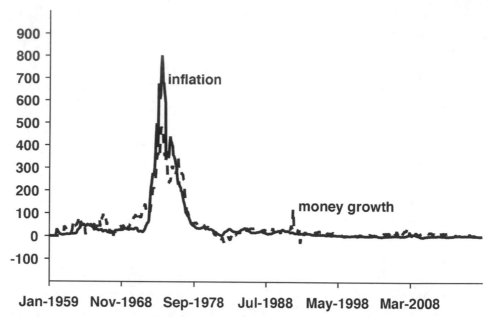

Figure 4. High-powered money growth and consumer price index (CPI) inflation (annual rates)

Sources: National Statistics Institute of Chile, Schmidt-Hebbel and Marshall (1981), Central Bank of Chile, https://www.bcentral.cl

"A Framework for Studying the Monetary and Fiscal History of Latin America," it considers the sources of fiscal financing: external debt, domestic debt, and seigniorage. The table also takes into account the main fiscal obligations: interest payments and the primary deficit. Both sources and obligations can change as a consequence of specific policies; hence, movements in these variables could reflect *ex professo* policy innovations. Sources and obligations, however, may also change as a result of exogenous shocks unrelated to policy. For instance, a decline in foreign funding could trigger a fiscal adjustment, which is a response induced by exogenous shocks rather than an explicit fiscal action. Now, we are able to compute independent measures of all components of the budget constraint. As a result, total sources and obligations will not necessarily coincide at any point in time.

The difference between the sources and obligations gives rise to the implicit transfer, which measures the excess or unrecorded spending in any given period (if positive), or it may reflect unaccounted income sources (taxes) when negative. In Table 1, we present sources, obligations, and implicit transfers. In general, periods of high volatility are associated with relatively high and positive implicit transfers. Figure 7 shows the implicit transfer as a percentage of GDP for every year in the period 1960 to 2016. Implicit transfers increase substantially in the early 1970s and the early 1980s. Both were periods of important macroeconomic volatility. In Figure 8 we present all the "off the books" measures that we could identify. As is clear, in different periods the implicit transfers play a role as an element that put pressure on the public finances. We can identify the

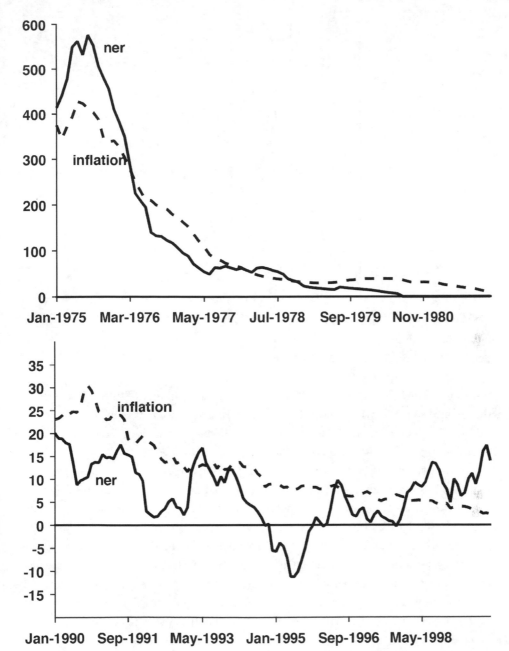

Figure 5. Stabilization phases: Inflation rates and rates of devaluation of nominal exchange rate (twelve-month rate of growth): top panel: 1975–81 (sample correlation: 0.96); bottom panel: 1990–99 (sample correlation: 0.41)

Source: Central Bank of Chile, https://www.bcentral.cl

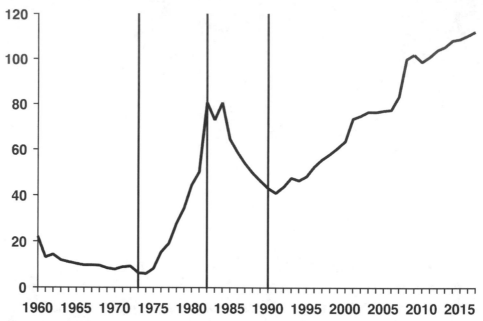

Figure 6. Credit to the private sector, percent of GDP (1960–2017)
Sources: World Bank, Central Bank of Chile, https://www.bcentral.cl

role of public deficits in the early 1970s or Treasury notes in the 1980s issued to rescue the private banks. We will describe in each period the determinants of the implicit transfers and to what extent they were the source of economic instability or a consequence of policy responses to attenuate exogenous shocks.

The role of public debt is also crucial to determine the magnitude and sources of implicit transfers. As seen in Figure 9, public total debt increased substantially in the early 1970s and early 1980s. This correlation does not necessarily reflect causation, as it may be driven by exogenous shocks. For instance, the exchange rate depreciation in the mid-1970s determined an increase in the ratio of external public debt to GDP; however, if we fix the exchange rate level and generate a counterfactual path for the external debt (see Figure 10), we can see that the increase in the debt position of the government is driven not only by policy decisions but also by exogenous shocks. Public debt is also influenced by the implicit transfers, as these represent a liability; they increase the debtor position of the government. To illustrate this point, in Figure 11 we present an exercise in which the level of implicit transfers, denoted τ_t in "A Framework for Studying the Monetary and Fiscal History of Latin America," is kept to zero in each period. As is clear, in this counterfactual scenario, the debt position of the government could have been substantially lower, especially in the 1960s and 1970s.

Now, we describe in more detail the main features that characterize each of the four phases. The 1960s was a period of relatively high inflation with mild fiscal deficits. The persistent inflation in the 1960s was, as in the previous periods of Chilean history, closely related to fiscal deficits and wage indexation. The beginning of the 1970s was a period of socialist reforms. In this period, fiscal deficits increased substantially and were financed by money issuance. As a consequence, the high inflation episodes of the previous decades

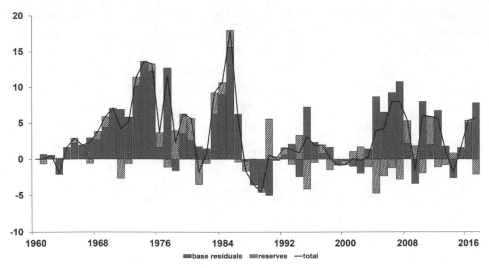

Figure 7. Budget constraint: Baseline scenario, percent of GDP

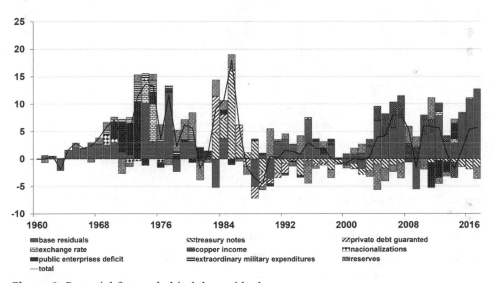

Figure 8. Potential factors behind the residuals

turned to hyperinflation. We think that in this first period, from 1960 to 1973, the main policy mistake was to rely on inflation taxes to finance an ambitious fiscal policy expansion that turned out to be unsustainable, because in the end the base over which the inflation tax was obtained (money) was reduced significantly during hyperinflation periods.

In the mid-1970s, market-oriented reforms were followed, and a period of fiscal adjustment began. The reduction of inflation was relatively slow in the second half of the 1970s, and a stabilization plan, based on fixing the nominal exchange rate, was implemented in 1978. This policy coincided with the opening of the capital account and the expansion of the financial sector. Credit was intermediated by private banks to households. Those credits were, in large proportion, denominated in foreign currency. Also, they were provided by foreigners through the local financial system. In this context, there was an increase in private absorption financed by banks. Eventually, the fixed exchange rate regime was abandoned, and the balance of payments crisis turned into a banking crisis: the private sector was unable to pay credits denominated in foreign currency once the devaluation materialized. In this context, the government and the central bank intervened in order to rescue the private sector. We should stress that this crisis was not generated by excessive fiscal deficits. In fact, the fiscal authority was able, from 1974 until today, to generate mild fiscal deficits and, in many cases, substantial fiscal surpluses. We think that a crucial policy mistake in this case was in the sequence of policy reforms. In particular, fixing the exchange rate indeed successfully stabilized inflation. The problem was to fix the exchange rate at the same time as the economy was completely open to foreign capital flows intermediated by the financial system.

The policy efforts after the financial crisis were concentrated on putting the country back on the growth path and fortifying the financial system. The contraction of GDP in 1982 and 1983 was severe, as shown in Figure 1. The main focus of the policies implemented soon after this recession was on solving the balance of payments crisis along with the financial crisis. To that end, the fiscal authority and the central bank designed a program to rescue the private banks. In this context, the central government implemented austerity measures with two objectives in mind: to prevent an increase in the fiscal deficit and to be able to support the rescue plans of the private sector. These austerity measures were difficult to implement and, of course, were very unpopular. In the end, however, these painful measures worked. In particular, from 1984 to 1990, the rate of growth in per capita output was positive and employment recovered. The emphasis on controlling inflation was diminished, and from 1984 to 1990, inflation was much higher than in 1982, when it reached single-digit values. Despite this fact, inflation was relatively stable and below the hyperinflation levels of the early 1970s.

In 1990 per capita GDP was already above, by 12 percent, the level of 1981. The economy was growing in a stable way, although inflation problems persisted. The central bank was granted independence in 1989, and from the early 1990s, it pursued an inflation-targeting regime. This regime was implemented even though there was, for most of the 1990s, an exchange rate band. The inflation target was set each year for the year-on-year inflation of the end of the year (December). The target was slowly declining from 1990 until 1999. In that year, Chile adopted a flexible exchange rate, and a full-fledged inflation-targeting regime was implemented. Specifically, since that year the central bank has set an inflation target of 3 percent, with a tolerance range of 1 percent (above or below), with the objective of anchoring market expectations in a two-year horizon. Also, since 1999 the fiscal authority has followed a structural balance fiscal rule, which despite many changes is countercyclical.

Now, there is a view among some economists, such as Calvo and Mendoza (1998), that the exchange rate appreciation helped stabilize inflation during the 1990s. We tend to disagree with this hypothesis and believe, as shown by Valdés (1998), that the nominal anchor from 1991 to 1999 was indeed the declining inflation target announced by the central bank. We will provide some evidence of the joint behavior of inflation and exchange rate that supports this hypothesis.

Slow Growth, Public Deficits, and Inflation: 1960–73

In the 1940s, Chile, as well as many Latin American economies, adopted an industrialization process based on import substitution. The idea was to promote the development of a domestic industrial sector. This, in turn, could be achieved if those industries were granted a high degree of protection in the form of import tariffs and quotas. The protection was supposed to be only a temporary measure. Protectionism, however, became a permanent feature of the Chilean economy. During the 1950s and early 1960s, this strategy began to run out of steam.[4]

During the 1960s, the fiscal authority mainly had access to foreign debt, which increased from 10 percent of GDP in 1960 to 22 percent in 1969. Internal public debt, on the other hand, was at 7 percent of GDP on average, well below the level it reached in subsequent years (Figure 9). Inflation was in general high, although below the hyperinflation levels reached in the mid-1970s (see Figure 4). It moved from 45 percent in 1963 to 30 percent in 1969 (see Figure 2).

Chile experienced high inflation levels starting in the 1940s, although during the 1950s this became a serious problem. In an effort to tackle this problem, in July 1955 the government hired the Klein-Saks consulting firm to provide technical advice regarding anti-inflationary policy. The mission's diagnosis of Chile's inflationary pressures

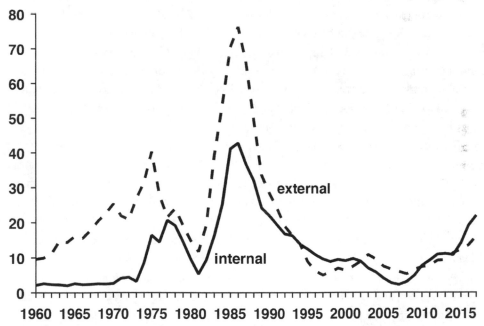

Figure 9. Public internal and external debt, percent of GDP
Sources: Central Bank of Chile (2002); Central Bank of Chile, "Chilean External Debt" (1977–2014); Central Bank of Chile, https://www.bcentral.cl; General Comptroller Republic of Chile, annual memories and annual Financial Management of the Public Sector Report; General Treasury of the Republic of Chile. Details on all of the data used in this chapter can be found in the online data appendix at http://manifold.bfi.uchicago.edu/.

revolved around four basic areas: (1) fiscal deficit, (2) monetary expansion, (3) exchange rate policy, and (4) wage rate policy. In addition, the mission forcefully argued that the state of government finances and, in particular, the extremely high fiscal deficit were at the heart of the inflationary process (Edwards 2007). In this context, when Jorge Alessandri was elected in September 1958, an inflationary stabilization policy was implemented. This policy consisted of reducing the fiscal deficit and fixing the nominal exchange rate to the dollar. The fixed exchange rate lasted until 1962, when a balance of payments crisis took place (this and 1979–82 are the only two periods of fixed exchange rates in the whole period of analysis; a short attempt took place in 1970). During 1959, the first year of Alessandri's government, the fiscal deficit, which averaged 2 percent of GDP in the previous administration, was drastically reduced and reverted. In that year, the government was able to generate a fiscal surplus of 1.6 percent of GDP. Besides the fiscal adjustment, Alessandri's administration pushed for (and succeeded in getting) wage adjustments that were well below past inflation. In particular, in 1960 wages increased by 10 percent, even though past (1959) inflation was 33 percent. These elements contributed to anchoring inflation expectations and increased the credibility of the stabilization plan. In 1960 and 1961, inflation declined to single digits: 5.5 percent and 9.6 percent, respectively.

The stabilization plan was apparently a success. The low level of inflation, however, was not going to last. In 1960 and 1962, the fiscal deficit increased to nearly 3 percent of GDP. At the same time, a balance of payments crisis took place in 1961 and 1962, inducing the abandonment of the fixed exchange rate, and the nominal exchange rate depreciated 33 percent in October 1962. Soon after the nominal depreciation, prices increased substantially. Inflation increased to 27.7 percent in 1962 (mostly explained by events during the last quarter), 45.3 percent in 1963, and 38.5 percent in 1964. Hence, inflation returned to its historical levels, with a fiscal deficit that, though not exorbitant, seemed to constitute a source of inflationary pressures in a context when fiscal debt was a stable proportion of GDP (around 3 percent).

Now, using the budget constraint in "A Framework for Studying the Monetary and Fiscal History of Latin America," we conclude that financing needs during Alessandri's administration were, on average, 2.68 percent of GDP. In the 1961–64 period, primary fiscal deficits constituted the main fiscal obligation. These deficits, representing 3.20 percent of GDP, were financed mainly by seigniorage (2.21 percent of GDP) and to a lesser extent by external debt (0.87 percent of GDP). Transfers, computed as residual, represented a very small proportion of overall financing needs: 0.24 percent of GDP. As can be seen in Figure 7, extraordinary transfers (which are calculated as the residual term of the budget constraint in "A Framework for Studying the Monetary and Fiscal History of Latin America") were close to zero during Alessandri's administration.

Overall, during Alessandri's administration, the modest contribution of external and internal debt to finance the public deficit generated a close link between public deficits, seigniorage, and inflation. Accordingly, the roots of inflation in that period could be traced back to persistent fiscal deficits, as was the case in the previous administrations.

Eduardo Frei was elected with 56 percent of the vote and took office in November 1964. The government's main economic focus was the implementation of basic structural changes, such as the land reform process and the Chilean participation in the owner-ship of the big copper mines. These reforms were slowly implemented in order to avoid impairing macrostability. There was a certain perception that structural reforms could generate short-run disequilibrium; hence, when there was an accumulation of inflationary pressures, priority was to be given to the restoration of macrostability.

Frei's program was, in terms of social policies, quite ambitious. The public sector was given a more active role in improving income distribution and increasing the investment capacity of the economy. Some of the goals of Frei's program were to increase real wages in the public sector, government expenditure in social areas (education and health, among others), and public investment in infrastructure and housing first, and then in other sec-tors of the economy. Public investment was expected to be financed by an increase in income taxes and more foreign debt.

In macroeconomic terms, Frei's administration faced significant challenges. One of them was to stabilize inflation from a level of 40 percent in 1964. The stabilization plan was to be gradual: the government expected to bring inflation down to 25 percent, 15 percent, and 10 percent in each of the first three years in office (Ffrench-Davis 1973). During the admin-istration's first year in office, 1965, inflation declined to 25 percent, and in 1966 inflation declined further, to 17 percent. The fiscal deficit was reduced to 1.5 percent of GDP in 1966 and continued to adjust in the following years. This occurred in a context in which GDP growth was, on average, 6 percent in 1965 and 1966. The stabilization program was, at least until 1967, successful. Two elements determined that, after 1967, the stabilization plan was no longer viable. First, although the fiscal authority increased its savings (the fiscal deficit declined significantly) and investment, the national level of investment did not increase enough. Second, wages adjusted much more than was initially expected. During these years, the exchange rate policy followed was of minidevaluations to prevent real exchange rate appreciation. These elements put upward pressure on inflation, which began to increase from 21.9 percent in 1967 to 34.9 percent in 1970, the last year of the administration.

During Frei's administration, financing sources increased, on average, to 4.52 percent of GDP. Compared with the previous government, the availability of foreign debt more than doubled, representing 2.13 percent of GDP, and the availability of domestic debt followed a similar increasing pattern. Frei's administration could not stabilize inflation, particularly at the end of this government period. On average, inflation was 25 percent, almost the same figure that prevailed during Alessandri's administration (see Figure 2). In this context, it is not surprising that seigniorage under Frei's and Alessandri's admin-istrations was nearly identical: 2.19 percent of GDP.

In terms of obligations, in this period there was a significant decline in the primary deficit, which moved from 3.2 percent of GDP during Alessandri's administration to 0.90 percent in Frei's administration. This decline in obligations, coupled with a sharp increase in funding sources, determined an increase in extraordinary transfers, τ_t, which on average represented 3.99 percent of GDP. As can be seen in Figure 7, these transfers increased systematically from 1965 to 1970.

Now, in order to identify the nature of the extraordinary transfers, we compute addi-tional obligations, not accounted in the central government primary deficit, taken during this administration. As seen in Figure 8, reserve accumulation, expenditures related to nationalizations, and the financing of public enterprise deficits could explain an important fraction of the extraordinary transfers, especially at the end of Frei's administration. In particular, reserve accumulation represents, on average, 0.8 percent of GDP in this period. Nationalizations and the financing of public enterprise deficits represent 0.42 percent and 0.53 percent of GDP, respectively, in the same period.

As documented in Reinhart and Rogoff (2009) and related to the balance of payments crises, during the 1960s three external debt restructuring episodes occurred. Those were implemented through International Monetary Fund programs in 1961 and in 1963 to 1965. They may explain the fact that in the first half of the 1960s, the external sources of funding were not very important (less than 1 percent of GDP).

The beginning of the 1970s was a period of great political instability: three years of a socialist government ended in 1973 with a military coup that put the armed forces into power until 1990. Even though different economic policies were implemented under each government, some economic problems were long-lasting. This decade witnessed high inflation, deep contractions in output (1972, 1973, and 1975), and high unemployment.

THE SOCIALIST EXPERIENCE: 1970–73

In September 1970, Allende was elected with 37 percent of the vote and took office in November 1970. His economic program was characterized by several left-wing-oriented structural reforms, including the nationalization of the banking sector and most industries. In terms of fiscal policy, an aggressive expansion of government spending generated an unprecedented increase in the public deficit.

An essential assumption of the economic program was that, in 1970, there was substantial underutilized capital capacity in the manufacturing sector. In this context, it was expected that an increase in aggregate demand could be accommodated without generating inflationary pressures in the short run. As a result, in 1971 an aggressive expansionary fiscal policy was implemented. The fiscal deficit, as a percentage of GDP, rose from 0.5 percent in 1970 to 7.3 percent in 1971, whereas nominal growth of high-powered money increased from 66 percent in 1970 to 136 percent in 1971. Not surprisingly, aggregate demand grew at double-digit rates—10.5 percent in 1971—while real GDP experienced an expansion of 9.4 percent with an important decline in the unemployment rate to 3.9 percent. In the first year of Allende's government, prices did not increase substantially. This fact is attributed to the existence of price controls as well as commodity and factor market rationing.[5]

The output expansion of 1971 was not to be sustained in the following years. In 1972, the fiscal deficit increased further, to 11.4 percent of GDP. The rate of growth of high-powered money was 178 percent, and prices, despite the official controls, could not be contained: inflation reached almost 255 percent on an annual basis.[6] In terms of real activity, a particularly serious problem evolved around the de facto process of expropriations of manufacturing firms implemented by Allende's administration. In particular, government interventions were usually preceded by long labor strikes and seizures of the firms' installations by their workers that generated significant output losses. In October 1972, a national strike generated a further decline in activity.[7] In 1972 real output declined by 1.2 percent, and the trade deficit reached 3.5 percent of GDP. In 1973, the economic crisis deepened. During that year, the fiscal deficit almost doubled, reaching 23 percent of GDP, the highest level experienced in the previous forty years (see Figure 3). At the same time, the signs were clear that the inflationary process was tending toward hyper-inflation. In 1973, inflation reached 433 percent on average, whereas the rate of monetary growth was 365 percent (see Figure 4).

The expansionary policies caused a progressive deterioration of the current account deficit, which was 3 percent on average in the 1971–73 period. In this context, the government used the large foreign reserves it had inherited from the previous administration to finance those deficits. As a consequence, foreign reserves declined significantly during Allende's administration.

From 1971 to 1973, nominal and real volatility increased substantially. Three elements characterized this period: first, a sequence of increasing fiscal deficits; second, an important expansion of high-powered money; and, finally, an inflationary process that became a hyperinflation. To understand the correlation among the previous variables and fiscal debt strategies, we follow Sargent (2013), who develops a framework to analyze the inflationary consequences of government deficits and alternative ways of financing them.

To see the extent to which the budget constraint in "A Framework for Studying the Monetary and Fiscal History of Latin America" can be used to understand the period of nominal volatility in Chile, we first analyze the relationship between money and inflation. From November 1970 to April 1972, the annual growth rate of high-powered money increased from 82 percent to 108 percent without inflation experiencing any substantial change (see Figure 4). In fact, in April 1972 inflation was 55 percent, a level higher than the one experienced during the previous decade.[8] In May 1972, however, inflation increased substantially, and from that date until December 1979, inflation and monetary growth tended to move together.

In November 1971, the government declared a moratorium on its existing external debt. This event implies a default, which is reported to have happened in 1972, according to Reinhart and Rogoff (2009). This moratorium implied no more external financing for Chile. In this context, in the absence of enough funding, both domestic and foreign, to cover both the fiscal deficit and the interest rate payments on the debt, the government had to rely on seigniorage as a source of funding (see Figure 12). As is clear, between 1971 and 1974 the fiscal deficit and seigniorage moved in the same direction. Furthermore, in quantitative terms, the magnitude of the increase is quite similar, with the exception of 1973, during which the fiscal deficit of 22.5 percent exceeded the seigniorage level by 5 percent of GDP. The evolution of debt, on the other hand, suggests that Allende's government was unwilling (or unable) to increase domestic and foreign borrowing considerably. Between 1970 and 1973, foreign public debt was almost constant at US$2 million. This means that, as a percentage of GDP, external debt actually declined in those years (see Figure 9). On the other hand, domestic debt increased, as a percentage of GDP, from 2.6 percent in 1970 to 3.2 percent in 1973 (see Figure 1A in the online appendix available at http://manifold.bfi.uchicago.edu/). This increase was, of course, not enough to finance a fiscal deficit that went, during the same period, from 0.5 percent to 22.5 percent of GDP.

The evidence presented thus far indicates that fiscal deficits, which increased substantially between 1971 and 1973, could not be completely financed by additional public debt (domestic and foreign). As a consequence, seigniorage became the most important source of funds for the fiscal authority. The implication of this strategy was that inflation became, in the end, a fiscal phenomenon. The fiscal deficit was, by far, the most important component of obligations in the 1971–73 period, whereas the sources of funds were seigniorage and, to a smaller degree, an increase in domestic public debt (see Figure 2A in the online appendix available at http://manifold.bfi.uchicago.edu/).

We construct the path of obligations and sources for this period. In the 1971–73 period, financing needs, compared with those in the 1960s, increased substantially, mainly by the increased importance of fiscal deficits, which averaged 9.10 percent of GDP. These needs were covered mostly by seigniorage, which represented 12.9 percent of GDP in that period. The availability of external funding and domestic funding in U.S. dollars declined greatly during Allende's administration. Domestic debt in local currency increased, although it could finance a small fraction of overall fiscal needs (representing 0.9 percent of GDP). Transfers, τt, were around 7 percent of GDP during this period (see Figure 7).

In Figure 8 we present the potential factors behind the residuals of the budget constraint (i.e., the transfers). We do so by calculating the transfers implied by the budget constraint considering counterfactual exercises. In these particular years, we can see that the transfers calculated considering the public enterprise deficits are much lower than the ones without considering them.[9]

Thus during these years, the deficits of public enterprises are the key factor in explaining the extraordinary transfers. In particular, they represent on average 7.2 percent of GDP, which is roughly the same value of transfers in this period.[10]

In aggregate terms, the 1960–73 period is characterized by the existence of important fiscal deficits financed by seigniorage. This is especially true in the 1970–73 period, so the average deficit from 1960 to 1973 of 3.44 percent of GDP, the seigniorage of 4.43 percent, and the implicit transfers of 3.67 percent in Table 1 underestimate the values observed in Allende's government.

From Stabilization to Balance of Payments Crisis: 1974–81

The armed forces, led by General Augusto Pinochet, took power in September 1973 after a military coup overthrew President Allende. Under Pinochet's administration, several structural changes were carried out. In 1974, Chile followed a stabilization policy based on a reduction of the government's deficit (from 22.5 percent of GDP in 1973 to 0.4 percent in 1975) through the elimination of subsidies and the increase in taxes (value-added tax [VAT], among others), the reduction of public employment, and the reprivatization of public companies that were in a precarious financial situation and required the permanent support of public funds. The government liberalized prices that were regulated, including a gradual unification of the multiple exchange rates in place (up to six during Allende's government). Inflation continued at high levels; in April 1974 the inflation rate (measured as a year-on-year variation) increased to more than 700 percent, reflecting in part the behavior of liberalized prices.

The monetary base was increased at high but declining rates in the first years of Pinochet's government. In 1973, the rate of expansion in nominal terms was 365 percent, while it was 320 percent, 283 percent, and 272 percent in 1974, 1975, and 1976, respectively. The monetary base in real terms contracted in 1973 by 34 percent, while it contracted by 11 percent in 1974 and 14 percent in 1975. In 1976, this monetary growth rate in real terms returned to positive values by increasing 24 percent. These variations are indicative of a reduction in the real demand of money until 1976. The monetary base continued increasing in real terms at positive (but lower) rates until 1981, the year when the financial crisis began.

In 1975, a severe crisis hit the economy, and real output growth declined by 13 percent. The recession of 1975 was generated by several factors. First, an important decline in terms of trade took place at the end of 1974, with copper prices falling by about 50 percent in real terms and the price of oil rising by a factor of 4. Second, the fiscal adjustment undertaken, which reduced the fiscal deficit to 0.4 percent of GDP, had an adverse effect on aggregate demand, which in 1975 declined by 21 percent. Inflation did not decline substantially from the previous year: it was 343 percent in December 1975. Despite the

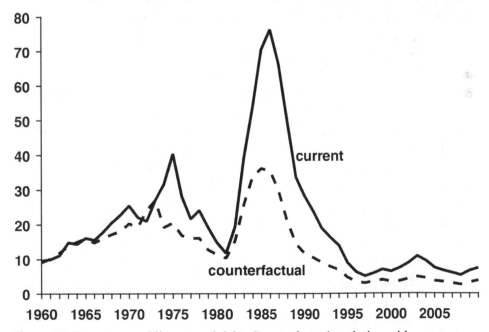

Figure 10. Long-term public external debt: Counterfactual evolution with constant real exchange rate at 1973, percent of GDP

Sources: Central Bank of Chile (2002); Central Bank of Chile, "Chilean External Debt" (1977–2014); Central Bank of Chile, https://www.bcentral.cl

recession, the reduction of fiscal deficits, the lower growth rate of the monetary base, and the openness of the economy, inflation continued to be high and erratic. This path was incorporated in inflation expectations. The economy was highly indexed; salaries and the exchange rate were indexed to past inflation.[11] This was the case until 1978, when the exchange rate followed a predetermined rate of devaluation in an effort to anchor inflation expectations and reduce inflation. This policy ended with a fixed exchange rate in June 1979. Between 1976 and June 1979, the reduction in inflation and the accumulation of reserves were the driving forces of monetary exchange rates and financial policies. It is likely that it took longer to reduce inflation because of the conflicting implications of policies directed at reducing inflation and increasing international reserves. In 1979 inflation, though not at the level of the early 1970s, was at double-digit levels: 39 percent at the end of 1979. Eventually, at the beginning of the 1980s, inflation was stabilized.

From 1974 to 1976, seigniorage was an important source of revenues, accounting for 7.4 percent of GDP on average in those years. Those revenue sources were important in a context in which the burden of foreign public debt increased. In particular, as a result of nominal exchange rate devaluations,[12] foreign public debt increased from 27 percent of GDP in 1973 to over 40 percent of GDP in 1975 (Figure 9). To assess the impact of the nominal devaluation on the public finances, we perform a counterfactual simulation of the foreign public debt. In particular, we allow the nominal rate to devalue, from 1973 onward, in a way in which the real exchange rate is constant at its 1973 level. In other words, we generate a counterfactual nominal exchange rate series that is adjusted by the inflation differential between Chile and its main trading partners. As shown in Figure 9, nominal devaluations between 1974 and 1975 increased the burden of public external debt by more than 20 percent of GDP. Nominal devaluations also increased the burden of domestic debt, which, after 1973, was denominated mainly in U.S. dollars (see Figure 1A in the online appendix available at http://manifold.bfi.uchicago.edu/).

To assess the impact of the devaluations on the external fiscal debt, we perform a counterfactual exercise in which we fix the level of the real exchange rate from 1974 onward and compute a counterfactual path for the nominal exchange rate according to the actual level of foreign prices and domestic inflation. As a result of this exercise, we obtain a counterfactual path for the evolution of debt. As shown in Figure 10, the devaluation of the exchange rate contributed to a significant increase in the external debt position of the fiscal authority.

From 1974 to 1981, the fiscal deficit was reduced substantially (Figure 3). This was determined by a combination of a sharp increase in fiscal revenues after 1974 and an important contraction in government expenditures (see Figures 3A and 4A in the online appendix available at http://manifold.bfi.uchicago.edu/). In the period 1974–81, there was a primary fiscal surplus of 0.6 percent of GDP. This determined that financial needs during that period declined significantly from those in the previous administration: 5.0 percent of GDP (Table 1). In this period, the country regained access to foreign financial markets, and as a consequence, both external debt interest payments (on average 0.8 percent of GDP) and external debt (0.3 percent of GDP) contributed as obligations and sources. In this period, and particularly between 1974 and 1981, inflation was at high levels and seigniorage was an important source of financing: 4.5 percent of GDP. Other sources of financing, external debt, and domestic debt denominated in U.S. dollars accounted for nearly 1 percent of GDP (Table 1).

The sharp contraction in fiscal deficits during this period, along with a positive source of financing, implied that transfers, τ_t, increased substantially from the previous administration. In particular, these transfers accounted for nearly 7 percent of GDP and were particularly important in 1974 and 1975 (Figure 7). Now, given that the real exchange rate depreciated substantially in 1974 and 1975, foreign debt could be contributing to the transfers' term in the budget constraint. To show the effects that the depreciations had on the transfers, we compute the contribution of foreign debt assuming that the nominal exchange rate between 1974 and 1975 evolves so as to keep the real exchange rate at the same level as the one observed in 1973. In this counterfactual scenario, transfers in 1974 and 1975 declined significantly. This can be seen in Figure 8, where the *exchange rate* bars in the years 1974 and 1975 refer to the transfer, assuming that the real exchange rate had been constant.

As discussed above, an objective of the government in the second half of the 1970s was to increase the level of reserves. Given that increases in the monetary base could be the consequence of this policy and that it would not have a correlation on the expenditure side of the budget constraint (thus affecting the transfers), we compare the increases in reserves as a share of output with the effective transfers that follow from the equation. As can be seen in Figure 8, the direction and size of the increase in reserves seem likely to have been important factors in the transfers in the years 1976, 1978, 1979, and 1980.

As a summary, we find that from 1974 to 1981, there was an important increase in seigniorage in a context in which the monetary base was still growing at high rates (although below the rate of growth reached in 1973). Given that fiscal deficits were drastically reduced, it follows that implicit transfers during this period were relatively large: on average, nearly 7 percent of GDP. Now we can identify two elements that could partially explain those residuals. First, the impact of large depreciations account for, on average, 1.34 percent of GDP in that period. Second, reserve accumulation, after the exchange rate was controlled (in 1978), could also explain an important fraction of transfers: 1.24 percent of GDP on average. Now, it is clear that, besides the elements just discussed, additional transfers may have contributed to the residuals. The unexplained fraction is relatively important in two specific years: 1974 and 1977. Two possible candidates could be related to contingent transfers associated with pension reforms,[13] to some fiscal expenses not explicitly stated in the central government budget, or to a combination of these. In this latter case, we follow Larraín (1991), Larraín and Vergara (2000), and Scheetz (1987), who provide information associated with defense expenses in the mid-1970s and contrast them with the ones provided by the fiscal authority. The difference between these two series, which is positive, is considered part of the transfers during the mid-1970s. As shown in Figure 8, that extra defense spending can account for a significant fraction of the transfers. On average, between 1974 and 1979, the unaccounted military expenses could represent 3 percent of GDP each year. One concern is that, given the existence of price controls from 1971 to 1973, the consumer price index could be underestimated (which in turn induces a seigniorage overestimation). To overcome this problem, we have used the CPI series computed by Schmidt-Hebbel and Marshall (1981), which aims to identify the true inflation rate. At least in the 1971 to 1973 period, seigniorage is used to fully finance the public enterprise deficits.

EXTERNAL FRAGILITY

In the context of a fixed exchange rate regime, the existence of wage and financial contract indexation to past inflation induced an important real appreciation. In fact, the real exchange rate declined from 92.1 in 1975 to 70.3 in 1979 and 60.9 in 1980. There is some consensus that the exchange rate policy and a domestic financial liberalization, carried out while the financial system was poorly regulated, were the main causes of the boom that developed between 1979 and 1981 and the severe recession that hit the economy in 1982–83.

The period between 1979 and 1981 was one of an economic boom with increasing consumption, investment, and asset prices financed by capital inflows intermediated by national banks. As shown in Figure 6, the credit to the private sector (intermediated mostly by financial institutions) increased by a factor of 14 between 1974 and 1982. In particular, this variable was 7 percent of GDP in 1974 and increased to 80 percent of GDP in 1982.

In addition to the expansion in credit, there was an increase in real wages, an indexation of salaries, and a reduction in taxes on labor. As a consequence, domestic demand expanded significantly: on average, it grew at 11 percent per year between 1979 and 1981. In the same period, the rate of growth in GDP was, on average, 7.8 percent. The widening gap between the rate of growth in GDP and aggregate demand generated persistent trade balance deficits that went from 1.7 percent of GDP in 1979 to 7.8 percent in 1981. Similarly, the current account deficit grew from 5.6 percent of GDP in 1979 to 14 percent in 1981. The behavior of the fiscal authority between 1979 and 1981 was very conservative. In fact, in that period there was on average a fiscal surplus of 4.1 percent of GDP. As is clear, private and public savings were moving in opposite directions. While the public sector was increasing its savings and reducing its debt (both external and domestic), the private sector was increasing its overall external debt (Figure 13).

After three years in which the exchange rate was fixed, inflation declined to single-digit numbers: 9.5 percent in 1981. The fact that the exchange rate was controlled helped explain the important decline in inflation. In particular, the nominal anchor of the economy was the nominal exchange rate. As shown in Figure 5, from 1975 to 1981 inflation and nominal devaluation, on a year-on-year basis, moved together. The contemporaneous correlation among these variables is high: 0.96. This behavior is determined by the introduction, in January of 1978, of a preannounced rate of devaluation, the so-called *tablita*. This system set the starting declining rate of devaluation at a lower level than ongoing inflation, with the aim of reducing inflation expectations and reducing actual inflation as long as the law of one price held. For instance, in 1978 the minister of finance, Sergio De Castro, announced that the rate of devaluation for 1978 had been determined at 21.4 percent and would decline further in the future. The *tablita* lasted until June 1979, when the nominal exchange rate was fixed.

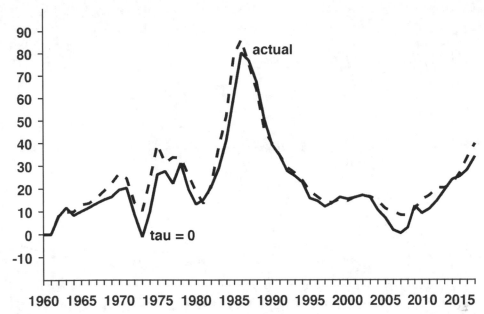

Figure 11. Counterfactual path for public debt, percent of GDP
Source: Authors' calculations

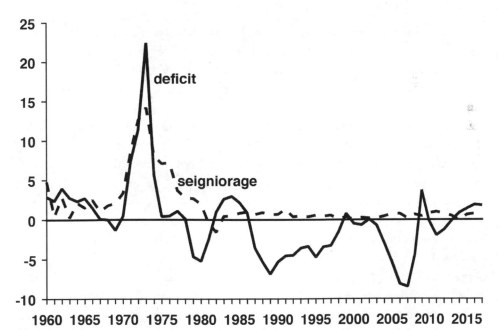

Figure 12. Seigniorage and public deficit, percent of GDP
Sources: Díaz, Lüders, and Wagner (2016); Central Bank of Chile (2002); DIPRES,
"Estado de Operaciones de Gobierno Central Total"; National Statistics Institute of Chile;
Schmidt-Hebbel and Marshall (1981)

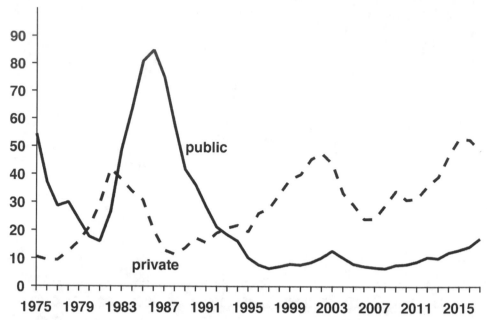

Figure 13. Public (with central bank) and private external debt, percent of GDP
Sources: Central Bank of Chile (2002); Central Bank of Chile, "Chilean External Debt" (1977–2014); Central Bank of Chile, https://www.bcentral.cl

The low inflation, however, was not going to last. Adverse external shocks—foreign capital reversals, an increase in international interest rates, and declining terms of trade—introduced some doubt regarding the sustainability of the fixed exchange rate policy. Once the exchange rate was devalued, there were no nominal variables to anchor inflation.

This business cycle related to a fixed exchange rate stabilization is documented in the literature. Kiguel and Liviatan (1990) note that the Chilean experience is shared by other countries with chronic inflation that stabilized inflation using the exchange rate as the nominal anchor. They note further that the response of the economy to such programs is an initial expansion of consumption and output, as well as appreciation of the real exchange rate, followed by a consumption and output contraction and by a depreciation of the real exchange rate. This business cycle behavior is rationalized by Calvo (1996), who argues that this is the consequence of the stabilization policy not being fully credible. If people think that the exchange rate will be abandoned in the future, they will increase consumption today to take advantage of the lower interest rates. In the context of some price stickiness, this produces an appreciation of the real exchange rate and a deterioration of the current account balance. In the Chilean case, a banking crisis also followed the abandonment of the fixed exchange rate. Velasco (1987) presents a model that explicitly includes a banking sector to study the interaction of macro and financial variables. In this economy, the fragility of the banking sector plus the government's (implicit) deposit guarantee plant the seeds of a crisis. The excessive rate of domestic credit creation does not come from a fiscal deficit, as in

Krugman (1979), but from the governmental commitment to guarantee the liabilities of the banking system.

In 1981 the world entered a recession, and Chile was hit by a negative terms of trade shock. Since the country had borrowed at floating rates, the interest rate rose, and by the end of that year, Chile was in recession. In June 1982, Chile had to abandon the fixed exchange rate, and in the following three months, the exchange rate went from 39 pesos to 63 pesos per U.S. dollar. After a period of instability that existed until August of that year, the exchange rate followed a crawling peg based on a purchasing power parity (PPP) rule, with some discrete and bigger devaluations (September 1984, 23 percent; in February and June 1985, 5 percent in each case). The initial devaluation increased the burden of foreign debt, deepening the financial crisis. Jointly with the abandonment of the fixed exchange rate, the compulsory wage indexation was eliminated. In 1982, the economy experienced a severe recession: output declined by 11 percent, and aggregate demand fell by 19 percent. Unemployment was nearly 20 percent, even after considering the emergency programs established by the government. The monetary base contracted in real terms by 15 percent in 1981 and by 41 percent in 1982 (in both years, the nominal monetary base also diminished). The stabilization plans of the late 1970s had failed.[14]

Saving the Banking System: The Fiscal Burden of the Debt Crisis (1982–90)

The crisis that followed the phase of economic euphoria described above put the banking system at severe risk. As noted previously, the main debtor with the rest of the world was the private sector. Between 1975 and 1982, the private foreign debt, as a percentage of GDP, increased from 10.5 percent to 41.8 percent. In the same period, the public external debt declined from 54.3 percent to less than 27 percent (see Figure 13). An important part of the private external debt was intermediated by domestic private banks, and a currency mismatch emerged in their balance sheets. The sharp depreciation of the peso, in the context of a severe recession, made many banks insolvent. They could not recover an important proportion of their credits and, as a consequence, were unable to repay their foreign loans.

In 1982 the Pinochet government approached the International Monetary Fund (IMF) in order to obtain financial assistance to service the foreign debt. Private banks were also approached, and a rescheduling of the foreign debt was proposed. A standby agreement with the IMF, which called for a new orthodox stabilization program, was signed. From the beginning of the debt crisis, the government developed a strategy of renegotiating the foreign debt, but with the declared goal of servicing it in full. The idea was to reestablish full access to international capital markets. As noted by Reinhart and Rogoff (2009), there were three debt restructuring episodes: in 1983, 1985, and 1989. In this context, Chile was not part of the "Brady bunch." In sharp contrast with other Latin American countries, default in Chile was never an option. The cost of this strategy was enormous and was borne by the fiscal authority and the central bank.[15]

To prevent widespread bankruptcies, the government introduced rescue programs, which were implemented, mainly, by the central bank.[16] As noted by Sanhueza (2001), the central bank undertook three sets of measures to save the banking system.

First, the central bank distributed subsidies to financial institutions in the form of contracts to buy foreign currency at a price below the market equilibrium (the so-called Dólar Preferencial program). Until September 1984, this subsidy corresponded to 17 percent of debt service and after that month was 35 percent until June 1985, when it ended. The losses of this program incurred by the central bank are estimated at US$2.4 billion.

Second, different debt restructuring programs were implemented to alleviate the situation of debtors. In August 1982, the central bank lent US$250 million directly to debtors to repay their debt with banks. In October of that year, the central bank issued money to buy long-term bonds from the banks, which used these funds to restructure their debt. In April 1983 and June 1984, two more debt restructuring programs were implemented. These last two programs did not imply an increase in the monetary base because central bank funds given to the banks had to be invested in central bank bonds, as required by the targets of the monetary programs agreed upon with the IMF.

Third, several private banks were liquidated, and the central bank provided the liquidity necessary to cover bank liabilities and expenses during the liquidation process. For financial institutions intervened and sold off between 1981 and 1982, the central bank provided special credit lines to pay off liabilities at 100 percent par value. Between 1982 and 1987, the central bank offered to buy part of commercial banks' and finance companies' risk portfolios, subject to an eventual buyback. The purpose of this measure was to avoid the insolvency of banks. The amount of these operations was the equivalent of 30 percent of the system's total outstanding loans for that period, representing 25 percent of GDP.

Because of the rescue plan, the central bank experienced heavy operational losses. In 1985, as a consequence of having assets with a low or zero return and liabilities generating large payments, the central bank experienced an operational loss equivalent to 18 percent of GDP in that year (see Figure 7A in the online appendix available at http://manifold.bfi.uchicago.edu/). The central bank was able to access domestic and foreign financial markets to finance its rescue operations. In practice, the central bank also relied on direct transfers from the Treasury in the form of long-term bonds. Those entered the balance sheet of the central bank as assets and appeared as domestic fiscal debt. In fact, in 1985, the fiscal debt was in large proportion the Treasury bonds that were transferred to the central bank, representing nearly 20 percent of that year's GDP (see Figures 1A and 8A in the online appendix available at http://manifold.bfi.uchicago.edu/).

The total net cost to the central bank of the portfolio purchase program was equivalent to 6.7 percent of the 1983 GDP when the social cost of capital is used as the discount rate, and it was equivalent to 5.4 percent of GDP when the cash flow is measured as a proportion of each year's GDP.[17]

The above strategy implied that the rescue plan was mainly financed by issuing domestic and foreign interest-bearing liabilities of the central bank and receiving transfers (long-term bonds) from the Treasury. For this strategy to be successful and coherent with price stability, the maturity of the central bank debt (and Treasury transfers) has to be such that it does not put too much pressure on public finances. In the literature there are two complementary ways in which this can be done. First, a long maturity debt contract can rule out an equilibrium in which default is expected and, as a consequence, funds cannot be raised and default materialized.[18] In the case of Chile, the increase in debt, by both the central bank and the fiscal authority, was concentrated in long-term bonds (see Figures 9A and 10A in the online appendix available at http://manifold.bfi.uchicago .edu/). As a consequence, the long maturity of debt has prevented the existence of an equilibrium in which deficits are financed by printing money. The same can be said regarding the public domestic debt. In this case, the bond transferred to the central bank was a twenty-seven-year Treasury bond. Furthermore, this bond was indexed to inflation and then converted to U.S. dollars in the late 1980s (see Figure 1A in the online appendix available at http://manifold.bfi.uchicago.edu/). As a consequence, debt repudiation was avoided by having an indexed bond or U.S. dollar-denominated bond.[19]

The financial crisis and its implications demanded that the focus of economic policies be concentrated on the recovery of the economy and a troubled financial sector. Regarding the inflation rate, the goal was to keep it under control without trying to reduce it significantly. After 1985, monetary policy involved periodic devaluations in order to avoid appreciation of the real exchange rate. The result of these policies was an annual average inflation rate of around 20 percent between 1982 and 1989. In 1988, elections took place, and the uncertainty about the change in the political regime may have affected the higher inflation rate observed in 1989.

As for the budget constraint accounting used in "A Framework for Studying the Monetary and Fiscal History of Latin America," during the period from 1982 to 1989, seigniorage reduced its relative importance as a source of financing, representing, on average, 0.5 percent of GDP. External debt, on the other hand, had a negative contribution of 1 percent of GDP (Table 1). In this period, the main source of financing is related to domestic credit in local currency (0.2 percent of GDP) and domestic credit in U.S. dollars (1.7 percent of GDP). In terms of obligations, the fiscal authority was able to generate a surplus of 1.3 percent of GDP. The difference between sources and obligations is such that transfers, τ_t, represented on average 3.8 percent of GDP.

Transfers were particularly important in the 1982–89 period (Figure 7). The Treasury bonds transferred to the central bank and the private debt guaranteed account for most of the transfers in this period (Figure 8). For example, in the year 1985, the transfers are almost completely explained by the issuance of Treasury notes.

To summarize, in the latter stage of Pinochet's government, fiscal financing needs were determined mostly by the fiscal debt the Treasury acquired with the central bank. With the exception of the years when the crises were at their peak, fiscal deficits were absent in this period. In the same way, external and domestic (private) debt were not important sources of funding (Table 1).

Fiscal Discipline, Fiscal Rules, and Inflation Targeting: 1991–2017

Chile avoided defaulting on its, mainly private, external debt. The cost of this strategy was assumed by the central bank and the fiscal authority (the Treasury), which assumed, de facto, the debt obligations of the private sector. As is clear, the rescue strategy implied an increase in the debt position of both the Treasury and the central bank. To avoid debt dilution and liquidity problems, debt obligations were indexed and set to long horizons. Now, those debts have to be paid eventually, and the only way to achieve this is by generating fiscal surpluses. This idea, present since the mid-1970s, was followed by the Pinochet administration in the late 1980s as well as by the democratic governments that came after. In fact, from 1987 to 2017, the fiscal authority has, in general, generated a surplus (see Figure 3). Net asset accumulation over time by the central government helped meet future public-sector commitments that grow at a higher rate than fiscal revenues and potential expenditures on contingent liabilities. Furthermore, they also helped finance central bank losses due to the carryover of quasi-fiscal costs incurred from the rescue of commercial banks in the early 1980s and the sterilization of large capital inflows in the 1990s.

Despite this prudent fiscal policy and the central bank's autonomy since October 1989, the reduction of the inflation rate during the 1990s was gradual in order to avoid the social costs of a stabilization plan. It is important to note that this gradual reduction in inflation rates was possible because of very favorable external conditions and, as discussed above, the fiscal discipline. Until 1999, there was an exchange rate band. During this period, there was a permanent appreciation pressure on the Chilean peso (it was regularly at the lower part of the band) because of the significant capital inflows and terms of trade levels. This implied a lower imported inflation. This crawling-peg system was in place until the Asian crisis. After that event, the appreciation of the peso dissipated.

The depreciation of the peso made it difficult to continue defending the band under conditions that were present after the Asian crisis (a decline in terms of trade and tighter credit conditions), and in September 1999, once uncertainty abated, the central bank announced the abandonment of the band, and inflation became the only explicit and formal target of the monetary authority.

There is a view among some economists—Calvo and Mendoza (1998), for example—that the exchange rate appreciation helped stabilize inflation during the 1990s. We tend to disagree with this hypothesis and believe, as shown by Valdés (1998), that the nominal anchor from 1991 to 1999 was indeed the declining inflation target announced by the central bank during the 1990s. To illustrate this point, it is useful to compare the evolution of the nominal exchange rate and inflation in the 1990s and the 1970s. In the top panel of Figure 5, we can see a close correlation between inflation and nominal devaluations from 1975 to 1981. The sample correlation among those variables is 0.96. In the bottom panel, we can see that this correlation is not as high in the 1991–99 period. In fact, the sample correlation is 0.4. In addition, at the end of the sample there is an important and persistent devaluation without inflationary consequences. In short, the stabilization experiences of the 1970s and the 1990s are very different. In the former, the exchange rate was the de facto nominal anchor of the economy, whereas in the latter case the nominal anchor was the inflation target announced by the central bank.

Summing up, fiscal discipline allowed a smooth transition from the troubled 1980s to the adoption of an inflation-targeting regime almost ten years later. This was true even though the central bank was experiencing operational losses (see Figure 7A in the online appendix available at http://manifold.bfi.uchicago.edu/) and had a net worth that has declined steadily since the mid-1980s. In particular, in 2010 the net worth of the central bank was −3.5 percent of that year's GDP (see Figure 11A in the online appendix available at http://manifold.bfi.uchicago.edu/).

An important fiscal institutional arrangement in Chile has been the adoption of a fiscal rule. In 2001, the government implemented a fiscal policy based on a yearly structural surplus of 1 percent of GDP. The basic logic of the rule is to stabilize public expenditures over the business cycle and fluctuations in the price of copper, preventing excessive adjustments in periods of recession or unsustainable expenditure levels in periods of prosperity. Hence, the rule is designed to generate savings in times of prosperity to pay debt contracted in times of recession, thus softening the economic cycle and granting sustainability to public finances. At the same time, because it is a known and transparent rule, it reduces uncertainty for economic agents regarding the future behavior of public finances and stabilizes public expenditure in economic and socially sensitive areas, such as investment and social spending. To establish the credibility of this rule, independent panels of experts have substantial influence in establishing the long-run reference value of the price of copper as well as the trend growth of GDP.

Going back to our budget constraint framework (in Table 1), from 1991 to 2016, the fiscal authority had managed to generate surpluses in a systematic way. On average, these surpluses represented 2 percent of GDP, relaxing the financing needs of the government. The rest of the obligations were, on average, a small fraction of GDP. Transfers represented 2.5 percent of GDP in the period from 1991 to 2016. As can be seen in Figure 8, fiscal incomes derived from copper seem to explain an important fraction of the transfers for the years around 2005. A potential additional explanation for these high transfers is that they may constitute assets accumulated by the state in order to be used when the cycle is adverse or the price of copper declines. In short, transfers in this period are going to wealth funds.[20]

FISCAL RULE

The structural balance fiscal rule followed by Chile has experienced several changes over time, although this policy has been, in theory, countercyclical.[21] In order to determine the de facto nature of the fiscal rule, we discuss some estimations of the fiscal rule in Chile performed by Caputo and Irarrazabal (2015). These estimations were made according to the specifications suggested by Fernández-Villaverde et al. (2011):

$$v_t = c + \alpha v_{t-1} + \beta(ym_t - ym) + \gamma(\tau cu_t - \tau cu), \qquad (1)$$

where $v_t = (g_t - tax_t) / ym_t$, g_t is government spending, tax_t is fiscal income, excluding copper-related revenues, ym_t is the real GDP noncopper, and tcu_t is the fiscal income (in real terms) related to copper. Variables without a time subscript represent the filtered variable (Hodrick-Prescott). If the fiscal authority is following a countercyclical fiscal rule, the coefficients β and γ are expected to be negative. The results for the whole sample indicate that the fiscal rule has been countercyclical in the case of noncopper GDP as well as in the case of the price of copper. From 1990 to 1999, the rule is almost neutral with a long-run response to the GDP cycle that is not different from zero and a response to copper-related income that is negative and statistically different from zero. For the latter sample period, 2000 to 2014, the responses to both the GDP cycle and the price of copper increase (in absolute value) quite significantly. This result suggests that in the last fourteen years, fiscal policy has been decisively countercyclical.

The countercyclical nature of the fiscal rule can explain to some degree the evolution of transfers since 2000: in times when the GDP cycle and the price of copper cycle are positive, the fiscal authority generates fiscal surpluses that are eventually used to increase the net asset position of fiscal authority. Hence, it is not surprising that during the 2000s, transfers increased significantly and were not only explained by revenues from higher copper prices.

To summarize, after the debt crisis of the early 1980s, it was clear that the only way to both service the debt and avoid nominal volatility was to generate fiscal surpluses. This has been done in a systematic way since 1987 and, as a consequence, enabled the Treasury to service its foreign and domestic debt (with the central bank). In recent years, the fiscal authority has followed a more countercyclical policy that can explain, to some extent, the important level that transfers have reached. This, in turn, enabled the central bank to pursue an inflation-targeting regime. One important consequence of this strategy is that it broke the correlation among fiscal deficits, seigniorage, and inflation that was prevalent in the 1970s (see Figure 12).

Conclusions

Over the last fifty years, Chile has experienced deep structural changes. In the 1960s, two different administrations, led by Alessandri and Frei, attempted to stabilize inflation. Inflation declined in some particular years, but it could not be permanently contained. During Alessandri's administration, there was a clear link between inflation and fiscal deficits. This link became less apparent during Frei's administration, which adjusted fiscal deficits but was not able to reduce inflation. According to our findings, in this period seigniorage was used to finance transfers not explicit in the central government deficits and related to the cost of nationalizations and the financing of public enterprise deficits.

In the early 1970s, a massive increase in government spending, which was not financed by an increase in taxes or debt, induced nominal instability in the form of high and unpredictable inflation. Between 1973 and 1974, Chile experienced a hyperinflation process that had no precedent in its past history. Between 1971 and 1973, seigniorage contributed to financing the central government deficit. In addition, it contributed to financing the public enterprise deficits, which represented, on average, 7.2 percent of GDP in that period.

After the military took power in September 1973, some attempts were made to stabilize the economy. However, inflation could not be stabilized until the late 1970s. The rate of growth in high-powered money, inflation, and seigniorage declined but remained at relatively high levels. Given that fiscal deficits were drastically reduced, it follows that implicit transfers during this period were relatively large: on average, nearly 7 percent of GDP. Reserve accumulations and the impact of large depreciations in the early 1970s can explain a fraction of these transfers. The rest could be related to contingent liabilities, expenses undertaken by the government and not fully reflected in the fiscal deficit.

In the early 1980s, after the exchange rate was controlled, inflation converged to lower levels. However, as a consequence of nominal wages that were indexed to past inflation, the real exchange rate experienced a sharp appreciation. This, in turn, generated external imbalances that could not be sustained once capital inflows reversed in 1982. In this context, the exchange rate regime had to be abandoned to restore the external equilibrium. This, however, came at a significant cost: the banking system collapsed and had to be rescued by the central bank and the Treasury. During this period, both seigniorage and the public deficit were very small. The implicit transfers in this period are related to actions taken by the government and the central bank to save the private banking sector.

During the 1980s, the government did not enter into debt default, but in order to service its debt, the fiscal authority had to generate surpluses consistently over time. Since 1987 this has been a systematic policy followed by all administrations. This policy helped achieve two different but related goals: it contributed to reducing the fiscal debt, and it enabled the central bank to pursue an independent monetary policy aimed at reducing inflation.

In terms of the accounting exercise we implement, we found that there were unaccounted transfers of 4 percent of GDP on average between 1960 to 2016. Once we include all the potential components associated with the transfers, the residual we obtained is close to 1 percent of GDP, and it fluctuates in a nonsystematic way.

Notes

We are grateful to Jorge Alamos, Luis Felipe Céspedes, José Díaz, Pablo García, Alfonso Irarrázabal, José Matus, Juan Pablo Medina, Juan Pablo Nicolini, Eric Parrado, Claudio Soto, Jaime Troncoso, Rodrigo Valdés, Gert Wagner, and seminar participants at the Central Bank of Chile, the University of Chicago, the University of Barcelona, LACEA 2017, the Becker Friedman Institute (BFI)–University of Chicago 2017 Conference, the BFI–Central Bank of Chile 2018 Conference, and the BFI Inter-American Development Bank (IDB) Conference in 2018 for helpful comments and discussions. We extend our gratitude to Roberto Álvarez, Manuel Agosín, José De Gregorio, Sebastián Edwards, Arnold Harberger, Rolf Lüders, Patricio Meller, Felipe Morandé, Gabriel Palma, Jorge Roldós, Andrés Velasco, and Pedro Videla, who discussed, extensively, a previous version of this chapter. Stefano Banfi, Rolando Campusano, Matías Morales,

Fabián Sepúlveda, Catalina Larraín, and Felipe Leal provided excellent research assistance in different stages of this project. Rodrigo Caputo is thankful for the hospitality of both the BI Norwegian Business School and the Nuffield College Center of Experimental Social Sciences, University of Oxford. The views expressed here are those of the authors and do not necessarily reflect the position of the Central Bank of Chile or its board members.

1 According to World Bank data, per capita GDP in Chile (purchasing power parity [PPP] in constant 2011 U.S. dollars) increased from US$8.995 in 1990 to US$22.707 in 2016. This is an increase of 153 percent. In the same period, per capita GDP in Latin America increased 48 percent.

2 See Velasco (1994).

3 The data on public deficits include the deficits of public-sector companies.

4 Further details can be found in Edwards and Cox Edwards (1987).

5 More details can be found in Edwards and Cox Edwards (1987) and Corbo and Fischer (1994).

6 For the period 1970–80, we use the alternative price series proposed in Schmidt-Hebbel and Marshall (1981), since the official series is somewhat unreliable.

7 Further details can be found in Edwards and Cox Edwards (1987).

8 Price controls and sticky prices may have contributed to a delayed response of prices to the increase in monetary growth.

9 In the basic framework, fiscal deficits do not include public enterprises deficits.

10 The dotted bars for the years 1971, 1972, and 1973 in Figure 8 explain almost all the transfers.

11 See Edwards (1985), De Gregorio (1991), and Corbo and Fischer (1994), who discuss the importance of wage indexation as a self-preserving device of inflationary pressures.

12 The nominal exchange rate increased from 0.11 in 1973 to 13.05 in 1976.

13 As noted by Diamond and Valdés-Prieto (1994), the program of fiscal tightening that started in 1977 had as its main purpose to finance the planned reform of social security. It was expected that, as a consequence of this reform, social security income (contributions) would decline significantly, whereas social security benefits (paid by the state) would remain constant as a fraction of GDP. This analysis, ex post, turned out to be accurate. In the 1970s, the social security deficit of the state was, on average, 2.6 percent of GDP. After the 1981 social security reform and until 1990, this deficit was, on average, 6.1 percent of GDP (see Figure 5A in the online appendix available at http://manifold.bfi.uchicago.edu/). The fiscal authority systematically generated fiscal surpluses that could more than compensate for the fiscal deficit related to social security (see Figure 6A in the online appendix available at http://manifold.bfi.uchicago.edu/). This fact could explain a fraction of transfers observed between 1974 and 1981.

14 Although during 1983 and 1984 the monetary base grew in nominal terms, it continued decreasing in real terms. It was in 1985 when the monetary base began to grow again in real terms.

15 For further discussion, see Edwards (1985) and Corbo and Fischer (1994).

16 The Chilean central bank has been autonomous since 1989.

17 This cost is computed by Sanhueza (2001). In this case, cash flow estimates are divided into two parts: flows from the central bank to financial institutions for payment of portfolio purchases, which reached 8.9 percent of GDP, and cash flows from financial institutions to the central bank for buying back portfolios, which reached 2.2 percent of GDP.

18 See Calvo (1995) and Cole and Kehoe (1996).

19 This point is stressed by Calvo (1988).

20 The fiscal responsibility law of 2006 allowed for setting up two sovereign wealth funds and establishing the basic institutional framework necessary for their management. These funds included the Pension Reserve Fund (PRF), created at the end of

2006, and the Economic and Social Stabilization Fund (ESSF), launched in early 2007.

21 See Tapia (2015), Ffrench-Davis (2016), and Céspedes, Parrado, and Velasco (2014).

References

Calvo, Guillermo A. 1988. "Servicing the Public Debt: The Role of Expectations." *American Economic Review* 78 (4): 647–61.

———. 1995. "Varieties of Capital-Market Crises." Working paper 4008, Inter-American Development Bank, Research Department, Washington, D.C.

———. 1996. "Exchange-Rate-Based Stabilization under Imperfect Credibility." In *Money, Exchange Rates, and Output*, 365–90. Cambridge, Mass.: MIT Press.

Calvo, Guillermo A., and Enrique Mendoza. 1998. "Empirical Puzzles of Chilean Stabilization Policy." Working paper 98-02, Duke University, Durham, N.C.

Caputo, Rodrigo, and Alfonso Irarrazabal. 2015. "The Business Cycle of a Commodity Exporter." Unpublished paper, Universidad de Santigo de Chile, Santiago.

Céspedes, Luis Felipe, Eric Parrado, and Andrés Velasco. 2014. "Fiscal Rules and the Management of Natural Resource Revenues: The Case of Chile." *Annual Review of Resource Economics* 6 (1): 105–32.

Cole, Harold L., and Timothy J. Kehoe. 1996. "A Self-Fulfilling Model of Mexico's 1994–1995 Debt Crisis." *Journal of International Economics* 41 (3–4): 309–30.

Corbo, Vittorio, and Stanley Fischer. 1994. "Lessons from the Chilean Stabilization and Recovery." In *The Chilean Economy: Policy Lessons and Challenges*, edited by Barry Bosworth, Rudiger Dornbusch, and Raúl Labán, 29–80. Washington, D.C.: Brookings Institution Press.

De Gregorio, Jose. 1991. "Indexación versus credibilidad en un programa de estabilización: La experiencia Chilena a mediados de los 70."

Latin American Journal of Economics (formerly *Cuadernos de Economía*) 28 (83): 189–99.

Diamond, Peter, and Salvador Valdés-Prieto. 1994. "Social Security Reform." In *The Chilean Economy: Policy Lessons and Challenges*, edited by Barry Bosworth, Rudiger Dornbusch, and Raúl Labán, 114–37. Washington, D.C.: Brookings Institution.

Díaz, Jose, Rolf Lüders, and Gert Wagner. 2016. *Chile 1810–2010: La república en cifras*. Santiago: Ediciones Universidad Católica de Chile.

Edwards, Sebastian. 1985. "Stabilization with Liberalization: An Evaluation of Ten Years of Chile's Experiment with Free-Market Policies, 1973–1983." *Economic Development and Cultural Change* 33 (2): 223–54.

———. 2007. "Establishing Credibility: The Role of Foreign Advisors in Chile's 1955–1958 Stabilization Program." In *The Decline of Latin American Economies: Growth, Institutions, and Crises*, edited by Sebastian Edwards, Gerardo Esquivel, and Graciela Márquez, 291–332. Chicago: University of Chicago Press.

Edwards, Sebastián, and Alejandra Cox Edwards. 1987. *Monetarism and Liberalization: The Chilean Experiment*. Chicago: University of Chicago Press.

Fernández-Villaverde, Jesús, Pablo A. Guerrón-Quintana, Keith Kuester, and Juan Rubio-Ramírez. 2011. "Fiscal Volatility Shocks and Economic Activity." Working paper 17317, National Bureau of Economic Research, Cambridge, Mass.

Ffrench-Davis, Ricardo. 1973. *Políticas económicas en Chile: 1952–1970*. Santiago: Ediciones Nueva Universidad, Universidad Católica de Chile, Santiago.

―――. 2016. "La experiencia de Chile con el balance fiscal estructural." *Cuadernos de Economía* 35 (67): 149–71.

Kiguel, Miguel, and Nissan Liviatan. 1990. "The Business Cycle Associated with Exchange-Rate-Based Stabilization." Policy Research Working Paper WPS513, World Bank, Washington, D.C.

Krugman, Paul. 1979. "A Model of Balance-of-Payments Crises." *Journal of Money, Credit and Banking* 11 (3): 311–25.

Larraín, Felipe. 1991. "Public Sector Behavior in a Highly Indebted Country: The Contrasting Chilean Experience." In *The Public Sector and the Latin American Crisis, 1970–1985*, edited by Felipe Larraín and Marcelo Selowsky, 89–136. San Francisco: ICS Press.

Larraín, Felipe, and M. Rodrigo Vergara. 2000. "Un cuarto de siglo de reformas fiscales." In *La transformación económica de Chile*, edited by Felipe Larraín and M. Rodrigo Vergara, 73–109. Santiago: Centro de Estudios Públicos.

Reinhart, Carmen M., and Kenneth S. Rogoff. 2009. *This Time Is Different: Eight Centuries of Financial Folly.* Princeton, N.J.: Princeton University Press.

Sanhueza, Gonzalo I. 2001. "Chilean Banking Crisis of the 1980s: Solutions and Estimation of the Costs." Working paper 104, Central Bank of Chile, Santiago.

Sargent, Thomas J. 2013. *Rational Expectations and Inflation.* 3rd ed. Princeton, N.J.: Princeton University Press.

Scheetz, Thomas. 1987. "Public Sector Expenditures and Financial Crisis in Chile." *World Development* 15 (8): 1053–75.

Schmidt-Hebbel, Klaus, and Pablo Marshall. 1981. "Revisión del IPC para el período 1970–1980: Una nota." Documento No. 176, Departamento de Estudios de Empresas BHC, Santiago.

Tapia, Heriberto. 2015. "Fiscal Rule in Chile: From Automatic Pilot to Navigation Device." Unpublished paper, United Nations Human Development Report Office, New York.

Valdés, Rodrigo. 1998. "Efectos de la politica monetaria en Chile." *Cuadernos de Economía* 35 (104): 97–125.

Velasco, Andrés. 1987. "Financial Crises and Balance of Payments Crises: A Simple Model of the Southern Cone Experience." *Journal of Development Economics* 27 (1–2): 263–83.

―――. 1994. "The State and Economic Policy: Chile 1952–92." In *The Chilean Economy: Policy Lessons and Challenges*, edited by Barry Bosworth, Rudiger Dornbusch, and Raúl Labán, 379–410. Washington, D.C.: Brookings Institution Press.

Discussion of the History of Chile

Sebastian Edwards
University of California, Los Angeles

Chile provides one of the most interesting experiences with monetary policy, fiscal policy, and inflation in Latin America. During the last six decades, the country has experienced almost every inflation-related phenomenon: persistent inflation throughout the 1960s and early 1970s, extremely high inflation in 1973 through 1975, and low and contained inflation starting in the early 1990s. The country went through periods of clear "fiscal dominance," as well as periods in which public finances were under control. The adoption of an explicit countercyclical "fiscal rule" in the early 2000s was a pioneering move around the world. In addition, Chile was an early adopter of central bank independence in 1990, the year the country returned to democratic rule.

The chapter by Caputo and Saravia is a welcome contribution to the literature on monetary and fiscal policies and inflation in Chile. It provides a useful description of different phases, presents the most relevant data, and offers reasonable interpretations of both the economic and political forces behind monetary and fiscal policies, exchange rate behavior, wage pressures, and inflation.

In this commentary, I would like to deal with two issues: first I would like to reference two very important classic studies of inflation in Chile, which are not mentioned by the authors. These works, by Albert Hirschman (1963) and Arnold Harberger (1963), are fundamental for putting Chile's macroeconomic history in perspective. I will then delve into a specific subperiod within the years analyzed by Caputo and Saravia: 1978–82. These were early years during the Augusto Pinochet dictatorship, when an attempt was made to use a strict exchange rate anchor to bring down an extremely stubborn inflation, which had its roots in the fiscal dominance episode that exploded during the Salvador Allende administration. The policy, however, did not work out as anticipated by its promoters, and it ended up in a major and very costly currency and banking crisis. In analyzing this episode, I relate the fixed-rate strategy to Milton Friedman's view on monetary regimes and stabilization.

Earlier Literature

In 1963 Albert Hirschman published, as chapter 3 of his *Journeys toward Progress*, a detailed analysis of inflation in Chile from the late nineteenth century through 1962.

The study is appropriately and simply titled "Inflation in Chile."[1] In the first table in this chapter, Hirschman presents data on accumulated and average inflation decade by decade between 1880 and 1960. These data clearly show the ratcheting up of inflation in Chile's history until the mid-twentieth century.

In this study, Hirschman elegantly analyzes the forces behind inflation in Chile, including disputes between gold and silver supporters, the role of paper money, and the increasing degree of fiscal dominance starting in 1940. He also goes through recurrent currency crises and the political economy of stabilization attempts. The chapter contains a fascinating analysis on the role of foreign advisers in developing countries in general and in Chile in particular. This discussion is carried out in light of the KleinSaks mission of 1955–56 and its failed attempt to bring inflation under control. The connection between the inflationary process and political developments is clearly captured by the title of the last section of his chapter: "Inflation, Revolution and Civil War."

Also in 1963, Arnold C. Harberger published his monumental article "The Dynamics of Inflation in Chile."[2] This chapter opens as follows: "[Chile's] history of inflation is long, and for practical purposes continuous. Its rate of inflation has varied greatly over time, permitting the testing of theories in which not only the level of prices but also the rate of change plays a role" (Harberger 1963, 219).

Harberger's study is a careful empirical investigation based on both quarterly and annual data and on a number of different price indexes. One of the notable aspects of this work is that it explicitly analyzes what Harberger calls "two extreme hypotheses. . . . one denying any true explanatory power to wage changes, and the other denying any true explanatory power to money supply changes" (Harberger 1963, 244).

Harberger's results suggest that neither of the two extreme hypotheses is supported fully by the data. His findings indicate that during the period under analysis (1939–58), both monetary changes and monetary conditions played a role in fueling and perpetuating inflation. After analyzing his regressions, Harberger writes, "These results suggest that one of the major roles of the wage variable was indeed as a 'transmitter' of inflation from one period to the next, responding to the monetary expansion of the past, and inducing monetary expansion in the subsequent" (Harberger 1963, 244).

Table 1. Inflation in Chile, 1880–1960

	Accumulated (%)	Annual average (%)
1880–90	57	5
1890–1900	58	5
1900–1910	109	8
1910–20	74	6
1920–30	30	3
1930–40	94	7
1940–50	412	18
1950–60	2,089	36

Given Chile's long history with inflation, it is not surprising that a number of Chilean doctoral students wrote their dissertations on inflation and stabilization. Out of the many works on the subject, two deserve particular attention. In his 1971 thesis at MIT, Vittorio Corbo constructed a small econometric model that, in the spirit of Harberger, combined monetary and wage rate pressures. A revised version of the dissertation was eventually published by North-Holland. In his 1973 thesis at Harvard, Tomás Reichmann emphasized (correctly) the role of expectations in inflationary dynamics in Chile.

Milton Friedman and Chile's Exchange Rate Anchor, 1978–82

In early 1978, with inflation at 57 percent per annum, Chile adopted an exchange-rate-based stabilization policy. The central bank preannounced the daily rate of the devaluation of the peso relative to the U.S. dollar for one year. The initial rate of devaluation was deliberately set below the ongoing rate of inflation. The economic authorities believed that this mechanism would generate a rapid convergence of domestic inflation to international inflation. This exchange rate scheme, known as the *tablita*, was supported by tight monetary and fiscal policies. This policy is discussed by Caputo and Saravia in the fourth section of their chapter. Surprisingly, however, the episode, including the ensuing currency crisis of 1982, is not given enough emphasis.

Eighteen months later, in June 1979, when inflation still stood at 35 percent per year, the government decided to put an end to the preannounced rate of the devaluation and to fix the exchange rate at 39 pesos per dollar. The authorities expected that this move would help rapidly reduce inflation to the one-digit range. At first the announcement was made that this fixed rate would last until February 1980. A few weeks before that date, however, the decision was made to maintain the fixed exchange rate (relative to the dollar) "forever." As Milton Friedman would point out later, fixing the peso to the dollar generated a serious problem, since around that time the U.S. dollar began to strengthen significantly in the international currency markets. While the nominal exchange rate with respect to the dollar stayed constant between the third quarter of 1979 and the second quarter of 1982, the multilateral, trade-weighted, nominal exchange rate with respect to a basket of currencies appreciated during that period by more than 30 percent.

Larry Sjaastad, a University of Chicago professor and a frequent visitor to Chile, was one of the intellectual fathers of the exchange rate anchor policy. Based on the then-popular "monetary approach to the balance of payments," he believed that purchasing power parity held in the short run and fixed exchange rates would provide almost instantaneous discipline and allow for rapid and low-cost stabilization. He explained the exchange-rate-based program as follows: "The rationale . . . was that once economic agents understood, or inferred, that the equilibrium between the prices of tradables and nontraded (home) good is neither random nor arbitrary, a change in the price of tradable goods will cause a revision of expectations concerning the equilibrium price of home goods. Under such circumstances, excess supply would not be required to drive down inflation; the change can occur spontaneously, as it were" (Sjaastad 1983, 12). Every month between June 1979 and June 1982, Chile's domestic inflation exceeded international inflation. This contributed further to real (as opposed to nominal) exchange rate appreciation. As a result, an increasingly large current account deficit developed; it was almost 6 percent of GDP in 1980, climbed to 8 percent in 1981, and reached the staggering figure of close to 10 percent of GDP in 1982. These deficits were largely financed with short-term, dollar-denominated bank loans and other forms of speculative capital. In mid-1982, the authorities could not hold the line any longer, and the peso was devalued. Many firms and families that had borrowed heavily in foreign exchange could not service their debts and went bankrupt. GDP declined by almost 15 percent, and unemployment exceeded 25 percent.

Why did Chile choose to have an exchange rate anchor in 1978? Did the authorities realize, at the time, that a growing and dangerous imbalance was developing? Did they foresee the massive and costly crisis? Why didn't the authorities think of an exit strategy from the fixed exchange rate?

These questions are of interest for at least two reasons. First, as is well known, during the early dictatorship, a group of economists known as the "Chicago boys" was very influential in Chile, with many of them holding cabinet-level positions. Second, and also well known, Milton Friedman, the economist most closely associated with Chicago, had for a long time advocated for (since at least the early 1950s) flexible exchange rates and was generally very critical of attempts to fix the currency value, especially if these efforts lacked credibility.

Milton Friedman visited Chile twice during Pinochet's dictatorship: the first time in April 1975 and the second in mid-November 1981.[3] During his early trip, Friedman met for about an hour with Pinochet. At the meeting—also attended by Arnold Harberger and some Chicago boys—Friedman told the general what he thought about Chile's economic situation and recommended implementing a drastic sterilization program based on a fiscal shock and monetary tightness. This visit was highly publicized and came to haunt Friedman a few months later when he was awarded the Nobel Prize in Economics. A number of renowned scholars and previous Nobel laureates in the sciences wrote letters to major media outlets decrying the award. They argued that Friedman was complicit in Chile's deep violations of human rights. During his second visit, in mid-November 1981, Friedman attended the regional meetings of the Mont Pèlerin Society. During this trip, he did not meet, officially, with any government authorities.

Figure 1 presents monthly data on the peso–U.S. dollar exchange rate between January 1975 and December 1982. The dates of Friedman's two visits (April 1975 and November 1981) are denoted by two vertical lines. Four phases of exchange policy in Chile during these years may be detected in the figure. The first phase goes from January 1975 to February 1978. During this period, Chile followed, for the most part, a passive, backward-looking, crawling-peg regime.[4] The nominal exchange rate was devalued frequently (daily) by the lagged (previous month) differential between Chilean and U.S. inflation. During the second phase, from February 1978 to June 1979, the *tablita*, or preannounced crawling peg, was in place. As may be seen, the slope of the peso-dollar curve becomes flatter, reflecting the deliberate slowing down of the rate of devaluation,

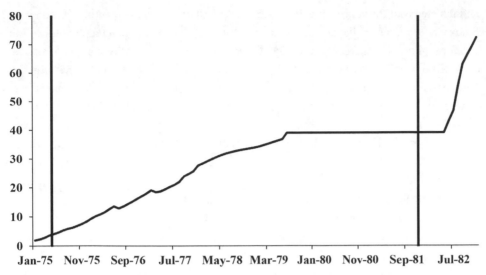

Figure 1. Peso-dollar exchange rate: January 1975–December 1982

below the ongoing rate of inflation. The third phase, from June 1979 to June 1982, is the fixed peso-dollar rate, and the fourth phase, after June 1982, is the devaluation crisis and the adjustable and managed peg.

During Friedman's first visit, the exchange rate was not at the center of policy discussions. It was taken as a given that with a three-digit rate of inflation, Chile could not have a completely fixed exchange rate. At the same time, it was thought that Chile (or any other developing country for that matter) didn't have the institutional capacity to adopt a truly market-determined, flexible rate. The crawling peg was considered, by most analysts, to be the natural answer to the exchange rate question.

In Friedman's main lecture in Chile in 1975, the term "exchange rate" did not come up even once. He talked about monetary policy, the fiscal deficit, the inflation tax, the merits of a "social market" economy, shock adjustment, and the experiences of Germany and Japan after World War II. But during his speech, he didn't say one word about currencies or exchange rates.[5]

The exchange rate issue was brought up briefly during the question-and-answer period. In his reply to a question on the connection between the degree of openness of the economy and monopoly power, Friedman intimated that, in his view, the authorities took into account market forces when determining the (sliding) value of foreign currency. He said, "If the exchange rate corresponds to a *market rate*—as is the *current policy* of the government—what would be the results [of a policy that opened trade fully]?"[6] He answered by saying that in those circumstances, an increase in the demand for foreign currency would lead to a depreciation of the peso.

The exchange rate was again raised in a question regarding the generalized indexation system that existed in Chile at the time.[7] A participant asked whether periodic and frequent adjustments of prices, wages, and the exchange rate could contribute to inflation by creating a "vicious circle." In his answer, Friedman dismissed the circularity argument and insisted that the source of Chile's very rapid inflation was the printing of money to finance a fiscal deficit that amounted to 10 percent of GDP. He then defended indexation as a form of facilitating the signing of contracts in an environment of rapidly rising prices.

A third (and last) exchange-rate-related question focused on the effects of the "minidevaluations" on costs and companies' profits. The participant also asked about the effects of very high interest rates on companies' ability to survive. Friedman began his answer by saying that there is a difference between nominal and real interest rates. He added that high nominal interest rates are a reflection of inflation and not a cause. He then said,

> The same is true about mini devaluations: they don't result in higher real costs. They are simply a response to price increases. . . . If prices in Chile increase by 10% each month, then it is necessary to devalue by 10% in order to maintain a stable *real* value of foreign currency. . . . And you already know the story: if you try to maintain a low price for foreign exchange [overvaluation of the peso], there would simply be a need to ration it. What happens then? Everyone would want to buy it [foreign exchange]. How would you decide who is allowed to buy [dollars]?[8]

To summarize, then, during Friedman's 1975 visit to Chile, he defended the sliding parity regime and explained that if inflation was high, fixing the rate would necessarily result in disequilibrium and rationing. He also praised, implicitly, the fact that the government was trying to maintain the official exchange rate close to its market value.

When Friedman arrived in Chile for his second visit, in November 1981, the fixed exchange rate experiment was entering its third year. There were clear strains and difficulties; the real exchange rate had appreciated significantly, as expected. However, and in contrast with Friedman's predictions six years earlier, there had been no need to ration foreign exchange. The very large and growing current account deficit was financed with ample monies coming from abroad. Most capital inflows took the form of syndicated bank loans.

Once he arrived in Santiago, Friedman was reluctant to talk about Chile. He told reporters that he "did not know enough about the Chilean economic situation" (*La Tercera*, November 18, 1981). One day later, at a press conference, he said, "I would like you to understand why I am in Chile. I am here to attend the Regional Meeting of the Mont Pèlerin Society, of which I have been [a] founding member for 34 years. I am not here to give advice, neither to analyze Chile's policies. I believe this country has been notably successful during the last years without my advice and I believe it will continue to be successful" (*Ercilla*, November 25, 1981, 21). Reporters, however, did not give up and continued to ask about Chile. Friedman finally agreed to answer a few questions. When asked about the fixed exchange rate, he replied that by fixing the value of the dollar, the government was imposing a constraint on money creation. That is, he answered the question in an indirect way: instead of tackling it directly, he pointed out that a truly fixed rate—by which he meant an irrevocably fixed one—acted as a constraint on the central bank in a way similar to the gold standard. The small group of supporters of flexible exchange rates was disappointed by his answers (*El Mercurio*, November 19, 1981).

Friedman's paper for the Mont Pèlerin Society Meeting was titled "Monetary System for a Free Society." But during his presentation, he did not talk about the paper. Instead, he divided his remarks into three parts: (1) the exchange rate issue in Chile; (2) the difficult economic situation in the United States, including the country's monetary policy; and (3) free markets and democracy, with an emphasis on Chile.

On Friday, November 20, 1981, the newspaper *La Segunda* partially reproduced Friedman's presentation.[9] With respect to the fixed exchange rate policy, Friedman expanded on what he had said during the press interview. He explained that there were two different types of pegged rates. One was the type of unilateral (soft) peg that the Bretton Woods system had instituted. These discretionary pegs had escape clauses and could easily be altered. They were usually unstable and in many countries had led to major financial crises. The second type of peg was hard. Under this system, a country irrevocably fixed the value of its currency to that of an important trade partner with a stable monetary policy and low inflation. Friedman explained, as he had already done in the press conference, that this second type of (hard) peg was similar to the gold standard or to what Panama had done by adopting the dollar as its currency. He went on to state that Chile had followed an "intermediate solution" through its fixed exchange rate relative to the U.S. dollar. By using the term "intermediate solution," he was implicitly being (somewhat) critical of the government policy. However, he didn't openly question the wisdom or sustainability of the policy.

In the years to come, Friedman would come back several times to the issue of the fixed exchange rate in Chile. For example, in a 1993 article, he compared Chile and Israel and explained that while in Chile the policy had led to a severe crisis, in Israel it had been successful. He also came back to this issue in 2001, during a debate with Robert Mundell, one of the staunchest supporters of fixed exchange rates (Friedman and Mundell 2001). Friedman said that Chile's 1979 "hard peg" policy was "disastrous" as a consequence of the strengthening of the U.S. dollar in 1980–81.

In his November 1981 remarks at the Mont Pèlerin meetings, Friedman also noted that if the currency is pegged, it matters with respect to which nation it is fixed. The reason is that, if the peg is durable, irrevocable, and credible, the monetary policy of the reference country would be imported. He recalled that when Australia decided to adopt a fixed exchange rate regime, he recommended a peg with respect to the Japanese yen.[10] This he did for two reasons: first, because Japan was Australia's most important trade partner, and second, because Japan's monetary policy had been, during the previous eight years, more stable and prudent than that of the United States. Given that the United States was Chile's main trading partner, pegging the peso to the dollar would, in principle, make some sense. However, Chile would have to accept what it implied in terms of monetary policy.

Toward the end of his presentation, Friedman stressed the fact that Chile had to "choose between the two alternatives: truly fixed or temporally fixed." He added that fixing with the option of abandoning the parity was a bad idea. If a fixed rate was chosen, it would have to be a firm fixed peg, one that would provide "credibility in the eyes of the world." Chile, he said, "has lived three or four years of extraordinary economic success, but could lose credibility" (*La Segunda*, November 20, 1981).

The discussion presented above indicates that during his 1981 visit to Santiago, Friedman was not openly critical of the fixed exchange rate policy in Chile. He didn't endorse it, but he didn't criticize it either. He covered himself by making a distinction between hard and soft pegs and by saying that if Chile decided to opt for fixity, it had to make sure that it was a credible, hard peg. In many ways, this ambiguity and evasiveness is surprising and is not consistent with Friedman's usual bluntness and directness. At this point, one can only speculate about his motives. A possible explanation is that after meeting privately with the authorities—with Minister of Finance Sergio de Castro and Central Bank President Sergio de la Cuadra, both of them Chicago boys—he realized that they would not alter their exchange rate policy. Thus under those circumstances, it would make little sense for him to openly criticize the exchange rate anchor. In fact, planting doubts about the sustainability and desirability of the fixed rate could have triggered major speculative moves and even a major currency crisis.

Seven months after Friedman's second visit, and in spite of his reluctance to openly criticize the policy, Chile could not defend herself from a massive speculative attack. On June 1982, the peso was devalued. The crisis that followed was one of the deepest ever faced by a Latin American nation.

Notes

1 An even earlier deep analysis of inflation in Chile was performed by Princeton's Frank Fetter and published in 1931. Fetter's work was initially undertaken as a PhD dissertation at Princeton, under the guidance of Edwin Kemmerer, the famous "Money Doctor" who helped found many of Latin America's central banks.

2 This paper was published in a volume titled *Measurement in Economics* (Stanford University Press), edited by Carl Christ. The contributors to this book include a number of luminaries of the economics profession, such as Milton Friedman, Jacob Mincer, Marc Nerlove, and Don Patinkin, as well as Harberger and Christ.

3 What follows is based on some research I have undertaken with Leonidas Montes, from the Centro de Estudios Públicos.

4 On two occasions, there were sharp, one-time, nominal appreciations of the peso. The purpose of these surprise adjustments was to break inertial expectations. However, after these occasions of abrupt strengthening of the peso, the crawling peg was resumed.

5 Milton Friedman, "Milton Friedman en Chile," Fundación de Estudios BHC, Santiago, May 1975.

6 Friedman, "Milton Friedman en Chile," 49. The transcript of the conference is in Spanish. This is question no. 9 (emphasis added).

7 Friedman, "Milton Friedman en Chile," 54 (question no. 12).

8 Friedman, "Milton Friedman en Chile," 57 (question no. 56; emphasis in the original).

9 Friedman himself shared his presentation with *La Segunda* and authorized its full publication.

10 Australia, since 1931, had its exchange rate pegged to the British pound; then in 1973 it changed the pegging to the U.S. dollar but in 1976 began using a crawling peg until free rate flotation was established in 1983. Friedman visited Australia in 1975, right after Chile, and then returned in 1981 (two private visits followed in 1994 and 2005).

References

Friedman, Milton. 1992. "Chile and Israel: Identical Policies—Opposite Outcomes." In *Money Mischief: Episodes in Monetary History*, edited by Milton Friedman, 234–48. New York: Harcourt Brace Jovanovich.

Friedman, Milton, and Robert Mundell. 2001. "One World, One Money?" *Policy Options–Montreal* 22 (4): 10–19.

Harberger, Arnold C. 1963. "The Dynamics of Inflation in Chile." In *Measurement in Economics: Studies in Mathematical Economics and Econometrics in Memory of Yehuda Grunfeld*, edited by Carl Christ, 219–50. Stanford, Calif.: Stanford University Press.

Hirschman, Albert. 1963. *Journeys toward Progress: Studies of Economic Policy-Making in Latin America*. New York: Twentieth Century Fund.

Sjaastad, Larry A. 1983. "Failure of Economic Liberalism in the Cone of Latin America." *The World Economy* 6 (1): 5–26.

Colombia

The History of Colombia

David Perez-Reyna
Universidad de los Andes

Daniel Osorio-Rodríguez
Banco de la República de Colombia

Major fiscal and monetary events, 1960–2017

1962	Balance of payments crisis Devaluation		Stabilization plan with exchange rate bands
1965	Balance of payments crisis Devaluation	**1999**	Balance of payments crisis, end of exchange rate bands
1967	Balance of payments crisis Adoption of crawling peg		Bank bailouts Establishment of floating
1982	Balance of payments crisis		exchange rate
1991	Central bank independence with low inflation mandate End of crawling peg	**2001**	Establishment of inflation targeting regime

Introduction

In this chapter, we characterize the joint history of monetary and fiscal policies in Colombia since 1960, following this volume's "A Framework for Studying the Monetary and Fiscal History of Latin America." Our analysis focuses on the joint evolution of inflation, economic performance, and the fiscal deficit of the Colombian central government and its sources of financing in the period between 1960 and 2017. As a first examination of our objects of interest, Figures 1, 2, and 3 present the evolution of the total fiscal deficit of the central government (as a percentage of GDP), consumer price index (CPI) inflation in Colombia, and real GDP per capita (against a counterfactual trend of 2 percent growth). With regard to the fiscal deficit, three periods can clearly be identified. In the first period, between 1960 and 1970, fiscal deficits were relatively small, averaging 0.43 percent of GDP. In the second period, between 1971 and 1990, fiscal deficits doubled on average (1.05 percent). Finally, during the third period, between the early nineties and the latest data available, deficits were the largest on average (3.27 percent between 1991 and 2017). We highlight the fact that the fiscal deficit peaked in the years during which banking crises occurred: 2.75 percent in 1982 and over 6 percent of GDP in 1999, during the year of the

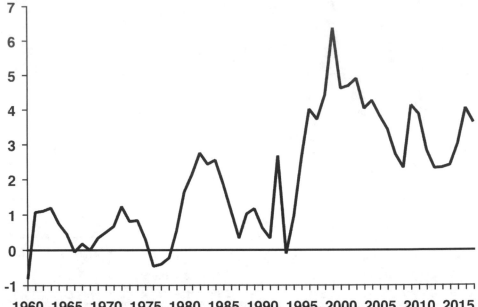

Figure 1. Fiscal deficit, 1960–2017

Sources: Junguito and Rincón (2007), Banco de la República Colombia

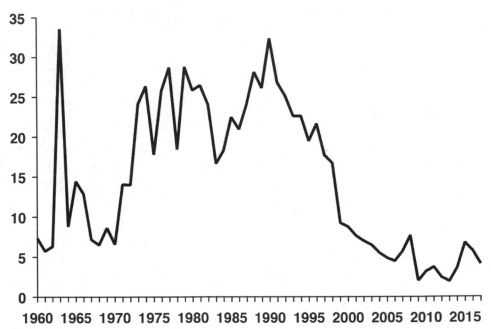

Figure 2. Inflation, 1960–2017

Sources: Banco de la República Colombia, authors' calculations

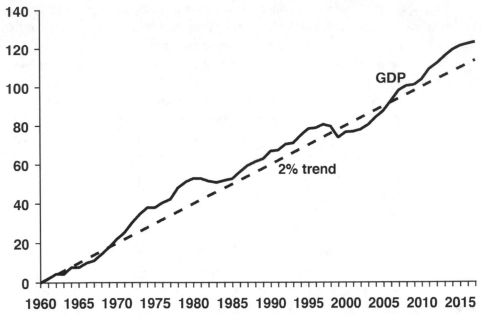

Figure 3. Real GDP per capita versus 2 percent counterfactual, 1960–2017
Sources: World Bank, authors' calculations

worst economic crisis since the beginning of the twentieth century. These three periods also translate into the evolution of inflation: between 1960 and 1970, inflation was low on average (excluding the unusual peak of 1963, inflation averaged 8.4 percent); between 1971 and 1990, average inflation persistently increased to an average of 23.1 percent; and finally, after 1991, inflation gradually and persistently decreased, reaching an average level of 3.9 percent after 2010, the lowest levels of our time window. Significantly, the recession of 1999 coincided with a rapid decrease in inflation.

Finally, real GDP per capita grew at an average pace of 2.16 percent for the period of analysis. This number, although above a benchmark rate of 2 percent for the United States, was not sufficient to allow the economy to achieve a perceivable degree of convergence. Figure 3 highlights the two major banking crises that Colombia experienced in 1982 and 1999.

Following from the previous analysis, we divide the Colombian experience after 1960 into three periods, which are differentiated by the financial structure of the fiscal deficit, the institutional setup of monetary and fiscal policies, the levels of inflation, and the relative economic performance against Latin American peers. The first period, from 1960 to 1970, was characterized by both a low average inflation rate and a low average fiscal deficit. During this period, monetary emission, through both increases in the monetary base and seigniorage, was the main source of financing. Foreign debt also played a role in financing toward the end of the period.

During the second period, 1971–90, the Colombian economy experienced high and persistent inflation and higher fiscal deficits, this time in the context of frequent use of monetary emission to finance government expenditures and heavily controlled foreign exchange markets, particularly after international finance dried up in the wake of the Latin American debt crisis of the early eighties. Throughout this period, the nominal exchange rate was heavily controlled, following a government-predetermined upward trend (crawling peg).

The third period, from 1991 to 2017, registered the highest average fiscal deficit, the highest peak in the deficit, and the worst economic recession since the early twentieth century, with the peak in the deficit and the recession occurring in 1999. Despite high deficits and a severe crisis, inflation kept a persistent downward trend, back to one-digit levels after 2010. This event occurred in the context of a newly independent central bank, increasingly flexible exchange markets, and a reorientation of deficit finance toward the domestic capital markets.

The division of our time window into three separate periods also allows us to illustrate the use of the conceptual framework in "A Framework for Studying the Monetary and Fiscal History of Latin America" to understand the evolving relationship between monetary and fiscal policies in Colombia. Specifically, the first two periods were characterized by fiscal dominance, institutionally defined as a nonindependent central bank. In the first period, fiscal discipline allowed inflation to be kept at relatively low levels. In the second period, an expanded fiscal deficit led to increased inflation under the frequent use of monetary emission to finance government expenditures.

In 1991, a new constitution enshrined monetary dominance via an independent central bank in charge of reducing inflation and accountable to Congress. Significantly, from 1993 to 1999, the central bank kept a managed floating scheme of currency corridors. In this context, the increased fiscal deficits of the early nineties did not lead to increased inflation (monetary emission to finance the fiscal deficit all but disappeared after 1991). Instead, large deficits created relatively large external imbalances, leaving the economy vulnerable to a sudden-stop shock of the sort that occurred in the late nineties, which drove the economy into a harsh recession without an easy resort to nominal depreciations or monetary finance. Since then, monetary independence, together with increased fiscal discipline and adoption of a floating exchange rate, allowed the economy to recover a certain degree of persistent macroeconomic stability, as evidenced by low historical inflation and fiscal deficits close to the average of our time window.

A key observation is that, for the period of analysis, large fiscal or monetary imbalances in Colombia, relative to other Latin American countries, were extremely rare in at least two aspects. First, fiscal deficits were generally small and peaked at only around 6 percent of GDP at the end of the 1990s. Second, although the use of monetary emission to finance the government was frequent, it was never sizable compared to other countries: monetary emission to finance fiscal deficits was more than 2 percent of GDP only during two small time windows, 1977–78 and 1991–92. Remarkably, the Colombian government did not default on its foreign or domestic debts during the period of study.

The rarity of large fiscal or monetary imbalances or extended periods of large monetary emission for budget finance purposes in Colombia could have contributed to a relatively stable macroeconomic environment during the period of analysis. The Colombian economy has been relatively less volatile than several of its Latin American peers: during this period, it has experienced no hyperinflationary episodes (although, as discussed, inflation was high and persistent during the seventies and the eighties). In addition, growth has been relatively stable: the worst recession since records began occurred in 1999, with a trough in real growth of −4.2 percent in 1999, a relatively small contraction compared to other Latin American economies.[1]

A more stable macroeconomic environment did not, however, foster long-term macroeconomic performance in Colombia relative to the rest of Latin America. As discussed before, real per capita GDP growth in Colombia was only slightly above the reference rate of 2 percent during the period. Figure 4 shows that the Colombian economy did not significantly outperform comparable Latin American economies. The growth experience reflected in Figure 4 also coincides with the division of our time window: during the first period, the Colombian economy diverged from other Latin American economies; by 1970, Colombian GDP per capita reached a minimum of slightly less than 0.8 times that of the region. We name this period divergent fiscal dominance. During the second period, the Colombian economy converged relatively quickly, especially during periods of coffee booms and after avoiding negative economic growth during 1980s. We name this period convergent fiscal dominance. Finally, the experience during the third period has been mixed: divergent during the first year and rapidly converging afterward (a trend that continues to this day). We name this period monetary dominance.

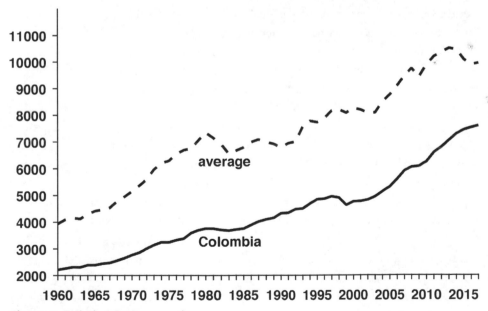

Figure 4. Relative GDP per capita

Source: Bolt et al. (2018)

Note: "Weighted average" is the average of GDP per capita for Argentina, Bolivia, Brazil, Chile, Colombia, Ecuador, Mexico, Peru, Paraguay, Uruguay, and Venezuela, in 2011 dollars, weighted by population.

Relative stagnation in Colombia amid a stable macroeconomic environment can possibly be understood if we consider the complex relationship between financial repression and fiscal or monetary imbalances throughout our period of analysis. Prior to 1991, as discussed, fiscal deficits and monetary finance were small but frequent. At the same time, existing evidence indicates that policy makers routinely employed heavy financial repression to control key monetary aggregates (Hernández Gamarra and Jaramillo Echeverri 2017). Convergence was thus a matter of commodity price shocks. After 1991, although financial repression was gradually abandoned, macroeconomic imbalances began to build up, creating the conditions for the financial crisis of the late nineties. Afterward, the solid and stable macroeconomic framework has allowed the economy to reach a relatively rapid degree of convergence.

Data

To understand the role that monetary and fiscal policy has played in Colombia, we focus on how the national central government has financed its fiscal deficit since 1960. We exclude local governments and government-owned firms from our analysis for three main reasons. First, Colombia has a centralized government in which local governments finance their expenses mostly with transfers from the central government. Since 1968 the central government has been required by law to transfer resources from value-added tax and social security to local governments, and with the new constitution of 1991, transfers increased. Local governments can levy particular local taxes, and some local governments even issue bonds that are publicly traded, but the latter sources are not the most important for financing.[2]

Additionally, the national central government is in charge of shaping fiscal policy and is the only governmental body that may be able to influence monetary policy. Finally, we are able to collect consistent data on how the national central government finances its fiscal deficit that go back to 1960. Therefore, when we refer to debt, deficit, expenditures, income, and so on, we are referring to claims on the central national government.

We use data from Junguito and Rincón (2007) for most data series since 1960. We are not able to identify indexed debt, so we can only discriminate between debt issued in Colombia, which we denote as domestic debt, and debt issued abroad, which we denote as foreign debt. We assume that foreign debt is issued in U.S. dollars and that domestic debt is issued in Colombian pesos, since debt issued in different currencies has little relevance.[3] Our data allow us to discriminate between interest rate expenditures on domestic debt and those on foreign debt. It is worth mentioning that interest on domestic debt includes interest on loans by the central bank to the government before 1991. Similarly to how we deal with domestic and foreign debt, we assume that interest payments on foreign debt are in U.S. dollars, while interest payments on domestic debt are in Colombian pesos.

We update most series from Junguito and Rincón (2007) using data from Banco de la República Colombia (the central bank). We also use data from the central bank for inflation and exchange rates. To update the series for interest payments on debt, we rely on the Ministerio de Hacienda.

Figure 5 shows the evolution of debt as a fraction of GDP. Three things are worth noting. First, since 1970 foreign debt has been greater than domestic debt, up until the 1990s. At that point, domestic debt surpassed foreign debt. This point marks the launch of the market for bonds issued by the government. Second, this point also coincided with a big increase in both domestic and foreign debt. Finally, during the last ten years, foreign debt has decreased, while domestic debt has continued increasing, although during the last five years, foreign debt has increased. As seen in one of the simulations below, this increase is not the result of a real exchange devaluation.

Periods of Analysis

We identify three main periods in Colombia since 1960 that correspond to different dynamics in inflation, the fiscal deficit, the structure of financing of the deficit, and the institutional structure of monetary policy. The first period, divergent fiscal dominance, covers the window from 1960 to 1970; the second period, convergent fiscal dominance, covers the nineteen years from 1971 to just before the promulgation of a new constitution in 1991; and the third and final period, monetary dominance, spans from 1991 to 2017, which is the latest data point in our analysis.

Table 1 summarizes the budget accounting for the three periods that we analyze. The economic institutions mainly determined the main source of government financing of its deficit: monetary emission in the first two periods and domestic debt in the final ones. Together with variations in the predominant source of financing, changes in the main

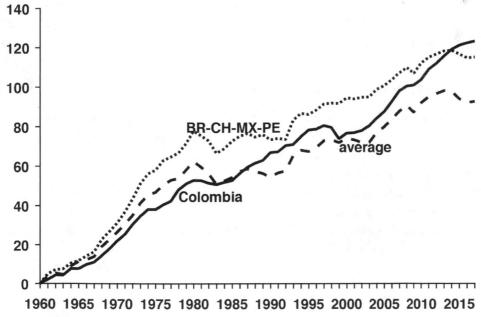

Figure 5. Debt to GDP in Colombia and in Brazil, Chile, Mexico, and Peru

Sources: Junguito and Rincón (2007), authors' calculations

components of the fiscal deficit took place over time. More specifically, we observe that until the early 1990s, most of the fiscal deficit was accounted for by the primary deficit. Beginning in 1992, interest payments on domestic debt as a share of the deficit increased, as did the share of interest payments on foreign debt a few years later (see Figure 6). Additionally, we observe that the maximum deficit reached in each of the three periods is increasing over time, which suggests increasing macroeconomic imbalances, although smaller than those observed elsewhere in Latin America. Both the primary deficit and the fiscal deficit peaked in 1999. Figure 7 shows the evolution of the fiscal deficit and its main sources of financing throughout our time window.

Before proceeding to a detailed analysis of the three periods, we provide some elements of the historical background of the joint determination of monetary and fiscal policies prior to 1960. Since the creation of the Banco de la República Colombia in 1923, the law opened the door to the possibility of the central bank extending direct loans to the central government. Despite the nominal independence of the central bank (the minister of finance only became a member of the board of directors of the central bank in 1931, and even then without the right to vote), in practice the borrowing limit was customarily bypassed by informal agreements between the government, Congress, and the central bank to enact laws that would allow the latter to directly purchase public debt instruments issued by the government (not included in the category of direct loans). This tradition persisted after the central bank was reformed in 1951, particularly after the minister of finance acquired veto power in the board at the same time as the composition of the latter was altered to include representatives from the productive sectors of the economy. The tradition also continued after 1963, when the board of directors was replaced by the monetary board, in practice composed entirely of members of the government, and it lasted until the constitution of 1991 made it harder for the central bank to make loans to the government (Hernández Gamarra and Jaramillo Echeverri 2017).

1960–70: DIVERGENT FISCAL DOMINANCE

The first period had the lowest average fiscal deficit of the three periods under analysis: 0.43 percent of GDP. Although characterized by fiscal dominance, inflation was also relatively low during this period, mainly because throughout the decade, the size of the government was small: its expenditures fluctuated between 5 and 7 percent of GDP. One reason why financing needs were small throughout this period was the steady increase in tax revenues (see Figure 8).

A notable exception to the low inflation during this period is 1963, a year that saw a one-off spike in inflation that reached the maximum observed for our sample (33.6 percent). This is also the year with the highest fiscal deficit: 1.2 percent. However, this deficit was financed mainly by foreign debt, and the monetary base even decreased.

During this period, a key change in the institutional structure of monetary policy was put into place. Specifically, the monetary reform of 1963 created the monetary board, which was in charge of monetary, credit, and exchange policy and aimed at contributing

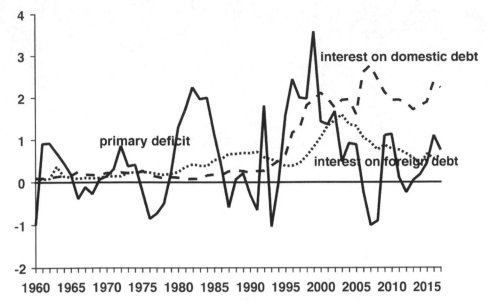

Figure 6. Primary deficit and interest payments

Sources: Junguito and Rincón (2007), Banco de la República Colombia, authors'
calculations

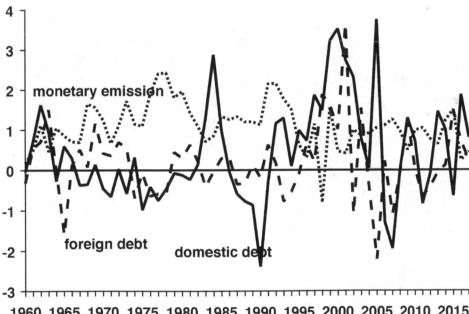

Figure 7. Financing

Sources: Junguito and Rincón (2007), Banco de la República Colombia, authors'
calculations

Table 1. Summary of budget accounting (percentage)

	$\Delta\theta^N$	$\xi\Delta\theta^*$	Δm	Seigniorage	Return on domestic debt	Return on foreign debt	T	D
Divergent fiscal dominance	0.25	0.28	0.07	0.83	−0.52	−0.19	2.01	0.15
Convergent fiscal dominance	−0.17	0.00	−0.09	1.48	−0.61	−0.32	1.65	0.50
Monetary dominance	0.97	0.30	0.16	0.79	0.19	0.14	1.11	0.78
1960–2017	0.44	0.19	0.06	1.04	−0.22	−0.09	1.47	0.56

Note: T is the transfer, and D is the primary deficit.

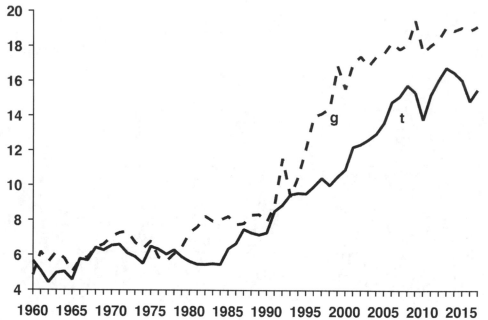

Figure 8. Government expenditures and tax revenue **g** is government expenditure; **t** is tax revenue.

Sources: Junguito and Rincón (2007), Banco de la República Colombia, authors' calculations

to the financing of those sectors of the economy considered crucial for long-term economic development.[4] The monetary board would remain in charge of monetary policy until the constitution of 1991. The switch toward a monetary policy with functions akin to those of a development bank and more directly controlled by the government naturally had implications for the financing of the fiscal deficit, as will be seen more clearly in the next subsection.

In terms of exchange policy, prior to 1967 Colombia had a complex system of multiple fixed exchange rates, which were often adjusted (Figure 9). This system was abandoned in 1967 in favor of a single, tightly controlled crawling peg with a positive slope. The change responded not only to the exchange anarchy of the previous period but also to a textbook first-generation balance of payments crisis in 1966: an increase in the central bank's credit to the government and a relative stagnation in foreign exchange reserves (see Figure 10). Naturally, a key ingredient of the regime was tight control of all transactions in foreign currency. This exchange regime lasted until the early nineties after the promulgation of a newly independent central bank.

1971–90: CONVERGENT FISCAL DOMINANCE

The second period of our analysis was characterized, first, by larger and more persistent inflation and fiscal deficits. During this period, average inflation increased to 23.1 percent and fiscal deficits doubled on average compared to the previous period (1.05 percent). Given the institutional structure brought about by the monetary board, this period can be understood as one in which fiscal dominance prevailed: increasing fiscal deficits during specific periods (particularly around the financial crisis of the early eighties) were matched by heavy use of credit from the central bank and high average inflation. During this period, monetary emission rose to prominence as the main instrument to finance the fiscal deficit, followed by foreign debt (0.31 percent).

Contrary to other emerging economies, foreign borrowing was not the rule during the second half of the seventies. There is a clear reason for this. After decades of stability

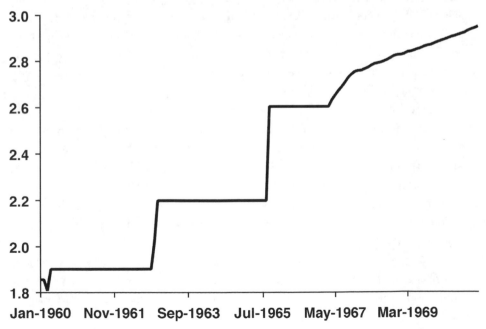

Figure 9. Nominal exchange rate, 1960–70
Source: Banco de la República Colombia

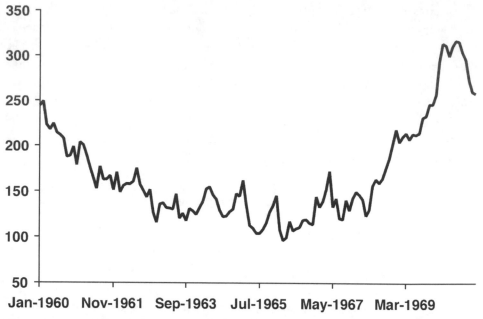

Figure 10. Foreign exchange reserves, 1960–70
Source: Banco de la República Colombia

around US$1 per kilo, the price of Colombian coffee rose almost six times in real dollars over the course of just two years, from 1975 to 1977 (see Figure 11). These developments helped bring about a period of fast economic growth (see Figure 12) and reduced external financing needs, for coffee was at the time the most important export commodity produced in a relatively undiversified Colombian economy. Figure 13 illustrates this fact: coffee exports accounted for over 10 percent of GDP in some years. At the peak of the boom in 1977, the economy grew at almost 8.5 percent in real terms. The coffee boom increased the tax revenue for the government via taxes on coffee exports.

After the coffee boom ended, the government resorted to international capital markets to fund increased government expenditures. From 1977 until 1982, government expenditures grew quickly, increasing the relative size of the state almost by half (the ratio of government expenditures to GDP grew from 5.6 percent to 8.2 percent during these five years). The main reason for this increase in government expenditures was the deep financial crisis that hit the Colombian economy in 1982, which led to the nationalization of banks and to the central bank using monetary emission to finance loans to credit-choked productive sectors.

According to Caballero Argáez and Urrutia Montoya (2006), the financial crisis was the result of increased financial repression during the coffee boom years, which led to financial innovations oriented toward speculative investments and occasionally evading regulatory controls.[5] When the Banco Nacional was intervened by authorities in June 1982 (and the Banco del Estado in October of the same year), the ensuing loss of public confidence in the financial system forced the central bank to use its facilities as lender of last resort,

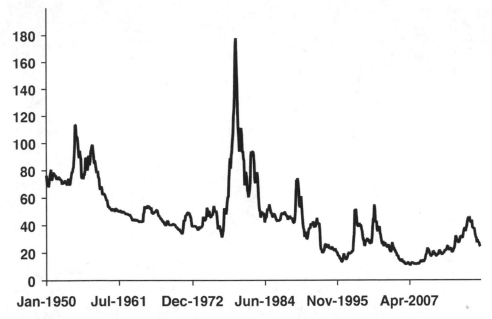

Figure 11. Price of Colombian coffee

Sources: Colombian Coffee Growers Federation, authors' calculations

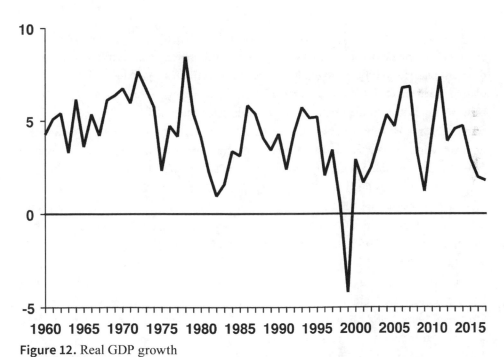

Figure 12. Real GDP growth

Sources: Junguito and Rincón (2007), Banco de la República Colombia, authors' calculations

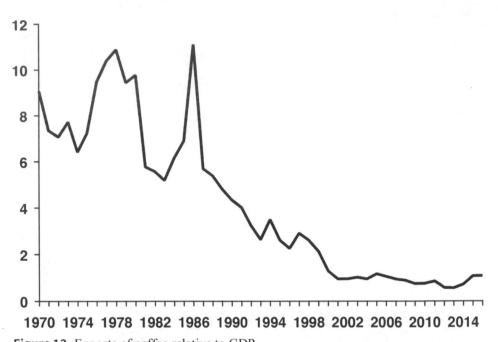

Figure 13. Exports of coffee relative to GDP
Sources: Banco de la República Colombia, World Bank, authors' calculations

in a first stage, eventually followed by the decree of outright nationalization powers to the central government. In early 1983, the monetary board used monetary emission to provide discount credit to credit-choked productive sectors as well, in a context in which the default of domestic banks to international financial institutions created additional hardship for the ability of the central government to obtain financial support abroad. In 1985, the government created the National Fund for the Guarantees of Financial Institutions (Fondo de Garantías de Instituciones Financieras—Fogafín), in charge of administering the deposit insurance fund and a resolution fund for financial institutions. Through Fogafín, the government nationalized, among other institutions, the largest bank of the system.[6] The nationalization operations consisted mostly of a bailout of financial institutions funded with monetary emission through the injection of fresh capital and the assumption (by the government) of earlier debts of banks with the central bank.

The financial crisis helps explain the increase in both the fiscal deficit and the stock of debt. The combination of these elements forced the Colombian government to rely heavily on monetary emission from the central bank as its main source of financing after 1982. After 1982, there was a prevalence of direct loans from the central bank to the government in the financing of the fiscal deficit: during the period between 1982 and 1986, an average fiscal deficit of 2.26 percent of GDP was mostly financed with credit from the central bank. Despite the financial crisis, it cannot be said that the decade of the 1980s was a lost decade for the Colombian economy, insofar as economic growth between 1980 and 1991 averaged 3.31 percent per year (more than double that of Latin America as a whole).

It is interesting to note that, even though fiscal deficits were relatively low, inflation averaged over 20 percent during this period. A possible explanation is related to the institutional setup at the time. The resources that the central bank generated (growth of monetary base and seigniorage) did not necessarily correspond to what it transferred to the government. To analyze this point further, we rely on García García and Guterman (1988) to account for the resources that the government used to finance its deficit, instead of implicitly deriving them from the series of monetary base and debt. Comparing Figures 7 and 14, we conclude that the actual resources that the government received from the central bank were greater than what was implied by the growth of the monetary base. This is consistent with the fact that the central bank lent directly to the government, besides transferring seigniorage.

Before proceeding to the next period of analysis, an important legacy of this period must be mentioned. An important consequence of an underdeveloped financial system was the absence of a well-developed mortgage credit market. To address this, in 1974 the Colombian government established special financial institutions named CAVs (Corporaciones de Ahorro y Vivienda, savings and home corporations), whose main goal was to supply mortgages. To address the negative effects of inflation, CAVs were authorized to issue loans denominated in UPACs (constant purchasing power units), indexed first to inflation and eventually to a measure of the nominal interest rate of the economy. CAVs funded these loans through deposits, whose return was also indexed to UPACs. At a point in time when deposit rates were capped, CAVs were able to increase their market share considerably. By 1985 they held 14.5 percent of all financial assets, just eleven years after coming into existence (Hernández Gamarra and Jaramillo Echeverri 2017).

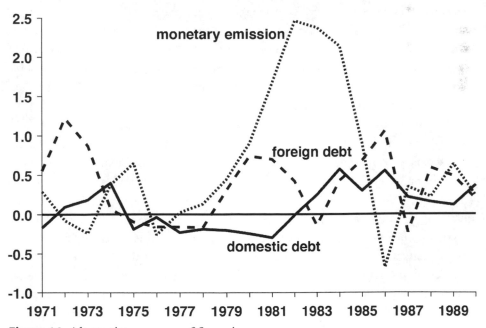

Figure 14. Alternative measure of financing

Sources: García García and Guterman (1988), authors' calculations

1991–2017: MONETARY DOMINANCE

The third period in our story begins in 1991, with the promulgation of the new political constitution of Colombia, and it includes the worst economic and financial crisis since the early twentieth century. This period was mainly characterized by the predominant use of domestic debt instruments to finance primary deficits, the virtual disappearance of monetary financing sources, and the gradual disinflation of the economy. Average inflation throughout this period fell to 10.12 percent (4.87 percent after 2000) despite fiscal deficits ballooning to an average of 3.27 percent. This period is characterized by an institutional switch of the Colombian economy to monetary dominance: larger fiscal deficits forced the government to resort to domestic and international capital markets and to respect a certain degree of fiscal sustainability, especially after the fiscal crisis of 1999. During this period, monetary financing was mostly in the form of transfers of profits from the central bank.

The promulgation of a new political constitution of Colombia in 1991 radically changed the set of institutions governing the design of and interaction between fiscal and monetary policies. Among these institutional reforms, the following two stand out as the most important for the topic of our chapter. First, the constitution entailed a new arrangement between the central and the regional governments regarding their economic and political role. In particular, the constitution committed the central government to transferring increasing resources to the regional governments, which would in turn spend them on public goods and services at the local level. Second, the constitution changed the nature and structure of the central bank, making it far more independent from the central government than at any time in its previous history. The central bank was given technical independence as to the instruments employed to achieve its main task, which was defined solely as the control of inflation. In addition, the monetary board was replaced by a board of governors in which the minister of finance had only one vote (of seven) and no veto power. Finally, the constitution prescribed that any direct loan from the central bank to the central government would require unanimous approval by the members of the board, thus all but forbidding monetary financing under this guise. To date, the independent central bank has never granted any direct loans to the central government.

One major change was the foreign exchange policy. After twenty-four years, the foreign exchange rate was allowed to be partially determined by market forces. Additionally, Colombia opened its borders to goods (import tariffs were lowered from an average of 43.7 percent in February 1990 to 11.7 percent by March 1992) and capital flows (Ocampo 1998). An important degree of exchange control was kept by the central bank in the form of crawling corridors for the nominal exchange rate, within which the nominal exchange rate was market determined, and the central bank intervened only if the rate got close to the corridor limits. Originally bands were specified to have a width of 7 percent relative to a medium level established by the central bank, as it was believed that this width was enough to adjust to shocks to the real exchange rate. The medium level was specified to crawl upward over time, according to the difference between expected domestic inflation and foreign inflation. In June 1999, the width of the bands was increased to 14 percent,

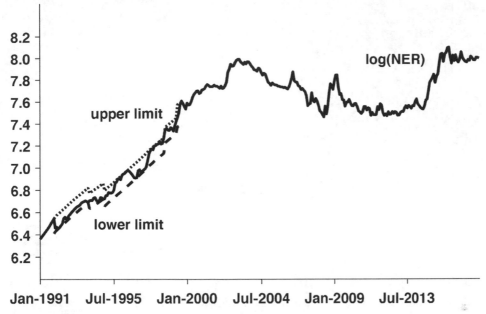

Figure 15. Log nominal exchange rate, 1991–2017
Source: Banco de la República Colombia

a few months before the band system was abandoned in September 1999 (see Figure 15, where the band is depicted by a dotted line). Since that time, the exchange regime has been (mostly) flexible, with occasional interventions from the central bank to mitigate excessive volatility in the foreign exchange market.

The transfers commitments provided by the constitution to the regional governments caused a rapid increase in central government expenditures (see Figure 8), mostly in social security (Ocampo 1997). The size of the government almost doubled between 1991 and 1999, as the ratio of central government expenditures to GDP increased from 8.9 percent to 16.9 percent. Tax revenues did not increase at the same pace, though, thereby generating an increasing primary deficit. In 1999, the fiscal deficit reached 6.4 percent of GDP, the highest mark in our sample.

During this period, inflation went from almost 30 percent to the low single digits (Figure 16). The fastest decreases in inflation occurred during the 1990s. The foreign exchange policy played a role in these dynamics. As Figure 17 shows, during the first years of the 1990s, the exchange rate bands caused expected devaluation to decrease. The nominal exchange rate followed this path as well. During the second half of the decade, this pattern reversed, but at this point, inflation was already in a decreasing pattern. In 2000, after the worst economic crisis in record (to be discussed shortly), inflation reached the single digits for the first time since the 1970s.

Figure 7 documents the financial structure that characterizes this period. First, as a result of the constitutional reform to the central bank, monetary financing decreased. According to the law, seigniorage financing is limited to the transfer of the profits of the central bank to the central government, which became positive (if small) only after

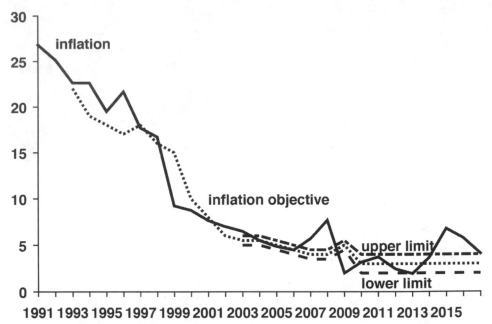

Figure 16. Inflation, 1991–2017

Source: Banco de la República Colombia

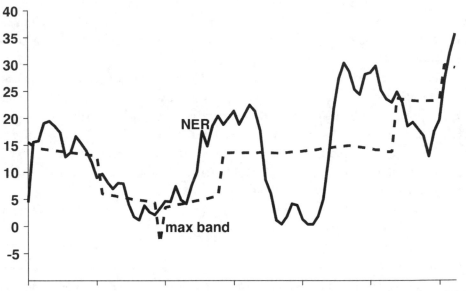

Figure 17. Expected and realized devaluation

Source: Banco de la República Colombia

1998. Second, and especially during the first half of the 1990s, the government decided to privatize key industries (mainly energy and coal), thus obtaining temporary financing worth up to 1.6 percent in 1996.

Last, and perhaps most important of all, early in the decade of the 1990s, the government decided to turn to the domestic financial market to finance its increasing primary deficit through the use of TES debt securities (Títulos de Deuda Pública Doméstica). These securities boosted the development of domestic money markets and became the predominant source of government finance until the present (by 2005, TES net emissions reached 3.7 percent of GDP). Given the high inflation prevailing at the time, the government had to pay a relatively high interest rate on domestic debt (26.7 percent implicit in 1995) in a context in which financial repression in the form of forced investments in public debt was gradually being abandoned. The increase in the stock of domestic debt went hand in hand with a sustained increase in foreign exchange reserves in the early 1990s (Figure 18).

In the transition between a fiscal deficit predominantly financed with monetary emission to one predominantly financed with domestic debt instruments, there is an important question with regard to the fate of the debt stock of the government to the central bank. In the case of Colombia, data from the balance sheet of the central bank indicate that the stock of government debt was progressively (that is, as payments to the central bank became due) swapped with TES, with which the central bank could perform monetary operations with financial intermediaries. As can be seen in Figure 19, the swap was completed in such a way that the participation of government debt securities in the assets of the central bank came to resemble almost exactly the share of outstanding government debt prior to 1991.[7]

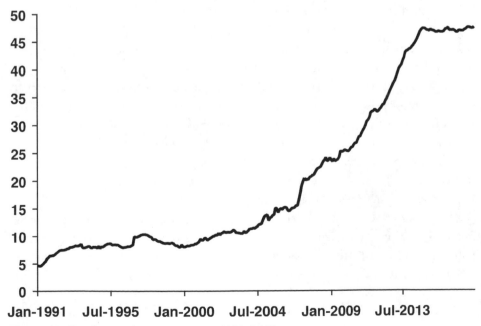

Figure 18. Foreign exchange reserves, 1991–2017
Source: Banco de la República Colombia

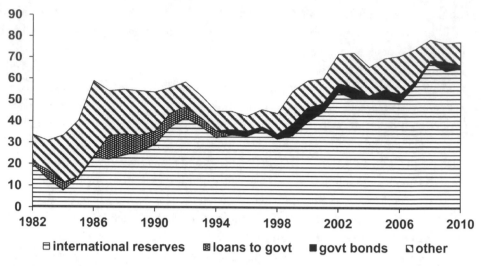

Figure 19. Balance sheet of the central bank
Source: Banco de la República Colombia

Since 1996, the symptoms of a massive crisis in external funding were being observed at the same time that a number of emerging economies were encountering difficulties in international capital markets. In particular, the government experienced an increase in the interest rate of foreign debt and a consequent increase in interest payments to international capital markets (Figure 6). The dramatic fiscal consequences of the eventual sudden stop are evident in Figure 20, with an abrupt reversal of the current account deficit. In fact, by the second quarter of 1999, there was a current account surplus.

The recession lasted from 1998 to 2000; real GDP fell by 4.2 percent in 1999, the worst contraction since records began. The central government entered a standby agreement with the International Monetary Fund, which forced a macroeconomic adjustment via the gradual reduction of the primary deficit. This was achieved through a reform of the transfers arrangements to regional governments and a series of tax reforms starting in April 2000, which gradually increased tax revenue (the effect of this reform on tax revenue is evident in Figure 8 as a change in the slope of the ratio of revenues to GDP). Both the interest expenditure and the stock of foreign debt fell gradually, whereas the interest expenditure and the stock of domestic debt stabilized, with net TES emissions fluctuating around 2.5 percent of GDP in subsequent years.

An important component of the recession was its coincidence with the deepest financial crisis in Colombian history. Because of the exchange rate bands, monetary policy naturally was partially subordinated to foreign exchange rate policy. The sudden stop that the country endured went hand in hand with devaluation pressures. The reaction of the central bank was twofold: first, it shifted upward the exchange rate bands (Figure 15), arguing that the fundamentals of the economy had changed because of the Southeast Asian and Russian crises of the late 1990s; second, the central bank defended the exchange rate band by intervening heavily in the foreign exchange rate market, which

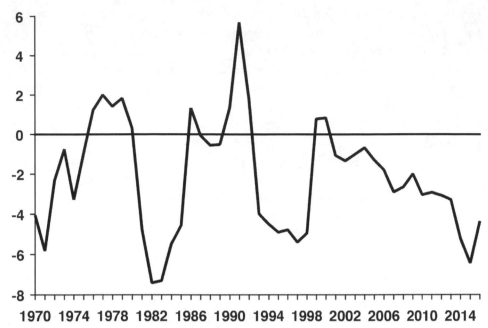

Figure 20. Current account as a share of GDP
Source: Banco de la República Colombia

led to an important decrease in foreign exchange reserves (Figure 18), and, crucially, by increasing the nominal interest rates of the economy.

As briefly discussed in the previous subsection, most of the mortgage credit market used loan instruments indexed to the nominal interest rate. The rise in real interest rates (accompanied by higher inflation and nominal depreciation) induced a large increase in nominal rates, leading to a sharp increase in the debt service ratios of a large number of Colombian households. The ensuing increase in the default rate of mortgage loans (the largest since records began) hit CAVs especially hard, leading to the bankruptcy of several of them, their acquisition by larger banks, and their disappearance as a class of financial institutions. To this day, mortgage credit as a share of GDP has not reached the levels observed previous to 1999.

The financial crisis of 1999 was thus fundamentally different from the crisis of 1982. It was especially different in a key aspect: in 1999, the central bank also heavily used its lender of last resort facilities, but unlike in the eighties, it was not allowed to finance bailout operations with monetary emission. The nationalization of banks (among them, Granahorrar—the largest CAV) was administered on this occasion by Fogafín, which capitalized troubled banks issuing bond instruments backed by the government.[8]

In 1999, the exchange rate was allowed to float (almost freely). The benefits of this floating have been twofold: monetary policy could focus on controlling inflation instead of reacting to the exchange rate, and the nominal exchange rate could respond to foreign shocks (Figure 15).[9]

After 1999, with an exchange rate that could adjust to market conditions, monetary policy could focus on achieving a low level of inflation. Beginning in 2001, the central bank adopted a full inflation-targeting scheme, established an explicit inflation target, and stated a long-term inflation goal of 3 percent. At the dawn of the twenty-first century, the Colombian economy entered a long expansionary period. Unlike the previous booms discussed in this chapter, on this occasion, economic growth was not accompanied by increasing primary deficits. This was probably the direct consequence of a new institutional arrangement introduced at the end of 2003—namely, the commitment to an explicit fiscal rule that constrains the exercise of fiscal policy to a ten-year horizon and presents the government with a debt ceiling. The success of this arrangement in ensuring the stability of public finance is perhaps evident in the stability of the implicit interest rate on public debt (domestic and foreign) amid the global financial crisis of 2008–9 and the continued ability of the central government to finance primary deficits throughout the period. In fact, for the first time ever, the central bank was able to implement a countercyclical policy and lower its policy rate as the growth of the economy decreased.

Debt Simulations

In analyzing how the government financed its fiscal deficit, we treat transfers as a residual. In this section, we analyze the role that these transfers played in the dynamics of debt. Figure 21 contrasts the observed evolution of debt to GDP with the implied evolution of debt had transfers equaled zero every year. The cumulative effect of transfers accounts for close to slightly over 60 percent of GDP by the end of the period of analysis, which implies average transfers of 1 percent of GDP.

We also analyze the role played by the real exchange rate in debt dynamics. In Figure 22 we compare the observed dynamics of debt to GDP with the implied evolution of debt with a fixed real exchange rate. The real exchange rate of 2007 is close to the average real exchange rate across our sample, so the implied evolution of debt keeps the real exchange rate fixed to the observed real exchange rate of that year. It is worth noting that both lines follow essentially the same path for most of the period, and at low levels. This is consistent with the fact that debt was low up until the early nineties. Episodes such as the real exchange rate appreciation of the late seventies and the real exchange rate devaluation of the mid-eighties are evident, but the disparity is not considerable.

The real exchange rate appreciation of the early nineties is not perceptible, since this event coincides with a surge in domestic debt. The real exchange rate devaluation after the economic crisis of the late nineties is evident, however, and accounts for slightly more than 6 percent of GDP in 2002.

Discussion

One implication of "A Framework for Studying the Monetary and Fiscal History of Latin America" is that inflation will naturally result as a consequence of fiscal deficits when there is fiscal dominance. When there is monetary dominance, fiscal deficits need to be

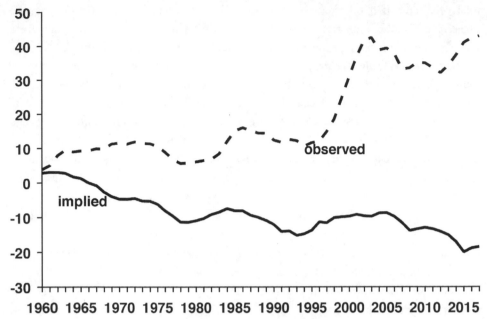

Figure 21. Isolating effect of transfers on debt dynamics

Sources: Junguito and Rincón (2007); Banco de la República Colombia, authors' calculations

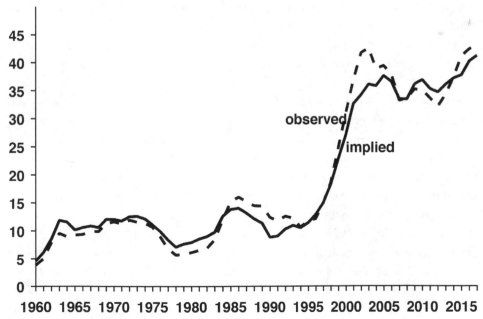

Figure 22. Isolating effect of real exchange rate on debt dynamics

Sources: Junguito and Rincón (2007); Banco de la República Colombia, authors' calculations

relatively controlled, otherwise risking costly fiscal or financial crises. In the end, the question of fiscal or monetary dominance is a question about the institutional structure (determined by historical, economic, and political factors) of a given country.

In the case of Colombia, the period between 1960 and 1990 is one in which the institutional structure of monetary policy clearly configured an equilibrium of fiscal dominance, chiefly through the lack of independence of the central bank from the government and its goal of promoting economic development in a context of heavily controlled foreign exchange markets. Within this period (1960–70), inflation was relatively low when fiscal deficits were low and duly increased under the expectation of widened fiscal deficits in the late seventies and early eighties. In contrast, the institutional reforms created by the constitution of 1991 promulgated monetary dominance in the form of a newly independent central bank. In this context, larger fiscal deficits could not be financed by monetary emission and left the economy exposed to external financing shocks. Since 2000, an equilibrium with monetary dominance and enhanced fiscal discipline mechanisms has allowed the Colombian economy to maintain macroeconomic stability and gradually lower inflation.

It has been argued elsewhere that a reason for the macroeconomic stability that Colombia endured throughout its history is the memory of a hyperinflation episode at the beginning of the twentieth century, during a civil war. In four years (1900–1903), inflation was over 50 percent per year, and in 1901 it reached 327.6 percent. This led the economic authorities of the time to create a new currency, also named the peso, by slashing two zeros from the previous currency. With this change, the new peso was at parity with the U.S. dollar (Junguito and Rincón 2007). A practical question that is left to be addressed is why and how, during the prolonged period of fiscal dominance between 1960 and 1991, inflation never increased to levels remotely comparable to those of other Latin American economies that suffered recurrent hyperinflationary episodes.

One potential explanation in this respect has been proposed by Hernández Gamarra and Jaramillo Echeverri (2017) in the form of the dynamic relationship between monetary discipline and financial repression in Colombia. Even though macroeconomic imbalances were not large prior to 1991, this was not necessarily because policies were prudent. Financial repression may have helped avoid large, undesirable macroeconomic fluctuations. This is consistent with the fact that although macroeconomic volatility was low, the Colombian economy did not catch up perceivably faster than other Latin American countries. It is also consistent with the fact that the Colombian experience of fiscal dominance only yielded convergence to other comparable Latin American economies as a consequence of commodity price shocks (particularly coffee booms).

Specifically, Hernández Gamarra and Jaramillo Echeverri (2017) argue that there is a historical, negative correlation between the growth of the monetary base and the money multiplier. This suggests that as the monetary base increased, the growth of credit did not necessarily follow suit, which might help explain why inflation in Colombia never went beyond 30 percent per year during this period. The reason for this negative comovement is consistent with the active use of reserve requirements throughout the period. In fact, the (inverse of the) money multiplier moves hand in hand with the reserve requirements (see Figure 24). Together, Figures 23 and 24 suggest that when the monetary base increased,

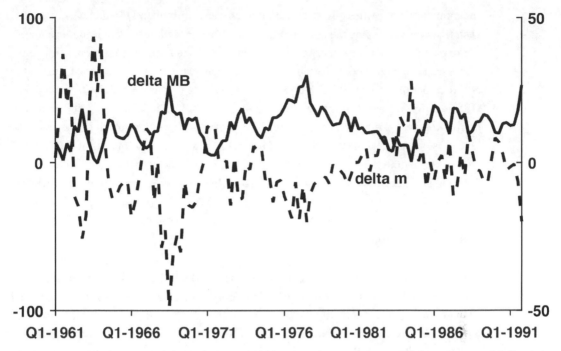

Figure 23. Annual growth of the monetary base (MB) and annual change of the money multiplier (m)
Sources: Hernández Gamarra and Jaramillo Echeverri (2017), authors' calculations

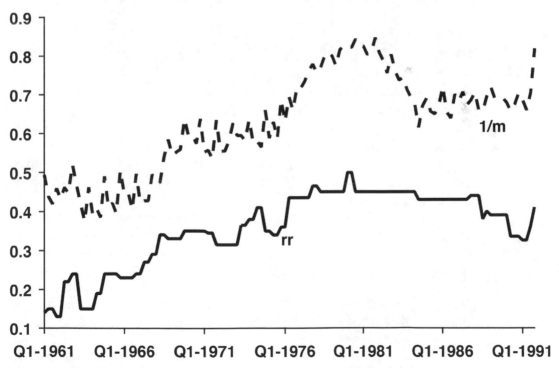

Figure 24. Reserve requirements (rr) and inverse of money multiplier (1/m)
Sources: Hernández Gamarra and Jaramillo Echeverri (2017), Avella Gómez (2007), authors'
calculations

the monetary authorities also increased the reserve requirements. In this way, the extra cash that was printed by the central bank did not necessarily translate into more loans.

In particular, reserve requirements were actively used to counteract economic events, which caused a rapid accumulation of foreign exchange reserves. For instance, during the coffee boom of the late 1970s, foreign reserves doubled from 1975 to 1976 and reached US$1.0 billion. Two years later, they reached US$2.5 billion. In 1977, the monetary board imposed a marginal reserve requirement of 100 percent on deposits over the level observed by January 31, 1977. Additionally, reserve requirements increased from 34 percent to 46.5 percent in various reforms in the following two years (Avella Gómez 2007). Consistent with this argument, the short-lived spike in inflation during the early 1980s may have been related to the fact that higher growth in monetary emission was not immediately accompanied by either rises in the reserve requirement or reductions in the money multiplier.[10]

Since 2000, the combination of monetary dominance and fiscal discipline has allowed the economy to achieve macroeconomic stability without the need for financial repression. The fact that GDP growth in Colombia remained well above zero during the global financial crisis of 2008–9 is indicative of the increased resilience of the economy to external shocks.

Together with fiscal discipline, an enhanced prudential financial regulation since 1999 has also been a key factor behind the macroeconomic stability in Colombia and behind a relatively rapid convergence to the GDP per capita of other Latin American economies.

Notes

We would like to thank Mauricio Avella, Ricardo Kerguelen, Johanna López Velandia, Ignacio Lozano, Marc Hofstetter, Laura Mojica, José Antonio Ocampo, Guillermo Perry, Hernán Rincón, Miguel Urrutia, Andrés Velasco, and the Centro de Apoyo a la Investigación Económica del Banco de la República Colombia. We also thank Jesahel Higuera for his work as research assistant. The views expressed herein are those of the authors and not necessarily those of Banco de la República Colombia or its board of directors.

1 Bértola and Ocampo (2012) and Kodama (2013) highlight the low macroeconomic volatility that Colombia has experienced.

2 According to the comptroller general of Colombia, by 2014 the debt of local governments represented around 3 percent of the debt of the national central government. Additionally, local governments are restricted regarding how much debt they can issue, as explained thoroughly in Sandoval, Gutiérrez, and Guzmán (2000).

3 The Colombian government issues bonds abroad, known as TES Global, that are denominated in Colombian pesos. Similarly, bonds have been issued in Colombia that are indexed to U.S. dollars. Unfortunately, we can only identify the currency of the bonds issued until very recently. Even so, since 2001 the share of domestic debt indexed to U.S. dollars was always below 9 percent and as of August 2009, all domestic outstanding debt has been in Colombian pesos. Foreign debt in Colombian pesos was first issued in November 2004 and has never represented more than 15 percent of the total. Also, since 2001 the share of foreign debt in U.S. dollars

has averaged more than 80 percent of the total outstanding debt.

4 According to Hernández Gamarra and Jaramillo Echeverri (2017), from 1951 to 1963, monetary policy was under the control of private entities (among them, private banks) delegated by the government to administer monetary and exchange policy in the interest of an "ordered development of the Colombian economy."

5 A favorite mechanism for regulated institutions to evade controls was the use of complex operations between financial and real sector firms belonging to the same financial conglomerate. Later in this chapter we will elaborate on the relationship between financial repression and monetary policy in Colombia.

6 At the end of 1983, the crisis hit the largest bank of the system (Banco de Colombia) after years of mismanagement, complex lending operations to firms belonging to the Banco's conglomerate funded with deposits, illegal foreign currency loans to the same firms through the Banco's branch in Panama, non-performing loans, and default to international financial institutions. The Banco de Colombia was finally nationalized in January 1986.

7 The ability of the central bank to purchase TES in secondary markets does not constitute seigniorage or monetary emission to finance the fiscal deficit inasmuch as interest rates are market determined.

8 The government also promulgated laws to alleviate the debt service ratio of mortgage borrowers. According to Caballero Argáez and Urrutia Montoya (2006), the total cost of the crisis to Fogafín reached 9.7 percent of the GDP in 1998. A total of thirty-five financial institutions were intervened for liquidation by the authorities.

9 It is interesting to note, though, that in 2016 the central bank had to increase its policy rate in part because of an important devaluation in the nominal exchange rate that resulted in a pass-through in inflation, even as the real growth of the economy was low.

10 The argument proposed here of a policy mix of money growth and financial repression implies a broader understanding of money supply in the context of a simple government budget constraint, as detailed in earlier sections. In this case, seigniorage revenues would be interpreted as also including those earned as credit expansion from a repressed banking system. In this sense, with higher financial repression, monetary emission would correspond to a larger share of seigniorage revenues.

References

Avella Gómez, Mauricio. 2007. "El encaje bancario en Colombia: Perspectiva general." Borradores de Economia 470. Banco de la República de Colombia, Bogotá.

Bértola, Luis, and José Antonio Ocampo. 2012. *The Economic Development of Latin America since Independence.* Oxford: Oxford University Press.

Bolt, Jutta, Robert Inklaar, Herman de Jong, and Jan Luiten van Zanden. 2018. "Rebasing 'Maddison': New Income Comparisons and the Shape of Long-Run Economic Development." Maddison Project Working Paper 10, Groningen Growth and Development Centre, University of Groningen, Netherlands. https://www.ggdc.net/maddison.

Caballero Argáez, Carlos, and Miguel Urrutia Montoya. 2006. "Las crisis financieras del siglo XX." In *Historia del sector financiero colombiano en el siglo XX: Ensayos sobre su desarrollo y sus crisis*, edited by Carlos Caballero Argáez and Miguel Urrutia Montoya, 641–60. Bogotá: Asobancaria and Grupo Editorial Norma.

García García, Jorge, and Lía Guterman. 1988. "Medición del déficit del sector público colombiano y su financiación: 1950–1986." *Ensayos sobre política económica* 7 (14): 115–33.

Hernández Gamarra, Antonio, and Juliana Jaramillo Echeverri. 2017. "La Junta Monetaria y el Banco de la República." In *Historia del Banco de la República, 1923–2015*, edited by José Darío Uribe Escobar, 185–274. Bogotá: Banco de la República Colombia.

Junguito, Roberto, and Hernán Rincón. 2007. "La política fiscal en el siglo XX en Colombia." In *Economía colombiana del siglo XX: Un análisis cuantitativo*, edited by James A. Robinson and Miguel Urrutia, 239–311. Bogotá:

Banco de la República and Fondo de Cultura Económica.

Kodama, Masahiro. 2013. "How Large Is the Cost of Business Cycles in Developing Countries?" *Review of Development Economics* 17 (1): 49–63.

Ocampo, José Antonio. 1997. "Una evaluación de la situación fiscal colombiana." *Coyuntura económica* 27 (2): 89–121.

———. 1998. "La política económica durante la administración Samper." *Coyuntura económica* 28 (4): 155–87.

Sandoval, Carlos Alberto, Javier Alberto Gutiérrez, and Carolina Guzmán. 2000. "Colombia y la deuda pública territorial." Estudios de Economía y Ciudad 8, Secretaría de Hacienda de Bogotá.

Discussion of the History of Colombia

Arturo José Galindo
Banco de la República de Colombia

David Perez-Reyna and Daniel Osorio-Rodríguez present an interesting description of the monetary and fiscal policies of Colombia since 1960. Their characterization of those almost six decades during three distinct periods—one of fiscal dominance with low inflation, a second one of fiscal dominance with higher inflation, and a third one of monetary dominance—seems accurate and uncontroversial.

The discussion presented in the chapter could be complemented along two fronts. First, because of their focus on central government finances, the authors understate the role of fiscal (or quasi-fiscal) matters in the rise and stabilization at moderate levels of inflation during their second period of analysis (1971–90). While the explanations provided by Perez-Reyna and Osorio-Rodríguez are accurate, the authors themselves question why, given a not-so-large increase in the fiscal deficit, inflation rises so much and continues in the 20 to 30 percent range. Part of the explanation comes from several institutional arrangements existing in Colombia that substituted for fiscal policies (with monetary implications), which are not captured in central government—or in some cases, any—fiscal data.

Two examples are the government substitute functions of the National Coffee Fund, a government fund managed by the private sector (National Federation of Coffee Growers), and the mechanisms developed in the financial sector and the central bank to foster home ownership. Through different mechanisms, which did not have a direct counterpart in the central government's fiscal accounts, expansionary fiscal policies that were financed through money issuance were carried out during several years of the second period of analysis. This happened thanks to the governance of monetary policy since the mid-1960s and up to the early 1990s. Beginning in 1963, the Junta Monetaria, the entity guiding monetary policy, was composed of the minister of finance, the minister of development (who led the housing initiatives), the minister of agriculture (recall that the major export was coffee), the chief of the National Planning Department, and the general manager of the central bank. In 1976, the director of the main government trade agency, INCOMEX (Instituto Colombiano de Comercio Exterior), was added to the junta. Without vote were the economic secretary of the president's office, the banking superintendent, and two technical advisers to the manager of the central bank. By design, the most important lobbies of the country made up part of the governing body of monetary policy. This arrangement had important consequences for how several sectors—particularly the coffee and the housing sectors—benefited from, at times, expansionary monetary policies.

As the authors discuss, coffee was the major export of Colombia throughout a significant part of the period analyzed. During many years, the expenditure of the National Coffee Fund, whose revenue was a tax on coffee exports, substituted for that of the government in many areas of the country. The Coffee Fund paid for the construction of infrastructure and provided various social security services in many areas of the country. To keep its levels of expenditure, the fund relied on the central bank's exchange rate management and its monetary consequences. For example, when the price of coffee rose and commodity revenue in foreign currency inflows increased, they were monetized by the central bank to avoid a currency appreciation and allow an increase in the fund's expenditure. With the bonanza of 1975–77, this mechanism led to inflationary pressures that later were perpetuated again through other indexation mechanisms. From this perspective, the expenditure of the Coffee Fund was inflationary, not because the central bank was lending to the public sector, but via the protection of the exchange rate and Decree 444 of 1967 (exchange rate regulation), which was designed with the coffee growers in mind.

In the early 1970s, the interests of the coffee sector were explicitly represented in the Junta Monetaria. But they were not the only major lobby that had a seat on the Junta. The interests of different parties supporting the development of a housing market (one of the key drivers of the National Development Plan of 1970–74—dubbed "the Four Strategies"), the minister of development, and the chief of the National Planning Department also sat on the Junta and had a say in the design of a potentially inflationary mechanism to develop mortgages. The view of the National Development Plan, inspired by Lauchlin Currie, a North American economist advising the government, was that housing shortages could be addressed by developing long-term mortgages. Given the risks associated with volatile interest rates and maturity risks because of the short terms of any savings instrument, developing mortgages would require some policy intervention.

The solution designed at the time was to index mortgages to inflation and have them supplied by financial intermediaries that could issue deposits in inflation-indexed units. So economic authorities created the Corporaciones de Ahorro y Vivienda—CAVs (savings and loans entities). The CAVs had no currency risk, since they issued deposits and loans in the same currency (inflation-indexed units [UPAC, Unidad de Poder Adquisitivo]), but they were still exposed to maturity risks coming from mismatches between the primarily overnight term of deposits and the longer terms of mortgage loans. This risk was dealt with through a convoluted arrangement with the central bank. The FAVI (Fondo de Ahorro y Vivienda), a fund to provide liquidity support to CAVs at the central bank, was created. This became an automatic facility through which CAVs could mitigate the risks of transforming short-term deposits, which competed with interest-rate-paying deposits at any other financial institution, into long-term inflation-indexed loans. When inflation was lower than interest rates, deposits in CAVs would fall and migrate to the rest of the financial system, causing liquidity problems in CAVs. At that point, the CAVs went to the FAVI, which compensated the fall in deposits via money issuance, which in turn would reduce interest rates and raise inflation until the CAVs deposits recovered. The opposite would happen when inflation was high. CAVs would have excess liquidity, which they would take to the FAVI, a monetary contraction would take place, inflation would fall, and interest rates would rise.

In the 1970s, because of the coffee boom, the interests of coffee growers represented in the Junta led to a monetary expansion and inflation. When the boom was over and the debt crisis hit in the early 1980s and interest rates rose, a monetary expansion through the FAVI took place to compensate the CAVs, in addition to a monetary-based rescue of the rest of the banking system, as mentioned by the authors.

Given the many interests prevailing in the governance of monetary policy, sector-specific shocks that in a way led to quasi-fiscal actions, and that would be reflected in a more comprehensive measure of the fiscal deficit, had overall inflationary consequences. These are not captured in any central government data. In addition, as noted by Carrasquilla (1999) in analyzing moderate inflation in Colombia, several indexation mechanisms were developed, which helped perpetuate any inflationary shock. Colombia ended up having a very convoluted policy framework incorporating several automatic mechanisms that conditioned monetary policy to fiscal (quasi-fiscal) pressure and that contributed to a rise in inflation during most of the 1970s and 1980s.

Interestingly, despite these mechanisms, inflation remained at moderate levels, in part because of the role of the advisers to the Junta. These advisers were usually very technically oriented central bank career economists, with a conservative view of monetary policy that designed instruments to keep inflation in line and counteract the expansionary mechanisms embedded in policy. The use of reserve requirements briefly discussed in the chapter is an example of one of these instruments.

The second complementary discussion to that of the authors, and one that is highly relevant in the recent history of Colombia's fiscal policy, pertains to the role played by the 1991 constitution in the fiscal deficit. The chapter explains in enough detail how the 1991 political constitution allowed for an independent central bank and documents how that relevant change led to a reduction in inflation. However, the chapter falls short in explaining the dynamics of the fiscal deficit during that period and deals only tangentially with how the same notorious institutional change that proclaimed the independence of the central bank also explains the large rise in the fiscal deficit.

The 1991 constitution imposed many mandates on the Colombian government without matching them to income generation. Several authors have documented the fiscal costs of many constitutional mandates regarding pension payments, provision of health services, wage indexation, provision of affordable housing, and subsidized mortgages, among others. While on the one hand, the constitution bought monetary stability, the fiscal cost was, however, substantial.

Overall, this chapter helps order the discussion and complements the existing literature well. Readers interested in inflation dynamics in the 1970s, 1980s, and early 1990s; the political economy during the reforms of the monetary system; other reforms of the

1990s, including the 1991 constitution; and the fiscal costs of the constitutional mandates would benefit from a reading of the references that follow.

References

Carrasquilla, Alberto. 1999. *Estabilidad y gradualismo: Ensayos sobre economía colombiana*. Bogotá: TM Editores.

Ecuador

The History of Ecuador

Simón Cueva
TNK Economics Ecuador and Laureate International Universities

Julián P. Díaz
Department of Economics, Quinlan School of
Business, Loyola University Chicago

Major fiscal and monetary events, 1960–2017

1971 Hydrocarbons law declares oil state property	**1999** Bank deposits frozen Nationalization of banking system
1982 Devaluation and crawling peg	
1983 Conversion of private foreign debt to sucres	Default on Brady bonds
	2000 Dollarization
1987 Default	Oil stabilization fund to promote government savings
1988 Tax reform	
1992 Law granting central bank independence	Restructuring of foreign commercial debt
Devaluation and fixed exchange rate to tackle inflation	**2002** Fiscal responsibility law
	2008 Suppression of central bank independence and fiscal stabilization funds
1994 Financial sector liberalization	
Foreign debt restructuring (Brady Plan)	
	2014 Return to international financial markets
1998 New constitution granting central bank independence	

Introduction

The recent economic history of Ecuador is marked by two crucial events. The first is the discovery of oil reserves in the late 1960s, which transformed the Ecuadorian economy from agrarian to oil-exporting (oil exports started in 1972). This shift produced a boom that lasted for almost a decade, with output growing at an average rate of nearly 9 percent between 1972 and 1981. More importantly, it radically changed the role of the government in the economy. Indeed, prior to 1972, the government (measured as the outlays of the central government) represented less than 10 percent of output. With oil as a new source of revenue, the size of the government doubled and has essentially remained at those high levels ever since, despite the large fluctuations in oil prices. The second event was the government's decision to officially dollarize the economy in 2000. The adoption of the U.S. dollar as legal tender ended a period of chronically high inflation that had lasted for almost three decades and has produced an environment of one-digit inflation since 2003.

Those two events in turn define three broad economic eras, as displayed in Figures 1 and 2. The first period, which goes from 1960—the initial year in our study—until the end of the oil boom in 1981, was characterized by rapid growth and low inflation. Prior to the oil boom, the country had been growing at an average rate of nearly 5 percent per year (and roughly 2 percent in per capita terms). The oil boom provided a further boost to the economy, and output per capita surged well above the 2 percent per year growth trend. Furthermore, inflation was low, averaging 8.6 percent per year during the 1960–81 period (and only 4.9 percent if the oil boom period is excluded). While the boost to the economy from the oil boom led to an increase in the inflation rate, which averaged 12.9 percent between 1972 and 1981, that value was not very different from the one registered in the United States during the highly inflationary 1970s.

The second era includes the two "lost decades" of the Ecuadorian economy, and it extends from the onset of the Latin American debt crisis in 1982 to the end of the twentieth century. This period is characterized by a stagnant economy, with an average GDP growth rate of only 1.9 percent per year (−0.5 percent in per capita terms). In fact, Ecuador's growth during this period was so dismal that it satisfies the definition of a "great depression" as described in Kehoe and Prescott (2007).[1] During this period, output per capita sank increasingly below the 2 percent trend, and by 1999 it was lower than in 1982. In addition to this poor economic performance, persistently high inflation became a trait of the Ecuadorian economy, averaging 39 percent per year between 1982

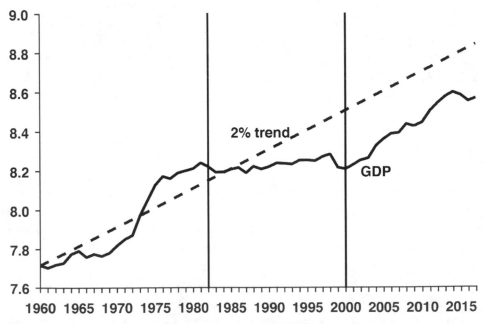

Figure 1. GDP per capita and 2 percent trend, 2010 US$, log scale

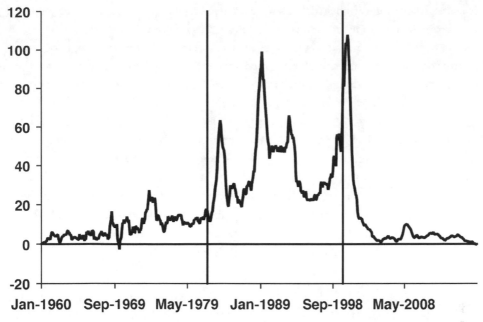

Figure 2. Inflation rate, percent

and 1999. While many countries in Latin America, such as Argentina, Bolivia, Brazil, or Peru, also suffered periods of high inflation—and even hyperinflation—during the 1970s and 1980s, by the 1990s those same countries had been able to restrain the rate of inflation. In Ecuador, however, it remained high—well in the two-digit range.

The third period is the dollarized era, which started in January 2000. Aided by a second oil boom fueled by historically high oil prices, the Ecuadorian economy started growing again, expanding at an average rate of 3.7 percent between 2000 and 2017. Output per capita experienced a noticeable recovery, although it has still not returned to the 2 percent trend. Perhaps more remarkably, it was only after dollarizing the economy that inflation fell back to the one-digit levels observed during the 1960–81 period. The fact that it was possible to attain a low inflationary environment only after Ecuador renounced its monetary independence is reminiscent of the findings in Sargent (1993), who documents how Austria, Germany, Hungary, and Poland were able to end their inflationary episodes during the 1920s only after they introduced significant policy regime changes in their governments' behavior.

Thus, broadly speaking, the economic history of Ecuador since 1960 can be summarized as nearly two decades of stagnation and chronically high inflation wedged between two periods of *relative* normality. Why did the Ecuadorian economy perform so poorly during the 1980s and 1990s? A common explanation for slow growth and price instability has been to attribute those undesirable outcomes to bad fiscal and monetary policies. To shed light on those linkages, we document the most salient features of the monetary and fiscal history of Ecuador during the 1960–2017 period and complement this review with a government budget constraint accounting exercise that follows Sargent (1993) in order to assess whether government deficits were financed with seigniorage revenues—instead of borrowing, for example—and consequently led to inflation.

As a preview to our findings, we present a summary of the government budget constraint accounting exercise in Table 1, which depicts the central government's obligations during the three periods and the different sources used to finance them (we have broken the first period into two parts in order to isolate the effects of the oil boom).[2]

Our analysis suggests that inadequate government policies indeed contributed to the disappointing performance of the Ecuadorian economy. According to the budget constraint accounting results, during the 1960–71 period, when the size of the government was relatively small, deficit financing needs were low as well, and the use of seigniorage was limited: seigniorage revenues during this era were the lowest for the entire period under analysis. These patterns coincide with a period of higher-than-average growth and low inflation.

The oil boom of the 1970s changed those trends and led to a disproportionate increase in the size of the government and a surge in government deficits, as shown in Figure 3.

Table 1. Central government budget accounting results, 1960–2017 (percentage of GDP)

| | Sources of central government financing | | | | | |
Period	Domestic debt	Foreign debt	Money issuing	Seigniorage	Assets in Central Bank	Total
1960–81	0.08	1.39	−0.03	1.40	−0.32	2.52
1960–71 (pre-oil)	1.26	0.38	0.14	0.85	−0.19	2.44
1972–81 (oil boom)	−1.34	2.60	−0.23	2.05	−0.48	2.61
1982–99	1.79	0.64	−0.02	1.82	−0.68	3.56
2000–2017	−0.08	−0.90			−0.17	−1.16

| | Central government obligations | | | | |
Period	Domestic return	Foreign return	Primary deficit	"Transfers"	Total
1960–81	0.64	0.89	0.60	0.39	2.52
1960–71 (pre-oil)	0.68	0.45	0.46	0.85	2.44
1972–81 (oil boom)	0.59	1.43	0.75	−0.15	2.61
1982–99	0.69	4.20	−2.47	1.13	3.56
2000–2017	0.59	1.31	0.31	−3.36	−1.16

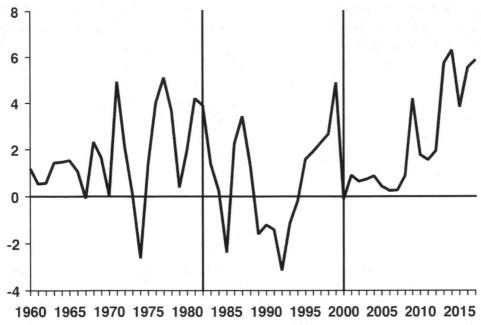

Figure 3. Central government deficit, percentage of GDP

In particular, the massive increase in the size of the government fueled by the oil boom was not accompanied by the creation of any substantial savings fund. This left the government's accounts vulnerable to unexpected declines in oil prices. When crude prices eventually stopped surging in the late 1970s, the government intensified its external borrowing to sustain its inflated spending patterns—amassing a large amount of debt in the process—instead of implementing a fiscal adjustment. The credit crunch derived from the Latin American debt crisis of the early 1980s in turn rendered that strategy unfeasible, but yet again there was no significant fiscal correction. The remarkable downward inflexibility of government expenditures, in spite of a series of negative shocks—severe weather phenomena, banking crises, and oil price collapses—resulted in large fiscal imbalances, which by then included the additional burden of the debt. To finance the deficits, the government relied on seigniorage, and inflation ensued. The lack of any substantial and lasting fiscal adjustment continued through the 1990s. High inflation became entrenched, and the economy stagnated. Inflation only returned to low levels when the discretion to finance the deficits using seigniorage was removed by the establishment of the dollarization system.

After the devastating financial crisis of 1999, the dollarization regime presented a second chance for the adoption of sounder government policies—and the abandonment of failed ones. Indeed, the size of the government briefly contracted during the early years of the 2000s, and fiscal responsibility laws were passed to ensure the long-term sustainability of the dollarization system. The resulting smaller deficits can easily be appreciated in Figure 3. However, this trend reverted after 2007, when government expenditures rose sharply again—aided by historically high oil prices—and reached levels similar to the ones observed during the oil boom of the 1970s. The windfall generated by the second oil boom, however, was not sufficient to produce balanced budgets, and the deficit surged again. Since the dollarization arrangement eliminated the ability of the government to turn to seigniorage to satisfy its obligations, the government has had to increase its indebtedness—both domestic and foreign—to cover its financing needs. Thus, in spite of large deficits, inflation has remained low during the dollarization era because the government cannot finance its expenditures with the inflation tax. However, the cycle of a boom in oil prices followed by a steep surge in government spending and a rapid rise in government borrowing (at increasingly onerous terms) is evocative of the policies followed during the 1970s and of their painful consequences. This in turn has raised concerns about the long-term sustainability of the dollarization scheme.

Finally, the budget constraint accounting analysis shows that primary deficits, at least as explicitly reported in Ecuadorian statistics, explain a portion but not the complete picture of the government's financing needs. In fact, "extraordinary transfers," as defined in "A Framework for Studying the Monetary and Fiscal History of Latin America," account for a significant fraction of the government's obligations. These transfers represent financing needs beyond primary deficits—not explicitly recorded in the officially reported fiscal figures—and reveal the untold story of hidden fiscal costs. Indeed, we find that transfers were especially large and positive during the most arduous periods of Ecuador's economic history, such as when the government decided to take over the private sector's foreign debt (thus assuming the exchange rate risk) in the 1980s, or when the government bailed out the banking system during the financial crisis of 1999. In that sense, the large extraordinary transfers reflect the consequences of the government's own mistakes, as well as the mistakes of others (e.g., the private sector), which eventually ended up becoming the government's responsibility.

The remainder of this study is organized as follows. In the second section, we provide a review of the most important facts of Ecuadorian macroeconomic history from 1960 to 2017. The third section reviews the main patterns of fiscal policy, and the fourth analyzes the evolution of government debt. The fifth section documents the main trends in monetary aggregates. In the sixth section, we present the budget constraint accounting methodology, discuss its results for the Ecuadorian case, and assess the role of the extraordinary transfers. Our conclusions appear in the seventh section.

The Three Eras of Ecuadorian Economic History

In this section, we document the most salient facts in Ecuadorian economic history for the period 1960 to 2017. We divide our analysis into the three aforementioned periods: 1960–81, the transition from the pre-oil economy to the oil boom of the 1970s; 1982–99, the two "lost decades"; and 2000–2017, the dollarized era. Additionally, we break down these periods into shorter subperiods because of the diverse approaches to economic policy adopted by the different governments.[3]

GROWTH AND THE OIL BOOM, 1960–81

The Pre-oil Economy, 1960–71

Prior to the discovery of its oil reserves in the late 1960s, Ecuador was primarily an agricultural economy with a small industrial sector. Exports, which averaged 16 percent of GDP during the 1960–71 period, were clustered around a handful of agricultural commodities, out of which bananas—the main export product—accounted for nearly 40 percent of total exports.

During this era, the government played a relatively small role in the economy. The revenues of the central government amounted to 10 percent of GDP. Of those, nearly 90 percent corresponded to taxes, with tariffs and export taxes accounting for over 40 percent of total revenues. However, in spite of their importance, the inability of the government to efficiently collect taxes limited its participation in the overall economy. On the other hand, the outlays of the central government represented, on average, 11.4 percent of GDP. Wages and salaries accounted for 42 percent of total expenditures, and purchases of goods and services claimed nearly another 30 percent. Taking into account revenues and outlays, the central government ran an average deficit of 1.4 percent of GDP between 1960 and 1971. This average is somewhat inflated because of the deficit in 1971 of 4.9 percent of GDP, when the government significantly increased its expenditures in anticipation of the oil revenues that it would be earning the following year. Excluding that year, deficits were even smaller, averaging 1 percent of GDP.

Throughout this period, the Central Bank of Ecuador—which had been founded in 1927—operated according to the Ley de Régimen Monetario (LRM, or Law of Monetary Regime) of 1948. The significant fluctuations in the stock of international reserves experienced during this period from the volatility in Ecuador's export prices required the central bank to routinely implement policies such as advanced deposit requirements for imports and import restrictions on selected products to contain the loss of reserves and preserve the stability of the exchange rate.[4]

The LRM of 1948 also required the central bank to "adapt the liquidity in the economy and the volume of credit to promote the growth of national output" and to "prevent and moderate inflationary or deflationary trends." To attain these objectives, the tool most commonly used by the monetary authority was to change the reserve requirement ratios. Similarly, to expand the money supply and to promote growth in industries deemed as important, the central bank would provide loans to both private banks and the private sector. The law also allowed the government to borrow from the central bank to finance its operations. In principle, the government would receive an advance from the central bank at the beginning of the year, which would be repaid during the remaining months.

In spite of the reliance of the Ecuadorian economy on just a few agricultural products and an incipient industrial base, output (measured in sucres) grew at an average annual rate of 4.7 percent, although strong population growth implied a per capita average rate close to 2 percent. Moreover, inflation was notably low—in particular when compared to the rates observed in the following decades—and averaged 4.9 percent per year.

The Oil Boom, 1972–81

Sizable oil reserves were discovered in the Amazon region in the late 1960s, which enabled Ecuador to start oil exports in 1972. This event radically transformed the Ecuadorian economy, with oil quickly becoming its main export product, accounting for over half of total exports between 1972 and 1981. This event changed not only the composition of exports but also their importance in the overall economy, and during this period, exports represented nearly 25 percent of total output. Moreover, the timing of the discovery of oil occurred at a crucial moment for the Ecuadorian economy. The world price of bananas had been dwindling since the mid-1960s. At the same time, the oil price—which had averaged US$3 per barrel (dpb) during the 1960s and early 1970s—started to consistently increase in 1973 until it reached 37 dpb in 1980, before dipping slightly to 36.7 dpb in 1981.[5]

The oil boom provided a boost for the Ecuadorian economy, and GDP (measured in sucres) grew at an average yearly rate of 8.8 percent (and nearly 6 percent in per capita terms). In 1973 alone, output grew at an impressive rate of 25 percent. Growth rates, however, declined over the period, and in 1981 the economy expanded at only a 3.9 percent pace.

The bonanza period coincided with a series of military regimes that ruled the country from 1972 until 1979; these regimes used the oil windfall to redefine the role of the state, making it an active participant in the economy and the leader of the development process. Indeed, the revenues of the central government averaged almost 21 percent of GDP during the 1972–81 period—more than doubling the corresponding value from the previous period—with oil revenues accounting for nearly a third of the revenues (tax revenues represented 44 percent of total revenues on average during the same span). The rise in total expenditures was even more pronounced, averaging 23 percent of GDP during the period. Those expenditures corresponded mainly to public-sector wages (42 percent of total revenues), purchases of goods and services (26 percent), and capital expenditures (17 percent), mainly in large infrastructure projects such as highway and hydroelectric plant construction.

The considerable increase in revenues was not sufficient to finance the expenditure expansion. As a result, the central government posted deficits in each year between 1972 and 1981 (with the exception of 1974). The average deficit during this period was 2 percent of GDP, more than twice as large as the deficits recorded during the previous period. The government, however, was able to finance the deficits relatively easily. Favorable conditions characterized by abundant liquidity in the international financial markets and very low interest rates allowed the government to fund the deficits by increasing its foreign indebtedness. Indeed, the public foreign debt went from $248 million in 1971 to $4.416 million by the end of 1981; that is, it grew by a factor of almost 18. As a percentage of GDP (measured in dollars), the public foreign debt increased from 9 percent to 20.2 percent of GDP during the same period.

The oil boom brought about another change in the Ecuadorian economy: the emergence of inflation, which averaged 13.2 percent per year between 1972 and 1981. Some Ecuadorian analysts attributed the increase in the inflation rate to the sudden increase in the demand for goods and services caused by the new oil wealth (a shift to the right in the aggregate demand curve, according to policy makers), which could not be matched by a commensurate increase in aggregate output. However, this was also a period marked by rapid growth in the monetary aggregates. The monetary base grew at an average annual rate of 21.9 percent between 1972 and 1981, while the annual average growth of M1 was 23.7 percent, much faster rates than the ones observed during the previous period (9.1 percent and 9.7 percent, respectively). Especially during the early part of the oil boom era, the increase in international reserves was the main contributor to the increase in the monetary base. The central bank tried to contain the expansion in the monetary aggregates by restricting the net domestic credit, more specifically the net credit to the public sector. In addition to the use of changes in the reserve requirement ratio, for the first time since its foundation, the central bank started conducting open market operations by issuing *bonos de estabilización monetaria* (BEMs, or monetary stabilization bonds) in order to withdraw liquidity from the economy. Additionally, the central bank imposed limits on the expansion of private bank lending and, to ease the pressure on prices, relaxed the restrictions on imports.

THE ECUADORIAN GREAT DEPRESSION, 1982–99

The Debt Crisis and the End of the "Golden Years," 1982–83

The favorable conditions enjoyed by the Ecuadorian economy during the 1970s would not last indefinitely. The growth in oil prices stagnated in 1981 and started a continuous decline throughout the remainder of the decade, falling from an average price of 36.7 dpb in 1981 to 19.6 dpb in 1989 (69.7 dpb to 31.3 dpb in 2010 dollars). Interest rates, which had been low—and even negative in real terms in some instances—started rising in 1981 as a reflection of the policies implemented by the Federal Reserve. Eventually, this would lead to the decision of the Mexican government to default on its external debt, which triggered a freeze on new loans to all countries in the region. This decision was particularly painful for the Ecuadorian government, which had been borrowing heavily from abroad to finance its expenditures.

On the domestic front, a border war with Peru in 1981 created an additional burden on the fiscal accounts and spread uncertainty and panic in the economy. Moreover, severe floods caused by the El Niño weather phenomenon in 1982 and 1983 destroyed agricultural crops, thus hurting primary exports, and destroyed the country's infrastructure, compounding the fiscal difficulties.

Facing this complicated scenario, in 1982 the government implemented a stabilization program that increased fuel and utility prices, eliminated subsidies, and cut expenditures. This adjustment plan—and the plans that would end up being put into practice during this decade—were part of the requirements in exchange for standby loans and foreign debt restructuring demanded by the International Monetary Fund and other multilateral organizations, which, because of the freeze in lending from private lenders, had become the only source of borrowing for the Ecuadorian government. In spite of these measures, the central government ran deficits averaging 2.6 percent of GDP in 1982 and 1983.

Additionally, the official exchange rate—which had been fixed since 1970—was depreciated from 25 to 33 sucres per dollar in May 1982. This decision was complemented with a scheme of daily *minidevaluaciones* (crawling peg) in 1983. These depreciations had multiple objectives: one was to correct the real appreciation of the sucre due to the prolonged fixed exchange rate coupled with persistently high inflation since the 1970s; another was to provide the government with more sucres per barrel of oil exported; and finally, they also were aimed at discouraging imports due to the necessity to generate current account surpluses.

The depreciations, however, severely hurt the private sector, which, like the government, had increased its foreign borrowing during the 1970s, encouraged by a fixed exchange rate regime in place since 1970, low inflation, and the abundance of liquidity in the international markets. Indeed, while at the end of 1971 the total private foreign debt amounted to barely $13 million, by the end of 1982, it had skyrocketed to $1,628 million. Fearing generalized bankruptcies and an eventual financial collapse, the government decided to implement the so-called *sucretización* mechanism of the private foreign debt. According to this arrangement, private foreign debt was converted into sucres and was to be paid to the central bank, which in turn assumed the responsibility to pay foreign creditors in dollars. As a result, by the end of 1984 the stock of private foreign debt fell to $227 million, with most of the reduction becoming public foreign debt. This decision proved to be extremely controversial and was labeled as a subsidy to private businesses. On the other hand, the authorities defended it, arguing that in the absence of such measures a financial crisis would have been inevitable.

All in all, output grew by only 1.2 percent in 1982 and contracted by 2.8 percent in 1983 (−1.3 percent and −5.2 percent in per capita terms, respectively). Inflation—fueled by the sucre depreciation, which made imported goods more expensive; the shortage of agricultural products due to El Niño; and rapid monetary aggregates growth—jumped to 16.3 percent in 1982 and 48.3 percent in 1983.

Two Approaches at Managing the Crisis: Economic Liberalization (1984–88) and Gradualism (1989–92)

León Febres Cordero took office in August 1984. His administration brought about a change in economic policy, promoting the implementation of market-oriented reforms, reducing the role of the state in the economy in favor of the private sector, eliminating price controls, and favoring private investment.

This term was marked by two distinct stages. The first half was characterized by economic growth. In 1985—the first full year of the administration—output expanded at a rate of 4.3 percent in 1985, in line with the growth rate of 4.2 percent observed in 1984. In 1986, output advanced further by 3.1 percent. The growth in 1985 was aided by an increase in oil prices, which pushed total revenues of the central government to reach nearly 25 percent of GDP—with oil revenues accounting for approximately half of the revenues—and to generate a surplus of 2.4 percent of GDP. Instead, the growth in 1986 occurred despite falling oil prices, which reduced the revenues of the central government to 19.7 percent of GDP and led to a deficit of 2.2 percent of GDP. During this first phase, the inflation rate declined to 28 percent by the end of 1985 (compared to 31 percent in 1984) and to 23 percent a year later. M1 also displayed slower growth, expanding by 24 percent in 1985 and 20 percent in 1986.

Despite its preferences for liberal economic policies, some of the government's actions seemed to contradict those beliefs. For example, in 1984 the government decided to extend for seven additional years the time limits granted to private businesses to repay their obligations to the central bank under the *sucretización* mechanism and to relax some of its terms. This was again criticized as a massive subsidy to the private sector.[6] Similarly, the expenditures of the central government increased, despite the desire of policy makers for a diminished role for the government in the economy.

The favorable environment observed during the first two years of this administration changed during the second half. Oil prices had started falling in late 1985 and by 1986 had reached one-digit levels, with a corresponding impact on the government's finances (oil revenues fell from 12.5 percent of GDP in 1985 to 6.5 percent in 1986). However, the most severe blow to the economy was dealt by the earthquake of March 1987. This earthquake destroyed the only oil pipeline in Ecuador and stopped oil exports for almost six months. The deficit of the central government reached 3.4 percent of GDP in 1987—the largest since 1982—and the economy contracted by 6 percent during that year. The government, facing such a critical situation, decided to suspend its external debt service. After that, Ecuador started accumulating significant arrears on its foreign obligations. In fact, the fiscal prudence exhibited during the first years of the administration was abandoned, and expenditures increased because of the upcoming presidential election of 1988.

Similarly, the relatively orderly monetary growth observed during the first half of the administration was completely abandoned during the second half. M1 grew by 32 percent in 1987 and 54 percent in 1988. While the central bank contracted its net credit to the financial and private sectors, it expanded its net lending to the public sector. Inflation, which had been on a declining path during the first subperiod, started rising again, closing at 30 percent in 1987 and 58 percent in 1988.

The new government, headed by Rodrigo Borja, faced a difficult situation at the beginning of its term in August 1988, with the largest contraction in output in recent history during the previous year, the fiscal accounts in deficit, negative international reserves, and disorderly money growth. In light of this scenario, the authorities implemented an emergency austerity plan—which included expenditure cuts, increases in fuel prices, and the suspension of net lending from the central bank to the government—aimed at reducing the deficit. Moreover, a tax reform was approved in late 1988, aimed at simplifying the tax structure and focusing tax collection on three sources: the income tax, the excise tax, and a newly created value-added tax (VAT). The establishment of the VAT proved to be of critical importance, as it eventually would go on to become the main source of tax revenue for the government. The government also embarked on a policy of reopening the economy by removing quantitative restrictions to foreign trade and consolidating the tariff schedule around three rates.

In order to tackle the high rate of inflation, the government introduced a crawling peg for the exchange rate, which had been allowed to float during the last years of the previous

Simón Cueva and Julián P. Díaz

administration. The crawling peg had the objective of guiding inflation expectations and driving the inflation rate down to 30 percent.[7] By then, the use of the exchange rate as a nominal anchor had become firmly established. The crawling peg arrangement, however, was never successful at reducing the inflation rate, which averaged 54 percent during the second year of the administration and 48 percent and 49 percent during the third and last years, respectively. Ecuador had become a country characterized by chronic inflation. Morillo (1996) attributes the failure of the gradualist approach to policy makers' inability to fully convince economic agents that they had macroeconomic management under control.

The fiscal position improved during the years 1990 and 1991, in part aided by an increase in oil prices due to the Gulf War. The increase in oil prices also helped revert the negative balance in the stock of international reserves, which became positive again during this administration. In turn, the accumulation of reserves led to increases in the monetary base, which the central bank tried to offset by restricting its net lending.

On the institutional side, in May 1992 a new Ley de Régimen Monetario (LRM) was passed. The new law conferred autonomy to the central bank—although some members of the monetary board were still appointed by the executive[8]—allowing it to conduct monetary policy to maintain price stability. In order to attain its objective, the central bank implemented its policies through money desk (*mesa de dinero*) and foreign exchange desk (*mesa de cambios*) interventions, in addition to conducting open market operations by issuing BEMs. Finally, the new legislation prohibited the central bank from lending to the government.

Orthodox Management of the Economy, 1992–96

In August 1992, Sixto Durán Ballén was sworn in as president. His administration's approach to macroeconomic management represented—yet again—a significant departure from that of the previous government and sought a smaller role of the state in the economy, fiscal discipline, a strengthening of the level of international reserves, and a decrease in inflation.

Briefly after taking office, the authorities decided to tackle the inflationary process by abandoning the crawling peg that had been set up by the previous administration and implementing a 35 percent depreciation of the sucre, with the commitment to keep the exchange rate fixed for a considerable time period. Despite the spike in the inflation rate following the depreciation, the government's policies proved successful, and the inflation rate dropped to 45 percent by the end of 1993 and 27 percent a year later—the lowest since 1986. Moreover, even though the price of oil had declined (relative to the levels observed in 1990 and 1991), the central government also posted surpluses in 1993 and 1994, with tax revenues accounting for a similar share in total revenues as oil revenues.

In 1994, the government approved a new banking law that liberalized the financial sector—including the establishment of foreign banks—and allowed banks to issue checking and savings accounts in dollars. Moreover, also in 1994, the government finalized a Brady agreement that restructured its foreign debt, which it had defaulted on in 1987. Since then, it had grown from nearly $9 billion to reach $13 billion in 1993 (or approximately 70 percent of GDP when measured in dollars), with most of the growth from the accumulation of arrears. The agreement—which normalized relations with Ecuador's foreign lenders—reduced the face value of the outstanding debt, increased its maturity, and, depending on the instrument, reduced the interest rates on the new debt.

The apparently promising path that the Ecuadorian economy had embarked on—output had grown by 2 percent in 1993 and 4.3 percent in 1994—suffered a major setback in 1995. A combination of negative shocks, including another war with Peru—which caused central government expenditures to increase from 19 percent to 23 percent of GDP between 1994 and 1995 to finance the purchases of military equipment—and a prolonged drought that led to electricity shortages and blackouts, significantly affected the economy and highlighted its vulnerability to external shocks. The central government posted a deficit of 1.6 percent of GDP, and the economy all but stagnated during the year. The uncertainty created by the war led to significant losses of reserves. Moreover, in order to defend the exchange rate—the fixed exchange arrangement had been replaced with a crawling band system with upper and lower bounds in December 1994—the government had to intervene through foreign exchange desk operations and by increasing interest rates until it was eventually forced to widen the range of fluctuations allowed for the exchange rate. On top of this delicate situation, Vice President Alberto Dahik—who was in charge of the administration's economic policy design—was charged with embezzlement in late 1995 and fled the country, thus deepening the feeling of uncertainty among economic agents.

Political Instability, External Shocks, and Financial Crisis, 1996–99

The second half of the 1990s saw an increase in political instability, with the two presidents elected during this period unable to conclude their terms. Indeed, between 1996 and 2007, Ecuador had seven presidents, five of whom were not able to finish their terms.

To tackle inflation, Abdalá Bucaram—elected in 1996—proposed to establish a currency board similar to the one in place in Argentina at the time. The currency board was supposed to start operating around July 1997, when the nominal exchange rate was expected to reach 4,000 sucres per dollar. In the meantime, however, Bucaram was removed from office after being declared mentally unfit by Congress in February 1997, and the currency board project was abandoned.

Between 1997 and 1998, Ecuador was affected by another harsh El Niño phenomenon, which, as in 1982–83, severely affected the agricultural sector and destroyed a significant portion of the country's infrastructure. This event coincided with a period of low oil prices, which drove down oil revenues to 4.6 percent of GDP in 1998. The combined effect of these negative shocks was clearly visible on the fiscal accounts, and the central government recorded deficits amounting to 2.3 percent and 2.7 percent of GDP in 1997 and 1998.

In August 1998, a new constitution was enacted. The institutional changes within it included granting the central bank technical and administrative autonomy from the government at the constitutional level. For the first time in its history, the constitution also defined price stability as the only objective of the monetary authority and prohibited it from lending to the government and financial institutions, except "in unavoidable cases to avoid liquidity issues." Additionally, the monetary board was replaced by a central bank board, composed of five members appointed by the president and confirmed by Congress.

GDP grew by only 0.4 percent in 1998, and the inflation rate had risen to 43 percent by the end of that year. More disturbingly, banks started exhibiting signs of distress and fragility, which would eventually turn into the worst financial crisis in Ecuador's history. Initially, the problems of the financial system were attributed to the inability of borrowers to repay banks because of the consequences of the El Niño phenomenon. However, authors such as de la Torre, García-Saltos, and Mascaró (2001) and Jácome (2004) identified serious flaws in the banking law of 1994—such as deficient banking supervision (in particular of offshore activities), the lack of adequate instruments to deal with bank failure resolution, and moral hazard derived from unlimited deposit insurance—as the main culprits of the crisis, combined with currency mismatch in the bank balances and fraudulent practices by bank owners. To avoid a financial meltdown, the central bank was forced to act as a lender of last resort. Net lending to the financial sector ballooned, and the monetary aggregates skyrocketed; the monetary base and M1 expanded by 137 percent and 90 percent in 1999, respectively. Moreover, the deposit insurance agency had only been created right before the onset of the crisis. Lacking resources, the agency had to issue bonds that in turn were purchased by the central bank, and it used those funds to repay depositors. This led to a massive increase in the government's domestic indebtedness.

By the end of the century, Ecuador was in the midst of the worst economic crisis of its history. Output contracted by 7 percent in 1999. Nearly half of the banks either shut down or were nationalized. A yearlong deposit freeze was decreed in March 1999. The deficit of the central government reached 4.9 percent of GDP, and the government decided it would not pay a tranche of its Brady bonds, thus triggering a default just five years after having restructured its debt. The fluctuation range for the exchange rate had been widened, and eventually the sucre was allowed to float freely, depreciating by 180 percent over the course of the year. Finally, inflation reached 67 percent by the end of 1999, with the distinct possibility of a hyperinflation looming on the horizon.

DOLLARIZATION, 2000–2017

The Initial Years, 2000–2006

With output collapsing, inflation rising rapidly, and the exchange rate plummeting, President Jamil Mahuad announced the adoption of the dollar in January 2000, thus officially dollarizing the economy. The exchange rate for the conversion of sucres to dollars was set at 25,000 sucres per dollar to ensure that the central bank possessed a sufficiently high level of reserves to implement the swap of currencies.

The decision to dollarize was received with widespread opposition—even from within the central bank—and the protests and social unrest that followed forced the resignation of Mahuad just two weeks after the dollarization announcement. In spite of this negative environment, Mahuad's successor, Gustavo Noboa, confirmed the dollarization process, and before the end of the year, the new monetary arrangement had been fully implemented.

To ensure the sustainability of the dollarization system, policy makers passed a series of fiscal responsibility laws that limited the annual growth rate of real central government expenditures to 3.5 percent and capped the debt-to-GDP ratio at 40 percent. Additionally, a number of oil stabilization funds were created in order to force government savings (though a portion of these funds were earmarked for a variety of projects other than savings; for details, see Cueva 2008). Finally, also in 2000, the authorities reached an agreement with international lenders to restructure the government's foreign debt, which Ecuador had defaulted on the year before. The restructuring lowered the face value of the debt by 40 percent.

The dollarization regime proved to be successful at reducing the inflation rate. After peaking at 108 percent in September 2000, the inflation rate started a consistent decline, and by 2003 it had dropped to one-digit levels, values not observed since the early 1970s.[9] Moreover, between 2003 and 2006, the inflation rate averaged 4 percent.

The reduction in inflation was accompanied by a restart in growth, and during the 2000–2006 period the average growth rate of GDP was 4.3 percent. On the fiscal side, the central government posted average deficits of 0.5 percent of GDP and average primary surpluses of 2.5 percent during the first six years of dollarization, a significant reversal from the patterns observed in the previous decade. The improvements in the fiscal accounts, coupled with the renewed growth of the economy, produced noticeable decreases in the debt-to-GDP ratios, with the foreign debt-to-GDP ratio dropping from 55 percent in 2000 to 21.5 percent in 2006 and the (central government) domestic debt-to-GDP ratio falling from 16 percent to 7 percent during the same interval.

A Second Oil Boom and an Increased Role of the State, 2007–17

In 2007, Rafael Correa took office. His election marked a departure from prevailing trends on two fronts. On the political side, it ended the era of political instability that had started in the late 1990s and had continued during the early 2000s.[10] On the economic side, Correa's administration promoted policies that highlighted the role and the participation of the state in the economy, increasing public expenditures and reverting the relatively disciplined fiscal stance observed during the previous period. Indeed, central government expenditures jumped from an average of 16 percent of GDP between 2000 and 2006 to 23.5 percent between 2007 and 2017. The increase in expenditures was driven by a second oil boom—which had started in 2004 but intensified during this period—characterized by historically high oil prices (even when adjusted by inflation) that boosted oil revenues during most of the 2007–17 period.

The increase in oil revenues was coupled with growth in tax revenues, which jumped from 9 percent of GDP in 2007 to an average of 13 percent of GDP between 2007 and 2017. The expansion in tax revenues was due to improved collection as well as to more than twenty tax reforms that expanded the tax base, increased existing taxes, and created new ones. However, in spite of the oil windfall and the increase in overall revenues—and the depletion of the stabilization funds created during the previous period—these factors were not enough to compensate for the increase in expenditures. Indeed, between 2007 and 2017, the average deficit jumped to 3.5 percent of GDP, compared to 0.5 percent during 2000–2006. To finance these deficits, the government increased its domestic and foreign borrowing, both of which had been on a declining path throughout the previous period. Total foreign debt jumped from $10.5 billion to $31.5 billion between 2007 and 2017, whereas domestic debt grew fourfold during the same period.

During the 2007–17 period, output continued expanding and inflation remained low, averaging annual growth rates of 3.3 percent and 3.8 percent, respectively. However, the fall in oil prices during the global financial crisis, and especially during the more recent one that began in 2014, affected the growth of the economy and underscored its chronic dependence on oil prices. Between 2015 and 2017, years with significantly lower oil prices, output grew at only 0.4 percent per year on average. Additionally, the inability of the government to reduce its expenditures to reflect the drop in revenues forced it to substantially increase its reliance on foreign borrowing. Indeed, the large increases in domestic and foreign indebtedness in such a short period of time—combined with their onerous conditions characterized by short maturities and high interest rates—have raised concerns about the long-term viability of the dollarization system because of fears that the government will not be able to obtain new credits and will cede to the temptation of abandoning the dollarization regime. Moreover, although in principle in a dollarized country the central bank is supposed to lose its ability to conduct monetary policy, "creative" measures recently devised, such as the central bank using bank reserves to lend to the government,[11] have not helped assuage the fears regarding the sustainability of the dollarization scheme.

Fiscal Policy: Revenues and Expenditures of the Central Government

We now document the main trends in Ecuador's fiscal policy during the 1960–2017 period. For the majority of this period, fiscal policy in Ecuador has been procyclical, as shown in Figure 4, where we plot the cyclical components of real government consumption expenditures and output. Indeed, the correlation coefficient between the two series is 0.7.[12]

Table 2 breaks down the cyclical behavior of fiscal policy across the different periods. Fiscal policy was highly procyclical during the pre-oil and oil boom periods. The procyclicality patterns somewhat decreased during the Great Depression years, and fiscal policy actually became *countercyclical* during the early years of the dollarization era. However, the rapid government expansion during the 2007–17 period turned fiscal policy procyclical again, reaching levels similar to those observed during the oil boom. This reversal is of particular importance, since, as a dollarized economy, Ecuador cannot use monetary policy as a stabilization tool. This, coupled with the highly procyclical current patterns of fiscal policy, implies that the country has become quite exposed to external shocks—a common recurrence in Ecuador's economic history—and thus faces considerable difficulties when trying to cope with those adverse events.

Figure 5 depicts total revenues and expenditures of the central government.[13] The effect of the discovery of oil is quite evident. Prior to the oil boom, total revenues and

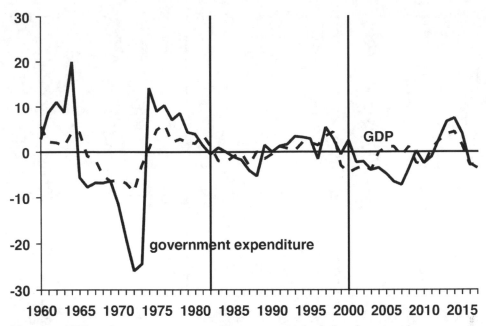

Figure 4. GDP and government expenditure, percent deviation from trend

Table 2. Correlation between the cyclical components of government expenditures and GDP

Period	Correlation coefficient between cyclical components
1960–81	0.78
1960–71	0.74
1972–81	0.85
1982–99	0.56
2000–2017	0.46
2000–2006	−0.75
2007–17	0.76
1960–2017	0.70

expenditures had averaged 10.1 percent and 11.5 percent of GDP, respectively. With the new oil wealth, the size of the government ballooned and has remained large ever since, representing 19.5 percent and 21.1 percent of GDP during the 1972–2017 period. The lack of downward flexibility of expenditures is particularly troubling, especially given the volatility in oil prices. For example, between 1982 and 1999, when the average price of oil was significantly below the one observed during the oil boom, total expenditures still represented 20.7 percent of GDP on average. Only during the first years of dollarization was there a noticeable decrease in expenditures, when they averaged 15.9 percent of GDP, reflecting the relatively disciplined approach to fiscal policy at the time. This

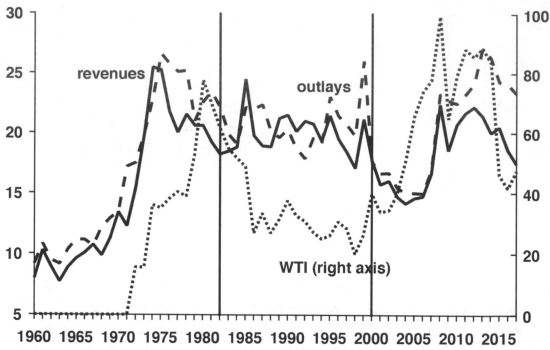

Figure 5. Revenue and outlays, percentage of GDP, and WTI (West Texas Intermediate) oil price, 2010 US$

trend clearly changed during the latter dollarization subperiod, when total expenditures averaged 23.5 percent of GDP, aided in part by the second oil boom that lasted until 2014.

Figure 6 shows the main components of total revenues and expenditures of the central government. Prior to the oil boom, the main source of revenues was tariffs, which accounted on average for 42 percent of total revenues, with income taxes and production taxes accounting for an additional 25 percent. This pattern was altered in 1972, when oil revenues went on to become the single largest source of revenue between 1972 and 1999, averaging more than a third of total revenues. However, the relative importance of the value-added tax has been rising since its establishment during the tax reform in 1988, and during the dollarization era it surpassed oil revenues as the main source of revenues, accounting for 30 percent of total revenues (with oil accounting for over a quarter of all revenues of the central government).

On the expenditures side, wages and purchases of goods and services were the main categories of expenditure during the pre-oil era. The oil wealth and heavy borrowing allowed the central government to undertake a number of large-scale projects, and consequently capital expenditures became the largest component of total expenditures during the oil boom period. The massive accumulation of debt during the 1972–81 period led to an increase in the relative importance of interest payments, which saw its share out of total expenditures grow to an average of 16 percent during the 1982–99 period. This fraction dropped to an average of 10.8 percent since the establishment of dollarization, although it has exhibited an upward trend since 2007 because of the rapid increase in government

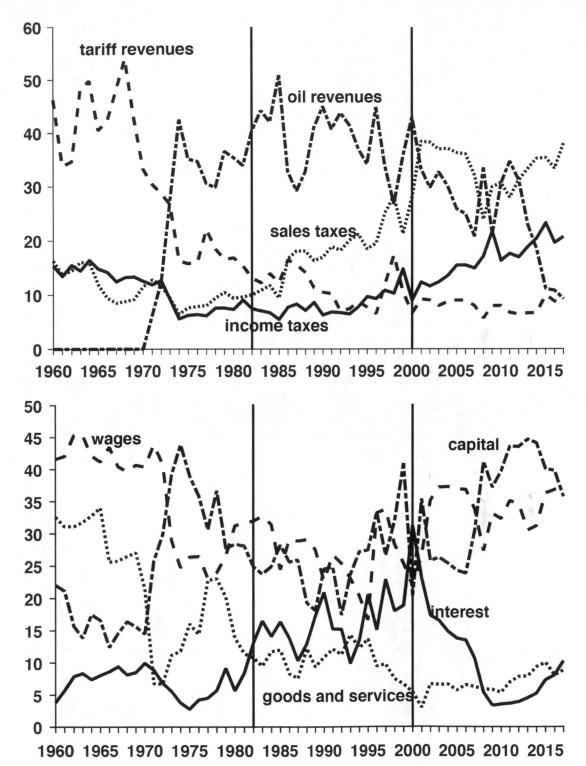

Figure 6. Central government: top panel: main sources of revenues, percent of total revenues; bottom panel: main sources of outlays, percent of total outlays

borrowing ever since. Lastly, the share of capital expenditures expanded from an average of 25 percent between 2000 and 2006 to 40 percent between 2007 and 2017, reflecting the Correa administration's efforts to improve and expand the country's infrastructure.

Finally, Figure 7 presents the deficit and primary deficit of the central government. The comparatively small deficits registered during the 1960–71 period—which averaged 1.4 percent of GDP—nearly doubled during the 1972–81 period and represented on average 2 percent of GDP. Between 1982 and 1992, the central government ran an average deficit of 0.25 percent of GDP, but this value hides a large volatility in the fiscal balance, with large deficits during the early years of the debt crisis and in 1987 (due to the earthquake that stopped oil exports) and surpluses between 1989 and 1992. A similar picture arises for the 1993–99 period: the early years—characterized by an orthodox management of the fiscal accounts—registered surpluses, but the fiscal position became negative as a consequence of the Cenepa War in 1995 and worsened significantly by the end of the decade because of low oil prices, the severe El Niño event of 1997–98, and the financial crisis of 1999. All in all, the average deficit during that period reached 1.7 percent of GDP. During the two "lost decades" period, it is also possible to appreciate the painful consequences of the heavy borrowing conducted during the 1970s: the government ran mainly primary surpluses between 1982 and 1999, but ultimately the deficits reflect the onerous burden of the interest payments.

The dollarization era is marked by nearly balanced budgets during the 2000–2006 period (with an average deficit of 0.5 percent of GDP) and large deficits between 2007 and 2017, reaching nearly 3.5 percent of GDP, in spite of a second oil bonanza for the better part of that interval. The 2007–17 period also marks a change in the patterns of the primary deficit: from 2000 until 2006, the central government had posted primary surpluses, while since 2007 those reverted to primary deficits of 2.1 percent of GDP on average.

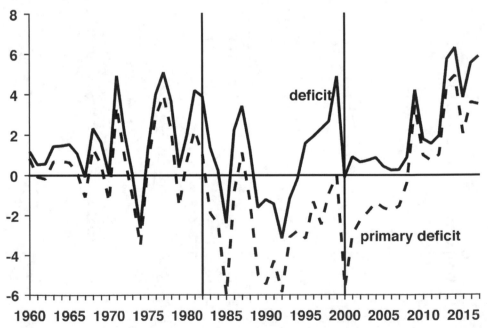

Figure 7. Deficit and primary deficit, percentage of GDP

The Evolution of the Public Debt

Prior to the oil boom, Ecuador's public debt was relatively low, although both foreign and domestic debt-to-GDP ratios had been growing since the 1950s, reflecting the recurrent deficits posted by the government. Foreign debt (measured in sucres) represented on average 12.4 percent of GDP during the 1960–71 period, and domestic debt represented a slightly larger share at 17.4 percent of GDP, especially during the final years of this period (see Figure 8).

The expansion of government spending during the oil boom, combined with the abundant liquidity and low interest rates prevailing in the international markets, led to an enormous increase in foreign indebtedness, which grew from $248 million in 1972 to more than $4,400 million by the end of 1981. The ratio of foreign debt (measured in sucres) to GDP doubled from 17.7 percent to 35.3 percent between 1972 and 1981. The easy access to external credits led to foreign borrowing replacing domestic borrowing as the main category of total debt. Indeed, during this period, the domestic debt-to-GDP ratio declined from 19.1 percent to 8.3 percent.

During the Great Depression, total foreign debt kept growing and reached $12.5 billion by the end of 1992. During the early years of this period, a significant portion of the increase in the stock of foreign debt was from the *sucretización* of the private foreign debt, which, as previously mentioned, reduced private indebtedness from $1,628 million in 1982 to $227 million in 1984, with most of this reduction becoming public debt. On the other hand, a large fraction of the increase in foreign debt during the latter years of this period was from arrears, which the government started accumulating after the earthquake of 1987. The magnitude of the arrears was massive,

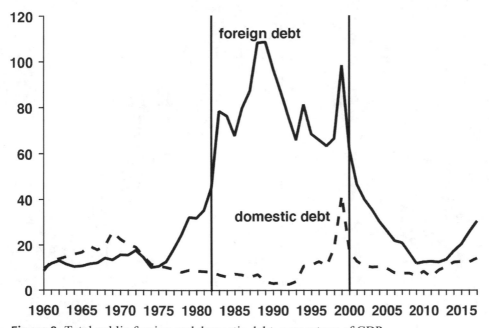

Figure 8. Total public foreign and domestic debt, percentage of GDP

and by the end of 1992, they amounted to $2.7 billion, or roughly 22 percent of all outstanding foreign debt.

As a result of these factors, the foreign debt-to-GDP ratio peaked at 109 percent in 1989 before eventually dropping to 76 percent in 1992. It is worth noting that, although the stock of foreign debt rose rapidly during this period, nominal output increased rapidly as well, and this should have curbed the growth in the debt ratio. Thus an important portion of the increase in the foreign debt-to-GDP ratio was from fluctuations in the real exchange rate. Figure 9 compares the path of the debt ratio when keeping the real exchange rate fixed.[14] On the other hand, the domestic debt-to-GDP ratio continued the declining trend exhibited during the previous period, and by the end of 1992 it represented less than 3 percent of GDP.

The composition of external creditors changed noticeably during the 1982–92 period, given Ecuador's inability to borrow from private sources after the freeze in lending triggered by the Mexican default in 1982. The share of private creditors, which in 1983 accounted for 75 percent of total public and publicly guaranteed (PPG) debt, fell to 60 percent in 1992, while the share of multilateral and bilateral creditors doubled during the same period (see Figure 10). The dependence on loans from multilateral institutions became a repetitive feature of the Ecuadorian economy during the debt crisis years.

After the Brady agreement in 1994, the foreign debt-to-GDP ratio kept declining until it reached 63 percent in 1997, its lowest level since the onset of the debt crisis. However, the slowdown in the economy during the last two years of the decade—and in particular, the large output contraction of 1999—combined with the fast depreciation of the sucre propelled the foreign debt-to-GDP ratio to nearly 100 percent in 1999. Moreover, the increase in domestic borrowing to rescue the failing financial system led to

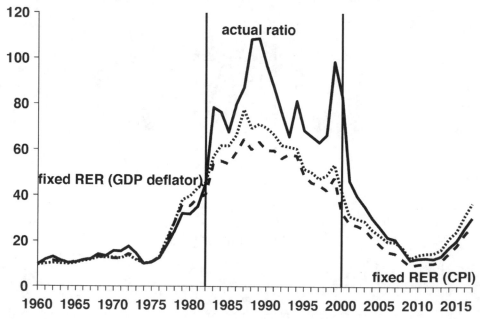

Figure 9. Foreign public debt: Actual and with fixed real exchange rate (RER), percentage of GDP

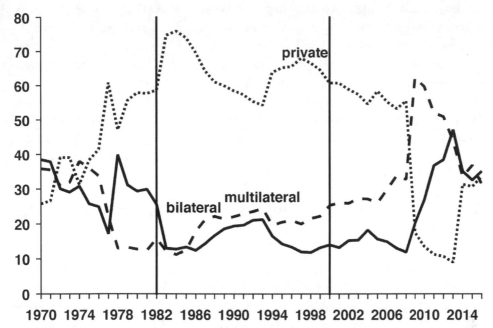

Figure 10. Composition of external creditors, percent of PPG debt

a rapid increase in the domestic debt-to-GDP ratio from 11 percent of GDP in 1997 to 41.5 percent of GDP in 1999.

The initial years of the dollarization regime were characterized by sustained reductions in the debt ratios. The small central government deficits, coupled with the reduction in the foreign debt stock due to the restructuring agreement in 2000 after the Brady default of 1999 and strong GDP growth averaging over 4 percent a year, led to a decrease in the foreign debt-to-GDP ratio (measured in dollars) from 62 percent in 2000 to 22 percent in 2006. Similarly, domestic debt fell from 15.5 percent to 7 percent during the same period.

The declining paths of the debt indicators observed during the early years of the dollarization era were reversed during the 2007–17 period. Since the government wanted to expand the participation of the state in the economy, it increased public spending substantially—well beyond the increase in revenues. Since seigniorage revenues were not an option for deficit financing because of the dollarization regime, the government resorted to increased borrowing, both domestic and foreign. This increase in indebtedness—which occurred during a period of historically high oil prices—could have been even larger if not for two events. One was the law passed in 2008 that unilaterally extinguished the government bonds—amounting to $1.1 billion—that had been purchased by the central bank from the deposit insurance agency during the financial crisis of 1999. Second, also in 2008, the government refused to pay a portion of the foreign debt that it had previously labeled—on ideological grounds—as "illegitimate" and that totaled nearly $3.2 billion. Later, in 2009, after the face value of this debt had collapsed, the government decided to repurchase it by paying about $900 million. Note that this default occurred during a period of abundance of resources, so it signaled a lack of willingness, rather than an inability, to pay. While this default had the short-run "benefit" of reducing the stock of foreign debt, its ulterior consequences have been costly: foreign lenders have been reluctant to extend new loans, and the ones that have done so—mainly China—have demanded onerous conditions in an era of historically low interest rates. The rapid expansion of government borrowing led to the foreign debt-to-GDP ratio reaching 30 percent by 2017, while its domestic counterpart stood at 14 percent in the same year—that is, the debt ratios doubled in only ten years. This in turn implies that the current borrowing levels exceed the debt limit imposed by the fiscal responsibility laws of the early 2000s, another indication of the lack of fiscal restraint that has characterized this last period.

Monetary Aggregates, the Nominal Exchange Rate, and Inflation

We now analyze the main trends in the monetary aggregates and the exchange rate and their comovements with the inflation rate. Figure 11 shows the year-to-year growth rate of Ecuador's monetary base and M1 and of the inflation rate (measured as the percentage change in the consumer price index) for the predollarization period. The averages for the subperiods are summarized in Table 3.

The table reveals that periods of faster monetary growth also exhibited higher inflation rates. Similarly, it shows that the correlation between inflation and the growth in monetary aggregates became stronger after 1982. Indeed, although between 1960 and 1971 monetary aggregates grew at double-digit rates on average, these rates were the lowest registered during the full 1960–99 predollarization period. In turn, inflation

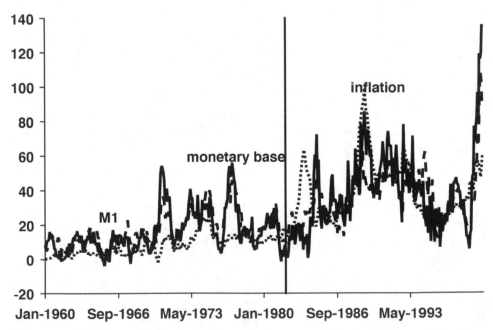

Figure 11. Inflation and annual growth rates of monetary base and M1, percent

Table 3. Annual growth rates of MB and M1 and correlation with inflation

Period	Average growth rate of MB (%)	Average growth rate of M1 (%)	Average inflation rate (%)	Correlation between MB and inflation	Correlation between M1 and inflation
1960–81	16.2	17.1	8.6	0.48	0.64
1960–71	11.8	11.7	4.9	0.37	0.37
1972–81	21.4	23.6	12.9	0.26	0.39
1982–99	38.8	36.0	39.1	0.55	0.47
1982–84	19.1	24.6	32.3	−0.20	−0.01
1985–88	36.2	32.4	34.4	0.57	0.77
1989–92	55.4	44.2	57.3	0.57	0.11
1993–96	31.4	35.7	30.3	0.72	0.47
1997–99	50.0	41.6	39.5	0.74	0.60

remained low, averaging 4.9 percent. The growth rates of monetary aggregates almost doubled during the oil boom, with an average growth rate of 21.4 percent for the monetary base and 23.6 percent for M1. This period marks the beginning of the inflationary years in Ecuador, with the average inflation rate growing threefold relative to the previous period, averaging 13 percent per year.

The Great Depression period recorded even faster growth in the monetary aggregates and an average inflation rate of nearly 40 percent. Indeed, the growth rate of monetary aggregates progressively increased between 1982 and 1992, and the rapid monetary increases were matched by a consistent rise in inflation. When monetary expansion slowed down between 1993 and 1996, a corresponding decline in inflation was observed, but the return of disorderly monetary growth between 1997 and 1999—especially in 1999 because of the financial crisis—produced a jump in inflation, which averaged almost 40 percent per year.

The sources of the changes in the monetary base are presented in Table 4.[15] Between 1960 and 1971, the largest source of the increase in the monetary base was the increase in domestic net credit, reflecting the traditional practice of the central government of borrowing from the central bank to finance its operations.

That trend reverted between 1972 and 1981, when the accumulation of international reserves during the oil boom accounted for the largest fraction of the increases in the monetary base. On the other hand, the sources of increases in the monetary base differ across subperiods during the Great Depression years. Indeed, between 1982 and 1988, increases in domestic net credit accounted for the observed expansion in the monetary base (in fact, reserves played a negative role), with increases in net credit to the financial sector (FS) dominating the 1982–84 period (when the *sucretización* mechanism was

Table 4. Growth rates of MB and its sources (percentage)

		MB growth due to		Growth of DNC components			
Period	Avg. growth of MB	Reserves	Domestic net credit (DNC)	To NFPS	To FS	Other assets	Other
1960–81	16.3	63.0	37.0	-32.6	29.4	−36.7	−11.3
1960–71	11.7	10.0	90.0	49.8	11.0	33.6	−11.4
1972–81	21.9	97.0	3.0	−131.5	51.4	−121.1	−11.1
1982–99	42.4	121.1	−21.1	−131.9	53.1	198.0	−244.4
1982–84	24.0	−11.0	111.0	−574.5	90.4	1209.5	−1124.5
1985–88	41.1	−57.5	157.5	8.3	−0.3	68.0	−74.8
1989–92	52.3	187.0	−87.0	−101.8	−19.6	50.3	−52.9
1993–96	27.4	264.1	−164.1	−26.3	−84.8	−38.2	8.8
1997–99	69.5	166.0	−66.0	−57.4	367.8	−128.3	−183.3

implemented) and increases in net credit to the nonfinancial public sector (NFPS) claiming the largest source of increases in net credit during the 1985–88 period. Finally, since 1988, increases in reserves accounted for the largest share of growth in the monetary base, with most of the contraction in domestic net credit due to reductions in the net credit to the NFPS (that is, the NFPS increased its deposits in the central bank).

As inflation became a defining feature of the economy, the currency composition of the monetary aggregates changed accordingly. Ecuadorian agents, attempting to avoid the ever-rising inflation, increased their money holdings in foreign currency—mainly dollars—significantly. While prior to 1984 the dollar-denominated share of M2 (composed of dollar-denominated checking and savings accounts, as well as time and other deposits in dollars) had remained relatively constant around 2 percent, it started a continuous increase, reaching 10 percent in 1994 and 45 percent in 1999. Thus while Ecuador *officially* dollarized in 2000, prior to that date the use of the dollar was already widespread, and the economy exhibited a high degree of informal, or de facto, dollarization.

Finally, in Figure 12 we show the evolution over time of the nominal exchange rate, a variable that has been widely believed to influence inflation in Ecuador, at least since the 1980s. Indeed, a variety of exchange rate regimes aimed at reducing the inflation rate were in place in Ecuador until the adoption of the dollar. Additionally, in Figure 13 we plot the comovements of the annual depreciation of the nominal exchange rate and the inflation rate. The depreciation rate corresponds to the year-to-year change in the average of the three types of exchange rates (official, intervention, and free market).

Table 5 summarizes the period averages and shows that periods with higher depreciation rates coincide with higher inflation rates. Moreover, until 1982 Ecuador operated

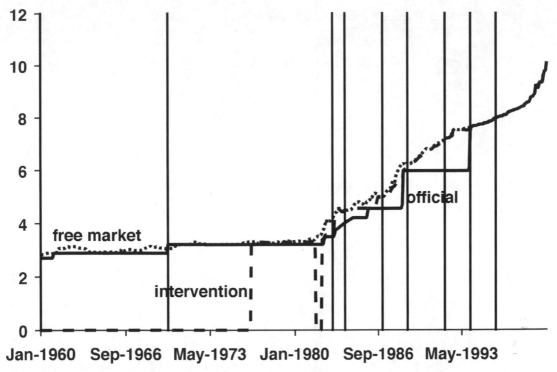

Figure 12. Official, intervention, and free market exchange rates, sucres per dollar, log scale

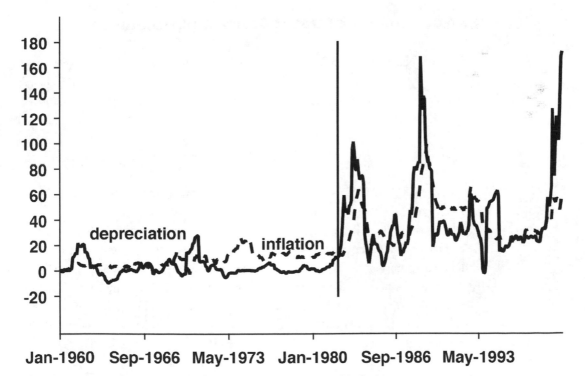

Figure 13. Annual nominal exchange rate depreciation and inflation rate, percent

Table 5. Average depreciation rate and correlation with inflation

Period	Depreciation rate (%)	Inflation rate (%)	Correlation between depreciation and inflation
1960–81	2.70	8.56	0.01
1960–71	4.01	4.93	0.23
1972–81	1.12	12.91	−0.06
1982–99	42.55	39.07	0.34
1982–84	47.03	32.26	−0.06
1985–88	41.56	34.36	0.69
1989–92	42.37	57.34	0.05
1993–96	29.50	30.32	0.54
1997–99	57.04	39.47	0.90

essentially under a fixed exchange regime, with a depreciation in 1961 and another one in 1970, and the correlation between the depreciation rate and inflation was very low. Since 1982, this correlation has intensified over time, with the brief exception of the 1982–84 and 1989–92 subperiods.

The Government's Budget Constraint Accounting

Having documented the main historical, fiscal, and monetary trends, we move on to quantifying the sources of deficit financing. To do so, we employ the framework developed in Sargent (1993) to assess the alternative sources available to the government to finance its obligations. The budget constraint of the government in period t is

$$B_t + b_t P_t + B_t^* E_t + M_t = (D_t + T_t) + B_{t-1} R_{t-1} + b_{t-1} r_{t-1} P_t + B_{t-1}^* R_{t-1}^* E_t + M_{t-1}, \quad (1)$$

where B_t, b_t, and B_t^* are total nominal, indexed, and dollar-denominated debt in period t, in that order, and R_t, r_t, R_t^* are their respective gross returns; M_t is the stock of money; D_t is the government primary deficit, and T_t are government transfers, which include transfers between the central government and the rest of the public sector, as well as the types of "extraordinary transfers" described in "A Framework for Studying the Monetary and Fiscal History of Latin America"; and P_t and E_t are the price level and the nominal exchange rate.

We modify (1) to incorporate two features relevant to the Ecuadorian case. First, since there are no publicly available statistics on Ecuadorian indexed government debt, we drop their corresponding terms from the budget constraint. Second, we include an additional option for financing deficits traditionally used in Ecuador: the use of previously accumulated assets of the central government. Essentially, these are deposits held in the Central Bank of Ecuador—usually in the form of money accounts—and thus the government earns no return on these assets. Including these two modifications yields a government budget constraint that can be written as

$$B_t + B_t^* E_t + M_t = (A_{t-1} - A_t) = (D_t + T_t)P_t + B_{t-1}R_{t-1} + B_{t-1}^* R_{t-1}^* E_t + M_{t-1}, \text{(2)}$$

where A_t represents the government's deposits in the central bank. Expressing (2) in terms of nominal GDP $(P_t y_t)$ and grouping terms yields

$$(\theta_t - \theta_{t-1}) + \xi_t(\theta_t^* - \theta_{t-1}^*) + (m_t - m_{t-1}) + m_{t-1}\left(1 - \frac{1}{g_t \pi_t}\right) + (a_{t-1} - a_t)$$

$$-a_{t-1}\left(1 - \frac{1}{g_t \pi_t}\right) = \theta_{t-1}\left(\frac{R_{t-1}}{g_t \pi_t} - 1\right) + \xi_t \theta_{t-1}^*\left(\frac{R_{t-1}^*}{g_t \pi_t^W} - 1\right) + (d_t + \tau_t) \quad , \qquad \text{(3)}$$

where $\theta_t = B_t / P_t y_t, m_t = M_t / P_t y_t, a_t = A_t / P_t y_t, \pi_t = P_t / P_{t-1}, P_t^W$ is the foreign price level and $\pi_t^W = P_t^W / P_{t-1}^W$ is foreign inflation, $g_t = y_t / y_{t-1}$ is the real GDP growth rate, $d_t = D_t / P_t y_t, \tau_t = T_t / P_t y_t, \xi_t = E_t P_t^W / P_t$ is the real exchange rate, and $\theta_t^* = (B_t^* / P_t^W) / y_t$.

The terms on the right-hand side of (3) denote the government's obligations in period t: the first two terms represent the returns on the two types of debt, while the last term is the government primary deficit, including transfers. The terms on the left-hand side include the sources to finance those obligations: the first two terms represent the changes in the debt-to-GDP ratios of the two types of debt; the third term represents the increase in the stock of money; the fourth term is seigniorage; and the last two terms are the use of assets in the central bank. Thus (3) suggests that sustained deficits need not necessarily lead to inflation if the government is able to borrow to finance its obligations. However, if the government is unable to borrow, then it will need to resort to seigniorage to balance the budget, and consequently deficits can lead to inflation.

In Table 6 we present the results of the budget constraint accounting exercise. Our definition of "the government" refers to the central government, since that is the fiscal level for which consistent statistics for the 1960–2017 period are available (data for Ecuador's nonfinancial public sector [NFPS]—a more comprehensive measure of the government—start only in 2000). The online appendix 3 (available at http://manifold.bfi .uchicago.edu/) details the data sources used in the analysis. Since there are no available data for the transfers term T_t, that term was calculated as the residual that makes the budget constraint hold in each period. Moreover, since Ecuador dollarized in 2000, the government cannot issue currency at its discretion (except for a small number of fractional coins, which by law must be fully backed by international reserves) and consequently does not receive seigniorage revenues.[16] Consequently, we set the corresponding terms in the budget constraint to zero for the 2000–2017 period.

Table 6. Central government budget accounting results, 1960–2017 (percentage of GDP)

Period	Sources						Obligations				
	Domestic debt	Foreign debt	Money issuing	Seigniorage	Assets in CB	Total	Domestic return	Foreign return	Primary deficit	"Transfers"	Total
1960–81	0.08	1.39	-0.03	1.40	-0.32	2.52	0.64	0.89	0.60	0.39	2.52
1960–71	1.26	0.38	0.14	0.85	-0.19	2.44	0.68	0.45	0.46	0.85	2.44
1972–81	-1.34	2.60	-0.23	2.05	-0.48	2.61	0.59	1.43	0.75	-0.15	2.61
1982–99	1.79	0.64	-0.02	1.82	-0.68	3.56	0.69	4.20	-2.47	1.13	3.56
1982–84	-0.85	7.93	-0.57	1.88	-0.42	7.98	0.51	7.02	-1.10	1.54	7.98
1985–88	0.66	1.34	0.09	1.96	-0.84	3.20	0.76	4.93	-1.75	-0.74	3.20
1989–92	-1.02	-2.26	-0.30	2.38	-1.18	-2.38	0.52	3.60	-5.13	-1.37	-2.38
1993–96	2.29	-3.84	-0.25	1.39	-0.24	-0.65	0.49	2.56	-2.58	-1.12	-0.65
1997–99	9.00	2.27	1.09	1.43	-0.64	13.14	1.26	3.42	-1.11	9.57	13.14
2000–2017	-0.08	-0.90			-0.17	-1.16	0.59	1.31	0.31	-3.36	-1.16
2000–2006	-1.24	-3.90			-0.49	-5.63	0.70	2.06	-2.48	-5.92	-5.63
2007–17	0.65	1.00			0.03	1.68	0.52	0.82	2.08	-1.74	1.68
1960–2017	0.56	0.45	-0.02	1.10	-0.39	1.70	0.64	2.05	-0.44	-0.54	1.70

We find that for the entire 1960–2017 period, the government's average financing needs represented 1.7 percent of GDP per year. Seigniorage was—by far—the most heavily used means to finance those obligations, representing, on average, nearly two-thirds of the sources of financing. In fact, that value understates the historic reliance on seigniorage, since that option became unavailable after the economy was dollarized in 2000. From Table 6 it is also evident that the financing needs—and the sources used to cover them—varied significantly throughout the periods covered in our analysis. We discuss the different trends across periods next.

ACCOUNTING RESULTS: GROWTH AND OIL BOOM ERA

As reported in Table 6, the 1960–81 period registered the smallest average obligations during the predollarization era at 2.52 percentage points (pp). The central government's primary deficit represented, on average, 0.6 pp and interest payments amounted to 1.53 pp, with domestic and foreign debt interest payments of relatively similar magnitudes. The pre–oil boom and oil boom subperiods, however, exhibited contrasting trends.

Prior to the oil boom, the central government's obligations were even lower than those for the entire period, averaging 2.44 pp. Primary deficits were smaller as well, standing at 0.46 pp, and interest payments represented 1.13 pp, with the share of domestic payments being slightly higher than the foreign one. During this subperiod, nearly half of the financing needs were covered by increases in domestic debt, while foreign debt accounted for about 16 percent of the financing needs. Moreover, even though seigniorage played a more significant role than foreign debt, it only averaged 0.85 pp. In fact, seigniorage revenues during these years were the lowest for the whole predollarization era. This period of a relatively small government, comparatively low financing needs, and limited use of seigniorage in turn coincided with the lowest average inflation.

On the other hand, the expansion of the government during the oil boom is quite evident: average financing needs jumped to 2.61 pp, and the average primary deficit rose to 0.75 pp. The way to finance these obligations significantly changed when compared to the previous period. Given the favorable prevailing external conditions, the government relied on external borrowing to cover its deficits. Indeed, foreign debt increases averaged 2.6 pp, while the role of domestic debt declined. The rapid increase in foreign indebtedness led to a large increase in the foreign debt interest payments, which more than tripled when compared to the 1960–71 period, averaging 1.43 pp. The rise in primary deficits and interest payments was coupled with a significant increase in the use of seigniorage, which more than doubled in magnitude when compared to the previous period. This increased reliance on seigniorage was accompanied by a sizable jump in inflation, which nearly tripled during this period, averaging 12.9 percent per year.

ACCOUNTING RESULTS: THE GREAT DEPRESSION

The accounting results for the Great Depression period show that, in spite of the collapse in oil prices and the deterioration of external conditions, the financing needs during this era actually increased relative to the 1960–81 period, averaging 3.56 pp per year. Although the government ran, on average, primary surpluses during this period—a departure from the trend observed between 1960 and 1981, when the government ran average primary deficits—the increase in obligations was driven, for the most part, by large interest payments—and more specifically by foreign debt interest payments, which averaged 4.2 pp between 1982 and 1999. This heavy burden was a direct consequence of the massive increases in the stock of foreign debt during the oil boom years.

How were these obligations financed? The strategy favored during the previous period of resorting to foreign borrowing was rendered unfeasible because of the credit crunch derived from the Latin American debt crisis.[17] Thus the government relied increasingly on seigniorage, which became the largest source of financing between 1985 and 1992. The growing dependence on seigniorage during the first half of the 1982–99 period was in turn matched by an increase in the average rate of inflation.

The latter years of this period exhibit two distinct phases. Between 1993 and 1996, the financing needs were negative, in line with primary surpluses that averaged 2.6 pp. This subperiod registered large reductions in the foreign borrowing component (mostly because of the debt restructuring contemplated in the Brady agreement), increases in domestic debt that averaged 2.3 pp, and the lowest seigniorage since the pre-oil period at 1.39 pp. On the other hand, the 1997–99 subperiod was characterized by increases in all the sources components (except for the term corresponding to assets in the central bank). In particular, domestic debt increases averaged 9 pp, reflecting the massive borrowing from the central bank as the government needed to bail out the banking system during the financial crisis of 1999. This in turn was materialized in the largest money-issuing component during the whole period under analysis, averaging 1.09 pp. In all, seigniorage dropped by nearly a third between 1993 and 1999, and the inflation rate also declined to an average of 34.2 percent per year.

To conclude the analysis of the predollarization years, in Figure 14 we plot the two main sources of financing during this period—namely, the changes in total debt $(\theta_t - \theta_{t-1}) + \xi_t(\theta_t^* - \theta_{t-1}^*)$ in equation (3) and seigniorage. We find that the two series are negatively correlated (with a correlation coefficient of -0.17), suggesting that debt and seigniorage were used as substitute—rather than complementary—sources of revenue.

ACCOUNTING RESULTS: DOLLARIZATION

The dollarization years are characterized by two distinct subperiods. During the first part (2000–2006), the relatively orderly management of the fiscal accounts led to average primary surpluses of 2.48 pp. In turn, both the domestic and foreign debt components experienced reductions of 1.24 pp and 3.90 pp, respectively.

On the other hand, the size of the government expanded significantly during the 2007–17 period, and the streak of primary surpluses dating back to the mid-1980s was turned into average primary deficits of 2.08 pp, the largest for the whole 1960–2017 period. Because of the dollarization regime, the government cannot turn to seigniorage to finance those deficits. However, it has been able to finance this expansion with increases

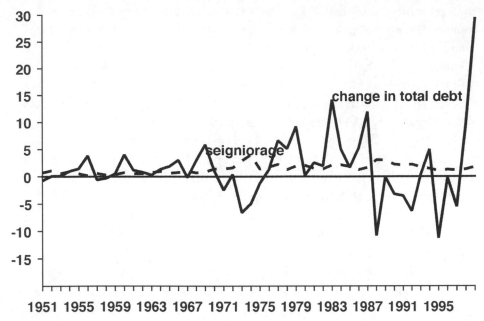

Figure 14. Change in total debt and seigniorage, percentage of GDP

in both domestic and foreign borrowing, which averaged 0.65 and 1.0 pp, in that order. (This last figure could have been larger, but recall that in 2009 there was a large decline in the stock of foreign debt due to the strategic default of 2008.) Note that in spite of the large fiscal imbalances, the inability to use seigniorage sources—combined with the ability to borrow domestically and externally—resulted in an average inflation of less than 4 percent per year, the lowest since the pre–oil boom period.

THE ROLE OF THE "EXTRAORDINARY TRANSFERS"

A noteworthy finding in the budget constraint exercise is the large size of the "transfers" component. Indeed, transfers accounted, on average, for nearly 16 percent of the obligations during the 1960–81 period and for almost a third of the financing needs between 1982 and 1999, and they were the largest component (although negative) of the obligations during the dollarized era.[18]

A natural question is, What constitutes these transfers? Certainly, a fraction of them could be from statistical discrepancies, errors, and omissions. Moreover, another portion of the transfers can be thought of as the deficit of the public sector beyond the central government. Indeed, in the online appendix 2 (available at http://manifold.bfi.uchicago .edu/), we perform the budget constraint analysis during the 2000–2017 period for the Ecuadorian NFPS, a broader definition of the government that, in addition to the central government, includes nonfinancial public enterprises, local governments, and the Social Security Institute, plus other smaller institutions.[19] Working with a wider definition of the government indeed reduces the size of the transfers component, which averaged

−2.93 pp between 2000 and 2017 for the NFPS instead of −3.69 pp for the central government. Unfortunately, the lack of consistent and comparable NFPS data precludes us from extending this analysis prior to 2000.

More importantly, we find that the peaks and troughs in the transfers term coincide with several of the most critical events in Ecuadorian history (see Figure 15). For example, the high level of transfers during the early 1980s coincided with the *sucretización* of the private foreign debt. Similarly, the steep rise in transfers in 1999 coincided with the financial crisis, when the government experienced massive financing needs owing to its decision to provide assistance to the banking system. This suggests that a further share of the "transfers" term corresponds to the deficit of the central bank.[20] On the other hand, the large negative transfers terms in 1995, 2000, and 2009 coincided with years when the stock of foreign debt decreased sharply, first from the restructuring of the foreign debt after the Brady agreement in 1994 and the default of 1999 and later due to the strategic default of 2008.

Thus these transfers most certainly represent expenditures not properly recorded—nor reported—in the government accounts and reveal the untold story of hidden fiscal costs. As such, they embody the consequences of the government's own policy mistakes—for example, the extreme dependence on oil revenues, the absence of any saving provisions to deal with the volatility in oil prices, and the massive external borrowing during the 1970s—as well as the mistakes of others (e.g., the private sector), which eventually ended up becoming the government's responsibility.

To assess the impact of those off-the-record expenses, we compare the actual path of the debt-to-GDP ratio with a hypothetical debt ratio computed under the assumption of transfers being zero in every year. This would reflect the borrowing needed to finance

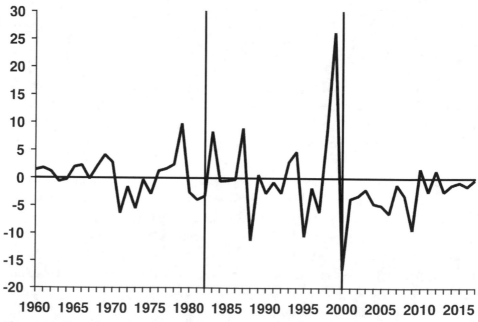

Figure 15. Transfers term, percentage of GDP

Figure 16. Total public debt, actual and without transfers, percentage of GDP

the deficits actually recorded. The two series are depicted in Figure 16. We find that prior to the establishment of the dollarization regime, the magnitude of the transfers term was significant (and positive), and thus the two series diverge noticeably, denoting the additional burden implied by the contingent liabilities. On the other hand, transfers have been negative on average since 2000, mainly because of the reduction in the stock of debt from the debt restructuring of 2001, the default of 2009, and the unilateral elimination of the debt with the central bank in 2008. Consequently, the actual debt ratio is significantly lower than the simulated one, denoting the "relief" provided by those events.

Conclusions

In this study, we document the main trends in Ecuador's fiscal and monetary history between 1960 and 2017. We also conduct a government budget constraint analysis following Sargent (1993) to identify the sources of deficit financing throughout that period. Since the economic history of Ecuador is characterized by disappointingly low output growth and high inflation for almost two decades, we ask whether the poor macroeconomic performance can be linked to bad fiscal and monetary policy.

We find that between 1960 and 1971, the size of the government and its financing needs were small, and the use of seigniorage to cover the government's obligations was the lowest for the whole period covered by this study. This coincided with an era of relatively high output growth and low inflation. When the government's size increased after the oil boom of the 1970s, those patterns changed abruptly. In particular, the government's financing needs increased significantly, and so did its reliance on seigniorage. The worsening of the fiscal and monetary variables coincided with a period of dismal economic growth—essentially, a Great Depression—and persistently high inflation. Finally, the establishment of the dollarization regime has proven successful at eliminating the inflationary environment that persisted for such a prolonged period. Indeed, although in recent years the government has run large deficits, the inability to use seigniorage to finance those imbalances because of the dollarization scheme has resulted in inflation rates at historically low levels.

We also find that "extraordinary transfers" account for a significant fraction of the government's obligations and that these transfers have been large during the most critical periods of Ecuador's economic history. Thus a sizable share of the "transfers" corresponds to additional burdens to the fiscal accounts (beyond deficits), such as the taking over of private liabilities during the *sucretización* mechanism or the agricultural sector's debt forgiveness granted by the public development banks, as well as the massive bailout of the banking system during the financial crisis of 1999. A more accurate decomposition of the "transfers" component of the budget constraint would suitably complement our work.

In all, the monetary and fiscal history in Ecuador reveals the country's failure to adequately manage fiscal and external booms and ensure mechanisms for long-term fiscal sustainability. The need to complement the benefits delivered by the dollarization system with strong, credible, and independent fiscal and monetary institutions conducive to desirable macroeconomic outcomes such as low inflation and indebtedness levels, as well as limited fiscal deficits, stands out as an important objective for the country in order to ensure a more stable macroeconomic environment over time.

Notes

We thank Roberto Mosquera for discussions and relevant contributions to earlier versions of this study and Paola Boel for her valuable comments and feedback. The views expressed herein are those of the authors and not necessarily those of their institutions.

1 Between 1982 and 1999, Ecuador's output per working-age person never grew at a rate higher than the 2 percent per year trend, except for the year 1988. Moreover, between 1982 and 1991, Ecuador's output per working-age person fell 19 percent below trend, and by 1999 it had fallen 35 percent below trend, reflecting a large and rapidly occurring contraction.

2 The sixth section of this chapter provides a detailed explanation of the government budget constraint accounting methodology.

3 A more detailed account of the recent economic history of Ecuador can be found in Díaz (2018). A timeline summarizing the most important events can be found in the online appendix 4, available at http://manifold.bfi.uchicago.edu/.

4 During this period, the exchange rate regime in place was a fixed arrangement. The official exchange rate was 15 sucres per dollar from 1950 until 1961, when the sucre was depreciated to 18 sucres per dollar. This rate lasted

Simón Cueva and Julián P. Díaz

312

until 1970, when it was further depreciated to 25 sucres per dollar, a value that remained in place until 1982.

5 These figures are in nominal terms and correspond to the price of the WTI crude oil, the grade of petroleum that serves as a reference for Ecuadorian oil.

6 For a detailed description of the *sucretización* program, see Bayas and Somensatto (1994).

7 The crawling peg also aimed at improving the real exchange rate to help the exporting sector.

8 Even more interestingly, until the approval of the constitution of 1998, some members of the monetary board represented the commercial banks and the chambers of commerce, with potential conflicts of interest when designing policy that affected the financial system.

9 Note that inflation actually *increased* after dollarization was implemented and remained high—above 10 percent—for almost three years. A similar pattern was observed in Argentina, where inflation remained above 10 percent for more than two years after the currency board was established in April 1991. A few explanations can account for the case of Ecuador. One is the exchange rate chosen for the currency conversion in January 2000 (25,000 sucres per dollar). Since the exchange rate in December 1999 was just below 18,000 sucres per dollar, the sizable depreciation implied by the conversion rate led to a large increase in the traded goods inflation rate. Moreover, the dollarization announcement was followed shortly by a fiscal adjustment program that included increases in utility rates and public transportation prices, which in turn affected the prices of related goods and services. Finally, the widespread practice of rounding up prices to the nearest dollar when converting prices from sucres contributed to the increases in the price level.

10 Correa governed uninterruptedly from 2007 to 2017, after gaining two reelections.

11 The constitution of 2008, sponsored by the Correa administration, removed the autonomy of the central bank and made it dependent on the executive branch, which became responsible for fiscal and monetary policy design.

12 The cyclical components were calculated using the Hodrick-Prescott filter. We work with data in dollars in order to use uninterrupted series expressed in a single currency.

13 We focus on the central government since it is the level of government for which the longest comparable time series are available.

14 In the online appendix 1, available at http://manifold.bfi.uchicago.edu/, we present the results of the budget constraint accounting exercise, keeping the real exchange rate fixed.

15 The average growth rates of the monetary base differ slightly relative to the values in Table 3 because the latter are based on annual values, whereas the former rely on monthly data.

16 In a dollarized economy, the changes in the stock of money are not determined by the central bank but instead by the overall balance of payments deficit or surplus.

17 Note that during the early years of the debt crisis, there were significant increases in the foreign debt component. However, a large fraction of those additions was actually from the *sucretización* arrangement, by which the government took over the foreign debt originally contracted by the private sector.

18 A positive value for the transfer term can be interpreted as additional obligations not recorded in the statistics. Similarly, a negative transfer can be thought of as sources not explicitly registered.

19 The NFPS deficit also includes crude oil derivatives subsidies, since the final price of fuels and cooking gas in Ecuador has

consistently been below import prices. This subsidy has been typically assumed by Ecuador's public oil enterprises.

20 Other sources of these "transfers" include the recapitalization of public development banks (for example, of the Banco de Fomento, a public bank that lends to the agricultural sector and has routinely granted farmers debt forgiveness); government support to the social security systems (both the general and the social security systems of the armed forces and the police); and floating debt, a term used in Ecuador to denote arrears with government suppliers.

References

Bayas, Santiago, and Eduardo Somensatto. 1994. "Programa de sucretización ecuatoriano: Historia de los efectos monetarios de la conversion de la deuda externa del sector privado." *Cuestiones económicas* 23:125–51.

Cueva, Simón. 2008. "Ecuador: Fiscal Stabilization Funds and Prospects." Country Department Andean Group Working Paper CSI-110, Inter-American Development Bank, Washington, D.C.

de la Torre, Augusto, Roberto García-Saltos, and Yira Mascaró. 2001. "Banking, Currency and Debt Meltdown: Ecuador Crisis in the Late 1990s." Unpublished manuscript, World Bank, Washington, D.C.

Díaz, Julián P. 2018. "La historia económica contemporánea del Ecuador, 1972–2015." In *Reformas y desarrollo en el Ecuador contemporáneo*, edited by Javier Díaz Cassou and Marta Ruiz-Arranz, 7–36. Washington, D.C.: Inter-American Development Bank.

Jácome, Luis. 2004. "The Late 1990s Financial Crisis in Ecuador: Institutional Weaknesses, Fiscal Rigidities, and Financial Dollarization at Work." Working paper WP/04/12, International Monetary Fund, Washington, D.C.

Kehoe, Timothy J., and Edward C. Prescott. 2007. "Great Depressions of the Twentieth Century." In *Great Depressions of the Twentieth Century*, edited by Timothy J. Kehoe and Edward C. Prescott, 1–20. Minneapolis: Federal Reserve Bank of Minneapolis.

Morillo Batlle, Jaime. 1996. *Economía Monetaria del Ecuador.* Quito: Libri Mundi.

Sargent, Thomas J. 1993. *Rational Expectations and Inflation.* 2nd ed. New York: HarperCollins.

Discussion of the History of Ecuador

Alberto Martin
European Central Bank, Center for Research in International
Economics, and Barcelona Graduate School of Economics

As its title suggests, this chapter provides an overview of the main fiscal and monetary developments in Ecuador between 1950 and 2015. Covering sixty-five years of history in forty pages is no small feat, particularly so for a country like Ecuador, which—like many of its Latin American neighbors—has been on an economic roller coaster over the last half century. During this period, Ecuador repeatedly experienced commodity booms and busts, sudden stops, large financial crises, and even two armed conflicts with neighboring Peru! In such a volatile economic environment, it is no wonder that fiscal and monetary policy also fluctuated wildly and included two large-scale government bailouts to the private sector, three sovereign defaults, and multiple changes in the monetary regime that ended in outright dollarization in 2000.

Let me therefore start by commending the authors on the great job that they have done in summarizing and analyzing this rich history. In these comments, I first provide a bird's-eye view of the history described in the chapter. I then discuss what, in my view, are the key takeaways from the analysis and the main questions that it raises.

A Bird's-Eye View of Ecuador's Recent Economic History

Based on the chapter, we can divide Ecuador's economic history since 1950 into four distinct periods, which I will refer to as pre-oil, oil, debt crisis and aftermath, and dollarization.

During the *pre-oil period*, which extends from 1950 to 1971, Ecuador mostly exported agricultural products (bananas made up 40 percent of its total exports). The country exhibited modest yet relatively stable growth (approximately 2 percent in per capita terms), and more importantly from the perspective of fiscal and monetary policy, it was characterized by a small government and relatively low inflation. During this period, the fiscal deficit averaged 0.9 percent of GDP, and average inflation was low at 3.7 percent.

In 1972, Ecuador began exporting oil and everything changed. During the *oil period*, between 1972 and 1981, the economy boomed. Per capita growth averaged 6 percent, and oil provided a substantial windfall for government finances. Despite the massive growth in revenues, spending increased even faster, and the fiscal deficit averaged 2 percent. In a world awash with liquidity, this deficit was largely financed by issuing foreign debt: as a result, total public debt increased by approximately 25 percent of GDP during the period (from 25 percent to 50 percent of GDP). Meanwhile, inflation also increased substantially to an average rate of 13 percent, fueled partly by the use of loose monetary policy to fund the fiscal deficit. In a nutshell, the oil boom brought about tremendous economic growth, but fiscal and monetary policies put the economy on a vulnerable path of rising imbalances.

These vulnerabilities surfaced in 1982, when Ecuador suffered the double blow of falling oil prices and rising interest rates in the United States. That is, just when they were most needed, the country found itself cut off from international financial markets. To make things worse, the private sector had also borrowed excessively from abroad during the boom years and now faced the specter of massive defaults and bankruptcies. The government intervened by partially nationalizing the private debt, which—coupled with the economic crisis—led to a discrete jump in public debt (approximately 30 percent of GDP in one year, from 50 percent to 80 percent) that ended with a sovereign default in 1982. The crisis also led to a large devaluation of the currency and to a spike in inflation, which rose to 48 percent in 1983.

This *debt crisis* had long-lasting reverberations on Ecuador's economy, and much of the following two decades was spent dealing with its legacy. Despite attempts at implementing reforms to boost growth and bring public finances in order, the 1980s were characterized by considerable fiscal deficits that were largely financed through seigniorage. Average inflation remained high, exceeding 34 percent throughout the decade. Public debt, meanwhile, grew as the country accumulated substantial arrears on foreign payments (by 1990, public debt stood at approximately 120 percent of GDP). During the 1990s, as elsewhere in Latin America, Ecuador embarked on a series of market-friendly reforms that included financial liberalization. Between 1997 and 1998, however, a sequence of natural and economic shocks—the El Niño phenomenon, low oil prices, and a tightening of international financial conditions following the East Asian and Russian crises—ultimately led to the worst financial crisis in the country's history. Output contracted by 7 percent in 1999, and the deficit of the public sector, which had to bail out the banking system, rose to 5 percent. Finally, inflation reached 67 percent by the end of the year.

By 2000, Ecuador's real GDP per capita was basically the same as in 1982. This year gave rise to the *dollarization period* as the country adopted the U.S. dollar and passed a series of fiscal responsibility laws to ensure the sustainability of the regime. This proved very successful in curbing inflation and jump-starting growth. Between 2007 and 2015, Ecuador experienced a new oil boom as commodity prices rose throughout the world. Once again, the boom was accompanied not only by economic growth but also by public deficits, which—given the lack of seigniorage in a dollarized regime—were financed with domestic and foreign debt.

What are the key takeaways from the chapter's analysis of sixty-five years of economic history? I divide my comments into three brief sections: what I knew, what I did not know, and what I would like to know.

What I (Thought I) Knew

This presumptuous title does not imply that I knew much about Ecuador before reading the chapter. It is instead meant to illustrate that the main guiding threads of Ecuador's economic history are common to many Latin American economies and not too surprising to anyone versed in the continent's recent past.

First, the country has persistently run fiscal deficits, which have been financed through the path of least resistance. During the 1970s, when international liquidity was abundant, the country financed deficits by issuing foreign debt; in the 1980s and 1990s, when access to international markets was curtailed, deficits were financed instead through seigniorage and, to some extent, through domestic debt.

Second, and contrary to what standard economic theory would suggest, fiscal policy in Ecuador has been largely procyclical with respect to the price of oil, its main export commodity. The oil booms of the 1970s and the 2000s were accompanied by large increases in government spending, fiscal deficits, and public debt. Jointly considered, these two points suggest that—in Ecuador—favorable economic conditions (e.g., high oil prices and abundant international liquidity) have not been used to correct but appear rather to have exacerbated fiscal and monetary imbalances.

Third, the high inflationary periods of the 1980s and 1990s were characterized by large increases in money supply, mostly from the monetization of the fiscal deficit. At least to a first approximation, Ecuador appears to confirm Milton Friedman's dictum that "inflation is always and everywhere a monetary phenomenon."

What I Did Not Know

Beneath the surface, however, this familiar story has some unexpected aspects. Perhaps the most surprising one uncovered by the chapter refers to the evolution of fiscal variables, especially the components of the deficit and the dynamics of public debt.

Between 1950 and 2000, the Ecuadorian government was consistently in the red: according to Table 1 in the chapter, its annual financing needs averaged 1.8 percent of GDP during the pre–oil boom period, 2.5 percent of GDP during the oil boom period, and 3.56 percent of GDP during the debt crisis and its aftermath. One may suspect that these needs were the result of irresponsible government spending. And yet, a relatively small share of them originated in *primary* deficits. During the debt crisis and its aftermath, in fact, Ecuador actually ran an average primary surplus of 2.47 percent of GDP! Where, then, did the financing needs originate? The chapter's answer is twofold: debt servicing and transfers.

Debt servicing is easy to explain. During the 1980s especially, as I have already mentioned, Ecuador's public debt grew as a consequence of high interest rates and accumulated arrears on foreign payments. Transfers are harder to pin down. Formally, they are defined as financing needs that go beyond the primary deficits and debt servicing. It is hard to know exactly what these transfers contain because they are not properly recorded in official statistics and are instead obtained as a residual in the authors' calculations. Some of the largest transfers coincide with Ecuador's hardest years, however, and they can be traced to large "fiscal shocks" such as the nationalization of private debt in the 1980s or the bailout of the banking system in 1999. To get a sense of these magnitudes, consider that Ecuador's debt-to-GDP ratio peaked at 130 percent in 1999: according to the authors' calculations, it would have been only 60 percent in the absence of transfers!

This is a fascinating and thought-provoking fact. Most theories of sovereign debt depict governments as borrowing to smooth consumption in the face of cyclical shocks or to increase the consumption of their constituents. This chapter, however, raises another possibility—namely, that a substantial share of countries' debt, in Latin America and elsewhere, is the result of financial crises and public bailouts. I am not aware of any systematic attempts to document the origin of public debt, but if this fact were verified for a broader set of countries, it could greatly influence our view of public debt. Traditional models of sovereign debt assume that countries face exogenous shocks and smooth them by issuing debt. According to these models, a central problem is that governments lack commitment, which may limit their ability to issue debt or expose them to costly debt crises: to solve this problem, countries should improve their "commitment technology" (e.g., by building institutions or exposing themselves to foreign sanctions). But Ecuador's experience suggests an alternative view, by which public debt is largely driven by financial crises. According to this view, the main problem is one of vulnerability to such crises, and the solutions lie in adequate crisis prevention and management.

What I Would Like to Know

As I said before, the chapter does a great job of documenting Ecuador's recent economic history. Yet two aspects leave the reader wanting more.

The first refers to data availability, and it largely escapes the control of the authors. All the statistics on fiscal policy refer to the central government because this is apparently the only level of government for which reliable data are available. This is unfortunate, because local finances (e.g., at the state or provincial level) have been important contributors to the aggregate fiscal deficit in many Latin American countries. It would be interesting to know how the primary deficit of the consolidated public sector behaves once other levels of government are taken into account and whether the needs of local governments can in part account for central government transfers. The composition of transfers is another aspect where perhaps more could be done. The chapter does a fantastic job of documenting the importance of transfers, their contribution to the buildup of public debt, and their relationship to major macroeconomic crises in Ecuador. But it would be interesting to know more. One possibility would be to complement the analysis in the chapter with archival work, which would enable the authors to identify the main drivers of transfers in years in which they were especially large.

The second aspect that could be further explored refers to the broader effects of dollarization. This is a recurrent debate in Latin America that resurfaces whenever a major crisis occurs. The chapter adequately documents the evolution of major macroeconomic, fiscal, and monetary variables during the dollarization period, but—given that Ecuador represents a fantastic case study—I was left wanting more. For instance, conventional wisdom suggests that dollarization enhances stability by providing a nominal anchor, but it may also be destabilizing by reducing the country's ability to respond to shocks. Can Ecuador's experience teach us anything about this trade-off? Also, given the large effect of financial crises in the past, how does a dollarized economy prepare for such crises? Can the central bank effectively fulfill its role as a lender of last resort? How has Ecuador dealt with these challenges?

But these are minor quibbles about an otherwise very thorough chapter Anyone interested in Ecuador's and, more broadly, in Latin America's recent economic history should definitely read it!

Note

This chapter should not be reported as representing the views of the European Central Bank (ECB). The views expressed are those of the author and do not necessarily reflect those of the ECB.

Mexico

The History of Mexico

Felipe Meza
Centro de Análisis e Investigación Económica and
Instituto Tecnológico Autónomo de México

Major fiscal and monetary events, 1960–2017

1976	Balance of payments crisis and devaluation	**1991**	Adoption of exchange rate band
	Discovery of oil fields	**1991–92**	Privatization of banks
1982	Balance of payments crisis and devaluation	**1993**	Central bank autonomy, mandate to preserve purchasing power of the peso
	Default	**1994**	Balance of payments and financial crisis
	Capital controls		Abandonment of exchange rate band
	Nationalization of banks		
1987	Stabilization plan, "Pacto Solidaridad"	**1995**	Debt crisis and Clinton bailout
	Establishment of exchange rate bands		Banks bailout
1989	Brady Plan	**2002**	Inflation targeting

Introduction

Between 1960 and 1982 Mexico went through a period of rapid growth and fiscal expansion, up to the 1982 crisis. The country then went through a period with crises in 1982 and 1994. During this period the government implemented major important reforms. Finally, Mexico experienced a period of slow growth and macroeconomic stability interrupted by the global recession of 2008–10. Figure 1 plots real GDP per capita and compares it to a trend line of growth of 2 percent per year.

The 1982 crisis was clearly a turning point in Mexico's economic history. The annual growth rate of real GDP per capita between 1960 and 1982 was 3.3 percent. Between 1982 and 2016, it fell to 0.7 percent. The drop in the growth rate during and following the 1982 crisis has had a major impact on Mexico's catch-up with the world economic leader, the United States. The real GDP per capita of the United States grew by approximately 2 percent per year between 1875 and 2010.[1] Between 1960 and 1982, Mexico grew faster than the United States, closing the per capita income gap between the two economies. Between 1982 and 1995, Mexico suffered what Kehoe and Prescott (2007)

323

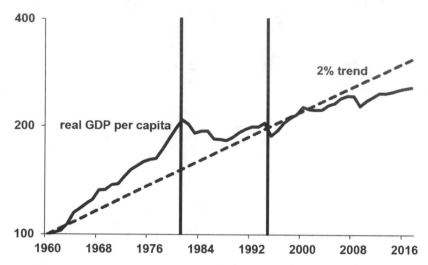

Figure 1. Real GDP per capita at 1993 pesos, 1960–2017, and 2 percent yearly trend, indexes 1960 = 100, vertical axis in logarithmic scale base 2
Sources: Author's calculations with data from Instituto Nacional de Estadística y Geografía (INEGI), World Bank

classify as a great depression. Finally, between 1995 and 2017, Mexico grew at a pace that was faster than, but roughly equal to, that of the United States. In short, in terms of catching up to the United States, by 2017 Mexico had still not recovered from the 1982 debt crisis.[2]

Figure 2 shows another crucial variable for the Mexican economy: the annual inflation rate measured using the GDP deflator. Mexico had low inflation up to 1972, when the rate was 4.6 percent per year. Between 1973 and 1981, inflation increased to levels around 25 percent per year. Then, in 1982, the year of the debt crisis, the annual inflation rate jumped to 61.8 percent. In the second period, 1983–94, there are two stages: first, Mexico had difficulties controlling inflation, as it reached its historical maximum of 142.8 percent in 1987; then inflation fell steadily, reaching 8.5 percent in 1994. In fact, except for the transitory impact of the 1994 crisis, inflation had a downward trend from 1988 until 2006. Between 2007 and 2016, inflation remained stable, having an average value of 4 percent per year. The data in Figure 2 make the important point that Mexico has never had hyperinflation according to the classic Cagan definition of 50 percent per month.[3]

Figure 3 reports several measures of the deficit of the public sector. "Public sector" is a broad definition of the government that includes the federal government plus other institutions such as the national oil company PEMEX.[4] "Financial deficit" is "public deficit" plus the financial intermediation deficit from development banks.

Mexico had a very small primary deficit up to 1971. In 1972, Mexico's primary deficit started to rapidly increase from less than 1 percent of GDP to 6 percent in 1975.

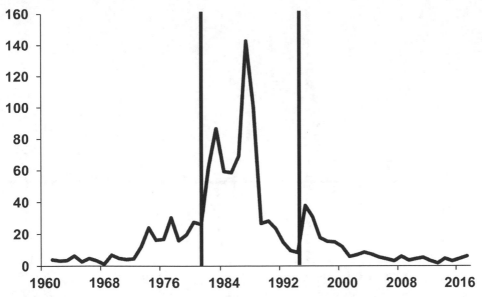

Figure 2. Annual inflation rate, percentage change in GDP deflator
Sources: Author's calculations with data from INEGI

This increase was financed with seigniorage and foreign debt. The growth in the deficit was not sustainable. Mexico devalued the peso in 1976 for the first time in twenty-two years. Afterward, there was a reduction and stabilization of the primary deficit to levels close to 3 percent. In the late 1970s, Mexico discovered a giant oil field at the same time that the international oil price rose. These events led to a new increase in the primary deficit. In 1981, it reached its historical maximum of 8 percent. This increase was again financed with seigniorage and foreign debt. The new indebtedness was unsustainable and increasingly dependent on the government's ability to finance debt payments in foreign currency. Following devaluations in 1982, which made it increasingly difficult for Mexico to service its debt, the government declared it could not pay part of the debt, starting the debt crisis.

Between 1983 and 1994, Mexico made a substantial effort to reduce the burden of the debt: large primary surpluses started in 1983. Then the 1994 crisis hit the economy. This crisis was not preceded by large fiscal deficits. It happened after a large increase in one type of dollar-denominated debt. I will discuss theories and evidence later on. The reaction to the 1994 crisis and the clear goal of achieving macroeconomic stability led to primary surpluses between 1995 and 2008.

I analyze the monetary and fiscal history of Mexico using a model of the consolidated budget constraint of the Mexican government.[5] In the model, when government policy is characterized by fiscal dominance, a debt crisis that is preceded by an increase in the primary deficit is then followed by an increase in inflation and the monetary base. I document that this narrative fits the events around the 1982 crisis.[6]

This fiscal dominance narrative does not account for the 1994 crisis, as I also document that monetary dominance prevailed after important changes in 1993. One important

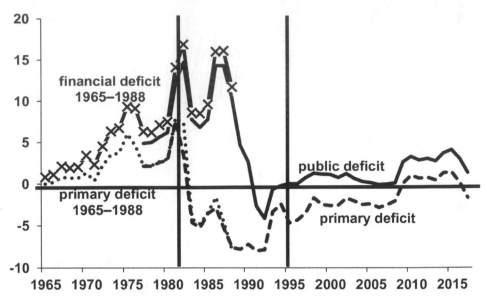

Figure 3. Different measures of the deficit of the public sector, percentage of GDP
Sources: Author's calculations with data from INEGI, Secretaría de Hacienda y Crédito
Público (SHCP), Banco de México

factor behind the crisis was the dollar-indexed *tesobono* debt. In late December 1994,
the central bank had very few international reserves. On December 22, the government
had to allow free floating, and the peso lost value. Investors refused to buy new issues of
tesobonos, which had become the largest portion of government debt. The government
had trouble financing debt that was increasing due to currency depreciations.

Analyzing fiscal and monetary policy around the 1994 crisis, I conclude that the
change in legislation that granted independence to the Banco de México in 1993 represented a credible change from fiscal to monetary dominance. The fact that the inflation tax remained low, compared to historical values, is consistent with such a change.
Inflation fell persistently after 1995, reaching values of 3 percent per year in mid-2016,
the target of the central bank (+/−1 percentage point). On the fiscal side, I observe a change
in the downward trend of the total debt ratio, as it fell between the 1980s and 2009, the
year in which it started to grow steadily until 2016.

Measurement: Model and Data

The model is a version of that in "A Framework for Studying the Monetary and Fiscal
History of Latin America." The budget constraint comes from consolidating the budget
constraints of the fiscal branch of the government, the Treasury, and the central bank
and using an equation that says that, for each kind of debt, total debt issued by the government BG is equal to a part bought by the central bank, BB, and a part bought by the
public, B. Therefore, $BG = BB + B$.

I include the international reserves of the central bank because reserves are an asset for the consolidated government. The reason for doing so is that the model includes foreign debt; therefore, for consistency, one should consider the role of international reserves as an asset.[7] In the model, the budget constraint of the government includes receipts from the central bank (RCB). "Receipts from Central Bank" is the label used by Walsh (2003) for receipts from the central bank to the fiscal branch of the government. In the United States, the Federal Reserve turns over to the Treasury most of its interest earnings from government debt. In the case of Mexico, the central bank, after determining its earnings and following rules legally specified, transfers resources to the Treasury. This is the Remanente de Operación de Banco de México.

I add to the Treasury's resources the revenue from oil. I make this addition because of the importance of PEMEX, Mexico's national oil company, for public finances. In 1938, the Mexican oil industry was nationalized, and PEMEX was granted a monopoly on all activities related to the oil industry: exploration, extraction, exporting, refining, distribution, and sales to consumers.[8] Mexico became a large exporter of oil in the late 1970s after an increase in the international oil price and the discovery of a giant oil field. These exports provided a cash flow to PEMEX. The Mexican Treasury has historically taxed PEMEX to obtain revenue from oil sales. PEMEX has historically provided a large fraction of all income of the public sector. In terms of the model, in an online appendix, I show how oil revenue is included in the basic budget constraint. I assume that the source of revenue is oil exports, excluding all other possible sources, such as domestic sales of refined products like gasoline. For simplicity, I do not model the particulars of the different ways in which the federal government has taxed PEMEX over time.

Given these considerations, the consolidated budget constraint of the government is

$$B_t + E_t B_t^* + M_t = D_t + T_t + \left(1 + r_{t-1}\right) B_{t-1} + E_t \left(1 + r_{t-1}^*\right) B_{t-1}^* + M_{t-1} \, ,$$

where B_t is the stock of domestic debt, B_t^* is the stock of foreign debt net of international reserves, D_t is the primary deficit of the consolidated government, M_t is the monetary base, E_t is the pesos per dollar nominal exchange rate, T_t are transfers, and the two kinds of debt have their respective nominal interest rates.

The fiscal and monetary branches of the government have two possible arrangements. One is fiscal dominance, in which case when the Treasury loses access to debt markets, the central bank has to adjust and create enough seigniorage to finance the gap in the government budget. The other arrangement is monetary dominance, in which case it is the Treasury, rather than the central bank, that adjusts in times of crisis.[9]

In the data analysis, I work with a broad definition of government. This means working with data from the federal government but also with data from the national oil company, PEMEX; the national electricity company, CFE; and the national social security institute, IMSS. Since the 1980s, the government has compiled statistics for the public sector. I describe its components based on Secretaría de Hacienda y Crédito Público (2010).[10] Table 1 shows a summary of the structure of the public sector. The public sector is A + B.

Table 1. Summary of components of the public sector

A. Public sector of direct budget control		B. Public sector of indirect budget control
A.1. Federal government	*A.2. Government enterprises and organizations of direct budget control*	*Government enterprises and organizations of indirect budget control*
	PEMEX	B.1 Development banks
	CFE	B.2 Nonfinancial
	IMSS	
	ISSSTE	

Source: Secretaría de Hacienda y Crédito Público (2010).

In turn, Part A has two main components: the federal government (A.1) and certain institutions and government firms (A.2). Part B has two main components: a financial and a nonfinancial one. The financial component (B.1) is the set of development banks. I exclude more detail, including in Table 1 the components of the government that are more relevant in terms of revenue and spending.[11]

To carry out the analysis, I choose three periods. The first one runs from 1960 to 1982, the year of the debt crisis. The second starts in 1982 and ends with the crisis in 1994–95. The third starts in 1995 and ends in 2017. I chose these periods based on the mechanism of the theoretical model. If the deficit plus transfers is larger than the sum of seigniorage and oil revenue, the consolidated government will have to issue a growing amount of debt until it hits an exogenous limit set by financial markets, and there will be a fiscal crisis. The last period, 1995–2017, includes the response to the 1994 crisis, as well as important changes in fiscal and monetary policy. It includes the impact of and the response to the international financial crisis. It also shows a change in the behavior of the debt-to-GDP ratio, which had fallen and remained stable for many years until it started growing in 2009.

1960–82: Rapid Growth and Monetary Expansion

Figure 4 shows the evolution of the consolidated budget constraint of the government. The primary deficit was close to zero in 1966. The period started with relatively low and stable levels of debt, but the fiscal situation deteriorated toward the second half of the 1970s. It would become even worse in the early 1980s. When computing seigniorage, I use the monetary base.[12] I focus the discussion on the last two presidential terms, 1970–76 and 1976–82, as those are the years for which I have more data. My main historical reference is Cárdenas (2015).

During the presidential term of Gustavo Díaz Ordaz, 1964–70, primary deficits were close to zero. There was an increase in the primary deficit to 1.3 percent of GDP in 1970, which was the last year he was in power.

The beginning of the term of Luis Echeverría, 1970–76, showed the first signs of instability. The peso suffered a devaluation in 1976 for the first time in twenty-two years. This crisis is an example of a first-generation balance of payments crisis. The government increased spending. This spending was financed with foreign resources and via money creation by the Banco de México. The growth of money was inconsistent with a fixed exchange rate, and therefore a crisis developed.

The year 1971 was one of low economic activity. President Echeverría decided to use public spending to stimulate growth. The economic team of the president opposed the large expansion, leading to the dismissal of the secretario de hacienda, Hugo B. Margáin. He was replaced by José López Portillo, who also used government spending as an instrument for growth when he became president in 1976. The deficit-to-GDP ratio went from 2.5 percent in 1971 to 4.9 percent in 1972.

The path to the crisis started in 1972, when the primary deficit ratio increased, as shown in Figure 4. There was a large increase in government consumption and public investment. The government bought private firms that had gone bankrupt or had financial problems. This policy of rescuing failing firms was a continuation from the 1960s, and by 1975, these firms, known as *empresas paraestatales*, had grown in number and industry scope. International financial markets went through important changes in the 1970s, including the collapse of the Bretton Woods system in the first years of that decade.[13] The peso had had a fixed nominal exchange rate with the dollar since 1954. The government borrowed in international markets to pay for the deficit, and there was an increase in the debt-to-GDP ratio. Figure 4 shows that the primary deficit reached

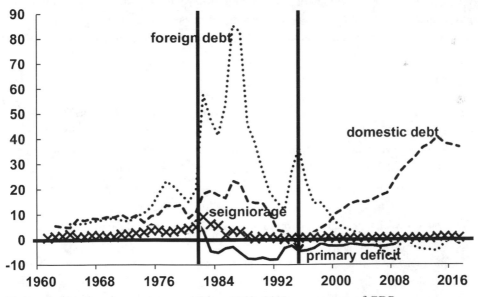

Figure 4. Fiscal and monetary variables, 1960–2017, percentage of GDP

Sources: For 1961–79, author's calculations with data from Banco de México, INEGI, SHCP, and Gurría (1993). For 1980–2017, calculations with data from Banco de México and INEGI. The falls in domestic and public debt ratios 1979–80 come from joining the two data sets.

6 percent of GDP in 1975, the highest value in the sample before 1981. In 1976, the government was unable to keep the exchange rate fixed. It went from 12.5 pesos per dollar in August to 19.4 in September, a devaluation of 55.2 percent. On the monetary side, Figure 4 shows a positive trend in seigniorage between 1970 and 1976, after having an average stationary value of approximately 2 percent of GDP from 1961 to 1969. In terms of the impact on prices, inflation and the growth rate of the monetary base had a correlation of 71.8 percent between 1961 and 1977, as shown in Figure 5. Inflation jumped from 4.6 percent to 12.1 percent; the growth rate of the monetary base increased from 19.2 percent to 23.6 percent.

Between 1960 and 1973, there was a roughly stationary current account deficit of 2.1 percent of GDP on average. In 1975, this deficit reached 4.5 percent and rapidly contracted to 1.8 percent in 1976. Even though the current account does not reverse its sign, it is clear that there was a large adjustment. The economy could not attract the capital flows necessary to maintain its level of expenditure. In 1977, real GDP per capita fell 4.1 percent below trend.[14]

1973 OIL CRISIS AND MEXICO AS A NET EXPORTER OF OIL

A key driver of Mexico becoming a net exporter of oil was the oil crisis of 1973. By 1968 Mexico had stopped exporting oil, limiting extraction to satisfy domestic demand. The oil embargo in 1973 generated a 70 percent increase in the international price to 5.1 dollars per barrel (dpb). In 1974, the price reached 12.0 dpb, at which point Mexico started exporting oil again. It is important to recall that the oil industry had been under the control of the government since 1938, when it was nationalized by President Lázaro Cárdenas. The international oil crisis had the effect on Mexico of incentivizing PEMEX to start exporting again.

BUILDING UP TO THE 1982 DEBT CRISIS

The 1982 debt crisis occurred in the final year of President José López Portillo's term. A crucial event during his term was the discovery of the massive oil field Cantarell in 1976. Proven oil reserves increased 151.2 percent between 1977 and 1978. Oil extraction started in 1979, and the government decided to invest in the infrastructure of the oil industry. Mexican oil exports grew very rapidly until 1982. To interpret this event in terms of a simple dynamic model, the discovery of Cantarell increased the permanent income of the economy, which caused an increase in foreign borrowing.[15] That is exactly what the Mexican government did.[16]

Other features of these years include an expansion of investment in health and education. Elementary school coverage and access to medical services increased significantly. The government created important policy tools, such as the value-added tax (IVA, *impuesto al valor agregado*) and the short-term bonds named CETEs (for *certificados de la tesorería de la federación*).

The administration of López Portillo is famous for the phrase "to manage abundance." The increase in oil reserves was seen as leading to a boom in the Mexican economy.

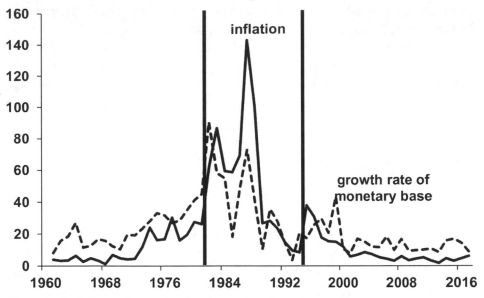

Figure 5. Inflation and growth rate of monetary base (percent)
Sources: Author's calculations with data from Banco de México, INEGI

However, the opposite occurred. I have mentioned some potentially productive investments made by the government in this administration. At the same time, there was a large increase in public spending unrelated to the oil industry. Total government spending increased from 30.9 percent of GDP in 1978 to 40.6 percent in 1981. Out of those approximately 10 percentage points, 7.3 came from increased spending in areas not related to the non-oil industry.

Figure 4 shows that the primary deficit increased to 7.6 percent of GDP in 1981. The figure also shows a substantial increase in borrowing prior to the 1982 crisis, particularly in foreign debt. In 1982, this administration would default on payments to the principal of foreign debt, though it would still pay interest. The government blamed Mexican banks for the capital leaving Mexico and chose to take control of them. Banks were nationalized toward the end of the presidential term of López Portillo. For approximately nine years, banks would be managed by the government.

1982–95: Crisis and Reform

The year 1982 saw large increases in the fiscal deficit and current account deficit. Interest rates in the United States had increased because of contractionary monetary policy. International banks reduced the amount of lending and shortened the maturity of loans. The oil price fell. Oil exports were a very important source of revenue for the government; therefore, this fall caused a further deterioration in public finances. The lack of fiscal adjustment led to expectations of devaluation and capital outflows. New debt could only be obtained at shorter maturities.

In 1982 the international reserves of the Banco de México had reached a low level. On February 5, President López Portillo gave a speech promising to defend the value of the peso. On February 17, the peso suffered a devaluation of 80 percent. Afterward, unions demanded wage increases, which were implemented. There was no fiscal adjustment because 1982 was a year of presidential elections. During the first half of 1982, foreign short-term debt grew by US$20 billion. International banks made lending more and more restrictive. After receiving a loan on June 30 from a group of international banks, Mexico suffered a total lack of access to more credit. By the end of July, with central bank reserves at a very low level, for the first time in the history of Mexico, capital controls were imposed. A system of dual exchange rates was created. On August 20, the secretario de hacienda (secretary of the Treasury), Jesús Silva Herzog, announced in New York that Mexico did not have the resources to pay the principal of debt due in the rest of the year. A moratorium was negotiated with international banks, and interest payments continued. The stock of foreign debt reached a level of $84 billion, of which 68.4 percent was public, 21.8 percent was private (excluding banks), and 9.7 percent was bank debt.

In summary, two external shocks severely deteriorated the fiscal and external balances in Mexico. One was the higher level of interest rates in the United States, which increased the opportunity cost of lending to Mexico. The other was the fall in the oil price, which was a crucial source of revenue for the government, in particular to make debt payments in dollars. The fiscal deficit increased, and in 1982 the government had to devalue the peso. Looking at yearly average data, the cumulative devaluation was 266 percent between 1981 and 1982. The burden of foreign debt on GDP increased dramatically, to the point that in August 1982, the government announced it would continue making interest payments, having negotiated a moratorium on payments of principal of foreign debt. The foreign debt-to-GDP ratio increased from 20.1 percent in 1981 to 57.6 percent in 1982. The moratorium lasted until successive rounds of renegotiation of the principal post-1982.

I consider a third factor as the cause of the crisis: the lack of financial planning by the government. There was no guarantee in 1980 that the oil price would remain high or that international interest rates would remain low. The economy did suffer two very important exogenous shocks, but the lack of anticipation and financial planning contributed to making the situation much worse. This myopic behavior managing public finances, in particular the growth of the primary deficit, set the stage for the external shocks to trigger the 1982 crisis.

CAUSES OF 1982 CRISIS

Throughout 1970–82, the Banco de México was controlled by the government. There were episodes in 1972 and in 1981 in which the Banco de México expanded the monetary base to finance growing deficits.

A prediction of the model is that, when there is fiscal dominance, the debt-to-GDP ratio increases when seigniorage is not enough to finance the primary deficit. Between 1965 and 1973, the domestic and foreign debt ratios were roughly constant. This is consistent with the fact that seigniorage was approximately equal to the primary deficit. In 1975, there was a spike in the primary deficit, as it jumped to 6 percent of GDP. At the same time, it became larger than seigniorage. The government had to issue more debt, leading to an increase first in the foreign debt ratio to 12.9 percent and in the subsequent years in the domestic debt ratio. Before 1980 the maximum values of the foreign and domestic ratios were 23.1 percent and 13.6 percent in 1977, respectively. Between 1977 and 1979, there was an effort to *reduce* the growth of the debt ratios. The primary deficit ratio had a smaller value of 2.2 percent in 1977. Additionally, seigniorage became larger than the primary deficit, reaching a value of 3.9 percent in 1979. The debt ratios stopped growing. In 1979, the foreign debt ratio actually fell to 17.9 percent, and the domestic debt ratio stabilized around 13.7 percent.

The fiscal situation deteriorated before 1982, as there was an increase in the primary deficit to 7.6 percent of GDP in 1981. In that year, the primary surplus became larger than seigniorage, and the government had to increase its borrowing. There were increases in both domestic and foreign debt between 1980 and 1981. Finally, the debt crisis took place in 1982.

DEVALUATION AND SPIKES IN THE FOREIGN DEBT-TO-GDP RATIO

An important force behind the increase in the foreign debt-to-GDP ratio was the large devaluation of the peso in 1982. Figure 6 shows the ratio of foreign debt to GDP fixing the nominal exchange rate to its 1981 value. The main source of the increase in the foreign debt ratio in 1982 is the devaluation of the peso. The story is different for the large increase in 1986. There is a sizable jump in the foreign debt ratio even when I keep the real exchange rate constant. This is also the case for 1994.

Zooming in on 1982 by looking at monthly average data, most of the increase in the foreign debt-to-GDP ratio was the result of devaluations in February, March, August, and December. I computed the *cumulative* devaluation during 1982 with respect to December 1981. With this metric, in February the devaluation was 24 percent. By March it was 75 percent. The peso stayed roughly constant for several months until August, when another devaluation brought the cumulative figure to 167 percent. The peso again stayed roughly constant until December, when the cumulative devaluation increased to 210 percent.

INFLATION AND INFLATION TAX

The consequences of the debt crisis parallel the predictions of the model regarding seigniorage. Figure 7 plots the inflation rate and the inflation tax. There was a large increase in inflation and the inflation tax between 1981 and 1983. Inflation went from 26.3 percent to 86.6 percent. The inflation tax as a percentage of GDP went from 4.1 to 8.5.[17] Figure 7 shows a strong correlation between inflation and the inflation tax between

Figure 6. Decomposition of foreign debt-to-GDP ratio keeping real exchange rate fixed at its 1981 value, index 1981 = 1
Sources: Author's calculations with data from Banco de México, INEGI

1977 and 2000. After 2000 both series become very stable, take low values, and show a smaller correlation.[18]

OIL PRICE AND U.S. INTEREST RATES

Measuring the contribution to the crisis of the two external shocks considered in this section is beyond the scope of this chapter; however, I argue that both are important factors and that both were likely contributing factors.[19]

Large falls in the price of oil took place between 1981 and 1982. The percentage yearly change in January 1982 was −14 percent, followed by −15 percent in February. Such falls put pressure on public finances.

If we use the model as a guide, the oil price that appears in the budget constraint is the *real* price.[20] Between 1980 and 1981, this price fell by approximately 10 percent. Between 1981 and 1982, this price increased. It did so because even though the dollar price fell, the exchange rate had a very large devaluation in 1982, and the domestic price level did not increase as rapidly. The fall in the international oil price in 1982 reduced the income *in dollars* of the Mexican government, therefore reducing its ability to repay foreign debt.

It is well known that oil revenue is very important for Mexican public finances. I compared the primary deficit to its value excluding oil revenue. The conclusion was that oil revenue is clearly a large contributor to having lower deficits and achieving surpluses. Focusing on the 1977–82 period, we can see that the deficit would have been much higher without the revenue coming from oil sales. In fact, the deficit excluding oil revenue

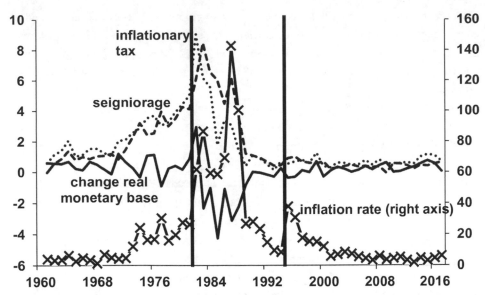

Figure 7. Change in real monetary base demand, inflationary tax, and seigniorage, as percentage of GDP, and inflation rate in percentage

Sources: Constructed with data from Banco de México, INEGI

Note: Inflation rate measured on right axis.

reached its highest value in that period, and in the entire sample 1977–2017, attaining a value of 15 percent of GDP in 1981.[21]

U.S. interest rates rose to historically high values and were very volatile between 1978 and 1982. These high and volatile rates were the result of tighter monetary policy to reduce inflation in the United States. The largest absolute yearly increase in interest rates took place between June 1980 and June 1981, when the rate went from 7.1 percent to 14.7 percent. The large increase in interest rates, especially during 1981, increased the cost of external funding for Mexico.

I calculate real interest rates by subtracting one of two measures of expected yearly inflation from nominal interest rates: inflation in the previous twelve months and inflation twelve months ahead. The message is the same: real interest rates in the United States jumped from values of around zero in 1980 to very high values between 1981 and 1986. The average value was, using both measurements, 4 percent. The values in this sample are the highest between 1960 and 2017. This increase in the real opportunity cost of investing in Mexico put pressure on the ability to repay and roll over foreign debt.[22]

POLITICAL FACTORS IN THE 1982 CRISIS

The same political party, the PRI, or Partido Revolucionario Institucional, ruled Mexico from the late 1920s until 2000. Each president handpicked his successor, who was part of the administration. There was little uncertainty about the characteristics of the newcomer. From 1976 to 1994, however, an economic crisis developed at the end of each presidential term. As mentioned earlier, 1976 was the year in which the peso was devalued after twenty-two years of being fixed. In 1982, Mexico suffered a debt crisis, and in 1994, it entered another crisis. In 1988, there was no large crisis, but there was a large devaluation of the peso in 1987.

In the case of the 1982 crisis, even though President López Portillo handpicked his successor, Miguel de la Madrid, the process was not exempt from political turmoil, particularly regarding the public deficit. The key participants in 1981 were Miguel de la Madrid, who was the *secretario* of the Secretaría de Programación y Presupuesto (SPP); David Ibarra Muñoz, who was in charge of the SHCP; José Andrés de Oteyza, who led the Secretaría de Patrimonio y Fomento Industrial (SEPAFIN); and Gustavo Romero Kolbeck, who was director general of the Banco de México. The issues were the following. First, the SPP reported a deficit of 9 percent of GDP, whereas the SHCP calculated 12 percent. Second, there was disagreement on the reduction of the deficit. The SHCP and the Banco de México wanted to reduce its growth. The SEPAFIN opposed. Third, there was disagreement on whether Mexico should devalue the peso. The SHCP and the Banco de México wanted to devalue to reduce the current account deficit. The SEPAFIN opposed, proposing instead restricting imports of consumption goods. The SPP mediated between the two sides. There was competition between these officials to become the presidential candidate of the PRI; my hypothesis is that this motivated the group to decide not to adjust the deficit, since it would have been an unpopular decision. The exchange rate remained fixed. Restrictions on imports were imposed to reduce the current account deficit. This politically motivated reluctance to reduce the deficit likely contributed to the origin of the 1982 crisis.

ECONOMIC REFORMS POST-1982

Part of the response of the government to the 1982 debt crisis was a sequence of primary surpluses. The presidential term of de la Madrid started in late 1982 and ended in 1988. Figure 4 shows that the government responded with a primary surplus of 4.6 percent of GDP in 1983 and an even larger one the following year. In fact, Mexico had primary surpluses throughout the entire period under analysis, 1982–94. Another crucial part of the response was the control of inflation, although this goal was difficult to accomplish. Figure 7 shows a high and volatile inflation rate during 1982–88. The inflation rate in 1987 was 142.8 percent.

Figure 4 also shows downward trends in the foreign and domestic debt ratios, as well as a fall in seigniorage, although in the case of foreign debt, the reduction is interrupted by devaluations of the peso. The reduction in debt ratios is consistent with the sequence of primary surpluses. This is a basic lesson of the model. A government can reduce the debt ratio by reducing the primary deficit to the point of having surpluses. Simultaneously, the figure shows that the government reduced its use of seigniorage. The fall in seigniorage, which went from 9 percent of GDP in 1982 to 1.5 percent by 1988, is consistent with the goal of reducing inflation. A government can obtain revenue through seigniorage, at the cost of increasing inflation.

A distinguishing feature of economic policy in the 1980s in Mexico is the use of *pactos*, literally "pacts," or agreements between the government and different economic agents. In December 1987 the government of de la Madrid created the Pacto de Solidaridad Económica, which had the goal of reducing inflation. The government insisted on consensus building (*concertación*) to achieve it. The government committed to a reduction in spending and a reduction in the number of government-owned firms (the *empresas paraestatales*). Workers committed to reducing wage increases in negotiations with business owners, and business owners committed to reducing price increases and increasing productivity. This *pacto* had limited success, as inflation was 100 percent in 1988.

Fiscal stability and the control of inflation were goals of the 1988–94 administration of Carlos Salinas. Figure 4 shows that the sequence of primary surpluses continued until 1994. The data used in the figure include revenue from privatizations of the national telephone company, TELMEX, and of the banks that had been nationalized in 1982. Additionally, there was progress in the control of inflation. Figure 7 shows a large fall in inflation in 1989 to 26.8 percent and a value of 8.5 percent in 1994. The previously mentioned trends in debt ratios and seigniorage are even clearer in these years. Figure 4 shows the debt ratios falling almost continuously. It also shows seigniorage taking values under 1 percent of GDP during the early 1990s. The Salinas government also used *pactos*. In December 1988, it created the Pacto para la Estabilidad y el Crecimiento Económico. The goal was to achieve one-digit inflation. This pact was again an agreement between the government, workers, and business owners.

The Salinas administration had two other important features. The first one was a continuation of the process of opening the economy to the rest of the world, which started in 1986 when Mexico joined the General Agreement on Trade and Tariffs. Under President Salinas, Mexico signed the North American Free Trade Agreement (NAFTA) with the United States and Canada, which went into effect in January 1994. The second was to regain access to international financial markets, which Mexico had lost after defaulting on its debt in 1982. As discussed in Kehoe and Meza (2011), the renegotiation of Mexican debt started in 1989. Negotiations with Mexico's creditors were successful, and in 1989 the United States announced the Brady Plan, which allowed Mexico and other countries to return to international financial markets.

INDEPENDENCE OF THE BANCO DE MÉXICO

In 1993 a constitutional reform specified the main task of the Banco de México and granted its independence from the government. Article 28 of the constitution now included the protection of the purchasing power of the peso as its main task. This article also states that no authority can force the Banco de México to provide credit. In 1993, the Banco de México Law was signed, specifying the rules under which it would relate to the government.[23] In particular, it specifies rules under which the central bank can give credit to the fiscal branch of the government.

The new independence of the central bank would be tested shortly after 1993: at the end of 1994, Mexico suffered a crisis. The monetary response had to be consistent with the goal of reducing inflation.

1994 Crisis

During 1994, several political and economic events took place in the months before the devaluation of the peso in December. This was the last year of the Salinas term. In January 1994, the Zapatista movement rose in southern Mexico. In March 1994, the ruling party's presidential candidate, Luis Donaldo Colosio, was murdered. Large capital outflows took place that put pressure on the exchange rate regime, which consisted of a predetermined band inside which the peso was allowed to fluctuate. Toward the last quarter of 1994, the political situation worsened. The secretary general of the ruling party, José Francisco Ruiz Massieu, was murdered in September. Capital outflows continued during the rest of the year.

During 1994, the government issued a growing amount of short-term debt with nominal value indexed in dollars and payable in pesos. Known as the *tesobono* debt, it became the largest source of short-term borrowing for the federal government, surpassing the amount of short-term peso debt in circulation, the CETEs debt.

These events preceded the collapse of the exchange rate regime and a large contraction in economic activity. In late December 1994, the government abandoned the exchange rate regime. The peso devalued considerably. In early January 1995, the government had difficulties rolling over the *tesobono* debt. During 1995, the economy suffered its worst yearly contraction since the 1930s. Between 1994 and 1995, GDP and private consumption per working-age person fell roughly 9 percent and 10 percent, respectively.

The 1994 crisis was not caused by accumulated deficits; as Figure 4 shows, the surplus was 2.4 percent of GDP. An important factor behind the crisis was the *tesobono* debt. At the end of December 1994, the government lacked the ability to service this debt. The cause of this lack of ability was the large decrease in the stock of international reserves. In turn, this decrease was driven in part by the exchange rate regime.

In the following subsection, I discuss complementary theories regarding expected future fiscal deficits. In the online appendix, I summarize alternative forces discussed in previous important texts on the 1994 crisis written by Cárdenas (2015), Gil-Díaz and Carstens (1996), Gil-Díaz (1998), Kehoe (1995), and Serra Puche (2011). This list is not exhaustive, as this crisis led to a large amount of research on its origins. A paper that expected difficult times for the Mexican economy was Dornbusch and Werner (1994). A seminal paper on understanding the origins of the 1994 crisis is Calvo and Mendoza (1996), which analyzes the mismatch between short-term debt and international reserves.

THEORIES BASED ON THE BANKING SECTOR

One theory is that the crisis happened because of *prospective deficits*. The existence of implicit bailout guarantees to failing banking systems and the expectation that at least part of the bailout would be financed by seigniorage could have led to a collapse of the exchange rate. Burnside, Eichenbaum, and Rebelo (2001) propose this theory to account for the 1997 Asian financial crisis. I would call this a classic, first-generation explanation for a balance of payments crisis. A second theory is that the crisis was *banking system self-fulfilling* that is, not based on public debt but on the characteristics of the liabilities of the banking system. In this theory, if banks had liabilities in dollars, a devaluation of the peso would hurt their balances. Assuming a bailout guarantee, the cost of rescuing the banks would reduce the ability of the government to defend the exchange rate regime. This sketch of a model would be an example of a third-generation explanation of a balance of payments crisis, in which the interaction between the financial system and the bailout guarantee of the government plays a crucial role.

As mentioned earlier, banks were nationalized in 1982. As part of the reforms during the term of President Salinas, banks were privatized. This happened between 1991 and 1992. At the same time, the financial system was liberalized, allowing for foreign capital flows. By 1994 three phenomena had taken place. The first was a large increase in the foreign short-term debt of the banking system. It increased from $8.6 billion in 1988 to $24.8 billion in 1994, as mentioned in Gil-Díaz and Carstens (1996). Banks had a large exposure to exchange-rate risk. Second, there was a large expansion of credit. From 1988 to 1994, bank credit had increased on average at a yearly rate of 25 percent. Third, there was an increase in delinquency rates. Past due loans relative to total loans increased from 4.1 percent in 1991 to 7.3 percent in 1994.[24] The problem was larger than reported with such statistics, as official accounting considered as a past due loan only the amount that had not been paid and not the entire amount lent.

There was a bailout guarantee in 1994–95. First, to be able to pay their debt in dollars, banks requested the Banco de México to act as a lender of last resort. The Banco de México created the Ventanilla de Liquidez, a mechanism through which it provided dollars to the banking system. It is important to note that the resources came from the financial aid provided by the United States and the International Monetary Fund. Second, Guillermo Ortiz, then secretario de hacienda in 1995, established three guiding principles. The financial system had to perceive determination from government authorities to solve the developing banking crisis. An additional principle was that the banking system was not going to be nationalized again, as in 1982. Finally, no saver should lose deposits. There was an implicit unlimited deposit insurance.

The principle that no saver should lose deposits prevailed before Ortiz became secretario de hacienda after December 1994. Ortiz's statement simply reinforced this idea. One important piece of evidence supporting this is the analysis of the banking crisis by Eduardo Fernández, who was president of the National Banking Commission in 1994. He oversaw the rescue of the banking sector from 1995 to 2000.[25] In 1990, the trust Fondo Bancario de Protección al Ahorro (Fobaproa) was established in the Banco de México with contributions from banks to provide deposit insurance. According to Fernández, the banking system worked under the assumption that the federal government would protect all liabilities. Cárdenas (2015) makes the same argument. Depositors assumed that deposits were fully insured by the government.

The bank bailout entailed a large fiscal cost. In the next section, I will provide some detail on how the government eventually became officially indebted because of the bank rescue. The debt the government issued was equal to 11.7 percent of GDP in 1999.[26] In 1998 the government, for the first time, asked Congress to approve the transformation of debt issued to rescue banks into public debt. The total cost has been estimated at 13.3 percent of GDP by adding to the previous number the cost during 1995–98.[27]

Burnside, Eichenbaum, and Rebelo (2001) look for evidence in favor of their hypothesis by plotting the monetary base, M1 and M2, for several Asian countries after the 1997 crisis. They also calculate the ratios of monetary aggregates using the value in 1999 relative to the one in 1997. In their theory, there is no immediate increase in monetary aggregates after a crisis. The increase happens with a lag. In my opinion, these tests are weak. A stronger test is to compute seigniorage and its components, the inflationary tax and the change in real monetary base. I plot them in Figure 7 relative to GDP. These are the empirical counterparts of theoretical variables in the consolidated budget constraint that I presented at the beginning.

There is some evidence in favor of the theory. According to it, seigniorage should increase with a lag. The value in 1995 is very similar to the one in 1994. The inflationary tax goes up, as inflation went from less than 10 percent in 1994 to almost 40 percent in 1995. At the same time, the change in the real monetary base is negative. Seigniorage does have a local peak in 1999, the value being 1.2 percent. At that point, it was the highest value since 1988. After 1999 it falls to persistently low levels.[28] The peak is due to an increase in the change of the real monetary base, not to an increase in the inflationary tax. To finish this discussion, more work is needed to disentangle whether there is strong evidence in favor of the prospective deficits theory. A specific model has to be chosen to test the predictions of a banking system self-fulfilling crisis.

THE ROLE OF INTERNATIONAL INTEREST RATES

The U.S. Treasury bill rate rose throughout 1994. The yearly absolute changes in interest rates grew during the year. This accelerated increase put pressure on public finances and was a contributor to generating the crisis.[29]

MONETARY AND FISCAL RESPONSE TO THE CRISIS

A crucial question at this point is whether Mexico went in practice from fiscal dominance to monetary dominance. I argue that the fact that in 1994–95 fiscal and monetary policies were procyclical indicates monetary dominance.

The primary surplus increased from 2.4 percent of GDP in 1994 to 4.7 percent in 1995, as Figure 4 shows. Additionally, the value-added tax was increased from 10 to 15 percent in early 1995. There was an increase in government-controlled prices. Real government consumption per working-age person fell 3.9 percent.[30]

Monetary policy was focused on reducing inflation. According to Ramos-Francia and Torres García (2005), who provide details on the implementation of that goal, the

objective of the central bank was to reduce inflationary pressures and prevent fiscal dominance. The devaluation of the peso at the end of 1994 and the beginning of 1995 slowed
convergence to low inflation. Nevertheless, the constitutional change of 1993 led Mexico
from fiscal dominance and high inflation in the 1980s to central bank independence and
low levels of inflation in 2016.

MARKET PERCEPTION OF MONETARY DOMINANCE IN 1995

There is evidence that, despite the crisis, inflation expectations did not increase. Figure 8
shows the term structure of interest rates around the crisis. Interest rates for short-term
debt increased more than those for longer maturity bonds.

   This behavior of the yield curve before and after December 1994 shows that markets expected inflation to rise in the short term and be lower in the medium term. This
is consistent with expectations that public finances would not resort to credit from the
central bank and that monetary dominance would prevail.

   The evidence presented above supports the hypothesis that a structural change happened in Mexico as monetary dominance prevailed after 1994. It is true that there was
an increase in monetary variables in 1999. For future research, it is important to look
at the sources of this increase in the monetary base, in particular the changes in the
components of credit of the central bank. Having said that, given the downward trend in
inflation that started in 1996 and led to a low and stable process, I argue that monetary
dominance has prevailed in Mexico.

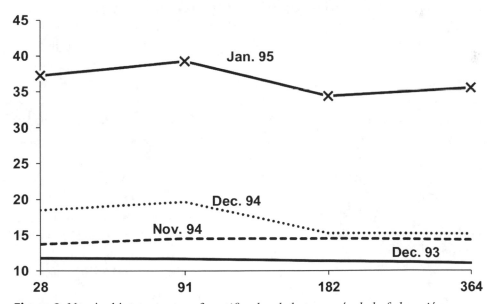

Figure 8. Nominal interest rates of *certificados de la tesorería de la federación*
(CETEs), in percentages, at maturities of 28, 91, 182, and 364 days
Source: Banco de México

1995–2016: Slow Growth and Macroeconomic Stability

The main goal of the post-1994 policy makers was macroeconomic stability. This was the case of the administrations of presidents Ernesto Zedillo (1994–2000) and Vicente Fox (2000–2006). It is important that stability was an important goal throughout two presidential terms, with presidents who came from different parties, the PRI and the PAN (Partido Acción Nacional). President Fox, from PAN, was the first opposition winner of a presidential election.

An important change took place during the presidential term of Felipe Calderón (2006–12, PAN) as Mexico reacted to the international financial crisis with expansionary fiscal policy. Finally, the first four years of the term of Enrique Peña (2012–16, PRI) showed a persistent increase in the debt-to-GDP ratio.

FISCAL POLICY

Figure 4 shows two facts for the subperiod 1995–2008: a persistent primary surplus and a substitution from foreign to domestic debt. In 2000, the ratio of domestic debt surpassed that of the net foreign debt position for the first time since the 1970s. An important force behind the drop in the latter is the accumulation of international reserves by the central bank. In fact, by 2006 the consolidated government has net assets, not net debt. The reason is the growth in international reserves of the Banco de México. Ramos-Francia and Torres García (2005) describe the policies leading to the accumulation of reserves by the Banco de México after the 1994 crisis.

The two facts previously mentioned had two consequences: a reduction in the burden of debt and a lower exposure to changes in the nominal exchange rate. This can be seen in Figure 4. Starting in 1997 and until 2008, the ratio of total debt to GDP is below 20 percent. The fact that Mexico had primary surpluses since 1983 contributes to this drop.

Additionally, the ratio is stable when compared with its behavior in the two periods analyzed before. Switching from foreign to domestic debt over time reduced the swings in the burden of the debt caused by sudden and large depreciations of the peso. Another factor that reduced the volatility of the debt ratio is the regime change to a flexible exchange rate at the end of 1994. The spike in 1982 is correlated with the adjustment in Mexico's fixed exchange rate regime. Notice that 1995–2008 is not exempt from large events in international financial markets. There was the 1997 Asian crisis, the 1998 Russian crisis, and the dot-com crash of 2000–2002. The exchange rate was volatile during those events; however, the total debt ratio showed a much smaller variation compared with previous years.

THE FISCAL COST OF THE 1994 BANKING CRISIS

One important event in the Mexican economy was the banking crisis that took place after 1994. Both borrowers and banks received financial support from the government.[31]

As mentioned earlier, in 1990 the trust Fobaproa was established to provide deposit insurance. At the beginning of 1995, high real interest rates produced an increase in past due loans. In 1995, the Programa de Capitalización y Compra de Cartera (PCCC) was created. Fobaproa cleaned up the assets of the banking system by buying loans; in exchange, bank owners provided new capital. The ratio was 2 pesos of loans per peso of capital. The loans were bought with promissory notes (*pagarés*) issued by Fobaproa and signed by the subsecretario de hacienda, the second highest ranking official in the SHCP, and by the tesorero de la federación, the official in charge of the financial management of the resources and assets of the federal government.

Fobaproa created several programs to provide financial support for different types of loans: credit to small and large firms, mortgages, credit to the agricultural sector, and credit to local governments, among others. In 1998, President Zedillo sent Congress an initiative to approve the recognition of Fobaproa debt, the promissory notes it issued, as public debt, which represented 15 percent of GDP. Political opposition was very strong. At the beginning of 1999, the Instituto para la Protección al Ahorro Bancario (IPAB) was created. Its goal was to complete the process of the bailout of the banking system. The IPAB assumed the liabilities created by the banking rescue. From a legal point of view, these liabilities were not public debt. In 2005, after a long legal process, the Fobaproa *pagarés* became public debt.

The debt originated by the rescue of banks and borrowers was 11.7 percent of GDP in 1999 and decreased steadily over time. In 2011, its value was 5.7 percent of GDP.[32] It is also important to say that this debt has been paid using three different sources: payoffs from loans bought from banks (as some bad loans produced payments), fees paid by banks, and government resources. The contributions from each of these sources have accumulated over time; 23.6 percent has come from loan payoffs, 15.8 percent from bank fees, and 60.6 percent from the government.[33]

THE EVOLUTION OF MONETARY POLICY

During the presidential term of Carlos Salinas, the nominal anchor was the nominal exchange rate; the regime was not a simple fixed exchange rate. The peso was allowed to fluctuate within a band, and monetary policy had to be consistent with the goal of keeping the peso within that band. When Mexico abandoned this exchange rate regime on December 22, 1994, choices had to be made regarding how to carry out monetary policy in a new environment with a floating exchange rate.

Starting in 1995, the Banco de México implemented monetary policy by affecting the cost of liquidity in the Mexican interbank market. This regime was informally known as *El Corto*, using the Spanish word for "short," referring to the fact that one or more banks would become "short on liquidity." The regime worked as follows. Private banks could borrow liquid resources from the Banco de México. The central bank chose a target for the cumulative balance (over a given number of days) of liquid funds provided to the banks. This target was called the Objetivo de Saldos Acumulados. A negative target meant that the central bank would carry out open market operations to reduce liquidity and cause one or more private banks to have a negative balance. The central bank would provide that liquidity at an interest double the market rate. Banks would try to avoid paying that penalty rate by raising interest rates on deposits or loans. A negative target implied a contractionary stance of monetary policy.

Starting in 1998, an important change in monetary policy was to provide more information to the public about decisions made by the central bank. Changes in the *Corto* target were discussed in official public documents, explaining the reasons behind them. This information strengthened the link between changes in the target and informing the public on the stance of monetary policy. In 1999, the Banco de México announced that the medium-term goal for inflation was convergence to external inflation by 2003. This goal turned out to be too ambitious. Below I will compare inflation to the target announced in 2002. In 2000, the central bank started publishing quarterly inflation reports, including a detailed discussion of the sources of changes in inflation. The central bank also introduced core inflation to its discussion of inflation dynamics. In 2001, the Banco de México announced it would implement an inflation-targeting regime. In 2002, the inflation target was announced: 3 percent annual inflation +/–1 percent. Since 2003, there exists an official public calendar of monetary policy decisions.[34] In 2005 the central bank started making policy announcements in terms of an interest rate. In 2008, the Banco de México announced that it substituted the *Corto* with having an operational target for the short-term interbank interest rate.

The persistent drop in inflation observed in Mexico since 1995 is the result of several factors, including two important ones: the adoption of an inflation-targeting regime and monetary policy decisions consistent with the regime. Figure 9 plots inflation of the consumer price index, which is what the central bank targets, and the 3 percent target and its band. There was a sizable drop in inflation between 2000 and 2002. Also, inflation remained inside the band for most months starting in 2006. It is worth mentioning that having a target is not useful unless the central bank responds to increases in inflation, or in inflation expectations, by tightening monetary policy.

FISCAL POLICY IN RESPONSE TO THE INTERNATIONAL FINANCIAL CRISIS

The period 2009–17 is one of primary deficits and increases in domestic debt. The first primary deficit took place in 2009. Deficits were persistent, reaching a maximum of 1.4 percent of GDP in 2015. There was a persistent increase in domestic debt, and at the same time, net foreign debt remained stable at values close to zero.[35] Total debt fell in the previous period. During 2009–17, its behavior changes, showing a large increase in 2009 and a persistent positive trend afterward.

The implementation of a deficit in 2009 was a change regarding Mexico's fiscal response to an economic crisis. In the past—for example, in 1995—the government reacted by increasing the primary surplus, as mentioned before. The response was the opposite. The switch from surplus to deficit in 2009 was a result of countercyclical fiscal policies aimed at responding to the 2008 financial crisis in the United States. One direct

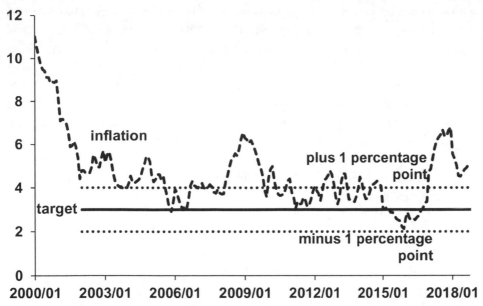

Figure 9. Annual consumer price index inflation versus inflation target with band, in percentages, monthly data

Source: INEGI

impact of the crisis in the United States was the drop in Mexican exports of durable goods. Kehoe and Meza (2011) report that Mexico was the Latin American country hit the hardest by the financial crisis because of its very close interaction with the United States. A specific goal of the government's response to the crisis was to increase investment in infrastructure. For more detail, see Banco de México (2009, 2010).

Two additional facts help explain the increase in debt during this period. The first is the implementation of the reform to the Ley del ISSSTE. The ISSSTE is the institution that provides health and other services to workers in the public sector. This institution had a pay-as-you-go pension system that was running into a financial crisis. The federal government implemented a transition to a fully funded individual account system and took charge of the pensions of the older ISSSTE workers. This cost represented 2.6 percentage points of the increase in total debt of 12.5 percentage points of GDP between 2008 and 2009. The second fact is the elimination of a special investment regime for PEMEX. This regime was called Pidiregas, which stands for *proyectos de inversión diferida en el registro del gasto*, or in English, "investment projects with a deferred expenditure registry." The registry of some investment projects carried out by PEMEX was deferred in time. Once the liabilities related to these investment projects were included in the total debt, the resulting increase accounted for 8.8 percentage points of the total increase in debt of 12.5 percentage points of GDP between 2008 and 2009. Thus the public deficit contributed, at most, 1.1 percentage points.[36]

To understand the reaction of financial markets to the increase in debt, I compare the Emerging Markets Bond Index spreads for Colombia, Mexico, and Peru. The comparison with other countries is important because Mexico and the rest of the world suffered the consequences of the international financial crisis of 2008. Therefore, it was not enough to look at Mexico to try to find evidence of a possible increase in the sovereign debt spread due to the increase in debt. The result is that there is no evidence of Mexico behaving much differently from Colombia or Peru in terms of the spreads during 2009 and 2010. There is a higher level of the Mexican spread relative to the other countries in 2012, but it is temporary. I interpret the data as saying that financial markets did not have a negative response in reaction to the increase in debt in Mexico.

Mexico showed a remarkable achievement generated by years of macroeconomic stability. Despite the increase in the government deficit, there was no negative reaction from markets. Fiscal policy evolved from relying on monetary policy during bad times in the 1970s and early 1980s to having the flexibility of policy in developed countries. Having said that, in 2016–17 the Mexican spread was several basis points above those of Colombia and Peru. This higher level is correlated with the persistent increase in the debt-to-GDP ratio of Mexico after 2009. In 2016, credit rating agencies announced a change in the perspective on Mexican debt, lowering it from stable to negative.

INFLATION AND THE REDUCTION IN EXCHANGE RATE PASS-THROUGH

Inflation during this period remained mostly within the range targeted by Banco de México, as shown in Figure 9. There is a deviation from this range in the aftermath of the 2008 financial crisis. Inflation increased to 6.5 percent at the end of 2008. Afterward, inflation went back to the previous range.

An important change during this period is the decline in the exchange rate pass-through. Figure 10 shows the percentage change in the nominal exchange rate and the inflation rate.[37] Between 1977 and 1994, there were large increases in inflation as the peso lost value in large devaluations. During 1995–2006, the correlation between the two variables seems to fall. During 2007–16, it is clear that despite large changes in the nominal exchange rate, inflation has become much less volatile.

Capistran, Ibarra-Ramírez, and Ramos-Francia (2011) and Kochen and Sámano (2016) do econometric estimations of pass-through in Mexico for the periods before and after the adoption of the inflation-targeting regime by the central bank and document its decrease after 2001. A simple statistic that indicates the fall in the pass-through is the correlation between inflation and the depreciation rate, which was 0.61 between 1976 and 2001 and close to zero, −0.04, between 2002 and 2017.

Another statistic that indicates the fall in the pass-through is the ratio of inflation to the depreciation rate in years of large depreciations. This ratio was 42 percent in 1995, 16.5 percent in 2009, and 16 percent in 2015. There were large depreciations in those years: 1995 is, of course, the year after December 1994, when Mexico had to float the peso; 2009 is the year in which the subprime crisis in the United States led to the international financial crisis; and 2015, in December, was the first time the Federal Reserve increased interest rates in nine years. The pass-through was large in 1995, as the exchange rate market produced the new equilibrium value. It was much smaller in 2009, despite the historical magnitude of the international financial crisis. It was also much smaller in 2015, compared to 1995, when markets adjusted expecting an increase in U.S. interest rates.

Here I use the Neo-Keynesian model laid out in Urrutia (2017) to analyze the change in pass-through. In that model, an expansionary monetary shock produces a depreciation of the peso and an increase in inflation. Therefore, the model predicts a certain pass-through after an expansionary monetary shock. The fact that the pass-through in Mexico has fallen could be accounted for by smaller monetary shocks.

Monetary policy in Mexico became credible in its goal of low and stable inflation in 2002. Starting that year, either inflation has remained within the band targeted by the Banco de México or deviations have been temporary and caused mainly by exogenous international and domestic shocks.[38]

FISCAL REFORM AND INCREASE IN NON-OIL REVENUE OF THE PUBLIC SECTOR

I want to highlight the recent increase in the size of the non-oil revenue of the public sector. Its components are tax revenue, nontax revenue of the federal government, and revenue of government institutions and firms. There was a fall in oil revenue after 2012, correlated with the decline in the oil price. At the same time, there was a large increase in tax revenue. Between 2012 and 2016, it increased by 6.4 points of GDP. In 2016, it reached the highest level in history, 16.2 percent of GDP. This historical increase in tax collection is related to the fiscal reform of 2014 undertaken by the Enrique Peña Nieto administration. This reform included several changes in taxation; however, it is beyond

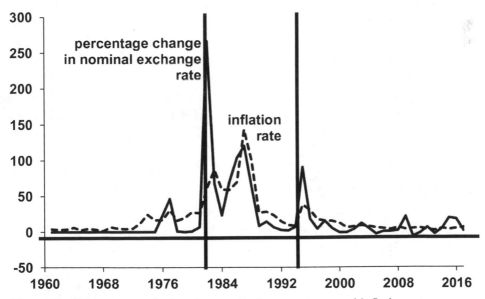

Figure 10. Change in nominal exchange rate in percentages and inflation rate
Sources: Banco de México, INEGI

the scope of this chapter to determine which change contributed the most to the increase in tax revenue.[39]

IMPLICIT TRANSFER IN THE BUDGET CONSTRAINT

The main tool in the project is the consolidated government budget constraint, in this case,

$$B_t + E_t B_t^* + M_t = D_t + T_t + \left(1 + r_{t-1}\right) B_{t-1} + E_t \left(1 + r_{t-1}^*\right) B_{t-1}^* + M_{t-1} ,$$

where B_t is the stock of domestic debt, B_t^* is the stock of foreign debt net of international reserves, D_t is the primary deficit of the consolidated government, and M_t is the monetary base.

The term T_t corresponds to transfers not registered in the primary balance. I use this residual term to make the budget constraint hold after plugging in the empirical counterparts of the theoretical variables. The existence of this residual could be due to particular transfers implemented in times of crisis and transfers that might not be registered completely or accurately in the data sources.

Figure 11 shows how debt would have evolved if this residual term were zero. The initial value of this debt and the observed one are the same. Afterward, debt fluctuates according to the budget constraint.

The residual term is small and positive for most years before 1982. My interpretation of these values is additional deficits, from either the central government or the other entities I include, that were not properly registered in the data. These missing deficits accumulate and imply a much lower counterfactual path for the debt in this exercise.

The residual term becomes large and volatile in periods with large exchange rate adjustments. The reason is that I use the same (period average) nominal exchange rate for different debt adjustments during the same year, which makes the calculation inaccurate in periods with high exchange rate volatility. It is positive when large devaluations occurred in 1982, 1986, and 1994 and during the large depreciation in 2008 due to the international financial crisis. It is large and negative in 1988 during an important appreciation of the exchange rate. It is worth noting that it is large and negative in 1983 despite a very large devaluation in that year, owing to the important fiscal shift from primary deficit to surplus during 1983.

Conclusions

For the 1982 debt crisis, I documented that higher primary deficits led to growth in debt, and, under fiscal dominance, the central bank adjusted its policy to satisfy public finances. In the data, this adjustment led to higher inflation.

This fiscal dominance narrative does not account for the 1994 crisis. An important force behind this crisis was the dollar-indexed *tesobono* debt. At the end of December, with very few reserves at the central bank and the peso allowed to float, investors refused

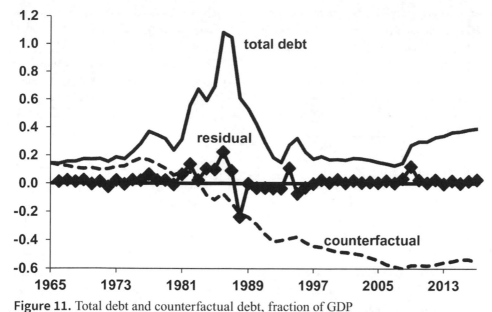

Figure 11. Total debt and counterfactual debt, fraction of GDP
Sources: Authors' calculations with data from Banco de México, INEGI, SHCP

to buy new issues of *tesobonos*, which had become the largest portion of government debt. The government had trouble financing debt that was increasing due to currency depreciations. Additionally, I showed evidence regarding two possible theories of expected future fiscal deficits that reconcile the 1994 crisis with the theory. One is expectations of a bank bailout by the government; the other is a self-fulfilling crisis created by the banking system's vulnerabilities.

Institutionally, there is evidence that the 1993 constitutional change, granting a goal and independence to the central bank, was actually a change from fiscal dominance to independence. Fiscal policy in 1995 was procyclical. The Banco de México had as its main goal a rapid control of inflation. There was no persistent high level of inflation in the late 1990s.

Solid public finances and an independent central bank are necessary to pursue other policy goals, such as poverty reduction and redistribution. As I have shown in this work, major economic crises in Mexico have been triggered by deviations (or expected deviations) from these policy principles. I hope this chapter contributes to understanding and preventing economic crises that resemble those of 1982 or 1994 in Mexico.

Notes

I thank seminar participants at the 2016 and 2018 Becker Friedman Institute (BFI) Conferences on the Monetary and Fiscal History of Latin America, the Banco de México, and the International Economic Association World Congress 2017— in particular, Rodolfo Manuelli and Enrique Mendoza, for their valuable comments. I also thank Alejandro Werner for his discussion of my paper at the 2018 Inter-American Development Bank Conference on the Latin American project. I especially thank participants at the Mexican Economic History Event held at ITAM in November 2017—in particular, Enrique Cárdenas, for his support and feedback on this chapter and his help in organizing the event. Rodolfo Oviedo, Rodrigo Morales, Fernando Aretia, Rubén García, Andrés Santos, and Diego Ascarza provided excellent research assistance. I especially thank Carlos Esquivel for detecting an error in the counterfactual debt calculation. Any errors are my own.

1 See, for example, Costa, Kehoe, and Raveendranathan (2016).

2 The Maddison Project Database shows that, up until the 1982 crisis, Mexico was catching up with the United States. Between 1960 and 1982, Mexican GDP per capita grew from 19 percent of U.S. GDP per capita to 39 percent. After the 1982 debt crisis, Mexico started lagging behind the United States, with its GDP per capita falling to 23 percent of the U.S. level in 1995. The Maddison Project Database shows Mexico catching up somewhat between 1995 and 2016, with its GDP per capita growing to 30 percent of the U.S. level. The Maddison Project compares GDPs across countries using a common purchasing power parity price index rather than calculating real GDPs in each country using a country-specific GDP deflator. Consequently, the comparisons do not exactly match those obtained by comparing growth rates of real GDP across countries.

3 A monthly inflation rate of 50 percent, if maintained over a year, would imply an annual inflation rate of close to 13,000 percent.

4 Data marked "1965–88" come from the Finance Ministry of Mexico, Secretaría de Hacienda y Crédito Público (SHCP). The rest of the deficit data come from the Banco de México. The financial cost of the debt is called *costo financiero*.

5 This includes both the Treasury and the central bank.

6 Throughout the chapter, I measure inflation using the growth rate of the GDP deflator, unless stated otherwise.

7 The Treasury cannot use the international reserves of the central bank at its discretion; their inclusion in the same budget constraint is to be consistent with the accounting of assets and interest payments implied by the model.

8 This changed with the energy reform of 2013. Today, foreign and domestic investments are allowed in the oil industry along the production and distribution chain. This is one of the major structural changes that has taken place in recent years. As of November 2018, there was uncertainty about whether the newly elected government would block the reform.

9 I exclude debt indexed to inflation from the model because the raw data I use do not report it separately. Indexed debt has been issued by the Treasury in the past, and today it sells *udibonos*. In the data, this kind of debt is included in domestic debt.

10 In particular, see page 9.

11 In 2013, as part of the energy reform that allowed the private foreign and domestic sectors to participate in the energy industry, PEMEX and CFE were assigned to the category Empresas Productivas del Estado.

12 I constructed a historical time series for the monetary base using INEGI and Banco de México data. In the online appendix, available at http://manifold.bfi.uchicago.edu/, I compare seigniorage and the inflation tax implied by the series I constructed and the ones using only Banco de México data. The conclusion is that seigniorage is basically the same. The inflation tax does show a difference for some years.

13 Mexico participated in the Bretton Woods Conference in 1944.

14 I show this in the online appendix, available at http://manifold.bfi.uchicago.edu/.

15 Arezki, Ramey, and Sheng (2016) document the effects of "giant" oil field discoveries on several macroeconomic variables in small

open economies. They find that borrowing, consumption, and investment rapidly increase following an oil or gas field discovery, which was also the case for Mexico in 1977.

16 In terms of theory, my framework is the dynamic endowment economy in Ljungqvist and Sargent (2004), chapter 10. The comments received from Manuel Ramos-Francia led me to analyze this episode with this tool.

17 Aspe (1993) also reports an increase in the inflation tax in the beginning of the 1980s.

18 I also calculated a monthly inflation tax *rate* and describe its behavior in the online appendix, available at http://manifold.bfi.uchicago .edu/. In general, it increases in the same years as the inflation tax *revenue* reported here.

19 Almeida et al. (2018) analyze the role of U.S. interest rates using a quantitative sovereign debt model.

20 By *real* I mean the international price in dollars multiplied by the exchange rate, then divided by the Mexican price index.

21 In the online appendix (available at http:// manifold.bfi.uchicago.edu/), I show that the average value of oil revenue to total revenue of the public sector is 31 percent for 1977–2016.

22 Notice that this rough calculation is not an exact match to the real interest rate that appears in the budget constraint. Having said that, given the sharp increase in the nominal interest rate, I would expect the real interest rate that is consistent with the model to increase post-1980.

23 In Spanish, the law is the *Ley del Banco de México*. It can be downloaded from Banco de México, http://www.banxico.org .mx/disposiciones/marco-juridico/ley-del -banco-de-mexico/ley-del-banco-mexico .html.

24 See Cárdenas and Espinosa Rugarcía (2011), vol. 5, table I.67.

25 See his chapter in Espinosa Rugarcía and Cárdenas (2011), vol. 1.

26 See Cárdenas and Espinosa Rugarcía (2011), vol. 5, table II.18.

27 Figure 4 shows that there is a small increase in the domestic debt-to-GDP ratio from 4.6 percent in 1998 to 6.4 percent in 1999. Recall that the data plotted in that figure are debt consolidated with the Banco de México. In the online appendix (available at http:// manifold.bfi.uchicago.edu/), I compare debt statistics that exclude or include this financial support, and without consolidation. Debt is significantly higher when this support is considered.

28 The behavior changes at the end of the sample.

29 I also looked at the oil price and found that it played no role in explaining the crisis.

30 The contribution to the fall in GDP of some of these changes in policy is quantified in Meza (2008).

31 The events regarding the rescue of the banking system after 1994 have been analyzed in exhaustive detail by Cárdenas and Espinosa Rugarcía (2011). These authors gathered a large amount of material on the privatization of nationalized banks starting in 1991, the impact of the 1994 crisis, and the subsequent rescue of the banking system.

32 See Cárdenas and Espinosa Rugarcía (2011), vol. 5, table II.18.

33 See Cárdenas and Espinosa Rugarcía (2011), vol. 5, table II.17.

34 Ramos-Francia and Torres García (2005) provide more detail on the evolution of monetary policy up to 2003.

35 Recall that this is a measure of consolidated debts and assets of the public sector and of the central bank, with international reserves generating a value close to zero.

36 This means that the cost of the ISSSTE reform, the change in the accounting of Pidiregas liabilities, and the deficit add up to 2.6 + 8.8 + 1.1 = 12.5 = increase in debt between 2008 and 2009. For a quick reference, see Banxico .org, "Sistema de Información Económica," http://www.banxico.org.mx/SieInternet/

consultarDirectorioInternetAction.do?sector
=9&accion=consultarCuadro&idCuadro=
CG7&locale=es.

37 Here I measure inflation calculated with the
GDP deflator. The figure is similar if I use
CPI inflation.

38 An example of the latter is adjustments to
energy prices, which have been managed by

the government. The increase in inflation
at the beginning of 2017 comes from the liberalization of the price of gasoline. Inflation
was persistently high in that year.

39 In the online appendix, available at http://
manifold.bfi.uchicago.edu/, I list the changes
that took place.

References

Almeida, Victor, Carlos Esquivel, Timothy J. Kehoe, and Juan Pablo Nicolini. 2018. "Default and Interest Rate Shocks: Renegotiation Matters." Unpublished paper, Federal Reserve Bank of Minneapolis.

Arezki, Rabah, Valerie A. Ramey, and Liugang Sheng. 2016. "News Shocks in Open Economies: Evidence from Giant Oil Discoveries." *Quarterly Journal of Economics* 132 (1): 103–55.

Aspe, Pedro. 1993. *Economic Transformation the Mexican Way.* Cambridge, Mass.: MIT Press.

Banco de México. 2009. *Informe anual 2008.* Mexico DF, Mexico: Banco de México.

———. 2010. *Informe anual 2009.* Mexico DF, Mexico: Banco de México.

Burnside, Craig, Martin Eichenbaum, and Sergio Rebelo. 2001. "Prospective Deficits and the Asian Currency Crisis." *Journal of Political Economy* 109 (6): 1155–97.

Calvo, Guillermo A., and Enrique G. Mendoza. 1996. "Mexico's Balance-of-Payments Crisis: A Chronicle of a Death Foretold." *Journal of International Economics* 41 (3–4): 235–64.

Capistran, Carlos, Raúl Ibarra-Ramírez, and Manuel Ramos-Francia. 2011. "El traspaso de movimientos del tipo de cambio a los precios: Un análisis para la economía Mexicana." Working paper 2011-12, Banco de México, Mexico DF.

Cárdenas, Enrique. 2015. *El largo curso de la economía Mexicana.* México CDMX, México: Fondo de Cultura Económica.

Cárdenas, Enrique, and Amparo Espinosa Rugarcía, eds. 2011. *La privatización bancaria, crisis y rescate del sistema financiero: La historia contada por sus protagonistas.* 5 vols. México, DF: Centro de Estudios Espinosa Yglesias.

Costa, Daniela, Timothy J. Kehoe, and Gajendran Raveendranathan. 2016. "The Stages of Economic Growth Revisited, Part 1: A General Framework and Taking Off into Growth." Economy Policy Paper 16–5, Federal Reserve Bank of Minneapolis.

Dornbusch, Rudiger, and Alejandro Werner. 1994. "Mexico: Stabilization, Reform, and No Growth." *Brookings Papers on Economic Activity* 25 (1): 253–316.

Gil-Díaz, Francisco. 1998. "The Origin of Mexico's 1994 Financial Crisis." *Cato Journal* 17 (3): 303–13.

Gil-Díaz, Francisco, and Agustín Carstens. 1996. "One Year of Solitude: Some Pilgrim Tales about Mexico's 1994–1995 Crisis." *American Economic Review: Papers and Proceedings* 86 (2): 164–69.

Gurría, José Ángel. 1993. *La política de la deuda externa.* Mexico: Fondo de Cultura Económica, S.A. de C.V.

Kehoe, Timothy J. 1995. "What Happened to Mexico in 1994–95?" In *Modeling North American Economic Integration*, edited by Patrick J. Kehoe and Timothy J. Kehoe, 131–47. Dordrecht, The Netherlands: Kluwer Academic Publishers.

Kehoe, Timothy J., and Felipe Meza. 2011. "Catch-up Growth Followed by Stagnation: Mexico, 1950–2010." *Latin American Journal of Economics* 48 (2): 227–68.

Kehoe, Timothy J., and Edward Prescott, eds. 2007. *Great Depressions of the Twentieth Century*. Minneapolis: Federal Reserve Bank of Minneapolis.

Kochen, Federico, and Daniel Sámano. 2016. "Price-Setting and Exchange Rate Pass-Through in the Mexican Economy: Evidence from CPI Micro Data." Working paper 2016-13, Banco de México, México CDMX.

Ljungqvist, Lars, and Thomas J. Sargent. 2004. *Recursive Macroeconomic Theory*. 2nd ed. Cambridge, Mass.: MIT Press.

Meza, Felipe. 2008. "Financial Crisis, Fiscal Policy, and the 1995 GDP Contraction in Mexico." *Journal of Money, Credit and Banking* 40 (6): 1239–61.

Ramos-Francia, Manuel, and Alberto Torres García. 2005. "Reducing Inflation through Inflation Targeting: The Mexican Experience." Working paper 2005-01, Banco de México, México CDMX.

Secretaría de Hacienda y Crédito Público. 2010. "Balance fiscal en México: Definición y metodología" (in Spanish). Downloaded in 2010 from https://www.shcp.gob.mx.

Serra Puche, Jaime. 2011. "Reflexiones sobre la crisis de 1994." In *Privatización bancaria, crisis y rescate del sistema financiero: La historia contada por sus protagonistas*, vol. 1, edited by Enrique Cárdenas and Amparo Espinosa, 177–79. México, DF: Centro de Estudios Espinosa Yglesias.

Urrutia, Carlos. 2017. "Modelo monetario con rigideces nominales y bienes diferenciados." Unpublished teaching material, Instituto Autónomo Tecnológico de México, México CDMX.

Walsh, Carl E. 2003. *Monetary Theory and Policy*. Cambridge, Mass.: MIT Press.

Discussion of the History of Mexico

Alejandro Werner
International Monetary Fund

This chapter does an impressive job of covering, with a significant amount of detail, the last half century of Mexico's macroeconomic history. The use of an analytical framework centered on the government's consolidated budget constraint gives the chapter a useful, but incomplete, structure for describing and analyzing such a long period. The chapter clearly establishes that the currency and financial crisis of 1982 was deeply rooted in fiscal mismanagement. However, after that period, the sources of the increase in inflation from 1986 to 1995 can hardly be associated with fiscal dominance. The chapter also does a very nice job of describing the transition of the monetary policy framework in Mexico toward an inflation-targeting regime during the last twenty-five years. Given the magnitude of the topic covered in this chapter, these comments will focus on complementing it by concentrating on the following seven themes.

First, a key feature of the monetary policy framework in a small open economy is its exchange rate regime. So describing how the exchange rate regime evolved in Mexico during this period is important, as it influences how the transmission from fiscal and monetary variables to inflation happened. During the period covered in the chapter, Mexico moved from a fixed exchange rate regime to a fully floating regime. During this transition, Mexico experimented with managed floating regimes, capital controls, crawling pegs, and crawling bands (see Table 1).

During the nonfloating periods, the transmission from fiscal dominance to inflation is diminished during a first stage by the control of traded goods prices implied by the fixed or predetermined exchange rate. Therefore, the nontradable goods component should be a better indicator to pick up this dynamic in the early stages of this process. However, the inconsistency between the fixed or managed rate and the expansion of the money supply needed to finance the public-sector deficit eventually shows up in a decline in international reserves. Once this process intensifies, the central bank is forced to devalue the currency, and inflation increases. This is the pattern present in the 1982 and 1994 crises. Although both these crises were preceded by a deterioration of the fiscal stance (see Figure 3 in the chapter), I concur with the author that in the second case, debt dynamics did not point toward unsustainability, and other factors were a more important source of the collapse of the peso. In future work, it will be useful to complement the analysis by including the

Table 1. Summary of Mexico's exchange rate regimes since 1954

Date	Regime	Exchange rates	Quotes* Beginning	End
April 19, 1954–August 31, 1976	Fixed	Fixed	$ 12.50	$ 12.50
September 1, 1976–August 5, 1982	Managed floating rate	Currency/ document transactions	$ 20.50	$ 48.79
August 6, 1982–August 31, 1982	Multiple exchange rate	General	$ 75.33	$ 104.00
		Preferential †	$ 49.13	$ 49.81
		Mexdollar ‡	$ 69.50	$ 69.50
September 1, 1982–December 19, 1982	Generalized exchange rates, control	Preferential	$ 50.00	$ 70.00
		Ordinary	$ 70.00	$ 70.00
December 20, 1982–August 4, 1985	Exchange's control	Controlled	$ 95.05	$ 281.34
		Special	$ 70.00	$ 281.51
		Free	$ 149.25	$ 344.50
August 5, 1985–November 10, 1991	Regulated float	Managed equilibrium	$ 282.30	$ 3,073.00
		Free	$ 344.50	$ 3,068.90
November 11, 1991–December 21, 1994	Exchange rate bands with managed slippage	FIX	$3,074.03	N$ 3.9970
December 22, 1994–present	Free float	FIX	N$ 4.88	-

Source: Banco de Mexico

Note: *Buy/sell average. Guide: $ = "old pesos"; N$ = "new pesos."

evolution of international reserves and breaking down the behavior of inflation into its tradable and nontradable components.

Second, the chapter points to two very interesting periods that might deserve further comments. The first period is the 1976 crisis, in which the Mexican peso was devalued by 55 percent and the pass-through to inflation was relatively low (compared with the 1982 and 1994 experiences). Therefore, a deeper discussion regarding the role of fiscal policies, external factors, the credibility of the central bank, and other issues in shaping this successful devaluation is needed. The second interesting period is from 1985 to 1987, when inflation accelerated while the primary surplus continued to increase. Again, an attempt to measure the role of policies and external factors such as the decline in the price of oil and the 1985 earthquakes would be needed. With respect to the role of policies, it is in this period when the central bank embarked on a more aggressive crawling-peg strategy, aimed at containing the appreciation of the real exchange rate. As a result, it might be possible that during this period, Mexico lost its nominal anchor.

Third, in the discussion of the period that followed the 1982 crisis, the author praises the fiscal effort made and implies that nominal instability was the product of other forces. However, the chapter does not attempt to undertake a debt sustainability analysis to establish that the fiscal effort was sufficient to stabilize the debt ratios. This exercise is needed because even after the important fiscal adjustment, many voices argued that the country was facing a debt overhang problem. Actually, it was only after the Brady Plan (1989) took place that Mexico was able to move forward and embark on a successful stabilization process.

Fourth, an interesting extension of the fiscal dominance model that is developed in the chapter to describe the 1994 crisis would be to allow for the materialization of contingent liabilities associated with financial system crises, as developed in Velasco (1987). In this case, it is the future monetization of this fiscal pressure that leads to the crisis. The chapter also discusses the possibility that the materialization of this financial crisis might be contingent on a discrete devaluation, opening the door to multiple equilibria. Another extension of the model that is not discussed is also related to third-generation models of speculative attacks that focus on the possibility of multiple equilibria associated with the foreign exchange market (FX) or short-term debt. All these issues were clearly present in Mexico at the time, as the financial sector was extremely vulnerable and public debt was short term and heavily dollarized.

Fifth, an interesting discussion in the chapter is the role played by central bank independence to achieve long-lasting nominal stability in Mexico. The chapter argues that the granting of constitutional independence was key to breaking fiscal dominance. However, as is clearly shown in the chapter, an important fiscal adjustment preceded the granting of independence to the central bank. And the additional effort undertaken after the currency depreciation is similar to that undertaken after the 1982 crisis, when the central bank was not independent. In addition, during 1995 Mexico entered into a large International Monetary Fund–U.S. Treasury financial support package that allowed the country to repay its future debt obligations and carried significant policy commitments. Thus it is difficult to establish causality from central bank independence to financial and policy variables when other important elements came into play. Moving a bit further from the 1995 policy reaction, the governments that were in place from 1995 to 2018 had a very defined orthodox bias regarding fiscal policy and low inflation. So in this period we might have seen an outcome that was more the product of fully aligned objectives between fiscal and monetary policies rather than the institutional strength granted to the central bank by its new charter. In this regard, the Latin American experience is interesting to study, since we can look at the case of fully independent central banks (Chile, Colombia, and Peru) as supporting the thesis that independence is key to breaking fiscal dominance on one side, but we can also look at the Brazilian experience with a less independent central bank achieving stability, even under a very weak fiscal stance.

Sixth, the chapter is silent regarding the evolution of fiscal institutions in Mexico. In 2006, Mexico passed a new fiscal responsibility law that included a balanced budget rule, a rule-based system to set the price of oil in the budget, and other fiscal discipline elements. This framework has been modified a few times since then. An assessment of the role of these adjustments to Mexico's institutions in the recent evolution of fiscal policy would be a nice extension to be undertaken in future work.

Finally, the section on the convergence to an inflation target concludes with the assertion that monetary policy in Mexico has become as credible as in any developed country. While I fully agree that the structural change that took place in the monetary framework, supported by fiscal sustainability, has anchored inflation expectations, at least three elements for Banco de Mexico to achieve a developed country's level of credibility are clear challenges. First, when confronted with negative supply shocks, Banco de Mexico still increases interest rates to avoid an unanchoring of inflation expectations, making monetary policy procyclical. Second, Banco de Mexico still overreacts to exchange rate movements, both with interest rates and with direct FX interventions, compared to advanced countries' central banks. This also calls for a deeper discussion of the FX intervention policies carried out by Banco de Mexico. Third and last, Banco de Mexico still needs to anchor medium-term inflation expectations to the inflation target. For a long time now, market participants' inflation expectations have been slightly above the target. This is the last frontier in Banco de Mexico's quest for full credibility, as its medium-term inflation target is not fully internalized by market participants and price setters in the economy.

Reference

Velasco, Andres. 1987. "Financial Crises and Balance of Payments Crises: A Simple Model of the Southern Cone Experience." *Journal of Development Economics* 27 (1–2): 263–83.

Paraguay

The History of Paraguay

Carlos Javier Charotti
Central Bank of Paraguay

Carlos Fernández Valdovinos
Central Bank of Paraguay

Felipe González Soley
Central Bank of Paraguay

Major fiscal and monetary events, 1960–2017

1956 Stabilization plan with exchange rate as monetary policy instrument	Change of the legal framework of the central bank
1962 Fixed exchange rate regime	**1997** Second financial crisis and bank bailouts
1974 Construction of hydroelectric plant of Itaipú	**2002** Third financial crisis and bank bailouts
1985 Debt crisis	**2003** Sovereign default
1988 Balance of payments crisis	Fiscal reform
1992 Central bank independence Target growth rate of monetary base	**2011** Inflation targeting
	2013 Fiscal rule with caps on fiscal deficit and on public expenditure growth
1995 First financial crisis and bank bailouts	

Introduction

The purpose of this chapter is to describe and analyze the monetary and fiscal history of Paraguay between 1960 and 2017 following the framework presented in "A Framework for Studying the Monetary and Fiscal History of Latin America." The analysis concentrates to a large extent on the historical evolution of the government's consolidated fiscal deficit, its sources of financing, the trajectory of inflation, and economic performance. We used these variables to explore the relationship between unfavorable fiscal and monetary policy and macroeconomic instability.

As a first approximation, Figure 1 introduces Paraguay's economic performance, measured by the change in GDP per capita. Average growth between 1960 and 2017 is

2.4 percent.[1] Although the economic performance has not been significantly different from Latin American countries, it is slightly higher than the Latin American average of 1.7 percent.[2] Figure 1 shows there was a period of high and persistent growth in the 1970s and a significant recovery recently in the 2000s. The unprecedented economic performance in the 1970s is mainly from the increase of the agriculture frontiers—especially fields dedicated to soya bean and cotton—and the investment made between 1974 and 1981 on the construction of the Itaipú hydroelectric power station.[3]

On the other hand, the period of analysis also includes two periods of relative decline in GDP per capita. The first one took place during the 1980s, which coincides with the conclusion of the construction of the Itaipú hydroelectric power station. This period was characterized by high and unstable inflation and a persistent deficit of the central government and public companies. The second one took place in the late 1990s, at a time when successive financial crisis episodes occurred, mainly because of a financial liberalization that was not followed by a proper change in the financial regulatory framework. Despite the absence of persistent macroeconomic imbalances and that average economic growth has been higher than the average for Latin America, the economic performance was not sufficient for the economy to catch up with the region's income levels. Currently, Paraguay remains among the countries with the lowest levels of income per capita in Latin America.

Paraguay has kept a record of nominal stability for more than seventy years, since the country has not experienced any hyperinflation episodes. Figure 2 illustrates this stability, and although inflation was high and volatile during certain years, average inflation was 11 percent between 1960 and 2017.

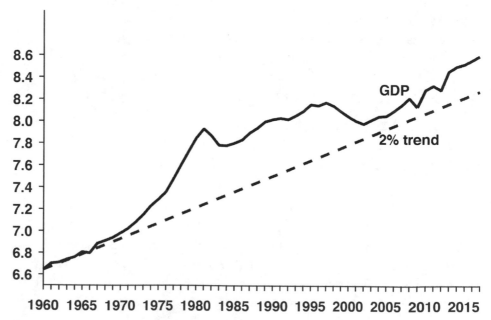

Figure 1. Log of real GDP per capita

Source: Central Bank of Paraguay

Note: Log (base 2) of real GDP per capita and 2 percent growth trend.

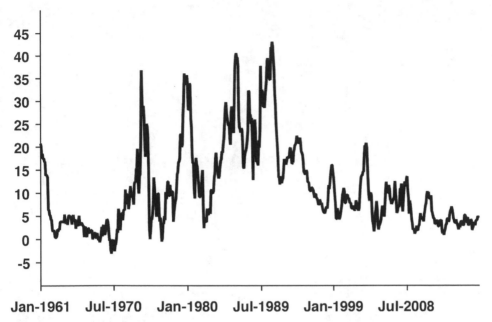

Figure 2. Annual inflation rate, percent

Source: Central Bank of Paraguay

Note: Twelve-month inflation rate measured by the change in the consumer price index.

During the 1960s, inflation remained below one digit (2.1 percent on average), supported by a stabilization plan initiated in 1956, when the central bank used the fixed exchange rate as the monetary policy instrument. In the following decade, inflation accelerated and fluctuated within a broader range. In particular, in 1973, 1974, and 1979, inflation was characterized as being quite high when compared to the 1960s average and also by the sharp decline that followed in 1975 and 1980. This pattern of high and volatile inflation persisted during the decade of the 1980s, which registered the highest average inflation (20 percent) relative to other decades. The highest record of the period was reached in 1990 (44 percent), which also marks a change in the inflation trajectory that coincides with a new legal framework of the central bank and the implementation of monetary aggregates as an instrument for monetary policy. Since then, there has been a persistent decline in inflation, and, except for some episodes that occurred in 1998 and 2003, inflation has maintained a downward trend.

Fiscal deficit outcomes evidence two different fiscal policy frameworks (Figure 3). The first was from 1960 until the end of the 1980s, when the operations of public companies played an important role in explaining the aggregate fiscal balance (Figure 4).[4] The second, since the beginning of the 1990s to the present, took place after a fundamental change in the legal framework of the central bank (Tables 2 and 3), which modified the relationship between the central government, public companies, and the central bank.

During the early years of the first fiscal policy framework, the deficit of the central government and the deficit of public enterprises were financed with external debt (Figures 5 and 6) and loans from the central bank. Once the government started to face

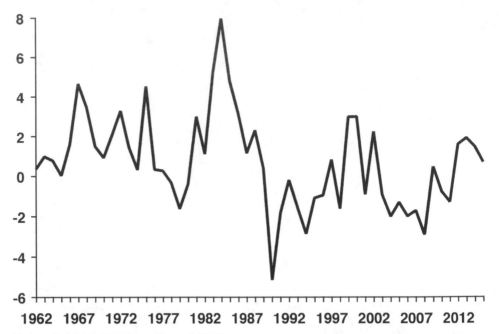

Figure 3. Total deficit, percent of GDP

Sources: Secretariat for Planning for the 1962–98 period; Ministry of Finance for the 1999–2015 period

Note: Total deficit of the nonfinancial public sector, which comprises the central government, decentralized institutions, municipalities, and public enterprises. Data for the 2016–17 period were not available for the nonfinancial public sector.

external financing constraints in the mid-1980s, the central bank's internal resources became its primary source of financing. At that time, the public-sector financial obligations were state-contingent debt for the central bank, and its assets served as collateral in public debt contracts.

The second fiscal policy framework has been in place since the 1990s. During this period, a change in the legislation of the central bank limited public-sector financing. Under this new configuration, central bank financing to the public sector was limited to short-term loans, and therefore fiscal policy needed alternative sources of financing. For this reason, the tariffs of public enterprises were adjusted, and since then, these enterprises have maintained a relatively balanced budget. Additionally, as Figure 4 shows, the central government became more relevant in explaining deficit outcomes.

The economic performance between 1998 and 2002, partially explained by a financial crisis, a weakening of regional trading partners, and the low prices of the main commodity exports, affected fiscal revenues. In addition, the central government significantly increased expenditures, especially capital expenditures in 1999, 2000, and 2002. During these years, central government deficits increased considerably (Figure 4), and the government defaulted partially on its debts in 2003. The new government, elected in 2003, inherited this crisis and implemented a set of fiscal reforms with the main objective of

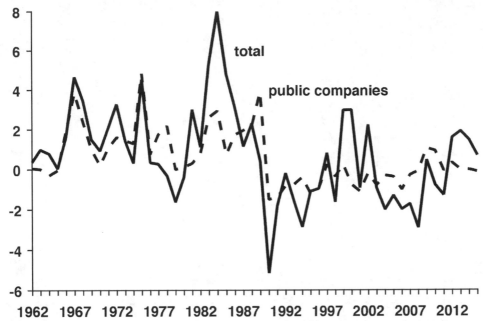

Figure 4. Total deficit and deficit of public companies, percent of GDP
Sources: Secretariat for Planning for the 1962–98 period; Ministry of Finance for the
1999–2015 period
Note: Total deficit comprises the nonfinancial public sector, which includes the central
government, decentralized institutions, municipalities, and public enterprises. Data for the
2016–17 period were not available for the nonfinancial public sector.

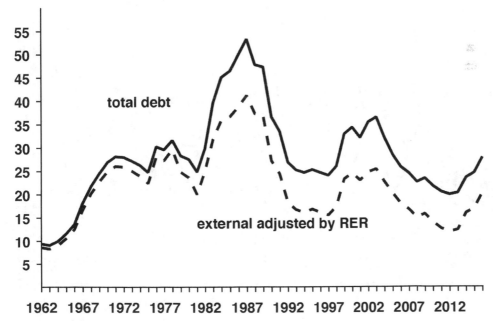

Figure 5. Public external debt, percent of GDP
Sources: Central Bank of Paraguay; Ministry of Finance

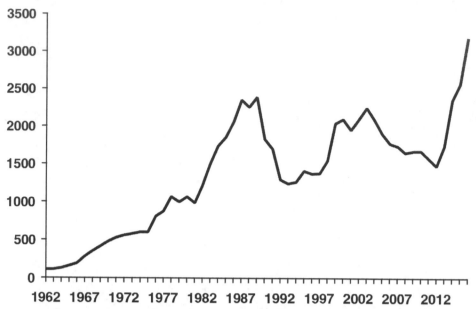

Figure 6. External public debt, millions of 1994 US$
Sources: Central Bank of Paraguay; Ministry of Finance

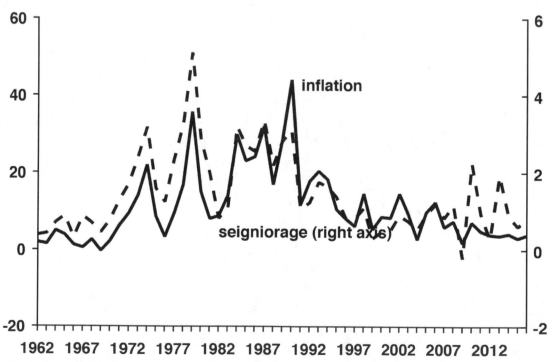

Figure 7. Annual inflation rate and seigniorage, percent of GDP
Source: Central Bank of Paraguay

Table 1. Changes in the Central Bank Legislation I

	Decree-Law Nr. 18 "That Creates the Central Bank of Paraguay [CBP]" (1952)	National Constitution (1992)	Law 489 "Organic of the Central Bank of Paraguay" (1995)
Government financing	The CBP may lend to the government and other institutions affected by public law, either with promissory notes or through purchase of government bonds. These operations will be approved by the executive power and are guaranteed by the Treasury (Art. 101).	The central bank must refrain from agreeing to provide credits (direct or indirectly) to finance the public sector's budget, except for short-term loans and in case of national emergency (Art. 286).	The CBP may provide short-term loans to the government based on the expected tax income stated in the budget. This amount cannot exceed 10% of the tax income and should be canceled by the end of the fiscal year (Art. 58).
Use of foreign reserves	The central bank will hold foreign reserves in gold and foreign currency. One of its purposes will be to ensure the external public debt service (Art. 83).		The foreign reserves are destined exclusively to ensure the stability of the free foreign exchange market, overcome transitory setbacks in the balance of payments, and preserve the external value of the currency (Art. 61).
Independence	If the central bank refrains from providing financing, this will be evaluated by the Economic National Council. The central bank will have to explain the potential impact of this financing to the economy. The recommendations adopted by the council will be binding (Art. 102).		The board of the CBP will determine the interest rate, maturity, and other required conditions to provide financing to the government (Art. 57).

Sources: Decree-Law Nr. 18/1952, "That Creates the Central Bank of Paraguay"; National Constitution of 1992; Law 489/95, "Organic of the Central Bank of Paraguay."

restoring fiscal balance and supporting an economic reactivation. To restore fiscal balance, the public sector exhibited six consecutive years of fiscal surplus until 2011. In 2012, a 30 percent adjustment in public wages put pressure on fiscal accounts, generating a deficit in recent years. In 2013, a fiscal responsibility law was passed in an attempt to prevent further deterioration of the fiscal balance.

It is important to note that there were some episodes when inflation did not seem to be related to the deficit of the public sector. As shown in Figures 2 and 3, there were high inflation levels in 1973, 1974, 1978, 1979, 1990, and 1991, with very low deficits or surplus. These events do not seem to conform to the conceptual framework followed in the chapter, and further analysis is needed to explain the reasons behind the high inflation and the increase in seigniorage (Figure 9) without a fiscal deficit. The next section provides an explanation for these episodes.

The remainder of the chapter is organized into two sections. The next section is based on the framework presented in "A Framework for Studying the Monetary and Fiscal History of Latin America." Its main purpose is to describe the evolution of the main macroeconomic variables and to present the results of the budget constraint exercise. The last section summarizes the main findings and conclusions.

Historical Perspective of Macroeconomic Variables and Budget Accounting Exercise

In order to properly characterize the monetary and fiscal history of Paraguay, the analysis is divided into subperiods that consider mainly two events. The first was the beginning, in 1989, of a positive and substantial flow of nontax revenues that the government received from the binational enterprise Itaipú. The second was the change in the legal framework of the Central Bank of Paraguay in the early 1990s (Tables 2 and 3). These changes were made by the newly democratic government that took power in 1989.[5]

Until the early 1990s, the central bank's legal framework established that the institution could provide financing to public institutions through the acquisition of government bonds or Treasury certificates. In addition, it allowed the use of foreign reserves to cover public debt service. The new national constitution of 1992 explicitly forbids the central bank from providing resources to cover public spending. In addition, in 1995, the new central bank's charter law established that foreign reserves can be used only to cover balance of payments deficits and ensure the proper functioning of the foreign exchange market. These changes modified the interaction between monetary and fiscal policy and ultimately induced a different debt management policy. Further, as we will illustrate, these changes explain the differences observed in the evolution of public debt in every subperiod. In addition, we will argue that these changes also explain the breaks in inflation and deficit that were described in the introduction (Figures 2 and 3). It must be noted, however, that the evolution of output per capita (Figure 1) does not exhibit a significant change, as compared with the other two variables.

Table 2. Changes in the Central Bank Legislation II

	Decree-Law Nr. 18 "That Creates the Central Bank of Paraguay (CBP)" (1952)	National Constitution (1992)	Law 489 "Organic of the Central Bank of Paraguay" (1995)
Central bank functions	Collaborate on the coordination between economic, financial, and fiscal policy of the government and monetary and credit policy of the central bank. Act as a banking agent and adviser of the government (Art. 4). Implement monetary and credit policy to maintain or reestablish the country's external balance and the competitiveness of domestic products on foreign and domestic markets (Art. 5).	Participate, with other public economic institutions, on the formulation of the monetary, fiscal, and exchange policy, being responsible for its implementation by preserving monetary stability (Art. 285).	The fundamental objectives of the central bank are maintaining the value of the domestic currency (Art. 3).
Guarantees	The central bank may provide guarantees to all public-sector financing contracts, using its assets (including foreign reserves) as collateral (Arts. 90 and 91).		The CBP may not provide guarantees to any public institution without explicit authorization of the law (Art. 59).

Sources: Decree-Law Nr. 18/1952, "That Creates the Central Bank of Paraguay"; National Constitution of 1992; Law 489/95, "Organic of the Central Bank of Paraguay."

Table 3. Summary of budget accounting (percentage of GDP)

Budget constraint	1960–80	1981–90	1991–2003	2004–15
Change in foreign debt	0.8	0.9	0.0	−0.9
Change in real monetary base	0.3	−0.5	0.0	0.2
Seigniorage	1.6	2.4	1.0	0.9
Total	**2.7**	**2.8**	**1.0**	**0.2**
Deficit	0.8	2.2	−0.2	−0.5
Interest on external debt	0.7	1.7	1.4	0.7
Transfers (residue)	1.1	−1.1	−0.2	0.0
Total	**2.7**	**2.8**	**1.0**	**0.2**

Sources: Central Bank of Paraguay, Ministry of Finance, Secretariat for Planning.

Note: Values expressed as percentage of GDP. Seigniorage is computed as $m_{t-1} (1 - \dfrac{1}{\pi_t g_t})$, where m_{t-1} corresponds to the real monetary-base-to-GDP ratio in $t-1$, π_t is the gross inflation rate, and g_t is the gross real growth rate of GDP. The deficit comprises the nonfinancial public-sector deficit, excluding external debt interest payments.

Thus 1990 splits the sample period we analyze in a natural way. Moreover, these two subperiods were again divided to account for two other events: the culmination of the Itaipú construction at the beginning of the 1980s and the policy reforms introduced in 2003. Again, these events coincide with relevant changes in the trajectory of debt, fiscal balance, and inflation. Looking at growth, there is some indication of a break point within the subperiods, which is not evident when we look at the two big periods. The remainder of this section will focus on the evolution of the main macroeconomic variables and the analysis of the four subperiods. Also, the results of the budget accounting exercise and the inflation outcomes are presented at the end of each subsection.

1962–80

During the early 1960s, the government in office continued implementing a stabilization plan initiated in 1956. According to this plan, the central bank used the exchange rate as the policy instrument. As can be seen in Figure 2, the plan was very successful, and inflation was substantially and rapidly reduced. Fiscal policy accompanied the effort: fiscal deficits were small and financed with external sources. Those same sources were used to finance the larger deficits of the late 1960s, so inflation remained at international levels until the early 1970s.

During the 1970s, we identify some episodes in which inflation does not seem related to deficit outcomes. Inflation in 1973 was 14 percent, with a fiscal deficit of 1.4 percent.

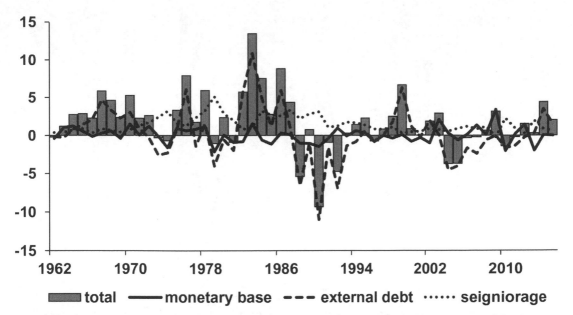

Figure 8. Public external debt, change in real monetary base, and seigniorage, percent of GDP
Sources: Central Bank of Paraguay, Ministry of Finance, Secretariat for Planning
Note: Results of the budget accounting exercise that correspond to the financing sources of the public-sector obligations.

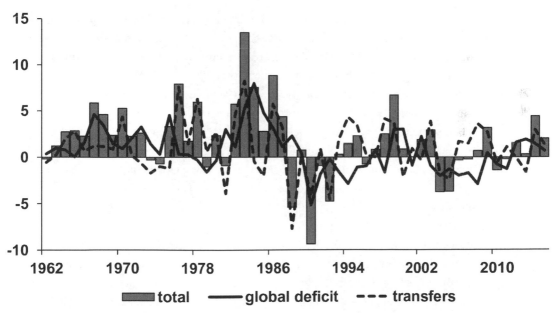

Figure 9. Deficit, interest on external debt, and transfers, percent of GDP
Sources: Central Bank of Paraguay, Ministry of Finance, Secretariat for Planning
Note: Results of the budget accounting exercise that correspond to the financial obligations of the public sector. The deficit comprises the nonfinancial public-sector deficit excluding external debt interest payments.

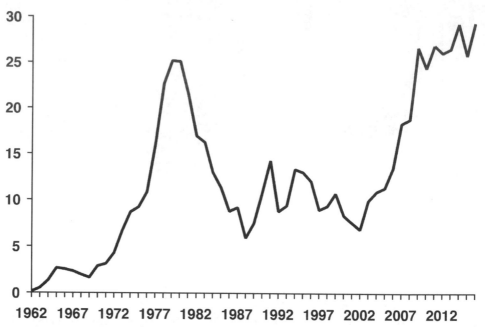

Figure 10. Net foreign reserves, percent of GDP

Source: Central Bank of Paraguay

Note: Foreign reserves of the Central Bank of Paraguay, net of foreign liabilities.

In the same way, in 1974, inflation was 24 percent, with a deficit of 0.3 percent. In 1979, we have the same pattern, even with a fiscal surplus. Official sources during those years argue that these episodes of inflation are to a large extent due to the importance that imported goods had in the consumer price index (CPI). In 1973, 1974, and 1979, imported goods and the oil crisis significantly affected the prices of local goods and services. This caused an increase of 24 percent in food and 46 percent in transportation in 1974.[6] These increases led the government to adjust salaries by 18 percent in that year. Additionally, this period coincides with a considerable increase in international reserves (Figure 10) due to the large inflow of foreign currency and a considerable increase in credits to the banking and private sector by the central bank, especially in 1974 and 1979, which partially explains the increase in M0 growth (Figure 8) during these years.

Additionally, in this period, despite the creation of new taxes, revenues grew below public spending (Figure 7). As a result, the central government reduced investment and financed its deficit with foreign resources. Also, there was an increase in the public tariffs of public enterprises to reduce the central government's external financing needs. However, the reduction in the deficit was only temporary, so it also increased its external financing needs. As a result, the size of external debt relative to GDP increased from 9.3 percent to 24.9 percent between 1962 and 1980 (Figure 5), respectively. This figure is particularly affected by the strong output growth at the end of this period. So when looking at the real value of external debt in 1994 U.S. dollars, we see an average annual increase of 13 percent during this period (Figure 6).

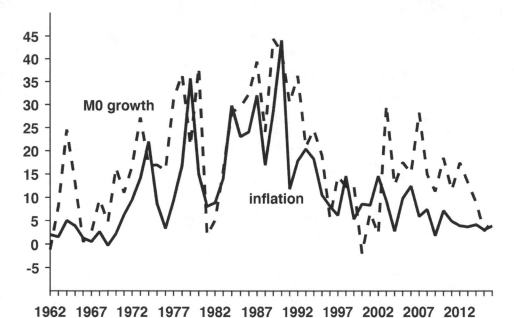

Figure 11. Annual inflation and M0 growth rate, percent

Source: Central Bank of Paraguay

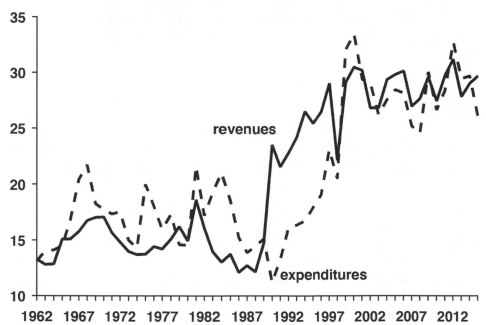

Figure 12. Revenues and expenditures of the public sector, percent of GDP

Sources: Secretariat for Planning for the 1962–98 period, Ministry of Finance for the 1999–2015 period

Note: Data for the 2016–17 period were not publicly available for the nonfinancial public sector.

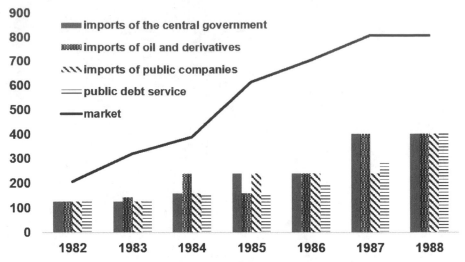

Figure 13. Multiple nominal exchange rate 1982–88, guaraníes per U.S. dollar

Sources: Central Bank of Paraguay, Otazú (1991)

Table 1 summarizes the results of the budget constraint exercise by following the conceptual framework of "A Framework for Studying the Monetary and Fiscal History of Latin America." On average, the public-sector deficit was 0.8 percent of GDP.[7] This result was mainly explained by the public enterprises result, as the central government partially offset this with surpluses at the end of the 1970s. The primary financing sources of these obligations were external debt (0.8 percent of GDP on average) and seigniorage (1.6 percent of GDP).

1981–90

The events that followed during this subperiod provide relevant evidence to test the hypothesis of the relationship between fiscal imbalances, nominal instability, and poor economic performance. In this subperiod, the central bank's legal framework (Tables 2 and 3) plays a key role because it shaped the interaction between fiscal and monetary policy, which ultimately helps us understand the evolution of macroeconomic variables. This section will follow the same structure as the previous one, presenting a narrative of the events, the evolution of debt, the results of the budget accounting exercise, and the inflation outcome. This will be complemented with an analysis that follows the balance of payments crisis model presented in "A Framework for Studying the Monetary and Fiscal History of Latin America" to account for the external imbalances that occurred at the end of the period.

In 1981, capital inflows experienced a significant reduction as the construction of Itaipú ended. In addition, the economic crisis of the main trading partners (Brazil and Argentina) put additional pressure on the trade balance. These two events contributed to a deceleration of economic activity, which caused a deterioration in the fiscal balance, specifically for the central government after consecutive years of surpluses. This result, in addition to the ongoing deficit of public enterprises, increased the demand for external debt financing. The government aimed to use these resources to fund investment projects from public enterprises as an attempt to sustain economic growth at levels similar to the previous decade.

The external resources, however, were not enough to cover the financing needs. So there was also a strong increase in the domestic financing of the central bank for both the central government and public enterprises. Moreover, the public sector covered its debt service with foreign reserves as the legal framework established that the public-sector obligations were state-contingent debt for the central bank. This put pressure on the fixed exchange rate regime and led the central bank to establish a multiple exchange rate regime (Figure 14). These were different exchange rate levels for exports, public-sector imports, oil imports, agriculture inputs, and public external debt service. In particular, the exchange rate for public-sector operations was lower than the market exchange rate, so implicitly, the central bank was providing exchange rate subsidies to the public sector that were not being computed in the fiscal accounts and represented, on average, 1 percent of GDP.

The implementation of this multiple exchange rate policy was a signal that the fixed exchange rate policy could not be sustained for long, since foreign reserves started to decrease in the early 1980s, mainly for two reasons. First, the government increased its domestic financing from the central bank to cover the persistent deficits from the public sector. So to maintain exchange rate parity, the central bank had to reduce its foreign reserves. The second reason relates to the public sector's obligations being state-contingent debt of the central bank. Then, foreign reserves were used to cover the external debt service. As a result, this put pressure on the nominal exchange rate, which experienced

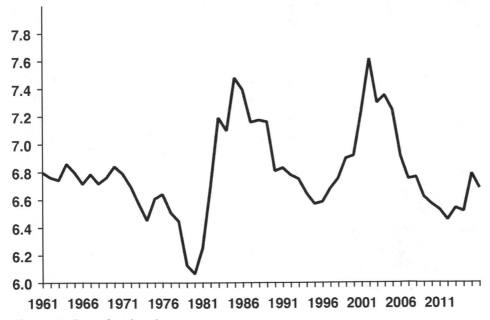

Figure 14. Log of real exchange rate
Source: Central Bank of Paraguay

Carlos Javier Charotti, Carlos Fernández Valdovinos, and Felipe González Soley

successive devaluations between 1981 and 1988 of 28 percent per year on average. Despite this devaluation, foreign reserves went from 26 percent to 8 percent of GDP between 1983 and 1988 (Figure 10), respectively.

These changes in exchange rate policy are relevant in understanding the macroeconomic outcomes of this period. Between 1981 and 1987, the relative size of external debt to GDP increased from 23 percent to 53 percent. To obtain this ratio, external debt was deflated using a U.S. price index and the nominal exchange rate, while GDP was deflated using the domestic consumer price index. As a result, Figure 5 is affected by movements in the real exchange rate—that is, changes between the guaraní (Paraguay's domestic currency) and the U.S. dollar—and the difference between domestic and external inflation. During this period (1981 to 1987), the average real devaluation was 12 percent, which contributed significantly to changes in the external financing ratio that were not related to deficit outcomes. To control for this effect, as Figure 5 shows, the external debt-to-GDP ratio was built holding the exchange rate constant and equal to the value in 1994. When considering this series, the increase went from 19 percent to 40 percent of GDP. In addition, there was also an increase in the net credit from the central bank from 0.3 percent to 6 percent of GDP between 1981 and 1985, respectively. Despite the availability of central bank resources to cover debt service, the public sector started accumulating arrears starting in 1985, which constrained the access to new foreign financing. As a result, external debt started to decline in 1988 (Figure 5).

The fiscal deficit (accounting for the exchange rate subsidies from the central bank) averaged 2.2 percent of GDP, mainly explained by the public enterprises accounts (1.6 percent of GDP on average).[8] This, according to Table 1, was financed mainly through seigniorage (2 percent of GDP on average) and external debt (1 percent of GDP on average). The increase in public-sector financing from the central bank was partially offset by the other components of the monetary base (a reduction of 0.5 percent of GDP on average). This increase in the financing of the central bank to public-sector deficits coincides with a period of relative nominal instability. Inflation accelerated during this period (23 percent on average) and remained above its historical mean. This narrative fits qualitatively with the theoretical framework from "A Framework for Studying the Monetary and Fiscal History of Latin America," which associates periods of nominal instability with persistent fiscal deficits that are financed through the central bank when the government is unable to borrow (Figures 2 and 3).

Two inflation figures, occurring between 1989 and 1990, do not fit qualitatively with the conceptual framework. One hypothesis that could explain these outcomes relates to the adjustment in tariffs to reduce public enterprises deficits in 1989 and 1990. An alternative explanation is related to the fact that, between 1989 and 1990, money (measured by M0) grew by 44 percent and 41 percent (Figure 8), respectively, as a result of an increase in foreign reserves.

In terms of economic performance, income per capita average growth was 1 percent during this period, lower than the historical mean, after a period of strong growth in the previous decade (Figure 1). It must be noted that this average is affected by the recovery of output in the late 1980s. Between 1982 and 1984, output per capita fell 3 percent on

376

average and recorded, in 1982 and 1983, two of the lowest levels of the series (−4 percent and −6 percent, respectively).

1991–2003

Following the crisis in the 1980s, at the beginning of 1989, a coup d'état ended a dictatorship that had lasted for thirty-four years. This period marked the starting point of the transition of Paraguay into a democracy, accompanied by a deregulation of the economy. In 1992, a new constitution was enacted that incorporated free-market principles and established the independence of the central bank.

The institutional changes induced a change in the interaction of fiscal and monetary policy, which resulted in a tax reform implemented in 1992 when the value-added tax (VAT) was introduced. In addition, there was an increase in the tariffs of public enterprises and a reduction in public investment. Previous to the legal modifications, the government had been renegotiating its public debt.[9] So in 1992 the government used foreign reserves to cancel its external arrears, converting foreign debt to domestic debt with the central bank.

In addition, changes related to monetary, exchange rate, and financial policy were made. First, in order to stabilize money growth and reduce inflation, the central bank established a ceiling on the growth of the components of the monetary base—that is, the net credit to the financial system and the public sector—as well as a ceiling on the accumulation of foreign reserves. From 1991 to 2003, monetary policy was conducted based on a monetary aggregates scheme by designing an annual monetary program with targets for money growth (specifically M0) but no explicit objective for inflation. The limits established were complemented by the issuance of central bank securities to control the monetary aggregates expansion in accordance with the targets established in the monetary program. These were short-term zero-coupon bonds with maturities that ranged from thirty days to one year, and financial institutions acquired these instruments through open market operations.[10]

Second, the new legal framework established a floating exchange rate regime with occasional interventions from the central bank to smooth sharp fluctuations. Foreign reserves accumulation was set mainly for these foreign exchange market interventions and in the case of a balance of payments crisis. Finally, there was a deregulation of the financial system, which will be described extensively below.

As a result of fiscal reforms, the public sector exhibited surpluses during the first years of the decade. However, starting in 1997, the combination of a financial crisis, political instability episodes, and a regional economic crisis had an adverse impact on economic growth, reducing tax revenues. At the same time, spending on wages and pensions increased, which put more pressure on fiscal accounts, and spending on public infrastructure increased through external debt financing. By 2002, the economy had accumulated five consecutive years of a decline in GDP per capita (−3 percent on average). At the beginning of 2003, the Ministry of Finance lacked the resources to cover wage spending and missed debt service payments with multilateral banks, and, as a result, credit rating agencies declared a selective sovereign default. As will be explained in detail below, this default was not associated with the monetary assistance provided to the financial system during the crisis, since most of those resources were provided by the central bank. There were disbursements made by the government and financed with domestic currency bonds; however, the default in 2003 was on foreign currency debt. Also, the definition of "deficit" in the budget constraint exercise considers the nonfinancial public sector. For this reason, this deficit does not incorporate the outlays made by the central bank.

Despite the deterioration of the fiscal balance by the end of this period, there was a 0.2 percent average surplus. The results in the first years and the balance of public enterprises contributed to this outcome. External financing did not change on average because it only increased at the end of the 1990s, and this was offset by the reduction in debt at the beginning of that same decade. The central bank financing to cover debt service was offset by a reduction in foreign reserves.

In terms of prices, inflation remained close to its historical mean at 12 percent, well below the levels of the previous period (Figure 2). At the beginning of the period, inflation dropped from 44 percent to 11 percent by the end of 1991, while money growth (measured by M0) was 30 percent (Figure 8). One explanation for this difference is the adjustments that were made on public tariffs and the minimum wage at the beginning of the 1990s. This can be confirmed when considering the average rates, which show that inflation and money growth were 25 percent and 26 percent, respectively. By the end of the period, there were two years (1998 and 2002) when inflation rose above average. In the first case, even though at the aggregate level the public sector ran a surplus, the central government recorded a deficit and received funding from the central bank of 0.4 percent of GDP. The second record in 2002 coincides with a public-sector deficit of 2 percent of GDP and an increase in the net credit of the central bank to the central government of 2 percent of GDP.

Financial Crisis

Until 1989, the financial system was subject to regulated interest rates, constraints on bank operations, reserve requirements up to 42 percent on deposits, and banks' loan portfolios determined according to government guidelines established by law. Within this setup, the financial deepening—measured by credits to GDP—peaked at 18 percent in 1978 but started declining in the 1980s, reaching 10 percent by the end of 1988 (Figure 15). The government that took office in 1989 implemented a set of policies in an attempt to deregulate the economy, including the financial sector. As a result, interest rates were determined by the market, banks were allowed to define their loan portfolios without government guidelines, reserve requirements were gradually reduced, and rediscounts were eliminated. Under these new rules, the financial deepening increased as credits peaked at 24 percent of GDP in 1997.

However, as argued by Braumann, Jaramillo, and Jenker (2000), the regulatory framework did not adapt to these new arrangements in the financial system. The entry requirements were lax, which led to a significant increase in new banks and finance

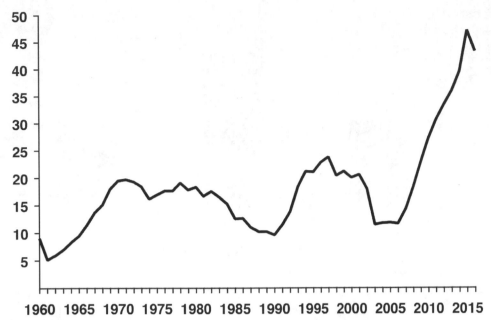

Figure 15. Credits of the banking system to the private sector, percent of GDP
Source: Central Bank of Paraguay

companies (Figure 16). Some institutions did not even comply with minimum capital requirements. In addition, these capital requirements did not consider the implicit risk taken by banks in their portfolio loans.

Banking practices were weak, particularly in locally owned financial institutions. There was no formal risk assessment framework, and granting credits to related enterprises was common, since the legislation at that time did not require registered shares in bank ownership. This, in turn, prevented banking authorities from identifying any links between banks and borrowers.

Even though rediscounts were eliminated, financial intermediaries maintained the same liquidity management framework, which resulted in an accumulation of negative cash flows that were hidden from the Superintendency of Banks, which is in charge of banking supervision. Furthermore, some institutions maintained off-the-books transactions, as there was no legal obligation for them to be subject to external audits. All these practices were mainly due to inadequate financial supervision that lacked the institutional and legal capabilities to enforce regulatory requirements (Braumann, Jaramillo, and Jenker 2000).

The combination of inappropriate banking practices and poor financial supervision led to the first financial crisis in 1995. It began with four locally owned banks (which accounted for 13 percent of the financial system's deposits in 1994) in which the government intervened after they were unable to comply with clearing obligations. Because there was no deposit guarantee scheme, and to prevent a potential bank run on other institutions, the government chose to cover the deposits of the affected banks through a credit provided by the central bank. These interventions led to the discovery of the

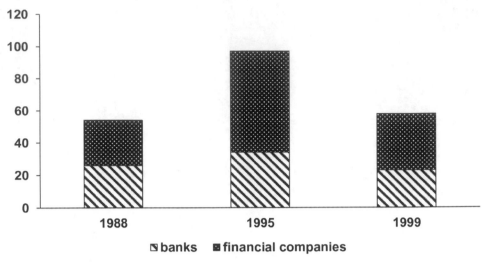

Figure 16. Number of financial intermediaries
Source: Insfrán (2000)

off-the-books deposits mentioned above, which were also covered by the government. Only in that year, the central bank disbursed funds that accounted for approximately 6 percent of GDP (Table 4). At the same time, other locally owned banks, which were perceived as being more vulnerable than foreign-owned banks in the financial system, started to raise interest rates to attract deposits. In addition, the government's decision to assist the banks in which it intervened prompted the public to perceive that deposits in the financial system were a risk-free asset.

The combination of these two events even though all the banks that ceased operations were local—seems to explain, to some extent, why there was no evidence of flight to quality (i.e., an increase in deposits to foreign-owned banks), as expected. On the contrary, the participation of foreign-owned bank deposits declined from 57 percent to 52 percent between 1995 and 1996.

Following these events, a new banking law was approved that set a limit on deposit insurance, which did not represent any cost to banks. These legal changes were complemented by financial support from the public sector. The central bank established a financial assistance program to institutions that exhibited higher levels of nonperforming loans relative to the financial system's average. In addition, the Social Security Institute (IPS, abbreviated by its Spanish name) acquired equities from a locally owned bank. Despite the financial support, between 1997 and 1998, a second wave of bank closures took place and led to the closure of locally owned, publicly owned, and foreign-owned banks that accounted for 21 percent of the financial system's deposits in 1996. In this case, even though the new banking law established a limit on deposit insurance, the law was subject to amendment, and the limit was increased (from ten times to one hundred times the minimum wage).[11] Again, the central bank was in charge of providing the resources to cover the deposits. However, when compared with the first crisis, the participation of foreign-owned bank deposits increased from 52 percent to 82 percent between 1996 and

Table 4. Estimates of direct costs of the financial crisis, percentage of GDP

Year	Annual cost (%)	Cumulative cost (%)
1995	5.6	5.6
1996	0.1	5.7
1997	3.4	9.1
1998	3.7	12.8
1999	0.5	13.3
2000	1.5	14.8
2001	0.1	14.9
2002	0.6	15.5
2003	0.2	15.7

Source: Mlachila (2010).

1998. In addition, IPS suffered a financial loss of 3 percent of GDP after it acquired the equities of a locally owned bank that had shut down (Mlachila 2010).

The last two episodes were recorded in 2002 and 2003. A foreign-owned and a locally owned bank exhibited liquidity problems and accounted for 16 percent of the financial system's deposits. After their intervention, their liquidity and solvency problems were attributed mainly to inadequate banking practices as well as to the impact of the financial crisis in Argentina and Uruguay, which affected the foreign-owned bank.

Mlachila (2010) quantifies the cumulative direct costs of the crisis at 15.7 percent of GDP (Table 4).[12] The disbursements made by the central bank are not reflected in the money growth series, since the central bank issued securities to restrict the growth of monetary aggregates in accordance with the targets established in its monetary program. Figure 17 shows the ratio of the stock of central bank securities to M0 between 1993 and 2003. In 1994, central bank securities accounted for 6 percent of M0, and by the end of the last financial crisis episode in 2003, this ratio climbed to 30 percent.

By the end of the last financial crisis episode in 2003, the financial deepening declined to 10 percent of GDP, a level similar to the levels recorded at the beginning of the 1990s (Figure 15). Between 1995 and 2003, output grew 1.4 percent on average (0 percent in per capita terms). This economic performance is the poorest relative to the other periods, and, although it cannot be attributed exclusively to the financial crisis, the uncertainty and instability derived from these episodes appear to have had a greater impact in terms of fiscal costs and economic performance when compared with the costs of the nominal instability experienced during the 1980s.[13]

Since 2003, the regulatory framework has been reformed to enhance the enforcement capabilities of the financial supervisor. Also, a deposit insurance scheme law was passed. It established a regime that is funded with private and public resources and covers up to an amount equivalent to seventy-five times the minimum wage (including principal and interest).[14] These changes appear to have contributed to the improvement of solvency

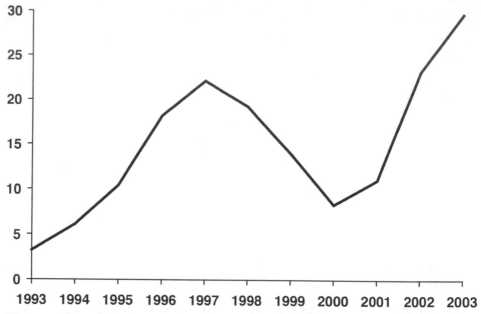

Figure 17. Central bank securities, percent of M0

Source: Central Bank of Paraguay

Note: Central bank securities are short-term zero-coupon bonds that financial institutions acquire through open market operations.

and liquidity indicators in the financial system, as well as to a higher financial depth (Figure 15).

2004–17

The fourth period begins with a set of structural reforms implemented by the government that took office in 2003. The first significant reform was the modification of the public-sector pension system, which generated a growing operating deficit for the central government in the last period. In addition, the new government implemented a tax reform that attempted to increase the formalization of the economy and fiscal pressure. This reform included changes in the income tax of businesses, agriculture, small business taxpayers, and the VAT on certain products.

The central government's main objective with this tax reform was to achieve a fiscal surplus of 0.2 percent of GDP in 2004. In addition, the government committed to covering its debt arrears by the end of the same year and to setting a limit on the financing of external debt. On the monetary side, it established a minimum level of foreign exchange reserves and a limit on the expansion of the central bank's domestic assets.

During this period, the central government recorded eight consecutive years of surplus. Given the accumulated savings, foreign debt exhibited a gradual reduction from 37 percent to 20 percent of GDP between 2003 and 2012, respectively (Figure 5). The fiscal balance deteriorated by the end of the period as a result of an increase in the wage bill in 2012. This was followed by a change in the debt trajectory, which began to increase as the central government issued bonds abroad, starting in 2013, to finance its deficit.[15]

To prevent a further deterioration of the fiscal accounts, the government that took office in 2013 passed a fiscal responsibility law, which established (1) a maximum annual fiscal deficit of the central government of 1.5 percent of GDP; (2) a maximum average fiscal deficit of the central government of 1 percent of GDP in the medium term (defined as three years); (3) a maximum annual increase in current real public expenditures of 4 percent; and (4) no increase in public wages, unless there is an increase in the minimum wage.

In 2004, the central bank initiated a gradual migration toward an inflation-targeting scheme. From 2004 to 2011, this institution adapted and modernized its operational instruments to change its monetary policy, which until then had been based on a scheme of monetary aggregates. At first, a 5 percent target was set for inflation within a range (+/−2.5 percent), but there was no explicit commitment until 2011 when it was formally announced.[16] Since then, the central bank has held monthly monetary policy meetings to set the level of the monetary policy rate, which was set as the new instrument instead of monetary aggregates. In order to provide the transparency that the scheme requires, the monetary policy committee regularly publishes press releases, minutes, and quarterly reports to communicate to the public the reasons behind various policy decisions, given the committee's expected outlook on macroeconomic variables.

These structural changes at the beginning of this period contribute to explaining the years of the surplus of the central government in the period 2004–11. The average surplus was 0.5 percent of GDP, and these savings led to a reduction in external debt (−0.9 percent of GDP on average).[17] Inflation, with the new monetary policy regime, averaged 5.4 percent with a decreasing trajectory at the end of the period. Our conjecture is that both central bank independence and balanced fiscal accounts contributed to keeping inflation low and stable.

Conclusion

This chapter has provided evidence that the Paraguayan economy follows the conceptual framework of "A Framework for Studying the Monetary and Fiscal History of Latin America" reasonably well, in that the high and volatile inflation that ensued since the mid-1970s to the late 1980s coincided with the period of large fiscal deficits that were partially financed by the central bank. In addition, the permanent reduction in inflation that started in the early 1990s coincides with a change in the institutional framework that made the central bank independent and with a more conservative fiscal policy stance that permanently changed a pattern of systematic deficits to a pattern of systematic surpluses.

However, the time series pattern does present some puzzles, according to the conceptual framework of "A Framework for Studying the Monetary and Fiscal History of Latin America," since some of the burst in inflation does happen in years of fiscal restraint, as, for example, the inflation spikes in the 1970s and in 1990. As mentioned above, one of the main factors explaining the increase in monetary growth (Figure 8) and inflation in those years without a fiscal deficit is the considerable increase in international reserves (Figure 10). In addition, other factors in each of these periods explain the increase in monetary growth and inflation. In the 1970s, there was a considerable increase in central bank lending to the banking and private sector. In 1990, interest rates were liberalized, legal reserves were reduced, and public-sector deposits (previously deposited in the central bank) were liberalized. This set of measures resulted in a strong increase in liquidity, which partly explains the increase in the monetary base and inflation during these years.

The instability of the 1980s did not seem to have a significant effect on economic activity, however, since it kept on growing as the trend. The main exception was the severe banking crisis of the late 1990s, a period of substantial income losses relative to trend. However, the crisis was not the result of fiscal imbalances, since after 1991, the government attained mostly surpluses. Improper banking regulation seems to have been the main cause of the crisis.

Compared with its peers in the region and with the exception of the 1980s, Paraguay has maintained low fiscal deficits. Inflation has also remained low, with no levels above 45 percent. This has allowed Paraguay to maintain the same currency for more than seventy years, an uncommon occurrence in the region. The legal framework allowed for the central bank's financing until the end of the 1980s, causing, in the decade of the 1980s, a period of fiscal imbalances and nominal instability. The successive modifications of the legal framework between 1989 and 1995 induced an important change in the interaction between fiscal and monetary policy. After this change, the central bank's main objective was to ensure price and financial stability, preventing it from financing the government deficit or public debt service. This modification of the legal framework ensured the independence of the central bank and allowed for the maintenance of nominal stability in the last two periods of analysis. Additional reforms were implemented to correct the inappropriate banking practices and poor financial supervision that led to the worst financial crisis in the history of the country.

Economic performance, on average, was not mediocre. However, this result is greatly affected by the construction of Itaipú in the 1970s. As mentioned, there is no record of sustained growth similar to that observed between 1974 and 1981. We believe that this situation is mainly a result of the various restrictions imposed on the financial system in the first two periods of analysis, as well as the successive financial crisis episodes between 1995 and 2003.

Paraguay, compared with most Latin American countries, has not experienced major macroeconomic imbalances. Nevertheless, it remains among the countries that have one of the lowest levels of income per capita, in addition to having a low-quality infrastructure and education system.[18] Although Paraguay has been able to narrow the income gap, especially relative to countries that have experienced significant output collapses, its efforts have not been sufficient. The analysis of this chapter suggests that macroeconomic instability, although present for several years, is not the likely reason for the country's lack of convergence.

Appendix

Itaipú Binational is an entity that was created in the 1970s by the governments of Paraguay and Brazil. Electric power production started in 1984, and since then Itaipú Binational has been selling power to the Administración Nacional de Electricidad (ANDE–Paraguay) and the Centrais Elétricas Brasileiras (Eletrobras–Brazil).

The installed capacity of the electric power plant is divided into equal parts. ANDE and Eletrobras hire fractions of the installed capacity based on their consumption. If a country does not consume all of its share of energy produced, Itaipú Binational may assign the surplus energy to other countries in exchange for compensation.

Nowadays, Paraguay consumes only a small percentage of its share of energy production, and as mentioned in the treaty, it receives payment for ceding energy to Brazil. Also, the government of Paraguay received financial transfers, called royalties, from the use of Paraguay's natural resource (Paraná River) for electricity production. In addition, ANDE received capital gains and compensation for management and supervisory duties.

The Itaipú Binational entity asked for loans to finance the dam's construction. The loans were mainly obtained from Eletrobras, the government of Brazil, and the Banco Nacional de Desenvolvimento Econômico e Social (BNDES). The funds raised for the construction, including financial extensions, totaled US$26.9 billion, in addition to US$100 million in shared capital. Currently, Itaipú Binational is still paying for the loans with revenues from electricity sales. It is estimated that by the year 2023, the company will finish paying its total debt.

Notes

We would like to acknowledge Andrea Szaran's remarkable work on the explanation of the database construction and her research assistance. The views expressed here are those of the authors and do not necessarily reflect the position of the Central Bank of Paraguay or its board members.

1 For a growth accounting analysis of the Paraguayan economy, see Fernández Valdovinos and Monge Naranjo (2005) and Castilleja, Garay, and Lovera (2014).

2 A simple average that includes Argentina, Bolivia, Brazil, Chile, Colombia, Ecuador, Mexico, Peru, Uruguay, and Venezuela for the 1960–2017 period.

3 For more details on the macroeconomic impact of Itaipú on the Paraguayan economy, see Charotti, Hevia, and Neumeyer (2017). Also, see the appendix to this chapter for an explanation of the Itaipú hydroelectric power station.

4 Cáceres (1991) assesses the impact of public enterprises deficits in the fiscal accounts during the 1980s.

5 Between August 1954 and February 1989, a dictatorship presided over by Alfredo Stroessner ruled Paraguay.

6 This is an example of some important items of 1974 where we have disaggregated data from the CPI index.

7 For this exercise, the deficit comprises the nonfinancial public sector and excludes external debt interest payments.

8 Excluding exchange rate subsidies, the deficit drops to 1.3 percent of GDP, which reduces

the transfers (residue) from −1.1 percent to −0.3 percent of GDP.

9 Páez (1993) summarizes the renegotiation process of the public external debt arrears.

10 These open market operations are still implemented under the inflation-targeting regime that has been the monetary policy framework since 2011, and their maturities have been extended up to 728 days.

11 In 1998, the minimum wage was equivalent to US$208.

12 These are computed based on the outlays made by the government.

13 As mentioned before, the fiscal deficit definition that is considered does not account for the central bank.

14 In 2003, the minimum wage was equivalent to US$160.

15 It must be noted that the legal framework only allows the government to issue debt for rollover and capital spending purposes. It explicitly forbids the issuance of debt to cover current expenditures.

16 After the implementation, the inflation target and the tolerance range have been gradually reduced since 2014. In 2017, the target was set at 4 percent within a +/-2 percent range.

17 The average is computed for the period 2004–15, since the deficit of the nonfinancial public sector was not available.

18 "Global Competitiveness Index Historical Dataset, 2007–2017," World Economic Forum.

References

Braumann, Benedikt, Juan Carlos Jaramillo, and Eva Jenker. 2000. "Paraguay: Selected Issues and Statistical Appendix." Country Report 00/51. Washington, D.C.: International Monetary Fund.

Cáceres, Rogelio. 1991. "Incidencia de las empresas públicas en el déficit fiscal. Caso paraguayo—Añõs 1980–1989." Banco Central del Paraguay, Asunción.

Castilleja, Liliana, Pedro Garay, and Diego Lovera. 2014. "Diagnóstico de crecimiento de Paraguay." Nota Técnica IDB-TN-666, Banco Interamericano de Desarrollo, Washington, D.C.

Charotti, Carlos Javier, Constantino Hevia, and Pablo Andrés Neumeyer. 2017. "The Macroeconomics of Itaipú." Paper presented at LACEA-LAMES 2017 Annual Meeting, November 9–11, 2017, Buenos Aires, Argentina.

Fernández Valdovinos, Carlos, and Alexander Monge Naranjo. 2005. "Economic Growth in Paraguay." Economic and Social Study Series RE1-01-009, Inter-American Development Bank, Washington, D.C.

Insfrán, Anibal. 2000. "El sector financiero paraguayo: Evaluando 10 añõs de transición." Banco Central del Paraguay, Asunción.

Mlachila, Montfort. 2010. "Crisis financieras recurrentes: Causas, costos y consecuencias." In *Paraguay: Haciendo frente a la trampa del estancamiento y la inestabilidad*, edited by Alejandro Santos, 43–78. Washington, D.C.: International Monetary Fund.

Otazú, Ovidio. 1991. "El déficit cuasifiscal en el Paraguay: 1982–1989." *Serie política fiscal* 24. Economic Commission for Latin America and the Caribbean, United Nations. https://repositorio.cepal.org/handle/11362/9260.

Páez, José Enrique. 1993. "El proceso de renegociación y regularización de atrasos de la deuda pública externa con la banca comercial internacional 1989/92." Unpublished paper, Banco Central del Paraguay, Asunción.

Discussion of the History of Paraguay 1

Roberto Chang
Rutgers University and National Bureau of Economic Research

Let me start by confessing that, before reading this chapter, I knew virtually nothing about Paraguay. Happily, that has now changed: after studying this chapter, I am now familiar with several interesting facts and issues about Paraguay's macrodevelopments since 1960. In this sense, I find the chapter rewarding and instructive. We should thank the authors for producing their work, which should become a reference for students of the region.

The chapter examines a time span of more than half a century, breaking that long period into four smaller subperiods. Focusing on the subperiods helps the analysis of short- and medium-term phenomena. One cost, however, is that it prevents a discussion of longer-term issues, which I would have enjoyed. I was surprised, for example, to learn that Paraguay's average growth rate during the whole period was 2.4 percent on average. This performance ranks in the middle of the Latin American pack, which I had not expected, having heard over the years that Paraguay's economy was a stagnating one because of political events combined with being landlocked. Perhaps those factors may have played a much smaller role than I would have guessed. On the other hand, as the authors remark at the end of the chapter, Paraguay's per capita income level remains significantly below the average level for the region: no Paraguayan growth miracle has occurred in the half century under study. This raises the question of the determinants of Paraguay's growth rate and, in particular, whether access to the sea has or has not been a significant obstacle.

Instead of exploring such long-run issues, the chapter's main focus is on how short-run macroaggregates, especially inflation, may be linked to fiscal imbalances and the way those imbalances have been financed. Figure 2 in the chapter shows how Paraguay's inflation rate, which averaged very small levels in the 1960s, exhibited two acute but short-lived bursts in the 1970s. Inflation became more of a chronic problem in the 1980s, settling in the 30–40 percent per year range. The beginning of the 1990s saw a drastic correction, to the 10–20 percent range; since then, inflation has fallen slowly but steadily, and now it is in the single digits.

Table 1 is suggestive of a link between the evolution of inflation and the financing of the budget. The table shows that the government's financing needs were about the same

(2.7–2.8 percent of GDP per year) during the 1960–80 and 1981–90 subperiods. There is a noticeable difference between the subperiods, however, in that seigniorage revenue increased from 1.6 percent per year in 1960–80 to 2.4 percent per year in 1981–90. A plausible conjecture, then, is that one should be able to find some econometric evidence of a connection between increases in seigniorage and inflation. Likewise, government finances have been roughly balanced since 1990, allowing seigniorage to fall to 1 percent of GDP. Again, this suggests searching for some correlation between the fall in seigniorage and the fall in inflation in the data for the subperiods after 1990.

As we review these statistics, we should note that the magnitudes are quite small. The increase in seigniorage revenue in the 1980s relative to the previous two decades is less than 1 percent of GDP. One wonders what kind of mechanism can amplify the increase in seigniorage so that it translates into 40 percent inflation. This is perhaps why the chapter offers only a few results in terms of formal statistical tests of the correlation between inflation and fiscal imbalances. One of them is a zero correlation between inflation and the total fiscal deficit in the 1980s and a 0.22 correlation between inflation and the deficit of public companies. These results indicate that the link between fiscal imbalances and inflation is quite weak, in spite of the less formal evidence in Figure 2 and Table 1.

In fact, the evolution of inflation in Figure 2 suggests that there may be other, more empirically important, factors underlying the increases in inflation before 1990. The first one is the behavior of oil prices. The two inflationary spikes in Paraguay in the 1970s coincide tightly with the first and second OPEC oil shocks, which also caused inflation to increase in the United States and elsewhere. The second factor was the Latin American debt crisis that started with the 1982 Mexican default. As we know, the 1980s was a lost decade for many Latin American countries, some of which experienced hyperinflationary episodes. It is hard to believe that Paraguay would have been immune to contagion effects during this period, even if its fiscal deficit had been in perfect balance.

All in all, the Paraguayan experience between 1960 and 1990 remains somewhat of a puzzle. But to me, in fact, the puzzle is not whether fiscal imbalances can explain the increase in inflation in the 1980s but, rather, how it was that Paraguay did *not* have triple-digit inflation and could limit seigniorage to *only* 2.4 percent. In this regard, I think that future research may benefit from a comparison of Paraguay's experience against others in the region.

The chapter's discussion of Paraguay after 1990 is dominated by policy reforms, especially those regarding the central bank's legal status, and by the impact of financial liberalization and crises. The 1992 constitution placed strict limits on the central bank's ability to finance government deficits. In 1995, a new central bank charter established "maintaining the value of the currency" as the single objective of the bank. More recently, starting in 2004, an inflation-targeting regime has been gradually implemented.

In view of the steady fall in inflation since the early 1990s, one is tempted to conclude that these reforms were instrumental in lowering inflation. Nevertheless, such a conclusion, while plausible, warrants more scrutiny, at least in view of two facts. First, Figure 2 shows that inflation already started a steep fall in 1991—that is, before the 1992 constitution—hence raising the question of whether the timing of the constitution and other legal reforms is consistent with the view that those reforms were the main drivers of the reduction in inflation. Second, inflation fell after 1990 in many Latin American countries, of which some did not reform their central bank frameworks. Here, once more, a comparative perspective may prove useful in future research.

The chapter stresses that a key development after 1990 was the growth of financial intermediation, made possible by deregulation aimed at overcoming financial repression. Starting in 1995 and until 2003, the financial system was hit by a sequence of runs and attacks, which according to one estimate resulted in the loss of more than 15 percent of GDP. The discussion in the chapter suggests that financial fragility and crises during this period mostly reflected policy errors following financial liberalization, including an inadequate deposit insurance policy and weak supervision and regulation. But this perspective by and large ignores that the period was characterized by financial instability in virtually all emerging markets, including Argentina, Brazil, and Uruguay, Paraguay's main economic partners. One then wonders to what extent the financial crisis in Paraguay was driven by contagion and the general retrenchment of capital flows from the region rather than by policy mistakes.

At the end, this chapter left me convinced that Paraguay has been surprisingly tranquil in macroeconomic terms since 1960, with the exception perhaps of the financial liberalization–growth–crash episode of 1995–2003. There were some fiscal and monetary imbalances, yes, but they seem to have been quite small, especially when compared with neighboring countries. And the outcomes, especially in terms of inflation, were correspondingly tame for Latin American standards. True, inflation rates rose to 40 percent in the eighties, but at that time Paraguay's neighbors were dealing with rates in the triple digits or worse.

From that viewpoint, I find somewhat strained the authors' conclusion that the evidence shows that Paraguay "follows the conceptual framework of 'A Framework for Studying the Monetary and Fiscal History of Latin America' reasonably well, in that the high and volatile inflation that ensued since the mid-1970s to the late 1980s coincided with the period of large fiscal deficits that were partially financed by the central bank . . . [and that] the permanent reduction in inflation that started in the early 1990s coincides with a change in the institutional framework that made the central bank independent and with a more conservative fiscal policy." To convince us that these are more than rough coincidences, future research should center on developing more formal evidence establishing the hypotheses that the authors maintain in this chapter and assessing their importance relative to other, natural alternatives.

Discussion of the History of Paraguay 2

Pablo Andrés Neumeyer
Universidad Torcuato Di Tella

Paraguay is the country with the best macroeconomic performance in the book's sample of eleven Latin American countries.[1] Figure 1 shows that, judging performance by the average inflation rate and the average per capita growth rate of each country in the sample, Paraguay is the clear winner. Paraguay's growth was a close second to Chile's. Per capita income grew from 26 percent of the eleven-country average in 1960 (the lowest in the sample) to 42 percent of the sample average. The average inflation rate for Paraguay in the sample period was the lowest in the region at 10.2 percent per year. This chapter on the monetary and fiscal history of Paraguay tells the story of the quest for stability of one of the poorest countries in Latin America.

A notable aspect of Paraguayan monetary history is its political will to keep inflation low. Figure 2 illustrates how low Paraguayan inflation was relative to its peers in the region. These comments center on the policies that allowed Paraguay to accomplish nominal stability. From an analytical point of view, it is useful to distinguish three monetary regimes in Paraguay. Between 1960 and 1980, there was a fixed exchange rate regime; between 1981 and 1990, the central bank financed government deficits; and after 1992, an independent central bank conducted monetary policy to keep inflation low.

Inflation under a Fixed Exchange Rate

The guaraní was officially pegged to the U.S. dollar at a rate of 126 guaraní per U.S. dollar between October 1960 and February 1984.[2] Despite the fixed exchange rate, Paraguay suffered two bouts of inflation during this period. These bouts of inflation were the result of real shocks accommodated by the monetary dynamics inherent in fixed exchange rate regimes. We can write the price level as $P = p_n \alpha E P^*$ where E is the exchange rate, p_n is the relative price of nontraded goods in terms of tradable goods, foreign prices are denoted by P^*, and α is the share of nontraded goods in consumer expenditures. Thus under a fixed exchange rate regime, fluctuations in domestic inflation are the result of real shocks affecting the relative price of nontraded goods (the inverse of the real exchange rate depicted in Figure 11 in the chapter) and of variations in foreign prices. Figure 3

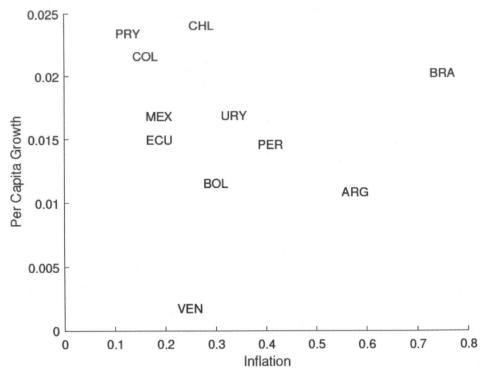

Figure 1. Inflation and per capita growth

Source: World Development Indicators from the World Bank

Note: Per capita growth is the average over the nonmissing values in the sample period 1960–2017 of the log difference between GDP per capita measured in local currency units in consecutive years. Inflation is the analogue for the consumer price index.

shows the evolution of inflation in Paraguay, the U.S. producer price index, and oil prices (right scale) while Paraguay was under a fixed exchange rate. It shows that the two large spikes in inflation in 1974 and 1979 are associated with imported inflation. Figure 11 in the chapter also shows a significant real appreciation of the guaraní between 1971 and 1981. This appreciation is likely to have been the consequence of large expenditures in nontradable goods associated with the construction of the Itaipú hydroelectric dam. Table 1 shows the magnitude of the expenditures made by the binational entity that built the Itaipú dam as a share of GDP as well as the evolution of aggregate gross fixed capital formation.

The endogeneity of the money supply inherent in a fixed exchange rate regime provided the monetary fuel for the inflation spikes. Under the rules of the fixed exchange rate regime, the increase in the nominal demand for money due to an increase in p_n and P^* is automatically translated into an increase in the money supply, implemented through the purchase of international reserves.[3] In the case of Paraguay, direct credit from the central bank to the private sector was also a source of expansion of the monetary base during the two spikes in inflation in the 1970s. On the liability side, commercial bank reserves

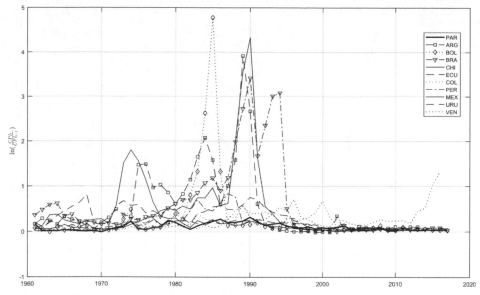

Figure 2. Inflation in Latin America

Source: World Development Indicators from the World Bank

Note: Inflation measured as the log difference of the consumer price index between two consecutive years.

at the central bank grew considerably as a share of the monetary base due to increases in reserve requirements (i.e., financial repression). Seigniorage during this period was quite high, averaging 1.9 percent per year (see Table 1 in the chapter), and was mainly used to accumulate reserves.[4] Deficits were financed with foreign debt, which started at around 10 percent of GDP in 1960 and practically doubled by 1980.

Monetary Financing of Deficits

Paraguay's nominal stability tumbled in the 1981–90 period as inflation averaged 23 percent in the decade with a peak of 44 percent in 1989. In spite of this, Paraguay's inflation was among the lowest in the sample of eleven Latin American countries during this period. For example, the average inflation for Paraguay's neighbors, Argentina, Bolivia, and Brazil, in this decade was in the triple digits (see Figure 2).

Several shocks disturbed the Paraguayan economy, putting it off balance. The end of construction in Itaipú and major devaluations in Brazil and Argentina increased pressure for a depreciation of the domestic currency. The debt buildup of the previous period, the real devaluation, and a drop in government revenues stressed public borrowing. As a result, the central bank financed the Treasury issuing money, and the Treasury used the central bank reserves to service the public debt. This simultaneous growth of domestic credit and the servicing of the public debt induced a rapid fall in international reserves and a succession of devaluations consistent with Krugman's balance of payments

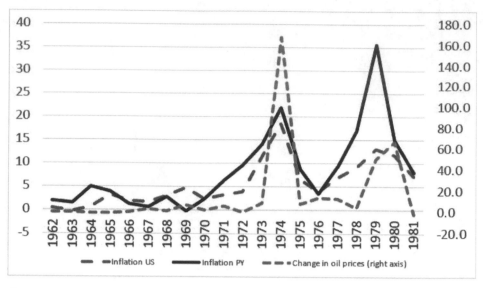

Figure 3. Oil shocks

Source: World Development Indicators from the World Bank

Note: U.S. Inflation is measured by the producer price index.

Table 1. Investment and other expenditures on Itaipú (% of GDP)

	1975	1976	1977	1978	1979	1980	1981	1982	1983	1984	1985
Itaipú	3.0	4.5	7.4	8.0	8.1	6.3	5.4	5.4	4.3	2.9	1.8
Investment	19	20	21	23	24	24	25	22	18	19	18

Source: Charotti, Hevia, and Neumeyer (2017).

Note: Itaipú is the ratio of investment and other operational expenditures of the Itaipú Binational entity to nominal GDP. It only includes expenditures paid in Paraguay. Investment is the ratio of nominal gross fixed capital formation to nominal GDP.

model (Krugman 1979). Between 1981 and 1985, the cumulative central bank credit to the Treasury added up to almost 6 percent of GDP.

The low inflation in Paraguay relative to its peers in the 1980s is explained by the relatively low deficits (2.2 percent of GDP on average for the decade) and by its decision to partially service the public debt. In 1985, the government decided to fall into arrears in servicing the public debt as a way of reducing public expenditures and, hence, the need for the monetary financing of deficits.

Paraguay's inflation could have been even lower. The ratio of the average seigniorage for this period, 1.9 percent of GDP, to the average monetary base, 11 percent of GDP, implies a steady-state annual inflation rate of 17 percent.[5] Inflation was higher due to a systematic fall of the monetary base from 15 percent of GDP in 1978 to 7 percent of GDP in 1991, a consequence of an increase in the cost of holding money and of a continuous reduction in reserve requirements. This is the flip side of the monetary dynamics of the previous two decades, when the monetary base was rising as a share of GDP. The government's revenues from money creation in this high-inflation period were the same as in the previous two decades of nominal stability.

Central Bank Independence

Paraguay initiated a series of economic reforms after a coup ended President Alfredo Stroessner's thirty-four-year dictatorship in February 1989. The most important of these reforms, from the perspective of this book, were the adoption of a new democratic constitution in 1992, which established the independence of the central bank, and a fiscal reform. Tax revenues increased by 3 percent of GDP in 1989 and by 9 percent of GDP in 1990. Thereafter, they grew at the same speed as expenditures, yielding ten years of budget surpluses. The government also negotiated a settlement on the arrears on the foreign public debt.

On the monetary front, Paraguay adopted a monetary-based stabilization plan with a floating exchange rate. After an initial jump in the price level associated with increases in public utility prices and the removal of price controls, inflation fell from 44 percent in 1989 to 8 percent in 1995. Inflation then remained under 10 percent until Paraguay started

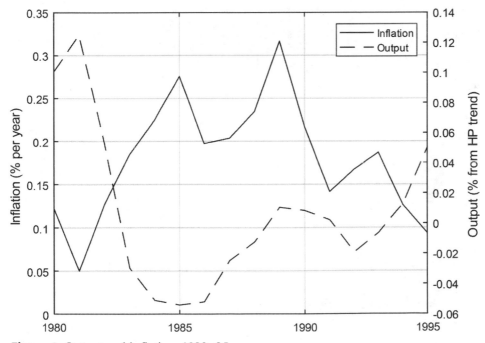

Figure 4. Output and inflation, 1980–95

Source: World Development Indicators from the World Bank

Note: Output is the logarithmic deviation from the Hodrick-Prescott (HP) trend, and inflation in year t is the logarithmic difference of the consumer price index between year t and year $t - 1$.

a gradual migration to an inflation-targeting regime in 2004. The initial inflation target was 5 percent plus or minus 2.5 percent, and the monetary policy instrument switched to the nominal interest rate. Contrary to conventional wisdom (see Calvo and Végh 1999), there is no evidence that this monetary-based stabilization plan was contractionary. Figure 4 shows that there is a mild V-shaped recession only three years after the beginning of the stabilization plan. Figure 5 plots output against inflation for the 1980–95 period. It shows a negative correlation between output and inflation.

The low-inflation regime survived two important challenges: a banking crisis and an increase of 50 percent in government expenditures.

The free market reforms that started in 1989 included a financial liberalization that freed interest rates and adopted a fractional reserve banking system. As was the case in the Southern Cone after the financial reforms in the 1970s (see Diaz-Alejandro 1985), the end of financial repression quickly turned into a financial crash. As in the Southern Cone before, an implicit deposit insurance without the appropriate institutions for effective bank supervision ended in a protracted banking crisis from 1995 to 2003. The cost of bailing out depositors in failed banks was almost 16 percent of GDP and was financed with central bank debt. GDP per person fell 12.5 percent between 1997 and 2002.

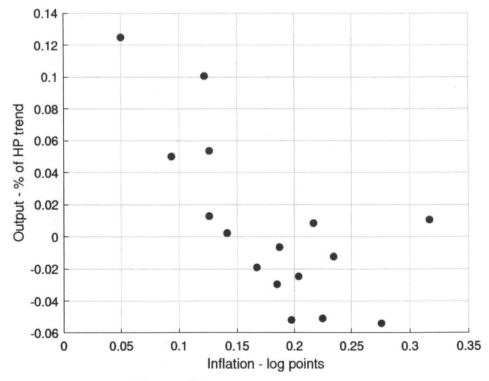

Figure 5. Output and inflation, 1980–95

Source: World Development Indicators from the World Bank

Note: Output is the logarithmic deviation from the Hodrick-Prescott (HP) trend, and inflation in year t is the logarithmic difference of the consumer price index between year t and year $t - 1$.

Starting in 1998, fiscal profligacy once again challenged monetary stability. Public expenditures climbed from 20 percent of GDP in 1998 to an average of 29 percent for the period 1999–2015 (see Figure 7 in the chapter), eliminating the primary surplus of the previous years.[6] The accumulated deficit between 1997 and 2002 was 7 percent of GDP. This led Paraguay to miss payments on its foreign debt. As was the case in the 1980s, the government decided not to raise revenues from inflation in order to pay foreign creditors. Paraguay emerged from this scenario under the umbrella of two successive precautionary standby agreements with the International Monetary Fund (2003–8). It adopted fiscal reforms to balance the budget and an inflation-targeting regime to consolidate price stability.

Final Remarks

My personal takeaways from reading about the Paraguayan experience are four. First, macroeconomic stability founded on small public deficits and conservative monetary policies enabled Paraguay to have the best macroeconomic performance in the eleven-country sample in this book. In times of financial stress, Paraguay chose to reprofile its foreign debt instead of abusing the monetary financing of government expenditures. Most notably, in 2003, the central bank managed to continue its disinflationary program in spite of the government's need to restructure its foreign debt. Second, fiscal deficits are not the only cause for inflation and money creation. In the 1970s, imported inflation and the fixed exchange rate regime brought about two inflationary spikes and a monetary expansion. Third, the control of monetary aggregates is an effective tool for managing inflation. Paraguay successfully lowered inflation after 1989 with a floating exchange rate and with no, or minimal, output costs. Fourth, Paraguay failed to learn from its neighbors the importance of bank regulatory and supervisory institutions to prevent banking crises. Unlike its monetary and fiscal policy, its banking policies in the 1990s replicated the mistakes of the liberalization of financial markets in Argentina and Chile two decades earlier.

Notes

1 The countries are Argentina, Bolivia, Brazil, Chile, Colombia, Ecuador, Mexico, Paraguay, Peru, Uruguay, and Venezuela for the period 1960–2017.

2 The source for the official exchange rate reported in the text is the International Monetary Fund. According to other sources, the exchange rate was pegged at 124 guaraníes per dollar between 1960 and 1975 and thereafter at 126 guaraníes per dollar. The exchange rate reported in the chapter differs from the official exchange rate because some restrictions on the foreign exchange market were in place. The average premium of the shadow exchange rate reported in the chapter during the period 1960–80 computed from yearly averages was 7 percent with a 4 percent

standard deviation. Starting in 1981, the black market premium was much higher, and the central bank introduced multiple exchange rates for different types of transactions.

3 To illustrate this, consider the following simple version of the quantity theory of money. The money demand is given by $Md = pnaEP^*y/v\,(i)$, where y is real output and $v\,(i)$ is the velocity of money, an increasing function of the nominal interest rate. Shocks to pn and P^* have a direct impact on the money demand.

4 I consider seigniorage to be

$$\frac{M_t - M_{t-1}}{Y_t} = m_t - m_{t-1} + m_{t-1}\left(1 - \frac{1}{(1+\pi_t)(1+g_t)}\right)$$

where M is the nominal quantity of money, m are real money balances, π is the inflation rate, and g is the growth rate of real output.

5 See endnote 4.

6 The increase in expenditures is from higher pensions and from public-sector wages. It excludes the cost involved in bailing out bank depositors.

References

Calvo, Guillermo A., and Carlos A. Végh. 1999. "Inflation Stabilization and BOP Crises in Developing Countries." In *Handbook of Macroeconomics*, vol. 1C, edited by John Taylor and Michael Woodford, 1531–614. Amsterdam: North Holland.

Charotti, Carlos Javier, Constantino Hevia, and Pablo Andrés Neumeyer. 2017. "The Macroeconomics of Itaipú." Paper presented at LACEA-LAMES 2017 Annual Meeting, November 9–11, 2017, Buenos Aires, Argentina.

Diaz-Alejandro, Carlos. 1985. "Good-Bye Financial Repression, Hello Financial Crash." *Journal of Development Economics* 19 (1–2): 1–24.

Krugman, Paul. 1979. "A Model of Balance-of-Payments Crises." *Journal of Money, Credit and Banking* 11 (3): 311–25.

Peru

The History of Peru

César Martinelli
George Mason University

Marco Vega
Banco Central de Reserva del Perú and Universidad Católica del Perú

Major fiscal and monetary events, 1960–2017

1967	Balance of payments crisis	**1988**	Hyperinflation
1975	Balance of payments crisis	**1990**	Hyperinflation
1978	International Monetary Fund (IMF) backed stabilization		Money-based stabilization
	Crawling peg	**1993**	New constitution, independence of central bank
1982	Default	**1997**	Brady Plan
1985	Heterodox stabilization attempt	**2001**	Inflation targeting

Introduction

Inflation in Peru has followed an extraordinary arc in the last half century, from a history of low inflation with periodic bouts of two-digit inflation, to chronic, accelerating inflation since the mid-1970s, to hyperinflation in the second half of the 1980s, culminating in the successful stabilization of the 1990s. By the turn of the century, deflation more than inflation was a worry for monetary authorities. The years of chronic inflation and hyperinflation were accompanied by a precipitous decline in GDP per capita, with a steady recovery in the last twenty-five years (see Figures 1 and 2). Thus the decade of the 1980s is marked by a hyperstagflation.

In this chapter, we provide an interpretation of these historical events through the lens of the monetarist approach developed in "A Framework for Studying the Monetary and Fiscal History of Latin America." From this perspective, inflation before the stabilization of 1990 reflects the fiscal need for inflationary taxation in a regime of fiscal dominance of monetary policy. Indeed, fiscal statistics reflect recurrent cyclical fiscal deficits up until 1990 (see Figure 3). Stabilization in the 1990s corresponds to a period of monetary policy independence and fiscal moderation.

We set the stage for the analysis with two accounting exercises. First, we perform a growth accounting exercise, breaking down changes in GDP per worker into several components. The exercise shows that a massive productivity slowdown coincides with

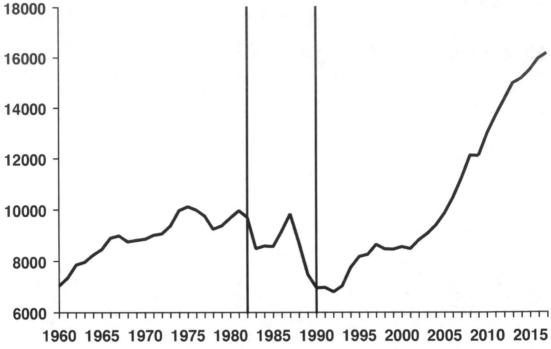

Figure 1. GDP per capita

Note: Measured in soles of 2007. (See online appendix available at http://manifold.bfi.uchicago.edu/ for data sources for this and other figures.)

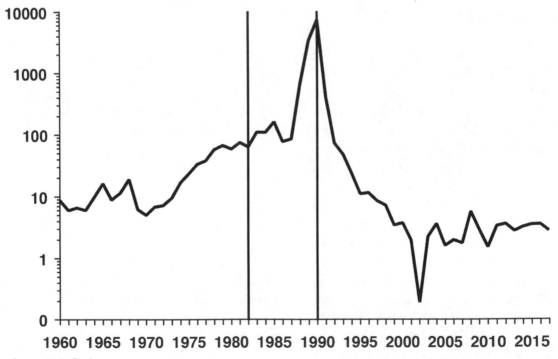

Figure 2. Inflation

Note: Inflation is measured in logarithmic scale.

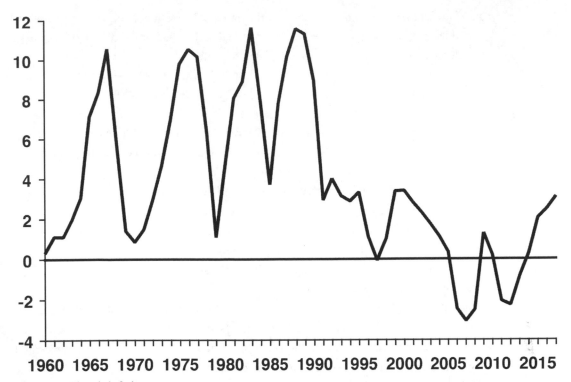

Figure 3. Fiscal deficit

Note: The fiscal deficit is defined as the negative of the economic result of the nonfinancial public sector as a percentage of GDP.

the stagflation. While unfavorable terms of trade, worse credit conditions for public debt, and unusual weather shocks contributed to the fall in GDP per worker, the productivity slowdown provides some evidence that there was a misallocation of resources as a result of the policies pursued, including extensive intervention of the state in the economy and the stop-and-go nature of fiscal policies before 1990.

Next, we perform a fiscal accounting exercise, breaking down financing of the government into several sources. The exercise shows that fiscal deficits were financed through inflationary taxation and through foreign debt accumulation, which over time yield an increasing need to rely on inflation. Correspondingly, seigniorage collected by the government increased until the second half of the 1980s. Consistent with a monetarist interpretation, the stagflation period exhibited larger seigniorage and a larger flow of government financing as a percentage of GDP than the preceding and subsequent periods. Stabilization in the 1990s corresponded to a fall in seigniorage to negligible levels, consistent with the interpretation of a regime change.

We then turn our attention to the policies adopted before, during, and after the stagflation, complementing the monetarist approach with an institutional perspective. We place the origin of fiscal difficulties in the pent-up demand for redistribution, for the provision of public services, and for public investment against the background of a small state with little tax collection and administration capabilities. To some extent, chronic fiscal difficulties and accompanying inflation reflect, from our point of view, a process of social learning to live within the realities of fiscal budget balance and the (still ongoing) development of modern monetary and fiscal institutions.

Two extreme policy experiments, in 1968–75 and in 1985–90, reflected a fundamental mistrust in market allocations and price incentives. There was demand by both large social groups and intellectual elites for the government to engage in fine-tuning the economy by providing "correct" incentives as opposed to those signaled by markets. The 1980s, in particular, correspond to a period of "heterodox" policies, including the attempted use of price controls and multiple exchange rates to abate inflation, with unintended, counterproductive results. The disastrous events of the late 1980s, including the hyperinflation, may have been determinant in the change in popular attitudes regarding economic policy. Expectations turned against interventionism first as revealed by the behavior of agents in the market, then in the climate of public opinion, and, last, in the plans of politicians.

The last quarter-century since the stabilization has witnessed for the most part macroeconomic stability and a robust resumption of the country's growth. Problems other than monetary mismanagement have become the focus of public opinion, notably the perennially difficult relationship between the executive and legislative branches and the remarkable extent of political and judicial corruption. One can only hope that the analogy of inflation as temporary growing pains in the development of modern institutions extends to other areas as well.

The remainder of this chapter is organized as follows. In the second and third sections we present our growth and fiscal accounting exercises, and the fourth discusses the onset of inflation. In the fifth section, we discuss the period of high inflation and the "policy follies" of the mid- to late 1980s, and the sixth addresses the end of the high inflation period and monetary policy since that time. The seventh section turns to conclusions and challenges suggested by the Peruvian experience. We describe our data sources in the online appendix available at http://manifold.bfi.uchicago.edu/.

Growth Accounting

It is tempting to directly relate the inflation and productivity performance evidenced in Figures 1 and 2 to the policy decisions taken in Peru. From this viewpoint, the damaging policies that begat high inflation and then hyperinflation would also be responsible for the decline in productivity. To explore this viewpoint, we follow Kehoe and Prescott (2007) to perform a growth accounting exercise. From an aggregate Cobb-Douglas production function with share of labor $1 - \theta$ and total factor productivity $A_t \gamma^{(1-\theta)t}$, we can derive the following expression for output per worker:

$$\ln y_t = (\gamma - 1)t + \frac{1}{1-\theta} \ln A_t + \frac{\theta}{1-\theta} \ln(k_t / y_t) + \ln h_t, \tag{1}$$

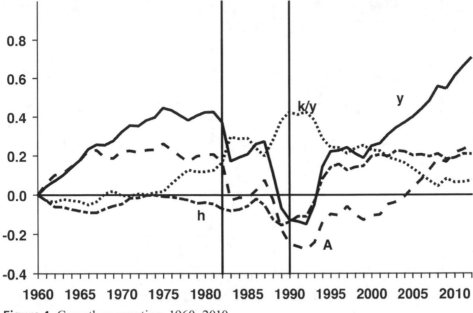

Figure 4. Growth accounting, 1960–2010

where y_t, k_t, and h_t are GDP, capital stock, and total hours worked per working-age person. The first two terms in the right-hand side of equation (1) describe the trend and stochastic productivity factors. In Figure 4 we use the decomposition given by equation (1) with data from Peru.[1]

In typical depressions, such as that in the United States in 1929–39 or Argentina in 1980–90, the ratio k_t / y_t rises because the denominator falls sharply while the capital stock remains stable (see Kehoe and Prescott 2007). Something similar happens in Peru, as observed in Figure 4. Depressions differ in the importance of productivity versus hours worked. In the case of the Peruvian depression, productivity fell way below the level at the starting point in 1960. While the contribution of total hours also fell during the recession, as in the case of Argentina in 1980–90, the bulk of the depression is explained by the massive productivity slowdown.

The growth accounting exercise illustrated in Figure 4 supports the idea that the radical reforms of the 1970s led to a misallocation of resources behind the massive drop in total factor productivity. They could be considered as a supply shock, affecting not only the cyclical component of output but also its trend (as in Aguiar and Gopinath 2007). A plausible channel is that the financing of the public sector crowded out the private sector. In the public sector, investment decisions may not have been led by efficiency considerations. Moreover, the financing of the private sector was distorted as the government put caps on interest rates and favored certain sectors. Government activity might have worsened the misallocation of resources typically observed in developing economies (Restuccia 2013), which in turn might have been behind the fall in productivity. The stop-and-go nature of fiscal cycles may have affected the quality of public investment, which was subject to deep cuts during fiscal adjustments. Finally, high inflation by itself may have

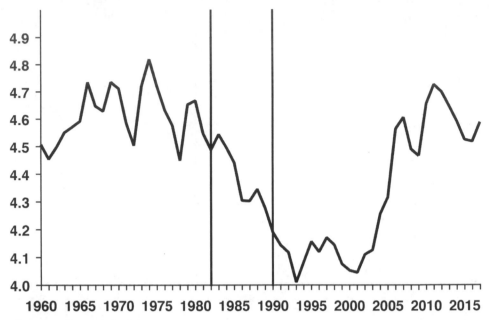

Figure 5. Terms of trade
Note: Calculated by the BCRP.

had consequences for productivity, since real resources were wasted as economic agents dealt with price volatility and exchange rate risk (see, e.g., Tommasi 1999).

The terms of trade series in Figure 5 may advise a somewhat nuanced stance. Movements in the terms of trade for Peru reflect mineral prices determined in world markets and largely exogenous from the viewpoint of the Peruvian economy. Terms of trade for Peru took a steep decline from the mid-1970s to the early 1990s. World interest rates also hiked in the 1980s. Thus the hyperinflation and the deep recession of the 1980s coincided with a very adverse external environment. To the extent that an important part of production is linked to the extraction of natural resources with prices set in international markets, a declining pattern of these prices over protracted periods weakened the economy by various channels. Government revenues fell, and concurrently foreign credit to the government became more expensive, which in turn dampened public investment. Private investment also suffered because of higher aggregate uncertainty and, in the case of the mining sector, lower income prospects. The fall in investment may also be linked to the fall in total factor productivity, as suggested by Castillo and Rojas (2014).

There has been some debate about the role of bad external conditions versus bad economic policies in the Peruvian depression.[2] In the words of Llosa and Panizza (2015), bad external conditions, mistaken policies, and supply shocks, such as El Niño of 1982–83, combined to create a "perfect storm." Note, however, that terms of trade remained stagnant until 2000, while growth resumed a decade before, after the change in orientation of economic policies. Our empirical exercise and available evidence indicate that policy responses to bad external conditions magnified the depression.

Fiscal Accounting, Public Debt, and Seigniorage

The increased role of the state in the economy and the implementation of the structural reforms attempted by successive administrations from the 1960s were in need of financing. The foremost preferred source of domestic financing was the central bank. At the time, this was perceived as a commonsense solution in Peru as everywhere else (see Goodhart 2011). In Peru, it was a customary role of the central bank to grant credit to state-owned sectoral banks with the ostensible purpose of promoting growth. These credit lines were a usual source of base money creation. Banks would then lend to private and public firms. Most of the central bank credit ended up as credit to the nonfinancial public sector.

The favored source of external financing was external debt, either in the form of bonds or as syndicated loans from governments, multinationals, and foreign private banks. This type of credit was relatively cheap in the postwar period; there was abundant dollar liquidity, which went toward developing economies and especially to Latin America. Peru and other countries committed what Hausmann and Panizza (2003) have called the "original sin" of taking debt in foreign currency instead of raising external debt denominated in their own currency. As in other cases, a determinant for the incapacity to take debt in its own currency was the relatively small size of the Peruvian economy.

To study the dynamics of public finance, we follow this volume's chapter "A Framework for Studying the Monetary and Fiscal History of Latin America" to perform a fiscal accounting exercise. Indexed debt has not been quantitatively important in Peru,[3] so for the purpose of the budget constraint analysis, we set it equal to zero. The budget constraint equation in that chapter can be arranged in terms of flows to obtain

$$\Delta\theta_t^n + \Delta\theta_t^*\xi_t + \Delta m_t + m_{t-1}\left(1 - \frac{1}{\pi_t g_t}\right) =$$

$$d_t + \theta_{t-1}^n\left(\frac{R_{t-1}}{\pi_t g_t} - 1\right) + \theta_{t-1}^*\xi_t\left(\frac{r_{t-1}^*}{\pi_t^\omega g_t} - 1\right). \tag{2}$$

The left-hand side of equation (2) represents the *sources of financing*. The term $\Delta\theta_t^n$ is the change in domestic gross debt as a percentage of GDP, $\Delta\theta_t^*$ is the change in foreign gross debt as a percentage of GDP (expressed in U.S. dollars), ξ_t is the real exchange rate, Δm_t is money creation as a percentage of GDP, and the term $m_{t-1}\left(1 - \frac{1}{\pi_t g_t}\right)$ is inflation tax, where m_{t-1} is the previous period money supply as a percentage of GDP, π_t is gross inflation (i.e., the ratio between current and past prices), and g_t is gross GDP growth. The sum $\Delta m_t + m_{t-1}\left(1 - \frac{1}{\pi_t g_t}\right)$ is seigniorage, and its main component is inflation tax.

The right-hand side represents the *overall fiscal deficit*. The term d_t represents an augmented primary deficit measured as a percentage of GDP and is equal to the primary deficit minus implicit or explicit transfers such as privatization proceeds,[4] which became relevant in the 1990s. The term R_{t-1} is the gross nominal interest rate on domestic debt, r_t^* is the gross nominal interest rate on foreign debt, and π_t^ω is gross tradable inflation, so the last two terms in equation (2) are the domestic and foreign public debt interest payments. In order for equation (2) to hold exactly, the level of transfers adjusts as a residual. This residual is obtained by comparing the total government financing on the left-hand side and the fiscal deficit—that is, the economic result of the nonfinancial public sector (with a sign change), which, in theory, should be the right-hand side of equation (2).

Figure 6 plots the total flow of government financing (left-hand side of equation (2)) and its two most important components for the Peruvian case: foreign debt financing (slashed line) and inflation tax (dotted line). During the stagflation period, the flow of government financing is both higher and more volatile than before and after this period. The volatility is explained in part by (1) real exchange rate volatility, affecting the valuation in soles of foreign debt financing, and (2) the behavior of GDP. During high to hyperinflation, measuring relative prices such as the real exchange rate becomes problematic. The peaks of government financing in 1983 and 1988 correspond to falls in GDP of 11.9 percent and 16.8 percent. (In 1989 GDP further shrinks by 14.7 percent.)

Before the stagflation of 1982–90, there is a slow buildup in government financing that is broken in 1978 as a reflection of stability measures adopted at the time. All sources of government financing shrink then, except inflation tax. which stabilized temporarily. After some respite in the early 1980s, inflation tax continues increasing until the late 1980s. As seen in Figure 7, hyperinflation coincides with very high levels of inflation tax, consistent with a monetarist view. After the stagflation, all sources of government financing, including inflation tax, fell sharply, consistent with the view of a regime change away from fiscal dominance around 1990.

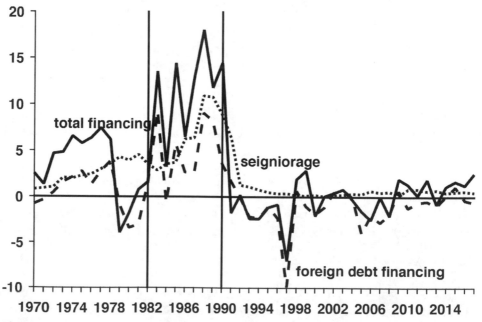

Figure 6. Government financing and selected components, percent of GDP

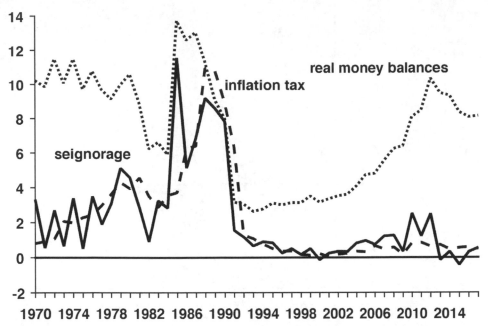

Figure 7. Real money balances, inflation tax, and seigniorage, percent of GDP

Understanding shorter-term fluctuations in the relation between inflation and sei-gniorage, of course, requires taking into account the role of expectations in the desire of the public to hold real money balances. In the mid-1980s, inflation abates temporarily during the initial phase of the heterodox plan as money balances increase, even though inflation tax is increasing. In the late 1980s, per contra, inflation tax starts falling while hyperinflation ensues, as the public flees the local currency in favor of foreign currency.

Figure 8 shows that domestic debt is negligible, while external debt grows from about 25 percent in 1975 to a peak above 75 percent at the end of the 1980s. As in the case of government financing, short-term fluctuations in external debt as a percentage of GDP in the 1980s are a consequence of movements in the real exchange rate and GDP. The three peaks observed in the solid line correspond to three real exchange devaluation years. The first occurs in 1978 with a real devaluation of 20 percent, preceded by two years of lower devaluations. The second peak occurs in 1985, corresponding to a 29 percent real devaluation. The last peak occurs in 1988 with a 35 percent devaluation.

Isolating the effects of movements in the real exchange rate, public debt grew through the stagflation (Figure 9). The country had been in arrears since the early 1980s, explicitly so since 1985, so there was no new foreign credit to the government. As argued in "A Framework for Studying the Monetary and Fiscal History of Latin America," higher debt ratios may hamper the capacity to rely on more debt financing. In a sense, there is a limit to the capacity of the government to rely on external debt; reaching the limit implies ever more reliance on seigniorage, which is the key source of inflation.

We can observe two periods of fiscal effort to reduce the debt ratio: a temporary one in 1978–82 and a persistent one from 1990 onward, which resulted in a sustainable debt

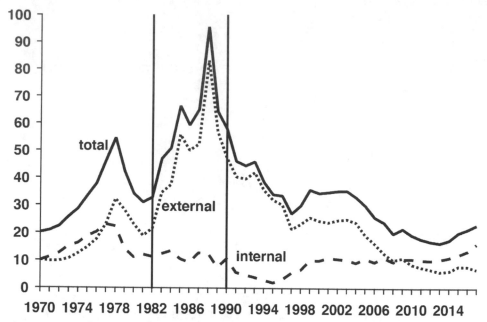

Figure 8. Domestic and external debt, percent of GDP

pattern. Public debt with foreign creditors was successfully renegotiated in the 1990s, with considerable help from foreign governments that were eager to ease Peru back into the global financial system after the period of default.[5] Given the high debt-to-GDP ratio, in relation to the ability of the government to collect taxes, the renegotiation of the debt appears as the linchpin of the successful stabilization effort. News about the start of the renegotiation contributed to the improvement of credibility of the stabilization program and the abatement of inflation expectations.[6]

The overall picture of government financing in Figure 6 is affected by the existence of transfers that are not fully accounted for in the official data and because of changes in the real exchange rate. Recall that transfers adjust in equation (2) as a residual. Moreover, regarding the debt service, the specific interest rates are not unique because of the various maturities and interest rates implied for each maturity.

Figure 10 plots the fiscal deficit and the total flow of government financing (left-hand side of equation (2)), and Figure 11 the transfers obtained as a residual. During the 1970s and the first half of the 1980s, the fiscal deficit is larger than the flow of government financing. This means that the government is financed from other sources; a key source is the credit of the financial public sector. As mentioned, the central bank would lend to state-owned banks, and these banks would lend to the nonfinancial public sector. In essence, this lending represents domestic debt that has not been properly recorded as such, nor repaid, and therefore acts as a hidden money source of financing. If we had included it in the overall debt position, total debt would have been much higher.

During the second half of the 1980s, per contra, the fiscal deficit is smaller than the flow of government financing. Some of the flow of government financing reflects hidden

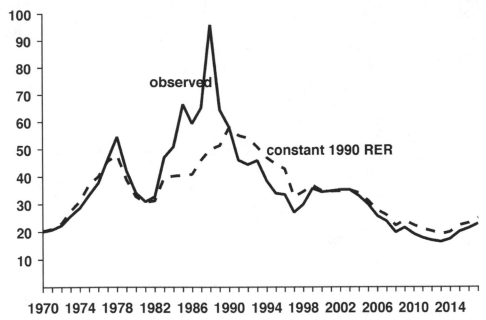

Figure 9. Counterfactual case of constant real exchange rate (RER), percent of GDP

subsidies by the central bank to imports and to credit transfers that were not properly accounted for as part of the fiscal deficit.[7]

During the 1990s, the fiscal deficit is again larger than the flow of government financing. The adjustment is made by privatization proceeds, as illustrated in Figure 11. The sale of state-owned enterprises is considered as a financing item "below the line" that implies less need for debt financing. Another important source of transfers since 1999 is a fiscal stability fund. We have performed a few counterfactuals regarding the level of debt, where transfers are kept at a level of zero, using information about transfers since 1990 (see online appendix available at http://manifold.bfi.uchicago.edu/).

The Onset of Inflation

Since independence, Peruvian economic history has been characterized by large export cycles linked to the boom and bust of the international prices of the raw materials exported by the country. At least until the 1960s, a small group of families, known locally as the *oligarquía*, owned the most important economic assets, sometimes in association with foreign capital. The oligarchy also held considerable political clout through patronage and influence over the army.[8]

In consonance with the concentration of wealth and political power, the Peruvian state was kept small. Fiscal revenue came from easy-to-collect taxes, such as import tariffs, fiscal stamps, and profit taxes. Until 1964, taxes were collected and government payments made through privately owned institutions. Official fiscal statistics were done

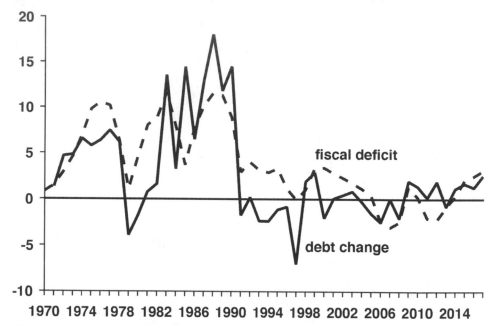

Figure 10. Fiscal deficit and government financing, percent of GDP

by the Office of the Comptroller General, which provided a monthly balance sheet of central government payments and cash receipts. Financial control over the decentralized agencies and public enterprises was difficult, for there was no standardized accounting.[9] Peru also lacked a tradition of government service.[10] In the terms of Besley, Ilzetzki, and Persson (2013), Peru was a "weak state," with a limited power to extract revenues from its citizens on a mass scale.

In spite of the apparent immobilism of Peru's economy and politics, the country underwent important changes in urbanization and education since the 1930s. The urban population went from 10 percent in 1930 to 47 percent in 1960 (United Nations 1969). Migration to the capital, Lima, from the highlands and the increase in the literacy rate deeply changed the franchise, since literacy was a requirement for voting. Reformist and radical ideas spread beyond intellectual elites, including to the upper echelons of the military. In 1963 a politician with an explicit reformist program, Fernando Belaúnde, was elected president.

The Belaúnde administration (1963–68) started an overhaul of public finance institutions, including the centralization of the financial management of the public sector in the newly created Banco de la Nación. The government engaged initially in a massive increase in expenditures for construction (roads and other public works) and outlays for education and health. The efforts of the administration to increase fiscal revenue were thwarted by the Congress, where the opposition was in the majority. The result was a "war of attrition" between the branches of government (see, e.g., Alesina and Drazen 1991; Martinelli and Escorza 2007). Efforts to attract long-term debt to finance public investment may have been thwarted by a conflict with a foreign oil company, IPC. Lacking

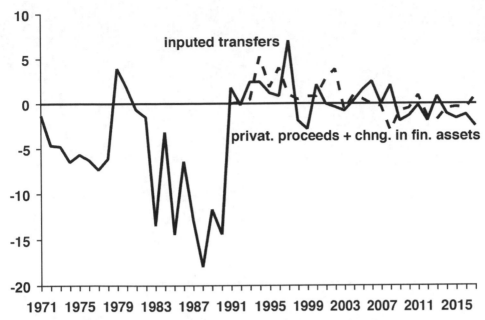

Figure 11. Imputed transfers and privatization proceeds, percent of GDP

any alternative, the expansion of public spending induced the central bank to increase domestic credit. With a regime of fixed exchange rates, inflation in domestic goods and losses in foreign currency reserves followed. A balance of payments crisis à la Krugman (1979) ensued, prompting a sizable exchange rate devaluation in 1967.

The devaluation of 1967 was the first in several years. A once-and-for-all devaluation episode works like a transitory shock on inflation. Given monetary conditions, inflation should have risen and fallen, as indeed was the case. From 1975 onward the exchange rate policy changed. Devaluations became more persistent and timed, as illustrated in Figure 12. Exchange rate increases no doubt fueled inflation in the tradable component of prices. An unfortunate consequence may have been the idea that devaluation and not monetary conditions *caused* inflation; later on, as we discuss, governments would try to curb inflation by fixing exchange rates and dealing with balance of payments difficulties via exchange controls.[11]

Congress finally relented and approved tax increases in 1968. The evolution of the fiscal deficit during the Belaúnde administration, including the closing of the fiscal gap starting in 1968, is the first cycle in Figure 3, and it is one of several such cycles. The economic crisis and frustration regarding unfulfilled promises by Belaúnde (such as land reform and a solution to the vexing conflict with IPC) contributed to a military coup in 1968.

The new military regime, the so-called Revolutionary Government of the Armed Forces (1968–75), started far-reaching institutional and structural reforms well beyond land redistribution. The role of the public sector in the economy expanded via the nationalization of private firms in oil, fishing, mining, food processing, and manufacturing. The reforms also included incentives to national investors to substitute imports and promote

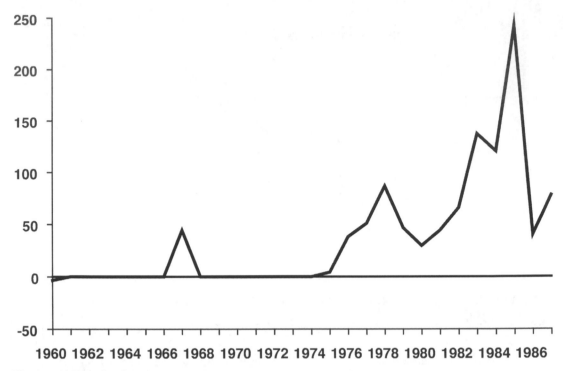

Figure 12. Devaluations

Note: Percentage increase in official exchange rate.

industrialization and extensive import controls. The ostensible purpose of the reforms was to broaden social and economic development and achieve social justice; indeed, the military dictatorship styled itself a "social democracy with full participation."[12] Though possibly well-meaning, the distortions introduced by extensive intervention[13] may help explain the dramatic fall in productivity in the economy in subsequent years.

During the first few years of the military dictatorship, current revenues remained stable, around 24 percent of GDP, while total expenditures rose from 25 percent of GDP to near 34 percent in 1974. Figures 13 and 14 illustrate the dramatic increase in expenditures and revenues of state-owned firms.[14] Behind the increase in expenditures was a major public investment effort, including big mining projects (Figure 15). Concurrently, financing of the public projects crowded out credit to the private sector.[15] Besides large public investment projects, a source of spending was an arms race between the military rulers of Peru and Chile, illustrated in Figure 16. Fiscal expansion was supported with inflationary financing and foreign debt accumulation.

Unfortunately, prices for Peruvian exports took a plunge, and balance of payments difficulties hit the country in 1974–75. Central bank reserves dropped, while the regime refused to contemplate a devaluation. A palace coup ensued, starting the so-called Second Phase of the Revolutionary Government of the Armed Forces (1975–80). The new military junta adopted a stabilization policy with the support of the International Monetary Fund, freeing the exchange rate and adopting drastic across-the-board spending cuts, including

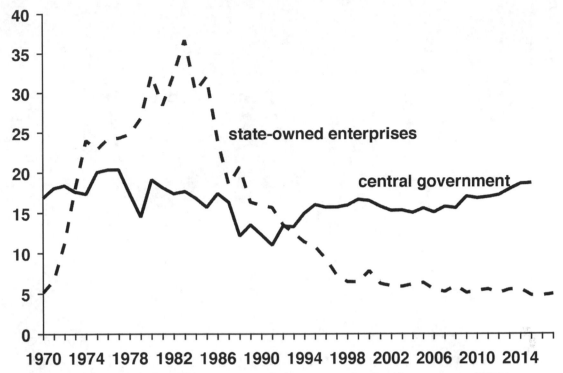

Figure 13. Expenditure of central government and state-owned enterprises, percent of GDP

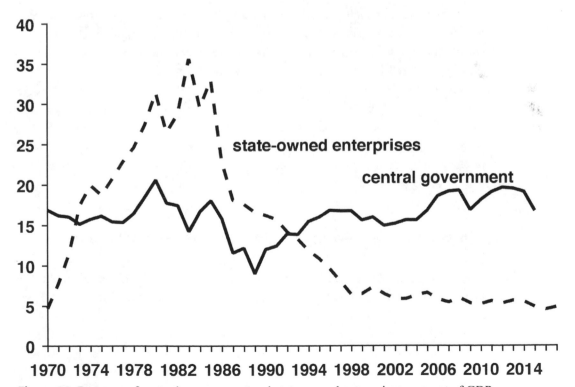

Figure 14. Revenue of central government and state-owned enterprises, percent of GDP

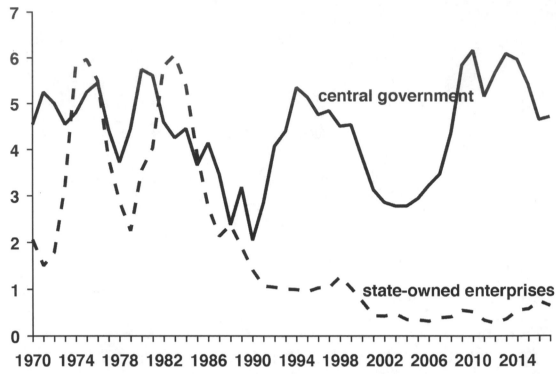

Figure 15. Capital expenditure of state-owned enterprises, percent of GDP

cuts in funding for ongoing investment projects. The cost of fiscal adjustment contributed to the increasing unpopularity of the government. After calling for elections to a constitutional assembly that was to enshrine the irreversible achievements of the military regime, followed by presidential elections, the military returned to the barracks in 1980.

The evolution of the fiscal deficit during military rule, lumping together both phases of the Revolutionary Government, corresponds to the second cycle in Figure 3. In spite of the fiscal effort, inflationary financing remained high during the Second Phase, corresponding to the plateau in the late 1970s in seigniorage in Figure 6. Accordingly, inflation remained high, reaching near 67 percent in 1979 and 59 percent in 1980. These were historical records for the country (see Table 3).

Supply Shocks, Policy Follies, and Hyperinflation

The elections of 1980 returned to government Fernando Belaúnde, the same politician that the military had deposed in 1968. The second Belaúnde administration (1980–85) started on a promising note, including recovering favorable international prices. As in the past, Belaúnde's second administration favored salary increases in the public sector and an increase in spending on some of the old favorite projects, this time financed with new foreign debt (see the uptick in Figure 9). From 1982 on, the government was hit by a combination of adverse shocks, including the drying out of foreign finance, worsening

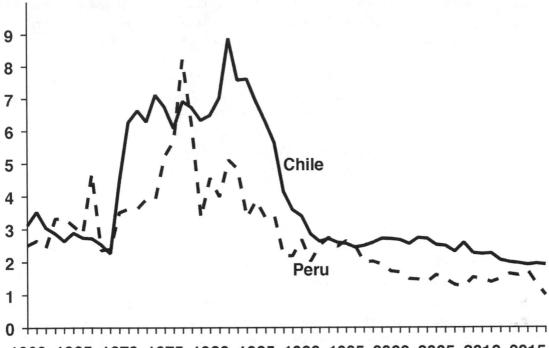

Figure 16. Military spending, percent of GDP

interest rates on the extant debt, and an extraordinary negative weather shock, El Niño of 1982–83. Policy responses included cuts in public investment, an undeclared policy of arrears in debt payments, and recourse to inflationary financing.

The rise and fall of the fiscal deficit during Belaúnde's second administration are visible as the third fiscal cycle in Figure 3. Inflation surpassed 100 percent in 1983 for the first time and reached 163 percent in 1985 (see Table 3). Though inflation became a concern of policy makers, a widespread view was that inflation was not necessarily a monetary phenomenon and could originate in cost pressure.[16]

The elections of 1985 installed the government of Alan García. The García administration (1985–90) embarked on an ambitious policy experiment dubbed the heterodox experiment or, as Dornbusch and Edwards (1990) put it, an experiment in macroeconomic populism.[17] Carbonetto et al. (1987) provide a blueprint for economic policy during the García administration. In their diagnosis, inflation on manufactured goods was a result of cost pressure. For those goods, the supply curve had a *negative* slope, with ample unused production capacity. A fiscal and monetary expansion, then, at the same time would increase production and reduce prices.

The Emergency Plan of 1985–86, detailed in Table 1, implemented the heterodox policies. The aim was to shut down inflationary expectations via a generalized price control and a freezing of the exchange rate while simultaneously easing credit to increase demand in the economy and achieve redistribution. In parallel, the policy of limiting debt payments contributed to relaxing the external constraint in the economy. The initial effect was a temporary recovery of GDP per capita and a lull in the inflation rate, both visible in Figures 1 and 2.[18] The initial lull in inflation is consistent with the idea of a cosmetic stabilization in the sense of Sargent, Williams, and Zha (2009)—that is, a reset in inflation and beliefs without a reduction in underlying seigniorage.

In fact, the heterodox program increased the need for inflationary financing through several channels. Freezing the prices of state-owned enterprises led to larger deficits of these firms. All exchange flows were controlled by the central bank; after the bank started losing reserves, it increased the exchange rate for exports above the one for imports. This was equivalent to a subsidy to imports, which was monetized. Interest rates to the Agrarian Bank were subsidized; the flow of credit to this bank was important.[19]

Monetizing the fiscal deficit and the losses of the central bank and state-owned enterprises were to have a strong impact on inflation, which rebounded from 1987 on, while international reserves were depleted. As a reaction, the government attempted to nationalize the banking industry, which was blamed for the failure of the program. Doubling down on failed policies seems to have been a version of the "gambling for resurrection" idea portrayed by Majumdar and Mukand (2004). In an extraordinary turn of events, popular resistance made impossible the takeover of the banking industry. The protests against the bank takeover seem to have been a turning point in popular opinion regarding the role of the state in the economy.[20]

Figure 17 illustrates the behavior of the official exchange rate and the black market exchange rate. The official exchange rate, known as Mercado Único de Cambios, was kept frozen until September 1988. Then an attempt to correct the exchange rate lag and lags in other controlled prices led to a 757 percent devaluation as part of a stabilization attempt popularly named "el Salinazo," after the then minister of finance, Abel Salinas. Successive devaluations reflect an attempt to correct the exchange rate gap. Multiple legal exchange rates other than the one still named Mercado Único de Cambios were introduced, with the central bank determining the appropriate rate for each transaction.

The monthly inflation rate in September 1988 was 114 percent (Figure 18). Peru had hit hyperinflation. Monthly inflation rates afterward hovered in between 23.05 percent and 48.64 percent. In July of 1990, the last month of the García administration, monthly inflation hit 63.23 percent.[21] The incoming administration of Alberto Fujimori implemented another large correction of exchange rates and controlled prices in August 1990, popularly named "el Fuji shock." The monthly inflation rate was 396.98 percent. We look at details of the stabilization of 1990 in the next section. It is instructive to notice, however, that unlike el Salinazo, el Fuji shock was followed by several weeks of deflation.[22] The reaction to the two big adjustments in controlled prices reflects different expectations; from our viewpoint, economic agents (correctly) anticipated a change in regime in 1990.

The conventional definition of hyperinflation is an inflation rate of at least 50 percent in a month. The hyperinflation ends when the monthly inflation falls below 50 percent and stays below that level for at least a year (Cagan 1956). Using such a metric, Peru experienced two hyperinflation episodes, September 1988 and July–August 1990.[23] In an environment of controlled prices, with rampant scarcity, black markets, and hoarding in anticipation of official price adjustments, the conventional definition may be inadequate.

Table 1. Heterodox Peru: August–September 1985

Fiscal policy	Monetary policy	Exchange rate policy
Reduction in selective taxes	Lending rate of commercial	Initial 12% devaluation and
Reduction in sales tax from	banks: gradual reduction	subsequent freeze of official
11% to 6%	from 280% to 40% annual	rate
Enhanced tax exemptions to	rate	Later, introduction of multiple
selected sectors on sales tax,	Saving rate (one-year deposits):	exchange rates for exports
import tariffs, and other taxes	gradual reduction from 107%	and finally for imports as
Freeze of public-sector prices	to 31%	well
and tariffs; in February	Lending rate by Agrarian	
1986, reduction in water and	Bank:	
electricity tariffs by 20%	Regular rate reduced from	
and in prices of petroleum	116% to 25%	
products by 10%	Zero interest rate for Andean	
Authorize Treasury bond	highland farmers	
issues		

Prices	Labor
Freeze of all prices	Periodic nominal hikes so as to reach a 7% annual increase in
Later periodic adjustments	real terms; in practice, minimum real wages rose 34% in the
and liberalization of most	seventeen-month period
agricultural prices	Tax exemption to employees on the share of income tax paid by
Creation of a price authority	them
(CIPA) coordinated by the	Two one-time interest-free loans to civil servants
Ministry of Finance	Reduction in probation period from three years to three months;
	stability laws
	Establishment of PROEM, allowing firms to hire temporary
	workers for up to two years without adhering to labor stability
	laws

Sources: Lago (1991), Velarde and Rodríguez (1992a)

It is worth noting that the expenditures and revenue of state-owned enterprises fell through the stagflation years (see Figures 13 and 14). State-owned enterprises were shocked on the revenue side by lagging prices and on the expenditure side, like the remainder of the public sector, by lagging salaries with respect to inflation. Tax revenues fell from about 12.20 percent of GDP in 1986 to 6.5 percent in 1989 as a consequence of the Olivera-Tanzi effect,[24] while expenditures fell because of lagging salaries. In a disorderly, painful way, fiscal adjustment started during the García administration, corresponding to the fourth and last fiscal cycle in Figure 3. The de facto retreat of the state from the economy during the hyperinflation is vividly described by Webb (1991).

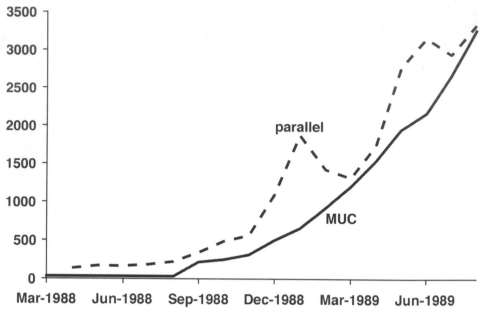

Figure 17. Official (Mercado Único de Cambios [MUC]) versus black market exchange rates

Inflationary expectations, however, would not budge until a perceived commitment to a regime change away from fiscal dominance of monetary policy.

Stabilization and Its Aftermath

By early 1990, the Peruvian economy and society were in disarray. Besides recession and hyperinflation, the country was hit by violent guerrillas, whose activities included murders, bombings, and blackouts. There was also considerable political uncertainty, with waning support for traditional political parties after the perceived failures of Belaúnde and García.

An unknown outsider, Alberto Fujimori, won the presidential runoff elections in June 1990. The Fujimori administration came to power without a coherent team of advisers, a program for governing, or any indication of who would hold the key positions in the government. In terms of the economic policy debate, two distinct sides emerged in the run-up to Fujimori's inauguration and the implementation of the economic program: one side favored an exchange rate–based stabilization program, while the other leaned toward a money-based program.

The monetary approach was not popular because it was associated with a deeper recession; the 1985 Bolivian stabilization, in particular, was a fresh case. Stabilization efforts in the early 1980s in the United States and the United Kingdom had relied on reducing the growth of the monetary base to fight relatively high levels of inflation for those countries, but these efforts were considered to have been costly. A hard exchange

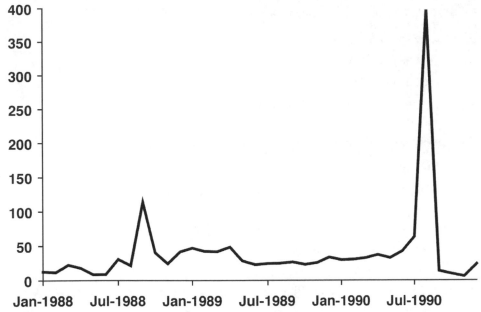

Figure 18. Monthly inflation and the hyperinflation episodes, percent

Note: Peaks in September 1988 and August 1990 correspond, respectively, to el Salinazo and el Fuji shock.

rate anchor, however, was hard to conceive given the demolition of government credibility during the preceding administration. There was also the perception that the correct exchange rate was hard to determine administratively, given the grave distortions during the previous years, so it was better to leave flexibility to the market. Without credibility and without reserves, the camp favoring a monetary-based stabilization, without any commitment to a particular number, predominated.

In August 1990, the long awaited stabilization program was announced via a national television broadcast. The dramatic closing line of the announcement, capturing the feeling of uncertainty about the results, was *"Que Dios nos ayude"* (May God help us). Key stabilization policies are detailed in Table 2. In contrast to other stabilization programs implemented in the region, the Peruvian program used a monetary anchor with an administered exchange rate. On the real side, the stabilization program took place along a drastic structural reform agenda aimed at deregulating markets and reducing the direct economic activity of the state. As a result, price controls were removed, along with subsidies and caps on interest rates. The capital market was liberalized, and the exchange market was unified.[25]

The stabilization program relied on two pillars. The first pillar was a strong commitment to cut inflationary fiscal financing. The government committed to not asking for any financing from the central bank, except for an emergency loan to cover the initial salary increases, which was repaid to the central bank in thirty days, as promised (Velarde and Rodríguez 1992a). Later, the Central Bank Organic Law of 1993 explicitly ruled out government financing by the central bank. The second pillar was a market-friendly

Table 2. Main stabilization policy measures, August 1990

Exchange rate policy
One-time exchange rate devaluation to a sufficiently high level
Since then, managed floating exchange rate regime
System of multiple exchange rates was unified
Most import restrictions were removed
The minimum tariff was set to 10% and the maximum to 50%

Monetary policy
A monetary anchor based on the control of the growth of base money, implemented through a yearly monetary program
A reduction in banking reserve requirements to alleviate financial repression; the marginal rate was reduced from 80% to 64%
Foreign currency deposits in domestic banks continued to be allowed
Interest rates for assets and liabilities in the banking system were allowed to be market determined

Fiscal policy
A set of fiscal austerity measures, including a ban on new procurement processes
Increases in regulated utility prices, controlled by state-owned enterprises: gasoline (3,040%), electricity (5,270%), water (1,318%), and others
Creation of the Budget Committee (Central Bank, Finance Ministry, and Revenue Authority) to ease the monetary control process
Removal of exemptions to value-added tax (VAT), excise taxes, and tariffs

Wages
Exceptional 100% bonus
Minimum wage was increased by 400%
Ban on new wage increases in the public sector until December

Source: Velarde and Rodríguez (1992b).

approach to policy that translated into freeing the exchange market after eliminating segmented (multiple) exchange rates, a reduction in tax and tariff dispersion, and the privatization of state-owned enterprises.

A new constitution, adopted in 1993, provided the institutional scaffolding for the change in policy regime. In the constitutional design, the budget sent by the executive branch to Congress has to be balanced. Loans from the central bank or from Banco de la Nación do not count as revenue, and new debt cannot cover current fiscal expenditures. Congress has no initiative to create or increase public spending, nor to pass taxes for predetermined purposes without a favorable report from the Treasury, and moreover the budget elaborated by the executive branch is enacted if Congress cannot pass the budget law in time. Autonomy of the central bank is asserted. The new constitution outlawed the use of social security surpluses for fiscal purposes and generally established that the state has only a subsidiary role in the economy.

The fast decline of inflation tax in the early 1990s is visible in Figures 6 and 7. A first phase of fiscal reforms included the measures outlined in Table 2, which were later accompanied by the modernization of the tax revenue authority and by successful external debt renegotiations. A second phase of reforms included the Law of Fiscal Prudence and Transparency of 1999. This law was intended to foster fiscal countercyclicality by allowing the government to accumulate buffers (for example, the Fiscal Stability Fund to be used in emergency cases) to smooth economic cycles.

A year after the Fuji shock, the monthly inflation rate was near 10 percent (Figure 19). In fact, the economy took five years to return to yearly inflation levels near 10 percent, even though the administration kept the promises of fiscal moderation and independence of the central bank. Why such a slow decline in inflation? We provide five plausible, complementary reasons next.

First, there was at the time considerable uncertainty about the commitment of the government to abandoning the fiscal dominance of the monetary policy. Fujimori had campaigned on the promise of not engaging in the sort of policies his administration promptly adopted. It was also unclear that Congress would go along with the stabilization effort. In 1992, Fujimori disbanded Congress and assumed legislative and judicial powers. The constitution of 1993, underpinning the change in policy regime, was approved by referendum, after the self-coup.[26] One may wonder whether policy reform, though increasingly popular, could have been processed without a breakdown in democratic normalcy.

Second, the intertemporal budget constraint that the government faced was unclear. Returning to normal relations with the international financial markets required dealing with the debt burden. Uncertainty about the terms of service of the public debt cast a shadow on the commitment of the government to not return to inflationary financing. News about debt renegotiation lowered inflation expectations the second semester of 1991.[27] A key for stabilization, then, was the successful renegotiation of the public debt with foreign creditors.

Third, and turning our attention to monetary policy, implementing a money-based stabilization was difficult given the uncertainty about the velocity of circulation of money. To get an idea of this problem, take Fisher's equation of exchange. In log terms, we have $m_t + v_t = p_t + y_t$, where m_t is the stock of money, v_t is the velocity of circulation, p_t is the price level, and y_t is real GDP. If real GDP growth is unrelated to monetary policy, we have

$$\pi_t = \Delta m_t + \Delta v_t - \Delta y_t. \tag{3}$$

The implementation of the monetary program relied on assuming a certain GDP growth rate for the planning year, a given velocity of money (implying $\Delta v_t = 0$), and an intended value for the inflation rate at the end of the planning year. The central bank could determine the growth of money compatible with the intended inflation target according to equation (3). The planned trajectory of the money growth rate became the intermediate target to achieve the desired inflation outcome. During the mid-1990s, the velocity of money became ever more unstable. In fact, the central bank did not publicly commit to any given money growth rate. The lack of clear targets may have hindered the building of credibility. Since 1994, the central bank started making annual inflation predictions, so to some extent, monetary policy had an implicit element of inflation-targeting.

Fourth, the central bank did not initially have the instruments needed to conduct an independent monetary policy. The purchase of U.S. dollars had to serve conflicting objectives: recovering the level of foreign currency reserves, managing the floating exchange rate regime, and serving as a means of monetary control. In the absence of a government bonds market, the central bank issued certificates of deposits (CDs), whose placement and repurchase served to implement the desired growth rate of money via open market operations. Monetary policy involved a delicate maneuvering between open market operations, the management of the administered exchange rate regime, and the consistency of the monetary program. To observers such as Mishkin and Savastano (2001), the monetary policy process was opaque, which made it difficult to signal intentions to the public.

Fifth, the high degree of dollarization of the economy as a result of the years of high inflation did not reverse during the stabilization. As pointed out by Kiguel and Liviatan (1995), the fact that money demand did not recover after hyperinflation left the economy vulnerable to a steep resumption of inflation if the government were to resort to inflationary taxation again, which may have weighed on inflation expectations. In the long run, however, dollarization may have discouraged politicians from inflationary taxation, precisely because relapsing would have been so costly.[28]

The Peruvian stabilization program did not work as fast as those programs based on hard exchange rate pegs, such as Argentinean convertibility or the Ecuadorian full dollarization program. Figure 19 depicts monthly inflation rates following the month of stabilization in the three countries. Inflation fell faster in Argentina and Ecuador than in Peru; convergence of inflation rates seemingly took four years. Though much harder to manage than a hard exchange rate peg, the monetary program would prove to be more resilient in the face of financial crisis originated abroad. Peru avoided currency crises of the sort that afflicted Argentina, which opted contemporaneously for a hard peg without full dollarization.

The global emerging market crisis of 1997 and 1998 prompted an outflow of U.S. dollars from emerging markets in general, and Peru was affected in turn. The monetary policy strategy and the instruments under disposal were not prepared for this shock. The result was a credit crunch with important consequences on the real side. As a result of the recession, inflation fell to about 0 percent by 2001. In fact, the monthly inflation rate was negative during some months in 2001. The time was ripe for a switch to a different monetary policy strategy.

Until 2001, monetary policy had been aimed at reducing inflation for a decade. By then it seemed necessary for the central bank to avoid the risk of deflation by means of an expansionary monetary policy. The policy problem involved doing so without jeopardizing the painfully built anti-inflationary credibility. It was believed that inflation-targeting provided the discipline the monetary authority needed at that moment. The Peruvian experience is unique in that inflation-targeting was adopted to move inflation

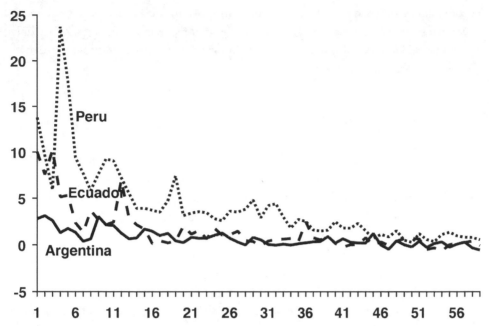

Figure 19. Monthly inflation during stabilization: Argentina, Ecuador, and Peru, percent

Note: The horizontal axis measures the number of months after the month the stabilization program takes place. In Argentina, the convertibility plan started in April 1991; in Ecuador, full dollarization started in January 2000; and in Peru, stabilization started in August 1990.

from below. Other experiences, especially in emerging market economies, featured inflation-targeting adoption to complete the convergence of relatively high inflation toward lower inflation levels.

As can be seen in Figure 1, the pace of GDP growth has been remarkably stable, featuring an average of 5 percent since the turn of the millennium. Although good external conditions are doubtless related to the GDP growth performance, it is hard to believe that the macroeconomic stability reforms and the liberalization of the economy implemented during the 1990s did not also play important roles.

Relatively free elections did not occur until the end of Fujimori's government in 2000. Yet, democratically elected administrations from 2001 onward have kept away from inflationary financing. Remarkably, for instance, Peru issued twenty-, thirty-, and thirty-two-year local currency bonds for the first time ever during a second García administration, headed by the same politician whose previous administration led the country to become a pariah in international financial markets.[29] As an explanation, the sustainability of the policy regime change may be linked to (1) the popular support for macroeconomic stability because of the traumatic effects of the hyperstagflation of the 1980s and also because of the good growth performance of the country after the stabilization; (2) the constitutional design, which has given autonomy to the central bank and has increased political accountability in giving key budgetary responsibility to the Ministerio de Economía y Finanzas (the Treasury); and (3) the presence of competent administrators not only in the central bank but also in the executive branch.[30] These are significant departures from the experience of the country in the 1960s.

Concluding Remarks

Recent Peruvian economic history is marked by an ambitious attempt to refashion the economy of the country through command-and-control policies adopted by a left-wing military dictatorship from 1968 to 1975. After the military returned to the barracks, they left as a legacy an expansive state, precariously financed through debt accumulation and inflation tax. The hyperinflation of the second half of the 1980s occurred in the midst of another radical policy experiment. The policies adopted by the populist administration then in office, such as pervasive price and exchange controls, were counterproductive by and large. These policies also made it hard or even impossible for the following administration to rely on an exchange rate peg to anchor expectations as part of the stabilization policies.

Looking back, it is hard to miss the fundamental mistrust in market allocations by economic and political actors in the run-up to hyperinflation.[31] Mistrust was compounded by wishful thinking by government authorities, in particular during the episodes of 1968–75 and 1985–90. Remarkably, a radical policy gamble attempted in the latter experiment was stopped by popular protest. In a way, society learned faster than the political elites, and the popular rejection of arbitrary government intervention in the economy preceded the stabilization of 1990.

The stabilization of 1990 was preceded by other attempts that looked ex ante similar. The question arises as to why this particular attempt was successful, leading to a persistent change in policy regime. Moreover, why did the same, or very similar, politicians behave more responsibly in fiscal and monetary matters after stabilization? The recent history suggests a process of social learning. From this viewpoint, the credibility of policy regime change in the 1990s may be linked ultimately to the change in public opinion giving proper incentives to politicians. Both the respect for central bank independence and the rejection of fiscal imprudence, which are currently characteristic features of Peru's economics and politics, can be traced back to some extent to the effect of the traumatic events of the 1980s. Borrowing the phrase of Malmendier and Nagel (2011), those who lived through those events are "hyperinflation babies."

In two previous occasions, in 1968 and 1992, disputes between the executive and legislative branches of government, motivated partly by conflicting views about policy and partly by political rancor, have led to the breakdown of democracy. The constitutional arrangement of 1993, with its checks on the spending ability of Congress and the delegation of monetary policy to an autonomous central bank, the popular support for fiscal prudence, and the presence of at least some competent administrators in the economic ministries, have isolated macroeconomic policies from the fractious and often

Table 3. Headline yearly inflation, 1901–2017

Year	Rate	Year	Rate	Year	Rate
1901	7.7	1940	8.2	1979	67.7
1902	−19.0	1941	8.4	1980	58.5
1903	13.2	1942	12.4	1981	75.4
1904	3.9	1943	9.0	1982	64.5
1905	31.3	1944	14.6	1983	111.2
1906	1.0	1945	11.6	1984	110.2
1907	1.9	1946	9.4	1985	163.4
1908	4.6	1947	29.4	1986	77.9
1909	−14.2	1948	30.8	1987	85.9
1910	−2.1	1949	14.7	1988	667.0
1911	3.2	1950	12.1	1989	3398.6
1912	−9.2	1951	10.1	1990	7481.7
1913	12.4	1952	6.9	1991	409.5
1914	4.0	1953	9.1	1992	73.5
1915	7.7	1954	5.3	1993	48.6
1916	9.8	1955	4.7	1994	23.7
1917	15.4	1956	5.5	1995	11.1
1918	15.5	1957	7.4	1996	11.5
1919	14.6	1958	7.9	1997	8.5
1920	11.7	1959	12.7	1998	7.3
1921	−5.2	1960	8.7	1999	3.5
1922	−4.5	1961	6.1	2000	3.8
1923	−5.3	1962	6.7	2001	2.0
1924	3.9	1963	6.0	2002	0.2
1925	7.0	1964	9.8	2003	2.3
1926	0.5	1965	16.3	2004	3.7
1927	−3.5	1966	8.9	2005	1.6
1928	−6.7	1967	9.9	2006	2.0
1929	−2.2	1968	19.2	2007	1.8
1930	−4.5	1969	6.3	2008	5.8
1931	−6.5	1970	4.9	2009	2.9
1932	−4.4	1971	6.8	2010	1.5

(*continued*)

Table 3. Headline yearly inflation, 1901–2017 (*continued*)

Year	Rate	Year	Rate	Year	Rate
1933	−2.6	1972	7.1	2011	3.4
1934	2.0	1973	9.5	2012	3.7
1935	1.3	1974	16.9	2013	2.8
1936	5.3	1975	23.5	2014	3.2
1937	6.3	1976	33.6	2015	3.5
1938	1.2	1977	38.0	2016	3.6
1939	−1.2	1978	58.1	2017	2.8

Source: Banco Central de Reserva del Perú, http://www.bcrp.gob.pe.
Note: 1901–49: Consumer price index collected by the Ministry of Finance and Commerce; 1950–2017: Lima consumer price index collected by the national statistics agency (INEI).

bitter nature of democratic politics in the country in the last two decades. If political infighting erodes the institutional setup for arbitrating disputes between the branches of government, it may end up endangering the country's hard-won macroeconomic stability.

Notes

We are grateful to Paola Villa and María Alejandra Barrientos for excellent research assistance. The authors alone are responsible for the views expressed herein.

1 The capital stock is from Seminario (2015); other data come from the Total Economy Database (see online appendix available at http://manifold.bfi.uchicago.edu/).

2 Mendoza (2013) and Dancourt, Mendoza, and Vilcapoma (1997) put emphasis on bad external conditions, while Hamann and Paredes (1991) and Lago (1991) put emphasis on policy mistakes. Gonzales de Olarte and Samamé (1991) and Wise (2003) attribute some of the blame for the poor performance to wide swings in economic policies.

3 No reliable data are available prior to the 1980s about public debt issued at a constant real interest rate. Since 2002, the government has issued inflation-adjusted sovereign bonds, but its stock has never been above 1 percent of GDP.

4 The usual statistical methodology, however, treats privatization proceeds as financing.

5 See Abusada-Salah (2000).

6 See Velarde and Rodríguez (1992b).

7 This is the quasi-fiscal deficit referred to in the fifth section.

8 Thorp and Bertram (1978) and Bourricaud (2017) are classic references for the economic history of the country and for a social and political portrait of the country in the 1960s.

9 This has made it difficult to extend backward our fiscal statistics.

10 See, for example, Kuczynski (1977).

11 Kuczynski (1977) provides an insightful insider look at the Belaúnde administration. According to Kuczynski, some officials in the Belaúnde administration perceived

Table 4. Monthly inflation, 1987–94

Month	Rate	Month	Rate	Month	Rate	Month	Rate
Jan-87	6.57	Jan-89	47.32	Jan-91	17.83	Jan-93	4.85
Feb-87	5.59	Feb-89	42.49	Feb-91	9.42	Feb-93	2.93
Mar-87	5.34	Mar-89	41.99	Mar-91	7.70	Mar-93	4.24
Apr-87	6.59	Apr-89	48.64	Apr-91	5.84	Apr-93	4.43
May-87	5.91	May-89	28.61	May-91	7.64	May-93	3.03
Jun-87	4.69	Jun-89	23.05	Jun-91	9.26	Jun-93	1.82
Jul-87	7.31	Jul-89	24.58	Jul-91	9.06	Jul-93	2.74
Aug-87	7.36	Aug-89	25.06	Aug-91	7.24	Aug-93	2.53
Sep-87	6.47	Sep-89	26.86	Sep-91	5.56	Sep-93	1.62
Oct-87	6.37	Oct-89	23.25	Oct-91	3.95	Oct-93	1.51
Nov-87	7.13	Nov-89	25.84	Nov-91	3.96	Nov-93	1.60
Dec-87	9.55	Dec-89	33.75	Dec-91	3.74	Dec-93	2.51
Jan-88	12.77	Jan-90	29.85	Jan-92	3.54	Jan-94	1.84
Feb-88	11.83	Feb-90	30.53	Feb-92	4.74	Feb-94	1.82
Mar-88	22.60	Mar-90	32.65	Mar-92	7.44	Mar-94	2.32
Apr-88	17.92	Apr-90	37.30	Apr-92	3.17	Apr-94	1.54
May-88	8.51	May-90	32.79	May-92	3.44	May-94	0.72
Jun-88	8.81	Jun-90	42.58	Jun-92	3.59	Jun-94	1.14
Jul-88	30.90	Jul-90	63.23	Jul-92	3.48	Jul-94	0.89
Aug-88	21.71	Aug-90	396.98	Aug-92	2.83	Aug-94	1.53
Sep-88	114.12	Sep-90	13.77	Sep-92	2.62	Sep-94	0.52
Oct-88	40.60	Oct-90	9.62	Oct-92	3.64	Oct-94	0.29
Nov-88	24.41	Nov-90	5.93	Nov-92	3.54	Nov-94	1.22
Dec-88	41.87	Dec-90	23.73	Dec-92	3.85	Dec-94	0.59

Source: BCRPData, Banco Central de Reserva del Perú, Gerencia Central de Estudios Económicos, https://estadisticas.bcrp.gob.pe/estadisticas/series/mensuales/resultados/PN01271PM/html.

Note: Lima consumer price index collected by the national statistics agency (INEI).

inflation as an inevitable collateral effect of development and not necessarily an evil. This corresponds to the Latin American "structuralist" view on inflation at the time. In that vein, Baer (1967) predicts that "runaway inflation" will not happen in the region.

12 The contributions to McClintock and Lowenthal (1976) provide an in-depth look at the military regime.

13 Documented by Schydlowsky and Wicht (1979) and others.

14 In the accounts of Peru's central bank, the nonfinancial public sector is equal to the general government plus state-owned enterprises; general government is equal to central plus local governments.

15 See, for example, Rivera (1979) and Pastor (2012).

16 In 1982, for instance, the central bank president, himself an accomplished economist, would write that stopping inflation necessitated a voluntary agreement among workers, business, and government, quoting approvingly that monetarism is a theology, and central banks are not theology schools (Webb 1985).

17 Heterodox policies have been studied by Lago (1991), Cáceres and Paredes (1991), Hnyilicza (2001), and Velarde and Rodríguez (1992a), among others.

18 Dornbusch and Edwards (1990) note a similar phase of initial success in other macroeconomic populist episodes in the region.

19 Choy and Dancuart (1990) calculate that the quasi-fiscal deficit, comprising import subsidies via the exchange rate differential by the central bank and credit subsidies by the Agrarian Bank, was 3.4 percent in 1986, 4.9 percent in 1987, 6.6 percent in 1988, and 2.7 percent in 1989.

20 The Peruvian writer Vargas Llosa (1993) provides a first-person account as one of the protagonists of the protest.

21 See the corresponding yearly and monthly inflation rates in Tables 3 and 4.

22 See Velarde and Rodríguez (1992a). Deflation was over before the end of September, so it is not captured by the monthly rates in Table 4.

23 Hanke and Krus (2013) rank them as twelfth and thirty-seventh among fifty-three hyperinflation episodes in the world.

24 The Olivera-Tanzi effect is the well-known decline of tax collection in real terms during high inflation episodes due to the fact that taxes are collected with a lag with respect to the economic activity taxed.

25 Accounts of the stabilization and monetary policy afterward include Terrones and Nagamine (1993); Kiguel and Liviatan (1995); Ishisaka (1997); Guevara (1999); Pasco-Font (2000); Velarde and Rodríguez (1992b); Rodríguez, Valderrama, and Velarde (2000); Mishkin and Savastano (2001); and Hnyilicza (2001).

26 Fujimori's *autogolpe* of April 1992 was supported by the military and had some popular approval. Its avowed aim was to give free rein to the executive branch in the stabilization effort and to implement more drastic measures in the fight against violent guerrillas.

27 Rodríguez, Valderrama, and Velarde (2000).

28 Pointedly, the constitution of 1993 enshrines the right of Peruvian citizens to hold foreign currency.

29 "Emerging-Market Debt: A Run for Your Money," *Economist*, August 26, 2010.

30 As an illustration, the key cabinet position of Ministro de Economía (formerly Ministro de Hacienda) was occupied in the 1960s by professional politicians, lawyers, and generals and from the 2000s to the present mostly by professional and academic economists.

31 See, for example, Sheahan (1999).

References

Abusada-Salah, Roberto. 2000. "La reincorporación del Perú a la comunidad financiera internacional." In *La reforma incompleta: Rescatando los noventa*, edited by Roberto Abusada-Salah, Fritz Du Bois, Eduardo Morón, and José Valderrama, 121–62. Lima, Peru: Universidad del Pacífico and Instituto Peruano de Economía.

Aguiar, Mark, and Gita Gopinath. 2007. "Emerging Market Business Cycles: The Cycle Is the Trend." *Journal of Political Economy* 115 (1): 69–102.

Alesina, Alberto, and Allan Drazen. 1991. "Why Are Stabilizations Delayed?" *American Economic Review* 81 (5): 1170–88.

Baer, Werner. 1967. "The Inflation Controversy in Latin America: A Survey." *Latin American Research Review* 2 (2): 3–25.

Besley, Timothy, Ethan Ilzetzki, and Torsten Persson. 2013. "Weak States and Steady States: The Dynamics of Fiscal Capacity." *American Economic Journal: Macroeconomics* 5 (4): 205–35.

Bourricaud, François. 2017. *Poder y sociedad en el Perú contempomráneo*. 3rd ed. Lima, Peru: Instituto de Estudios Peruanos.

Cáceres, Armando, and Carlos E. Paredes. 1991. "The Management of Economic Policy, 1985–1989." In *Peru's Path to Recovery: A Plan for Economic Stabilization and Growth*, edited by Carlos E. Paredes and Jeffrey D. Sachs, 80–116. Washington, D.C.: Brookings Institution.

Cagan, Phillip. 1956. "The Monetary Dynamics of Hyperinflation." In *Studies in the Quantity Theory of Money*, edited by Milton Friedman, 25–117. Chicago: University of Chicago Press.

Carbonetto, Daniel, M. Inés C. de Ceballos, Oscar Dancourt, César Ferrari, Daniel Martínez, Jaime Mezzera, Gustavo Saberbein, Javier Tantaleán, and Pierre Vigier. 1987. *El Perú heterodoxo: Un modelo económico*. Lima, Peru: Instituto Nacional de Planificación.

Castillo, Paul, and Youel Rojas. 2014. "Terms of Trade and Total Factor Productivity: Empirical Evidence from Latin American Emerging Markets." Working paper 2014-012, Central Bank of Peru, Lima.

Choy, Marylin, and Alfredo Dancuart. 1990. "Una aproximación al déficit cuasi-fiscal en el Perú." Sede de la CEPAL en Santiago (Estudios e Investigaciones) 33548, Comisión Económica de las Naciones Unidas para América Latina y el Caribe (CEPAL).

Dancourt, Oscar, Waldo Mendoza, and Leopoldo Vilcapoma. 1997. "Fluctuaciones económicas y shocks externos, Perú 1950–96." *Revista Economía (Pontificia Universidad Católica del Perú)* 20 (39–40): 63–102.

Dornbusch, Rüdiger, and Sebastian Edwards. 1990. "Macroeconomic Populism." *Journal of Development Economics* 32 (2): 247–77.

Gonzales de Olarte, Efraín, and Lilian Samamé. 1991. *Péndulo peruano: Políticas económicas, gobernabilidad y subdesarrollo, 1963–1990*. Lima, Peru: Instituto de Estudios Peruanos.

Goodhart, Charles A. 2011. "The Changing Role of Central Banks." *Financial History Review* 18 (2): 135–54.

Guevara, Guillermo. 1999. "Política monetaria del Banco Central: Una perspectiva histórica." *Revista Estudios Económicos, Banco Central de Reserva del Perú* 5:24–72.

Hamann, A. Javier, and Carlos E. Paredes. 1991. "Economic Characteristics and Trends." In *Peru's Path to Recovery: A Plan for Economic Stabilization and Growth*, edited by C. E. Paredes and J. Sachs, 41–79. Washington, D.C.: Brookings Institution.

Hanke, Steve H., and Nicholas E. Krus. 2013. "World Hyperinflations." In *The Handbook of Major Events in Economic History*, edited by Randal E. Parker and Robert Whaples, 367–77. London: Routledge Publishing.

Hausmann, Ricardo, and Ugo Panizza. 2003. "On the Determinants of Original Sin: An Empirical Investigation." *Journal of International Money and Finance* 22 (7): 957–90.

Hnyilicza, Esteban. 2001. *De la megainflación a la estabilidad monetaria: Política monetaria y cambiaría, Perú, 1990–2000.* Lima, Peru: Banco Central de Reserva del Perú, Fondo Editorial.

Ishisaka, Susana. 1997. "Política monetaria y desarrollo del mercado secundario de Certificados de Depósitos del Banco Central de Reserva del Perú: 1995–1996." *Revista Estudios Económicos, Banco Central de Reserva del Perú* 1:51–72.

Kehoe, Timothy J., and Edward C. Prescott, eds. 2007. *Great Depressions of the Twentieth Century.* Minneapolis: Federal Reserve Bank of Minneapolis.

Kiguel, Miguel A., and Nissan Liviatan. 1995. "Stopping Three Big Inflations: Argentina, Brazil, and Peru." In *Reform, Recovery, and Growth: Latin America and the Middle East,* edited by R. Dornbusch and S. Edwards, 369–414. Chicago: University of Chicago Press.

Krugman, Paul. 1979. "A Model of Balance-of-Payments Crises." *Journal of Money, Credit and Banking* 11 (3): 311–25.

Kuczynski, Pedro-Pablo. 1977. *Peruvian Democracy under Economic Stress: An Account of the Belaunde Administration, 1963–1968.* Princeton, N.J.: Princeton University Press.

Lago, Ricardo. 1991. "The Illusion of Pursuing Redistribution through Macropolicy: Peru's Heterodox Experience, 1985–1990." In *The Macroeconomics of Populism in Latin America,* edited by R. Dornbusch and S. Edwards, 263–330. Chicago: University of Chicago Press.

Llosa, Luis G., and Ugo. Panizza. 2015. "La gran depresión de la economía peruana: ¿Una tormenta perfecta?" *Revista Estudios Económicos, Banco Central de Reserva del Perú* 30:91–117.

Majumdar, Sumon, and Sharun W. Mukand. 2004. "Policy Gambles." *American Economic Review* 94 (4): 1207–22.

Malmendier, Ulrike, and Stefan Nagel. 2011. "Depression Babies: Do Macroeconomic Experiences Affect Risk Taking?" *Quarterly Journal of Economics* 126 (1): 373–416.

Martinelli, César, and Raul Escorza. 2007. "When Are Stabilizations Delayed? Alesina-Drazen Revisited." *European Economic Review* 51 (5): 1223–45.

McClintock, Cynthia, and Abraham F. Lowenthal, eds. 1976. *The Peruvian Experiment Reconsidered.* Princeton, N.J.: Princeton University Press.

Mendoza, Waldo. 2013. "Contexto internacional y desempeño macroeconómico en América Latina y el Perú: 1980–2012." Documento de Trabajo No. 351, Departamento de Economía, Pontificia Universidad Católica del Perú.

Mishkin, Frederic S., and Miguel A. Savastano. 2001. "Monetary Policy Strategies for Latin America." *Journal of Development Economics* 66 (2): 415–44.

Pasco-Font, Alberto. 2000. "Políticas de estabilización y reformas estructurales: Perú." Cepal Serie Reformas Económicas No. 66.

Pastor, Gonzalo C. 2012. "Peru: Monetary and Exchange Rate Policies, 1930–1980." Working paper 12/166, International Monetary Fund, Washington, D.C.

Restuccia, Diego. 2013. "Factor Misallocation and Development." In *The New Palgrave Dictionary of Economics, Online Edition,* edited by Steven N. Durlauf and Lawrence E. Blume. London: Palgrave Macmillan. https://doi.org/10.1057/978-1-349-95121-5_2870-1.

Rivera, Iván. 1979. "La crisis económica peruana: Génesis, evolución y perspectivas." *Revista Economía (Pontificia Universidad Católica del Perú)* 2 (3): 117–46.

Rodríguez, Martha, José Valderrama, and Julio Velarde. 2000. "El programa de estabilización." In *La reforma incompleta: Rescatando los noventa,* edited by Roberto

Abusada-Salah, Fritz Du Bois, Eduardo Morón, and José Valderrama, 91–119. Lima, Peru: Universidad del Pacífico and Instituto Peruano de Economía.

Sargent, Thomas J., Noah Williams, and Tao Zha. 2009. "The Conquest of South American Inflation." *Journal of Political Economy* 117 (2): 211–56. ISSN 00223808, 1537534X.

Schydlowsky, Daniel M., and Juan J. Wicht. 1979. *The Anatomy of an Economic Failure: Peru 1968–78*. Boston, Mass.: Center for Latin American Development Studies, Boston University.

Seminario, Bruno. 2015. *Breve historia de los precios, población y actividad económica del Perú: Reconstrucción de las cuentas nacionales, 1700–2013*. Lima, Peru: Universidad del Pacífico.

Sheahan, John. 1999. *Searching for a Better Society: The Peruvian Economy from 1950*. University Park: Pennsylvania State University.

Terrones, Marco E., and Javier Nagamine. 1993. "Reorientación de la política monetaria en el Perú: Avances y problemas." *Notas para el debate (GRADE)* 11:9–42.

Thorp, Rosemary, and Geoffrey Bertram. 1978. *Peru, 1890–1977: Growth and Policy in an Open Economy*. New York: Columbia University Press.

Tommasi, Mariano. 1999. "On High Inflation and the Allocation of Resources." *Journal of Monetary Economics* 44 (3): 401–21.

United Nations. 1969. *Growth of the World's Urban and Rural Population, 1920–2000*. New York: United Nations Department of Economic and Social Affairs.

Vargas Llosa, Mario. 1993. *El pez en el agua*. Barcelona, Spain: Editorial Seix Barral, S. A.

Velarde, Julio, and Martha Rodríguez. 1992a. "De la desinflación a la hiperestanflación, Perú: 1985–1990." Documento de Trabajo No. 5, Universidad del Pacífico, Lima, Peru.

———. 1992b. "El programa económico de agosto de 1990: Evaluación del primer año." Documento de Trabajo No. 2, Universidad del Pacífico, Lima, Peru.

Webb, Richard. 1985. *Por qué soy optimista*. Lima, Peru: Ediciones Virrey.

———. 1991. Prologue to *Peru's Path to Recovery: A Plan for Economic Stabilization and Growth*, edited by Carlos E. Paredes and Jeffrey D. Sachs, 1–12. Washington, D.C.: Brookings Institution.

Wise, Carol. 2003. *Reinventing the State: Economic Strategy and Institutional Change in Peru*. Ann Arbor: University of Michigan Press.

Discussion of the History of Peru 1

Mark Aguiar
Princeton University

The chapter on Peru by Martinelli and Vega provides a comprehensive and fascinating overview of Peru's monetary and fiscal transition from high inflation to stabilization and then to several decades of low inflation and economic growth. In this discussion, I present a framework that links the political progress discussed in the chapter with positive economic outcomes. In particular, the simple model provides an explanation for why political reform, debt reduction, enhanced credibility, and growth are inextricably linked. I conclude by placing Peru's experience in context with other emerging markets.

Figure 1 replicates the authors' Figure 1 and depicts Peru's GDP growth over the last half century. Peru's post-1990 growth experience is striking. Figure 2 replicates the authors' Figure 3, which documents the fiscal consolidation that took place in the 1990s and 2000s. Associated with this consolidation is a dramatic decline in debt, particularly external debt, as a fraction of GDP. This is depicted in Figure 3, which is the same as the authors' Figure 8. At the same time as the fiscal and monetary stabilization, Peru began reforming its private sector, including a major privatization program. One result of this combination of policies was a sharp increase in inward foreign direct investment as a percentage of GDP, depicted in Figure 4.

This discussion provides a framework for understanding why this prudent fiscal policy led not only to monetary stability but also to a period of sustained growth and investment. To do so, I build on Aguiar and Amador (2011).

Consider a deterministic, discrete time environment in which a small open economy (SOE) operates a neoclassical production function. Specifically, output is $f(k)$ when k is the stock of capital, all expressed in per capita terms, with $f'(k) > 0$ and $f''(k) < 0$. The SOE's government has enough policy tools to choose per capita consumption c and the level of capital k each period. To simplify the exposition, suppose the capital is rented from a world market each period at a rate $r + \delta$, where r is the world risk-free interest rate and δ is the rate of capital depreciation. See the Martinelli and Vega chapter for a more general framework in which capital is accumulated via investment. The important element is that capital is mobile between periods but is vulnerable to expropriation within a period.

The government finances consumption and capital expenditures through current output and net borrowing and lending with foreign debt markets. In particular, external debt b_t evolves according to the law of motion:

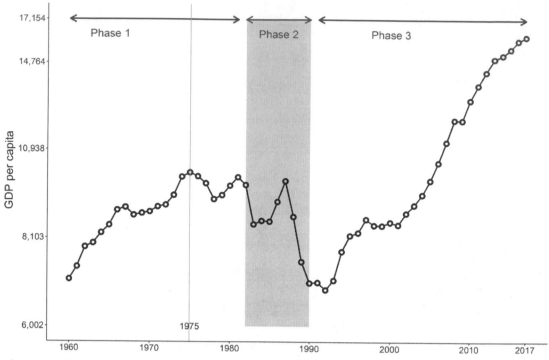

Figure 1. GDP per capita

Note: The figure replicates Figure 1 in the chapter by Martinelli and Vega; GDP is in 2007 soles.

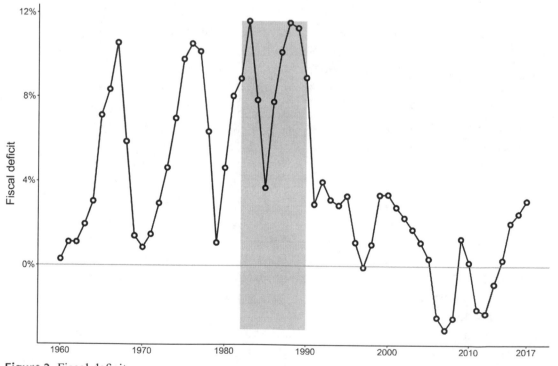

Figure 2. Fiscal deficit

Note: The figure replicates Figure 3 in the chapter by Martinelli and Vega; see that chapter for details.

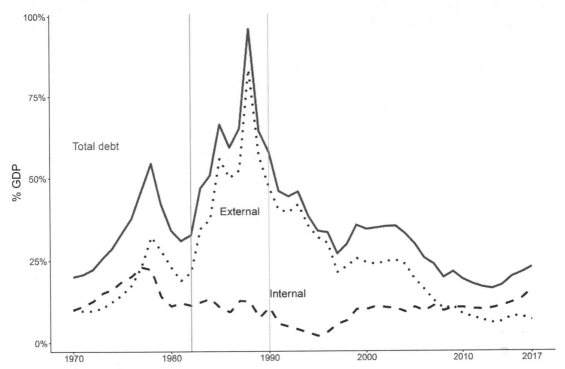

Figure 3. Domestic and external debt

Note: The figure replicates Figure 8 in the chapter by Martinelli and Vega; see that chapter for details.

$$b_{t+1} = R(c_t + (r + \delta)k_t + b_t - f(k_t)),$$

where $R = 1 + r$. Summing this equation forward from initial debt b_0 and imposing a no-Ponzi condition, we obtain a present value "resource constraint":

$$b_0 = \sum_{t=0}^{\infty} R^{-t}(f(k_t) - (r + \delta)k_t - c_t). \tag{RC}$$

Any allocation $\{c_t, k_t\}$ that satisfies (RC) is feasible for the government to implement.

The representative domestic agent has preferences over consumption sequences, given by

$$\sum_{t=0}^{\infty} \beta^t u(c_t), \tag{1}$$

where $\beta \in (0,1)$ is the discount factor and $u(c)$ is a strictly increasing function. For simplicity, we shall assume $\beta R = 1$, although this rules out some interesting debt dynamics that are discussed in Aguiar and Amador (2011).

The environment has two main frictions. The first is a political economy friction. In particular, suppose political parties randomly rotate in and out of power. Following the tradition of Alesina and Tabellini (1990) and Persson and Svensson (1989), a party prefers spending to occur while in power. In particular, suppose that the political incumbent

Mark Aguiar

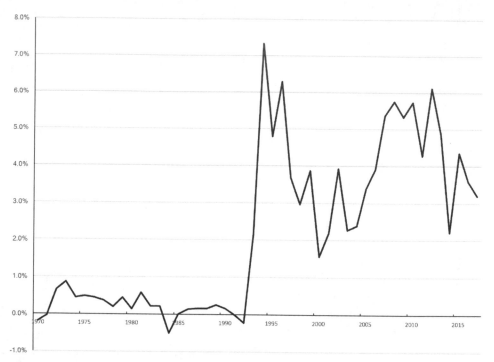

Figure 4. Foreign direct investment
Source: World Development Indicators
Note: The figure depicts net foreign direct investment as a percentage of GDP.

enjoys utility $\tilde{\theta}u(c)$ while in power, where $u(c)$ denotes the utility of the domestic representative agent. The incumbency bias is represented by $\tilde{\theta}>1$. Assume there are N political parties, and with probability $\gamma \equiv 1/N$, party $n \in \{1,2,...,N\}$ is in power. Transitions are independent and identically distributed, and hence there is a constant hazard γ that party n will be in power next period regardless of current incumbency. Aguiar and Amador (2011) implement a more general formulation in which incumbency affects the probability of being in power next period.

Given a sequence of consumptions $\{c_t\}$, the incumbent at period t has value

$$\widetilde{W}_t = \tilde{\theta}u(c_t) + \sum_{j=1}^{\infty} \beta^j \left[\tilde{\theta}\gamma + 1 - \gamma\right] u(c_{t+j}),$$

where the term in square brackets in the continuation value captures the uncertainty regarding future incumbency. As this value is a constant, we can express the current incumbent's value in normalized form:

$$W_t \equiv \frac{\widetilde{W}_t}{\tilde{\theta}\gamma + 1 - \gamma} = \theta u(c_t) + \sum_{j=1}^{\infty} \beta^j u(c_{t+j}), \tag{W}$$

438

where $\theta \equiv \tilde{\theta} / (\tilde{\theta}\gamma + 1 - \gamma)$ is a parameter that summarizes the preference for incumbency combined with the probability of losing office. Note that aside from the risk of political transitions, the current incumbent shares the same discount factor as private agents, β. This construction results in political preferences that have a hyperbolic (or quasi-geometric) discount factor in the spirit of Laibson (1994). An increase in $\tilde{\theta}$ or an increase in turnover ($\gamma \downarrow$) both increase θ, making the government more present biased.

In addition to the political economy friction, the other inefficiency in the environment is due to limited commitment. In particular, the government cannot commit to repaying debt and respecting capital property rights. The incumbent at time t always has the option of deviating from an allocation to increase current consumption. The consequence is a lower continuation value, as foreigners are no longer willing to trade financial assets or physical capital once the government has deviated. Aguiar and Amador (2011) specify microfoundations for the punishment. For this discussion, it suffices to posit a deviation value $\underline{W}(k)$, with $\underline{W}'(k) > 0$.

The environment builds on the neoclassical growth model, and hence capital is a focal variable that is subject to expropriation. That is, private investors are concerned about capital taxation or expropriation. It is not conceptually difficult to extend this environment to inflation and money balances. The mechanism described below that links debt reduction with enhanced credibility can therefore easily encompass Peru's inflation stabilization as well.

We now characterize constrained efficient allocations in this environment. Specifically, consider allocations that maximize the representative domestic agent's initial welfare subject to the resource constraint and a sequence of constraints that ensure each incumbent does not deviate:

$$v(b_0) = \max_{c_t, k_t} \sum_{t=0}^{\infty} \beta^j u(c_t)$$

subject to:

$$b_0 \leq \sum_{t=0}^{\infty} R^{-t}(f(k_t) - (r+d)k_t - c_t$$

$$\underline{W}(k_t) \leq W_t, \forall t. \tag{P}$$

Let $\mu_0 > 0$ be the multiplier on the resource constraint and $\lambda_t R^{-t} \mu_0$ be the multiplier on the sequence of political participation constraints. The first-order condition for k_t is

$$\lambda_t = \frac{f'(k_t) - (r+\delta)}{\underline{W}'(k_t)}. \tag{2}$$

The numerator on the right-hand side is the wedge between the marginal product of capital and the rental rate. The denominator is a strictly positive number. Hence, capital is distorted down if $\lambda_t > 0$. That is, if the political participation constraint strictly binds, capital is depressed. This implies that lack of commitment to debt repayments and property rights puts downward pressure on the level of economic activity.

The first-order condition for c_t is

$$1 = u'(c_t)\left(\frac{1}{\mu_0} + \sum_{s=0}^{\infty} \lambda_{t-s} + (\theta - 1)\lambda_t\right). \tag{3}$$

The first term in the brackets on the right is the role the resource constraint plays in determining the level of consumption: more initial debt implies a greater μ_0 and a lower c_t, all else constant. The second term sums the multipliers λ_s over $s \leq t$. This sum is weakly positive and hence raises c_t, all else constant. This reflects that c_t enters the value for all previous political incumbents, and hence raising c_t relaxes the political participation constraint for all prior governments. This is the usual "back-loading" incentive in models of limited commitment. The final term reflects that consumption in period t is of particular value to the incumbent in that period due to the political friction $\theta > 1$.

An interesting implication of (3) is that $\lambda_t \to 0$ as $t \to \infty$. If this were not the case, then $\sum \lambda_t$ would diverge, violating the first-order condition. Hence, the economy eventually saves its way out of the constraints. From (2), this implies that $f'(k_t) \to r + \delta$, and capital achieves its first-best level.

The fact that the steady state is the efficient level of production stems from the strong incentives to delay consumption in models of limited commitment when $\beta R = 1$. However, the speed at which k_t converges to the efficient level depends on θ_t. To see this, suppose u is linear: $u'(c_t) = 1$. The first-order condition (3) then traces out the following first-order difference equation:

$$\lambda_{t+1} = \left(1 - \frac{1}{\theta}\right)\lambda_t. \tag{4}$$

The greater the political economy wedge θ, the slower the rate of convergence to the first-best level of output. Hence, more distorted political economy environments have slower growth.

To bring the model back to the discussion of fiscal and monetary stabilization, under some concavity assumptions on $\underline{W}$, equation (2) implies that as $\lambda_t \to 0$, capital is increasing to its first-best level. This implies that the political deviation value $\underline{W}(k_t)$ is increasing over time. One can show that to ensure participation, this requires that consumption is growing and debt is declining. That is, as debt declines over time, both capital and consumption increase.

Credibility in this environment is earned by the reduction of debt, and the payoff is greater growth. This mimics the experience of Peru depicted in the figures above.[1] A theme throughout this volume is the role that credibility of fiscal prudence plays in inflation stabilization. The same credibility plays a role in encouraging greater private-sector economic activity.

Peru's growth experience via debt reduction is not unique. Gourinchas and Jeanne (2013) document that high-growth emerging markets tend to run current account

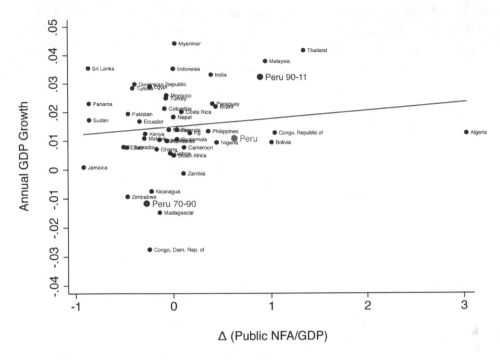

Figure 5. Growth and net foreign assets (NFA)

Source: Data from the World Development Indicators

Note: Public NFA is defined as government foreign reserves minus external public and publicly guaranteed debt. The vertical axis is log change in real GDP between 2011 and 1970 divided by 41. The horizontal axis is the change over this period in U.S. dollar–denominated NFA divided by mean dollar-denominated GDP.

surpluses; that is, growth is associated with net capital *outflows*. Aguiar and Amador (2011) dig deeper and document that this pattern is driven by the public sector reducing external indebtedness (or increasing foreign reserves, or both), combined with private-sector capital inflows. Figure 5 depicts the pattern for forty-five developing economies. On the horizontal axis is the change in public-sector net foreign assets (NFA) between 1970 and 2011 normalized by average U.S. dollar-denominated GDP, where public NFA is defined as foreign reserves minus public external debt expressed in dollars. On the vertical axis is annual average growth in real GDP over the same period. The positive slope indicates that countries that grow relatively fast also have increases in net foreign assets. That is, countries grow by reducing their net indebtedness.

The three large dots in Figure 5 depict Peru's experience. The dot labeled "Peru" is the data point for Peru over the entire sample. The two dots labeled "Peru 70–90" and "Peru 90–11" represent the subperiods 1970–90 and 1990–2011, respectively. The robust growth that Peru has experienced since 1990 coincides with a significant reduction in external debt. Viewed through the lens of the model above, the political stabilization post-1990 led to a coincident decline in debt overhang and faster growth. The chapter by Martinelli and Vega documents that the same forces led to inflation stabilization. While the political frictions in the model are taken as primitive, the exercise highlights that Peru's improved political economy environment is consistent with the host of good economic outcomes discussed briefly above and in great detail in the fascinating analysis by Martinelli and Vega.

Note

1 The chapter by Martinelli and Vega emphasizes growth through productivity. The simple framework of this discussion exhibits growth through capital intensity. However, the mechanism applies to any output-enhancing activity that is vulnerable to government expropriation or taxation. Many productivity-enhancing investments fit this class of activities.

References

Aguiar, Mark and Manuel Amador. 2011. "Growth in the Shadow of Expropriation." *Quarterly Journal of Economics* 126 (2): 651–97.

Alesina, Alberto, and Guido Tabellini. 1990. "A Positive Theory of Fiscal Deficits and Government Debt in a Democracy." *Review of Economic Studies* 57 (3): 403–14.

Gourinchas, Pierre-Oliver, and Olivier Jeanne. 2013. "Capital Flows to Developing Countries: The Allocation Puzzle." *Review of Economic Studies* 80 (4):1484–1515.

Laibson, David. 1994. "Hyperbolic Discounting and Consumption." PhD diss., Massachusetts Institute of Technology, Cambridge, Mass.

Persson, Torsten, and Lars E. O. Svensson. 1989. "Why a Stubborn Conservative Would Run a Deficit: Policy with Time-Inconsistent Preferences." *Quarterly Journal of Economics* 104 (2): 325–45.

Discussion of the History of Peru 2

Saki Bigio
University of California, Los Angeles

The chapter on the monetary and fiscal history of Peru by César Martinelli and Marco Vega is among the best available narratives addressing one of the most painful lessons from economic policy experimentation. I was born and raised in Peru during the time when those policy experiments were being carried out. Perhaps that is the reason why I am a macroeconomist. Today, it has been almost twenty years since I took my first macroeconomics course, and I can still remember my favorite readings: Sargent (1986) on the history of hyperinflations in Eastern Europe and Velarde and Rodríguez (1992a, 1992b) on the Peruvian hyperinflation.[1] What is good about this chapter is that the story is illustrated with calculations that employ the government budget constraint. The beauty of a budget constraint is that it is transparent but also agnostic about theory. But in the end, it is always the task of the author to interpret an insipid account. I have a few comments on the interpretations of Martinelli and Vega.

Martinelli and Vega interpret the accounting in a way that coincides with the most common narrative of the period. The synopsis is that a sequence of populist governments, which began with the coup of 1968, consistently ran primary deficits. The source of those deficits was subsidized prices by state-owned enterprises (SOEs). The authors label this period as phase 1. SOE deficits were mainly financed externally but also set the stage for money financing. Phase 2 during Alan García's government, the story goes, took those policies to an extreme and triggered a multiple crisis of default and stagflation. I think the history is more complex than that.

Figures 13 to 15 in the chapter show the evolution of fiscal deficits. My reading of the series differs slightly. In Figure 1, I plot the economic results of SOEs. The top panel shows that the overall deficits coincide with two waves of capital formation by the public sector. What the money was invested in, I cannot tell. The waves of capital investment at the SOEs coincide with a similar pattern for the central government: a primary-surplus cycle (bottom panel) coincides with the capital formation. I interpret from these pictures that the two large waves of public investments reflect a national policy of large capital formation that led to dramatic deficits. The figure also shows that each wave led to substantial increases in interest payments, which reflects that the capital formation waves were primarily funded externally. I see these waves of capital formation in phase 1 as the original sin of what would eventually happen during phase 2. The point I want to emphasize is that the driver of fiscal deficits was not

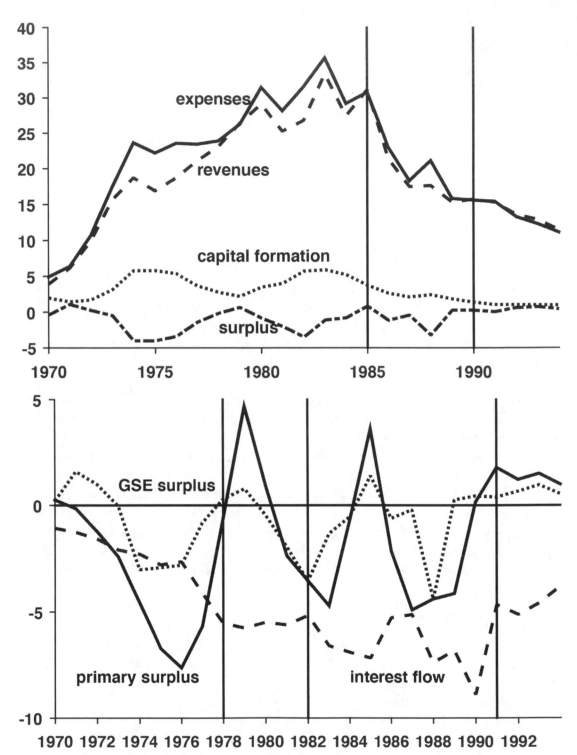

Figure 1. Capital formation waves: top panel: financial results of government-sponsored enterprises; bottom panel: financial surplus of government-sponsored enterprises vs. central-government surplus

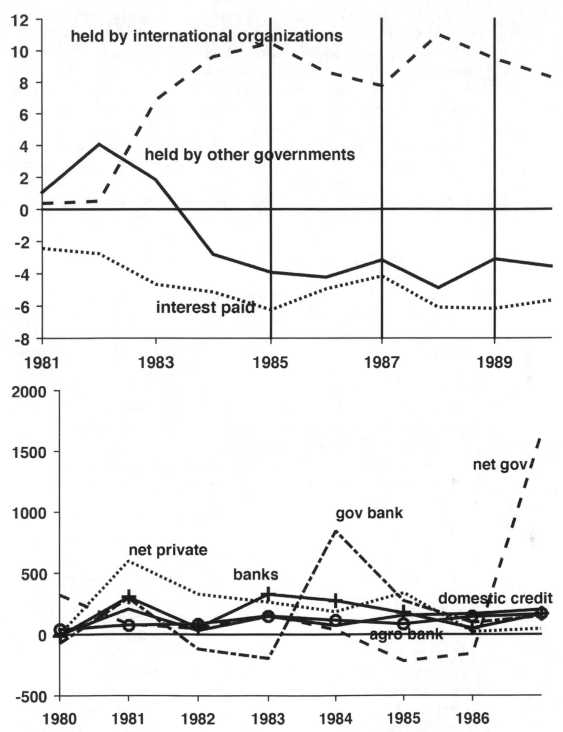

Figure 2. Balance of payments and central bank assets: top panel: key components of balance of payments; bottom panel: central bank assets

the poor performance of state enterprises but rather a failed macroeconomic program of capital investment at the national level.

An analysis of the balance of payments is always complicated because of the multiple components. However, one thing you can also read, through an inspection of Peru's external account, is that the waves of large infrastructure investments coincided with current account deficits. This added pressure to the currency pegs. The resulting exchange-rate depreciations increased the real fiscal burden of external debt. By the beginning of phase 2, in the early eighties, Peru had de facto defaulted, as many countries had done explicitly at the time. García would be the first to be explicit about the default, but the country was already in financial autarky for any practical purpose. I make this argument because Peruvian bond holdings had shifted from private hands to international organizations (Figure 2). Importantly, throughout the eighties Peru increased its overall debt stock because it was rolling over debt at high interests, not because it was obtaining more funding. By the middle of phase 2, the main source of deficit financing was left to seigniorage.

One thing I find missing from the computations of seigniorage revenues in the chapters in this volume is the role of publicly held banks. In fact, in Figure 2, bottom panel, we see a large increase in credit by the central bank to state-owned banks. This expansion corresponds to an increase in the monetary base, but the effect on M1, coming from cheap credit and deposit creation by government-owned commercial banks, could have been much more important. The national monetary statistics fail to capture a hidden component of the consolidated government's deficit: if government-owned banks issue deposits to grant low-quality loans, this operation will not be picked up by the national accounts because nonperforming loans take time to appear in income statements.

García's government had a chance to reverse courses, but it failed and triggered the hyperinflation of phase 2. García was misled by theories that would be proven wrong. In the book by Carbonetto et al. (1987), which was very influential in García's regime, you can even find an IS-LM diagram where the IS curve has a downward-sloping portion! This is a reflection of the beliefs of that time: that a monetary stimulus could increase output without inflation. In other words, the main trigger of the hyperinflation during phase 2 was an attempt to boost aggregate demand with a monetary expansion in the context of an international recession.

The final point I want to make is that the government's budget constraint is silent about whether it is easy to cut the deficit. The standard monetary-fiscal theories assume that it is, but I think that the Peruvian case study reveals that it isn't. I believe that García's government learned its lesson quickly. If you inspect the path of revenues and expenditures, you see a clear picture: in the period between 1987 through 1989, the government was trying hard to cut its deficits by reducing expenditures. That is my interpretation of Figure 1 (top panel), where you see a strong reduction in the size of government expenditures during phase 2. This was not a situation in which expenses were increasing; there was a reduction in both government income and expenses together. Further evidence is found in Figure 3(bottom panel), which shows a dramatic shift in the composition of the sources of government income. Here we find a shift away from income taxes and

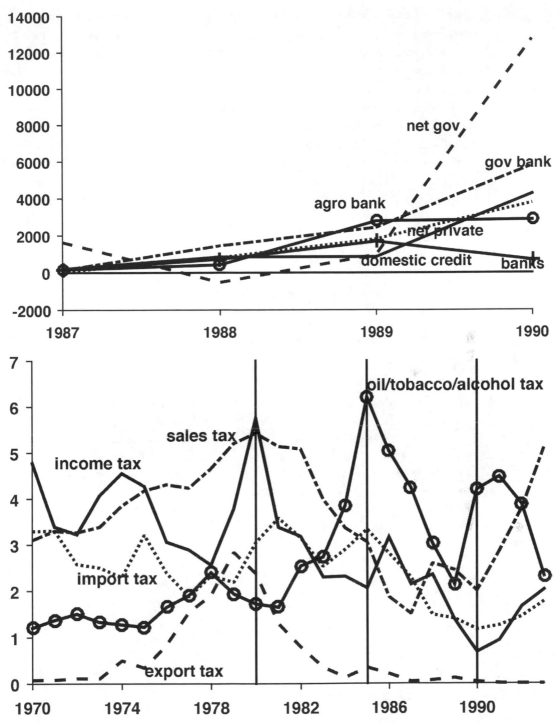

Figure 3. Central bank assets and sources of revenues: top panel: central bank assets; bottom panel: sources of revenues

toward excise taxes, which are easier to collect in a hyperinflationary environment. The government's budget constraint is silent about how inflation erodes tax collections or how an austerity plan can backfire as a reduction in revenues. It is easy to blame one government, but the blame should be placed on a sequence of governments and the institutions that let them fail.

Today, Peru is back on track. For the most part, it has learned its lesson the hard way and has achieved macroeconomic stability through institutional change. The challenge now is to increase microeconomic efficiency and taper corruption in a country where every living president since I was born is either being prosecuted or has been convicted for corruption. Let's hope it doesn't take another hard lesson to further improve Peru's institutions.

Note

1 I had the good fortune later on to have Velarde and Sargent as undergraduate and graduate thesis advisers.

References

Carbonetto, D., M. I. C. de Ceballos, O. Dancourt, C. Ferrari, D. Martínez, J. Mezzera, G. Saberbein, J. Tantaleán, and P. Vigier. 1987. *El Perú heterodoxo: Un modelo económico.* Lima, Peru: Instituto Nacional de Planificación.

Sargent, Thomas J. 1986. "The Ends of Four Big Inflations." In *Rational Expectations and Inflation.* New York: Harper & Row.

Velarde, Julio, and Martha Rodríguez. 1992a. "De la desinflación a la hiperestanflación, Perú: 1985–1990." Documento de Trabajo No. 5, Universidad del Pacífico, Lima, Peru.

———. 1992b. "El programa económico de agosto de 1990: Evaluación del primer año." Documento de Trabajo No. 2, Universidad del Pacífico, Lima, Peru.

Uruguay

The History of Uruguay

Gabriel Oddone
Universidad de la República and Centro
de Investigaciones Económicas, Uruguay

Joaquín Marandino
Universidad Torcuato Di Tella, Argentina

Major fiscal and monetary events, 1960–2017

1965 Banking crisis	**1991** Brady Plan
1967 Creation of Central Bank of	Stabilization plan with crawling peg
Uruguay as an "autonomous	**1995** Central Bank Act limits assistance
state entity"	to public sector
1968 Stabilization plan	Social security reform
with mandatory price	**2002** Balance of payments crisis and
fixing	devaluation
1974 Financial liberalization	Banking crisis and default
1978 Stabilization plan with crawling	**2003** Public debt restructuring
peg (*tablita*)	**2005** Inflation targeting
1982 Balance of payments crisis and	**2008** New Central Bank Act sets
devaluation	restrictions to bailout
1983 Banking crisis and default	operations

Introduction

During the last half of the twentieth century, Uruguay opened commercially and financially to the international economy, became progressively more stable, and abandoned the interventionist policies that had prevailed since the 1930s. However, during this period, the country suffered three banking crises (two of which became public debt crises), recorded double-digit chronic inflation for more than three decades, and was unable to reverse its long economic decline.[1]

The inflationary financing of deficits in the late 1950s explains the origin of the nominal instability (i.e., high inflation) that lasted until the end of the twentieth century. This chronic inflation affected the credibility of macroeconomic policy, which contributed to demonetizing the economy. As a result, macroeconomic instability consolidated,

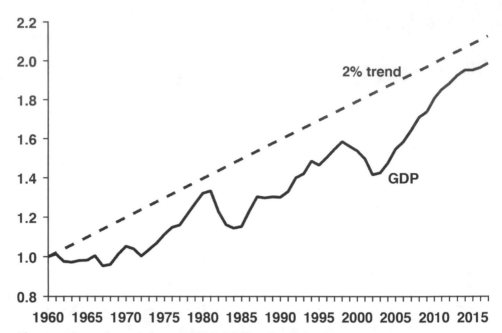

Figure 1. Log of per capita real GDP (1960 = 1)
Sources: Bonino, Román, and Willebald (2012); Central Bank of Uruguay

making agents more impatient for their expected returns and affecting investment and thus growth (Oddone 2008).

Between 1960 and 1973, the economy stagnated (Figure 1) with high and volatile inflation (Figure 2) and persistent fiscal deficits (Figure 3).

In 1974, GDP started to converge slowly to the 2 percent annual growth trend, while inflation and the fiscal deficit began to fall. This process went on until 1982, when the second major crisis—in banking, balance of payments, and public debt—hit.[2]

Between 1983 and 1990, the economy stagnated again, inflation increased to three-digit rates, and the fiscal deficit remained high because of large interest payments.

In 1991, after several measures and reforms, GDP growth started to converge to its trend, and the inflation rate began to decline. In addition, since the beginning of the 1990s, the fiscal deficit remained significantly lower than in the previous decades.[3]

In 2002, a third banking crisis took place. Compared with the 1982 crisis, the drop in GDP was similar, but the recovery was faster. Likewise, the fiscal effect of the crisis was smaller, and the impact on inflation was substantially lower and less persistent.

In summary, Uruguay made a significant macroeconomic change in 1974 by opening the economy through the liberalization of the current and capital accounts of the balance of payments. From there, successive governments reduced the monetary financing of fiscal deficits, as had been the norm up to that point. Nonetheless, during the transition, the country had to endure two major crises: the first in 1982 and the second in 2002. The significantly lower fiscal and inflation effects of the second crisis suggest that governments have slowly understood the importance of fiscal constraints to guarantee nominal

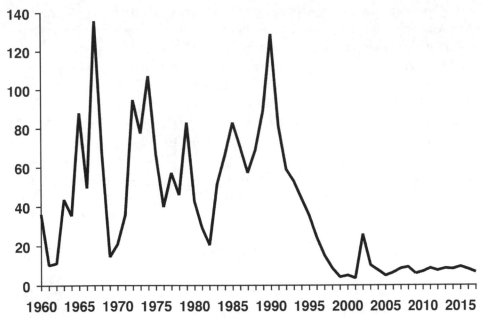

Figure 2. Consumer price index (CPI) inflation

Source: Instituto Nacional de Estadística (INE)

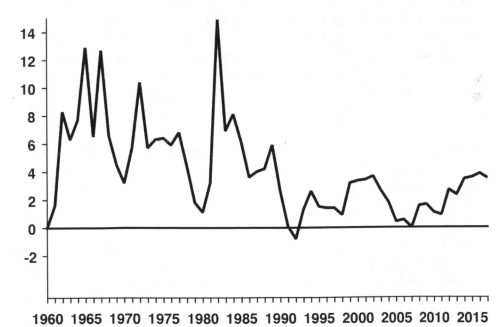

Figure 3. Overall deficit of the public sector as percentage of GDP

Sources: Banda and Onandi (1992); Borchardt, Rial, and Sarmiento (2000); Licandro and Vicente (2006); Ministerio de Economía y Finanzas (MEF)

instability. Institutional changes and economic reforms also helped improve the overall macroeconomic discipline. As a result, Uruguay has experienced fifteen years of uninterrupted growth and macroeconomic stability since 2003.

This chapter is organized into an introduction, two main sections, and a conclusion. The first main section shows the results of the budget constraint analysis for Uruguay for the 1960–2017 period based on the framework of "A Framework for Studying the Monetary and Fiscal History of Latin America." The second contrasts the stylized facts of the monetary and fiscal history of Uruguay during the same period with the main conclusions from the budget constraint analysis. In addition, some theoretical models were used to achieve a better understanding of critical episodes, such as the crises of 1965, 1982, and 2002. Finally, the chapter presents conclusions and final remarks.

The Budget Constraint: Framework and Overall Results

This section describes the results of the budget constraint framework for the case of Uruguay.[4] Table 1 shows the main results for the 1960–2017 period.[5] Three subperiods were considered in analyzing these results. The first one (1960–73) comprises the stagflation years. The second (1974–90) includes the phase of the first trade opening (i.e., regional integration), financial liberalization, and the severe consequences of the banking and balance of payments crisis of 1982. The last subperiod (1991–2017) includes the second trade opening, the price stabilization plan (1991–2002), the 2002 banking crisis, and the years of strong growth and macroeconomic stability (2003–17).

The results in Table 1 show that the financing of Uruguay's public sector in 1960–2017 was mostly inflationary: two-thirds of the sources came from an inflation tax and one-third from the public debt. Nevertheless, the monetization and the inflationary financing of fiscal deficits (monetary issuance plus inflation tax) fell throughout the whole period.

Between 1960 and 1973, the main source of financing fiscal deficits was the inflation tax, as public debt issuing was limited because of financial repression (real interest rates in pesos were negative) and lack of access to external financing. The financial liberalization in Uruguay since 1974 and the greater access to external financing from emerging markets in the early 1970s increased the weight of public debt as a source, although the inflation tax remained significant. Since the 1990s, inflationary financing was discarded because of greater access to public debt, lower obligations, and macroeconomic reforms. Since 2004, further improvements in public debt management kept the need for inflationary financing relatively low.

On the obligations side, the primary fiscal deficit decreased continuously in every subperiod (Table 1). After the second half of the 1980s, the deficit remained relatively low, reflecting greater government commitment to macroeconomic stability. However, primary deficits in the late 1990s and since 2012 suggest that this commitment is still weak (Figure 4).

In 1982 and 2002, the end of the price stabilization plans based on exchange rate anchors provoked strong currency devaluations. As shown later in section 3, these

Table 1. Consolidated budget constraint of the public sector, 1960–2017 (% GDP)

	1960–73	1974–90	1991–2017	1960–2017
Sources				
Local currency public debt (var.)	−1.1%	0.4%	0.2%	0.0%
Foreign currency public debt (var.)	0.9%	4.4%	−0.8%	1.1%
Inflation-indexed public debt (var.)			0.8%	0.4%
Wage-indexed public debt (var.)	0.1%	0.1%	−0.1%	0.0%
Monetary base (var.)	−0.2%	−0.4%	0.0%	−0.2%
Inflation tax	4.7%	3.6%	0.8%	2.6%
Total	**4.4%**	**8.0%**	**1.0%**	**3.9%**
Obligations				
Public-sector primary deficit	5.9%	1.8%	−1.1%	1.4%
Local currency return			0.0%	0.0%
Foreign currency return	−0.1%	2.8%	0.9%	1.2%
Inflation-indexed return			−0.1%	0.0%
Transfers	−1.4%	3.5%	1.3%	1.3%
Total	**4.4%**	**8.0%**	**1.0%**	**3.9%**

Note: Transfers are estimated as a residual.

devaluations severely weakened public finances (Figure 5) given the highly dollarized public debt and the central bank's contingent liabilities (dollarized bank deposits). This is why the returns on that type of debt were large in the 1974–90 subperiod (Table 1).

Transfers (t_t) are, by definition, the residual of the budget constraint. They capture data limitations (estimation errors) as well as missing sources or obligations ("A Framework for Studying the Monetary and Fiscal History of Latin America"). The residual shows an erratic path throughout the entire period, although a negative sign prevails in the 1960s and the 1990s and a positive one in the 1970s, the 1980s, and the last decade (Figure 6). When there is a negative sign, there are missing *sources* in the budget constraint. Conversely, when the sign is positive, there are missing *obligations*.

An *adjusted residual* was estimated to interpret the budget constraint residual (transfers). Factors likely to be included in the budget constraint residual were identified and then extracted from the original residual. The result, the adjusted residual, allows analysis to the extent that the residual can be explained by such factors.

Three main terms were identified that are omitted from the budget constraint identity and thus end up in the residual: (1) international reserves, (2) reserve requirements, and

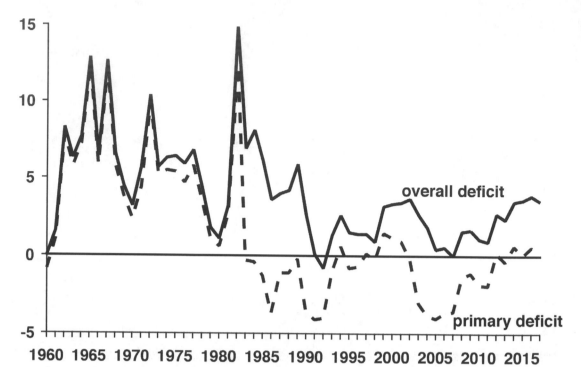

Figure 4. Overall and primary deficit of the public sector as percentage of GDP
Sources: Banda and Onandi (1992); Borchardt, Rial, and Sarmiento (2000); Licandro and Vicente (2006); MEF

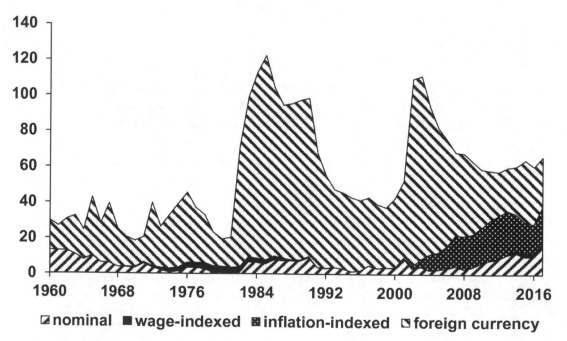

☑ nominal ■ wage-indexed ▦ inflation-indexed ◪ foreign currency

Figure 5. Gross public debt by currency (% GDP)
Sources: Azar et al. (2009), Central Bank of Uruguay

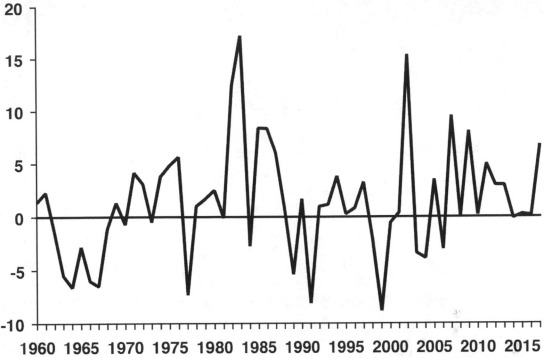

Figure 6. Residual, percent of GDP

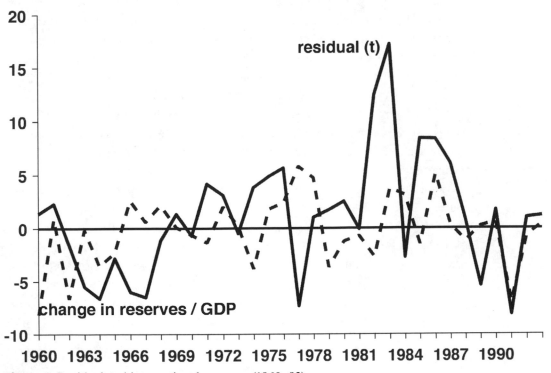

Figure 7. Residual and international reserves (1960–93)

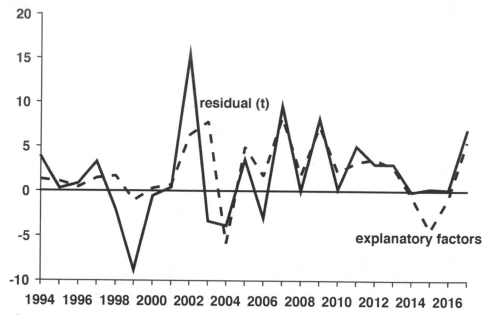

Figure 8. Residual and explanatory factors (1994–2017)

Source: Central Bank of Uruguay

Note: Between 1994 and 2017, the "explanatory factors" include net-of-credit deposits, financial assets, and other extraordinary transfers.

(3) transfers. Then, data were collected on these variables and subtracted from the original residual.[6] The results in Table 2 show that, on average, the absolute value of the adjusted residual is lower than the absolute value of the budget constraint residual. This suggests that the residual can be partially explained by international reserves, reserve requirements, and extraordinary transfers. However, it remains relatively large in the 1960s, in 1977, around the 1982 crisis, in 1999, and around the 2002 crisis (Figure 9).

Following are some explanations for the remaining residual. First, the way the implicit interest rate is constructed for the period 1960–93 (interest payments in $t + 1$ over the stock of debt in t) may not be precise. That means estimation errors end up in the adjusted residual. Second, when estimating the implicit interest rate in 1960–2002, all public debt is assumed to be denominated in foreign currency. As a consequence, foreign currency returns may be inaccurate, and the ones denominated in other currencies are missing. The net effect of these errors is also contained in the adjusted residual. Third, some transfers associated with the 1982 and 2002 debt crises remain out of the budget constraint. For instance, transfers from the central bank to Banco Hipotecario during the 1982 crisis are not included in the deficit.[7] Fourth, residuals may also arise from appending different data sets. For example, the adjusted residual is significantly large in 1999, the year when estimates and official data on public debt are joined.

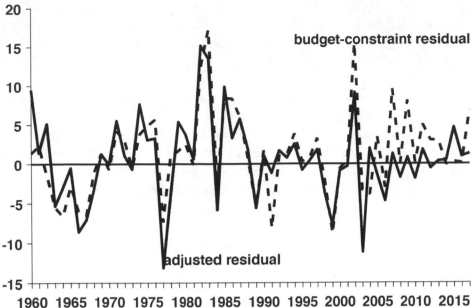

Figure 9. Adjusted and original residuals (% GDP)

Note: "Adjusted residual" is defined as the budget constraint residual minus the explanatory factors.

Table 2. Original and adjusted average residual by subperiod, percent of GDP

	1960–73	1974–90	1991–2017
Original residual	−1.4%	3.5%	1.3%
Adjusted residual	−0.3%	2.7%	−0.2%

Stylized Facts and the Budget Constraint

The economic history of Uruguay between 1960 and 2017 includes first a brief stage where interventionism and import-substitution policies predominated (1960–73). After 1974, and especially since 1991, more market-oriented policies stimulated the opening of the economy.

To contrast the stylized facts with the budget constraint results for Uruguay, the 1960–2017 period has been divided into three subperiods: (1) stagflation (1960–73); (2) opening, liberalization, and balance of payments crisis (1974–90); and (3) boost, halt,[8] and the golden years (1991–2017). Each of the following parts is devoted to analyzing these subperiods using the conceptual framework described above.

STAGFLATION (1960–73)

The 1960s was the end of a growth period as the economy stagnated and inflation remained high in historical comparison. The magnitude of the economic failure led to a social and

459

political crisis in 1973 that ended the long democratic stability of the country. GDP per capita grew 2.2 percent on average in the 1950s and only 0.5 percent between 1960 and 1973. Annual inflation reached 51.7 percent on average in 1960–73 (it was 6.4 percent in the 1940s and 13.0 percent in the 1950s; Figure 2).

The economic decay of the late 1950s had political consequences. In 1958, the Colorado Party lost the presidential election for the first time in the twentieth century at the hands of its secular opponent, the National Party.

In 1959, the new government approved the Monetary and Foreign Exchange Reform law, which was the first attempt to liberalize the economy since 1929. The aim was to restore the internal and external balances of the economy. The reform simplified and reunified the various types of exchange rates, dismantled trade controls, and put an end to the tendency toward bilateral trade agreements. It also imposed drawdowns on exports and surcharges on imports. The reform restricted the expansion of payment methods by establishing an issuance regime based on gold and the rediscounting of private documents, thus eliminating other issuance props such as the assets of the state-owned commercial bank (Banco República).[9] Under the reform, in 1960 Uruguay signed the first agreement with the International Monetary Fund (IMF). Even though most of the initiatives included in the reform were abandoned in the 1960s, some of them started to be implemented after 1974.

Between 1960 and 1973, under the low-growth situation, primary fiscal deficits were sustained (5.9 percent of GDP on average) as expenses grew more rapidly than revenues. This was because the public expenditure structure was very rigid, while revenues stopped growing because of stagnation (Figure 10).[10]

The debt-to-GDP ratio remained stable in this period, since the increase in dollar-denominated debt was offset by a fall in peso-denominated debt (Table 1; Figure 5). The latter began in the 1950s when negative real interest rates made peso-denominated debt unattractive for the private sector.[11] The government began to issue dollar-denominated Treasury bonds, but it was not enough to finance the large fiscal deficits. A solution was to increase the debt held by the public sector, particularly by social security institutions. Nevertheless, this financing source wore out as social security institutions weakened in the 1960s because of the economic stagnation and the negative real return on public debt.

Therefore, the financing of obligations in this period was inflationary.[12] The results of the budget constraint showed that deficits were financed with the inflation tax (4.7 percent of GDP on average) and other sources captured in the residual as negative obligations (1.4 percent of GDP on average; Figure 3). The following explanation is offered for this negative residual. Since no data are available on peso interest rates for the 1960s, debt obligations in pesos end up in the residual. Real interest rates were negative in this period, so debt obligations in pesos were likely to be negative. Thus our conjecture is that the residual is negative (that is, a missing source) because it contains transfers from debt holders to the public sector due to inflating away public debt in pesos. In other words, if data on interest rates in pesos were available, debt obligations in pesos would more likely be negative, increasing the sources and reducing the negative residual.

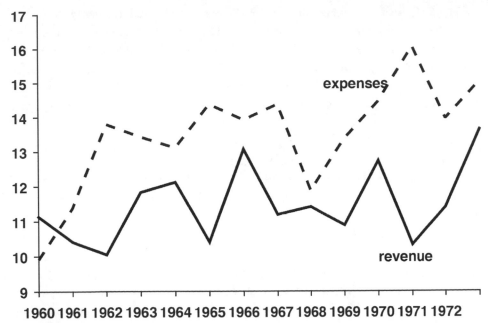

Figure 10. Central government: Revenue and expenses 1960–73 (% GDP)
Source: Instituto de Economía (IECON)

In 1965, a banking crisis occurred, which contributed to nominal instability (Vaz 1999). In December 1964, a bank run on the Transatlantic Bank of Uruguay began and spread to the other private banks. In April 1965, Banco República decided to rescue the bank, for which a significant monetary expansion was necessary.[13] This fueled the speculation against the peso: the official exchange rate depreciated 25 percent in March and the gap with the parallel exchange rate still remained above 40 percent (Vaz 1999).[14] The shortage of international reserves increased at the beginning of 1965 to the point that in April a commitment to Chase Manhattan was breached. In addition, the private sector's peso-denominated time deposits fell by 36 percent in real terms between 1964 and 1965 (Vaz 1999).

Amid this large bank run, the government created an explicit insurance scheme on peso-denominated bank deposits, converting them into contingent public debt. Also, there existed an implicit insurance on dollar-denominated deposits, so the total contingent liabilities for the monetary authority depended on the exchange rate as well.[15] So once bank runs intensified in 1965, the monetary authority had to monetize the deposits. And although deposits were falling, the frequent devaluations of the peso implied an increase in the number of pesos to be monetized.

Moreover, the banks' weak position impeded the restriction of secondary money creation, which could have been done by increasing reserve requirements or eliminating the inflation tax subsidy in rediscounts.[16] Therefore, the monetization of bank deposits and the decision not to restrict money creation contributed to the growth of monetary issuing, and thus nominal instability, by the mid-1960s.

Monetary issuing promoted currency devaluations and pushed inflation even further, provoking a vicious circle. In addition, the reserves-to-GDP ratio fell constantly in the first half of the 1960s and remained low until the first part of the 1970s (Figure 11). This was due to large capital outflows, the defense of the exchange rate, and the scarce issuing of dollar-denominated public debt. Therefore, the monetary authority was forced to devalue the peso several times, creating further inflationary pressures through higher import prices (Figure 12).

Therefore, the first half of the 1960s was marked by chronic inflation, scarce international reserves, the aftermath of the 1965 banking crisis, and the inflation-devaluation spiral. This scenario encouraged a political consensus to create a specialized institution to oversee monetary policy and the banking system's regulation and supervision. In 1967, the Central Bank of Uruguay was created.[17]

Nevertheless, erratic monetary policy and nominal instability remained in 1967 and 1968. For instance, the monetary base continued growing at three-digit figures at the beginning of 1968, and annual inflation reached 183 percent by midyear (Banda, De Brun, and Oddone 2017). In this situation, the social and political unrest became the main concern for the government, which led to implementing a price stabilization plan based on mandatory price fixing.

The plan chose wages as the nominal anchor, given that other instruments were unavailable under the prevailing macroeconomic policy conditions. First, interest rates were set by law, so they could not be used as a monetary target. Second, commitments on the exchange rate and monetary aggregates were not credible, given the large primary

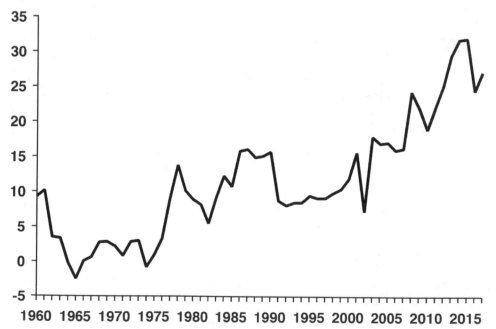

Figure 11. International reserves (% GDP)
Sources: Central Bank of Uruguay, IECON

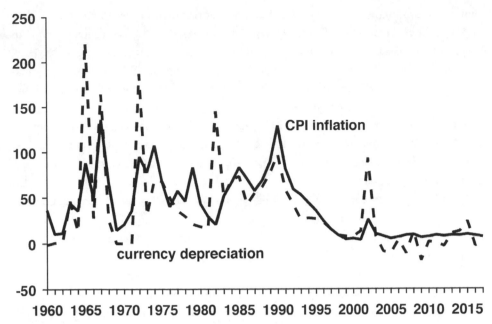

Figure 12. Currency depreciation and CPI inflation
Sources: IECON, INE

fiscal deficit (12.2 percent of GDP in 1967) and scarce international reserves (0.6 percent of GDP in 1967).

The plan also included a significant fiscal adjustment. The primary fiscal deficit shrank continuously to 2.4 percent of GDP between 1967 and 1970. Consequently, the need for inflationary financing was reduced (Figure 3), consistent with a fall in annual inflation (Figure 12). The stagnation period ended in 1968–70 as GDP grew 4.1 percent on average, in contrast to just 0.1 percent in 1958–67.

In 1970, Argentina abandoned the price stabilization plan that started in 1966. As a result, Uruguay received an external shock, which caused a GDP contraction in 1971 and 1972. The central government primary deficit started growing as revenues decreased (Figure 10), creating incentives for inflationary financing (Figure 3). A larger deficit (9.9 percent in 1972) in a context of a fixed exchange rate with a negative external shock put an end to the stabilization plan that began in 1968. Annual inflation rose back to three-digit figures by the end of 1972.

OPENING, LIBERALIZATION, AND BALANCE OF PAYMENTS CRISIS (1974–90)

In 1973, amid growing political and social tensions that had persisted for almost a decade, the constitutional government fell, and a de facto government was instituted, which remained until 1985.

The economic policy of this period had three stages. The first one in 1974–78 focused on stabilizing the external sector and starting to dismantle the closed-economy model.

Some of the initiatives were, as mentioned before, included in the Monetary and Foreign Exchange Reform law of 1959. Among these changes were greater integration with Argentina and Brazil, export promotion, and financial liberalization. During these years, sustained fiscal deficits remained, reaching on average 5 percent of GDP. Average annual inflation was 62.7 percent, and most of the deficit was financed with the inflation tax (3.9 percent of GDP on average).

During the second stage in 1979–82, the government implemented an anti-inflationary plan based on a preannounced crawling peg. The plan managed to reduce annual inflation from 83 percent in December 1979 to 11 percent in November 1982 (Figure 2) amid real currency appreciation (Figure 13) and strong GDP growth.

Nonetheless, in a context of a crawling peg and positive shocks from Argentina and Brazil, two of Uruguay's main trading partners, the fiscal contraction was not enough to offset private demand. This caused a significant deterioration of the current account balance, which reached −10.7 percent of GDP in 1982.

The expansion of the aggregate demand was boosted by an increase in private spending, especially real estate investment and consumption of durable goods. This was stimulated by a significant growth in private debt because of the financial liberalization initiated in 1974. By the end of 1981, 53 percent of the foreign currency debt was held by the private sector, something unprecedented in the history of Uruguay (Antía 1986).

Between 1978 and 1982, the primary deficit followed a U-shaped path. In the first three years, the overall deficit-to-GDP ratio fell from 4.4 percent to 1.1 percent amid a strong economic expansion. The debt-to-GDP ratio shrank while a significant amount

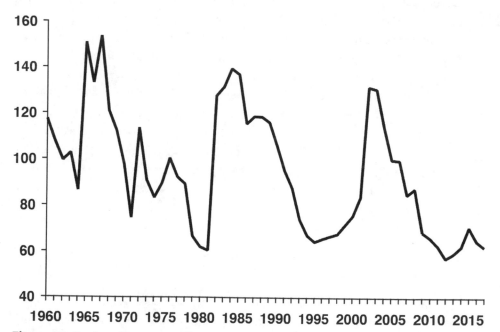

Figure 13. Real exchange rate, Uruguay–United States
Sources: Authors' elaboration based on data from Federal Reserve Economic Data (FRED), Federal Reserve Bank of St. Louis; INE

of inflation tax was still collected (annual inflation was 59 percent on average) and used to increase the stock of international reserves (Vaz 1999). However, in 1981 real GDP growth slowed after Argentina abandoned its price stabilization plan and contracted 9.4 percent in 1982. As a result, government revenue was affected, and the overall fiscal deficit of the public sector increased by 2.1 percent of GDP between 1980 and 1981 (Figure 4).

The simple version of Krugman's balance of payments crisis model (Krugman 1979) allows for a more precise interpretation of these events. Krugman's argument is that sustained fiscal deficits within a context of restrictions to external financing force the central bank to increase domestic credit. Under a fixed exchange rate, the increase of domestic credit leads to a loss of international reserves, which may cause a balance of payments crisis, currency devaluation, and an increase in inflation.

In 1982 Uruguay suffered a balance of payments crisis. The year before, external financing became more restrictive (Figure 14), so given a current account deficit of 5 percent of GDP, international reserves began to fall. In addition, net domestic credit started to increase to finance the fiscal deficit, which led to a further decline in international reserves (Figure 15). In November 1982, the stabilization plan was abandoned, and the peso was devalued by 149 percent against the U.S. dollar. Annual inflation climbed from 20.5 percent in 1982 up to 51.5 percent in 1983 (Figure 12). The large stock of dollar-denominated debt of the private sector quickly caused serious solvency problems for debtors, which triggered a banking crisis.

The banking crisis became a public debt crisis, since an implicit deposit insurance scheme existed. In other words, the banking system's liabilities were, at the end of the day, the central bank's liabilities. The adapted-for-Uruguay "Calvo ratio,"[18] which relates these liabilities to the government's capacity to comply with them, grew slowly between 1978 and 1980 and more rapidly in 1981 and 1982 once international reserves began to fall (Figure 16). After the currency devaluation, the central bank had to bail out commercial banks, as a large portion of debtors defaulted on their commercial credits. Therefore, the liberalization of the financial sector in Uruguay since 1974 led to a significant increase in contingent public debt and, soon after, a public debt crisis.

The third stage of the period began with the end of the stabilization plan in November 1982 and lasted until 1985. During these years, the public debt-to-GDP ratio rose from 20 percent in 1981 to 122 percent in 1985 (Figure 5) for three reasons. The first is the private debt restructuring after the crisis. The central bank purchased nonperforming assets from four failed banks and exchanged dollar-denominated public debt for nonperforming assets with Citibank and Bank of America.[19]

The second reason was the need for the central bank to recompose its stock of international reserves (Figure 11). Therefore, the reserves-to-GDP ratio grew from 5.5 percent in 1982 to 12.3 percent in 1984. This may partly explain the size of the budget constraint residual in 1982 and 1983 (12.4 percent and 17.2 percent of GDP, respectively).

The third reason was the effect of the currency devaluation on public debt, as it was mostly denominated in U.S. dollars (Figure 17).[20]

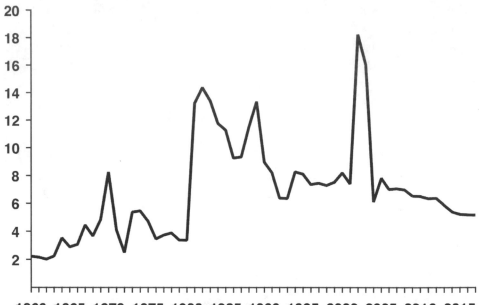

Figure 14. Interest rate of public debt in foreign currency (%)

Sources: Authors' elaboration based on data from IECON; Central Bank of Uruguay; MEF; República Administradora de Fondos de Ahorro Previsional (RAFAP); Borchardt, Rial, and Sarmiento (2000)

Note: 1960–93: implicit interest rate = interest payments in $t + 1$ / stock of debt in t; 1994–2003: estimated using the Uruguay Bond Index (RAFAP); 2004–14: dollar interest rate from the Debt Management Unit—MEF.

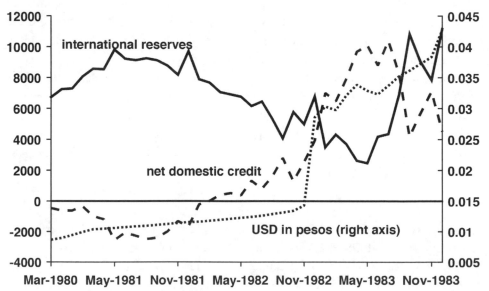

Figure 15. 1982 balance of payments crisis

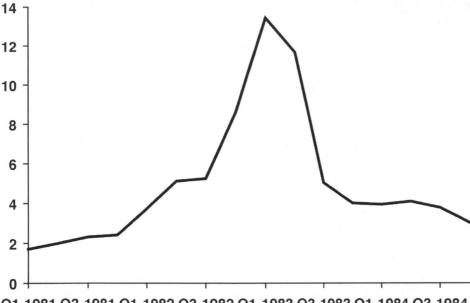

Figure 16. Adapted Calvo ratio

Note: Foreign currency bank deposits of the nonfinancial private sector / international reserves.

Source: Central Bank of Uruguay

Therefore, after the 1982 crisis, the public sector's budget constraint was dominated by public debt service and international reserve accumulation (Table 1). Public debt returns, especially in foreign currency, became the main obligation, reaching 11.6 percent of GDP in 1982–85. The large residuals may reflect the recovery of international reserves (Figure 6). At the same time, primary expenses were reduced. Regarding the sources in the budget constraint, even though public debt issuing was the main one, the rising inflation after the end of the stabilization plan allowed collecting an inflation tax of 3.3 percent of GDP in 1983–85.

In 1986, after the end of the de facto government, the economy began to recover. Real GDP expanded 8.9 percent and 7.9 percent in 1986 and 1987, respectively, due to a sequence of positive external shocks: a fall in oil prices, lower dollar interest rates, and strong demand from Argentina and Brazil because of price stabilization plans. In addition, there was a positive net wealth effect on debtors, given the fall in the real value of dollar-denominated loans.[21]

During these years, the public sector achieved a primary surplus, consistent with a heavy public debt service. This, together with strong GDP growth, allowed a reduction of the public debt-to-GDP ratio and the need for inflationary financing. As a result, twelve-month inflation dropped from 84 percent in January 1986 to 54 percent in March 1988.

Nonetheless, as of 1988 Argentina's performance was no longer favorable, and Uruguay's GDP stagnated. Argentina contracted 10 percent between 1987 and 1990, while

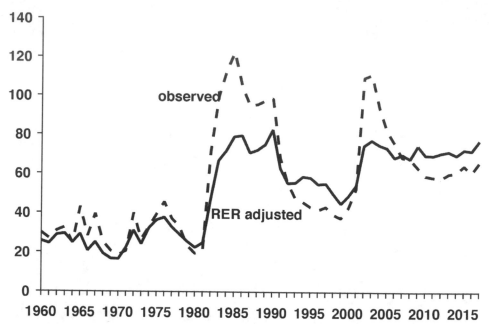

Figure 17. Real exchange rate (RER)–adjusted gross public debt (% GDP; based year = 2008)

Sources: Authors' elaboration using data from Central Bank of Uruguay, FRED, IECON, INE

Uruguay grew only 0.5 percent on average in 1988–90. The overall deficit stood at 5.9 percent of GDP in 1989, which consisted mostly of debt service (real returns on public debt reached 9.7 percent of GDP between 1988 and 1990). As a result, inflation rose back to almost 90 percent by the end of 1989.

BOOST, HALT, AND THE GOLDEN YEARS (1991–2017)

In the 1990s, governments carried out an array of measures and reforms geared to making public finances sustainable and guaranteeing nominal stability.[22] These measures were the Brady Plan in 1991, the price stabilization plan in 1990–2002, the first central bank act in 1995, and social security reform in 1996.

The large overall deficit, mostly due to a heavy public debt service, explains the persistence of nominal instability in the second half of the 1980s. Debt service exceeded primary surpluses, giving rise to inflationary financing. In addition, weak public finances limited access to external financing, forcing the government to issue money to purchase U.S. dollars and thus comply with debt payments. After a long negotiation period, in January 1991 Uruguay reached an agreement on its external debt in the context of the Brady Plan. This agreement reduced the debt stock by 5 percent of GDP (Rial and Vicente 2003) and reprogrammed short-term debt.[23]

In the last quarter of 1990, the government began another price stabilization plan. The plan consisted of a deep fiscal adjustment (around 6 percent of GDP in 1990–91) and a preannounced crawling peg. The exchange rate anchor was maintained for the whole decade, and the primary fiscal deficit remained balanced until 1999 (Figure 4). The latter reduced the need for an inflation tax as well as access to external financing (Figure 3). As a result, in 1998 inflation reached a one-digit figure for the first time in thirty years: it went from 133.7 percent in January 1991 to 9.9 percent in October 1998 (Figure 2).

In 1995, the Parliament approved a new central bank act that strengthened the commitment to avoid inflationary financing.[24] This new act set a limit on the assistance the central bank could offer to the rest of the public sector. First, it limited the stock of public debt the central bank could hold to 10 percent of the primary budget of the previous year. Also, it allowed the central bank to grant loans ("temporary transfers") for an amount not greater than 10 percent of the primary budget of the previous year. The former remains in force, and the latter was derogated by law in 1997.

The social security system weakened persistently before the 1990s for administrative, demographic, and structural reasons (Laens and Noya 2000). In addition, in 1989 a referendum determined that social security pensions be indexed to the Average Wage Index. In the context of disinflation, this indexation led to significant real growth of pensions and an increase in the deficit of the social security system from 2.2 percent of GDP in 1989 to 5.7 percent of GDP in 1997. In 1995, the government carried out a reform to ensure the long-term sustainability of the pension system and public finances.[25, 26] As discussed in the last part of this section, the sufficiency of benefits and the sustainability of the pension system are still part of Uruguay's political debate.

In terms of the budget constraint, there is relative stability between 1990 and 1998. The public sector's obligations decreased after both the fiscal adjustment and the Brady Plan. On average, the primary surplus stood at 1.5 percent of GDP, and the real returns on foreign currency debt were 0.2 percent of GDP during these years. Regarding the sources, public debt decreased by 2.7 percentage points every year, while the inflation tax fell from 3.4 percent to 0.6 percent of GDP. These results suggest that lower obligations and greater access to public debt reduced the need for inflationary financing.

The real currency appreciation favored the consolidation of a public debt profile in foreign currency (91.3 percent of total public debt in 1998).[27] By the end of the decade, features of the economy were an exchange rate commitment, a high share of public debt in foreign currency, and an implicit deposit insurance scheme (Figure 18).[28, 29] Thus international reserves were the key to guarantee the exchange rate commitment; ultimately, public debt service; and implicitly, bank deposits.

Between 1999 and 2001, the economy received an array of external shocks amid gradual restriction to external financing. At the beginning of 2002, the end of the convertibility in Argentina led to a run on bank deposits, especially from nonresidents, which caused a loss of international reserves (Figure 19). Lower international reserves threatened the credibility of the exchange rate commitment and thus public debt service.

This scenario led to abandonment the exchange rate commitment in July 2002. On the one hand, the devaluation had slowly favored the growth of exports since the end of 2002. On the other, given the high share of dollar-denominated public debt, the currency

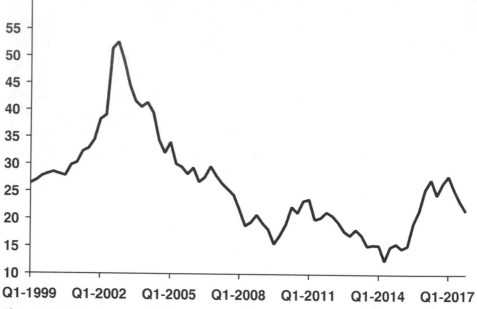

Figure 18. (M3—international reserves)/GDP
Source: Data from Central Bank of Uruguay

devaluation severely increased the vulnerability of public finances (Figure 5) and placed public debt on an unsustainable path (Rial and Vicente 2003).

The government's strategy to overcome the crisis was organized into three phases: stop the bank run, stabilize the exchange rate, and restructure public debt (Banda, De Brun, and Oddone 2017). The resolution of the banking crisis was the central bank's priority. For this crisis, on the one hand, measures were taken to maintain the continuity and liquidity of the payment chain.[30] On the other hand, the central bank proceeded to liquidate the three suspended banks and created a *new bank* based on the assets of the liquidated banks.[31, 32] The second priority was to stabilize the exchange rate: the central bank defined a policy based on a target for the monetary base and a fixed quarterly pre-announcement rule with annual horizons.

The third phase was the restructuring of public debt. After the devaluation, the debt service due in 2003 was US$471 million, equivalent to 4.4 percent of GDP in 2002 (De Brun and Licandro 2005; Figure 20). Thus the market and the IMF expected a default on public debt. In other words, the fiscal adjustment necessary to comply with debt service obligations and make public debt sustainable was too large to be reachable without provoking a strong recession (Calvo 1998). Given the debt service due in 2003 and the primary surplus in 2002 (0.2 percent of GDP), it was necessary to make a fiscal adjustment of at least 4 percent of GDP.

In May 2003, the government conducted a restructuring, which reprogrammed the maturity of 50 percent of the total public debt.[33] The swap obtained 93 percent of the proposed amount, while the 7 percent that did not adhere received the payments under the conditions originally agreed upon (De Brun and Della Mea 2003).[34]

As in the 1970s, the *boost* of the 1990s ended with a sudden *halt*. However, as opposed to 1982, the 2002 crisis originate not in a balance of payments crisis but in a bank run (Figure 19). Notwithstanding the severity of the 2002 crisis that had significant economic, social, and political consequences, many changes made before 2002 laid the foundation for a stronger economy. This explains part of the recovery as of 2003.

In the second half of 2003, Uruguay left the crisis behind and began the longest growth period since the 1940s. In the period 2004–14, the GDP compound annual growth rate was 5.4 percent, three times the growth in the second half of the twentieth century. This growth originated in the supercycle of commodity prices, strong external demand, and extraordinary financial conditions for emerging markets, especially after the 2008 international crisis. In addition, structural policies and reforms helped create a favorable business climate.

The economic policy implemented since 2003 attempted, in the first place, to reduce those macroeconomic fragilities that amplified external shocks in 1982 and 2002. The pillars of the strategy were to consolidate exchange rate flexibility, reduce the financial vulnerability of the public sector, and strengthen the prudential regulation of the financial system. For this, the macroeconomic policy scheme adopted was based on inflation targets (since 2005), the consolidation of a primary fiscal surplus (Figure 4), and stronger management of the public sector's assets and liabilities, especially public debt (Table 3).

In parallel, the central bank was granted greater independence.[35] As a result, it strengthened banking regulations to manage the risks of currency mismatch and liquidity, improving capital requirements and reducing exposure to nonresident operations. The

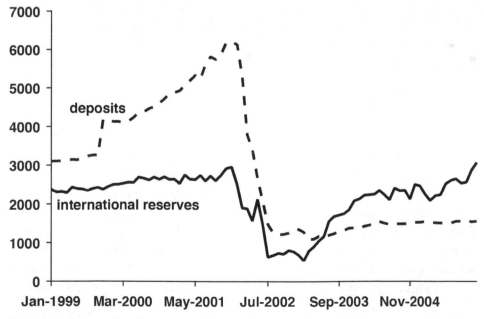

Figure 19. International reserves and nonresident nonfinancial private sector deposits in foreign currency (US$ millions)
Sources: IECON, Central Bank of Uruguay

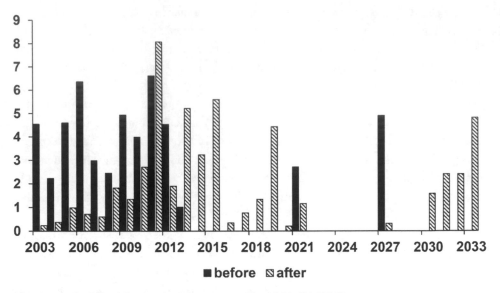

Figure 20. Public debt service restructured in 2003 (% GDP)
Source: Central Bank of Uruguay
Note: Estimated using GDP of 2002 and peso-dollar exchange rate of May 2003.

Table 3. Public debt profile, 2001 vs. 2017

	Share of public debt (%)	
	2001	*2017*
Debt with maturity < 1 year	13	19
Foreign currency public debt	82	42
Fixed-rate public debt	43	88

Source: Central Bank of Uruguay.
Note: Public debt includes reserve requirements on bank deposits.

combination of a favorable external environment with a risk-oriented macroeconomic management policy returned the investment grade to Uruguay's public debt in 2012.

Regarding budget constraint results, relatively low obligations and access to external credit markets guaranteed a relative nominal stability. Primary surpluses during the first few years allowed compliance with the 2002 crisis debt service and accumulation of international reserves. Since 2004, foreign currency public debt was partly substituted by peso-denominated and CPI-indexed public debt (Table 1; Figure 5). This was stimulated by relatively low inflation, real currency appreciation, and debt de-dollarization policies. As a result, the financial vulnerability of the public sector decreased.

Nonetheless, since 2008, and especially after 2011, the primary surplus dropped (Figure 4) in a context of strong GDP growth (5.1 percent in 2008–14). That is, fiscal policy was not tight during the expansive phase of the cycle, while the wage policy attempted higher nominal rigidity in a context of full employment.[36] All this contributed to the end of the golden years in 2014 with the consolidation of two imbalances: primary fiscal deficit and inflation above the central bank's target range. The primary deficit averaged 0.3 percent of GDP in 2015–17, and inflation remained above the target range between September 2011 and February 2017. In addition, the RER-adjusted public debt shows that the debt-to-GDP ratio is higher than the unadjusted one (Figure 17), which implies that the effort to comply with public debt obligations could be larger than the observed one.

Regarding the social security system in Uruguay, the current structure may be a threat to fiscal sustainability. Although only a few studies quantify the potential effects of contingent liabilities (associated with the sufficiency of contributions and the sustainability of the pension system) on public finances, there are reasons to believe that the pension system should be reformed.

First, the increase in life expectancy and the decrease in the birth rate are putting pressure on the sustainability of the system. In a recent work, Camacho (2016) shows that the financial deficit of the pay-as-you-go system has two long-term trends: it will fall to 0.2 percent of GDP by 2030 but then will rise to 2.2 percent of GDP by 2050 because of the aging population. This suggests a reform is needed to reduce disbursements, increase future revenues, or both.[37]

Second, many reforms, such as the reduction in the minimum number of years of contribution from thirty-five to thirty, the doubling of the minimum amounts of retirements under the mixed regime, and changes in the distribution of contributions between systems of distribution and capitalization, could affect the sustainability of the system.

Lastly, in 2017 the Parliament approved a change to the system that would allow a nonnegligible group of system assets to abandon the mixed regime. This would cost between 7 percent and 10 percent of GDP (at 2017 prices) over a forty-year horizon.[38]

Conclusions and Final Remarks

The budget constraint analysis shows that from 1960 to 2017, the financing of Uruguay's public sector was mostly inflationary. On average, two-thirds of the total sources came from the inflation tax and one-third from public debt.

Between the 1960s and the late 1980s, chronic inflation was associated with large fiscal deficits. This caused nominal instability, which ended up triggering nominal rigidities (prices/wage indexation) and dollarization of financial assets. Both increased the financial vulnerability of the public sector and limited the ability of macroeconomic policies to stabilize the economy. Nonetheless, since the 1970s, but especially after 1991, the opening of the economy, financial liberalization, greater access to external financing, stabilization plans, and the more restrictive institutional framework of the central bank decreased the inflationary financing of fiscal deficits. Moreover, after the 2002 crisis, the lower share of foreign currency public debt reduced the vulnerability of the public sector.

During this transition, Uruguay had to endure two major crises: one in 1982 and the second in 2002. The former was very costly in fiscal terms and brought back the monetization of deficits, while the latter had significantly lower effects on the deficit and inflation. This suggests that governments have slowly understood the importance of fiscal constraints to guarantee nominal stability.

Uruguay's trade and financial integration with Argentina influenced the development and outcome of these two crises. First, the devaluation of the Argentine peso in September 1981 worsened the balance of payments problems that ended with the devaluation of the Uruguayan peso in November 1982. Second, the bank run in 2002 began with a massive exit of Argentine depositors after the risk of contagion increased. Once again, the situation in Argentina precipitated the currency devaluation of 2002.

This chapter offers some lessons that can be learned from the case of Uruguay and may be helpful in explaining the performance of other Latin American economies. Stabilization plans based on exchange rate anchors with insufficient fiscal adjustments could induce, under certain circumstances, balance of payments crises, currency devaluations, banking crises, and increases in the central bank's liabilities, which, eventually, can lead to public debt crises and cyclical volatility. In addition, implicit insurance on bank deposits, public and private debt dollarization, and commitments on the exchange rate require a strong and consistent fiscal policy. This seems to be common to Argentina (1981, 2001), Chile (1983), and Uruguay (1982, 2002).

Notes

We would like to thank Alfonso Capurro, Juanpa Nicolini, Timothy Kehoe, and Santiago Rego for their valuable comments and Germán Deagosto and María José Fernandez for their research contributions.

1 Uruguay's per capita GDP fell from a level similar to that of the United States at the end of the nineteenth century to almost one-third of U.S. GDP in the second decade of the twenty-first century.

2 The first banking crisis occurred in 1965 and had no significant consequences on public debt (see section 3).

3 On average, the deficit of the public sector was 5.9 percent of GDP in 1960–90 and 1.9 percent of GDP in 1991–2017.

4 See "A Framework for Studying the Monetary and Fiscal History of Latin America" in this book for a complete description of the conceptual framework.

5 The "consolidated budget constraint" includes the general government, state-owned enterprises, and the financial public sector. See appendix 2 in the online appendix, available at http://manifold.bfi.uchicago.edu/, for a complete description.

6 See appendix 4 (online at http://manifold.bfi .uchicago.edu/) for a detailed explanation of this estimation.

7 See the next section for further explanation.

8 "Boost and halt" is a translation from the Spanish *El Impulso y su Freno*, a book written by Carlos Real de Azúa, that used the phrase to refer to the import-substitution period between the 1930s and 1950s (Real de Azúa 1964).

9 Between 1896 and 1967, Banco República was both the state-owned commercial bank and the monetary authority.

10 The financial balance of the central government was mostly negative from the beginning of the 1930s. Nonetheless, it was not necessary to monetize the deficits at least until the second half of the 1950s, when the financial repression began.

11 The executive branch set bank interest rates by law (Act No. 9756 of 1938) until 1968. We assume bank interest rates in pesos were not significantly different from public debt interest rates in pesos.

12 Azar et al. (2009) arrive at the same conclusion.

13 Deposit withdrawals from the Transatlantic Bank on April 20 and 21 amounted to 10 percent of Banco República's cash availability at the end of March.

14 Although the Monetary and Foreign Exchange Reform law of 1959 imposed a single exchange rate, regulated "by the free play of supply and demand," in May 1963 a double exchange market was reestablished.

15 "In this situation, the inflationary impact of having a lender of last resort or a deposit insurance facility increases" (Vaz 1999, 102).

16 Commercial banks charged investors a discount for amortizing debt in advance, collecting part of the inflation tax (Vaz 1999).

17 Until 1967, the state-owned commercial bank Banco de la República Oriental del Uruguay had the role of monetary authority. During the transition time (1967–71), Banco República and the Central Bank of Uruguay shared the functions of a monetary authority.

18 The ratio of foreign currency deposits over international reserves is an adapted version of the "Calvo ratio" from "A Framework for Studying the Monetary and Fiscal History of Latin America." In a highly dollarized economy such as Uruguay's, the contingent liabilities of the central bank were mostly foreign currency deposits of the nonfinancial private sector in the banking system.

19 The central bank purchased nonperforming assets for US$1,141 million and issued US$755 million in public debt to Citibank and Bank of America (Vaz 1999). These agreements caused an increase in the quasi-fiscal deficit that reached 3.7 percent of GDP in 1984, almost half of the overall deficit of the public sector (Roldós 1994).

20 Appendix 2 (see at http://manifold.bfi .uchicago.edu/) describes the procedure followed to estimate RER-adjusted public debt.

21 The government had proposed to keep a stable real exchange rate against the currencies of Uruguay's major trading partners. The sharp international weakening of the dollar strengthened the peso and ended up generating a positive net wealth effect for debtors in dollars. Borrowing from the private sector was mainly in dollars. Noya and Rama (1987) conclude that this effect was 14.7 percent and 10.9 percent for private companies and the public sector, respectively, between 1985 and 1986. In addition, given the high level of public debt in dollars, real currency appreciation also had a significant positive net wealth effect on the public sector. According to Noya and Rama (1987), it was 15 percent of GDP between 1984 and 1985.

22 The definition of the 1991–2017 period is controversial. From the perspective of the economic history of Uruguay, the crisis of 2002 is a milestone that should define two subperiods: 1991–2002 and 2003–17. However, from the perspective of the conceptual framework of this project, the relevant change occurs at the beginning of the 1990s when the fiscal restriction becomes an anchor of macroeconomic policy.

23 The Brady Plan was preceded by the Baker Plan, which was launched by the secretary of the U.S. Treasury in October 1985. The Baker Plan sought to make the refinancing conditions of the highly indebted emerging countries more flexible. Within its framework, Uruguay, on the one hand, reprogrammed around 70 percent of its debt payments. On the other hand, it agreed with creditor banks on a three-year payment period, longer than the one agreed to with the IMF.

24 A 1964 law allowed the monetary authority to assist the Treasury with up to one-sixth of the annual budget (Banda and Onandi 1992).

25 Laens and Noya (2000) estimate that at the time of the reform, the implicit public debt

was around 2.5 times Uruguay's GDP, one of the largest implicit debts in Latin America. They conclude that the reform reduced the system's primary deficit by 2 percent of GDP in the long run.

26 The system covers the risks of disability, old age, and survival. It is a mixed system, as it has two pillars: intergenerational solidarity and compulsory individual saving. The former is a defined benefit, and the benefits of the liabilities are financed by contributions from active workers, employers, taxes affected, and, if necessary, the state's financial assistance. The second pillar is a defined contribution: each worker accumulates individual contributions and returns in a personal savings account. At the time of cessation of activities for cause (thirty-five years of contribution), or when reaching sixty years of age, the worker has the right to receive a monthly income that is determined by the amount accumulated in the individual account, the worker's sex and age, and a technical interest rate determined by the regulator. Likewise, the second pillar has a collective capitalization insurance, with a defined benefit, which covers the risks of disability and death in activity.

27 Data are from the Central Bank of Uruguay.

28 "There was the perception among economic agents that, should anything happen in the banking system, the government would bail them out. This implicit guarantee, in turn, became a potential liability of the state" (De Brun and Licandro 2005, 7).

29 As Figure 18 shows, the central bank's contingent liabilities (estimated as the difference between M3 and international reserves as a percentage of GDP) became an additional source of risk by the end of 2001.

30 For example, (1) access to current accounts and savings accounts was restored to the clients of the suspended banks with funds from the Banking System Stabilization Fund; (2) the validity terms of the checks issued by the suspended banks were extended so that holders could claim from the drawer their payment or substitution by others against other banks; and (3) it was provided that the transfers ordered from and to the accounts in the suspended banks that had been accepted before the suspension had to be fulfilled in full.

31 The creditors of the banking companies in liquidation received shares in proportion to their credits, and a public auction enabled the purchase of the assets of the new bank.

32 The legal framework approved in order to make the liquidation operation of the suspended banks feasible gave the central bank powers for the first time since its creation in 1967 to supervise and sanction state-owned banks.

33 All dollar-denominated bonds were eligible, except for short-term instruments issued since January 2003 (De Brun and Licandro 2005).

34 The rating agencies considered it a default. S&P downgraded Uruguay's public debt to Selective Default and Fitch downgraded to DDD in 2003. Uruguay inserted a collective action clause in the new bonds as well, which many believed would trigger a credit default swaps event because it changed the underlying structure of the debt.

35 In 2008, the Parliament approved a new central bank act that included the creation of the Macroeconomic Coordination Committee and the Monetary Policy Committee and set restrictions on the type of bailout operations for the central bank. Also, the Banking Supervision and Regulation Committee was granted greater technical autonomy from the central bank.

36 Collective bargaining has been active in Uruguay since 2005. Wage agreements in force since 2012 and 2013 have established clauses of periodic adjustments based on past inflation. This, together with a 10 percent inflation clause that triggers automatic wage increases in several sectors of the economy, resulted in a rigid nominal environment that favored inflationary inertia.

37 In September 2017, the annual deficit of the general regime of the pension system was

1.8 percent of GDP. The general regime excludes the retirement funds of the military, police, and bank officials, which have a deficit of 1.7 percent of GDP and are assisted by the government.

38 According to estimates by República AFAP, one of the main pension fund managers, this change would affect between forty thousand and seventy thousand people.

References

Antía, Fernando. 1986. *Endeudamiento externo, crisis financiera y política económica (1979–1983)*. Revista Suma 1. Montevideo: CINVE.

Azar, Paola, Ulises García Repetto, Reto Bertoni, Claudia Sanguinetti, Mariana Sienra, and Bertino Magdalena. 2009. *¿De quiénes, para quiénes y para qué? Las finanzas públicas en el Uruguay del siglo XX*. Montevideo: Facultad de Ciencias Económicas y de Administración Universidad de la República, Instituto de Economía.

Banda, Ariel, Julio De Brun, and Gabriel Oddone. 2017. *Historia del Banco Central del Uruguay*. Online ed. Montevideo: Banco Central del Uruguay. Accessed October 21, 2018. https://www.bcu.gub.uy/Acerca-de-BCU/50Aniversario/Libros/Historia%20BCU_FINAL.pdf.

Banda Ariel, and Dionisio Onandi. 1992. *El déficit parafiscal en Uruguay: 1982–1990*. Serie Política Fiscal. Santiago de Chile: CEPAL, Naciones Unidas.

Bonino, Nicolá, Carolina Román, and Henry Willebald. 2012. "PIB y estructura productiva en Uruguay (1870–2011): Revisión de series históricas y discusión metodológica." Series Documento de Trabajo, 05/12, Instituto de Economía (FCEA-UdelaR), Montevideo.

Borchardt, Michael, Isabel Rial, and Adolfo Sarmiento. 2000. *La evolución de la política fiscal en Uruguay; ¿Cómo armar el rompecabezas fiscal?* Washington, D.C.: Banco Interamericano de Desarrollo.

Calvo, Guillermo A. 1988. "Servicing the Public Debt: The Role of Expectations." *American Economic Review* 78 (4): 647–61.

———. 1998. "Varieties of Capital-Market Crises." In *The Debt Burden and Its Consequences for Monetary Policy*, edited by Guillermo A. Calvo and Mervyn King, 187–207. Proceedings of a conference held by the International Economic Association at the Deutsche Bundesbank, Frankfurt, Germany. Houndmills, Basingstoke, Hampshire: Palgrave Macmillan/International Economic Association.

Camacho, Luis. 2016. *Análisis global sobre posibles cambios paramétricos del régimen de reparto administrado por el Banco de Previsión Social*. Asesoría General en Seguridad Social, Comentarios de Seguridad Social No. 52, Segundo Trimestre, Montevideo.

De Brun, Julio, and Umberto Della Mea. 2003. "Una aproximación de mercado a la reestructuración de la deuda Soberana: Lecciones de la experiencia uruguaya." *Revista de economía*, 2nd época (Banco Central del Uruguay), 10 (2): 97–142.

De Brun, Julio, and Gerardo Licandro. 2005. "To Hell and Back: Crisis Management in a Dollarized Economy: The Case of Uruguay." Documento de Trabajo N° 004/2005, Banco Central del Uruguay, Montevideo.

Instituto de Economía. 1969. *Uruguay estadísticas básicas*. Montevideo: Facultad de Ciencias Económicas y Administración, Universidad de la República.

Krugman, Paul. 1979. "A Model of Balance-of-Payments Crises." *Journal of Money, Credit and Banking* 11 (3): 311–25.

Laens, Silvia, and Nelson Noya. 2000. "Efectos fiscales de la reforma de la seguridad social en

Uruguay." Paper series. Santiago: Ministerio de Hacienda Chile/CEPAL.

Licandro, Gerardo, and Leonardo Vicente. 2006. "Incentivos fiscales e inconsistencia temporal: Uruguay 1970–2006." *Revista de economía*, 2nd época (Banco Central del Uruguay), 14 (1): 97–154.

———. 1987. *¿Quién financió la reactivación?* Revista suma 3. Montevideo: CINVE.

Oddone, Gabriel. 2008. "Instituciones y políticas en el declive económico de Uruguay durante el siglo XX." *Revista de Historia Económica—Journal of Iberian and Latin American History* 26 (1): 45–82.

Real de Azúa, Carlos. 1964. *El impulso y su freno: Tres décadas de batllismo.* Montevideo: Ediciones de la Banda Oriental.

Rial, Isabel, and Leonardo Vicente. 2003. "Sostenibilidad y vulnerabilidad de la deuda pública uruguaya: 1988–2015." *Revista de economía*, 2nd época (Banco Central del Uruguay), 10 (2): 143–220.

Roldós, Jorge. 1994. "A Long-Run Perspective on Trade Policy, Instability, and Growth." In *The Effects of Protectionism on a Small Country: The Case of Uruguay*, edited by Michael Connolly and Jaime De Melo, 150–72. Washington, D.C.: International Bank for Reconstruction and Development, World Bank.

Vaz, Daniel Enrique. 1999. "Four Banking Crises: Their Causes and Consequences." *Revista de economía*, 2nd época (Banco Central del Uruguay), 6 (1): 29–346.

Discussion of the History of Uruguay 1

Eduardo Fernández-Arias
Inter-American Development Bank

The chapter by Oddone and Marandino is a comprehensive account of the evolution of fiscal and monetary policy in Uruguay since 1960. It highlights major macroeconomic crises that disrupted the process and often led to stages with distinct policy regimes. This is a systematic and serious analysis of Uruguayan economic history that provides a solid background for understanding policy regimes over time and how lessons have been learned the hard way. It should become mandatory reading for economists interested in Uruguay's macroeconomic experience and a useful reference for current policy debates.

The authors open with a decomposition of the budget constraint of the consolidated public sector based on the accounting framework of the introductory chapter and then move on to examine the monetary and fiscal policy regimes throughout the period. From my understanding of the framing chapter of this book, the purpose of the project is to test the hypothesis that bad fiscal policy, at the macroeconomic level, was a main cause responsible for macroeconomic instability: the balance of payment crisis, financial crisis, defaults, and hyperinflation. While the authors do not test that hypothesis explicitly, they do attempt to integrate both parts of the analysis and trace macroeconomic events to the budget constraint. In my view, however, the prevalence of macroeconomic crises associated with the balance of payments and the richness of these key experiences discussed in the second part far exceed what can be accounted for by the budget constraint. In my reading, the second part contains the meat, and the first part is background. Consequently, my comments will focus on the second part.

Before moving on to my main points, I would like to mention that the budget constraint decomposition elaborated by the authors is a welcome extension of the limited accounting scope usually found in other analyses—namely, the nonfinancial public sector (or the general government, which leaves aside state-owned enterprises, which are crucial to having an accurate fiscal picture of Uruguay). The authors should be commended for usefully supplementing the basic accounting framework of the introductory chapter with an adjustment to take into account international reserves, reserve requirements, and transfers, producing a finer decomposition that would merit a full-fledged presentation in the chapter. This extended accounting framework can be fruitfully used by itself and in conjunction with the conventional nonfinancial framework. Having said that, it is important to remember that accounting is informative but not conclusive because it is consistent with multiple interpretations of the driving forces. For example, the chapter tends to focus on the importance of the inflation tax as a gauge of fiscal policy, while high inflation may be simply the mechanical consequence of persistence in the context of costly disinflation. I found that the attention given to the inflation tax as a smoking gun was overemphasized.

The authors organize their analysis into three subperiods: stagflation (1960–73); opening, liberalization, and the balance of payments crisis (1974–90); and boost, halt, and the golden years (1991–2017). This published version successfully incorporates some of the comments made by me and other participants in the Inter-American Development Bank conference "Monetary and Fiscal History of Latin America," held in September 2018 in Washington, DC. In this updated chapter, I will focus my comments on the last subperiod, "boost, halt, and the golden years," and organize them under three headings: (1) "Boost and Tripping over the Same Stone (1991–2002)," (2) "The Golden Years (2003–17)," and (3) "What's Next?" My comments are broadly complementary to the authors' points except in relation to the pre-2002 period, on which I have a somewhat different assessment.

Boost and Tripping over the Same Stone (1991–2002)

The public external debt restructuring under the Brady Plan in 1991, with the financial support of multilateral institutions after carrying out a deep fiscal adjustment, allowed Uruguay to finally emerge from the lost decade of the debt crisis, regain access to external financing, and boost the economy. Over the decade, and with the help of a benign external economic environment, the fiscal deficit remained balanced, and inflation decreased from very high to tolerable levels. Social security reform and the approval of the central bank act further helped macroeconomic stability going forward.

Despite these achievements, however, a macroeconomic crisis visited Uruguay again shortly thereafter, in 2002. What went wrong? In a nutshell, continued vulnerability to the external opening and financial liberalization in the context of a rigid exchange rate regime—a preannounced crawling peg in this case—led to a major macroeconomic crisis, when external shocks hit, that was reminiscent of the 1982 balance of payments crisis. The increase in financial dollarization, in both the public and private sectors, and an implicit deposit insurance on dollar deposits multiplied potential claims to international reserves and made macroeconomic stability fragile. This otherwise successful period of the 1990s continued with many of the vulnerabilities of the past and tripped over the same stone. The authors did not highlight this fatal flaw of the policy framework, which failed to incorporate past lessons regarding macroeconomic stability risks and continued deepening financial liberalization without proper concern for Uruguay's vulnerabilities.

The currency appreciation against the dollar created by the crawling-peg policy was possible only because Argentina and Brazil, the main trade partners, embarked on a similar policy of exchange rate appreciation. In fact, extraregional currency overvaluation led to an increase in the already high exposure to regional trade as well as intense financial flows. The risk of a negative regional shock was clearly in play. After Brazil devalued in 1999 and Argentina, chained to the fixed exchange rate of the currency board, entered a recession, exchange rate pressures in Uruguay mounted without a corresponding adjustment in the crawling peg. The crawling peg was sustained as if regional shocks were temporary. The exchange rate commitment was abandoned only by mid-2002 after Argentina imploded following the abandonment of the currency board, and all the elements for a macroeconomic triple crisis in Uruguay (balance of payments, public debt, and banking) were in place.

While it is always difficult to disentangle multiple crises because of their positive feedback loops, I do not concur with the authors that the macroeconomic crisis of 2002 originated in a bank run. The root problem was not in banking but in the multiple vulnerabilities to a currency depreciation originating in a balance of payments shock. While it is clear that many of the successful policy changes made before 2002 helped sustain the golden years in the subsequent period, I disagree with the authors' conclusion that these changes laid the foundation for a stronger economy after 2003. I think that such a foundation can be found elsewhere—a point to which I now turn.

The Golden Years (2003–17)

In my view, the golden years should not be lumped together with the period prior to the 2002 crisis, as the authors do, for the fundamental reason that policies after 2003 substantially fixed the previous policy pitfalls leading to the crisis. This true foundation of the golden years was accomplished in two stages: first, through a model resolution of the 2002 crisis, which had the potential to become a second Argentina debacle and was successfully reduced to a deep but short downturn; and second, with policies going forward designed to minimize the vulnerabilities that led to the crisis. (For more details, see Fernández-Arias 2007.)

The crisis resolution rested on four pillars that signaled Uruguay's commitment to a sustainable recovery and earned multilateral support, in stark contrast to Argentina's experience. The first pillar was a minimalist bank resolution strategy prioritizing the payment system; organizing a friendly, value-preserving reprofiling of time deposits only in banks lacking access to liquidity; and facilitating bilateral loan renegotiations abstaining from legal imposition. The second was a minimalist and friendly public debt reprofiling designed to substantially preserve the value to investors. The third pillar was a decisive fiscal adjustment based on wage austerity that counted on broad political support across the spectrum. And finally, the fourth pillar was careful monetary policy to keep inflation low.

Once the crisis was resolved in 2003, macroeconomic policies were set to support a new policy regime designed to reduce the underlying vulnerabilities. Exchange rate policy was made flexible, consistent with inflation control. Regional trade vulnerabilities were reduced through diversification, and regional financial vulnerabilities were addressed through regulation. The deleterious risk impacts of financial dollarization in banking and real activity were recognized and addressed through a range of prudential-financial policies aimed at reducing those impacts. An active prudential management of public debt produced a substantial shift toward less dollar debt and longer terms, as well as advancing debt issuance and contracting international lines of credit to be used contingently. Finally, fiscal policy was restrained using self-imposed bounds to ensure acceptable sovereign credit ratings.

In addition, as the authors mention, structural policies and reforms helped create a favorable business climate. This is not to say that the policy shift was entirely responsible for the miraculous recovery. In part, it was sustained by good luck. For example, international interest rates quickly declined to a point where bondholders participating in the debt exchange actually made money, as country risk fell to a record low. As mentioned by the authors, commodity prices helped Uruguay. But it is clear that it was a positive policy shift that addressed some of the endemic macroeconomic risk factors. Furthermore, once implemented, it was not backtracked despite favorable winds—yet another virtue of the new policy regime.

Nevertheless, the authors perceptively point to signs of possible exhaustion of fiscal discipline in recent years. As in most Latin American countries, fiscal expansion associated with the global crisis of 2009 was not shed as expected once the business cycle turned positive (see Fernández-Arias and Pérez Pérez 2014), and debt appears to be on an upward trend. The key question is what is next, to which I now turn.

What's Next?

The main element missing from making fiscal policy reliable and placing it beyond the point of no return is the lack of appropriate fiscal rules and supporting institutions (see Fernández-Arias 2007). As of now, policy performance rests on the exercise of fiscal restraint to avoid large deficits. Self-discipline may fail under pressure, and even if unwavering, it may create overspending in good times.

Uruguay needs a structural approach to fiscal management, meaning considering fiscal accounts and public debt purged from the effects of the business cycle and temporary valuation fluctuations (such as real exchange rates and interest rates). Structural measurements reveal the true stance of fiscal policy and the real content of debt, avoiding the illusion that debt is lower when the currency is appreciated and that spending can be expanded without risk when fiscal revenues rise. They are needed for a correct assessment of fiscal sustainability and prudent fiscal policy as well as macroeconomically efficient fiscal decisions over time.

Structural accounting requires independent and reliable institutions to produce estimations and forecasts as well as ex post verification. Within a structural fiscal policy framework, Uruguay needs appropriate fiscal rules and processes to define targets that account for parameters such as the debt level and social security spending projections. These are some of the pending items in the reform agenda.

References

Fernández-Arias, Eduardo. 2007. "Algunas enseñanzas de la crisis financiera de 2002." In *¿Uruguay: Qué aprendimos de la crisis financiera de 2002?* Conference proceedings. Montevideo: World Bank and Ministerio de Economía y Finanzas, Uruguay.

Fernández-Arias, Eduardo, and Jorge Eduardo Pérez Pérez. 2014. "Grading Fiscal Policy in Latin America in the Last Decade." Policy Brief 216, Research Department, Inter-American Development Bank, Washington, D.C.

Discussion of the History of Uruguay 2

Carlos A. Végh
World Bank and Johns Hopkins University

It has been a pleasure to read this chapter on the monetary and fiscal history of Uruguay over the last sixty years. It is highly informative and clearly written, and it does an excellent job of linking fiscal deficits to monetary instability, a trait that has clearly dominated the fiscal-monetary landscape of Uruguay in the last sixty years.

The Missing Link in the Fiscal Story

Rather than marginally adding to this well-known link, let me address the issue of how fiscal policy has been conducted over the business cycle in Uruguay. For some reason, the chapter completely abstracts from this phenomenon, which, in my view, is as critical to understanding fiscal policy in Uruguay as is the link between fiscal deficits and monetary instability. Specifically, the issue is whether fiscal policy has been procyclical, acyclical, or countercyclical. By definition, procyclical fiscal policy (i.e., expansionary fiscal policy in good times and contractionary fiscal policy in bad times) reinforces the business cycle. If anything, standard Keynesian prescriptions would call for exactly the opposite policies (i.e., countercyclical fiscal policy to stimulate the economy in bad times and cool it down in good times), and neoclassical fiscal policy prescriptions (à la Lucas and Stokey 1983) would, under separable preferences, imply acyclical fiscal policy.

Since a picture is worth a thousand words, let me illustrate this critical issue with Figure 1.

Each bar represents one of 123 countries: 22 industrial (black bars), 77 emerging markets (gray bars), and 24 nonemerging Latin American and Caribbean (LAC) countries (striped bars). The bars (which vary between −1 and 1) indicate the correlation between the cyclical components of real GDP and government spending. As indicated in the figure, a positive correlation implies procyclical public spending, since public spending increases (falls) in good (bad) times.[1] The opposite is true in the case of countercyclical policy. The sample period covers 1960–2017. Several key observations follow from this plot:

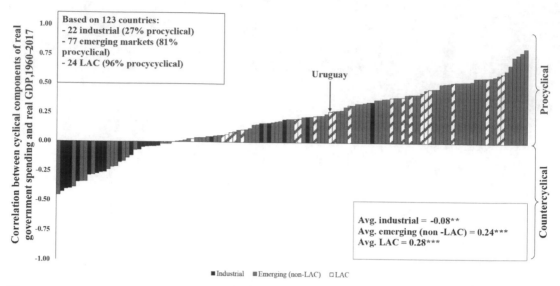

Figure 1. Correlation between government spending and GDP, 1960–2017
**significantly different from 0 at 0.05 confidence level
***significantly different from 0 at 0.01 coincidence level
Source: Kaminsky, Reinhart, and Végh (2005, updated)
Note: Total expenditure consists of total expense and new acquisition of nonfinancial assets.

- Seventy-three percent of industrial countries have been countercyclical, with an average correlation of −0.08 (and significant at the 5 percent level).

- Seventy-seven percent of non-LAC emerging markets have been procyclical, with an average correlation of 0.24 (and significant at the 1 percent level).

- All but one of the LAC countries have been procyclical, with an average correlation of 0.28 (significant at the 1 percent level). The arrow indicates Uruguay, which has been procyclical throughout this period.[2]

Breaking the Sample: Before and After 1999

Figure 2 breaks the sample into two (before and after 1999) for LAC countries.[3] Interestingly enough, as a whole, the LAC countries have become less procyclical: the number of countercyclical countries has increased from 8 percent during 1960–99 to 33 percent after the year 2000. The other side of the coin is that the average correlation has fallen from 0.29 to 0.14. A big exception to this otherwise good news is Uruguay, which has become more procyclical both in absolute terms (with the correlation increasing from 0.26 to 0.58) and in relative terms (from twelfth most procyclical country in the LAC countries to fourth most procyclical). At the other extreme, Chile is the best-behaved country in the LAC countries. As illustrated in Figure 2, in the post-2000 period, Chile has become the most countercyclical of the LAC countries (with a correlation of −0.68).

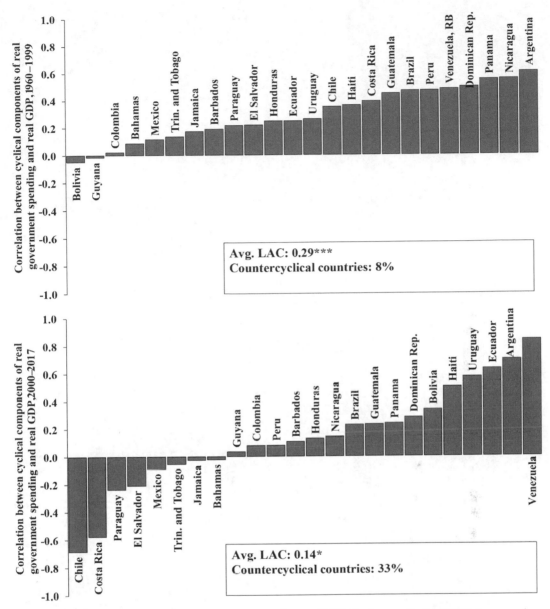

Figure 2. Correlation between government spending and GDP before and after 2000: top panel: 1960–99; bottom panel: 2000–2017

*significantly different from 0 at 0.10 confidence level

***significantly different from 0 at 0.01 coincidence level

Source: Végh, Lederman, and Bennett (2017, updated)

What may lie behind different degrees of cyclicality? Figure 3 points to institutional quality (which includes the quality of fiscal institutions) as a key determinant, by comparing Chile and Uruguay. The plot shows a twenty-year rolling window for an index of institutional quality and the correlation between the cyclical components of government spending and real GDP. In the case of Chile, the large improvement in the quality of

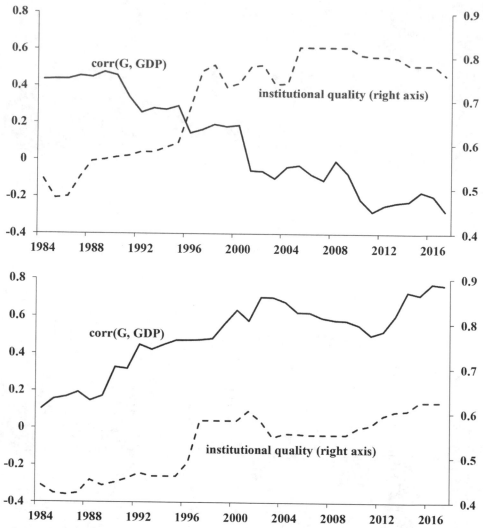

Figure 3. Cyclicality of government spending and institutional quality: top panel: Chile; bottom panel: Uruguay

Source: Frankel, Végh, and Vuletin (2013, updated)

institutions and the beneficial effects of the structural balance budget rule introduced in the year 2000 are readily apparent, as fiscal policy has become clearly countercyclical over the last two decades. In sharp contrast, Uruguay has become more and more procyclical over time, reaching a correlation of 0.77 in 2017.

One Hundred Years of Fiscal Policy Cyclicality

Finally, we take a really long-run view and compute fiscal cyclicality based on one hundred years of data for both Chile and Uruguay (Figures 4 and 5).[4] The plot illustrates

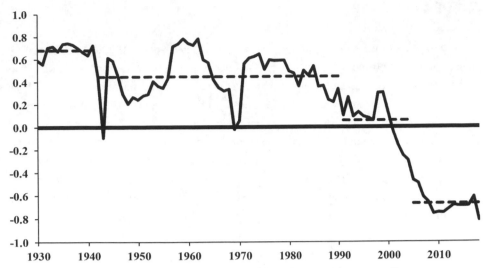

Figure 4. Chile: One hundred years of cyclicality of government spending

Source: Camarena et al. (2018)

Figure 5. Uruguay: One hundred years of cyclicality of government spending

Source: Camarena et al. (2018)

ten-year rolling windows of the correlation between the cyclical components of government spending and GDP. Further, we use the PELT algorithm (pruned exact linear time) to look for multiple change points in the fiscal cyclicality regime. In the case of Chile, we observe that the algorithm detects four different regimes, which become progressively more countercyclical over time, ending with an extremely countercyclical policy (partly reflecting the sharply countercyclical reaction to the global financial crisis of 2008–9). The case of Uruguay is the opposite. After alternating regimes, Uruguay has been consistently procyclical for almost four decades. The contrast with Chile could not be starker.

Why?

Why would a country follow procyclical fiscal policy? This is the key public policy question. More and more, countries in LAC are escaping the fiscal procyclicality trap thanks to better fiscal institutions, including fiscal rules and fiscal councils (such as those in Chile, Colombia, and Peru). But most continue to reinforce the business cycle in a suboptimal way. The two most plausible explanations found in the literature are (1) frictions in (or incomplete) capital markets and (2) political-economy pressures to spend in good times. In my view, these are complementary explanations, since the first one is more likely to apply in bad times, while the second would come to the fore primarily in good times. The urge to spend in good times is legendary in emerging markets, whether to solidify power or buy constituencies' favor (including future votes) or as the result of viewing temporary shocks as permanent. In bad times, international creditors (with the possible exception of official multilateral organizations) are typically reluctant to lend, given the long history of defaults in emerging markets.

Uruguay has not been able to escape these forces and, hence, the procyclical trap. The fiscal authorities either seem unaware of the simple idea of saving in sunny days for rainy days or, much more likely, conveniently choose to ignore such an elementary dictum to reap the political benefits of spending temporary windfalls. In fact, this misguided fiscal behavior has taken place irrespective of the political party in power, which suggests that the roots go deeper. But, eventually, common sense and good economics will hopefully prevail, and Uruguay will follow the sensible cyclical path of industrial countries and an increasing number of LAC countries.

Notes

This chapter represents a written version of comments delivered on September 25, 2018, at the Inter-American Development Bank (IDB) regarding "The Monetary and Fiscal History of Uruguay, 1960–2017," by Gabriel Oddone and Joaquín Marandino. These comments draw heavily on the author's joint work with various coauthors (see references), particularly José A. Camarena, Jeffrey Frankel, and Guillermo Vuletin. The views expressed in this note are the author's own and do not necessarily represent those of the World Bank, its staff, or its executive board.

1 Even though we are implicitly assuming that fiscal policy reacts to GDP, correlation does not, of course, imply causation. Ilzetzki and Végh (2008), however, use instrumental variables to show that there is indeed causality from GDP to fiscal policy.

2 Uruguay has also been procyclical on the tax side, tending to increase tax rates in bad times and lower them in good times. In fact, Végh and Vuletin (2015) report a correlation of -0.38 for a tax index comprising corporate income, personal income, and value-added taxes that covers the period 1969–2013.

3 See Frankel, Végh, and Vuletin (2013) and Végh, Lederman, and Bennett (2017) for detailed analyses of fiscal policy graduation in developing countries (i.e., the switch from procyclical to countercyclical fiscal policy).

4 Based on Camarena et al. (2018).

References

Camarena, J. A., J. Frankel, C. Végh, and G. Vuletin. 2018. "Procyclical DNA." World Bank, Washington, D.C.

Frankel, Jeffrey, Carlos Végh, and Guillermo Vuletin. 2013. "On Graduation from Fiscal Procyclicality." *Journal of Development Economics* 100 (1): 32–47.

Ilzetzki, Ethan, and Carlos A. Végh. 2008. "Procyclical Fiscal Policy in Developing Countries: Truth or Fiction?" Working paper 14191, National Bureau of Economic Research, Cambridge, Mass.

Kaminsky, Graciela L., Carmen M. Reinhart, and Carlos A. Végh. 2005. "When It Rains, It Pours: Procyclical Capital Flows and Macroeconomic Policies." In *NBER Macroeconomics Annual 2004*, vol. 19, edited by Mark Gertler and Kenneth Rogoff, 11–82. Cambridge, Mass.: MIT Press.

Lucas, Robert E., Jr., and Nancy L. Stokey. 1983. "Optimal Fiscal and Monetary Policy in an Economy without Capital." *Journal of Monetary Economics* 12 (1): 55–93.

Végh, Carlos, Daniel Lederman, and Federico Bennett. 2017. *Leaning against the Wind: Fiscal Policy in Latin America and the Caribbean in a Historical Perspective.* LAC Semiannual Report. Washington, D.C.: World Bank.

Végh, Carlos A., and Guillermo Vuletin. 2015. "How Is Tax Policy Conducted over the Business Cycle?" *American Economic Journal: Economic Policy* 7 (3): 327–70.

Venezuela

The History of Venezuela

Diego Restuccia
University of Toronto and National Bureau of Economic Research

Major fiscal and monetary events, 1960–2017

1976	Nationalization of oil industry	**1986**	Default
1983	Balance of payments crisis and devaluation	**1990**	Brady Plan
		1994	Banking crisis
	Capital controls	**2016**	Hyperinflation

Introduction

In the postwar era, Venezuela represents one of the most dramatic growth experiences in the world. Measured as real gross domestic product (GDP) per capita in international dollars, Venezuela attained levels of more than 80 percent of that of the United States by the end of 1960. It has also experienced one of the most dramatic declines, with levels of relative real GDP per capita now reaching less than 30 percent of that of the United States. Understanding the features—institutional or policy driven—that determined such dramatic episodes of growth and collapse is of great importance. The purpose of this chapter is to take a small step toward understanding some aspects of the institutions and policies that may have contributed to these experiences. The focus is on the monetary and fiscal outcomes during the period between 1960 and 2016. While the connection of monetary and fiscal policies to long-run growth may seem tenuous, in the case of Venezuela, they provide a perspective on the extent to which the government was involved—directly or indirectly—in the determination of prices, the allocation of resources, and therefore, the outcomes.

Venezuela became an oil economy after the discovery of crude oil around 1913; today it has one of the largest proven oil reserves in the world. During the 1920s, oil production, at the time mostly done through concessions to foreign companies, was an important contributor to Venezuela's structural transformation and development. Over time, discussions about the nationalization of the oil industry in the late 1960s and early 1970s brought a halt to this development even though nationalization was only formalized in 1976. For instance, total crude oil production declined substantially (55 percent) from its peak in 1970 to the mid-1980s, and labor productivity in the oil industry declined by more than 70 percent in that period. In addition, the nationalization of the industry and its impact on fiscal policy implied that distortions accumulated over time as vast

495

amounts of resources were being allocated by government officials and disparate policies, not by market forces. These distortions were exacerbated by the increase in oil prices in 1974—which led to a windfall in government revenues—and the larger volatility observed in oil prices since then. Oil represents an average of around 90 percent of all exports and almost 60 percent of government revenues during the period between 1960 and 2016. But contrary to some theories, such as that of "Dutch disease," oil is not the problem of the Venezuelan economy; the problem lies in how the vast amounts of resources generated from oil were utilized.[1] Other economies, such as Norway, have managed their oil wealth properly, with diametrically different economic outcomes.

Figure 1 documents the (log) real GDP per capita in Venezuela from 1960 to 2016. The figure illustrates the positive growth process between 1960 and 1977 and the subsequent decline and volatility. To put this growth process in perspective, note that between 1960 and 1977 average annual growth was only 2.3 percent, lower than the growth achieved by Venezuela in the decades prior and also lower than that observed for the United States during the same time period. An important element in this relative low growth is the process of nationalization of the oil industry. The period between 1978 and 1989 had a negative average annual growth of −2.6 percent, a remarkable economic collapse. From 1990 to 2016, annual average growth was −0.2 percent, with dramatic declines in output per capita of −19 percent between 2001 and 2002 (declines associated with political uncertainty and an oil strike) and of −30 percent between 2013 and 2016.

Venezuela is also distinct from many other Latin American economies in that for much of the economic decline, Venezuela enjoyed a period of relative macroeconomic stability. Figure 2 documents the yearly inflation rate from 1960 to 2016. From 1960

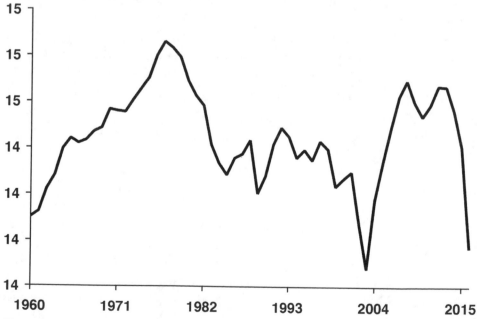

Figure 1. The log of real GDP per capita

Note: The logarithm of real GDP per capita; 1997 base prices in millions of bolivares.

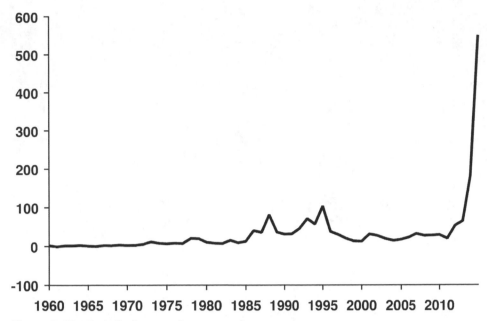

Figure 2. Yearly inflation rate (percentage)

Note: The inflation rate is the percentage change in the consumer price index.

to 1986, inflation was almost always below 30 percent, but since 1987 inflation has almost always been above 30 percent, with 80 percent in 1989, more than 100 percent in 1996, and more than 500 percent in 2016.

Only in recent years has Venezuela been suffering a more standard period among Latin American economies of hyperinflation, fueled by a substantial and systematic process of government deficits, which, in the absence of external credit, are being financed by seigniorage and the inflation tax. Figure 3 documents the government deficit as a proportion of GDP from 1960 to 2016. It also reports the primary deficit, which excludes interest payments on public debt. In the 1960s and early 1970s, government deficits or surpluses represented around 2 percent of GDP (an average surplus of 0.9 percent of GDP), but starting in 1974, movements in government deficits were as high as 6 and 7 percent of GDP, with year-to-year variations of around 5 percentage points. Government primary deficits have become systematic and large in magnitude starting only around 2006, with an average of 3.6 percent of GDP between 2006 and 2016.

To make a systematic analysis of monetary and fiscal outcomes, I follow the conceptual framework of this volume's chapter "A Framework for Studying the Monetary and Fiscal History of Latin America," the consolidated government budget equation, to account for the events that led to episodes of substantial inflation or a run-up in debt. Interestingly, and contrary to many other Latin American economies, the contribution to financing needs of the government does not rest with primary deficits or even commitments on government debt. Instead, a large number of transfers to other decentralized agencies accounts for all the financing needs, which paradoxically usually occur during periods of oil revenue booms. During the entire time period between 1960 and 2016,

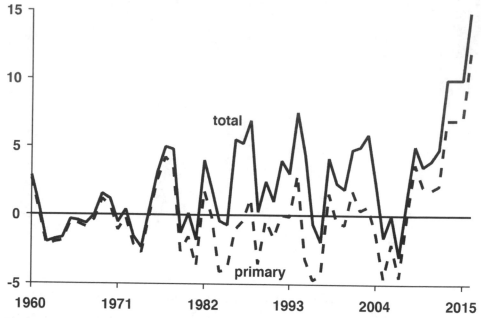

Figure 3. Government deficit to GDP (%)

Note: Positive numbers represent a deficit and negative numbers a surplus. The primary deficit is the deficit minus the interest payments of public debt. Total deficit numbers for 2013 to 2016 are estimates.

seigniorage is the source of funds that accounts for most of the financing needs, while increases in internal and external public debt account for a substantial portion during some periods.

This chapter is broadly related to the literature analyzing the growth experience of Venezuela, such as Hausmann (2003); Bello, Blyde, and Restuccia (2011); and Agnani and Iza (2011), although the present analysis focuses on fiscal and monetary outcomes rather than specifically on growth.[2]

Da Costa and Olivo (2008) study monetary policy in the context of oil economies with an application to Venezuela. The paper is also broadly related to the literature on the resource curse—for example, Manzano and Rigobon (2001) and Hausmann and Rigobon (2003).

The chapter is organized as follows. In the next section, I present a background of the macroeconomic history of the Venezuelan economy, while the third contains the analysis from the accounting framework. The fourth section concludes.

Economic Background

I discuss the evolution of the main macroeconomic variables of the Venezuelan economy during the period 1960 to 2016, starting with a brief historical description. Bello, Blyde, and Restuccia (2011) also provide a detailed description of Venezuela's economic policies during this time period.

HISTORICAL PERSPECTIVE

Venezuela represents one of the most interesting growth experiences of Latin America. From the early twentieth century, Venezuela has experienced both a rapid and sustained period of income growth and a prolonged period of economic decline. To put these experiences in perspective, Figure 4 documents the time path of real GDP per capita in Venezuela relative to that of the United States from 1900 to 2016. The series are from the Maddison Project Database, version 2018, which represents an update of the well-known historical data in Maddison (2010); see Bolt et al. (2018). As in Maddison (2010), the main series are constructed by taking GDP per capita from the latest round of international prices—in this case, the International Comparison Program (ICP) 2011 benchmark (solid line)—and extrapolating across years using constant-price GDP per capita growth in each country from national accounts. As a result, the time path of relative income closely reflects the actual growth process of Venezuela relative to the United States. However, the implied level of relative income depends heavily on which set of international prices is used to aggregate output, and, as a consequence, relative income levels can vary substantially with different benchmark prices. For this reason, the new version of the Maddison data includes series of real GDP per capita that take into account multiple rounds of international prices. While it is meant to more accurately reflect differences in income at a point in time, it does not accurately reflect the process of growth in each country. Figure 4 reports GDP per capita in Venezuela relative to multiple benchmarks (dashed line).

From 1900 to 1920, GDP per capita fluctuated around 30 percent of that of the United States, but since then it has increased substantially to almost 80 percent in the late 1950s. Starting around 1960, relative income per capita declined systematically to levels that are now around 30 percent. Many observers associate the decline of the Venezuelan economy with the first oil price shock in 1974, but from this perspective of relative income growth, we see that the decline started much earlier. Note that when we use the multiple benchmarks of the ICP, we see that relative income levels in Venezuela were much lower, around 10 percent between 1900 and 1940, rising to 40 percent in the late 1980s, and later declining to levels between 15 and 30 percent. While the focus of the present study is to document and analyze the history of monetary and fiscal outcomes in Venezuela from 1960 to 2016, it is important to keep in mind the potential relationship among the events, policies, and institutional features that could have partly determined the economic performance of the Venezuelan economy in the more recent past.

As discussed in Figure 1 in the introduction, the growth of real GDP per capita shows periods of positive performance as well as periods of strong volatility and decline. In describing the specific monetary and fiscal outcomes below, keeping in mind the following three broad periods in the Venezuelan economy is useful. First, from 1960

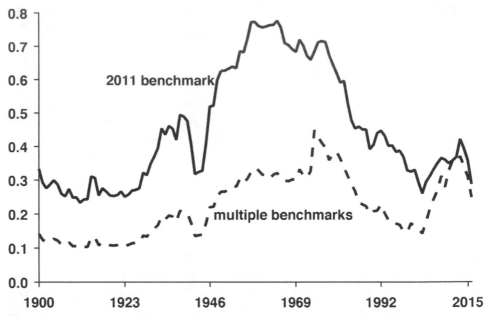

Figure 4. Venezuela real GDP per capita (relative to United States)
Note: GDP per capita from the Maddison Historical Statistics Project; see Maddison (2010) and Bolt et al. (2018), Venezuela relative to the United States. The solid line is based on the 2011 ICP and growth rates in each country from national accounts, and the dashed line considers multiple ICP benchmark rounds.

to 1977, real GDP per capita increased by 2.3 percent annually. It was a period of relative macroeconomic stability with negligible or low fiscal deficits and low inflation, and although debt was rising toward the end of the period, it was still relatively low. As I discuss below, this relative macroeconomic stability hides the strong changes that were occurring in oil production around the nationalization of the industry and with oil revenues that may have set the stage for worsening outcomes in later years. Second, from 1978 to 1998, real GDP per capita declined by about 1 percent annually, and the economy went through substantial instability. This cycle of rising debt and inflation mitigated toward the end of the period. Third, from 1999 to 2016, real GDP per capita declined by −0.8 percent annually. It was a period of strong political and economic instability, with episodes of strong decline in economic activity accompanied by a large and sustained oil price boom. An interesting natural question that arises is, What happened around 1977 to determine the fundamental change in relative macroeconomic stability? More research on this topic may be required, but the undercurrent from the analysis below hints at the important fall in oil production starting around 1970, associated with discussions of nationalization that were partially hidden in the macroeconomic accounts through large increases in real oil prices during the time. In fact, the failure of real oil prices to continue their previous growth appears to have triggered an important reduction in government spending and fiscal deficits, which may have brought the growth of economic activity to a halt.

GROWTH, VOLATILITY, AND OIL

The overall process of income per capita growth between 1960 and 2016 documented in Figure 1 is associated with a noticeable change in the volatility of economic activity. I use the Hodrick-Prescott filter on the series for real GDP per capita to separate trend and cycle.[3] I calculate that starting around 1974, economic fluctuations, defined as the difference between actual and trended real GDP, show a substantial increase. Between 1960 and 1974, the standard deviation of detrended real GDP per capita was 2.1 percent and increased to 6.8 percent for the period 1975 to 2016.[4] To put these fluctuations in GDP in perspective, recall that the typical business cycle in the United States amounts to a standard deviation of filtered log real GDP of slightly more than 1 percent for the yearly series. Hence, economic fluctuations are orders of magnitude larger in Venezuela than in the United States, particularly for the period starting in 1974.

Three major changes provide context for the economic performance of Venezuela. First, the discovery of oil reserves in the early 1910s promoted a strong process of structural transformation whereby economic activity was reallocated from agricultural and rural areas to the oil industry and urban areas. For instance, the share of agriculture in GDP declined from more than 30 percent in 1920 to currently less than 5 percent, whereas the share of oil production in GDP sharply increased from almost zero in the 1920s to around 35 percent in 1930, fluctuating around that level between 1930 and 1970 and then declining to levels around 20 percent during the process of nationalization of the oil industry in the early 1970s.

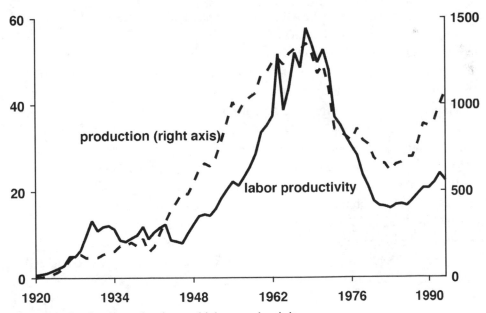

Figure 5. Crude oil production and labor productivity

Source: Baptista (1997)

Note: Production of crude oil is in millions of barrels. Labor productivity is the production of crude oil relative to employment in the oil sector.

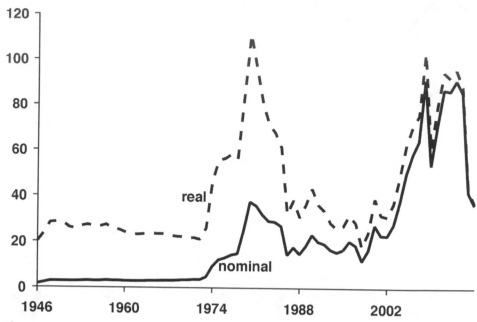

Figure 6. Crude oil prices

Note: The price of oil is expressed in US$ per barrel. "Nominal" refers to current prices, and "real" refers to the price deflated by the U.S. consumer price index (CPI). The data are from Inflation-Data.com, "Historical Crude Oil Prices (Table)," https://inflationdata.com/ Inflation/Inflation_Rate/Historical_Oil_Prices_Table.asp.

Second, nationalization, which formally took place in 1976, generated an important change in the operation and efficiency of the oil industry. To illustrate this process, Figure 5 reports the production of crude oil in Venezuela (right axis) and labor productivity as barrels of oil per worker (left axis). Note the strong and systematic increase in oil production and productivity from 1920 until about 1970. The growth process of the oil industry is broken precisely around the time when discussions of nationalization took place in the late 1960s and early 1970s. For instance, in the decade between 1960 and 1970, oil production increased by 30 percent and labor productivity increased by 125 percent, whereas in the decade between 1970 and 1980, oil production declined by 41 percent and labor productivity declined by 59 percent. The decline in economic activity associated with the nationalization process is substantial: crude oil production declined by 55 percent from 1970 to the mid-1980s, and labor productivity in the oil industry declined by 72 percent.

Third, as Venezuela became fundamentally an oil economy—weakened by the nationalization of the industry—it also became exposed to fluctuations in commodity prices. Crude oil prices were fairly stable, around US$2 per barrel, until about 1974 (see Figure 6). Since then, crude oil prices have fluctuated tremendously, reaching almost US$60 in 1974 in real terms and US$110 by 1980, then dropping to US$20 in 1998, up again to US$100 in 2008, and then down to below US$40 by 2016.[5] Note the tight association between oil prices and real economic activity, documented in Figure 7. But the

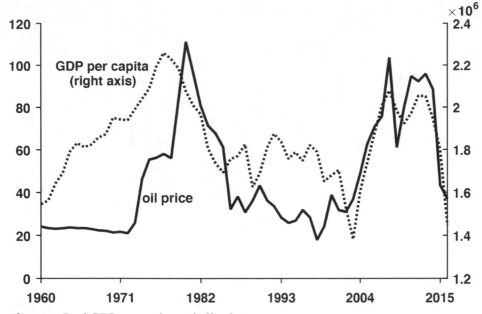

Figure 7. Real GDP per capita and oil prices
Note: Real GDP per capita is in constant 1997 prices. Oil prices are deflated by the CPI in the United States.

transmission of oil price shocks to economic activity is not through fluctuations in the oil industry, as discussed earlier; instead, it is through fiscal policy broadly defined. By law, the oil industry must supply all revenues in foreign currency to the central bank in exchange for domestic currency, and taxes are imposed on the industry that leave minimal margins for investment in the sector.

FISCAL ACCOUNTS

To illustrate the importance of oil revenues in the public finances of Venezuela, Figure 8 documents the ratio of government revenues to GDP from 1960 to 2012.[6] The figure also shows the oil and non-oil components of government revenue. In the 1960s, government revenues were about 16 percent of GDP, but in 1974, as a result of the first big oil price shock, revenues increased to more than 30 percent of GDP and have fluctuated around 25 percent since then, with positive and negative variations of more than 10 percentage points in a given year. On average, oil represents around 60 percent of total government revenues. Figure 9 illustrates how oil revenues are related to government expenditures. Again, we see a substantial jump in government expenditures in 1974 and substantial fluctuations since then.

In contrast to many other countries where government expenditures appear counter-cyclical, in Venezuela government expenditures are procyclical.

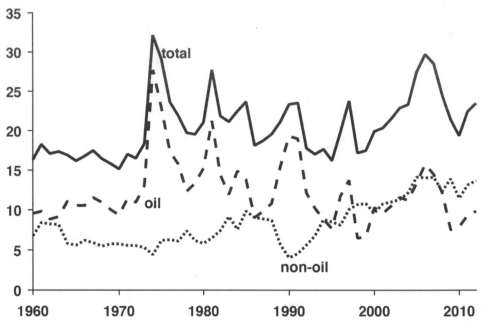

Figure 8. Government revenues to GDP

Note: Revenues of the central government expressed as a percentage of GDP.

PUBLIC DEBT

The larger income proceeds from oil generated a rapid increase in government expenditures and public expenditures more broadly defined. The public sector committed resources to large long-term expenditure projects such as establishing public enterprises in the mineral industry (aluminum, iron, steel, and coal). Heavy borrowing and the instability in oil revenues led to a rapid rise in public debt. Figure 10 reports the nominal stock value of total public debt to GDP and the value of internal public debt as a proportion of GDP. Public debt includes the central government and public enterprises whose debt is guaranteed by the central government, such as ALCASA, BAUXILUM, CADAFE, CAMETRO, and EDELCA, among others. It does not include the oil company (PDVSA), the central bank (BCV), and other financial public enterprises. There is no indexed debt and no zero coupons; bonds pay coupons every semester. The public debt in Venezuela is classified in two forms—internal and external—essentially differing on whether the debt is denominated in local currency or in U.S. dollars. Traditionally, internal debt was contracted with domestic residents and external debt with foreign residents, but this distinction has blurred over time as domestic residents have used external bonds as an instrument to bypass foreign exchange controls. I follow the fiscal budget convention of valuing the stock of external debt at the end of each year at the official exchange rate. But in this context, it is important to note that in some periods, the wedge between the official and market exchange rates can be very substantial, and, as a result, the ratio of debt to income can understate the real burden of the debt.

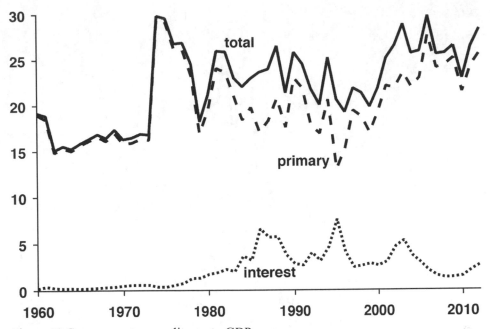

Figure 9. Government expenditures to GDP
Note: Expenditures of the central government expressed as a percentage of GDP. Primary expenditures exclude interest payments on public debt.

Figure 10 documents that between 1960 and the mid-1970s public debt was less than 10 percent of income, and a large fraction of the total debt was internal debt. This characterization changed dramatically after the first oil price shock, and the debt-to-income ratio increased to almost 100 percent in the mid-1980s. Most of the increase is accounted for by external debt. To illustrate the importance of the exchange rate in the valuation of external debt, note that in the mid-1980s if the market exchange rate is used instead of the official rate, the debt-to-GDP ratio reaches more than 150 percent in 1986; and similarly, at the end of 2016, the wedge between the black market exchange rate and the official rate is a factor of 320-fold, which implies that the debt-to-income ratio exceeds 600 percent using the market rate instead of 6.3 percent under the official rate. Movements in the real exchange rate also play an important role in accounting for the variation in the debt ratio. Figure 11 shows the role of the movement in the real exchange rate in debt ratios by reporting the debt ratio using a constant 1960 real exchange rate. An important portion of the run-up in the 1980s is associated with changes in the real exchange rate.

Just as with real GDP per capita, there is a close association between the increase in the external public debt and oil prices. Figure 12 documents the amount of external public debt in real U.S. prices in 1960 and real crude oil prices, with the substantial increases in oil prices in the mid-1970s and late-1970s slightly preceding the sharp increases in real debt.

Also note the close association between the increase in public debt and international reserves. To put this link in context, Figure 13 documents the debt-to-GDP

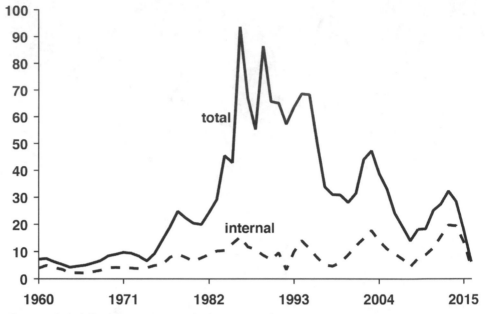

Figure 10. Public debt-to-GDP ratio (percentage)

Note: External debt is valued at the official exchange rate at the end of each year.

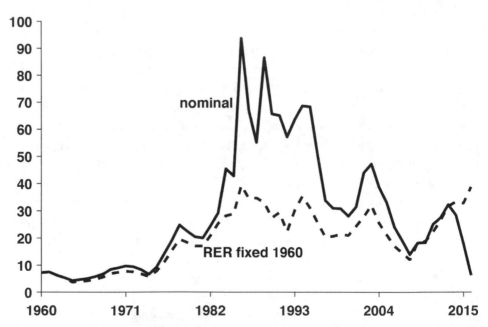

Figure 11. Public debt-to-GDP ratio (percentage)—constant real exchange rate (RER)

Note: External debt is valued at the official exchange rate at the end of the period. The constant real exchange rate keeps the real exchange rate at the level in 1960.

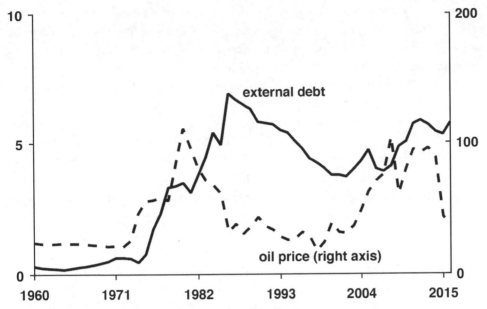

Figure 12. Real public external debt and crude oil prices
Note: External debt is expressed in U.S. dollars at constant 1960 prices. The crude oil price is also expressed in 1960 U.S. dollars per barrel.

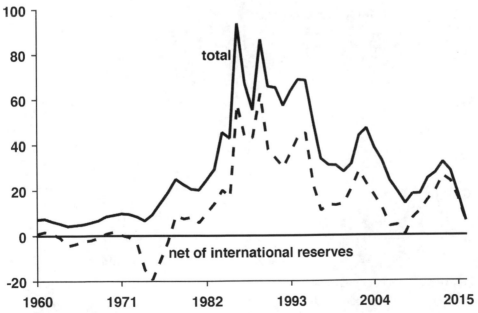

Figure 13. Public debt-to-GDP ratio (percentage)—net of international reserves
Note: External debt is valued at the official exchange rate at the end of each year. Net of international reserves is internal debt plus external debt minus international reserves valued at the official exchange rate.

ratio net of international reserves. While the level of debt ratios is lower when taking international reserves into account, the increase in debt ratios between the mid-1970s and mid-1980s is almost as substantial when neglecting the increase in reserves during the period.

In the 1960s and early 1970s, external debt represented around 50 percent of international reserves, increasing to more than 100 percent in the 1980s. The external debt reached more than twice the amount of international reserves at the end of 1986, increasing to more than 3.5 times by the end of 1988. This substantial run-up in debt by the government affected government finances because of the heavy load that the payments of principal and, to a lesser extent, interest represented as part of overall income. In particular, Figure 14 shows the amount of public debt service as a proportion of government revenue. Debt service includes all payments related to public debt, inclusive of principal, interest, and commissions. The service of the debt represented less than 5 percent of government revenues between 1960 and 1974, increasing systematically after 1974 and reaching levels of 70 percent in 1986 and 90 percent in 1995. Similarly, Figure 14 also shows the burden of external debt service as a proportion of international reserves. The level of external debt service to international reserves in 2016 is similar to that during the crises in 1989, which involved a severe adjustment of the nominal exchange rate.

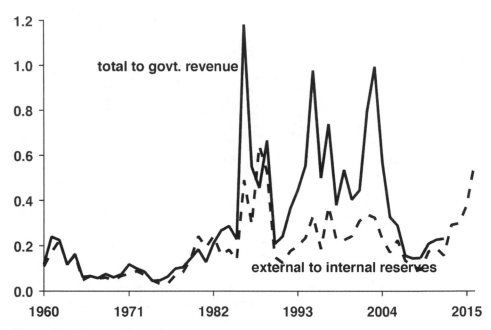

Figure 14. Debt service ratios

Note: Debt service includes all payments related to internal and external public debt inclusive of principal, interest, and commissions. External debt service payments are valued at official exchange rates following the reporting of the interest payments in the government fiscal statistics. Total debt service is expressed relative to government revenues, and external debt service is expressed relative to international reserves.

EXCHANGE RATE

Venezuela has experienced several exchange rate systems, from long periods of fixed exchange rates—in some cases, with multiple rates—to some periods of floating exchange rates. It has also experienced long periods with capital controls. A key feature of the exchange rate market in Venezuela in the last four decades is the fact that most of the supply of foreign currency is under the control of the central bank, since the state oil company is required by law to sell all receipts in foreign currency to the central bank in exchange for local currency. This implies that even in periods of exchange rate flexibility, public officials have substantial discretion in determining the exchange rate. Figure 15 documents the lowest official nominal exchange rate at the end of the period between 1960 and 2016. This is the rate that prevails in fiscal accounts, and in particular for the valuation of external debt and associated payments, as well as for the conversion of foreign exchange revenues from oil exports. In some periods, this rate also prevails for imports of goods considered essential, and the administration of the allocation of foreign currency at this preferential rate has been a substantial source of corruption in the last four decades.

The two decades before 1960 represented a period of relative stability in foreign exchange in Venezuela. The exchange rate was unique and fixed during this period, owing to the positive capital flows from many European immigrants and the cumulative increase in oil production. Positive capital flows also came from new oil concessions granted by the government after the Suez Canal crisis in 1956. But the reopening of the Suez Canal in 1958, the fall of the ten-year Jiménez dictatorship, and uncertainty surrounding the new democratic government meant that capital flows reversed, and in 1960, the government imposed the first capital controls, adopting a dual exchange rate. Pressure from negative capital flows meant that the government had to move the majority of imports to the higher exchange rate, effectively devaluating the currency. By 1964, the government abandoned capital controls by unifying the exchange rate at a higher rate of 4.45 bolivares per U.S. dollar. From this point until February of 1983, Venezuela had a fixed exchange rate system with a single rate against the U.S. dollar. This rate changed marginally from 4.5 to 4.25 to 4.3 bolivares per U.S. dollar at different times. In February of 1983, a period now called *Viernes negro* (Black Friday), the government was forced to recognize the misalignment in exchange rate valuation and devalued the exchange rate to 7.5 bolivares per U.S. dollar. The government maintained the fixed exchange rate system but established capital controls and multiple rates, with some activities remaining at the rate of 4.3 bolivares per U.S. dollar.

From February 1989 to September of 1992, a floating exchange rate system was established. This period deserves special attention because 1989, at least from the official statistics, looks like a dismal year, with strong depreciation of the currency, high inflation, and economic contraction. A new government took office at this time, and paradoxically this is the period during which Venezuela had the most coherent economic policies in recent history. A key limitation in the implementation of the economic policies was that the new government inherited essentially a broken economy from the previous government: liquid international reserves were essentially nil compared with the large short-term

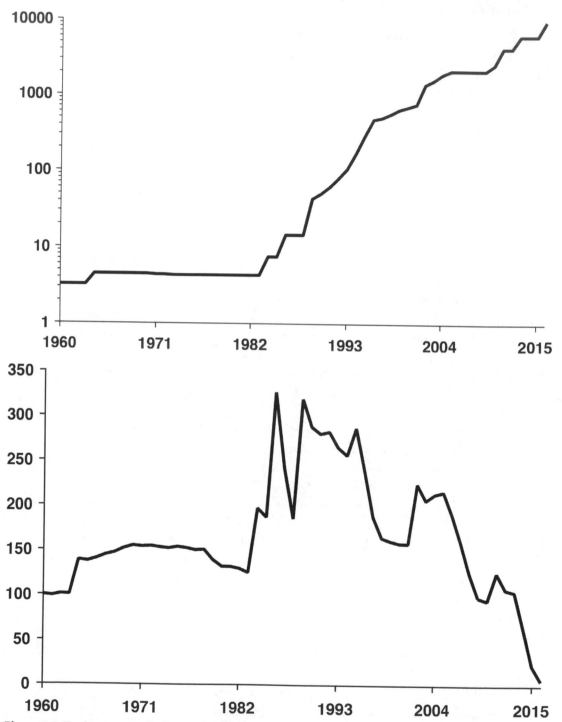

Figure 15. Exchange rate (bolivares/US$): top panel: nominal, log scale; bottom panel: real
Note: Official exchange rate in bolivares per U.S. dollar. Exchange rate value at the end of the period.
The real exchange rate is calculated as the nominal exchange rate times the price index in the United
States relative to the price index in Venezuela and is normalized to 100 in 1960.

obligations due in that year and the large deficits in fiscal and current accounts. This left no room for the new government to implement a more gradual adjustment in the severe misalignment of the exchange rate. Similarly, other key prices, which were repressed for many years, allowed for little maneuvering in the price adjustment. To lend some viability to the economic reform program, Venezuela signed an agreement with the International Monetary Fund and in February 1990 signed the Brady Plan. The Brady Plan provided a restructuring of the debt, reducing the external debt by almost 30 percent, extending the maturity of the debt, and reducing interest payments.

From 1994 to 2003, several systems were tried, among them multiple exchange rates with capital controls and exchange rate bands, but in February of 2003, a fixed exchange rate system with a single rate was established. Strict capital controls were also established. The rate was changed from time to time. An important event during this period was a banking crisis that started in January of 1994 and extended to 1996. The origins of the crisis have been debated, but political turmoil from two military coups in 1992, the eventual impeachment of President Pérez in 1993, and a transition government with a newly elected government in 1994 provide a background for the events that unfolded. The banking system suffered from a loss of public confidence, and the lack of a coherent plan from the new government generated a remarkable drop in the demand for money and capital flight pressures, which eventually led to more than seventeen failed financial institutions (representing 60 percent of the assets of financial institutions and 50 percent of the deposits). Conservative estimates put the total cost of bailouts at 10 percent of GDP, but more careful estimates put this figure at 20 percent of GDP; see, for instance, García, Rodríguez, and Salvato (1998).

In the last few years, multiple rates, as well as different administrative units, have been established, all involved in corruption scandals in the allocation of foreign currency at preferential rates. The misalignment of the official exchange rate and the black market rate has been so large—reaching factor differences of more than one hundred times between the market rate and the official rate—that the assignment of preferential dollars has been a contentious issue in Venezuela for more than a decade.

MONEY AND INFLATION

Figure 16 reports the yearly inflation rate and the yearly growth in the monetary base for the Venezuelan economy. It is important to note that in many respects, the Venezuelan economy during the sample period was, and continues to be, a heavily regulated economy, including the implementation of price controls, especially for basic food and other essential products, interest rates, and exchange rates, among many other prices. Specifically related to inflation, the Venezuelan economy has experienced many episodes during which price controls resulted in severe shortages of essential food products in supermarkets. As a result, the spikes in inflation rates in some years have more to do with the relaxation of price controls (repressed inflation) than with current monetary and fiscal policies.

Figure 16 has two notable features. First, from 1960 to about 1984, the pattern of inflation resembles that of the United States, the country with which Venezuela has the highest share of

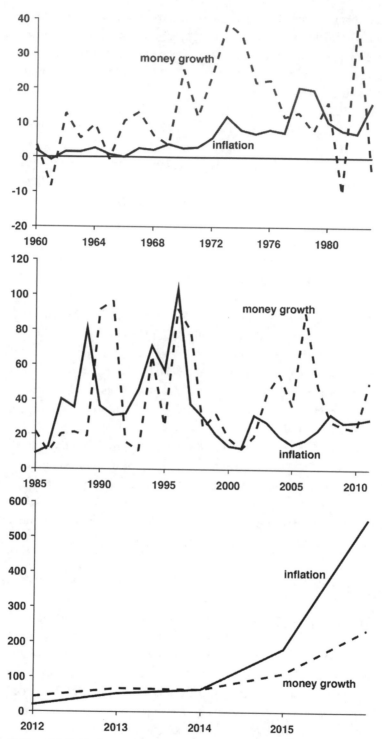

Figure 16. Inflation and money growth (percentage): top panel: 1960–84; middle panel: 1985–2011; bottom panel: 2012–16

Note: The inflation rate is the percentage change from the consumer price index. Money growth is the percentage change in the monetary base.

imports and the country against which Venezuela has fixed its currency for long periods of time. Second, between 1985 and 1998, inflation has been persistently above 30 percent (in some years, more than 100 percent), and between 1999 and 2010, inflation has been persistently below 30 percent (even below 20 percent in some years). But starting in 2012, inflation and money growth have been on a different scale, reaching more than 200 percent in 2016. Starting in 2012–13, and accelerating since then, is a substantial process of money growth and inflation, reaching monthly rate changes of more than 20 percent by the end of 2016.

Analysis

THE BUDGET EQUATION

Since Venezuela has two main classifications of debt, internal and external, I modify the consolidated budget equation in "A Framework for Studying the Monetary and Fiscal History of Latin America" to incorporate those two classifications. Indexed debt has not been used in Venezuela. The lack of data on the maturity structure of debt prevents a more disaggregated analysis. However, while short-term debt was used in some periods, the majority of debt issuance was long term (more than a year). In addition, available data from the World Bank's world debt tables indicates that the average maturity of Venezuelan external debt was fairly constant at around ten years.

As discussed in "A Framework for Studying the Monetary and Fiscal History of Latin America," the consolidated budget constraint can be written in terms of real GDP and in differences as follows:

$$(\theta_t - \theta_{t-1}) + \xi_t(\theta_t^* - \theta_{t-1}^*) + (m_t - m_{t-1}) + m_{t-1}(1 - \frac{1}{g_t \pi_t}) =$$

$$d_t + t_t + \theta_{t-1}\left(\frac{R_{t-1}}{g_t \pi_t} - 1\right) + \theta_{t-1}^*\left(\frac{r_{t-1}^*}{g_t \pi_t^W} - 1\right), \tag{1}$$

where θ is real internal debt to real GDP, $\theta*$ is real external debt to real GDP, ξ is the real exchange rate calculated as $(E \cdot PW)/P$, m is the ratio of monetary base to GDP, d and t are the primary deficit and transfers to GDP, π and πW are the gross domestic and imported inflation, and g is gross real GDP growth. The first four terms on the left-hand side of equation (1) represent the sources of financing for the consolidated government: internal debt, external debt, seigniorage, and the inflation tax; the four terms on the right-hand side represent the obligations: the primary deficit, transfers, internal debt payments, and external debt payments.

Note that transfers t are an important component of the consolidated budget and represent more than just extraordinary transfers. Part of these transfers include discounted debt issuance or repurchases that should be included in the returns to internal and external debt, R and r. It also includes a wide array of transfers between the central government and the nonfinancial public sector. Lack of disaggregated data prevents me from allocating these individual components into the appropriate terms in the budget equation. The approach I follow is to calculate these transfers as a residual: essentially, the residual that validates the budget equation every period.

ACCOUNTING RESULTS

In each year, I compute the terms in equation (1). Table 1 reports the averages of the sources and obligations across subperiods and for the sample period between 1961 and 2016.

Sources of Financing

For the entire period, average financing needs are 2.5 percentage points, but this magnitude changes dramatically across subperiods. From 1961 to 1974, the financing needs were small, an average of 0.7 percentage points (pp), and all these needs were covered by the inflation tax. Note that, on average, seigniorage was slightly negative (−0.03) and that inflation was moderate despite substantial money growth (recall Figure 16). Strong positive growth in real GDP was also a factor. The period from 1975 to 1986 represents a major change in financing needs, with an average of more than 5 pp, and two-thirds of these needs were financed with external debt issuance. The inflation tax accounted for a much smaller proportion than in the previous period but nevertheless still accounted for more than 18 percent of the overall needs. In the period from 1987 to 2005, financing needs declined substantially on average relative to the previous period to 0 pp. However, substantial variations can be seen across years, with increases of up to 10 pp in 2003 and decreases of −9 pp in 1992. The inflation tax represented the only positive source of financing on average in this period: more than 2 pp. The period between 2006 and 2016 represents a return to large amounts of financing needs on average, with 7.6 pp. Note that this period, like 1975–86, is a period of a substantial and prolonged boom in oil prices. But, distinct from the earlier period, external debt is not a substantial source of financing; instead, seigniorage and especially the inflation tax are the sources that account for all the financing needs, with 1.4 and 5 pp, respectively.

Figure 17 reports the time path in each year for each of the four terms on the left-hand side of equation (1). The top two panels report the change in internal and external debt ratios, and the bottom two panels report seigniorage and the inflation tax. While external debt represents a substantial source of funds in some periods, seigniorage and especially the inflation tax are the most important systematic sources of funds in the sample period.

Obligations

I now analyze the elements that account for the changes in financing needs. Overwhelmingly, real transfers tt are the most important obligation, accounting for all the government's financing needs. On average, they represent more than 3 pp, whereas the primary deficit was negligible on average. Across subperiods, during the 1961 to 1974 period, 1.9 pp of transfers were compensated by close to 1 pp of government surpluses and negative

Table 1. Accounting results across subperiods

Sources	1961–74	1975–86	1987–2005	2006–16	1961–2016
(1) Internal debt	0.01	0.94	−0.23	−0.61	0.01
(2) External debt	−0.02	3.44	−1.93	−0.24	0.03
(3) Seigniorage	−0.03	0.26	−0.16	1.36	0.26
(4) Inflation tax	0.71	1.03	2.25	5.49	2.24
Total	0.67	5.67	-0.07	6.00	2.54
Obligations					
(1) Internal return	−0.17	−0.25	−1.53	−2.76	−1.16
(2) External return	−0.12	0.78	0.54	0.32	0.38
(3) Primary deficit	−0.90	−0.41	−0.90	3.29	0.03
(4) Transfers	1.87	5.56	1.82	5.15	3.29
Total	0.67	5.67	−0.07	6.00	2.54

Note: Numbers represent percentage points of items in equation (1).

returns to debt of 0.3 pp, to reduce the overall financing needs to only 0.7 pp (see again Table 1). In the 1975 to 1986 period, the large financing needs of 6 pp are accounted for by transfers (5.6 pp) and payments on external debt (1 pp) and partly mitigated by primary surpluses of the government (−0.4 pp) and negative real internal debt payments (−0.3 pp). During the 1987 to 2005 period, the much smaller financing needs are explained by smaller transfers (1.8 pp versus 5.6 pp in the previous period), primary surpluses (−0.9 pp), and roughly offsetting real returns on government debt. For the 2006–16 period, the much larger financing needs of 6.0 pp are accounted for by transfers of 5.2 pp and primary deficits of 3.3 pp, with real returns to debt mitigating the burden of obligations.

Figure 18 reports the time path of each of the four terms on the right-hand side of equation (1). Note how real returns on external debt are substantial burdens during the 1980s, 1990s, and early 2000s; the Brady Plan, signed in 1990, provided important relief in terms of real payments of external debt. Note also how primary deficits are not a systematic obligation component: most periods experienced a surplus, a pattern that clearly changed in the late 2000s and persists today, and primary deficits became a systematic and substantial component of the overall obligations of the government. The figure also shows how real transfers make up the large and systematic component that accounts for most of the financing needs.

Discussion

The last period, from 2006 to 2016, deserves special discussion because the unfolding crisis is much more closely aligned with the typical crises in Latin America where the logic of the budget accounting in "A Framework for Studying the Monetary and Fiscal History of Latin America" holds—that is, the link between systematic government

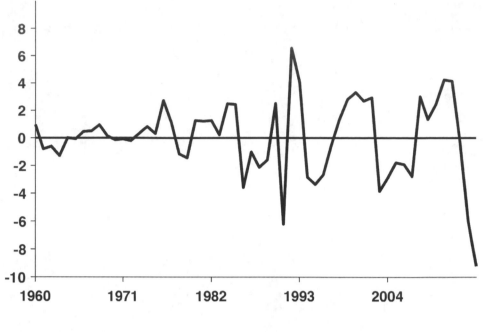

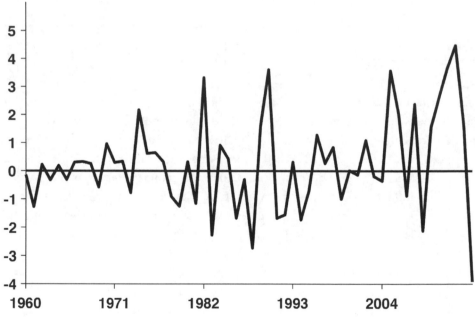

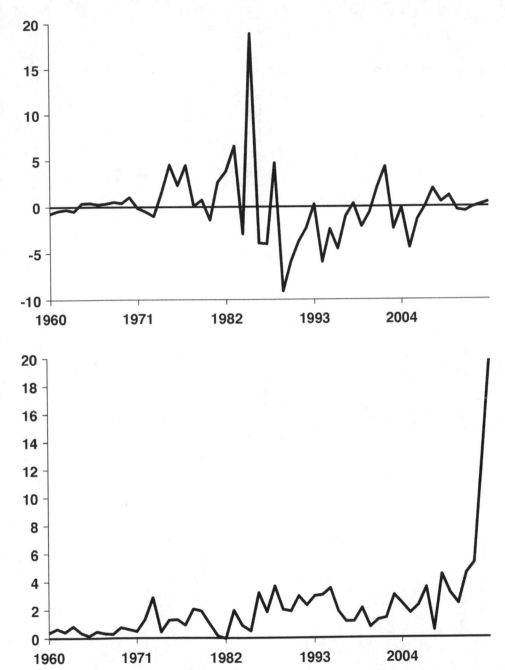

Figure 17. Sources of consolidated government funds: top left panel: internal debt; top right panel: external debt; bottom left panel: seigniorage; bottom right panel: inflation tax

Note: The figure documents each element on the left-hand side of equation (1). The top left panel is the period-by-period change in the ratio of real internal debt to real GDP ($\theta_t - \theta_{t-1}$). The top right panel is the change in real external debt to real GDP using the real exchange rate $\xi_t(\theta_t^* - \theta_{t-1}^*)$. Panel C is seigniorage ($m_t - m_{t-1}$). Panel D is the inflation tax $m_{t-1}\left(1 - \dfrac{1}{g_t\pi_t}\right)$.

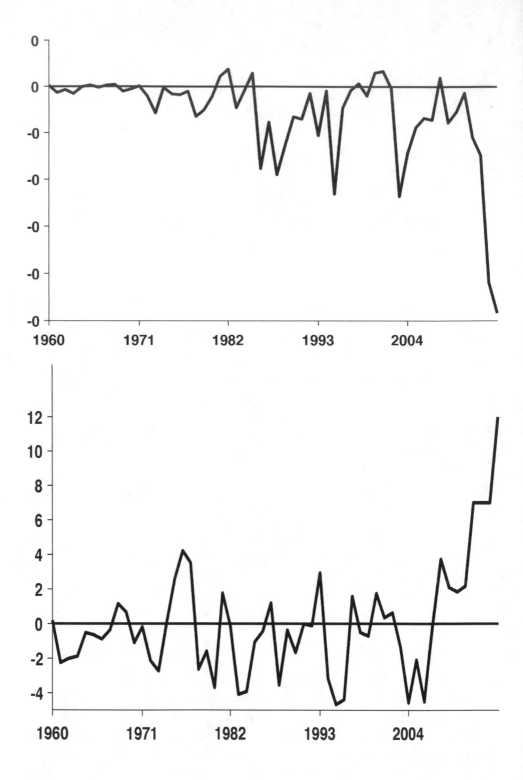

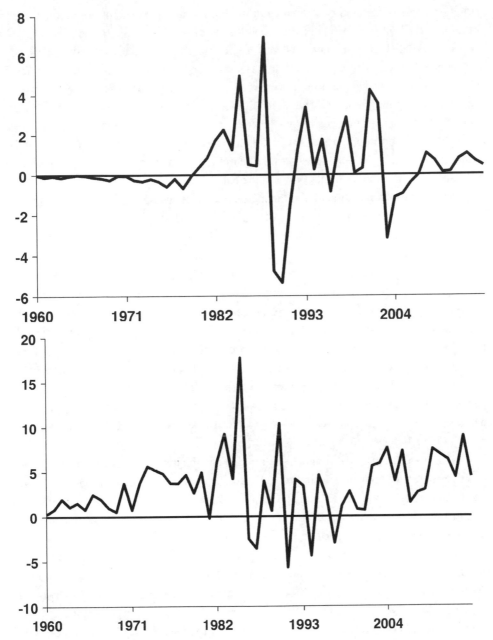

Figure 18. Contributions to consolidated government obligations: top left panel: internal debt return; top right panel: external debt return; bottom left panel: primary deficit; bottom right panel: transfers

Note: The figure documents each element on the right-hand side of equation (1). The top left Panel panel shows the period-by-period real interest payments of internal debt $\theta_{t-1}\left(\dfrac{R_{t-1}}{g_t\pi_t}-1\right)$.

The top right panel shows the real interest payments of external debt $\theta_{t-1}^*\left(\dfrac{r_{t-1}^*}{g_t\pi_t^W}-1\right)$. The bottom left panel shows the real primary deficit to real GDP d_t. The bottom right panel shows the ratio of real transfers to real GDP t_t.

deficits, the eventual inability to finance those deficits, and subsequent seigniorage and inflation. This is also a period during which the distortions to economic activity, which have accumulated since the late 1990s, were drastically expanded. Several aspects of the economic environment are worth mentioning. First, note the extreme intervention of the public sector in economic activity through the expropriation of private enterprises and government intervention in the distribution system of goods. A decline in private production and the failure of expropriated enterprises have exacerbated the dependence of the economy on imports. Second, this is a period of rising debt, both internal and external, with the internal debt becoming the majority of new debt as external sources of financing became more limited toward the end of the period.

Third, there was a decline in the transparency of debt statistics because a substantial portion of new debt was not accounted for in official statistics (e.g., loans from China in exchange for future oil and the fast-rising new debt of the state-owned oil company, PDVSA). Fourth, a partial reform of the central bank allowed for the discretionary use of foreign reserves. Fifth, there was a changing role in PDVSA's activities involving large transfers via *misiones* (off-budget programs) and FONDEN (the Fondo de Desarrollo Nacional, or National Development Fund) for social programs. In addition, government intervention in the company's activities meant shrinking production capacity and cash flows. As a consequence of these characteristics, and despite one of the largest oil price booms in recent history, the government found it harder to obtain new loans with mounting fiscal deficits, resorting to much more substantial seigniorage. This is also a period during which real GDP per capita and labor productivity were contracting: for example, real GDP per capita in 2013 was essentially the same as in 2007, and it declined by 30 percent between 2013 and 2016.

As discussed earlier (see Table 1), seigniorage and the inflation tax were the only two positive sources of financing during the 2006 to 2016 period. The much larger financing needs in this period—of 6 percentage points—are accounted for mostly by the inflation tax. Primary deficits and transfers account for all the obligations. But in particular, note that, unlike in the other subperiods, primary deficits represent a substantial 3.3 percentage points, more than 50 percent of the financing needs of the period. This changing role of primary deficits starting around the mid-2000s is illustrated in Figure 19, which documents the primary deficit and the primary deficit plus transfers as a proportion of GDP over time. Between 1961 and 2005, primary deficits were not a systematic component of the obligations of the government, since they represented −0.7 percentage points (a surplus) on average. During this span, deficits were important in some short-lived periods in the late 1970s and around the 2000s. But the picture looks different in the mid-2000s, when government primary deficits became systematic and large and were exacerbated when including the transfers. The strong financing needs generated during the 2006–16 period and the restricted ability of the government to borrow in domestic and international markets imply that the government turned more systematically to seigniorage and inflation as the primary sources of financing.

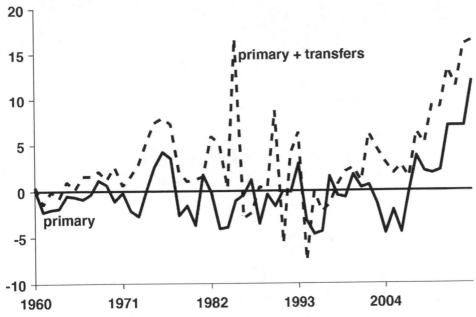

Figure 19. Primary government deficit and transfers to GDP (percentage)
Note: Positive numbers represent a deficit and negative numbers a surplus. The primary deficit is the total deficit minus the interest payments of public debt. Primary deficits for 2013–16 are estimates. Transfers are the residual estimates from the accounting.

Counterfactual Transfers

Transfers are an important component of the government accounts and help account for much of its financing needs. But as depicted in the bottom right panel of Figure 18, the magnitude of the transfers shows a lot of volatility, making it difficult to appreciate the cumulative effect of transfers on the dynamics of debt. To assess the impact of transfers on total debt, I make a counterfactual simulation of debt, assuming that transfers are zero during the entire period. I use the government budget equation (1) to solve for the amount of debt (or sovereign fund) that would result as a consequence of no transfers, assuming all the other variables are the same (seigniorage, inflation tax, returns to debt, and primary deficit). For this counterfactual simulation, I assume that the composition of debt between internal and external remains the same as in the actual data in each period. The top panel of Figure 20 reports the amount of cumulative real transfers as a fraction of GDP (the cumulative of *tt*) and the bottom panel reports the debt-to-GDP ratio in the counterfactual and the data. Because Venezuela's financing needs arise from large transfers in the late 1960s and early 1970s, without transfers, the debt would have quickly turned into a positive asset account, representing more than 180 percent of GDP by 2016. The cumulative effect of transfers is very large and rises quickly starting in the mid-1970s, as documented in the top panel of Figure 20, implying that debt quickly transforms into a positive sovereign fund of substantial size, as illustrated in the bottom panel of Figure 20, reaching 50 percent of GDP by 1990, 100 percent of

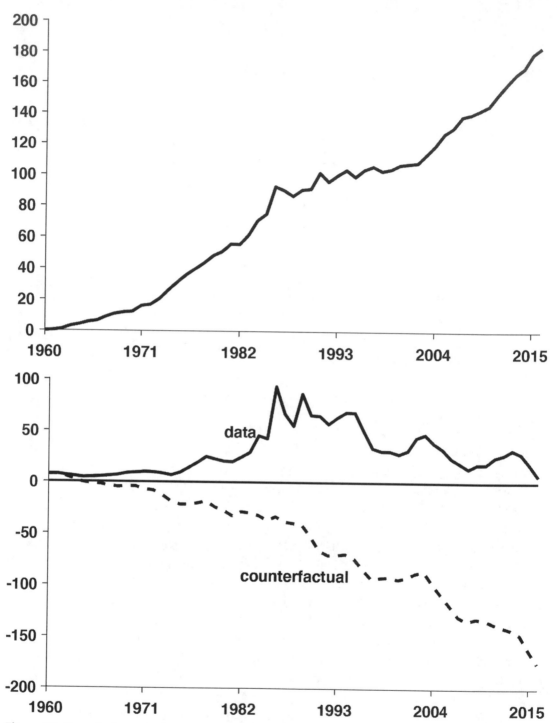

Figure 20. Cumulative transfers and counterfactual debt: top panel: cumulative transfers; bottom panel: counterfactual debt

Note: The top panel reports transfers accumulated over time. The bottom panel reports the debt-to-GDP ratio in the data (solid line) and in the counterfactual situation of no transfers from equation (1), other things being equal (dashed line).

GDP around 2000, and more than 180 percent of GDP in 2016, just short of the current 200 percent sovereign wealth fund of Norway as a fraction of their GDP.

Conclusions

I document the salient features of monetary and fiscal outcomes for the Venezuelan economy during the 1960 to 2016 period. Using the consolidated government budget accounting framework of "A Framework for Studying the Monetary and Fiscal History of Latin America," I assess the importance of fiscal balance, seigniorage, and growth in accounting for the evolution of debt ratios. I find that extraordinary transfers, mostly associated with unprofitable public enterprises and not central government deficits, account for the increase in financing needs in recent decades. The inflation tax has been a consistent source of financing needs, especially in the last ten years, with increases in debt ratios being particularly important in some periods. Interestingly, debt exposure has increased in periods of oil price booms.

Notes

Many thanks to several individuals who have provided assistance with data, especially Fernando Alvarez-Parra, Maria Antonia Moreno, Victor Olivo, and Flor Urbina. All remaining errors are my own.

1 Dutch disease refers to the consequence of a sharp increase in foreign currency inflow that leads to currency appreciation, making the country's other products less price competitive in export markets and in domestic markets against imports; see Corden and Neary (1982). The term was used by the *Economist* magazine in 1977 to characterize the decline of the manufacturing sector in the Netherlands around the discovery of the large Groningen natural gas field in 1959.

2 For a thorough discussion of the economic environment during the period of study, see Hausmann and Rodríguez (2014) and the references therein.

3 I use $\lambda = 100$ for annual series; see Hodrick and Prescott (1997).

4 Note that oil represents about 20 percent of GDP, and almost none of the fluctuations in aggregate GDP are accounted for by fluctuations in economic activity in the oil sector. The transmission mechanism seems to be an ill-suited fiscal policy, as I discuss below.

5 It is interesting to note that since 1974, several attempts have been made to institutionalize macroeconomic stabilization funds in Venezuela, with no success. This situation contrasts sharply with the success of Norway in dealing with oil price booms. An important context may be that Norway was a much richer country when it discovered oil in the 1970s.

6 Notice that detailed fiscal data in Venezuela have not been published since 2012, and hence the series for government revenues and expenditures stop in 2012. Data for the total government deficit are estimates from the International Monetary Fund and other institutions. The primary deficit is estimated from the total deficit minus interest payments of public debt, which is available for the entire period.

523

References

Agnani, Betty, and Amia Iza. 2011. "Growth in an Oil Abundant Economy: The Case of Venezuela." *Journal of Applied Economics* 14 (1): 61–79.

Baptista, Asdrubal. 1997. *Bases cuantitativas de la economía venezolana, 1830–1995.* Caracas, Venezuela: Fundación Polar.

Bello, Omar D., Juan S. Blyde, and Diego Restuccia. 2011. "Venezuela's Growth Experience." *Latin American Journal of Economics* 48 (2): 199–226.

Bolt, Jutta, Robert Inklaar, Herman de Jong, and Jan Luiten van Zanden. 2018. "Rebasing 'Maddison': New Income Comparisons and the Shape of Long-Run Economic Development." Maddison Project Working Paper 10, Groningen Growth and Development Centre, University of Groningen, Netherlands. https://www.ggdc.net/maddison.

Corden, W. Max, and J. Peter Neary. 1982. "Booming Sector and De-industrialisation in a Small Open Economy." *Economic Journal* 92 (368), 825–48.

Da Costa, Mercedes, and Víctor Olivo. 2008. "Constraints on the Design and Implementation of Monetary Policy in Oil Economies: The Case of Venezuela." Technical report, International Monetary Fund WP/08/142, Washington, D.C.

García, Gustavo, Rafael Rodríguez, and Silvia Salvato. 1998. *Lecciones de la crisis bancaria de Venezuela.* Caracas, Venezuela: Ediciones IESA.

Hausmann, Ricardo. 2003. "Venezuela's Growth Implosion: A Neoclassical Story?" In *In Search of Prosperity: Analytic Narratives on Economic Growth,* edited by Dani Rodrik, 244–70. Princeton, N.J.: Princeton University Press.

Hausmann, Ricardo, and Roberto Rigobon. 2003. "An Alternative Interpretation of the 'Resource Curse': Theory and Policy Implications." Technical report, National Bureau of Economic Research, Cambridge, Mass.

Hausmann, Ricardo, and Francisco R. Rodríguez. 2014. *Venezuela before Chávez: Anatomy of an Economic Collapse.* University Park: Penn State University Press.

Hodrick, Robert J., and Edward C. Prescott. 1997. "Postwar U.S. Business Cycles: An Empirical Investigation." *Journal of Money, Credit and Banking,* 1–16.

Maddison, Angus. 2010. "Historical Statistics on World Population, GDP and Per Capita GDP, 1–2008 AD." Maddison Project Database, University of Groningen. https://www.rug.nl/ggdc/historicaldevelopment/maddison/original-maddison.

Manzano, Osmel, and Roberto Rigobon. 2001. "Resource Curse or Debt Overhang?" Technical report, National Bureau of Economic Research, Cambridge, Mass.

Discussion of the History of Venezuela 1

Luigi Bocola
Stanford University

The chapter on Venezuela tells the story of a country that, despite having good initial conditions and large endowments of natural resources such as oil, is currently experiencing one of the deepest social and economic crises documented in history. Diego Restuccia gives an excellent account of the broad macroeconomic trends over the 1960–2016 period and provides a measurement of the driving forces behind the fiscal and monetary outcomes of Venezuela during this period.

The main results of the accounting procedure for Venezuela can be seen in Table 1 in the chapter. There, we can see the main components of the consolidated budget equation averaged across four subperiods: 1961–74, 1975–86, 1987–2005, and 2006–16. Three main patterns emerge. First, and with the exception of the last subperiod, most of the increase in the obligations of the public sector in Venezuela is accounted for not by increases in primary deficits but rather by "transfers"—the residual component in the accounting exercise. Second, we can see that the increase in public-sector obligations observed over this time period took place during two specific periods: 1975–86 and 2006–16, with the remaining periods displaying a roughly constant share of obligations over output. Third, the public sector financed these obligations initially by issuing debt. From the late 1980s onward, however, most of the financing occurred with seigniorage and the inflation tax.

Thus the bottom line in the accounting exercise is that transfers were the prime driver of the obligations of the public sector, a point that is strikingly reinforced by Restuccia's counterfactual in Figure 20. Unfortunately, these transfers are the residual component in the accounting exercise, and it is hard to pinpoint what they stand for. They could stand for actual transfers between the central government and nonfinancial public firms that are not consolidated in the fiscal accounts, or they might even capture misspecifications in the budget equation. Given the lack of transparency in the debt statistics, Restuccia cannot assign this component to something tangible. This is a limitation of the current analysis because the most important driver of fiscal and monetary outcomes in Venezuela is not measured directly.

Restuccia's interpretation of the residual, however, is sensible. His interpretation is that this component does reflect actual transfers to pseudo-private entities, and it could be used by the Venezuelan government for fiscal policy purposes. For instance, the author

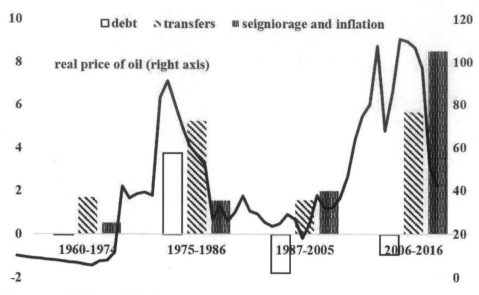

Figure 1. Oil prices, obligations, and sources

mentions the case of the state-owned oil company, PDVSA, which holds a monopoly over the production and exports of Venezuelan oil. The company under the Chavez presidency has engaged in the direct financing of different social and investment programs through FONDEN (the Fondo de Desarrollo Nacional, or National Development Fund), a private corporation controlled by the Finance Ministry of Venezuela. This move has been interpreted as a way for the Venezuelan government to engage in discretionary spending with little oversight from Congress.[1]

To the extent that transfers capture discretionary spending by the fiscal authority, their pattern over time conforms to the experience of other Latin American economies. Gavin and Perotti (1997), for instance, document that fiscal policy in these countries has been mostly procyclical during the postwar period, with expenditures and fiscal deficits rising during good times. In the case of Venezuela, endowed with large oil reserves, those good times coincide with periods of oil price booms. Figure 1 plots real oil prices over the 1960–2016 period, along with the key elements of the budget equation for Venezuela: transfers, the sum of internal and external debt, and the sum of seigniorage and the inflation tax. From the figure we can see that the two cycles of expansionary transfers coincide with sizable increases in oil prices. As the good times end, however, the government has a hard time cutting back on those obligations, which pushes the economy toward fiscal or monetary crises (or sometimes both).

Let me conclude the discussion with more general thoughts about what the Venezuelan experience tells us about fiscal and monetary policy. The first takeaway is that careful case studies, such as the ones presented in this volume, are clearly needed. The case of Venezuela shows that official statistics might not deliver an accurate account of the policy stance, and efforts should be directed toward studying local accounting practices and institutions.

The second takeaway is that researchers should devote more effort toward incorporating political economy considerations into models of determination for fiscal and monetary policy. The Venezuelan experience points toward features that make governments increase financial obligations during good times, making it hard to subsequently cut back on those obligations when the cycle turns bad—a behavior at odds with the standard tax-smoothing model of Barro (1979). Models of sovereign borrowing, such as Arellano (2008) and Aguiar and Gopinath (2006), can generate this comovement by having a myopic government, but more research is needed to understand the underlying frictions determining this behavior and which institutions could potentially tame the tendency to generate fiscal deficits.

Finally, governments have chosen different instruments during different time periods to finance their fiscal obligations. In the case of Venezuela, the government mostly relied on debt issuances and defaults in the 1970s through the 1980s, whereas it reverted to money supply and inflation in the 2000s. Few studies in the literature compare these different ways through which the intertemporal budget constraints are satisfied in practice (see, for instance, Du and Schreger 2016). More research is needed to understand the trade-offs that these alternatives bring.

Note

1 See, for example, Brian Ellsworth and Eyanir Chinea, "Special Report: Chavez's Oil-Fed Fund Obscures Venezuela Money Trail," Reuters.com, September 26, 2012, available at https://www.reuters.com/article/us-venezuela-chavez-fund-idUSBRE88P0N020120926.

References

Aguiar, Mark, and Gita Gopinath. 2006. "Defaultable Debt, Interest Rates and the Current Account." *Journal of International Economics* 69 (1): 69–83.

Arellano, Cristina. 2008. "Default Risk and Income Fluctuations in Emerging Economies." *American Economic Review* 98 (3): 690–712.

Barro, Robert. 1979. "On the Determination of the Public Debt." *Journal of Political Economy* 87 (6): 940–71.

Du, Wenxin, and Jesse Schreger. 2016. "Sovereign Risk, Currency Risk, and Corporate Balance Sheets." BGIE Unit Working Paper No. 17–024, Harvard Business School, Boston, Mass.

Gavin, Michael, and Roberto Perotti. 1997. "Fiscal Policy in Latin America." In *NBER Macroeconomics Annual 1997*, vol. 12, edited by Ben S. Bernanke and Julio J. Rotemberg, 11–72. Cambridge, Mass.: MIT Press.

Discussion of the History of Venezuela 2

Fabrizio Perri
Federal Reserve Bank of Minneapolis and Center for
Economic and Policy Research

Introduction

This very interesting chapter on Venezuela by Diego Restuccia is part of an ambitious and important project that can help us understand the impact of monetary and fiscal policy on the macroeconomic fortunes (or misfortunes) of Latin America. Venezuela is an especially relevant country because of the extraordinary amount of variation in its economic performance over time. In these comments, I will do two things. First, I will provide some simple measures of the economic performance of Venezuela and compare them with the same measures for other Latin American countries, suggesting that indeed Venezuela stands out as the only country in Latin America that experienced, over the course of a century, both a growth miracle and a growth disaster. The second is to provide some cursory evidence on the connection between economic performance and policies. In the conclusion, I will briefly discuss why the early discovery of oil, rather than fiscal or monetary policy per se, might have had an important role in shaping the economic destiny of Venezuela.

The Macroeconomic Performance of Venezuela in Perspective

A LONG-RUN VIEW

Figure 1 plots long-run series (from 1900 to 2016) of GDP per capita for Venezuela, Argentina, Brazil, and an average of the seven major Latin American countries, all relative to U.S. GDP per capita.[1] The top panel of the figure uses data that are based on multiple purchasing power parity (PPP) benchmarks, which are supposed to capture well the level of GDP per capita. The bottom panel uses a more traditional constant price series (based on a single PPP benchmark) and thus is a better measure of the growth experience of these countries.[2] The top panel shows how, at the beginning of the century, Venezuela's GDP per capita is significantly lower than that in Argentina and also below

529

the average GDP per capita in Latin America. By the 1970s, however, probably owing to oil discoveries and to an increase in the price of oil, income per capita in Venezuela is significantly higher than the Latin American average. At the end of the sample, however, Venezuelan income has returned to below the Latin American average. This peculiarity of Venezuela's experience is probably better appreciated by looking at the bottom panel of Figure 1, which gives us a better picture of the growth patterns. First, focus on the Latin American average GDP per capita, which is remarkably constant around 30 percent of U.S. GDP per capita. This shows that, throughout the last 115 years, Latin America has grown at the same rate as the United States; that is, it has failed to catch up. Two types of experiences are behind this average lack of convergence. One is exemplified by the constant decline (relative to the United States) of GDP in Argentina and the other by the very mild catch-up (relative to the United States) of GDP in Brazil. Figure 1 shows that Venezuela is different from both cases. Venezuela starts out poor, below the Latin American average, but experiences a growth miracle from 1930 to 1970, significantly outpacing U.S. growth. From the 1970s on, however, Venezuela's growth performance turns into a disaster that pushes the country below the Latin American average. So although Venezuela in 2016 is essentially in the same position (relative to the United States and to the rest of Latin America) as it was in 1900, a lot of action has taken place in the middle.

Next, I will focus on the postwar experience and explore whether Venezuela's poor performance after 1970 is associated with especially poor fiscal or monetary policies or both.

THE POSTWAR PERIOD

Figure 2 plots the volatility, over the period 1950–2016, of per capita annual GDP growth against the average growth, over the same period, for the twelve major Latin American countries and, for reference, the United States and Canada.[3] The figure displays a few interesting features. All Latin American countries (with the exception of Colombia) feature a much higher GDP volatility than the United States and Canada. In terms of average growth, quite a few countries (such as Colombia, Mexico, and Paraguay) display no or minimal catch-up to the United States; some countries (notably Brazil and Chile) show a mild catch-up; and others (notably Argentina, Bolivia, and Venezuela) feature relative decline. Putting the two indicators together, we see that Venezuela clearly stands out in the northwest quadrant, displaying dismal average growth over the period (less than 1 percent per year), coupled with very high volatility.

FISCAL AND MONETARY POLICIES

Is Venezuela's poor macroeconomic performance associated with particular poor fiscal and monetary policies? We start by looking at a broad measure of fiscal policy—that is, the government primary surplus.[4] Figure 3 plots the average fiscal surplus, together with its volatility for the same set of Latin American countries, and again with the United States and Canada as a reference.

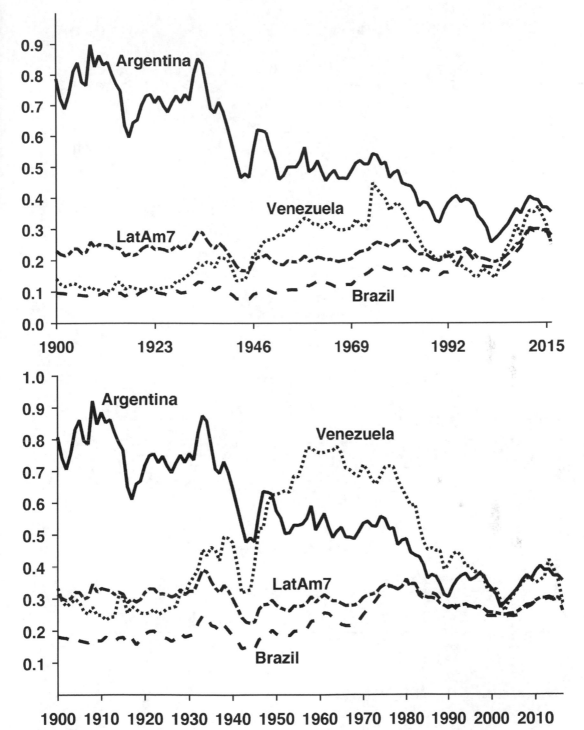

Figure 1. GDP per capita in Venezuela, Argentina, Brazil, and Latin America, 1900–2016: top panel: multiple PPP benchmarks; lower panel: single PPP benchmark (constant 2011 prices)

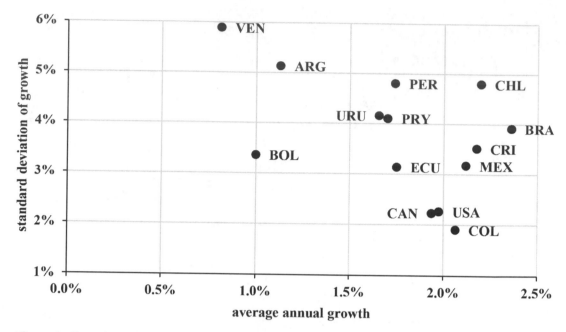

Figure 2. Growth and volatility in twelve Latin American countries, 1950–2016

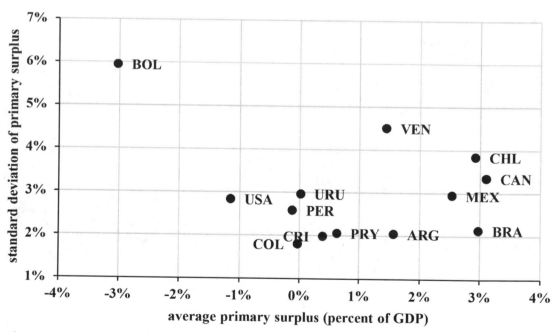

Figure 3. Fiscal surplus in eleven Latin American countries, 1974–2011

The figure shows that Venezuela stands out as displaying a rather high surplus volatility. As discussed in the Venezuela chapter, this feature is probably due to the volatility of oil revenues. In terms of average surplus, however, Venezuela does not stand out. Comparing Figure 2 with Figure 3 suggests that for Bolivia the low average growth over the postwar period might be related to its fiscal profligacy, but for Venezuela that does not seem to be the case. Moving now to monetary policy, Figure 4 shows inflation in Venezuela from 1960 to 2016, compared to median inflation in the group of Latin American countries considered above.[5] The figure reveals an interesting pattern, with Venezuela displaying a level of inflation considerably below the Latin American median until the 1980s and then switching to having higher inflation in the second part of the sample. Indeed, in the final years of the sample, Venezuela is the only Latin American country in hyperinflation territory. The figure suggests that monetary policy during the years of Venezuela's growth disaster might indeed have been an exacerbating factor.

A Concluding Story

Venezuela's growth disaster after the 1970s is often cited as a textbook example of the so-called resources curse (see Sachs and Warner 2001). One caveat for this interpretation is that oil in Venezuela was discovered and developed early (in the 1920s), and, from 1930 to the 1970s, abundant oil resources have been associated with Venezuela's fast growth (see Figure 1). Venezuela thus serves as an example of both a resources blessing

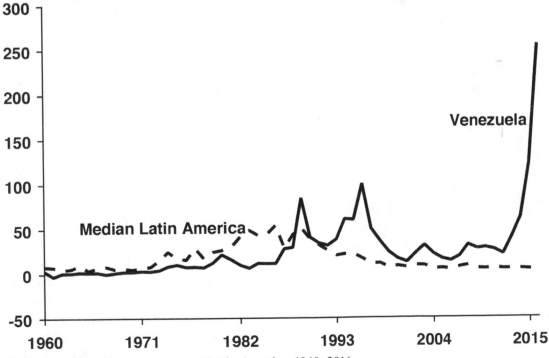

Figure 4. Inflation in Venezuela and Latin America, 1960–2016

and a resources curse. Indeed, as noted in Torvik (2009), "For every Nigeria or Venezuela there is a Norway or a Botswana." This is why the resources curse literature is now moving beyond explaining whether resources are good or bad for an economy and toward examining under what conditions resources help growth and under what conditions they hinder it. The evolution of monetary policy described in Figure 4 suggests that resources in Venezuela might have played a different role over time. Early on, oil wealth might have reduced the need for bad policies in a developing economy—as reflected by an inflation well below the Latin American median—and enabled faster growth than other Latin American countries at a similar stage of development. Over time (and possibly because of oil shocks; see, for example, Tornell and Lane 1999) the volatile oil wealth might have increased power struggles instead of investment in institutions, which resulted in worse policies, possibly less democratic institutions (see Caselli and Tesei 2016), and exceptionally poor growth in the second part of the sample.

Notes

The views expressed herein are those of the author and not necessarily those of the Federal Reserve Bank of Minneapolis or the Federal Reserve System.

1 The seven countries are Argentina, Brazil, Chile, Colombia, Mexico, Peru, and Uruguay. The data are from Bolt et al. (2018) and are the same data used in Figure 4 of Restuccia's Venezuela chapter.

2 Pinkovskiy and Sala-i-Martin (2016) also show that single measures of growth based on a single PPP benchmark correlate better with measures of GDP growth based on measures of light from satellite imaging.

3 The countries (with codes in parentheses) are Argentina (ARG), Bolivia (BOL), Brazil (BRA), Chile (CHL), Colombia (COL), Costa Rica (CRI), Ecuador (ECU), Mexico (MEX), Peru (PER), Paraguay (PRY), Uruguay (URU), and Venezuela (VEN).

4 Data on annual primary fiscal surplus are from Mauro et al. (2015). The set of countries is the same as in Figure 2, with the exception of Ecuador, for which no data are available. The time coverage is the same for all countries: 1974–2011.

5 Data for CPI inflation are from the World Bank's World Development Indicators.

References

Bolt, J., R. Inklaar, H. de Jong, and J. L. van Zanden. 2018. "Rebasing 'Maddison': New Income Comparisons and the Shape of Long-Run Economic Development." Research Memorandum 174, Groningen Growth and Development Centre, University of Groningen, Netherlands.

Caselli, Francesco, and Andrea Tesei. 2016. "Resource Windfalls, Political Regimes, and Political Stability." *Review of Economics and Statistics* 98 (3): 573–90.

Mauro, Paolo, Rafael Romeu, Ariel Binder, and Asad Zaman. 2015. "A Modern History of Fiscal Prudence and Profligacy." *Journal of Monetary Economics* 76 (c): 55–70.

Pinkovskiy, Maxim, and Xavier Sala-i-Martin. 2016. "Newer Need Not Be Better: Evaluating the Penn World Tables and the World Development Indicators Using Nighttime Lights." Working paper 22216, National Bureau of Economic Research, Cambridge, Mass.

Sachs, Jeffrey D., and Andrew M. Warner. 2001. "The Curse of Natural Resources." *European Economic Review* 45 (4–6): 827–38.

Tornell, Aaron, and Philip R. Lane. 1999. "The Voracity Effect." *American Economic Review* 89 (1): 22–46.

Torvik, Ragnar. 2009. "Why Do Some Resource-Abundant Countries Succeed while Others Do Not?" *Oxford Review of Economic Policy* 25 (2): 241–56.

Lessons from the Monetary and Fiscal History of Latin America

Carlos Esquivel
Rutgers University

Timothy J. Kehoe
University of Minnesota, Federal Reserve Bank of Minneapolis,
and National Bureau of Economic Research

Juan Pablo Nicolini
Federal Reserve Bank of Minneapolis and Universidad Torcuato Di Tella

Introduction

When we started the project, our hypothesis was that the inability, or unwillingness, of governments to limit their spending to their own ability to raise tax revenues was the driving force behind the macroeconomic instability that prevailed in Latin America during the last quarter of the twentieth century.

In 2019, at the end of the road, after overseeing the application of our common framework to the recent macroeconomic history of our group of eleven countries, we conclude that our hypothesis is correct. Seven of our eleven countries have learned the lesson and have run conservative fiscal policy for more than a decade. This decision has allowed all of them to run monetary policy so as to achieve the macroeconomic stability that they had not attained for decades, in spite of the global financial crisis of 2008–12.

In contrast, the region currently includes one dramatic case of a country that has not learned that lack of fiscal discipline leads to bad economic outcomes—namely, Venezuela—and three problematic cases: Argentina, Bolivia, and Brazil. The problems in each of these four countries reinforce our conclusion that our hypothesis is correct in the sense that the underlying cause of their problems is lack of fiscal discipline:

- The virulent economic crisis that has led to hyperinflation, economic misery, and political chaos in Venezuela, which unravels as we write these concluding lines, started when the government did nothing to rein in spending in spite of a sharp fall in oil revenues.

- During 2018, Argentina went through a recession that followed a run on its currency and a dramatic increase in country risk that led the country to ask for International Monetary Fund (IMF) support, a very unpopular measure. The fiscal deficit in Argentina, which had been either negative or small until 2010, started to grow at that point. The principal condition of the IMF's assistance was that Argentina rapidly reduce its deficit.

- Brazil, a country that was considered one of the giants of the emerging world a decade ago, is agonizing over a high deficit that has persisted for several years. The probability that the newly elected government will succeed depends, to a large extent, on its ability to tame the fiscal deficit.

- Bolivia is less problematic than Argentina and Brazil. Nonetheless, the increase in external debt caused by increasing deficits since 2012, coupled with a loss of foreign reserves, is reminiscent of policy mistakes in the region that led to debt crisis and inflation.

Thus the current state of affairs in the region suggests that the main lesson of the last decades has not been learned by some of the countries. The amount of pain and misery imposed on the people of Venezuela and the uncertainty faced by Argentineans and Brazilians has a feeling of déjà vu about it, and, as opposed to natural disasters such as hurricanes and earthquakes, it is self-inflicted.

This is not a statement regarding left versus right, more government or less government, or more or less redistributive policies. To be precise, the key variable in our main hypothesis is not the size of government. What matters is not how much the government spends; rather, what matters is the difference between how much the government spends compared to how much it raises in revenues. Norway provides an example that clarifies this distinction: its government spends more than any Latin American government as a fraction of total output, but it raises even more revenues, to the point that it owns assets that are worth about three times the yearly GDP of the country. No fiscal clouds appear on Norway's horizon.

The cross-country analysis in this volume makes clear that those countries with large and sustained deficits ended up having substantially more macroeconomic instability than the countries that did not. For instance, Chile and Argentina ran large deficits in the first half of the 1970s, compared, for example, to Paraguay and Peru, and therefore faced much more macroeconomic instability during that decade. Chile made structural changes to its fiscal policy following its debt crisis in the early 1980s, while Argentina did not. Sure enough, while Chile managed to have very stable macroeconomic indicators, the 1980s brought a sequence of crises for Argentina. Eventually, in the 1990s, Argentina did make a structural change to its deficit and managed to stabilize the economy, albeit only for a decade. By 2001, after several years of recession, the government defaulted on its debt once again.

Paraguay and Peru, as mentioned above, had relatively conservative fiscal policies in the 1970s. As a consequence, macroeconomic instability was relatively low. For example, inflation in Paraguay was, on average, 11 percent per year, while in Peru it was 26 percent per year. While Paraguay maintained fiscal discipline, Peru started spending beyond its means during the 1980s, a process that led to hyperinflation.

The lesson seems to have been learned in most of the region. It is worth mentioning an interesting anecdote from Paraguay, which we learned when we visited Asunción, its capital, for the local workshop. The government, at the time managed by a center-right party, prepared and eventually launched its first issue of bonds into the market. Before that, all government debt had been with international organizations or foreign governments. The fiercest opponents to the executive branch were the congress members from the left parties, worried that the possibility of issuing bonds would induce a spiral of overspending, as had happened in too many of the countries in the region. This anecdote highlights the fact that fiscal discipline is a virtue that need not be associated with right-wing policies.

The histories told in these chapters, while reinforcing our hypothesis that lack of fiscal discipline has been responsible for the macroinstability in Latin America, also provide interesting examples of other ways that economic policies can lead to poor economic outcomes. In particular, some crises occur even without large government deficits. Lack of fiscal discipline is sufficient for generating crises, but not necessary. These exceptions allow us to draw some useful lessons.

The rest of this chapter is organized as follows. In the next section, we provide an application of the budget accounting framework developed by the editors of this volume to provide a narrative about the policy mistakes in Mexico that led to its great depression in the 1980s. We illustrate the role of bad fiscal policy in the crisis, but we argue that other factors were also important.

The Mexican crisis that erupted in 1982 was a perfect storm of lack of fiscal discipline combined with the external shocks of falling oil prices and rising international interest rates and a series of devaluations that sharply increased the value of dollar-denominated public and private debt. The crisis simultaneously involved a default on sovereign debt and a domestic banking crisis, which resulted in the Mexican government taking control of the banking system and paying for some of the banks' losses by reducing the value of dollar-denominated deposits with a system of multiple exchange rates. We study Mexico's 1982 crisis because these elements were repeated over time and across countries in Latin America.

We then move to discuss other factors that interact with lack of fiscal discipline in generating crises. In the third section we discuss the role of banking crises, and in the fourth we discuss how denominating sovereign debt in dollars left Latin American countries vulnerable to debt crises. The fifth section studies transfers, the discrepancies that our budget accounting produces, where borrowing needs do not match the fiscal deficit even after we take into account all the available data on transfers, profits and losses of government enterprises, and so forth. We find that discrepancies tend to be large during crises and often involve policies like multiple exchange rates that make transfers to groups favored by the government at the expense of taxpayers and groups who see their benefits cut. The sixth section discusses external factors, mainly the role of international banks and foreign bank regulators. Finally, we discuss some general lessons that we can draw from the country cases that we have studied. The seventh section looks at the impact of inflation stabilization on output, and the eighth section discusses the role of primary commodity price movements. The ninth, concluding section of the chapter considers some lessons for policy.

Budget Accounting for Mexico in the 1980s

In August 1982, Mexico defaulted on payments on its dollar-denominated foreign debt. This led to Mexico being excluded from international financial markets until it was able to renegotiate this debt under the Brady Plan in 1989. Kehoe and Prescott (2007) classify the period 1982–95 in Mexico as being a great depression, meaning that the fall in GDP per working-age person from its long-term trend was at least 20 percent in total and 15 percent during the first ten years of the period.

We use the budget accounting framework from "A Framework for Studying the Monetary and Fiscal History of Latin America" to develop a narrative for the role of monetary and fiscal policy in Mexico during its 1982 debt crisis. The budget accounting provides guidance for our narrative and suggests that factors besides large fiscal deficits played important roles in causing the crisis and delaying the subsequent recovery.

In "A Framework for Studying the Monetary and Fiscal History of Latin America," Kehoe, Nicolini, and Sargent develop the budget accounting framework starting with the government budget constraint:

$$B_t + B_t^* E_t + M_t = P_t(D_t + X_t) + B_{t-1}(1+r_{t-1}) + B_{t-1}^*(1+r_{t-1}^*)E_t + M_{t-1}.$$

On the left-hand side of this equation, B_t is the stock of peso-denominated domestic debt; B_t^* is the stock of dollar-denominated foreign debt; E_t is the pesos-per-dollar nominal exchange rate; and M_t is the stock of high-powered money. On the right-hand side, $D_t + X_t$ is the total primary deficit of the government, where D_t is the deficit as is recorded in the national budget, X_t is a residual term that makes the budget constraint hold, and P_t is the domestic price level in the form of the GDP deflator; $B_{t-1}(1+r_{t-1})$ is the value of domestic debt and debt service requirements inherited from the previous year; and $B_{t-1}^*(1+r_{t-1}^*)E_t$ is the corresponding term for foreign debt. A series of simple algebraic steps transforms the budget constraint into our budget accounting equation:

$$(\theta_t - \theta_{t-1}) + \xi_t(\theta_t^* - \theta_{t-1}^*) + (m_t - m_{t-1}) + \left(1 - \frac{1}{g_t \pi_t}\right)m_{t-1}$$
$$= d_t + \left(\frac{(1+r_{t-1})}{g_t \pi_t} - 1\right)\theta_{t-1} + \xi_t\left(\frac{(1+r_{t-1}^*)}{g_t \pi_t^*} - 1\right)\theta_{t-1}^* + x_t.$$

Here we have redefined terms as fractions of GDP:

$$\theta_t = \frac{B_t}{P_t Y_t}, \theta_t^* = \frac{B_t^* / P_t^*}{Y_t}, m_t = \frac{M_t}{P_t Y_t}, d_t = \frac{D_t}{P_t Y_t}, x_t = \frac{X_t}{P_t Y_t},$$

where P_t^* is the U.S. price level, and we let

$$\xi_t = \left(\frac{E_t P_t^*}{P_t}\right), g_t = \frac{Y_t}{Y_{t-1}}, \pi_t = \frac{P_t}{P_{t-1}}, \pi_t^* = \frac{P_t^*}{P_{t-1}^*}.$$

In our discussion of the terms of this budget accounting equation, we will focus considerable attention on the term x_t. We will often refer to it as a transfer because it includes losses of public enterprises and government-operated development banks that are ignored, or poorly accounted for, in the budget or implicit transfers to private agents who benefit from increases in inflation or from systems of multiple exchange rates.

Table 1 presents this accounting for 1982 in Mexico as well as the three years before the crisis and the three years after.[1] The numbers are flows as a percentage of GDP, which we refer to as percentage points (pp). To put these flow numbers into perspective, the stock of debt in 1978 was 34 percent of GDP.

We see in Table 1 that the Mexican government ran large primary deficits up until 1982 and subsequently ran primary surpluses. Notice that in 1981, the primary deficit

Table 1. Budget accounting for Mexico, 1979–85

	1979	1980	1981	1982	1983	1984	1985
Sources							
Domestic debt issuance	0.52	−5.13	2.51	7.11	1.10	−1.59	−1.24
Foreign debt issuance	−1.21	−0.60	6.38	6.05	−5.82	2.95	7.79
Money issuance	0.42	0.18	0.89	2.94	−2.33	−1.01	−4.26
Seigniorage	3.48	4.25	4.12	6.10	8.47	6.58	6.03
Total	3.21	−1.29	13.90	22.20	1.42	6.94	8.32
Obligations							
Primary deficit	7.10	2.86	7.61	3.37	−4.62	−5.21	−3.49
Domestic debt service	−3.14	−1.88	0.23	3.85	−0.33	0.47	0.87
Foreign debt service	−3.03	−1.40	−0.29	1.39	4.15	1.20	1.09
Transfer	2.28	−0.87	6.35	13.59	2.23	10.47	9.85
Total	3.21	−1.29	13.90	22.20	1.42	6.94	8.32

was 7.61 pp. One narrative that we could tell is that the 1982 debt crisis was the result of lack of fiscal discipline.

There is some validity to this narrative, and the government deficits played a central role in the balance of payments crisis and the debt crisis of 1982. This simple narrative leaves out other factors, however, that caused the crisis to escalate to devastating proportions for the Mexican economy. As we have explained, the crisis in 1982 in Mexico was a perfect storm of lack of fiscal discipline combined with external shocks and a series of devaluations that sharply increased the value of dollar-denominated public and private debt compared to output. The devaluations of the peso that occurred in August 1982 and afterward were part of the debt crisis, which started in August, but the large devaluation in February 1982 was an attempt to avert a crisis. Unfortunately, the increase in the value of dollar-denominated private debt compared to output caused by the February devaluation led to a banking crisis, and the Mexican government nationalized the banks and assumed their debts. The Mexican government resorted to increasing inflation and imposing multiple exchange rates, which led to large transfers to some economic agents at the expense of others and distorted incentives, thereby prolonging the crisis. We see evidence to support this perfect storm narrative in Table 1 in the large values of transfers starting in 1981, in the foreign debt service terms that become positive starting in 1982, and in the increasing importance of seigniorage starting in 1982. We discuss each of these patterns in the data in Table 1 in turn, although they are all related.

Although the Mexican government's primary budget deficits were large in the late 1970s and early 1980s, it is worth putting these numbers in some perspective. Between 2009 and 2014, the Spanish government ran primary deficits that averaged 8.8 percent of GDP per year, and Spain's government debt went from 39.5 percent of GDP in 2008 to 100.4 percent in 2014. The period 2011–13 was one of crisis for Spain, but nowhere near as severe as Mexico's crisis of the early 1980s.

Notice in Table 1 that the debt service terms for both domestic debt and foreign debt go from negative in the late 1970s to positive in the 1980s. Our measures of debt service include changes in the ratio of domestic debt to GDP due to Mexican inflation and changes in the ratio of foreign debt to GDP due to U.S. inflation and devaluation. In Mexico and the United States, inflation was higher than interest rates in the later 1970s, but this changed, particularly in the United States, during the early 1980s with the sharp increase in U.S. interest rates to combat inflation. Our budget accounting also includes changes in the ratio of both domestic debt to GDP and foreign debt to GDP due to Mexican GDP growth. Mexican GDP was growing up until 1982, reducing the debt service terms, but then it started to contract, increasing the debt service terms.

Notice that the transfers during 1981–85 were much larger on average than were the primary deficits during 1979–82. Transfers not included in the government's budget of expenditures and receipts increased the government's need to borrow more than did the primary deficits. Parts of these transfers are easy to identify. Some of the 13.59 pp transfer in 1982 was the cost of nationalizing the failing banks. Other parts of the transfers are harder to identify, but we can hypothesize about them.

Some of the transfers were the result of multiple exchange rates imposed by the Mexican government starting in August 1982 and continuing through November 1991. Figure 1 presents data on the exchange rates. Overall, there were nine different exchange rates, with some overlapping periods, but at any point in time, there were no more than three. Consequently, there is no easy way to distinguish all nine in the same figure. As an indicator of how complex the exchange rate regime was, we note that there were three exchange rates during part of August 1982 and from December 1982 through March 1983. The system of three exchange rates officially continued through August 1985, but the two lower rates, the special rate and the controlled rate, were virtually identical after March 1983 and were lower than the free rate. As an indicator of how different the prevailing exchange rates were during some periods, we note that during most of December 1982, the free rate was more than 100 percent higher than the special rate (Banco de México 2009). The Mexican government forced exporters in the *maquiladora* sector (in-bond manufacturers who purchased intermediate inputs for processing and reexport) to do all transactions on imports and subsequent reexports at the controlled rate rather than the higher free rate official rate; this was an implicit tax on their net exports (Gómez-Palacio 1984). The government also allowed some importers to buy dollars at the controlled rate; this was an implicit subsidy on their imports. We do not have data on these taxes and subsidies, so they end up in the transfer. If we redo the budget accounting using the controlled exchange rate rather than the free exchange rate, we find the transfer declines from 13.59 pp to 12.06 pp in 1982, giving us a very rough estimate of 1.53 pp as the transfer generated by the multiple exchange rate system. Since the Banco de México intervened in all three exchange rate markets simultaneously, the transfer could have been much higher.

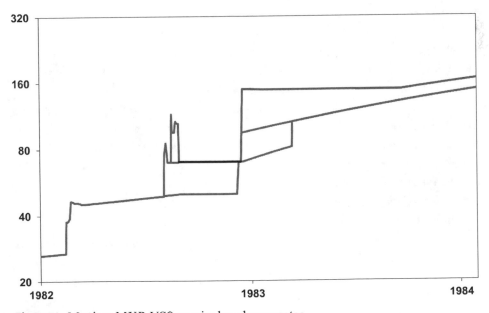

Figure 1. Mexico: MXP-US$ nominal exchange rates

Another transfer related to the multiple exchange rate system was the liquidation of Mex-dollar accounts in the banking system. The Mexican government had encouraged banks to set up dollar-denominated accounts to allow middle-class Mexicans to keep their savings in domestic banks in spite of their fears of devaluation. In August 1982, the Mexican government authorized the banks to convert these accounts into peso-denominated accounts at a special Mex-dollar rate of 69.5 MXP per US$ rather than the fluctuating rate of more than 100 MXP per US$ prevailing in the free market. This meant that Mexican depositors lost more than 30 percent of the value of their savings and paid much of the costs of the nationalization of the banks that took place immediately after the liquidation of the Mex-dollar accounts (Serrano 2015). It is worth noting that the Argentinean government resorted to a similar mechanism, called "pesification," in 2002 to pay for most of the cost of a bailout of the banking system.

Our examples show that some transfers were positive and others were negative, but, as the data in Table 1 show, they tended to be positive during the early 1980s. It is worth noting that transfers averaged 5.58 pp per year during the 1980s, while afterward they averaged 0.62 pp. In particular, the large transfers that the residual in our budget accounting identifies are much larger in periods of crisis than in normal periods.

A major element of our perfect storm narrative for Mexico's debt crises was the series of devaluations in February and August 1982 that continued during the rest of 1982. This increased not only the foreign debt of Mexican banks but also that of Mexico's government. We have seen that most of the increase in debt to GDP in Mexico between 1981 and 1982 was due to devaluation, not to more borrowing. To see how this fits into our budget accounting, let us decompose the foreign debt issuance term:

$$\xi_t(\theta_t^* - \theta_{t-1}^*) = (\xi_t\theta_t^* - \xi_{t-1}\theta_{t-1}^*) - \theta_{t-1}^*(\xi_t - \xi_{t-1}).$$

The first term in this decomposition tells us how much the value of foreign debt as a fraction of GDP changed from year $t-1$ to year t. The second term tells us how much of this change in value was due to the change in the real exchange rate. In 1982, the value of the ratio of external debt to GDP, $(\xi_t\theta_t^* - \xi_{t-1}\theta_{t-1}^*)$, increased by 17.19 pp, but 11.14 pp were due to the real devaluation that occurred between 1981 and 1982, $\theta_{t-1}^*(\xi_t - \xi_{t-1})$, leaving 6.05 pp as the value of the increase in foreign debt deflated by inflation in the United States and real GDP growth in Mexico. It is noteworthy that foreign debt increased in Mexico in 1982, 1984, and 1985, even though Mexico was excluded from private international debt markets because it received loans from the U.S. Treasury and the International Monetary Fund, most of which were intended to help it continue to pay debt service on its debt to U.S. banks.

During the 1980s, the inflation rate in Mexico increased from an average of 24 percent per year during 1979–81 to an average of 66 percent per year during 1982–85. (It was even higher in 1986 and 1987, before starting to fall rapidly in 1988.) The increase in inflation allowed some agents to reduce their real tax payments by paying as late as possible, and it made it possible for the government to reduce real expenditures also by paying as late as possible. The primary deficit data mix early expenditures with late expenditures and early revenues with late revenues. In principle, it is possible to do a careful accounting of the deficit considering the dates of expenditures and revenues, but using the data that we have, we can just say that the difference between the ideally measured deficit and that in the data shows up in the residual.

Banking Crises

A common and sometimes recurrent phenomenon in the histories of these countries, which almost always has a large fiscal impact, is the eruption of banking crises like that in Mexico in 1982. These crises are typically characterized by runs on bank deposits that lead a sizable fraction of the banks to either fall or be forced to merge. Examples of this phenomenon abound in the chapters of this book. The typical outcome of this sort of crisis involves some form of public bailout of the banks' liabilities and some form of confiscation of deposits. Also typical is some sort of debt reduction to those who had bank loans.

Briefly, the crises follow the same general pattern. Starting from a heavily regulated financial sector a—typically new—government administration would decide to reform the capital markets. This happened in most countries, since these markets were heavily regulated in the early 1960s. The reforms often involved liberalizations of the financial sector and the opening of the current account. These two reforms were regarded as desirable and defended by supporters of the Washington Consensus, which served as a role model of reforms for developing countries in the 1990s. The outcome was typically a large inflow of private borrowing, channeled through a vibrant and growing banking sector. Following several years of boom, the fraction of nonperforming loans would build up to the point at which a run on bank deposits would lead to a full-blown banking crisis. The resolution of the crisis typically included nationalization of private debts. This happened frequently all over the region. Even countries with conservative fiscal policy relative to the region, such as Paraguay and Colombia, faced that problem. Most experiences of liberalization of the financial sector and opening of the current account ended in a banking crisis and a bailout of private debt.

In some cases, the crisis can be associated with banks having high exposure to government debt. This would typically be the result of government policy: unable to raise enough to finance expenditures, the government would pass a regulation forcing the banks to buy its bonds. The likelihood of a default of the government on its own bonds would raise doubts about the solvency of the banks and increase the probability of a run. The experience of Argentina in 2001 features these characteristics.

In several of the cases, however, such as in Chile in 1982, the crisis appears not to be the result of profligate spending by the government. Rather, it is private spending that explains most of the borrowing. But it turns out that after the crisis, the government nationalized the private debt. The occurrence and recurrence of these crises in Latin America led to the notion of "excessive borrowing" as one of the causes of the region's economic problems. An interesting question raised by these experiences is, Why would the private sector borrow beyond its means, risking its own bankruptcy? The resolution of the crises points to a hypothesis: it is the probability of a future bailout that gives the private sector the incentive to borrow. To the point where agents can anticipate that, in the event of a crisis, the government would bail out the financial sector if the problem was large enough, a coordination problem arises. If enough agents are borrowing enough funds, the problem of nonperforming loans becomes a social problem rather than a private problem. It may be individually rational to borrow more than what the private return suggests. Bailouts have been too frequent in the region to assume that agents would not take that possibility into account in making their economic decisions.

As mentioned above, the reforms of the financial sectors would typically be accompanied by the deregulation of the capital account. The access to foreign borrowing would exacerbate the excessive borrowing, making the crisis of a substantially larger magnitude.

These experiences suggest that prudential regulation measures such as limits on debt-to-asset ratios and restrictions on foreign currency–denominated borrowing by individuals, together with capital requirements and liquidity provisions much larger than the ones adopted in developed economies for banks, ought to be considered. Opting for a gradual liberalization, in which restrictions are high initially or even phasing in the deregulation, starting with the financial sector first and then deregulating the current account later on, could be desirable. Regrettably, we do not yet have quantitative models that have been tested enough so as to provide clear answers to these problems. Nonetheless, the evidence points out clearly that the frictionless models that imply that the immediate joint liberalization of the financial sector and the current account are sound policy decisions, as the Washington Consensus recommended, are clearly at odds with the evidence. Prudent and gradual deregulation seems to be the safe choice. (See Nicolini 2018 for further details.)

Denomination and Maturity of Sovereign Debt

Another feature that also had a large fiscal effect, and has been present in all the countries analyzed in this volume, is that the government issued debt instruments denominated in foreign currency. The degree and the persistence of this phenomenon have varied substantially across countries and over time for each country. For example, Brazil has mostly issued domestic currency–denominated debt, with some form of indexation during the high inflation years. While Brazilian dollar-denominated debt was zero for most of the period, it did reach 30 percent of total federal government debt in some years. In contrast, Argentina's dollar-denominated debt has always been over 60 percent of the total, reaching values higher than 95 percent in some years. The comparison between these two countries is particularly interesting, since they had very similar inflation histories. Both countries had very long periods with high chronic inflation with recurrent bursts of hyperinflation, and both countries eventually conquered high inflation during the 1990s.

It has long been recognized that a major source of volatility has been the sensitivity of debt-to-output ratios to variations in the real exchange rate. The series of studies in this book provide a quantitative measure of this by comparing the measured debt-to-output

Table 2. Ratio of standard deviation of debt–output ratio to standard deviation of simulated series

VEN	MEX	CHL	ARG	PER	ECU	BRA	URU	PAR	BOL	COL
2.8	2.0	1.9	1.6	1.5	1.4	1.3	1.3	1.2	1.1	1.1

ratio to a simulation in which the real exchange rate is maintained constant at a specific value. The data in Table 2 show the ratio of the standard deviation of the debt-to-output ratio as observed in the data to the standard deviation of the simulated series maintaining a fixed real exchange rate.

The relevance of the numbers in Table 2 lies in the role that the debt-to-output ratio plays in the conceptual framework that guides the explorations performed in this book. The total obligations for a government in a particular period are given by the primary deficit and by the interest payments on the existing debt. Those interest payments are high when the debt-to-output ratios are high. It is the sum of these two concepts that the government must finance by printing money or by issuing new debt.

At the same time, in many models of sovereign debt, the ability of the government to borrow is lower—or the interest rate it must pay on newly issued debt is higher—when the debt-to-output ratio is higher. Thus variations in the real exchange rate can have a substantial impact on the amount the government needs to finance at the precise moment in which floating bonds becomes particularly expensive.

The quantitative implications of this discussion become evident once we notice that the volatility of the real exchange rate is very high in general, and particularly so for these countries. In Figure 2, we plot the evolution of the debt-to-output ratios for several countries, normalizing then to be equal to one in 1980.

All the countries in the figure defaulted in the early 1980s. And all the countries had substantial depreciations of their currencies. For each country, we show the evolution of the debt-to-output ratio as in the data and also as simulated assuming that the real exchange rate remains constant at its value of 1980.

Exchange rate volatility combined with a high degree of debt dollarization can have dramatic effects. For example, the debt-to-output ratio went from 0.15 in 1980 to 0.68 in 1983 in Argentina, mostly due to the effect of the exchange rate depreciation. To achieve the same effect through primary deficits, it would require a yearly deficit of more than 17 percent of GDP for those three years. There has never been a period of three consecutive primary deficits of that magnitude for any of the eleven countries covered in this volume during the almost seventy-year period considered.

Following the international financial crisis of 2008, the United States and many European countries ran very large deficits for several years. Spain's debt, for example, went from 36 percent of GDP in 2007 to 88 percent in 2012; Portugal's debt went from 68 percent to 126 percent; and Greece's debt went from 103 percent to 126 percent.

For the countries whose data are depicted in Figure 2, the exchange rate movements achieved the same effect in just a couple of quarters, without any fiscal expansion.

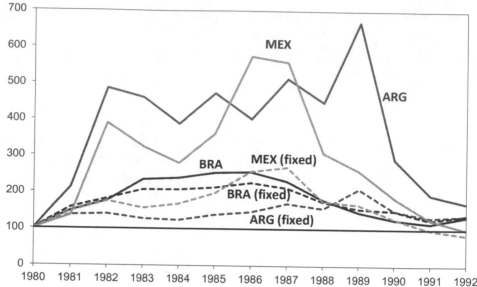

Figure 2. Evolution of the debt-to-GDP ratio observed and with fixed real exchange rate (RER), 1980 = 100

In Mexico in December 1994 and January 1995, a devaluation coupled with the short maturity of its dollar-indexed debt, *tesobonos*, caused a balance of payments crisis and would have caused a default if not for the bailout put together by U.S. President Bill Clinton and offered to Mexico in January 1995. Mexico had a primary surplus in 1994, making it difficult to ascribe the 1994–95 debt crisis to lack of fiscal discipline. The problem was that the Mexican government had allowed most of its debt that was not in Brady bonds to become dollar-indexed *tesobonos* with very short maturities during 1994. In fact, the average maturity of the debt that was not in Brady bonds was nine months by the end of 1994 (Cole and Kehoe 2000). The short maturity of the debt meant that, although the *tesobono* debt was relatively small, much of it became due every week. This made Mexico vulnerable to a self-fulfilling crisis, as discussed in Cole and Kehoe (1996): investors believed that if they did not buy new *tesobonos* at the weekly auctions held by the Banco de México, the government would not be able to pay off the old *tesobonos* becoming due. The beliefs of these investors seemed to be realized until President Clinton intervened with a US$50 billion loan package with funds put together from the U.S. Treasury, the International Monetary Fund, and other official lenders. The loan had a high-penalty interest rate and relied on the receipts from Mexico's oil exports as collateral. Mexico borrowed only US$22 billion of the loan offered and had no problem paying off the loan early.

The Transfer

From the budget constraint accounting exercises, three cross-country patterns emerge. First, with the exception of Ecuador and Peru, the sign of the transfer term is, on average, positive. Second, the transfer is much larger in times of economic distress. For example, the average of the transfer term in Argentina and Mexico is 1.9 and 0.5 percent of GDP, respectively, but it was 35 percent for Argentina in 2002 and 22 percent for Mexico in 1982. Third, the accumulation of the transfer term over time explains a substantial portion of the debt-to-GDP ratios in 2017. For example, Argentina's debt-to-GDP ratio would have been half of what it was in 2017 had the transfer term been zero; however, there are cases like Ecuador, where persistently negative transfer terms imply that debt would have been twice as large had these transfers been zero.

The positive sign of the transfer term means that governments find ways to increase spending and keep it outside the reach of their national congresses, which typically approve the budget. In the eleven country chapters of this book, we identified some of the sources of these hidden expenses. One of the most important is the bailout of the banking sector, a recurrent pattern in most countries. In some cases, the bailouts were the natural result of previously announced government-sponsored deposit insurance. In others, the bailouts were decided ex post. More generally, due to the recurrence of crises, these governments are exposed to contingent liabilities that are absent from studies of debt sustainability and, in some cases, are hard to measure.[2]

In other cases, positive and large residuals are present. Sometimes it was through relatively large deficits in government-owned enterprises, as in the cases of Bolivia and Argentina in the 1970s and the 1980s. The most common mechanism, however, was the losses incurred by government-owned development banks.[3]

The main channel through which spending could be increased while bypassing Congress was through direct transfers from the central bank to the development banks. In some cases, the banks would have an account at the central banks, with instantaneous credit. For instance, the authors of the Brazil chapter discovered that the Bank of Brazil, which managed most of the government's operations for subsidized credit, had the ability to make automatic withdrawals from its account at the central bank, without any authority from either the executive or the legislative power to authorize those transactions. Even though the balance of this account was meant to average zero, in practice this mechanism gave the Bank of Brazil control over money issuance, since it could withdraw funds that would automatically be matched with an expansion of the monetary base.

Another source of transfers represents recognition of debts incurred in periods of fiscal hardship and therefore high inflation. When inflation is high, just delaying payments is a way to reduce the real value of expenditure. Another is to delay increases in compensation of public servants or pensioners. In many circumstances, however, these practices ended up in the courts. Legal resolutions in these countries take several years. Thus there may be issuances of bonds in a particular period that are unrelated to expenditures of that period. Rather, they are the explicit recognition of implicit arrears. The issuance of several series of bonds in Argentina during the early 1990s provides a clear example.

In many cases, however, the authors of the chapters have not been able to identify the origins or the recipients of these transfers, even though these transfers do account for a sizable fraction of the increases in the debt-to-output ratios on many occasions. An important implication of our analysis of transfers is the conclusion that running a responsible fiscal policy goes beyond the debate about the budget in Congress. Effectively controlling spending requires a transparent relationship between government-owned banks and enterprises and the Treasury and, most importantly, the central bank.

A large body of literature has stressed the importance of central bank independence in the conquest of inflation. This literature stresses the time inconsistency problem of a centralized government. The experience of some of these countries suggests that it may also be important as an effective tool to control spending by individual units in a multiunit government, a feature that has not been addressed in the literature.[4]

These increases in net spending without any oversight by Congress also have important implications for redistribution and growth. Episodes of high spending typically end up in either hyperinflation or large devaluations, accompanied by severe measures such as capital controls, dual exchange rates, and pesification of deposits. The fact that the transfer term is large in these distressed periods implies that these severe measures create large transfers of resources from the government to some private agents—resources that are being redistributed to these specific agents from the rest of the population as in a zero-sum game.

Our guess is that these zero-sum games played by private agents in times of economic distress imply that talent is allocated not to lower production costs—which increases productivity, making it a positive-sum game—but rather to rent-seeking activities to capture large government transfers that are not closely scrutinized. The way to become rich is not through the creation of wealth but by being the winner of a zero-sum game by outsmarting the typical working-class family that is saving in simple instruments. This, in turn, implies there is no net wealth creation, which transforms into poor total productivity performance. This may explain the severity and length of crises in Latin America, especially the one that occurred during the 1980s.

A silver lining from this analysis of the transfer term is that it became significantly lower for some countries after 1989. The most drastic changes have been in Brazil, Mexico, and Uruguay, where the average transfer term went down from 3.4, 5.6, and 4.7 percent of GDP on average during the 1980s to 0.5, 0.6, and 1.3 percent, respectively, from 1990 onward. Argentina, Chile, and Paraguay are also in this group of countries where the transfer term has been low in recent years. Our interpretation is that these economies have somewhat successfully moved away from institutional environments that incentivize rent-seeking activities, especially during periods of economic crisis.

International Banks and U.S. Banking Regulators

We now discuss the role of external factors in the evolution of the region. The eleven countries studied in this book can be modeled as small open economies, which means they are exposed to international shocks that are beyond their control but affect their economic performance to varying degrees. (Of our eleven Latin American countries, the one for which the small-open-economy assumption is least applicable is probably Chile because of its importance in the world copper market.)

During the 1970s, there was a substantial increase in credit to emerging economies, including Latin America. The banking sector in the United States went through major structural changes that reduced profit margins in the domestic market. For example, the rapid growth of the commercial paper market implied that banks that were losing big clients sought other forms of financing.[5] At the same time, important financial liberalizations in Latin America opened the door to foreign financial flows, which allowed U.S. banks to allocate credit there.

The oil boom in the 1970s increased the liquidity of banks in the United States and thus the size of the credit flows to Latin America and other emerging economies. Additionally, near-zero real interest rates on short-term loans allowed U.S. banks to provide credit to foreign countries at a very low cost. Even though economists and some authorities were concerned, most of their warnings were frequently disregarded as exaggerations, and the general opinion of U.S. regulators was that the likelihood of a banking crisis was low.[6]

By the end of the 1970s, concerns about high inflation in the United States rose, and in 1982 then Federal Reserve chairman Paul Volcker decided to raise the federal funds rate. This decision increased the funding costs of commercial banks, which restricted the amount of credit that could flow to Latin America. This reduction in credit availability put significant stress on public finances in most countries in the region.

Almeida et al. (2018) show how high risk-free interest rates induce countries to default on their debt because they expect favorable renegotiation terms in the future. When the reference rates are high, the opportunity cost of banks holding up renegotiation on defaulted loans is higher, inducing them to accept higher haircuts when renegotiating defaulted debt. In August 1982, Mexico defaulted on most of its loans from U.S. commercial banks, an action followed by Argentina and Venezuela and, later in the same decade, Brazil.

Reference interest rates in the United States, however, remained high for only a short period of time, going back to pre-1982 levels by the end of 1983. Through the lens of the mechanism in the paper by Almeida et al. (2018), this implied less favorable renegotiation prospects for the Latin American governments in default. Additionally, as documented on the Federal Reserve History website (Sims and Romero 2013), U.S. banking regulators allowed lenders to delay recognizing the full extent of the losses on defaulted loans. They were worried that, had the losses been fully recognized, the banks would have been deemed insolvent, which would have led to potential bank runs and a financial crisis in the United States. This relaxed regulation delayed the renegotiation of Latin American debt until the Brady Plan was enacted in 1989. In effect, the loans from the U.S. Treasury and the International Monetary Fund to countries such as Mexico were a stopgap that gave vulnerable U.S. banks time to build up their capital before they had to renegotiate their debt with Latin American countries, but they also left these Latin American countries frozen out of international capital markets until the enactment of the Brady Plan.

The loans to Latin American governments were, at the time of the debt crisis of 1982, very similar to the total capital of the banks that issued the loans. This risk exposure clearly reflects bad bank supervision. Still, an interesting question remains: Why did the individual banks put themselves in that position? These were large, nondiversified syndicated loans, suggesting that defaults would put the system in jeopardy. Were these banks making the decision to lend to these few governments under the veil of the "too big to fail" doctrine? The intervention of the monetary and regulatory authorities in the United States postdefault suggests that this may well have been the case.

The chapters in this book offer multiple examples of how bad economic policies by Latin American governments generated crises in the region. Nevertheless, from this section we conclude that U.S. economic policies set the table, triggered, and amplified the Latin American debt crisis of the 1980s, a period of time often referred to as "the lost decade" because of its length and severity.

The Real Effects of Inflation Stabilization

The eleven countries studied in this volume provide a large variety of experiences in inflation episodes, both across countries and over time for any single country. Consequently, the eleven stories combined contain a very rich set of experiences on inflation stabilization. The list of successful stabilization plans to stop inflation is almost as large as the list of stabilization plans that failed. The experience of these countries makes clear the need for fiscal adjustment as a means of stopping inflation permanently, while other policies, such as fixing the exchange rate, can be very effective at stopping very high inflation temporarily. These two policy measures, fiscal restraint and a fixed exchange rate, proved to be a powerful combination: they are behind many of the successful stabilization plans (although fixing the exchange rate was not always used).

Besides being laboratories to evaluate policies to stop inflation, the histories of these countries can also be used to make a first evaluation of a notion that has become conventional wisdom in many policy and academic circles: reducing inflation has large real costs. This conventional wisdom was born out of the evidence relating reductions in the rate of inflation to increases in the rate of unemployment, the Phillips curve. This wisdom was consolidated following the 1982 recession in the United States, associated with the inflation stabilization plan successfully undertaken by the Fed under the leadership of Paul Volcker—so much so that the 1982 recession is too frequently called the "Volcker recession."

An alternative interpretation was provided by Sargent (1986) in the same book that set the foundations of the conceptual framework that we have used in this book. Thus the argument can be laid out using the government budget constraint and the money demand equation, which are the two main foundations of the conceptual framework discussed in "A Framework for Studying the Monetary and Fiscal History of Latin America." At the time the Federal Reserve announced that it was vigorously tightening its policy, the Treasury increased its deficit as a result of both a reduction in taxes (supply-side economics) and an expansion in military spending (the Star Wars program). The natural consequence of the reduction of seigniorage on the one hand and the increase in the deficit on the other was a rapid increase in government debt. This rapid increase in debt, Sargent argued, would strain the relationship between the Fed and the Treasury and would put pressure on one of them to switch its policy. A reasonable probability that the Fed would relax its policy tightening reduced the credibility of its plan to defeat inflation. It is this increase in macroeconomic uncertainty that may have been responsible for the "double-dip" recession of 1980–82. The persistently high long-term nominal rates following the inflation stabilization provide some evidence of lack of credibility in the long-run success of the Volcker strategy.

We certainly lack enough theory to provide a quantitative appraisal of that debate. But Latin America offers five episodes of successful stabilizations of extremely high inflation (from over 600 percent per year in Chile in 1973 to over 10,000 percent in Bolivia in 1985) and six instances of successful stabilizations of more moderate inflations (from about 25 percent per year in Chile in 1990 to 130 percent in Uruguay, also in 1990). As a first approach to the debate, we take a simple look at the data.

The top panel of Figure 3 plots the evolution of real GDP per capita after the stabilization of chronic inflation for six Latin American countries as well as for the United States. For each country, we set the year before the stabilization plan to be time zero. We then plot the evolution of per capita income for the next eight years. The number that accompanies the name of the country refers to the year the stabilization plan was launched. In all countries, output expanded after stabilization. For the three countries that launched their plan with inflation close to or above 100 percent per year (Mexico 1988, Uruguay 1990, and Ecuador 2000), growth was very fast during the years following the plan. The three countries chose to control the nominal exchange rate as the policy instrument to lower inflation, but whereas Mexico and Uruguay chose a gradual plan that brought inflation to one digit in six and eight years, respectively, Ecuador did it by adopting the U.S. dollar as its currency, so inflation was at one digit by year 2. In terms of the evolution of income per capita, Mexico and Ecuador behaved similarly in the first few years following the stabilization, but Uruguay did even better. Mexico then had a severe crisis in 1994 (year 7); that crisis, however, was related notto the stabilization plan but rather to the dollar indexation and short maturity of its debt, as we have discussed. The three countries that launched their stabilization plans starting from much lower inflation rates chose a gradual program. To bring inflation down to one digit, Chile took five years and Paraguay six, and Colombia still had two-digit inflation (around 15 percent) by year 8. No evidence of real costs associated with reducing inflation can be detected.

The bottom panel of Figure 3 presents the evidence for the five extreme inflation episodes. Hyperinflation was conquered and its control immediately spurred in Argentina and Brazil. In both countries, the hyperinflations were ended successfully and quickly: in less than several months, monthly inflation went from almost 100 percent in Argentina and 42 percent in Brazil to 5 and 15 percent, respectively. By the third year, yearly inflation was one digit in both countries. In both cases, output grew as a result of the stabilization. The other three countries followed a more gradual policy. In Bolivia and Peru, inflation was still very high one year after the plan (around 280 percent for Bolivia and 410 percent for Peru). Only in the second year was inflation brought down to two digits, and it took the countries eight and seven years, respectively, to bring inflation down to one digit. It took Peru three years to start growing and five

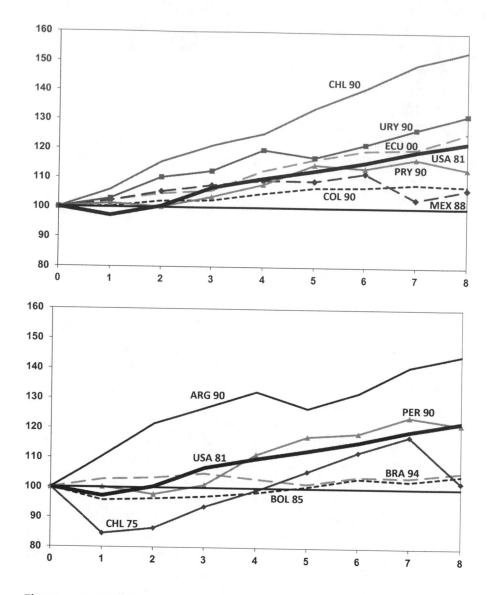

Figure 3. Real GDP per capita, year of inflation stabilization = 100: top panel: after stabilization of chronic inflation; bottom panel: after stabilization of extreme inflation

years for Bolivia, though its growth rate was very low. In Bolivia, the hyperinflation was accompanied by a long-lasting banking crisis that was not necessarily associated with the stabilization plan. The case of Chile, the country that chose a very gradual strategy, is the most dramatic: it took four years for Chile to bring inflation down to two digits—to about 40 percent per year. The stabilization plan started while the country was undergoing a major recession, emerging from the high level of social unrest that led to the coup of 1973. Overall, the experiences of these countries suggest that neither a gradual reduction of moderate inflation nor a sudden stabilization of high inflation is associated with output costs.

The Role of Primary Commodity Prices

A common theme in the discussions we had with economists and policy makers from these countries was the role of primary commodity prices. All eleven countries are net exporters of primary commodities. Invariably, the fate of these countries was associated with the price behavior of those commodities. They play no role in the framework used in this book, except in relation to the direct impact they may have in the evolution of the fiscal deficit. Indeed, in many cases, the government is directly involved in the production of the export commodity, such as oil in Mexico, which owns Pemex, the only oil company, or copper in Chile, where the state company, Codelco, has a large share of copper production. But primary commodity prices can also affect total revenues through their effect on royalties from the direct taxation of these activities. We have explored whether commodity-exporting countries exhibit different price behavior, especially during commodity booms. We have classified the eleven countries into three groups according to the importance of their commodity exports to GDP, and Table 3 summarizes this classification.

In Figure 4, we plot the evolution of real GDP per capita for each of the three groups and an index of international prices for a basket of primary commodities.

The top panel of Figure 4 shows the evolution of per capita GDP for the four highest commodity exporter countries. The most striking feature of the data in the figure is the behavior of output in Venezuela, which exhibits a very close relationship with the swings in the price of oil. Note an important exception, though: the peak per capita income in Venezuela is in 1975, several years before the peak in the price of oil. In 1976, Venezuela nationalized the oil industry, and oil production steadily declined for many years after

Table 3. Importance of commodity exports

| Group | Country | Commodity exports (percentage of GDP) | |
		2000	Average 1989–2017
Top 4	Venezuela	23.6	20.8
	Ecuador	21.9	17.7
	Chile	14.8	17.3
	Bolivia	8.0	15.8
Medium 4	Colombia	7.7	11.3
	Peru	7.4	11.2
	Paraguay	6.5	7.7
	Uruguay	4.6	7.1
Bottom 3	Argentina	3.8	4.5
	Mexico	3.0	4.1
	Brazil	2.4	3.8

that. In comparison, the evolution of output in Chile is much less closely correlated with the prices, and Ecuador, the other big commodity exporter, is somewhat in between. In the top and bottom panels of Figure 4, we show the data for the other countries. There seems to be some correlation between the long period of low prices in the 1980s and poor output performance and the period of high prices in the first years of this century and good economic performance. With the exception of Venezuela, however, there is little evidence that the swings in commodity prices are the most relevant determinant of the fate of these countries. For example, income per capita in Mexico (bottom panel of Figure 4) did decline with the drop in oil prices after 1981. The recovery started in the late 1980s, however, coincidental with the years in which Mexico started a successful plan to stabilize its macroeconomy, not the years in which oil prices recovered. The 1995 crisis was unrelated to commodity prices, and the 2009 recession coincided with a drop in the price of oil, but it also coincided with a world recession. In any case, both events were highly transient. It is also the case that the recoveries for Argentina in 1991 and for Brazil in 1994 (bottom panel of Figure 4) coincide with the periods in which they finally controlled inflation, and those were the years with the lowest prices for commodities during the period. Finally, note also that both Chile and Bolivia started growing in the middle and late 1980s, respectively, once they stabilized their economies when commodity prices were at very low levels and declining.

To explore the role that commodity prices may have played through their impact on the government's revenues, in Figure 5 we show the relationship between the movements in primary commodity prices and the sum of total fiscal deficits plus the transfer term from the budget accounting exercises, grouping countries the same way we did in Figure 4. These sums of total deficits and transfers are rather volatile, but a careful inspection of the three panels in the figure shows no evident worsening of fiscal policy during primary commodity price booms, with the clear and single exception of Venezuela.

To a lesser extent, Brazil and Argentina also show a deterioration in their fiscal position that follows the boom in primary commodity prices. Those countries were precisely the ones in trouble by the end of 2018. For the other countries, we can find no evidence of a worsening in their fiscal accounts during booms in primary commodity prices.

As we have pointed out, the policy mistakes that led to—or worsened—crises are common to all countries, regardless of how dependent they are on exploiting natural resources. The downward phase of commodity prices goes from 1980 to 2000. It is indeed the case that the period of the 1980s was a lost decade. By 2000, however, almost all countries had recovered what they had lost in the 1980s. The link that we can clearly identify in each country is from macrostability to output growth. In fact, on average, commodity prices were higher in the 1980s than in the 1990s. The first of the two decades, however, was much worse than the second for all the countries.

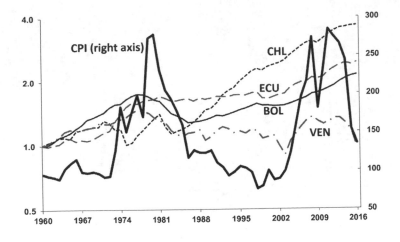

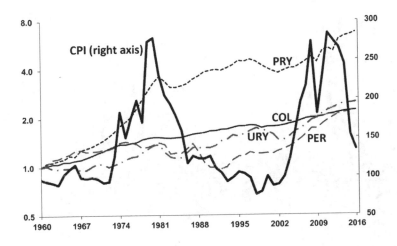

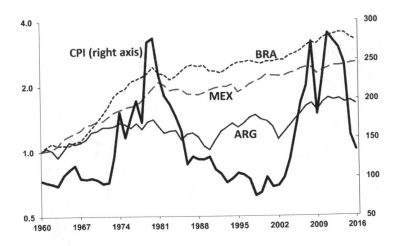

Figure 4. Real GDP per capita, 1960 = 1, and primary commodity price index, 1960 = 100: top panel: top four; middle panel: middle four; bottom panel: bottom three

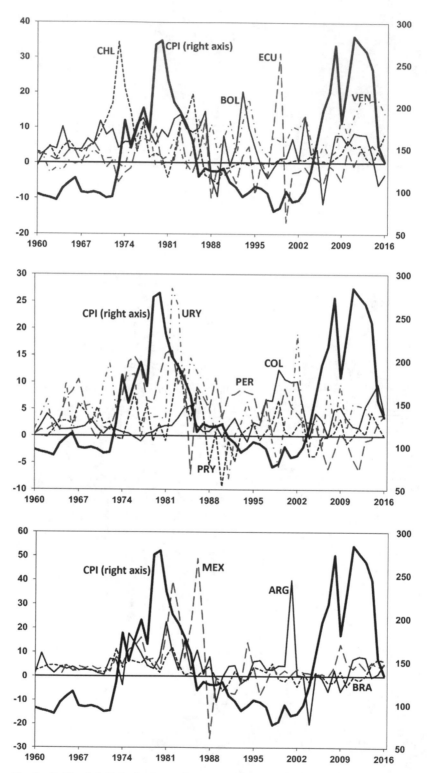

Figure 5. Total deficit plus transfers, percentage of GDP, and primary commodity price index, 1960 = 100: top panel: top four; middle panel: middle four; bottom panel: bottom three

Lessons Learned

What have we learned by studying all these countries together? We have isolated economic forces behind the major macroeconomic events. In many cases, the causes were common—such as crawling pegs in the 1970s, exchange rate controls and stabilization attempts in the 1980s without any fiscal adjustments, and banking crises in the 1990s. Experts in each country believe that their problems are unique and their causes specific to that country. The first lesson we take away from this book is that this belief is misguided: during the last fifty-seven years, most of the economic problems in Latin America—as well as their causes—had several common factors.

When this project started, we focused on the six largest countries in South America and Mexico. Later we expanded to include the ten largest South American countries and found many common factors in their economic crises and causes. An interesting topic for future research would be to expand this framework to the rest of Latin America and potentially to other regions where the idea of problems being country specific may also be misguided. We started our analysis in 1960 so we could have ten years of data before things started to go wrong. We considered starting in 1950, but we were limited by data availability for some of the countries.

Similar to the case of high inflation episodes, most balance of payments crises were the result of high sustained deficits. There are also some exceptions, such as Mexico during 1994–95; however, the common pattern suggests that lack of fiscal discipline can also result in important external imbalances, with the subsequent costly adjustments.

Another important lesson is related to the series of debt defaults that started with Mexico in 1982. Ex post, we suspect the defaults were not entirely justified, especially considering the huge costs that ensued. The role of U.S. regulators and policy makers before, during, and after the crisis is key to understanding its buildup as well as its long duration. Structural changes in the U.S. financial sector, along with a worldwide oil boom and financial openness in Latin America, fueled the flow of lending into the region. Then, drastic policy changes to tame inflation in the United States triggered a series of defaults whose costs and duration escalated because of relaxed regulation in the U.S. banking sector. These events indirectly prevented the Latin American governments from successfully renegotiating their debt until the enactment of the Brady Plan in 1989.

To conclude, based on the common elements that we identified as causes of poor economic performance, we identify four conditions that could avoid future crises that resemble those from the 1970s and 1980s:

- solid fiscal policy

- gradual and prudent liberalization of financial markets and the current account

- low exposure of government debt to real exchange rate movements

- careful monitoring and control of the expenditure of independent government institutions

Those countries that satisfy these policy guidelines will continue to have stable and good economic performance in the long run.

There is no reason to limit the discussion above to the countries studied in this project. The conceptual framework used to study the history of these eleven Latin American countries has no specific element that is exclusive to the region. Rather, it identifies policies that make countries more prone to macroeconomic instability. As it turns out, many countries in the region adopted those policies at one or more points in their recent histories. As we mentioned above, some countries learned the lesson early on, others later, and others are still struggling with it. What makes these countries similar in some—but not all—periods of their histories are the macropolicies they adopted, not the continent to which they belong.

One could, of course, adopt an alternative view that focuses on some Latin American virus whose origin could be found in the common history of centuries as a Spanish colony, the distance from the rest of the world, or some other fateful common feature. Under this view, the Latin American dummy in cross-country regressions does indeed account for that unobserved structural feature.

We believe that the studies in this volume show that there is enough cross-country and within-country variation in the macropolicies adopted and the macroeconomic outcomes to enable us to disregard that view. Therefore, the lessons drawn from these experiences are not limited to the region. We now briefly discuss a few examples.

THE EUROPEAN DEBT CRISIS

In the first months of 2012, the spread between the interest rate of sovereign bonds in Italy, Portugal, and Spain against the German sovereign bond, which had been very small since the adoption of the euro, started to go up, reaching a staggering five hundred basis points. These dramatic changes in sovereign spreads did not seem to be accompanied by a corresponding change in fundamentals.

This fact led many to argue that multiplicity of equilibria could be behind the unraveling debt crisis. Essentially, the argument boils down to a shift in expectations that increases the interest rate, which imposes a higher fiscal burden on the country, increasing the probability of default and thereby confirming the shift in expectations.

As it turns out, theories that rationalize this behavior also imply that deep-pocket lenders can adopt policies that rule out the bad-expectations equilibrium at no fiscal cost (see, for instance, Lorenzoni and Werning 2013 and Ayres et al. 2015).

This is a possible interpretation of the end of the European debt crisis, marked by a sustained drop in spreads following the announcement by the European Central Bank (ECB) that it would lend to troubled countries to end the crisis. An interesting feature is that the policy announcement alone was enough to end the crisis, as is implied by the theory.

As Meza shows in "The History of Mexico" in this book, this phenomenon is not a novel one. The financial crisis experienced by Mexico following the devaluation of December 1994 ended after the so-called Clinton bailout with the announcement of a debt relief package that was close to US$50 billion. Mexico borrowed less than half of the package and returned the funds in less than three years, well before the due date.

A reasonable conjecture is that the debt relief packages that Mexico received from the United States, and that Italy, Portugal, and Spain received from the ECB, avoided defaults that could have been very costly. Is it possible that without those relief packages, those three European countries could have been dragged into a lost decade, similar to the one endured by several of the Latin American countries? We believe so. If this were the case, belonging to the European community and the euro system may have substantial benefits that are not always acknowledged.

Though some details of the Mexican crisis are different from the European one, the same logic of a policy action by a large lender solving a multiple-equilibria-driven crisis lies behind the Mexican crisis (see Cole and Kehoe 1996). A reasonable conjecture is that the success of the Clinton bailout, now well understood by the profession, played some role in the decision of Mario Draghi, then president of the ECB, to grant the debt relief packages for Italy, Portugal, and Spain.

THE ASIAN FINANCIAL CRISIS

The outbreak in balance of payments and banking crises that hit the fast-growing econo-mies of Southeast Asia in 1997 took everyone by surprise. The understanding was that these systemic crises seemed to grow only on Latin American soil. At first sight, the nature of the crises seemed to be different from those that plagued Latin America in the early 1980s, since the measures of deficits were much smaller than the ones observed in Latin America during those years. Upon closer scrutiny, however, we see that the cri-ses share several features. One important contribution to understanding the Asian crisis points out that, once prospective deficits are taken into account, a crisis may unravel through essentially the same mechanism that allows current deficits to cause a crisis, as demonstrated by the conceptual framework used by the country cases in this book (see Burnside, Eichenbaum, and Rebelo 2001).

As it turns out, the role played by prospective deficits already has been pointed out as a potential cause of the Mexican crisis of 1995 (Calvo and Mendoza 1996). Those two contributions suggest that we can draw useful lessons from the crises in Mexico and Asia.

FINANCIAL MARKET AND CAPITAL ACCOUNT LIBERALIZATIONS

All too often, as illustrated in this book, financial liberalizations ended in banking crises with very large fiscal costs. In many of those cases, countries were unable to finance those sudden increases in spending, so the financial crisis was accompanied by defaults on government debt. Most of the time, these defaults were very costly with respect to output performance. This was particularly the case for financial liberalizations that were adopted at the same time that capital controls were eliminated, allowing both the govern-ment and the private sector to start borrowing heavily in international financial markets.

A remarkable feature of the Latin American debt crises is that they occur at levels of debt to total output that are much lower than those observed in many developed economies. In "A Framework for Studying the Monetary and Fiscal History of Latin America," Kehoe, Nicolini, and Sargent briefly describe theories that could rationalize this feature based on the credit history of these countries. All the countries studied in this volume were isolated from international financial markets until the early 1970s. The theories described in "A Framework for Studying the Monetary and Fiscal History of Latin America" imply that in the early stages of participation in credit markets, participants are constrained by how much debt they can raise in a single period. Eventually, after a long period of compliance with debts, those constraints cease to bind. An "emerging" economy would thus be one that is still in transition, with tight debt limits that eventually disappear once the economy becomes "developed."

Currently, a few countries in Asia have started a growth process that nurtures the hope that poverty rates will fall dramatically in the next couple of decades. And many of us hope to live long enough to see many countries in Africa follow that path. The Industrial Revolution has been spreading at a remarkable rate in the last few decades, and if the world maintains that pace, we may end the twenty-first century living on a planet where poverty is studied only in history courses.

We do not know what ignites an industrial revolution in a particular country. But the case studies in this book suggest that some combination of policies can kill an industrial revolution once it has started. Clearly, more research is needed in order to provide more conclusive evidence. We believe, however, that the Latin American experience suggests that governments should be very cautious before proceeding with a joint and sudden liberalization of the financial market and the capital account in the early stages of a country's development.

MODERN MONETARY THEORY

As a final example of the lessons that the experiences of these countries have to offer for other countries, we now use a couple of examples, described in detail in this book, that shed light on a current debate in the United States. Recently, some politicians in the United States have proposed increasing spending on social programs, detaching that decision from taxation, based on some academic formulations that have collectively been called "modern monetary theory" (MMT).

What MMT accounts for is not precisely defined. The discussion in policy circles does not necessarily reflect what is being discussed in academic circles. Our purpose is not to debate the merits of the academic discussions on the topic, about which we have far too many reservations. Rather, we want to consider two examples discussed in the chapters for Argentina and Chile.

Briefly, one of the first major policy implications of most versions of MMT is that countries whose governments issued debt in domestic currency may never default, since they can print the money they need to pay for their debt. A second main implication is that those governments can finance social spending by issuing money and that, to the extent that output is below potential, this policy will not generate increases in the rate of inflation.

Our conceptual framework allows a government to inflate away the domestic currency–denominated debt and allows the government to raise revenue by printing money—although limited by the interest rate elasticity of the demand for real money. It also implies that inflation will follow and that it can be stopped by raising taxes or issuing bonds (albeit limited by the willingness of credit markets to lend to this government). However, our conceptual framework is not consistent with the latter part of the second implication, since the economy, being at full employment, is not a prerequisite for inflation.

The key assumption in MMT is that government debt must be denominated in its own currency. This assumption clearly omits from consideration most of the crises that plagued Latin America starting in the early 1980s, since in most cases the share of dollar-denominated debt was sizable. Nonetheless, this assumption is a good description of the state of affairs in Argentina and Chile in the early 1970s. In both countries, government debt was very small and mostly denominated in local currency. Both countries ran rampant deficits for two years in a row and financed those deficits by printing money. Neither of the two governments defaulted on their debt, since they inflated away the debt. Inflation in Chile was over 700 percent during 1973, however, and it was over 500 percent in Argentina in 1975. In both cases, total output and total labor experienced severe drops, as documented in the corresponding chapters, showing that full employment is not a prerequisite for inflation. The experiences of these countries clearly show that following the tenets described above will seriously jeopardize the price stability mandate of the Federal Reserve.

Notes

We thank Lars Hansen and a referee for comments. The views expressed herein are those of the authors and not necessarily those of the Federal Reserve Bank of Minneapolis or the Federal Reserve System.

1 A detailed description of all the data in this chapter can be found in the data appendix available at http://manifold.bfi.uchicago.edu/.

2 This is not exclusive to developing countries. Government finances in the United States, for example, do not explicitly account for the contingent liabilities implied by the current social security system.

3 These banks were popular during the period of import substitution, a strategy that dominated economic policy making after the Great Depression. In many countries, these banks started to be closed or privatized in the 1980s. Currently, although government-owned banks still represent a large fraction of the banking system in some countries, these development banks no longer exist or are unimportant.

4 An exception is the work of Zarazaga (1993), who uses a game-theory approach to model the behavior of different government entities competing to appropriate seigniorage.

The positive probability of very high inflation periods acts as a self-enforcing mechanism to restrain this competition for seigniorage and support periods of relatively low inflation.

5 This topic is discussed in detail in Federal Deposit Insurance Corporation (1997).

6 In 1977, in a speech at Columbia University, Arthur Burns, chairman of the Federal Reserve Board, criticized commercial banks for assuming excessive risks. Also, a 1977 published staff report from the Senate Subcommittee on Foreign Relations noted its concern about the exposure of U.S. commercial banks to loans in emerging economies.

References

Almeida, Victor, Carlos Esquivel, Timothy J. Kehoe, and Juan Pablo Nicolini. 2018. "Default and Interest Rate Shocks: Renegotiation Matters." Unpublished paper, Federal Reserve Bank of Minneapolis.

Ayres, Joao, Gastón Navarro, Juan Pablo Nicolini, and Pedro Teles. 2015. "Sovereign Default: The Role of Expectations." Working paper 723, Federal Reserve Bank of Minneapolis.

Banco de México. 2009. "Regímenes Cambiarios en México a partir de 1954." Accessed April 22, 2019. http://www.banxico.org.mx/mercados/d/%7BC260B142-835E-2F6B-D7BD-3C9E182BB8B9%7D.pdf.

Burnside, Craig, Martin Eichenbaum, and Sergio Rebelo. 2001. "On the Fiscal Implications of Twin Crises." Working paper 8277, National Bureau of Economic Research, Cambridge, Mass.

Calvo, Guillermo A., and Enrique G. Mendoza. 1996. "Mexico's Balance-of-Payments Crisis: A Chronicle of a Death Foretold." *Journal of International Economics* 41 (3–4): 235–64.

Cole, Harold L., and Timothy J. Kehoe. 1996. "A Self-Fulfilling Model of Mexico's 1994–1995 Debt Crisis." *Journal of International Economics* 41 (3–4): 309–30.

———. 2000. "Self-Fulfilling Debt Crises." *Review of Economic Studies* 67 (1): 91–116.

Federal Deposit Insurance Corporation. 1997. "The LDC Debt Crisis." In *History of the Eighties—Lessons for the Future.* Vol. 1, *An Examination of the Banking Crises of the 1980s and Early 1990s*, chap. 5. Washington, D.C.: Federal Deposit Insurance Corporation.

Gómez-Palacio, Ignacio. 1984. "Mexico's Foreign Exchange Controls. Two Administrations: Two Solutions. Thorough and Benign." *University of Miami Inter-American Law Review* 16 (2): 267–99.

Kehoe, Timothy J., and Edward C. Prescott, eds. 2007. *Great Depressions of the Twentieth Century.* Minneapolis: Federal Reserve Bank of Minneapolis.

Lorenzoni, Guido, and Ivan Werning. 2013. "Slow Moving Debt Crises." Working paper 19228, National Bureau of Economic Research, Cambridge, Mass.

Nicolini, Juan Pablo. 2018. "Access to International Capital Markets: A Blessing or a Curse?" Unpublished manuscript, Federal Reserve Bank of Minneapolis.

Sargent, Thomas J. 1986. *Rational Expectations and Inflation.* Princeton, N.J.: Princeton University Press.

Serrano, Alejandro. 2015. "Banking History of Mexico and the 1982 Nationalization of Banks." *Journal of Emerging Issues in Economics, Finance and Banking* 4 (2): 1554–77.

Sims, Jocelyn, and Jessie Romero. 2013. "Latin American Debt Crisis of the

1980s." Federal Reserve History. Accessed April 22, 2019. https://www.federalreserve history.org/essays/latin_american_debt _crisis.

Zarazaga, Carlos. 1993. "Hyperinflations and Moral Hazard in the Appropriation of Seigniorage." Working paper 93-26, Federal Reserve Bank of Philadelphia.

Contributors

Mark Aguiar is a professor of economics and international finance at Princeton University.

Fernando Alvarez is a professor of economics at the University of Chicago.

Manuel Amador is a professor of economics at the University of Minnesota and a monetary advisor at the Federal Reserve Bank of Minneapolis.

Joao Ayres is an economist at the Research Department at the Inter-American Development Bank.

Saki Bigio is an assistant professor of economics at the University of California, Los Angeles.

Luigi Bocola is an assistant professor of economics at Stanford University.

Francisco Buera is a professor of economics at Washington University in St. Louis.

Guillermo Calvo is a professor of economics at Columbia University.

Rodrigo Caputo is an associate professor of economics at the Universidad de Santiago, Chile.

Roberto Chang is a professor of economics at Rutgers University.

Carlos Javier Charotti is a PhD candidate at the University of Manchester, UK.

Simón Cueva is a director at TNK Economics, Ecuador.

Julián P. Díaz is an associate professor of economics at Loyola University Chicago.

Sebastian Edwards is a professor of international economics at the University of California, Los Angeles.

Carlos Esquivel is an assistant professor of economics at Rutgers University.

Eduardo Fernández-Arias is a regional economic advisor at the Inter-American Development Bank.

Contributors

Carlos Fernández Valdovinos is a member of the board of Banco Basa, Paraguay.

Arturo José Galindo is a governor at the Central Bank of Colombia.

Márcio Garcia is a professor of economics at Pontificia Universidad Catolica-Rio, Brazil.

Felipe González Soley is a PhD candidate in economics at the University of Southampton, UK.

Diogo Guillen is a lecturer at Pontificia Universidade Católica do Rio de Janeiro and Insper Instituto de Ensino e Pesquisa, Brazil.

Lars Peter Hansen is a professor and director of the Becker Friedman Institute's Macro Finance Research Program at the University of Chicago.

Patrick Kehoe is a professor at Stanford University and a monetary advisor at the Federal Reserve Bank of Minneapolis.

Timothy J. Kehoe is a professor of economics at the University of Minnesota and an adviser to the Federal Reserve Bank of Minneapolis.

Carlos Gustavo Machicado is a senior researcher at the Institute for Advanced Development Studies, Bolivia.

Joaquín Marandino is an adjunct professor at Universidad Torcuato Di Tella in Argentina.

Alberto Martin is currently a senior research adviser at the European Central Bank.

César Martinelli is a professor of economics at George Mason University.

Felipe Meza is a professor of economics at Instituto Tecnologico Autonomo de Mexico.

Pablo Andrés Neumeyer is a professor of economics at Universidad Torcuato Di Tella in Argentina.

Juan Pablo Nicolini is a senior research economist with the Federal Reserve Bank of Minneapolis and a professor of economics at Universidad Torcuato Di Tella in Argentina.

Gabriel Oddone is a professor of economic policy at the Universidad de la República and a partner of the Centro de Investigaciónes Económicas in Uruguay.

Daniel Osorio-Rodríguez is the head of the Financial Stability Department at the Banco de la República, Colombia.

José Peres-Cajías is an assistant professor at the University of Barcelona, Spain.

David Perez-Reyna is a professor of economics at Universidad de los Andes, Colombia.

Fabrizio Perri is a monetary advisor in the Research Department at the Federal Reserve Bank of Minneapolis.

Andrew Powell is the principal advisor in the Research Department at the Inter-American Development Bank.

Diego Restuccia is a professor of economics at the University of Toronto in Canada.

Diego Saravia is the manager of economic research and senior advisor at the Central Bank of Chile.

Thomas J. Sargent is a professor of economics at New York University and a senior fellow at the Hoover Institution, Stanford University.

José A. Scheinkman is a professor of economics at Columbia University.

Teresa Ter-Minassian is an international economic consultant.

Marco Vega is the deputy manager of economic research at the Central Bank of Peru.

Carlos A. Végh is a professor of international economics at Johns Hopkins University.

François R. Velde is a senior economist and research advisor in the Economic Research Department at the Federal Reserve Bank of Chicago.

Alejandro Werner is the director of the Western Hemisphere Department of the International Monetary Fund.